MW01630060

RoRoR 05

NEW HALL PORCELAINS

Frontispiece. *A small porcelain tureen from a New Hall dessert service painted by Fidelle Duvivier for John Daniel, the manager of the factory, c.1785-90. Many pieces from this important and magnificent service are illustrated in Chapters V and VI.* Private collection

NEW HALL PORCELAINS

by

Geoffrey A. Godden, F.R.S.A.

ANTIQUE COLLECTORS' CLUB

ISBN 1 85149 463 4

British Library Cataloguing-in-Publication Data.
A catalogue record for this book is available from the British Library.

Printed in England
by the Antique Collectors' Club Ltd., Woodbridge, Suffolk

Antique Collectors' Club

THE ANTIQUE COLLECTORS' CLUB was formed in 1966 and quickly grew to a five figure membership spread throughout the world. It publishes the only independently run monthly antiques magazine, *Antique Collecting*, which caters for those collectors who are interested in widening their knowledge of antiques, both by greater awareness of quality and by discussion of the factors which influence the price that is likely to be asked. The Antique Collectors' Club pioneered the provision of information on prices for collectors and the magazine still leads in the provision of detailed articles on a variety of subjects.

It was in response to the enormous demand for information on 'what to pay' that the price guide series was introduced in 1968 with the first edition of *The Price Guide to Antique Furniture* (completely revised 1978 and 1989), a book which broke new ground by illustrating the more common types of antique furniture, the sort that collectors could buy in shops and at auctions rather than the rare museum pieces which had previously been used (and still to a large extent are used) to make up the limited amount of illustrations in books published by commercial publishers. Many other price guides have followed, all copiously illustrated, and greatly appreciated by collectors for the valuable information they contain, quite apart from prices. The Price Guide Series heralded the publication of many standard works of reference on art and antiques. *The Dictionary of British Art* (now in six volumes), *The Pictorial Dictionary of British 19th Century Furniture Design*, *Oak Furniture* and *Early English Clocks* were followed by many deeply researched reference works such as *The Directory of Gold and Silversmiths*, providing new information. Many of these books are now accepted as the standard work of reference on their subject.

The Antique Collectors' Club has widened its list to include books on gardens, garden design, garden history and architecture. All the Club's publications are available through bookshops world wide and a full catalogue of all these titles is available free of charge from the addresses below.

Club membership, open to all collectors, costs little. Members receive free of charge *Antique Collecting*, the Club's magazine (published ten times a year), which contains well-illustrated articles dealing with the practical aspects of collecting not normally dealt with by magazines. Prices, features of value, investment potential, fakes and forgeries are all given prominence in the magazine.

Among other facilities available to members are private buying and selling facilities and the opportunity to meet other collectors at their local antique collectors' club. There are over eighty in Britain and more than a dozen overseas. Members may also buy the Club's publications at special pre-publication prices.

As its motto implies, the Club is an organisation designed to help collectors get the most out of their hobby: it is informal and friendly and gives enormous enjoyment to all concerned.

For Collectors — By Collectors — About Collecting

ANTIQUE COLLECTORS' CLUB
www.antiquecollectorsclub.com

Sandy Lane, Old Martlesham, Woodbridge, Suffolk, IP12 4SD, UK
Tel: 01394 389950 Fax: 01394 389999
e-mail: info@antique-acc.com
or
Eastworks, 116 Pleasant Street – Suite #60B, Easthampton, MA 01027, USA
Tel: (413) 529-0861 Fax: (413) 529-0862 Orders: (800) 252 5231
e-mail: info@antiquecc.com

This book is dedicated to my fellow New Hall enthusiast and author, the late
DAVID HOLGATE

In appreciation of his kind assistance and helpful advice,
so generously offered and readily given, a belated

'Thank you', David

Contents

Author's Note		8
Prelude		10
Colour Plates		17
Preface		65
Chapter I	The West Country Connection	68
Chapter II	The Patent comes to Staffordshire — The Tunstall Period	88
Chapter III	The New Hall, Marks, Markets and Prices	125
Chapter IV	The New Hall Works and the Partners	143
Chapter V	Fidelle Duvivier and other Decorators	159
Chapter VI	The New Hall Porcelains, c.1784-1812	191
Chapter VII	The Blue Printed Designs and Blue Painted Patterns	277
Chapter VIII	The 'Cottagy' Oriental Style Designs	316
Chapter IX	The On-glaze Bat-printed Designs	329
Chapter X	The Bone China Wares, c.1812-1835	361
Chapter XI	Post-1835 Developments on the New Hall Site	406
Appendix I	The Patents	416
Appendix II	The Land Tax Returns	422
Closing Notes, Resumé of Dates and Selected Bibliography		425
Checklist of Illustrated Patterns		433
Acknowledgements		435
Index		437

Author's Note

NEW HALL. With regard to New Hall, little need be said as the ware which emanated therefrom is of little importance and has so far shown no evidence of becoming valuable.

So wrote H. Mordaunt Rogers, F.R.I.C.S. in *The Making of a Connoisseur* in 1925 (republished in 1951). I need not at this stage comment on the commercial aspect, or on the idea that certain types of porcelain are of 'little importance' because they had shown no evidence of becoming valuable! Yet it is true that many present-day collectors, myself included, were initially attracted to New Hall for that very reason – it was modestly priced in relation to more traditionally collectable classes of old pottery or porcelain.

As to the claim that New Hall was of little importance, I hope to show that this factory and its several partners played a very large part in the development of British ceramics, a fact that the several post-war specialist reference books and learned papers (as listed in the Bibliography) have underlined. In recent years we have come to see that New Hall and its contemporary commercial rivals producing similar fashionable and popular designs form one of the most interesting classes of collectable English porcelain which conveniently links the eighteenth century with the nineteenth. There is today a large, dedicated, group of collectors of New Hall porcelain. Such collectors are by no means limited to the British Isles; the appeal is international and growing as research shows the quality and variety of these once almost despised unpretentious Staffordshire porcelains.

You may well be surprised that I have chosen to write on New Hall porcelains when there are already excellent books about this factory. The answer is simple. I believe I have much to contribute and to add to the information already published. We all look at a subject from a different viewpoint and place emphasis on different aspects of a complicated story. Also, within recent times important, hitherto unrecorded New Hall shapes and patterns have been discovered which tend to show the New Hall porcelains in a new light.

These porcelains are also of great personal interest to me. I have collected New Hall for over half a century and, as a trader in and a collector of these Staffordshire porcelains, I have handled thousands of specimens and held seminars to study such porcelains and discuss the many problems that baffle collectors. It is also true that the later bone chinas of the post-1815 period have interested me as much as the earlier hybrid hard-paste porcelains, which have been the main concern of earlier writers.

I have also been extremely interested in the many makes of contemporary porcelains which were the New Hall partners' commercial competition and which have been the subject of lengthy research, both by specialist 'study groups' and individuals. I have therefore studied New Hall porcelains in a very broad context, one which I feel is interesting and rewarding.

Over the years I have not been afraid to rethink old problems and to re-examine long accepted beliefs. In so doing I have advanced new theories, some (but not all!) of which have now been widely acknowledged and accepted. This new book also breaks new ground and, I believe, advances still further our understanding of the very varied porcelains produced by a changing partnership which prospered for most of the fifty and more years of its existence. The fact that so much that was not made by the company is widely classed as 'New Hall' or as 'New Hall type' surely underlines the popularity of these porcelains or at least the charm of the range of less expensive formal floral patterns that are almost universally classed as 'New Hall'.

My approach to this new study may at times be unconventional and I trust that I will not upset too many purists. My aim has been to put over my points and personal views and the complex story in a clear and perhaps novel manner. Over the years so much nonsense has been written about these pioneer Staffordshire porcelains that there is a need to separate the wheat from the chaff. I will, therefore note the errors which I believe exist in some earlier works, although I would say at this point that I am in general agreement with the published thoughts of my friends the late Geoffrey Grey and Tony de Saye Hutton and my fellow researcher and helper David Holgate.[1] This book aims to add to their studies, to complement their writings and to add to the range of illustrated New Hall porcelains available to new and established collectors.

It is interesting to reflect how our conception of New Hall porcelain has changed over the years. When I commenced dealing in and collecting such wares in the late 1940s every simple, cottagy, formal floral design was termed New Hall. The idea was also afoot that no gilding appeared on New Hall teawares. The picture was gloriously simple, but completely incorrect! The belief that New Hall porcelain was 'Unsophisticated and intended for the cheaper market'[2] was widespread.

One of the greatest collectors of New Hall porcelain was the late Geoffrey Grey – a great researcher. His superb collection was sparked by the chance gift of a so typical 'New Hall' creamer. On this 'starter' he built a reference collection which was to lead him to the conclusion that his first 'so typical' creamer was not made at the New Hall factory. It was an impostor! – well, perhaps not an impostor because the original maker would merely have been making his version of a popular design and fashionable silver-like creamer shape. Mr. Grey initially loved that gift piece – he was quite right, but perhaps very wrong if later he had discarded this cream jug which had only suffered a change of attribution. We now know that over twenty other porcelain factories produced the simple New Hall-like patterns, simply because they were in demand.

We also are now aware that the New Hall partnership produced some very richly decorated, often ornately gilded, porcelains. These designs, which I call the 'Drawing Room' New Hall, outnumber in terms of pattern numbers, if not in output, the traditional simple floral designs.

Our understanding of New Hall porcelains is now far clearer than it was only twenty-five years ago. The range of known shapes and patterns has been greatly extended. Other contemporary firms have been rediscovered and researched, although much still awaits our attention. Research is by no means finished, the subject is vast and complicated. This interest is good, it is healthy. Collecting would be very dull if we already were in possession of all the answers.

I trust you will enjoy your collecting and your collection of the varied and interesting New Hall, as I have done over the years.

Geoffrey A Godden
Findon,
West Sussex

1. David unfortunately died in December 1999, having just previously completed his most helpful checking of my initial manuscript. His loss will be long felt by all New Hall collectors, indeed by all interested in British ceramics.

2. *The Antique Collector's Handbook* by S.C. Johnson (W. Foulsham, & Co., n.d., c.1950).

Prelude

The recent chance discovery of the 'Draft Minutes' covering the initial meeting of the Staffordshire potters gathered together to discuss with Richard Champion, the Bristol porcelain manufacturer, the possibility of producing his patented true (or hard-paste) porcelain in Staffordshire within a new co-partnership agreement enables me to show briefly the outline story of how an amended novel new type of ceramic came to be made in the Staffordshire Potteries and how a completely new company was eventually set up to manufacture such wares under unique circumstances – as a form of potters' co-operative.

The resulting new Staffordshire partnership changed its trading style several times and is now conveniently called the New Hall Company and its products 'New Hall'. This company was to prosper, or at least last, for over fifty years, from 1781 to the closure in 1835. More importantly, its success was greatly to encourage other potters and firms to produce porcelains in a district which in the early 1780s was almost entirely concerned with the manufacture of earthenwares. Richard Champion succeeded in encouraging the Staffordshire potters to take up the manufacture of chinaware or porcelain whereas Josiah Wedgwood had failed in his similar efforts some five years earlier. It must not be forgotten that there had been earlier efforts to produce porcelains in Staffordshire, at Newcastle-under-Lyme in the 1740s and slightly later William Littler's more successful attempts at Longton Hall (c.1749-60) with perhaps the so-called Baddeley-Littler porcelains of c.1777-90 – but these represent ventures that were not commercially successful and therefore tended to delay further other attempts, rather than encourage them. Information on both these early concerns is given in *Staffordshire Porcelain* (under my editorship and published in 1983 by Granada Publishing Ltd.).

The first meeting and the subsequent ones held at the Swan Inn at Hanley were substantially to change the whole history of English ceramics. The original 'Draft Minutes' are unfortunately not complete and are slightly torn so that some portions are missing, particularly those on the damage prone first page. The Minutes, too, are only in draft form and some minor amendments may have been made before the fair and final copy was submitted for approval at the following meeting. Yet the all-important gist of the business is, I believe, here recorded.

DRAFT MINUTES

Meeting held at the Swan Inn, Market Place, Hanley on [corner of page here missing] 1781 to discuss the formation of a Joint Stock Company to produce Mr Champion's respected and Patent Real Porcelain in the Staffordshire Potteries under License, using native raw materials.

The company present comprise the substantial and enterprising local adventurers – Anthony Keeling, John Turner, Joshua Heath, Thomas Heath as well as John Hollins, Samuel Hollins, Jacob Warburton, Charles Bagnall, ... [page here torn] with Mr Richard Champion in attendance by invitation.

Anthony Keeling of Tunstall was elected Chairman of the meeting, by general approval. John Turner offered to act as Clerk, on a temporary basis until such time as permanent officers were elected, if such a Company be agreed to be formed.

The Chairman invited Mr Champion to address the meeting and to outline his proposals.

Mr Champion stated that he had called on most of the persons present, either on his first visit to the Potteries in November 1780 or during his later visits earlier this year, and that he had published a broadsheet setting out the basic details of his wish to move his manufactory from the City of Bristol to the Staffordshire Potteries and to permit others to join the Venture. Copy of this Notice was deposited with the Secretary and is affixed to the Minutes.

Mr Champion stated that at great expense (he mentioned the sum of fifteen thousand pounds) he had perfected the production of true porcelain after the manner of the Chinese and German Dresden or Meissen porcelains and that as was well known he now owned the assigned Patent Rights originally granted to William Cookworthy of Plymouth in 1768 which reserved the use of the vital Cornish raw materials (the Petuntse and the Kaolin of the Chinese) necessary to produce real porcelain and that such rights had been extended by Act of Parliament to 1796, that is the protection has a further fifteen years of life.

Mr Champion then showed an assortment of his Bristol porcelains comprising in the main figures and groups with some vases, also ornamental fancies and cabinet pieces all decorated to a very high standard with a selection of tablewares, dessert services, sauceboats and tea equipages, mostly embellished with burnished gold. It was conceded that these porcelains were of a very high order.
Mr Champion stated that these samples evidenced the fact that he had perfected the technique and that his recipe was capable of producing prime-quality true porcelains equal if not excelling in goodness all imported and native porcelains His teapots and other articles would not fly – but would withstand boiling water as did the Oriental imports.
He foresaw a great expansion in the market as the popularity of the tea as a middle-class beverage increased and as the population of the British Isles was now expanding to a remarkable degree. He also foresaw that most of the upper ranks of society would demand porcelain rather than earthenware teawares, and yet none or very little[1] of this type was, he believed, currently produced in this neighbourhood, which depended on the production of various types of refined earthenwares. Our Staffordshire potters were, he correctly stated, leading the world in that branch of the trade and were enjoying a large export trade but were as yet neglecting the potentially vast and prosperous trade in dependable true porcelains.
Mr Champion then stated that as the Patent holder and the licensee of mines from which the raw materials could be obtained he sought to permit a group of leading and prosperous Staffordshire Potters of standing to form a Company to exploit the Patent and to produce Real Porcelains in Staffordshire. He proposed to sell shares in such a Company, co-partnership or combination. Such shares or Licenses would enable himself to recoup some of the considerable expense which he had vested in the search for the correct method of manufacturing true Porcelain.
He in turn would supervise the setting up of the new manufactory, instruct any new hands in the manufacturing and firing processes and in general pass on his vast experience of the Art or Craft. He was also in a position to guarantee an adequate supply of the necessary raw materials. Having set up the concern and sold the Licenses or shares, he would stand aside and permit the new owners to reap the full benefit of their adventure.
The Staffordshire potters or their friends or partners would furnish the necessary funds, find and acquire the premises and the work-force and be responsible for the sale of the finished Articles. He understood that the prosperous and well-known Worcester Company had years ago been formed in a similar manner by a group of adventurers purchasing the small Bristol works of Benjamin Lund and transferring the concern to the City of Worcester, where it still flourished to their great benefit.
He suggested that the Staffordshire potters were even better placed to reap their own similar rewards. The porcelain body was novel, but tested and true. The potters had vast experience of their Trade and they had at their command a vast network of retail and wholesale outlets all of whom must surely be ready customers for neat new porcelain tea equipages and other saleable articles.
He likened his proposed sale of the manufacturing expertise to a franchise and suggested that such a venture would be beneficial to all concerned, provided that the potters were prepared to work harmoniously together for the common good of all share-holders.
Mr Champion also suggested that alternatively he could manufacture and supply the mixture to individual potters who would then be able to manufacture what he termed 'Real Porcelain' using the Cornish china stone and china clay under his license. However, if he were to take this step he could not restrict the sale of the mixture to the Staffordshire potters. Other enterprising potters and adventurers would doubtless commence production in other centres, giving rise to commercial competition and price cutting.
The Chairman, after thanking Mr Champion for his proposition, opened the discussion to the attending potters. He suggested that for the purposes of this initial meeting they should consider the advantages (or disadvantages) of forming a local partnership to work Mr Champion's Patent. The disadvantages of permitting individuals outside The Potteries to enjoy the Rights were obvious and even if such rights were confirmed to the locality, the cost of adapting several potteries to produce the new porcelains, would be great and the production of their own earthenwares would be interrupted. Also, each manufacturer would need to employ extra hands capable of manufacturing and decorating the new porcelains.
Sam Hollins rose to state that he favoured the formation of a single manufacturing and trading Company. He thought it advantageous to employ a capable manager so that he and the other potters could continue to manage their own Potteries and business without need to attend or supervise the new porcelain venture about which they had no specialised knowledge. He would not wish to give up part of his existing Pottery to produce Porcelain which he assumed would require the erection of new and special kilns. He would however, venture upon a share or shares in such an enterprise provided that a capable manager and trained hands could be found to work a new or enlarged existing manufactory.
Mr John Hollins of Newcastle-under-Lyme, rose to enquire of Mr Champion the cost of the proposed shares in any new Company. Mr Champion replied that he sought only to recoup a portion of his total outlay. He probably would be content to raise the sum of six thousand pounds. The price of each Share therefore depended on the number issued and on the number of potters or others who were interested in joining the adventure. He thought that the number of share-holders should be small – the better to agree the various matters that would undoubtedly arise. Also the greater the individual holding the greater the incentive to make the venture a profitable one. The owner of a single one guinea share would have little interest in the manufactory but a gentleman vesting five hundred guineas would obviously be concerned in its lasting success. If ten persons were pleased to join the Company and hold one share each their individual holding would be six hundred pounds. If the meeting so wished however, the shares could be smaller value

say one hundred pounds each – providing all the necessary sixty were taken up. Such shares, Mr Champion pointed out would be affected by market forces – if they were offered for sale and if the venture proved a profitable one (as he had no doubt it would) these shares would rise in value – to perhaps double or even treble their original cost It was not he conceded, for him to suggest how the profits should be distributed but it seemed obviously beneficial to link such payments to the number of shares taken up by each holder. The more ventured the greater the gain. Or loss, murmured Mr Charles Bagnall, to the amusement of the meeting.

John Turner, speaking as a potential share-holder, asked what type of porcelains it was proposed to manufacture. Mr Champion had shown a varied assortment of decorative 'fancies' – figures and such like. These were all very well but seemingly they had been produced at a loss. It was well known that Mr Champion had sunk thousands of pounds in perfecting such 'toys'. Would not the same fate overtake any other manufacturing of the seemingly troublesome True or Real Porcelains.

In answer to this Mr Champion assured the company that the money had been spent in over-coming the early difficulties, in perfecting the techniques, and that they could now reap the reward of his labours and endeavours. Also, as he had indicated in his broadsheet the locality of the original manufactory at Plymouth and later at Bristol had proved very costly and that the Staffordshire Pottery towns enjoyed the advantage of having less expensive but skilled labour, willing to work for little more than half that which he paid in wages at Bristol. But of greater importance was the low cost of the coals. Here in Staffordshire it was readily available at a quarter of the cost charged in Bristol. He had, he claimed, greatly reduced the necessary firing temperature so that his new porcelains could be fired in the kilns in which white stonewares were fired and he hoped to reduce the needed temperature still further – even to that necessary for the cream-coloured earthenwares. In this way the cost of manufacture here in Staffordshire would be very much less than that with which he was burdened in Bristol. They were, he pointed out, extremely fortunate that the Grand Trunk Canal had been recently completed and that consequently the clays from Cornwall could be transported by sea to Liverpool and thence via the canal to the Potteries, in bulk and at a very reasonable cost. The finished goods as the Potters know well would also be distributed nationally and indeed overseas in a like inexpensive and dependable way.

While he considered he was merely moving a proven and established works from one county to another, it was possible – as he had indicated in his broadsheet – that the new management and experienced share-holding potters might well introduce an amended system of manufacture; in the management of the Fire the construction of the Kilns and in the use of new materials, so reducing the risks of manufacture and of cost still further.

The Clerk [John Turner] stated that such claims were all very well but the fact remained that Mr Champion was proposing to charge an enhanced price for his Cornish raw materials. Mr Wedgwood and the writer had travelled to Cornwall and would obtain the necessary clays for a considerably lower price per ton than that quoted by Mr Champion.

Mr Champion conceded this and pointed out that he himself was governed in this matter by a binding agreement entered into many years ago between William Cookworthy and Mr Pitt – the landowner. Mr Champion hoped to ease the present contract but reminded the meeting that although they might well be able to arrange for a supply of the clays, they could only use it under license for the manufacture of true porcelain according to his deposited specification. He could only remind the meeting that he sought not gain for himself but rather to make the name of Staffordshire China as well known – both here and abroad – as they had made the name Staffordshire pottery.

Mr Champion further pointed out that the proposed new Company, having in effect purchased the Patent rights when they acquired the new shares could in turn if they so wished refranchise the right to produce similar porcelains to other potters. His draft agreement had a clause in it giving liberty to every potter to make porcelain in his own works on payment of a fee. He could also, of course, resell the special mix – the 'composition' to other individuals.

Mr Turner intervened to state that so far as he could understand, the Patent Rights claimed by Mr Champion were by no means watertight even when related to transparent, non-earthenware bodies. Surely, he observed, the mix could be amended by other manufacturers using other proportion of China Stone and China Clay or by the simple means of adding other ingredients. The Chairman observed that this sort of question should be left for determination at a later stage by their legal representatives if the project was to be embarked upon by a new Company of Staffordshire potters and other interested parties.

Mr Turner further asked, if it was agreed to purchase the Patent Rights, could we then call the new Staffordshire wares 'Patent Porcelain'? Mr Champion, in reply, stated that neither he nor Mr Cookworthy before him had found it necessary to so designate their porcelains but as the raw materials specified in the Patent were the same as were used by the Oriental potters, he thought that the new Staffordshire Company could well claim to manufacture 'Real China'.

Mr Champion also added that the Staffordshire Potters might well wish to amend the manufacturing process, which had already been changed on several occasions. Mr Cookworthy had originally fired his ware in the Oriental style, using wood as the fuel and firing the body and glaze together in a single firing. He [Mr Champion] at Bristol used Coal and employed a biscuit-firing to mature the body before it was glazed and fired again. This permitted him to use underglaze-blue printing techniques which now seemed so popular and convenient. He suggested other amendments in the body, the firing temperature and the glaze could well be made – especially if the Staffordshire potters favoured their traditional lead-glazes which would require a softer fire. The Chairman here interrupted – stating that at this initial meeting they should not get bogged-down in technical details, Mr Champion would no doubt oversee production and demonstrate this technique should a jointly owned pottery be established in the Potteries. Sam Hollins asked what designs it was proposed to ornament the new wares with. He did not wish the chinas to compete with his (and other potters) earthenwares. Mr Champion stated that such matters would be in the hands of the Potters themselves – they or their manager would decide such day-to-day questions. He further stated that porcelains called for gold ornamentation and that such finery was not normally applied to earthenwares. The porcelains should augment their range of productions, not clash with existing lines.

Mr Hollins further asked what name or mark device they would use and whether the different designs would be classified and numbered. Mr Champion again stated that this would be open to the new management, but he suggested that at least initially no name or clear device should be affixed to the chinas – they would obtain greater wholesale and retail sales without such a hindrance and at first their products would not have any reputation. As to the numbering of the patterns – this he considered was unnecessary – certainly in their early years. He did not use numbers at Bristol, nor did the Worcester, Caughley or Lowestoft managements and of course the East India Company's imported Oriental porcelains did not bear any design number. As the range of designs increased they might feel it advantageous for pricing, invoicing and reordering to mark the larger pieces in each set with such a number but such minor matters should not trouble the meeting at this early stage.

The Chairman at this point stated that Mr Champion had ably explained his objective and had answered the various questions in a fair manner, it was now up to the Potters to decide if they collectively wished to establish a Company to work Mr Champion's Patent in the Potteries. He suggested that the meeting now be terminated and that interested parties meet again at the Swan Inn, at the same hour in two weeks time after considering the matter at length and perhaps after ascertaining if the necessary funds were available with which to purchase the shares.

At this point Mr Thomas Heath asked if the full price of the share had to be paid before the Company was trading. He thought that a ten per cent deposit would be fair, the remainder to be paid in two or three further instalments once the products were selling and income was coming to hand. Mr Champion stated in reply that he had to have the full amount within three months as he had other plans awaiting fulfilment. The shares were so priced as to repay him only a small part of his total outlay, and it would be unreasonable of the potters to delay payment until such time as the shares were earning dividends. He suggested that the potters could perhaps bring their own backers to raise the necessary funds and such gentlemen would also hold shares in the proposed company and reap their own just rewards for the investment.

The Chairman closed the meeting at ten minutes past four, praying that his fellow potters give earnest consideration to Mr Champion's plans. His proposal to make the new Staffordshire china the standard consumption both at home and overseas and undersell the importations of the East India Company must appeal to potters and investors alike.

The foregoing 'Draft Minutes' are, of course, a complete spoof.[2] They were made up by me in an attempt concisely to put over the general situation obtaining when Richard Champion came from Bristol to Staffordshire to sell his patent rights in true porcelain manufacture to the local potters. Made up as they are, some sort of initial meeting must have been arranged and, as a result of this or a series of such meetings, the various individuals did agree to purchase the patent rights and form their own Joint Stock Company to work the 'Franchise', the right to produce a type of porcelain using the two basic and all important raw materials – the China Clay (Kaolin) and the China Stone (the Petuntse) which had been found and identified in Cornwall – the subject of William Cookworthy's original patent which formed the patent number 898 of 1768.

I believe all the points made in my spoof 'Draft Minutes' can be substantiated by recorded facts or are a matter of sound commercial sense and the various aspects of the story will be detailed in subsequent chapters.

Subsequent quotations are all correct and seemingly factual, although of course individual interpretations of original source material may well vary or be amended in the light of the later discoveries or re-thinking of the problem.

It is convenient to incorporate in the 'Prelude' the text of an important broadsheet or address issued by Richard Champion apparently after he had first visited the Staffordshire Potteries attempting to interest the local potters in the patent rights. This document (a copy of which is in the Wedgwood archive now housed at Keele University Library) was first found by Mr. Rodney Hampson and published by David Holgate in his 1987 book *New Hall.* It is a most interesting and unique document conveniently linking the Bristol venture with its proposed removal to Staffordshire. This address is dated April 1781. It is well worthy of your attentive study today over two hundred years later. The hand-written notation (this pencilled note is not necessarily contemporary, but it could well be so) on this printed notice reads:

MR CHAMPION'S ADDRESS TO THE POTTERY
APRIL 1781

Richard Champion's printed broadsheet reads:

> A Consideration of the disadvantages which the Proprietor of the Bristol China Manufactory labours under, from the situation in which his Works are placed, has induced him to compare the prices he pays for Labour and Materials, with those of other established Potteries. On the comparison he finds, that their workmen are not only better, but their Wages little more than one half, the price of the essential Article of Coal a fourth part alone, and raw Materials in general, in the same proportion. Such a very great difference has determined him to change his situation, being fully

convinced that, manufacturing now to advantage in as simple a manner as Earthern Ware and with a little Risque, the savings alone will be a capital Sum. He has two Situations in view. The one is a neighbouring County, where Manufactures of Earthen Ware, similar to this Pottery, are carried on, where Coal is still cheaper,[3] workmen and raw materials good and in plenty, with the advantage of being nearer the Sea for Export; and attended with this additional and weighty circumstance, that all Countries, where Manufactures have been newly and successfully established, are continually desirous of Increase, and peculiarly favourable to rising Works. The other is the old and experience'd Potteries in Staffordshire, where Coal and raw Materials are also cheap, where there are Numbers of workmen of excellence in every Branch. The observations which he has made since he has been in Staffordshire, seem to point it out to him as a very eligible Situation for his Manufactory to be removed to. His Sentiments have been considerably strengthened by the options of many very respectable Potters, who are not only desirous of encouraging it, but have express'd their wishes that it may be extended on the most enlarged Scale; that the whole Pottery, and of course the Neighbourhood, may reap the greater Benefit from it. The Public Utility he shall very chearfully give up every contracted Plan of his own; for, from his first application to the discovery, the improvement, and the Perfection of the Manufacture, he has spared neither time, Pains, or Expence, his first Object having been to make it a great National concern. If he should not be so fortunate, during the term which has been granted him, as to be repaid the very great but necessary Expences which he has been at in bringing so important a Manufacture to Perfection, his country will be the Gainer; for his Ware must be as common in England as it is in China itself. Nor has he a doubt, should he come to an agreement with the Potters, but that Staffordshire China will not only be the common Consumption of the Kingdom, but of every part of Europe and America to which the Cream Coloured Ware is exported, made with a little Trouble and Expence, and sufficiently cheap to prevent all future importations from the East Indies. He shall on his part very readily concur with the Pottery at large, in forming an extensive work in Shares by Subscription, open to the County, or in any other manner that may forward an undertaking as productive of advantages, not only in a National View, but to the Parties who may be concern'd in it. He therefore submits to them the following Considerations.

FIRST That this Porcelain or China Ware is manufactured from a Native Clay, of a hard and firm Texture, the Glaze smooth, and of a beautiful White. The enamelled Colours in Great Perfection, the blue and white very good. It will boil Water, and is not injured by the most frequent Use. It resembles more nearly the Dresden, being superior to East India China Ware. The fine Fabric of Sève in France, the Chelsea, Derby, Worcester, Salopian, Leostoffe and all other Wares in England, called English China, are frit Bodies, which the Scratch of a Knife, hot Water, or even the Change of Weather will affect, and may be thus distinguished from this Manufacture they will melt into a glass or vitreous Substance, and lose their form and original appearance in a degree of heat, which this china Ware, agreeing in all properties with the East India and Dresden, will not only bear, but which is necessary to manufacture it.

SECONDLY That the Clay used in manufacturing this China Ware is of the most tenacious Nature, and may be worked on the Wheel and Lathe, or pressed in Moulds, with the same ease as the common Clay from which the Earthern Ware of this country is made.

THIRDLY That although the Fire, which is necessary to bring so fine a Body to Perfection, is much greater than what is requisite for the Manufacture of Cream Coloured Ware, yet it is not carried to the Height of the White Stone Kilns. Besides there is a great Probability of lessening it in time to having been reduced within a very short Period nearly one half. Another circumstance strengthens this Opinion – there is a Species of Nankin China Ware, which is of a similar Nature to this, yet does not to appearance receive a greater degree of Heat than the Cream Coloured Ware, the Body (which is of a real China Ware, and which a greater degree of Fire will make transparent) having a Suction, yet it is perfect, and of a fine Quality.

FOURTHLY That this China Ware is manufactured with as much certainty, and the Kilns are as productive, in proportion, as the Cream Coloured Kilns an equal quantity of good Ware being produced from them.

FIFTHLY That all the Disadvantages which have occurred in the discovery and Progress of this Work, now of above Thirty Years Continuance, and at the Expence of near Thirty Thousand Pounds, have been for some time wholly at an end, and a great and extensive Sale has been made, both in elegant Table and Desert Services; and all sorts of useful and ornamental Ware, with an increasing Reputation. The Manufacture therefore is not to be considered as an Experimental one, but as an Established Work, removing from one Country to another, merely for the Benefit of better and cheaper Workmen and Materials; and with this advantage to those who receive it, that they have no Share in the heavy Burden which has attended its formation.

SIXTHLY That the Establishment of the Manufactury in the Potteries, by introducing a different system of Manufacture, in the management of

> Fire, the Construction of Kilns, and the use of new Materials, will make such essential Improvements in all kinds of Earthen Ware as will form an entire System of Pottery; and will be the means of preventing the considerable Expence which every Potter is at in Experiments, amounting annually amongst the whole to a very large Sum of Money'.[4]

Richard Champion may not have been a particularly successful businessman or potter but he certainly worked several important points or claims into this broadsheet.

The basic costs would be lower if the manufactory was moved to Staffordshire. The new porcelain could be as cheap and dependable in its manufacture as the all successful Staffordshire creamwares. He even claimed that it could be 'sufficiently cheap to prevent all future Importations' of the Chinese porcelains into Great Britain.

In fact, as we now know, the company was set up in the Staffordshire Potteries in or about 1781. In general it proved a great success and continued for over fifty years, until the mid-1830s. The porcelains, which came to be generally called 'New Hall', quickly established a firm commercial reputation and led to the establishment of several small partnerships endeavouring to produce similar useful porcelain tablewares. The Staffordshire Potteries were to become as famous for porcelains as they had been for the centre of English earthenwares. The English East India Company even ceased its bulk importations of Chinese porcelain some ten years after the New Hall Company had been established, although the reason for this cessation of imports was not due to the success of the New Hall porcelains.

These events, however, owe little or nothing to the instigator, Richard Champion, who suddenly left the newly formed Staffordshire consortium in April 1782. The later success was due to the Staffordshire potters and other backers who had formed and taken shares in the new adventure.

I shall be listing and discussing these persons on later pages but it must be remembered that they had other interests and businesses. They were shareholders in the new company, not necessarily concerned with the day-to-day running of the porcelain works. They employed a manager, or rather a succession of managers, and of course a sizeable workforce to produce and decorate the new porcelains which have in recent years become so collectable, some two hundred years after they were made for everyday use.

I do need in this Prelude to mention briefly the types of body that we shall be discussing and our present descriptions. The pre-war authorities were of the opinion that the New Hall partners produced true hard-paste porcelain in the Plymouth and Bristol manner. The early, and indeed some recent, books state that only three English porcelain factories produced hard-paste porcelain – Plymouth, Bristol and New Hall.

Most authorities do not now accept that the New Hall partnership produced true hard-paste porcelain. Mr. David Holgate coined the new description 'hybrid hard-paste' to cover the post-1780 New Hall porcelains and a quite large grouping of other porcelains of the pre-1810 period which seem to be of a very similar type. These include Chamberlain-Worcester and Coalport as well as Wolfe's Liverpool porcelains and various Staffordshire porcelains of this interesting transitional period before the post-1800 bone china was taken up by most manufacturers.

The hybrid hard-paste porcelains appear hardish, but they are not as hard as the Chinese, the Continental porcelains or as Plymouth and Bristol. They were seemingly fired at a lower temperature, at about 1150 to 1200° centigrade rather than at 1350° centigrade or more required for the true hard-paste mixes.[5] It is also believed that the Staffordshire potters forming the new partnership amended the firing sequence, using a high fire for the first (biscuit, or unglazed body) firing and a lower temperature when the body had been glazed. This reverses the system generally employed for true hard-paste porcelains. The Staffordshire potters also incorporated lead in their glaze. For these three basic reasons it is not considered that the new partnership produced true hard-paste porcelain but a compact relatively high-fired mixture of china stone and china clay which we now refer to as hybrid hard-paste porcelain.

The rather heavy, slightly greyish, hybrid hard-paste body, however, gave way to a bone china type mix at an unknown period between 1810 and 1814. Details of this are given in Chapter X, but in general terms the new bone china was whiter, less heavy and compact and was cheaper to produce on account of the rather lower firing temperature and thinner potting.

We therefore have the New Hall manufactory producing a hybrid hard-paste china, which the partners termed 'Real China', and from about 1812 bone china. In reality, however, there may not have been any clear-cut cut-off point between the two as accumulated stocks of undecorated hybrid hard-paste may have been decorated early in the bone china period. It also has to be said that wares produced quite late in the bone china period appear to be much harder than other standard Staffordshire bone chinas and it could be that for certain objects, such as jugs, a convenient mixture of the two bodies was employed. Few aspects of New Hall are straightforward! Yet that is what makes the study of these wares so interesting.

I must not write of 'Taste' – an ever-changing and certainly very personal aspect of collecting. Let me merely cite the views of Marc Louis Solon, of Minton's pâte-sur pâte fame, a Frenchman who was to set himself up as an authority on British ceramics. Writing in his A *Brief History of Old English Porcelain and its Manufacturers,* which was published in 1903 (Bemrose & Sons Ltd.), he wrote of 'the debased productions of the New Hall works':

> Hunting for specimens of New Hall ... a pursuit once indulged in by collectors – is now out of fashion. It is scarcely worth the trouble, for the best representative of the ware, if it may be of some value to complete a comprehensive collection of English china, will certainly not embellish it.

This is one famous ceramic authority's opinion, written at a time when his own painstaking, time-consuming ceramic relief figure decoration, pâte-sur-pâte, was receiving widespread, indeed international, praise, helped by Solon's own writings and high judgement of his own craftsmanship.

It is, however, pertinent, rather than impertinent, to cite also the later views of one great international potter on Solon's own masterpieces. Bernard Leach wrote of Solon's pâte-sur-pâte technique: 'It would be difficult to find a better example of what should not be done with clay.'[6]

I must not take sides. It is not a question of which is right or wrong. It is perhaps a question of what criterion one employs, but one can certainly admire different objects or styles – for different reasons.

I happen to collect Solon's much despised New Hall. I have also collected and admire Bernard Leach's pet dislike, Solon's pâte-sur-pâte. Currently Leach's own Oriental inspired Studio Pottery has attracted criticism from some modern potters. I happen to collect and admire that also. They are all so different, but all have attractive features and to me great charm and interest.

In defence of Solon's 1903 views of 'debased' New Hall, however, I can point out that the then view of New Hall porcelain was not complete. The better quality pieces and the early specimens were not then recognised as New Hall – because of that very feeling that it was mediocre and ordinary. Today, I and other collectors regard New Hall as a market leader. As the factory continued in production for over fifty years, it must surely also be considered as a success story, hardly 'the abortive New Hall factory' as one writer was pleased to describe my pet manufactory.

But, form your own judgement from the following account and my selection of illustrations.

---

1. Champion may have had in mind the small group of soft-paste porcelains now called 'Baddeley-Littler' which were probably being produced in Staffordshire in the early 1780s.

2. I did not submit these made-up minutes to David Holgate fearing that, as a former schoolmaster, he might not have approved of my approach!

3. The 1783 sale notice of the Swansea Pottery cited coal at 'Less than 5/-. a ton'.

4. The original printed notice now housed in the Keele University Library in Staffordshire with other Wedgwood archives is here reproduced courtesy of The Trustees of the Wedgwood Museum, Barlaston, Stoke on Trent, Staffordshire.

5. See *Godden's Guide to English Porcelain*, Chapter 6 (W.H. Smith exclusive book, 1992).

6. *A Potter's Book* (Faber & Faber, 1940).

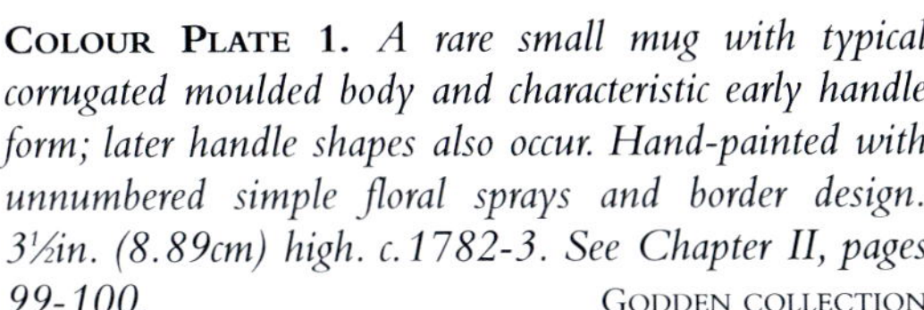

Colour Plate 1. *A rare small mug with typical corrugated moulded body and characteristic early handle form; later handle shapes also occur. Hand-painted with unnumbered simple floral sprays and border design. 3½in. (8.89cm) high. c.1782-3. See Chapter II, pages 99-100.* Godden collection

Colour Plate 2. *A moulded corrugated bodied teapot and coffee cup from an early Tunstall period tea service shown in Plates 21-7. The teapot has thirty ribs, the cup twenty-eight. 6¼in. (15.88cm) high. c.1782-3. See Chapter II, pages 101-107.* Godden collection

Colour Plate 5. *A very rare early period moulded teapot with oval floral-type knob (see Plate 28A). Twenty-eight ribs to wide corrugated style body. Various slightly different versions of this early (usually pre-1790) pattern are to be found. These designs were later given the number 3. The front with larger spray is shown in Plate 28. 6¾in. (17.15cm) high. c.1782-3. See Chapter II.* Godden collection

---

Colour Plate 3. *An oval relief-moulded teapot, with knob form linking with Plates 28 and 28A. The handle shape is similar to that in Plates 21 and 64. This brightly enamelled and gilt relief-moulded teapot is unlike any other acknowledged New Hall examples, but it is submitted as a strong contender. 7½in. (19.05cm) long, 5in. (12.7cm) high. c.1783-5.* Godden collection

Colour Plate 4. *A very rare form of moulded corrugated bodied drum-form teapot of the first (or Tunstall) period. Painted with a version of pattern number 3. 6½in. (16.51cm) high. c.1782-3. See Chapter II.*
Private collection. Photograph Charnwood Antiques

Colour Plate 6. *A rare early large jug (or coffee pot, if it originally had a cover) with moulded, corrugated body and characteristic Tunstall period handle. See also Colour Plate 7. 8¾in. (22.23cm) high. c.1782-3. See Chapter II.* Godden collection

---

Colour Plate 7. *A fine Tunstall period so-called 'cabbage leaf' moulded jug, with hand-painted overglaze decoration. The moulded handle matches that on the jug shown in Colour Plate 6. 8¾in. (22.23cm) high. c.1782-3. See Chapter II. A later version is shown in Colour Plate 46.* Godden collection

Colour Plate 8. *A group of corrugated moulded Tunstall period teawares. All decorated with early, unnumbered, gilt patterns in a simple but tasteful style. Diameter of saucer 5in. (12.7cm). c.1782-3. See Chapter II.* Godden collection

Colour Plate 9. *The twice-signed Duvivier decorated New Hall mug. The inn scene is taken from a Hogarth engraving. The fineness of decoration shows the high quality of the individual, perhaps special order, pieces. 5⅝in. (14.29cm) high. c.1785-90. See Chapter 5.*

Godden collection

Colour Plate 10. *The centre section of the New Hall mug shown in Colour Plates 9 and 11. It bears F. Duvivier's signature on the left and on the right sides. 5⅝in. (14.29cm) high. c.1785-90.*

Godden collection

Colour Plate 11. *The right side of the New Hall mug shown in Colour Plates 9 and 10. The signature clear of the painting reads 'F. Duvivier pinx'. 5⅝in. (14.29cm) high. c.1785-90.*

Godden collection

Colour Plate 12. *The interior view of the footed centrepiece to the Duvivier-decorated dessert service shown in Plates 65-7 and 195-201 and Colour Plates 13 and 39-44. 11¾in. (29.85cm) long. c.1785-90. See Chapters V and VI.* Godden collection

Colour Plate 13. *One of the dessert service dish forms from the service painted by Fidelle Duvivier for John Daniel, the New Hall factory manager. See also Plates 65-7, 195-201 and Colour Plates 12 and 39-44. 9¾ x 7¼in. (24.77 x 18.42cm). c.1785-90.* Godden collection

Colour Plate 14. *A New Hall moulded dessert plate of characteristic form – see also Colour Plate 44. Well painted in Fidelle Duvivier's typical style (see Chapter V). Diameter 8¼in. (20.96cm). c.1785-90.* Private collection

Colour Plate 15. *The side view of the New Hall covered milk jug illustrated in Plates 72-3 and 114. This illustration shows the stippled effect of Fidelle Duvivier's monochrome ceramic painting. See Chapter V. 5¼in. (13.34cm) high. c.1785-90.* Godden collection

Colour Plate 16. *The front of a magnificent New Hall, clip handled teapot, painted by Fidelle Duvivier. The figures may well be John Daniel (the factory manager) and his sister, as possibly also depicted in Colour Plate 12 (see Chapter V). 6½in. (16.51cm) high. c.1785-90.* Formerly Godden collection

Colour Plate 17. *The reverse side of the New Hall Duvivier decorated teapot shown in Plate 76. Again the good three-dimensional effect can be seen. The choice of subject underlines Duvivier's unconventional approach. 6½in. (16.51cm) high. c.1785-90.* Formerly Godden collection

Colour Plate 18. *A New Hall clip-handled teapot and stand painted by Fidelle Duvivier in a typical monochrome style. Note the typical three-dimensional effect and the windmill or kilns introduced into the background. A trio from the same service is shown in Colour Plate 19. Teapot 6in. (15.24cm) high. c.1785-90.*

Formerly Godden collection

Colour Plate 19. *A New Hall trio of saucer, teabowl and slip-handled coffee cup painted by Fidelle Duvivier in his typical monochrome technique. The three-dimensional style is shown to good effect. These pieces match the teapot and stand shown in Colour Plate 18. Diameter of saucer 5⅛in. (13.02cm). c.1785-90.*

Formerly Godden collection

Colour Plate 20. *A rare New Hall globular teapot (shape as Plates 117-8) well painted by Fidelle Duvivier in his Continental style – see Chapter V. Other pieces from this splendid tea and coffee service are shown in Plate 81. 6¼in. (15.88cm) high. c.1785-90.* Private collection. Photograph Messrs. Phillips

Colour Plate 21. *A silver shape New Hall teapot, dated on the reverse side '1796' (see Plate 85A). The good quality painting is probably by Fidelle Duvivier, although he had reputedly left the factory's full-time employment by this period. See Chapter V and page 183. 6¼in. (15.88cm) high. 1796. A coffee cup from this service is shown in Plate 86.* Roderick Jellicoe

---

Colour Plate 22. *A rare form of early New Hall or perhaps Tunstall period teapot. The moulded handle matches the jugs illustrated in Colour Plates 6-7 and that on the teapot shown in Colour Plate 4. The saucer form shown in Plate 40 may also relate to this shape. The unnumbered pattern is also featured in Plates 42, 97, 99 and 133. 6½in. (16.51cm) high. c.1782-5.* Private collection

Colour Plate 23. *An attractive and well-decorated New Hall teabowl and saucer, showing the quality of potting and design reached at quite an early stage in the factory's development. Diameter 5in. (12.7cm). c.1784-7.* Private collection

Colour Plate 24. *A New Hall tall version of a popular moulded cream jug form known as a 'Chelsea Ewer', made at several factories, in the 'low' (as Plate 92) and 'tall' version. Early moulded handle form. Painted standard design, later numbered 20. 3¾in. (9.53cm) high. c.1783-6.* Godden collection

Colour Plate 25. *Three small so-called 'Robin' cream jugs, decorated with different early enamelled patterns and with two handle forms. Even the simplest of basic shapes can be treated in many different ways. See Chapter VI. 2½ and 2¾in. (6.35 and 6.99cm) high. c.1785-90.* Godden collection

COLOUR PLATE 26. *Two early New Hall cream or milk jugs. The one with the exterior top border has its cover, see page 195. Note the characteristic painted decoration or trim on the handles. 4¼ and 5½in. (10.8 and 13.97cm) high. c.1784-8.* GODDEN COLLECTION

COLOUR PLATE 27. *A large size tea service plate and a trio showing the rare moulded forms matching those blue and gilt teawares in Plates 102-5. The pattern number for this design is not at present known. Diameter of plate 8½in. (21.59cm). c.1784-8.*
GODDEN COLLECTION

COLOUR PLATE 28. *A rare New Hall globular teapot with moulded ribbed handle (see also Plates 99, 107 left, 118 and 229). Enamelled early pattern (a version of that numbered 3). Firing fault to knob, later repair to tip of spout. 6½in. (16.51cm) high. c.1784-8. Shown with an early ribbed-handled coffee cup, with variant border on inside.* GODDEN COLLECTION

COLOUR PLATE 29. *A New Hall ribbed coffee pot with moulded spout of the type found on some teapots (Plates 147-8). The simple enamelled pattern was later numbered 20. 9¾in. (24.77cm) high. c.1785-90.* PRIVATE COLLECTION

COLOUR PLATE 30. *A faceted New Hall so-called silver shape teapot (with four applied floret feet, as Plates 138, 141 or 145). Moulded spout with leafage under and herring-bone style handle. Shown with its stand. Enamelled pattern, later numbered 22. Teapot 8¾in. (22.23cm) long. c.1785-90.* GODDEN COLLECTION

COLOUR PLATE 31. *A New Hall globular teapot with Derby-style inset footrim. Moulded spout and handle of conventional type with pierced knob – see also Plate 148. Enamelled popular early pattern later numbered 121. 6½in. (16.51cm) high. c.1785-90.* GODDEN COLLECTION

COLOUR PLATE 32. *A large New Hall silver shape teapot from a service each piece of which is hand painted with Kent views copied from a book published in 1793. Richly gilt ornamentation – see Plates 157-8. 6¼in. (15.88cm) high. c.1793-6.* GODDEN COLLECTION

COLOUR PLATE 33. *A well-decorated New Hall fluted bread and butter plate from a tea service of pattern 160. See also Plate 156. The quality of the painting and gilding perhaps suggests Fidelle Duvivier as the artist. Painted pattern number N160. Diameter 7¼in. (18.42cm). c.1790.* GODDEN COLLECTION

COLOUR PLATE 34. *A New Hall globular teapot with plain (non-moulded) spout and inset cover – compare with the earlier version shown in Colour Plate 32. Enamelled pattern 195, with inscription, names and date 1798. Painted pattern number N 195. 5¾in. (14.61cm) high. 1798.* GODDEN COLLECTION

COLOUR PLATE 35. *A late New Hall silver shape teapot of conventional type, close copies having been produced at several contemporary English factories. Enamelled pattern 660 (?), inscribed and dated '1804'. 6¼in. (15.88cm) high. 1804.* GODDEN COLLECTION

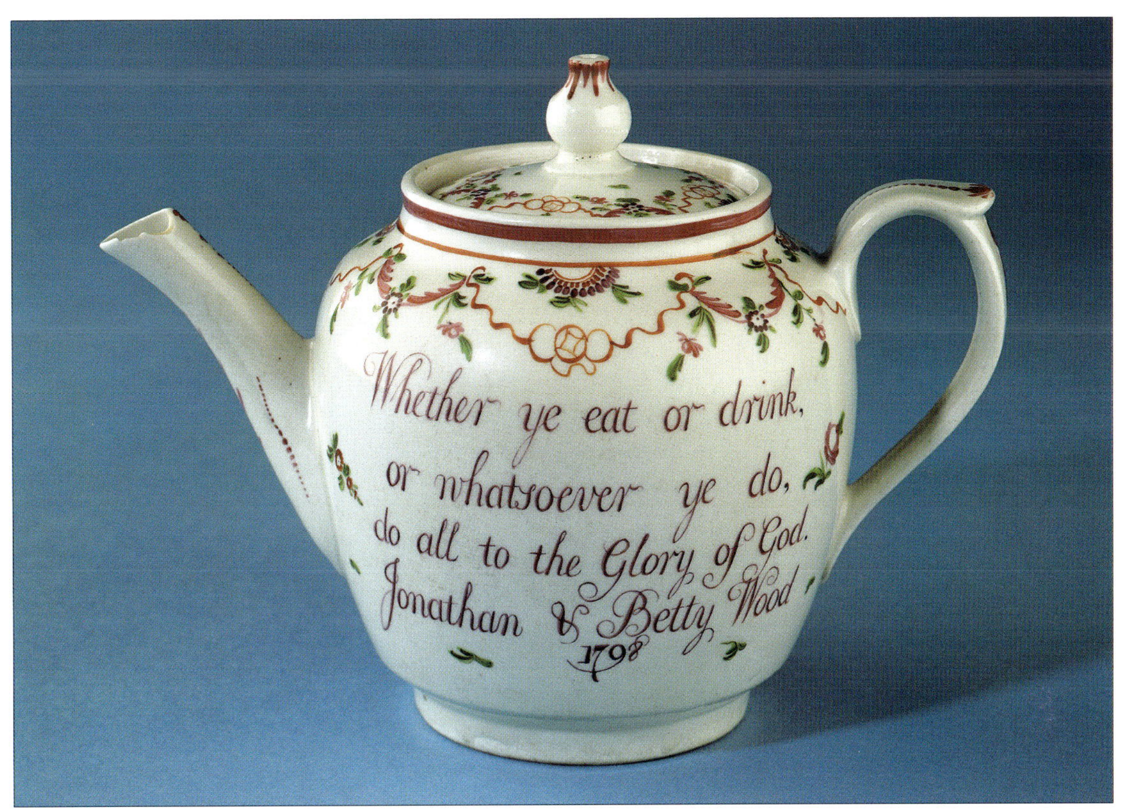

Whether ye eat or drink,
or whatsoever ye do,
do all to the Glory of God.
Jonathan & Betty Wood
1798

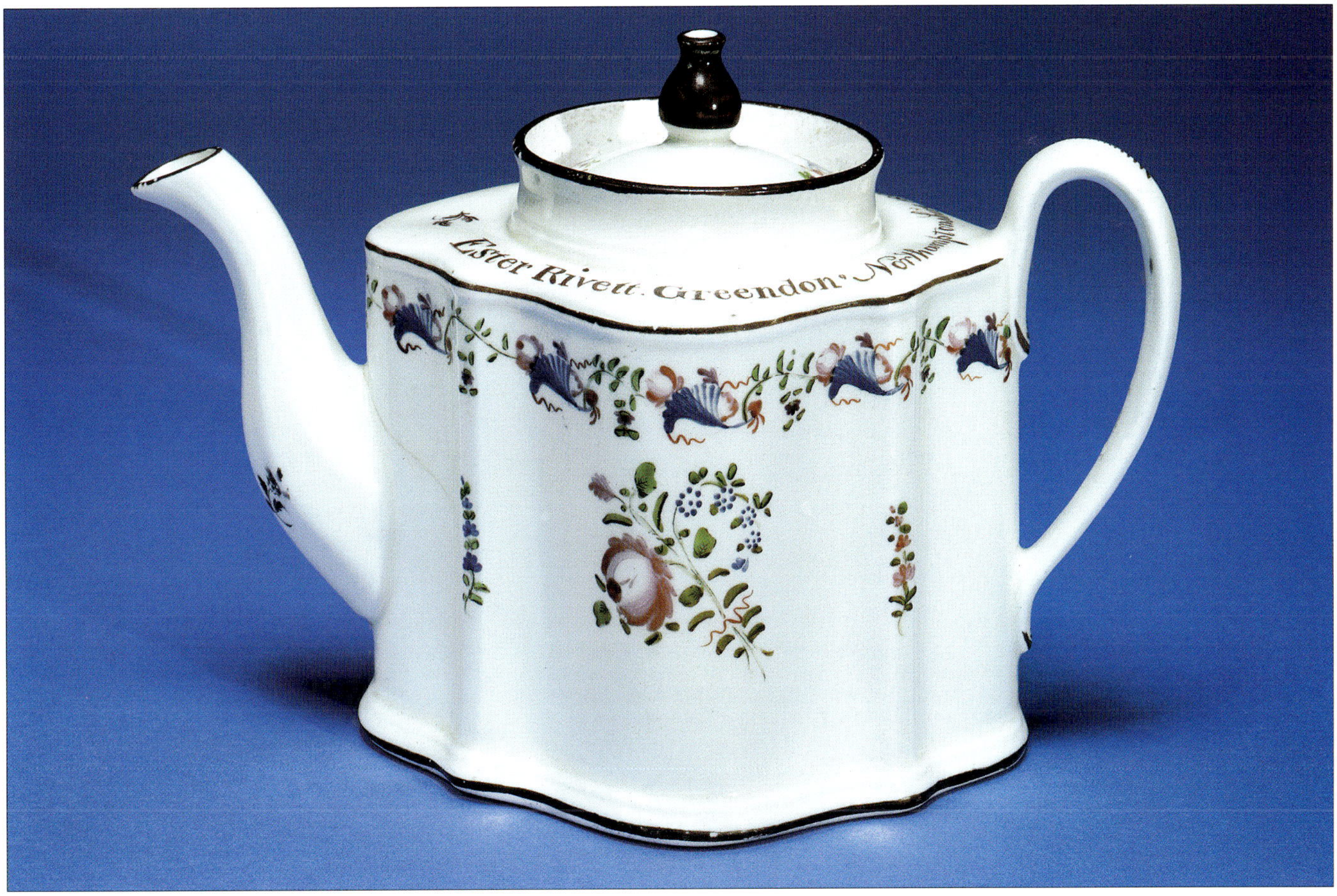
Ester Rivett. Greendon.

Colour Plate 36. *New Hall teawares decorated with pattern 446 (as ordered by Wedgwoods in 1812 – see page 251). This and other patterns can occur with slightly different gilt trim (see Plate 187). Prow-form teapot 10½in. (26.67cm) long. c.1810-5.* Godden of Worthing

Colour Plate 37. *Representative pieces of a New Hall tea service of pattern 571, with prow-form teapot, but loop handles to the cups and cans. Painted pattern number on teapot and sugar basin. Teapot 10½in. (26.67cm) long. c.1810-15.* Godden of Worthing

Colour Plate 40. *The stand to a dessert tureen (or basket) being part of the dessert service made for John Daniel, the New Hall factory manager. See Chapter V. Repair to left edge. 9¼ x 7¾in. (23.5 x 19.69cm). c.1785-90.* Private collection

---

Colour Plate 38. *A superb quality New Hall prow-form teapot from a service of pattern number 611, each piece painted with a slightly different basket of flowers. Painted pattern number 611. 10¼in. (26.04cm) long. c.1810-5.* Godden of Worthing

Colour Plate 39. *The smaller of two covered tureens (for cream and for sugar) in the New Hall dessert service painted by Fidelle Duvivier for John Daniel. See Chapter V and Plates 65-7 and 195-201. 6¼in. (15.88cm) high. c.1785-90.* Private collection

Colour Plate 41. *One of four deep, side dishes with very well modelled handles, being part of the New Hall dessert service painted by Fidelle Duvivier. See Chapter V and Plate 195. 8¾ x 8½in. (22.23 x 21.59cm). c.1785-90.* Private collection

---

Colour Plate 42. *One of the shaped edged side dishes (of slightly different sizes – see Plate 197) being part of the dessert service painted by Fidelle Duvivier. See Chapters V and VI. 11½ x 8½in. (29.21 x 21.59cm). c.1785-90.* Private collection

Colour Plate 43. *One of a pair of New Hall side dishes being part of the dessert service painted by Fidelle Duvivier with local contemporary views. See Chapters V and VI. The pair to this dish, showing a horse-racing scene, is shown in Colour Plate 13. 9¾ x 7¼in. (24.77 x 18.42cm). c.1785-90.* Private collection

Colour Plate 44. *One of the twelve moulded, ribbed, dessert plates being part of the New Hall service shown in Plate 195. Painted in Fidelle Duvivier's typical style – see Chapter V. Other pieces from this service are shown in Plates 65-7 and 195-201. Diameter 8¼in. (20.96cm). c.1785-90.* Private collection

---

Colour Plates 45 and 45A. *A rare New Hall footed centrepiece with openwork edge. Such a piece (or a pair) could have been included in some dessert services of the type shown in Plate 195 and discussed in Chapter VI. 4in. (10.16cm) high. c.1785-90.* Private collection

Colour Plate 46. *A rare New Hall moulded cabbage-leaf jug, with a slightly different and rather later handle form than that shown in Colour Plate 7 – see Plate 213. 8¼in. (20.96cm) high. c.1784-8.*
Godden collection

Colour Plate 47. *A large New Hall clip handled jug, painted with the popular early pattern later numbered 20. See Plate 217 for the front side. 7¾in. (19.69cm) high. c.1790-5.* Godden collection

Colour Plate 48. *A very rare form of New Hall jug, incorporating earlier spout and moulded handle shapes. Painted with neat landscape panels on each side. 6in. (15.24cm) high. c.1790-5.*
Messrs. Phillips

Colour Plate 49. *A New Hall clip handled jug of a very popular type – see Plates 219-26. These were often used for presentation gifts and several bear initials – see Colour Plates 50-2. These jugs were made in different sizes. 7½in. (19.05cm) high. c.1795-1800.*
Private collection

Colour Plate 50. *A typical New Hall clip handled jug, the top border enamelled and gilt with pattern 436. Initials within gilt framework under spout. 7½in. (19.05cm) high. c.1795-1800.*
Godden of Worthing

Colour Plate 51. *A typical New Hall presentation jug with gilt initials to the front. Each side painted with a bold floral spray. 7½in. (19.05cm) high. c.1800-10.* J.A. Ward

Colour Plate 52. *A magnificent New Hall presentation jug with initials under the spout and superb floral painting under gilt Greek key border. 7½in. (19.05cm) high. c.1800-10.* Private collection

Colour Plate 53. *A rare New Hall moulded jug (as Colour Plate 46) decorated with an underglaze blue printed version of the 'Gazebo' pattern (see Chapter VII and Plates 241-9). See Colour Plates 54-5 for other views of this jug and its prints. 5½in. (13.97cm) high. c.1784-8.* Godden collection

Colour Plate 54. *The reverse side of the rare moulded jug illustrated in Colour Plate 53 showing the remaining parts of the popular early blue printed 'Gazebo' pattern, as shown in Plates 241-9. 5½in. (13.97cm) high. c.1784-8.* Godden collection

Colour Plate 55. *The front view of the New Hall moulded jug illustrated in Colour Plates 53-4, illustrating some of the small sprays of flowers used as space fillers. These can occur on other early New Hall porcelains such as Plate 265. See also Plates 237-9. 5½in. (13.97cm) high. c.1784-8.* Godden collection

Colour Plate 56. *A New Hall teapot as Plates 147-8, bearing a rare underglaze blue print, as Plate 268. The reverse side is shown in Plate 270. 6½in. (16.51cm) high. c.1785-90.* The late A. de Saye Hutton

Colour Plate 57. *A New Hall teapot stand (to a silver shape pot) decorated with a typical but not common Oriental style underglaze blue landscape print including two moths or butterflies. See also Plate 287. 7¾ x 6½in. (19.69 x 16.51cm). c.1795-1805.* Godden collection

COLOUR PLATE 58. *A New Hall lobed edge dish from a dessert service decorated in blue (in the Sèvres style with gilding). See Plate 208 for related shapes. 10¾ x 8¾in. (27.31 x 22.23cm). c.1790-5.*

THE LATE A. DE SAYE HUTTON

COLOUR PLATE 59. *A New Hall oval form teapot and stand (see Plates 166 and 168-9 for related teaware shapes) decorated with the popular 425 pattern. This is based on a printed outline coloured over by hand. See Chapter VIII. 6¾in. (17.15cm) high. c.1797-1803.*

GODDEN OF WORTHING

Colour Plate 60. *A hand-painted New Hall Chinese style cup and saucer of superb quality. The simpler and the printed outline designs were less expensive to produce and therefore sold in larger quantities. Note the circular ring handle to the upturned Bute shape teacup (see Plate 362). Diameter of saucer 5½in. (13.97cm). c.1810-15.*

Godden of Worthing

Colour Plate 61. *The interior view of a New Hall large bowl, often termed 'punch bowls', painted with the popular figure design numbered 20. The border is taken from New Hall's pattern 195. See Chapter VIII and Plate 310 for the exterior view. Diameter 9in. (22.86cm). c.1795-1805.*

Godden of Worthing

Colour Plate 62. *A bat-printed New Hall coffee can and saucer, with gilt border. Part of a service of pattern 511, most pieces of which would have different bat-printed designs within the same border. See Chapter IX. Can 6¼in. (15.88cm) high. c.1805.*

W.A. Brown collection

Colour Plate 63. *A rare form of New Hall jug or coffee pot, bearing one of a popular series of figure subject bat prints. See also Colour Plate 64 for a coloured-in version. 9¾in. (24.77cm) high. c.1805-10.*

Private collection

Colour Plate 64. *One of two plates from a New Hall bone china tea service bearing a coloured-in version of the popular children bird's nesting subject bat print. See also Colour Plate 63. Painted pattern number 984. Diameter 8¼in. (20.96cm). c.1814-6.*

Godden collection

Colour Plate 65. *A New Hall bone china coffee pot of a standard shape. Decorated with a coloured-in bat print. One of the many popular prints used with this gilt trim to make up services of pattern 1053. See Chapter IX and Plate 339 for the reverse side. 9in. (22.86cm) high. c.1814-8.* Godden of Worthing

Colour Plate 66. *The interior view of a decorative blue ground New Hall bone china punch bowl. The reserves decorated with various coloured-in bat printed designs. See Chapter IX and Plate 342 for the exterior view. Painted pattern number 1277. Diameter 9in. (22.86cm). c.1815-20.* Godden of Worthing

Colour Plate 67. *The main pieces from a New Hall bone china tea service, showing typical London shapes (first version, see Chapter X). This set of pattern 1092 shows a selection of coloured-in bat-printed designs on a light blue ground with gilding. See also Plate 345 for tally marks on the cans. Painted pattern number 1092 on these major pieces but not on the cup and saucers. Diameter of plate 8¼in. c.1814-8.*

Godden of Worthing

Colour Plate 68. *Three New Hall bone china London shape milk jugs bearing typical bat-printed designs. The trim or border patterns relate to different patterns; left to right 1140, 984, 1357. For matching teaware shapes see Colour Plate 67 and Plates 336-7. 4in. (10.16cm) high. c.1815-20.*

Godden collection

Colour Plate 69. *A New Hall bone china bread and butter or cake plate from a service decorated with different coloured-in bat-printed fruit compositions. See Plate 352 for a related London shape cup and saucer. Unknown pattern but similar to 1357. Diameter 8¾in. (22.23cm). c.1820-5.* Private collection

Colour Plate 70. *Representative pieces from a New Hall bone china London shape tea service. The popular so-called 'Japan style' pattern incorporating underglaze blue with overglaze enamels and gilding is pattern number 1153. Painted pattern number on major pieces. Teapot 5¾in. (14.61cm). high. c.1815-20.*

Godden of Worthing

Colour Plate 71. *A New Hall moulded bread and butter plate of pattern 1944. For related teawares see Plates 373-4. Painted pattern number. Diameter 8½in. (21.59cm). c.1823-8.*
Private collection

Colour Plate 72. *The smaller of two bread and butter or cake plates from the New Hall bone china London shape (second version, see Chapter X) tea service shown in Plate 378. This is a particularly well decorated late New Hall pattern. Painted pattern number 2215. Diameter 8in. (20.32cm). c.1825.* Private collection

Colour Plate 73. *A New Hall bone china teapot decorated with pattern 3050. This form was popular at all factories and similar shapes were made at most factories – Ridgways, Rockingham etc. Painted pattern number 3050. 6½in. (16.51cm) high.* Private collection

Colour Plate 74. *A moulded New Hall bone china milk jug and a coffee cup and saucer decorated with pattern 4/3753. Incised dated (?) '1831' under the cup. Jug 3½in. (8.89cm) high. 1831.* Dr. G. Audley

Colour Plate 75. *A New Hall two-handled chocolate or caudle cup (missing the stand and cover). Typical coloured-in bat-printed fruit composition. The reverse side is shown in Plate 405. 2⅞in. (7.3cm) high. c.1810-20.* Private collection

Colour Plate 76. *A New Hall bone china dessert service tureen, with typical relief moulding shape 'B' (see page 388). Related services are shown in Plates 413-8, often with coloured backgrounds. Pattern probably 2239. 5¾in. (14.61cm) high. c.1818-25.* The late A. de Saye Hutton

Colour Plate 77. *A New Hall bone china dessert plate, shape 'B'. Each piece in a service would have slightly different coloured-in bat-printed designs but with the same borders and gilt trim. Pattern 1706, as Plates 415-7. Diameter 8½in. (21.59cm). c.1818-25.* David Golding

Colour Plate 78. *A decorative New Hall dessert dish of shape 'C' (see page 390). Relief moulded border. The centre painted with one of many popular designs relating to Dr. Syntax's adventures. See Plate 425 for a grouping of similar dessert wares. Pattern 2623. 12in. (30.48cm) long. c.1822-7.* W. Kirkby

Colour Plate 79. *A well-decorated New Hall dessert plate of pattern 3664. Moulded shape 'D' (page 391) as also illustrated in Plates 431-4. The hand-painted centres would be different on each piece in the service. Painted pattern number 3664. Diameter 9½in. (24.13cm). c.1828-33.* Private collection

Colour Plate 80. *A rare form of New Hall bone china jug, decorated with coloured-in standard bat-printed designs. Inscribed and dated 1814 in gold. The reverse side is shown in Plate 330. 6in. (15.24cm) high. 1814.* Private collection

Colour Plate 81. *A large New Hall inscribed presentation jug, well painted each side with floral sprays. The front is illustrated in Colour Plate 82. Moulded handle of standard type, see Plates 438-42 and 446. 9½in. (24.13cm) high. c.1816-22.* Messrs. Bonhams

Colour Plate 82. *The front of the New Hall bone china presentation jug illustrated in Colour Plate 81. Made for the Cambridge Cricket Club and sold in 1992 for £4,000. 9½in. (24.13cm) high. c.1816-22.* Messrs. Bonhams

Preface

Having established that Richard Champion, the Bristol porcelain manufacturer, was successful in selling his patent rights to produce translucent porcelain using china stone and china clay to a consortium of Staffordshire potters and other backers, we might first briefly consider the situation in the market which the new partnership was to join and later influence.

If we take the position in 1780, the china dealers and therefore the private buyers would have enjoyed a wide choice of decorative tablewares, especially the popular porcelain tea services. We have the major English firms such as Caughley, Derby, Lowestoft and Worcester supplemented by imports from France and Germany and, of course, the vast quantities imported from China.

In addition there were smaller concerns which must have seemed large and threatening to a partnership about to enter the market. Of these smaller firms we should especially remember the so-called Baddeley-Littler porcelains, Hugh Booth's wares, the Isleworth porcelains and the various porcelain makers at Liverpool – Philip Christian and Co., John Pennington and probably Pennington & Part – to name only the manufacturers known to us today.

Details of these and other firms are listed in my general book *The Encyclopaedia of British Porcelain Manufacturers* (Barrie & Jenkins, 1988) and in some specialist works or learned papers. I must resist the temptation to illustrate here typical products made by these other firms, but the competition facing the New Staffordshire partnership in the 1780s was very strong.

Obviously, some of the fashionable shapes and styles of decoration that were to be employed by the new firm were already in production and had been tried and tested by existing porcelain manufacturers.

Equally clearly, new enterprising manufacturers would amend some traditional forms and designs and gradually introduce their own styles. The most successful of these would in turn be copied by their competitors, new and old. This proved to be all too true and in later years everybody seemed to be copying traditional New Hall forms – such as the so-called silver shaped teapots and the simple, if cottagy, New Hall floral designs. The New Hall firm turned out to be a market leader within a few years of its establishment in 1781 or 1782.

We can to some extent gauge the market position from contemporary archives or letters. When Richard Egan was establishing his retail business in Bath in the early 1790s, his son-in-law Joseph Lygo, the manager of the Derby showrooms in London, gave him in a series of letters much good advice on the most saleable stock to order for his new business.

Pride of place in a letter dated 13 November 1792 was 'Foreign China': 'The six boxes you mention being come are full of Foreign China from Fleet Street, they are our boxes which I sent them – there is more of theirs coming'. Whilst these porcelains could have been French porcelains, the description 'Foreign' is more likely to have been ascribed to Chinese porcelains – ever fashionable in the eighteenth century. Plates 1-7 show just a few examples of the East India Company's bulk importations of Chinese porcelains. The scale and range of these eighteenth century imports from China is explained in my book *Oriental Export Market Porcelain and its Influence on European Wares* (Granada Publishing Ltd., 1979).

In a letter dated 25 January 1793 Joseph Lygo mentions sending 'a few things from Turners'. It was, I feel sure, Turners' London premises at 82 Fleet Street which supplied the 'Foreign China'. Lygo did considerable business with Messrs. Turner & Abbott and with the succeeding firm of Abbott and Newbury. Their stock of Chinese and French porcelains was sold by Harry Phillips in April 1799, after which this large firm of retailers concentrated on marketing English goods. Good details of these London retailers and of the Turners' products are given in Bevis Hillier's standard book *Master Potters of the Industrial Revolution, The Turners of Lane End* (Cory, Adams & Mackay, London, 1965). Joseph Lygo's letter of November 1792 also noted 'five crates full of Blue and white Staffordshire ware from Spodes'. This admittedly was earthenware rather than porcelain but the blue designs of the 1790s would have been in the Oriental style and would have competed with, and undersold, the New Hall blue and white porcelains. Richard Egan was also advised to order 'black teapots' (basalt ware) from Mr. Yates.[1] Whilst the new Staffordshire partnership was formed solely to produce a new type of porcelain (related to the hard-paste Bristol porcelains of the c.1770-80 period), it must be remembered that several of the partners were leading earthenware manufacturers of the period (see Chapter IV). They produced and continued to produce good quality fashionable earthenwares, creamwares, pearlwares, coloured bodies such as jasper or the black basalt teapots which Richard Egan, the new Bath retailer was advised to stock.

The better quality up-market porcelains were supplied from the Derby shop in London: 'I have sent you 9 boxes full of Derby China'. It would seem that the less expensive porcelains, the standard tea services, were to be supplied by the New Hall Company – by 1792 well known by this name, if not by reference to the personal names of the partners: 'I do not know the names of the People at the New Hall China works but if you direct a letter to the Proprietors it will be the same, order their goods by the waggon immediately.'

Other china sellers ('Chinamen') in Bath or in other fashionable towns would also have stocked the standard Chinese porcelains, Derby or assortments from other factories – Flight at Worcester, the Chamberlain works also at Worcester, the Caughley porcelains from Shropshire or even, as I previously suggested, some late Liverpool or Lowestoft porcelains.

The competition which the New Hall management had to contend with has been greatly underestimated. Some of these firms were to produce a type of hard-paste porcelain which we now tend to term 'hybrid hard-paste' porcelain. I believe this description was coined by David Holgate, to define the New Hall porcelain body which had usually been referred to as a hard-paste porcelain. We now consider the only eighteenth century English true hard-paste porcelains were those produced at Plymouth (c.1768-70) and at Bristol (c.1770-81).

It is important to quote David Holgate's definitions of what we now term 'hybrid hard-paste' for that is the body the new Staffordshire partnership produced from the early 1780s up to about 1812.

> ...Any porcelain which is composed principally of china-stone and china clay must be called 'hard-paste,' but in order to distinguish those factories like Plymouth and Bristol which used the same process as the Chinese from those like New Hall, Coalport and Chamberlain, which used the earthenware and soft-paste porcelain firing sequence, a sub-set can be named 'hybrid hard-paste' porcelain – a hybrid between the hard-paste composition and the soft-paste process...

The soft-paste process was, of course, a high first firing before the piece was glazed and a lower second firing which was merely needed to melt and mature the glaze. The traditional hard-paste technique was either to use only one firing for the glazed body or to set the biscuit (unglazed body) with a low first firing and to resubmit the glazed article to its highest temperature (some 1350°C or higher) which matured the body and glaze together.

It must not be thought that the New Hall partners were to be the only firm to produce this hybrid body, which can appear quite hard. By the 1790s several rival firms were producing a similar type of porcelain and used similar styles of decoration – to our great confusion today, for all these wares are unmarked.

There were at least two ways in which other potters could produce porcelain using the two basic true porcelain ingredients – china clay and china stone (covered by Cookworthy's patent up to 1796).

First, the New Hall partners could have licensed others to produce similar porcelains on the payment of a suitable fee or royalty. Richard Champion of Bristol in his letters makes it clear that he would be open to such arrangements. He or the new owners of the patent could then receive licence income without the risk of producing the porcelains and having to find buyers! We also have no knowledge of the arrangements made between the remaining partners and their former colleagues, Anthony Keeling and John Turner. These two potters, who were later to make their own porcelains, had after all been parties to the purchase of the patent rights from Champion.

Secondly, the patent could be disregarded or circumnavigated. The Act published in 1775 and dated 29 November 1774 contains the following important clause:

> Provided also, that nothing in this Act contained shall be construed to hinder or prevent any Potter or Potters, or any other Person or Persons, from making use of any such raw materials or any Mixture or Mixtures thereof (except such mixture of Raw materials, and in such proportion, as are described in the specification herein before directed to be enrolled), any thing in this Act to the contrary notwithstanding.

The official margin note (or Summary) to this clause

reads: 'No Potter, etc. hindered from using the same in different proportions'.

Whilst Richard Champion undoubtedly did his utmost to give his 'specification of the mixture and proportions of the raw materials of which his porcelain and glaze is composed' in wide terms, it was probably still possible for others at least to claim that different proportions were used. Also, other ingredients could be added to make a new mix unique to another maker.

It is now generally accepted that various English porcelains of the late 1780s and the 1790s were of the hybrid hard-paste type containing, like the New Hall mix, the china clay and china stone. This is not to state, however, that all manufacturers of this period favoured this basic class of porcelain. Several did not make hybrid hard-paste porcelains; these included Derby, Isleworth, Lowestoft, Pinxton and Worcester.

We can now proceed to discover how this all came about, how William Cookworthy's original patent, sold to Richard Champion of Bristol, came to be resold in Staffordshire and how the resulting partnership produced attractive and serviceable porcelains that were widely acknowledged as 'New Hall'. This enterprise lasted (with several changes within the partnership) from the early 1780s to the mid-1830s, from George III's time nearly into the Victorian era.

---

1. These black basalt teapots would have been from John Yates of Shelton. The Yates basalt was highly regarded over a long period, but at this period was seemingly unmarked.

CHAPTER I

The West Country Connection

It can be fairly claimed that the story of Staffordshire's 'New Hall' porcelain commenced in the West Country in the 1760s. One might also assert that it dated back to the seventeenth and early eighteenth century Chinese porcelains that were flooding into Europe and, in so doing, set totally new standards for the production of this wonderful new white translucent material – true porcelain.

One certainly cannot compare the late eighteenth century so-called 'New Hall' porcelains to the finest of the Chinese but, on a lower plane, some of these Staffordshire porcelains can be comparable to the later mass shipments of Chinese wares imported by the English East India Company. I have in mind the popular Chinese export market types represented by Plates 1-7. Certainly, the Oriental hard-paste porcelain imports inspired the search for the necessary raw materials in the British Isles and then the mastery of the many manufacturing difficulties in order to produce a native British china that could compete on equal terms with the Oriental importations.

Most of my readers will no doubt be aware that the first successful efforts to produce porcelain in England dated from the mid-1740s when manufactories at Bow, Chelsea and Limehouse in London produced their own reasonably good, semi-translucent body of the soft-paste type. Lacking the availability of the *Kaolin* (silicate of alumina) and *Petuntse* (silicate of alumina, potash and soda) of the Chinese or, in other words, the Cornish 'china clay' and 'china stone,' the early English porcelain makers could only produce various types of artificial porcelain containing varying clays, glass, soaprock, bone ash and suchlike materials that would fire, or mature, at a relatively low temperature before collapsing into a shapeless mass. The average soft-paste or artificial English porcelain was fired at approximately 1200°C as opposed to the hard-paste or true porcelain bodies which matured and became vitrified and translucent at 1350°C or at a still higher temperature.

Plate 1. *A standard hard-paste Chinese export market globular teapot, enamelled with typical figure panel and borders. 6¼in. (15.88cm) high. c.1770-80.* Private collection

Although the early European soft-paste porcelains were fired at a lower temperature than the true porcelains, they were nevertheless extremely unstable in the kiln and the firing losses were high; even the best examples usually displayed some faults in the body in the form of tears, cracks or warping. It was, I believe, obvious to the manufacturers, if not to the buying public, that the English porcelains were technically inferior to the Oriental which were always held up as the ideal.

The secret of Chinese porcelain was well known to Europeans in the eighteenth century through the letters of Father d'Entrecolles, a Jesuit missionary in China, which contained descriptions of the basic raw materials and the methods of manufacture. These letters (of 1712 and 1722) were later published in France and subsequently translated into English. The great difficulty was to discover deposits of the vital raw materials, the Kaolin and the Petuntse. Attempts had been made to obtain the clays from China but the Chinese naturally sought to prevent this and, as the English were restricted to a few ports (mainly Canton), they were unable to obtain the raw materials located thousands of miles inland. Nevertheless, some attempts to smuggle Kaolin or Petuntse out of China were seemingly successful, although it is doubtful whether European porcelain was ever made from this Chinese material.

Plate 2. *A Chinese export market saucer shape plate enamelled with European style simple floral design. This style was to be much copied by English manufacturers. Diameter 8in. (20.32cm). c.1775-85.*

PRIVATE COLLECTION

Plate 3. *A simple Chinese export market hard-paste teabowl and saucer, with slight ribbing. Such teawares flooded into Europe and were widely copied in England. Diameter of saucer 5¼in. (13.34cm). c.1780-90.*

J. NEWTON COLLECTION

PLATE 4. *Two Chinese export market saucers with typical simple floral enamelled designs, of the type copied by New Hall and other English porcelain manufacturers. Diameter of slightly ribbed saucer 4¾in. (12.07cm). c.1780-90.* GODDEN COLLECTION

However, the following quotations do illustrate the European's quest for the all-important raw materials. My first, taken from the 1705 sale of the goods from the East Indiaman *The Fleet:,* 'One parcell China earth'. This lot was valued or reserved at £3 but sold for £16, much more than was expected. This entry may not refer to *Kaolin* or *Petuntse* imported from China with other eastern goods from this East Indiaman, but it is interesting to note that William Cookworthy used the same description, 'China-earth', when writing of its discovery in North America, see page 72.

In December 1716 an essay was published in London explaining 'a try'd and infallible method' of making china as fine as the East India imports from China. The method was simply to grind up broken Chinese porcelains and mix with quicklime dissolved in 'Gum Water' and to add burnt oyster shells to the mix. Wares were then to be formed and fired. Later accounts relate that mills were at work around London grinding up Chinese porcelain for resale.

Such ground Chinese porcelain may well have been added to earthenware mixes, but it is highly unlikely that any true china would have been made by this method and I merely mention the 1716 essay so as to underline the general desire to emulate the Chinese wares.

An interesting entry occurs in the Court Minutes of the English East India Company of May 1720: 'Letter dated 12th instant directed to the Secretary of the Company and signed "S S" was read relating to earth discovered alledged to be the same sort with that china is made.' Alas, this is only a minuted note and the original letter has not been preserved. We therefore do not know where this clay was discovered – in China, on the Continent, in North America or in Cornwall?

Du Halde's 1738 work *A Description of the Empire of China,* being a translation of the 1735 French original, wherein the letters from Father d'Entrecolles explaining the Chinese methods of porcelain manufacture are quoted, also contains the following statement showing that Chinese clays had found their way to France:

> I have produr'd samples of them from China and put them into the hands of M. de Reamur, one of the members of the Academy of Sciences, who is capable of discovering whether there are any of the same kind in the Provinces of France?[1]

Plate 5. *Hard-paste Chinese porcelain globular teapot of standard export shape and style of decoration. Repaired by a china mender in Bristol and dated 1779. 5¾in. (14.61cm) high. c.1770-77.*
GODDEN COLLECTION

Later it seems that samples were also sent to the Secretary of the Society of Arts in London and these were forwarded to Josiah Wedgwood for a report of the properties. An account of this importation of Chinese raw materials by J. Bradley Blake, the East India Company agent in Canton, was reported in *The Gentleman's Magazine* in 1776.

The English translation of Abbé Grosier's *A General Description of China,* published in London in 1795, contains yet another long account of the Chinese methods of producing porcelain and includes the following observation:

> It is from the Kaolin, that fine porcelain derives all its strength ... It is very extraordinary, that a soft earth should give strength and consistency to the Petuntse, which is procured from the hardest rocks. A rich Chinese merchant told Father d'Entrecolles that the English and Dutch had purchased some of the Petuntse, which they had transported to Europe, with a design of making porcelain; but, having carried with them none of the Kaolin, their attempt proved abortive, as they have since acknowledged. They wanted, said this Chinese, laughing, to form a body-the flesh of which would support itself without bones.'

As reasonably full descriptions of the raw materials needed to make true porcelains were freely available in Europe, and partly because some samples had been imported, interested persons in England would have had a good inkling of what to seek as well as a knowledge of the general properties and appearance of the Chinese *Kaolin* and *Petuntse,* the vital raw materials necessary to produce true porcelains.

No doubt several Europeans were seeking such materials, but the one destined to recognise them in Cornwall was William Cookworthy, born of Quaker parents on 12 April 1705. He was later, after the death of his father, apprenticed to two successful chemists in London, Timothy and Silvanus Bevan. On completing this apprenticeship he moved to Plymouth to manage at the age of twenty a new pharmacy under the style Bevan and Cookworthy. I do not propose to dwell on Cookworthy's early career for two excellent books detail his life: John Penderill-Church's *William Cookworthy 1705/1780* (Bradford Barton, Truro, 1972) and A. Douglas Selleck's *Cookworthy 1705-1780 and his Circle* (Baron Jay Ltd., Plymouth, 1978). Dr. F. Severne MacKenna's paper

'William Cookworthy and the Plymouth Factory; An Updating', as published in the *Transactions of the English Ceramic Circle* Vol. II, Part 2 (1982), is also of great interest. However, I must mention that William Cookworthy was no mere country chemist interested only in local affairs or in making a living. Jabez Fischer, a visitor from America, noted on 1 January 1775: 'Spent the whole day ... with William Cookworthy, canvassing politics, religion, history, etc. etc. The most sensible, learned, kind man I ever knew, the history of every nation is familiar to him, he has explored every country, understands many languages, an amazing memory ... Catholic in the extreme (deep in argument) meek, humble and divested of the least particle of vanity, pedantry or any one disagreeable sentiment, in short the most refined and accomplished man...'. And all this recorded in a personal diary, not in a sweeping obituary.

As early as 1745 William Cookworthy had shown a keen interest in producing porcelain or at least in the search for the raw materials. In a now famous letter written from Plymouth in 1745 to Richard Hingston he wrote:

> ...I had, lately with me, the person[2] who hath discovered the China-earth. He had several samples of the china ware, of their making, with him; which were, I think, equal to the Asiatic. T'was found in the back of Virginia, where he was in quest of mines; and having read Du Halde, discovered both the Petunse and Kaulin [*sic*] 'Tis this latter earth, he says, is the essential thing towards the success of the Manufacture. He is gone for a cargo of it, having bought the whole country of the Indians, where it rises. They can import it for £13 the ton; and by that means afford their china as cheap as common stone ware. But they intend only to go about 30 per Cent under the Company. The man is a Quaker by profession but seems to be as thorough a Deist, as I have ever met with. He knows a good deal about mineral affairs, but not *funditus*...

(I have used the rendering of this letter as given by Dr. MacKenna in his 1982 paper. This differs from other versions of the now destroyed original in several respects.)

The 'Company' was no doubt the East India Company whose imports from China they hoped to undersell. It is also possible that the intended manufacturers were the Bow partnership who reputedly used 'unaker' from America. Can this 'person who has discovered the China Earth' have been the 'S S' who wrote to the East India Company in 1720, about newly discovered 'earth ... the same sort with what china is made'? However, it should be stated that there is a very strong case for believing that Cookworthy's visitor was Andrew Duché who seemingly had made true porcelain in America in the early 1740s. The background to this belief was given by Dr. F. Severne MacKenna in his *Cookworthy's Plymouth and Bristol Porcelain* (F. Lewis, Leigh-on-Sea, 1946), pages 21-6. However, that writer later slightly modified his views and pointed out that Cookworthy did not state that his visitor was a true Quaker, only that he professed to be one, quite a different matter. Again the reader is referred to Dr. MacKenna's 1982 E.C.C. paper.

In about 1755 William Cookworthy discovered (or later claimed to have discovered) in Cornwall first the *Kaolin* and then the *Petuntse* (the Cornish moor-stone, a form of decomposed granite). Of this discovery Cookworthy was later to record in an undated account:

> It is now nearly twenty years since I discovered that the ingredients used by the Chinese in the composition of their Porcelain were to be got, in immense quantities, in the County of Cornwall...
> I first discovered it in the parish of Germoe, in a hill called Tregonnin Hill...
> Caulin [Kaolin] ... constitutes the bones as the Petuntse does the flesh, of chinaware. It is a white talcy earth, found in our granite country in both the counties of Devon and Cornwall ... the sort I have chiefly tried is what is got from the side of Tregonnin Hill, where there are several pits of it ... I have lately discovered that, in the neighbourhood of the parish of St Stephens in Cornwall, there are immense quantities both of Petuntse stone and the Caulin [Kaolin] ... by the

PLATE 6. *A large Chinese export market mug, hand-painted in underglaze blue with a typical landscape with water. 8in. (20.32cm) high. c.1770-80.* J.A. HAMPTON COLLECTION

experiments I have made on them, they produce a much whiter body, and do not shrink so much, by far, in baking nor take stains so readily from the fire...

Our method of dipping (glazing) was just the same as is used by the Delft-ware people, We first baked our ware to a soft biscuit which would suck [the water in the glaze]; then, painted it with blue, and dipped them with the same ease; and the glazing goes hard and dry, as soon as it does in the Delft ware ... the Jesuits observe that the Chinese paint and glaze their ware on the raw body. I know, this can be done, for I have done it...[3]

In regard to burning ... coal, will not do for our body, at least when it is composed of the materials ofTregonnin Hill ... the only furnace or kiln, which we have tried with any degree of success is the kiln used by the potters who make brown stone. It is called the 36 hole kiln. Wood is the fuel used in it.

William Cookworthy closed his account of his manufacturing processes by discussing the 'safeguards' or saggars and writes of the 'tingeing vapours, which have given us so much trouble. Experience must determine the best form and way of using this kiln...'.

This memorandum preserved at the Swedenborg Institute is, as I have stated, undated, but it was probably written between a possibly early experimental period at Bristol late in 1765 and his taking out the Patent to 'make, use, exercise and vend a Kind of Porcelain newly Invented by me, compos' d of Moorstone or Growan and Growan clay' at Plymouth early in 1768 (Patent 898 of 1768 – see Appendix I). I have considerably abbreviated the full text which is given *in toto* in various specialist books such as *Cookworthy 1705-80 and his Circle* by A. Douglas Selleck. The statement that 'coal will not do for our body' is interesting for in a letter dated 21 December 1766 he had stated 'we have no reason to question but that we shall be able [to] use Newcastle Coals as fuel which will be vastly cheaper than wood'.

It would appear that William Cookworthy had experimented with the use of these native raw materials in or before 1758 for Borlase's 1758 work *Natural History of Cornwall* records that the moor-stone '...if I have been rightly informed by a gentleman who has tried many experiments this way is most proper for making porcelain'. A footnote names the gentleman as a 'Mr Cookworthy of Plymouth'.

There are other and rather later contemporary references to porcelain-making in Bristol before the Plymouth period and the 1768 patent. These references occur in a series of letters written by Richard Champion. One dated 7 November 1765 refers, in part, to 'a new work, just established. This new work is from a Clay and Stone discovered in Cornwall, which answers the description of the Chinese. But in burning there is a deficiency; though the body is perfectly white within, but not without which is always smoky'. In a further letter dated 15 December 1765, Champion stated 'The Cornish materials are ... not so pure as the Cherokee (American) ... as they meet with many difficulties with the Cornish... I have had your clay tried at the Works here, which is now given up, as they could not bum the ware clean...'. In another letter dated 28 February 1766 he wrote of 'a Manufactory set up here some time ago, on the principal of the Chinese Porcelain; but not being successful is given up ... the Proprietors of the Works in Bristol imagined they had discovered in Cornwall all the materials similar to the Chinese, but though they burnt the body part tolerably well, yet there were impurities in the Glaze or Stone which were insurmountable, even in the greatest fire they could give it and which was equal to a Glass-house heat'.

PLATE 7. *A Chinese export market milk jug and cover. Painted in underglaze blue with a pattern copied at New Hall. Additional gilding added in England. 5in. (12.7cm) high. c.1780-90.*

P. HOPKINS COLLECTION

I think that these letters written by Richard Champion in 1765 and 1766 evidence at least an interest in porcelain

PLATE 8. *Plymouth hard-paste mask-head jug painted in a blackish-blue with a mock Oriental scene and border. The handle has sprung away from the body during firing. 6½in. (16.51cm) high. c.1768-70.*
GODDEN COLLECTION

and its manufacture and even show an understanding of the inherent difficulties. I make this point as Josiah Wedgwood was later to remark on Champion's lack of manufacturing know-how. Richard Champion seems to have had several interests – political, commercial and maritime. He was also involved in two dissolutions of non-ceramic partnership at Bristol in 1768, quite apart from his association with William Cookworthy's porcelain venture.

What is vitally important to the main theme and subject of this book is that on 17 March 1768 William Cookworthy was granted a patent giving him exclusive rights to produce china or porcelain using the Cornish raw materials, the china clay and china stone. Correspondence published by Cyril Staal (under his pen name Geoffrey Wills) in the *Apollo* magazine of December 1980 and January 1981 show that there was in fact a close-run race to perfect his wares before others, in particular Comte de Lauragais, were successful. As William Cookworthy noted in a letter to Thomas Pitt on 20 December 1767, '...If Lauragais succeeds in getting his Patent ... it will prevent our getting a Patent for the exclusive use of Moorstone which is our main point...'.

William Cookworthy did obtain his patent in March 1768. This was assigned to Richard Champion in May 1774 after the works had been moved to Bristol in 1770. The Plymouth works were closed late in 1770 and a

Plate 9. *A Plymouth hard-paste jug, showing slight turning (or wreathing) marks. Hand painted in underglaze blue with typical mock Chinese scene. 6½in. (16.51cm) high. Mark 2 and 4 joined. c.1768-70.* Godden Collection

contemporary note records 'the last burning of enamels November 27th 1770.' Some shares in the Plymouth concern were sold on to the 'New China Manufacturers at Bristol where the work is intended to be carried on' in September 1770.[4]

The short-lived Plymouth venture certainly provided a vital first link in the chain of English porcelain manufactories producing a type of true porcelain, but it cannot be considered to have been a resounding commercial success. The main difficulties arose from the high temperature needed to fire and mature the body and glaze. Plymouth figures tended to warp and lean out of true, open cracks developed and discoloration of the glaze, due apparently to smoke-staining, are all fairly normal faults. The handle on the jug shown in Plate 8 has come completely away at its bottom junction with the body, the top of the handle too shows a heat fracture, yet it was seemingly put on the market. Obviously not all pieces were as badly damaged in manufacture as this example, but it does serve to show the basic difficulties which William Cookworthy encountered at Plymouth. The underglaze blue also suffered in the high temperature firing; it is usually an unpleasant dark blue-black tint, not equal to the Chinese or indeed to any other English class of underglaze blue decoration then in production.

After the transfer to Bristol, Richard Champion took an

increasingly important part in the new porcelain works and by at least September 1773 it was trading as Richard Champion & Co. William Cookworthy's patent was officially assigned to Champion in May 1774, having been agreed in, or by, October 1773, but Cookworthy retained for himself a royalty payable on the china stone and china clay used. This was later to cause difficulty when Champion sought to resell his patent rights.

The full terms of the agreement under which William Cookworthy assigned his patent rights to Richard Champion in 1774, when the patent had some eight years to run, is not known. Perhaps Champion was able to buy out Cookworthy, perhaps a complicated series of payments was arranged, maybe Cookworthy received payment in the form of a royalty, his remuneration depending on the success of the Bristol porcelain works under Champion's management.

A large initial payment by Champion seems unlikely, as the manufacturing difficulties were apparently not fully overcome by 1774. Indeed, a letter quoted in part by Hugh Owen[5] suggests strongly that William Cookworthy reserved for himself a type of royalty payment. This Victorian author obviously had access to original Champion correspondence. The agreement on the assignment was mentioned in a letter written by Richard Champion's sister in October 1773 relating to a meeting between Cookworthy and Champion in Bristol, following a series of letters on the subject – a 'debate by correspondence' to use Owen's term. The letter, as quoted by Hugh Owen in 1873, read:

> I am glad I have it in my powers to add that the China business which brought him [W. Cookworthy] to Bristol is settled. I hope satisfactorily to both Parties, indeed I had always hoped when they met it would be so. My Brother often represented to him the great injury he imagined would attend a Tax for ever on a work, left it entirely to himself to make his own terms to which he promised to abide, William Cookworthy immediately determined that he would give up the perpetual claim, and fix it to ninety nine years, the time of the Lease for the Clay.

If Champion was prepared to leave the terms to Cookworthy and to agree a ninety-nine year term, it seems to me likely that Champion paid little or no money directly to Cookworthy for the right to produce true porcelain under Cookworthy's original 1768 patent. I must acknowledge, however, that later in November 1790 Thomas Pitt, who had been, it would seem, a partner, wrote: '... we had procured a patent for the use of our materials, and expended on it between two and three thousand pounds. We then sold our interest to Mr Champion of Bristol'.

The all-important lease for the milling of clay entered into between William Cookworthy and Thomas Pitt (later Lord Camelford) provided not only for Cookworthy to pay for the materials extracted for a period of ninety-nine years but also it limited the landowners from selling the said moor-stone to others for the same long period. Both parties and their successors were bound to each other subject to high penalties. Complications obviously arose when others discovered different sources of the same china clay and china stone in Cornwall. Cookworthy and Champion were locked into an expensive agreement with one supplier whilst other would-be manufacturers could purchase their materials from a different source at a cheaper price.

Plate 10. *A Bristol hard-paste 'low Chelsea ewer' of a form copied by the New Hall partnership and several other firms. 4½in. (11.43cm) long. Overglaze mark a cross and 'B'. c.1775-80.* Godden collection

Plate 11. *A Bristol hard-paste spoontray of a shape produced in China and copied by most late 18th century English porcelain factories. Unglazed base. 6in. (15.24cm) long. c.1775-80.*

Dr. T. Darling collection

In our study of the later Staffordshire story the history of the Bristol factory under Richard Champion is more important than the pioneering endeavours of Cookworthy, important as these undoubtedly were.

Richard Champion's Bristol manufactory seemingly did not open with any great fanfare or publicity. The former Plymouth mark, the sign for tin (a '2' and '4' conjoined), was probably soon discontinued and when a Bristol mark did appear it was usually merely a simple cross. This occurs in underglaze blue on blue decorated pieces or painted in overglaze enamels or gold on surface decorated pieces. This simple device was often accompanied by a painter's or gilder's number, but on very many examples no mark at all was employed. It should be noted also that on many objects a close imitation of the Dresden crossed swords device occurs painted in underglaze blue. It is a regrettable fact that this fake mark was carefully painted when just as easily a special 'Bristol' publicity mark could have been employed.

Even in the city of Bristol, the local manufactory – the only one in the British Isles then to be making true (hard-paste) porcelain – seems to have been little known, for Felix Farley's *Bristol Journal* of 28 November 1772 carried the following advertisement:

China
At the Manufactory in Castle-Green Bristol,
Are sold, various Kinds of
The True Porcelain
Both useful and Ornamental
Consisting of a New Assortment.

The figures, Vases, Jars and Beakers are very elegant, and the useful Ware exceedingly good. As this Manufactory is not at present sufficiently known, it may not be improper to remark, that this Porcelain wholly free from the Imperfections in Wearing, which the English China usually has, and that its Composition is equal in Fineness to the East Indian, and will wear as well. The enamell's Ware, which is rendered nearly as cheap as the English Blue and White, comes very near, and in some Pieces equal the Dresden, which this Work more particularly imitates.

N.B. There is some of the old Stock, which will be sold very cheap, Two or three careful Boys are wanted...

The 'very cheap' old stock could well have been Plymouth porcelains or slightly faulty Bristol 'seconds'. In general, however, the Bristol hard-paste porcelain of the early or mid-1770s is extremely good in body and glaze. The old difficulties which Cookworthy experienced with firing cleanly seem to have been overcome. In fact, although tears in the body occur, I have never seen a Bristol piece that showed any of the glaze defects – the dullness and smoke-staining – that is so evident on much Plymouth. The Bristol glaze is extremely clear and glossy with a good Dresden-like sheen. Considerable play was made in advertisements that the glaze was very hard and resisted scratching – 'The Polish is so fine as to resist every scratch...'.

Whilst some of the decoration on Bristol porcelain can be very fine, showing the influence of leading Continental manufactories, most of the standard designs were quite simple but neat. Floral swags (Plate 12), often in monochrome, were much favoured, as were floral sprays – see Plates 10 and 13-14.

The cost of such teawares – the staple of most porcelain factories – was, however, very modest. An April 1775 account for a tea service of now unknown pattern, supplied to a George Hunt, is in the Bristol Museum collection. This 'complete [forty-three piece] set of tea china' comprised:

1 coffee pot, cover and stand
1 teapot, cover and stand
1 slop basin
1 sugar box and cover
1 milk pot and cover
1 spoontray
1 bread and butter plate
12 teacups with saucers
6 coffee cups

This set, made in the difficult hard-paste porcelain, was priced at only 2gns., surely not permitting Champion a large profit. The make-up of this set varies somewhat from the standard late eighteenth century English porcelain service. First, we have the inclusion of a coffee pot and its stand.[6] Secondly, only six coffee cups were included, although there were twelve teacups and saucers. Still, such variations, which may have been dictated by the buyer, matter little. I have only been endeavouring to show the modest cost of a complete Bristol tea service. It seems that the market did not permit a premium to be charged for the real or hard-paste porcelain body; it had to compete in price with the standard English soft-paste porcelains.

Champion's patent rights to produce such true or hard-paste porcelains were, however, highly valued by Champion for he was to enter into long and costly endeavours to extend the period of the patent, giving him more time in which to recover the cash he had expended in purchasing the patent. William Cookworthy's original patent was due to expire in 1782, after which any manufacturer would be free to use the Cornish raw materials and produce true porcelain. The competition would be weighted against Champion as the others would not be burdened with the royalties he had to pay Cookworthy.

Richard Champion therefore sought in 1775 to extend his assigned patent for a further term of fourteen years from the original termination in 1782, that is up to 1796. This attempt, however, was strongly opposed by many of the Staffordshire potters, ably led in this matter by Josiah Wedgwood who had several influential friends in both Houses of Parliament. I cannot in this brief outline detail the whole story and quote the lengthy correspondence, etc. relating to this matter, one of principle and great commercial consequence to the Staffordshire potters, but the events are well documented in Chapter V of Hugh Owen's *Two Centuries of Ceramic Art in Bristol* (Bell & Daldy, London, 1873) and to a lesser degree in later more readily available books on Bristol porcelain. In the event Champion gained his extension, but only, it has been stated, to use the Cornish raw materials to produce a translucent porcelain and mixing the ingredients in the proportions that he had to specify. It is widely believed that all other potters were free to use the china stone and china clay in earthenware-type (opaque) bodies. It is very unlikely that any English manufacturer sought to challenge the patent and produce a type of hard-paste porcelain during the Bristol period, that is before 1780. The manufacture of what we now call 'hybrid hard-paste' porcelains arose in the later Staffordshire period, after about 1781.

In seeking the extension to the term of the patent in the mid-1770s, it was claimed that Champion 'hath been at a very considerable expense and at pains and labour in prosecuting the said invention and by reason of the great difficulty attending a manufacture upon a new principle, hath not been able to bring the same to perfection until within the last year; and it will require further pains, labour and expense to render the said invention of public utility...'.

A witness, John Britain, gave evidence to a Committee of the House of Commons which had been set up to consider the extension of the Cookworthy/Champion patent. The report, presented in April 1775, stated that 'Mr. John Britain had great Experience in several China Manufactures' and has made 'several Trials upon all those which had been manufactured in England, and finds that all of them, except that of Bristol, were destroyed in the same Fire that brings the Bristol to Perfection'.

Plate 12. *A Bristol teapot (missing the cover) painted with Chinese figure designs. Emulating in style the contemporary Chinese imports – see Plate 1. 4¼in. (10.8cm) high. Crossed swords mark (of Dresden). c.1775 80.* FJ Houseman Collection

And he produced to your Committee several Samples of the said kinds of China, which showed the effects upon china severally; and said, that they had not been able to bring the Bristol China to a marketable commodity, so as to furnish an Order, until within the last Six months, but that sometimes they succeeded, and at other Times not, but that now they can execute any order.'

That they have lately made considerable Improvements in the said Manufacture, and particularly are endeavouring to perfect the Blue, in which they have not as yet entirely succeeded, though they have now a Gentleman who has succeeded in a small Way, in which they have been at a considerably Expense; that the witness thinks the manufacture is capable of further improvements; that they can afford it at a price equal to Foreign China of equal Goodness, and that they have made some specimens equal to good Dresden; that he had not seen any Dresden ornamental China equal to the Vases produced to your Committee, nor any Thing in Biscuit [unglazed porcelain] equal to the Biscuit in those Vases, and other Ornaments; that the Gilding stands well; and the Sève [Sèvres] China differs from this; the Ornamental is more of a Cream Color, but the Glaze is so soft that it will not bear using; that he believed the Enamel of the Bristol China is as hard as the Dresden, and harder than the Chinese; that they can make it of any Degree of Thickness required, and there is the Difference between the Bristol China and the Sève, and several other kinds, that when they are broke they seem as dry as Tobacco Pipe, that this is the case of all the English China; but the Dresden, the Bristol and the Asiatic China, have, when broken a moist and lucid appearance; in proof of which he produced Fragments of the several kinds; that the Bristol China will stand hot water without splitting, that he has never known an instance of it splitting, though he has known several pieces of the Asiatic split; that the Gold does not come off the Bristol; that there are some China which frequent use turns brown, and cracks, which the witness thinks arises from there not being a proper Union between the Body and the Glaze; that the Manufacturers have their Glaze made into a Glass previous to its being applied to the Body; but that is not the case with the Bristol; that they can make Plates, but have had great Difficulties; that they have not hitherto much attended to that Object, but have applied themselves to perfecting the Body as a Body, and the Glaze as a Glaze; that they can render this China in most Articles as cheap as the Asiatic, and much cheaper than the Dresden.

Then the witness produced to your Committee, Specimens of the Asiatic and Chinese Materials and said, he found no Difference, except that the Materials of the Asiatic shrunk in the Burning One 42nd. Part more than those of Bristol and judges the Bristol Materials to be better ... Ordered, That Leave be given to bring in a Bill for enlarging the Letter patent.'

This was, however, but the first stage. The troubles arose when the Bill was debated in the House. Josiah Wedgwood was greatly put out by Champion's endeavours to extend the period of the patent. In reply to Wedgwood's 'Memorial relative to a Petition from Mr Champion for the extension of a Patent', as quoted by Hugh Owen in *Two Centuries of Ceramic Art in Bristol,* Champion claimed that he had:

> no objection to the use which potters of Staffordshire may make of his or any other raw materials, provided earthenware only, as distinguished by that title, is made from it. He wants to interfere with no manufacture whatever, and is content to insert any clause to confine him to the invention which he possesses, and which he has improved. He is contented that Mr Wedgwood, and every manufacturer, should reap the fruit of their labour; all he asks is, such a protection for his own as the legislature, in its wisdom, shall think its merits...

Champion further stated:

> He has been many years concerned in this undertaking; nearly from the time that Patent was granted to Mr Cookworthy, in whose name it continued till assigned over to Mr Champion. To deny the advantage of any part of Mr Cookworthy's merits, to his assignee, is to deny that advantage to Mr Cookworthy himself. One part of the benefit of every work, from whence profit may be derived, is the power of assignment; and if, in fact, the manufacture could not be completed, nor the inventor, of course, derive any profit from it, without the expense, care and perseverance of the assignee and once partner, the merit of that assignee, who both completes the manufacture and rewards the discoverer, is equal in equity to that of the discovered himself – equal in every respect, except the honour that attends original genius and power of invention.
>
> Mr Champion can assert, with truth, that his hazard and expense were many times greater than those of the original inventor. Mr Champion mentions this without the least disparagement to the worthy gentleman, Mr Cookworthy, who is his particular friend; he gives him all the merit which is due to so great a discovery; he deserved it for finding out the means of a manufacture, which will, in all probability, be a very great advantage to this country; but yet, Mr Champion claims the merit of supporting the work, and, when the inventor declined the undertaking himself, with his time, his labour, and his fortune, improved it from a very imperfect to an almost perfect manufacture; and he hopes, soon, with proper encouragement, to one altogether perfect...

In the end, after great difficulty and because of the help of many friends, some of whom had received presents of Bristol porcelain, Champion was granted the extension of his patent to run until 1796. As one of the conditions, however, he had to deposit the specification for his porcelain mix and for the glaze – see page 417. This then became public knowledge, but the amounts of the various raw materials were given in imprecise terms – the patent would be stated to have been extended in more than its term!

The specifications were deposited by Champion (see page 417) but were very wide (not exact) so as to better deter others who might wish to slightly vary an exact specification. The proportions of china stone to china clay were stated to be from four parts stone to one of clay, to at the other extreme sixteen parts clay to one part of stone. Surprisingly, it was stated that with 'all this variation I make without taking away from the ware the distinguishing appearance and properties of Dresden and Oriental porcelains...'. It would have been difficult for any other manufacturer to have made a workable and presentable porcelain using proportions outside those claimed by Champion!

Champion's extended patent protection does not seem to have gained him the profits one would expect from such a monopoly. This was doubtless due to the fact that the patent did not prohibit the manufacture by others of porcelain, only of a certain expensive type that had inherent difficulties in its manufacture. The East India Company was still importing vast quantities of durable Chinese porcelain tablewares, some Continental porcelain was also available in at least the London china shops, and the porcelains made by several English factories were of a high standard. The Worcester and Derby factories rightly enjoyed a very large share of the market, particularly in the more expensive ranges, while the Liverpool manufacturers catered for the less demanding classes. The Caughley factory too from 1775 was producing very workmanlike Worcester style porcelains which almost certainly undersold the Bristol productions.

The Plymouth and Bristol works could never have been large prosperous concerns, rivalling Worcester or Derby. Cookworthy and Champion were seemingly under-financed and always seeking to overcome the difficulties of producing high-fired porcelain for a market that was not willing to pay a premium for such a product.

In order to raise funds, both Cookworthy and Champion had sought backers and in effect endeavoured to sell shares in their enterprise to various merchants and investors. They probably lost all or most of their investment. Hugh Owen in his 1873 study *Two Centuries of Ceramic Art in Bristol...* quoted a long letter written by Champion to his friend William Burke in June 1776. In part this reads:

> ... as the increased sale has entailed an extension of the works, together with an enlargement of expense, a greater capital is necessary. I must therefore procure the assistance of a man of fortune, which makes me give you the trouble again of requesting the favour of your sentiments concerning Mr

PLATE 13. *A selection of typical Bristol porcelain teaware shapes. Some cups and the milk jug show handle forms similar to the later Tunstall period Staffordshire porcelains. The cup form was also copied. Teapot 5½in. (13.97cm) high. c. 1775-80.* BRISTOL MUSEUM COLLECTION

Kendall. From your description he is a Man of Spirit and Sense, and knows the value of an affair of this great sort, which with a proper Capital, without doubt, must become an object of the utmost extent and profit The ware is much superior to the Asiatic, – equal in strength to the Dresden – and in elegance, perfectly resembling the beautiful manufacture of Sèvres, – and in texture, far exceeding it. The materials are cheap and the manufacture now reduced to certainty. This work, therefore, possessed of these advantages, may be rendered so cheap as to be within the reach of all persons, for common use; and at the same time, by the addition of elegant ornaments, be rendered equal to the French, at a much less expense; as we can afford to sell for less than half their price, and yet at a very good profit. Bristol is not the place to find a man of fortune and spirit to give it its due extent, so as to supply the market. We have no such men, and to divide it out in shares I do not like. Our sale is greatly increased, and may be still more, immediately could I extend It. The profit is now very considerable. The extension will make it very great. Ten thousand pounds addition would make a capital concern. The future profits would annually increase. The terms, I should not be unreasonable in. ...any Gentleman joining me, has the greatest advantage, I have borne the fatigue and risks, and I have brought it to perfection, he receives the advantage alone.

We do not know how many other would-be backers Richard Champion had approached before or after this letter was written in June 1776, but at this period he was obviously seeking one or more backers and was embarking on an exercise that was to be enlarged upon in Staffordshire some four or five years later.

In August 1778 Richard Champion was at least temporarily financially embarrassed, for he had then 'assigned his property to Trustees for the benefit of his Creditors'. He seems, however, to have survived without bankruptcy proceedings being finalised. This was vitally important for if Champion had been declared a bankrupt his patent rights would have lapsed. In a letter dated 3 September 1778 he admitted '... I carry on the smallest work...'. This is not to say that no Bristol porcelain was produced after 1778. The situation was one of decline rather than cessation, although this final stage was probably reached by 1780.

It would seem that before December 1778 Richard Champion had laid or considered plans for further activities to be undertaken in 1780. Hugh Owen in 1873 published a letter written by the Duke of Portland to Champion. This letter commenced:

Dec. 1st 1778

My dear Sir,

If my name can be of any use to you with regard to the engagements you wish to enter into for April and October, 1780, command it freely...

Can Champion have already planned to move the manufactory from Bristol?

The *Public Advertiser* in January and February 1780 carried the following advertisement or notice of a forthcoming sale comprising 'The valuable Stock of the Bristol China Manufactory':

BRISTOL PORCELAINS
To be Sold by Auction
by Messrs. CHRISTIE & ANSELL,
At their Great Room (Next Cumberland House) in Pall-Mall, on Monday, the 21st of February and the two following Days,
The Valuable Stock of the BRISTOL CHINA MANUFACTORY; consisting of an extensive Variety of elegant Patterns in Tea and Coffee Equipages, Cabinet and Caudle Cups, Dejeunes, Desert Services &c in the newest and most approved Taste. Likewise an Assortment of Medallions of curious China Flowers, accurately modelled and highly finished.
To be viewed on Friday and Saturday proceding the Sale.
Catalogues may be then had.

It is true that within a few days a correction was issued stating:

N.B. In the former advertisement there was a mistake in mentioning this to be the Stock of Bristol China Manufactory, it being only a Collection of very valuable pieces manufactured at that Place.

But I believe this statement was only issued because Champion early in 1780, for good commercial reasons, did not wish to give the impression that he was selling the Bristol concern or was in financial difficulties. The original wording 'The valuable stock of the Bristol China Manufactory' certainly tends to give such impressions.

Stock or collection, the contents of the London sale, held not in 'The Season' but in February, was quite extensive. The sale was scheduled to last for three days. Although not all the lots were of Bristol origin, they comprised quite ordinary articles as well as the finer styles. For example, the first two lots comprised thirty-seven piece tea services decorated with a standard Bristol 'green festoon' pattern which is found without gilding. Each of these services sold for £1.16s.0d. The next lot comprised only twelve blue and white coffee cups. It is interesting to read that the sale contained several lots decorated only in gold, for such gilt designs featured largely in the early productions made in Staffordshire in the next partnership two or three years later. For example, in February 1780 the London sale included 'A white and gold teapot, slop basin, sugar dish and milk pot' [Lot 68, third day]. This group sold for 9s. The white and gold Bristol teapot shown in Plate 17 could well have been of a similar type.

Plate 14. *A Bristol enamelled globular teapot, with moulded spout form later copied in Staffordshire. Note the typical hard-paste wreathing or turning marks. 5in. (12.7cm) high. Blue enamel cross mark and '11'. c.1775-80.* Godden collection

For further details of this catalogue, still preserved at Christie's, the reader is referred to W.J. Pountney's book *Old Bristol Potteries* (J.W. Arrowsmith, Bristol, 1920) and to J.E. Nightingale's *Contributions towards the History of Early English Porcelains from Contemporary Sources* (privately printed Salisbury, 1881, reprinted by E.P. Publishing, Wakefield, 1973). It is noteworthy that Bristol figures, groups and vases were not included in this Christie sale held in February 1780; it comprised useful tablewares.

The final chapter in the history of Bristol hard-paste porcelain was delayed until after Richard Champion had entered into his arrangement with the Staffordshire potters and after he had settled in Newcastle-under-Lyme, once called the capital of the Potteries. Indeed, he had already left there to take up his political post in London some three weeks before a sale was held in Bristol of 'the remaining stock'.

The closing sale was first advertised in *Felix Farley's Journal* on 27 April 1782:

> To be sold by hand on Monday, 29th April inst. At the Manufactory in Castle Green, the remaining stock of Enamel, Blue and White and White Bristol China.
> The Manufacturers being removed to the North. The time of the sale each Day from Ten to One and from Two till six.

This may not have been a sale by auction (for it was again advertised on 1 June and on 8 June) but rather the sale by normal person-to-person methods of the remaining Bristol porcelains. The term 'sold by hand' could, however, have meant sale by the raising of a hand at auction as opposed to the auction 'sale by candle' method when verbal bids were made.

In whichever way the sale was conducted, the April 1782 notice is important showing, as it does, that the Bristol stock was unlikely to have been moved up to

Plate 15. *A selection of Bristol teawares of typical type. The moulded spout to the cream jug is repeated in some early New Hall – see Plate 23. Teapot 5½in. (13.97cm) high. Crossed swords mark in blue, '6' in gold. c.1775-80.* Messrs. Christie's

Staffordshire and that even the 'White Bristol China' was offered for sale locally. This 'white china' presumably consisted of undecorated blanks left over in the warehouse, not having been called forward for decoration before Champion closed the manufactory. Regarding these remaining white Bristol porcelains, the possibility exists that former Bristol decorators purchased such blanks at the closing down sale and added enamel decoration before re-selling the now finished articles. It should be noted that the Bristol sale notice also mentioned 'Blue and White', another general style to be taken up by the new Staffordshire Company, 'the manufacturers being removed to the North'.

Apart from the sale 'at the Manufactory in Castle Green', the main local china dealer, Elliott at 53 Clare Street, also closed and advertised in June 1782 that 'The Goods in the said warehouse will continue … to be sold very cheap'.

It will be seen, therefore, that, as the new owners of the hard-paste patent were striving to establish the porcelain works in the Staffordshire Potteries, the remaining stocks of Bristol porcelains were thrown on the market 'very cheap'. It should, however, be noted that The Bristol China Warehouse owned by Joseph Hancock at 17 Salisbury Court, Fleet Street, London also remained open until at least 1782.

We now have no record of the sale locally of the Bristol factory's working materials, the moulds, the copper plates, etc. and no doubt there would have been little or no demand for such articles in Bristol. Perhaps Champion moved many of the materials up into Staffordshire with him? I must record in this regard that none of the overglaze or underglaze printed designs used at Bristol seems to occur on New Hall porcelains. This suggests that at least the Bristol engraved copper plates were not available to the new partnership. These copper plates would have had a scrap value and they also could have been reissued after the engraved surface was smoothed or planed.

The Bristol porcelain manufactory lasted for ten or eleven years, initially under William Cookworthy and then under Richard Champion. In manufacturing terms I regard it as a success. The body and glaze represent a distinct improvement over the so often faulty Plymouth porcelains. The technical difficulties seem to have been almost entirely overcome.

If one views a good collection of Bristol porcelain, such as that housed in the Bristol Art Gallery and Museum or in the Victoria & Albert Museum, one will surely be amazed by the individuality of the porcelains, the novel shapes and the high standards of the decoration. The body is of good colour, the glaze clear and glass-like, free from the discoloration or speckles of the Plymouth glaze. The gilding can be superb. Many of the styles of decoration were inspired by fashionable Continental prototypes, both in the Dresden and in the Sèvres taste. In regard to the cheaper lines the underglaze blue was a distinct improvement over the smoky-blackish Plymouth tint. Richard Champion, too, seems to have overcome the difficulty of applying underglaze blue prints to hard-paste porcelain.

Whilst I cannot prove the following points I believe that these undoubted improvements were occasioned by a radical rethinking of the manufacturing technique – the kilns, the firing sequence and perhaps the composition of the body and glaze. William Cookworthy on his own admission (see page 73) fired with wood fuel and used the Continental method of a low biscuit firing before applying the glaze and re-firing at the higher temperature, some 1350°C.

Most writers have assumed that Richard Champion fired his Bristol porcelains in the same manner. I do not believe that this was the case, particularly in the later years of the factory's life. There is evidence that from time to time improvements were made in the manufactory. One vital step would have been a fundamental change in the firing methods. Champion's experienced manager, John Britain, testified in 1775 '...That they have lately made considerable improvements in the said Manufacture and particularly are endeavouring to perfect the Blue, in which they have not as yet entirely succeeded, though they have now a Gentleman who has succeeded in a small way...'. Perhaps the references to the improvement in the Bristol blue and white designs reflect amendments being made. For example, *Aris's Birmingham Gazette* on 1 February 1779 carried the following blurb :

> Genuine China (established by Act of Parliament) at the China Manufactory in Castle Green, Bristol ... The blue and white is now brought to the greatest perfection equal to the Nankeen, which with the very great strength and fine polish renders it the best for use of any china now in the world.

It has often been stated that the Bristol management could not print in underglaze blue as the low-fired biscuit (unglazed) body could not withstand the process of applying and pressing on the pigment-charged transfer paper. However, underglaze blue printed patterns certainly occur on Bristol porcelain, even on thinly potted leaf dishes (Plate 16), on delicate cups (Plate 18), as well as on plates, teapots, jugs and other articles. Furthermore, several of these printed designs are of a very simple nature, of the type of floral or sprig design that could very easily have been hand painted by semi-skilled child painters or apprentices if the printing had in fact presented difficulties.

I believe that this blue printing was possible and even favoured over hand painting because the firing sequence had been amended to that employed by most, if not all, other English porcelain manufacturers. I refer to the now standard method of raising the first (biscuit) firing to the highest temperature to completely set or vitrify the body before glazing and refiring at a lower temperature to melt and mature the added glaze. The success of the blue printed Bristol porcelains on quite delicately potted objects points strongly to this basic change in technique.

We are on reasonably firm ground in suggesting that the all-important kiln fuel was changed from wood to coal for when Champion, writing as 'the Proprietor of the Bristol China Manufactory' in his address to the Staffordshire potters (see page 13), compared his costs in Bristol with those obtaining in Staffordshire he remarked '...the price of the essential article of Coal a fourth part alone ... such a very great difference has determined him to change his situation...'. Champion further stated in 1781 'That all the disadvantages which have occurred in the Discovery and Progress of this Work, now of above Thirty Years Continuance and at the Expense of near Thirty thousand Pounds, have been for some time wholly at an end...' – see page 14.

I believe that the reasons given by Richard Champion for wishing to move from Bristol to the Staffordshire Potteries were correctly stated – see page 14. He had

Plate 16. *A simple Bristol leaf-shape dish of the type made by most English manufacturers. This bears underglaze blue printed sprays; others are shown in Plate 18. 4¼ x 4½in. (10.8 x 11.43cm). c.1775-80.*
Godden collection

Plate 17. *A fluted barrel shape Bristol teapot decorated with a simple gilt design. Several early designs introduced by the post-1781 Staffordshire partnership were only worked in gold. 4¾in. (12.07cm) high. Gilder's number '2'. c.1777-80.* Godden Collection

perfected the manufacturing processes, he possessed the patent rights and a supply of the raw materials, but the costs of coal and materials plus the potters' wages (and the royalty he still had to pay William Cookworthy) made the Bristol porcelain uneconomical. He had to sell his porcelains in competition with all other English manufacturers as well as with the imported Chinese and to some extent the Continental wares. The Bristol porcelains were too costly and consequently the venture was failing. The only practical course open to Champion was to cut his costs and move to an area where labour and fuel were cheaper. Fuel is vital in the production of all ceramics, Josiah Wedgwood calculating that it took ten tons of coal to produce one ton of earthenware. The proportion would be even greater with highly decorated porcelain requiring a higher firing temperature than most earthenwares and bearing more decoration and gilding which in turn required re-firing at progressively lower temperatures.

Richard Champion's great success was undoubtedly the sale of the franchise to a group of Staffordshire potters, enabling him to recoup some of his losses and leaving them to establish new works and employ a new labour force and, in general, to take the future risks and expenses while he became Assistant Deputy Paymaster General in London (for only a few months) before emigrating to America where he died in October 1791. This brief obituary appeared in London's *The Gentleman's Magazine:*

> Oct. 7th near Camden in South Carolina, Richard Champion Esq late Deputy Paymaster General of his Majesty's forces, and proprietor of the China Manufactory formerly carried on in Bristol.'

His ceramic successes were to be continued in Staffordshire where an adaptation of his and William

PLATE 18. *A Bristol leaf dish and coffee cup both printed in underglaze blue, showing the process could be used on hard-paste porcelain. The cup design is in the Chinese fashion. Cup 2½in. high c. 1775-80.*
GODDEN COLLECTION

Cookworthy's true hard-paste porcelain was produced into the nineteenth century until the 'evergreen bone-china' body finally won the day in about 1812. This change too was undoubtedly due to financial reasons and the need of the new proprietors to compete successfully with the competition from other manufacturers.

In this first chapter I wished to tell in a brief form the story of the establishment of hard-paste porcelain manufacture in England, for without this phase the New Hall Company as such would not have been established and in turn many of the other contemporary porcelain factories might not have flourished. The story has, however, been much abbreviated and those wishing to delve deeper into the story of Plymouth and Bristol porcelains or to learn more of William Cookworthy or of Richard Champion should consult the following books, papers or articles:

Two Centuries of Ceramic Art in Bristol by Hugh Owen (Bell & Daldy, London, 1873)

Old Bristol Potteries by W.J. Pountney (Arrowsmith Ltd., Bristol, 1920, reprinted by E.P. Publishing Ltd., East Ardsley, 1972)

Cookworthy's Plymouth & Bristol Porcelain by F. Severne MacKenna (F. Lewis, Leigh-on-Sea, 1946)

Champion's Bristol Porcelain by F. Severne MacKenna (F. Lewis, Leigh-on-Sea, 1947)

'The End of Bristol. The Beginning of New Hall: Some fresh evidence' by R.J. Charleston, *The Connoisseur,* April 1956

William Cookworthy 1705-1780 by John Penderill-Church (Bradford Barton, Truro, 1972)

English Blue and White Porcelain of the 18th Century by B. Watney (Faber & Faber, London; revised edition 1973)

Cookworthy 1705-80 and his circle (also titled 'Cookworthy – a man of common clay') by A. Douglas Selleck (Baron Jay Ltd., Plymouth, 1978)

'William Cookworthy and the Plymouth Factory; an updating' by Dr. F. Severne MacKenna, a paper published in the *Transactions of the English Ceramic Circle,* Vol. II, Part 2, 1982.

'The Plymouth Porcelain Factory – Letters to Thomas Pitt, 1766-69' by Geoffrey Wills (Cyril Staal) published in *Apollo,* December 1980 and January 1981

1. Deposits were later found in the Limoges district.

2. Probably Andrew Duché – see F. Severne MacKenna's *Cookworthy's Plymouth and Bristol Porcelain* (F. Lewis Ltd., 1946), pages 21-6.

3. In a letter to Thomas Pitt dated 2 July 1768 William Cookworthy, stating that his methods were different from those used at Worcester, wrote 'we burn up our Ware and glaze it by the same fire'.

4. See W.J. Pountney's *Old Bristol Potteries* (J. Arrowsmith, Bristol, 1920). The shares were seemingly sold at a loss.

5. *Two Centuries of Ceramic Art in Bristol* (Bell & Daldy, London, 1873).

6. It is interesting to note that this Bristol set included a stand for the coffee pot, as the later Staffordshire New Hall coffee pots often had stands.

CHAPTER II

The Patent comes to Staffordshire

The Tunstall Period

Our study of the early history of Richard Champion's efforts to establish a porcelain manufactory in the Staffordshire Potteries is built upon a few firmly bedded rocks, although in some cases the foundations are less well established and the date of the successful launching of the new venture is not exactly known.

We are not clear how Champion surmounted the several legal difficulties that governed the sale or assignment of a patent and the foundation of a new company. After the South Sea Company's 'bubble' burst, official Government difficulties were placed on the sale of shares to the public in a new venture. Certainly the wording of a patent made it quite clear that the patent would be cancelled if the holder sold the rights, etc. to more than five persons. Yet we believe that Champion dealt with eight or ten. It may be significant that the new company seemingly never claimed to own a patent or referred to the porcelain as being protected by such rights. They did not trade on past history, only to the extent of using the term 'Manufacturers of Real China' on their bill-head. I have also been unable to trace any record of an assignment of the patent from Champion to any single, or group of, Staffordshire potters. This is in contrast to the previous official assignment from William Cookworthy to Richard Champion.

We need not now worry unduly on the details concerning the setting up of a new, but not the first, porcelain producing company in the Staffordshire Potteries. The new partnership was undoubtedly formed but still the views of different authors are varied and not all can be correct.

Several very misleading accounts of the situation have been published. I quote below just two very different statements to illustrate the contrasting views. For example John Penderill-Church's 1972 specialist book on Cookworthy states, in part:

> ...in December 1780, he [that is Richard Champion] formed a company made up of eight potters, and this company bought the patent from him. They began once again manufacturing hand [*sic,* presumably a typographical error for 'hard'] porcelain to the Cookworthy formula, slightly modified ... Shortly after the formation of the company, originally known as Hollins, Warburton, Daniel & Co., Turner and Keeling withdrew, leaving the other six to carry on. The Company later became known as the New Hall company of Shelton, taking its name from Shelton in Staffordshire...

On the other hand that distinguished authority F. Severne MacKenna, writing in *Champion's Bristol Porcelain* (F. Lewis, Leigh-on-Sea, 1947), remarked:

> ... it is frequently stated that the patent was bought and worked by the New Hall company. This however, is certainly not borne out by any of the concrete evidence now remaining to us, for no specimen of New Hall porcelain has ever come to light which could in any way be claimed as showing the close affinity to Bristol which would inevitably result from employment of the same process, particularly as it is asserted that Champion went to New Hall to supervise the working of his Patent. He certainly did go there, after leaving Bristol on November 5th, 1781, and left again in the following April. During the period of his stay there is no doubt that negotiations were afoot for the purchase, and equally probably certain trials were made, but the whole matter terminated when he left the district and went to London. It is quite certain that the patent was never acquired by the New Hall firm and worked by them...

I think that few present-day authorities would agree with

this 1947 statement and possibly Dr. Severne MacKenna later amended his early view. It is surely relevant to recall that in February 1786, within five years of the setting-up of the company, the all-knowing Josiah Wedgwood informed a Parliamentary Committee that he was speaking 'in the name of the [earthenware] Potters and of the proprietors of Mr Champion's Patent…'. However, it seems to be true that there is no firm evidence to support a sale or assignment of the patent.

I cannot find myself in full agreement with Mr. Penderill-Church's 1972 statement. Quite apart from fixing the date for the formation of the new Company at an unlikely December 1780, I do not think that Richard Champion himself 'formed a Company'. This, I believe, was left to the Staffordshire potters once they had purchased the right to manufacture under Champion's patent. Champion was, I believe, seeking to recoup his expenses by selling his rights. He was surely not interested in investing more money in establishing another porcelain factory with all the expenses that would have entailed. Wedgwood clearly stated 'He has come amongst us to dispose of his secret…'. Champion's name was not used in any Staffordshire firm or partnership.

The company was certainly not 'originally known as Hollins, Warburton, Daniel & Co.'. We may not now know the first trading style which may have been Hollins & Co. but that of Heath, Warburton & Co. was recorded in Tunnicliffe's 1786 *Directory,* a style that dated back to 1784. By at least December 1789 the style was Hollins, Warburton & Co. John Daniel's name was seemingly not included in the trade style until 1797 or later, although he had undoubtedly been associated with the company for several years, acting as its manager.

As to the New Hall name, taken from the renamed new Shelton Hall, this was most certainly not used by the original partners who established themselves at Tunstall, only moving later to Shelton and the New Hall property and outbuildings which they adapted to their requirements.

The fact that Richard Champion sought 'to dispose of his secret – His patent etc.' in Staffordshire is clearly defined in Josiah Wedgwood's last letter to his partner Thomas Bentley written just before the latter died in Liverpool. Wedgwood, in a letter dated 12 November 1780 stated:

> Amongst other things Mr Champion of Bristol has taken me up near two days. He is come amongst us to dispose of his secret – His patent etc., and, who could have believed it? Has chosen me for his friend and confidante. I shall not deceive him for I really feel much for his situation. A wife and eight children (to say nothing of himself) to provide for, and out of what I fear will not be thought of much value here – The secret of China making. He tells me he has sunk fifteen thousand pounds in this gulf, and his idea is now to sell the whole art, mystery, and patent for six, and he is now trying a list of names I have given him of the most substantial and enterprising potters amongst us, and will acquaint me with the event.'
>
> I gave him reasons why I could not be concerned in such a partnership which I believe were satisfactory even to himself.

Some few months later, probably in April 1781, Richard Champion published in Staffordshire what amounts to a prospectus for selling shares in the new concern which he hoped to transfer from Bristol to the Potteries. This statement setting out the advantages of the adventure is reproduced in my 'Prelude', on page 13. It is, however, by no means certain or probable that this form of disposal by 'shares by subscription, open to the country' was decided upon or would have been legal under the restrictions then in force to protect the public from dubious enterprises. However, there were independent (non-potter) shareholders in the former companies at Plymouth and Bristol, see Chapter IV.

Family correspondence quoted by Hugh Owen confirms that late in 1780 Richard Champion had spent 'a month or two in Staffordshire on account of the china manufactory' (Sarah Champion's letter dated 14 January 1781). He again visited the Potteries during the early summer for on 9 June Sarah wrote 'my Brother … returned the 4th of this month from London, on their way from Staffordshire, intending for some time to come, to make Newcastle in Staffordshire the place of their residence, he, being in a way of profitably disposing of the china manufactory, reserving a part to himself…'.

Richard Champion enlarged to some small degree on his sister's simple statement when he wrote two letters later in the year. The first important letter setting out his plans was written to James Fox on 6 August 1781, whilst Champion was staying with Lord Rockingham at Wentworth Woodhouse in Yorkshire. The whole letter (with other correspondence in the series) was published by Mr. R.J. Charleston in *The Connoisseur* of April 1956. The important sections are here quoted:

> You know that I exchanged the old terms of the China for the same amount that was paid Mr Pitt for the materials, of which some was paid to the late Mr Cookworthy…
>
> …I designed to have wrote you from thence where I was about a week, but was prevented by continual Imployment amongst the Potters (with whom I was in the Spring above two months negotiating a Plan for the introduction of my Porcelain Manufactory), and therefore took the opportunity whilst I am here and more at leisure. I have made Proposals,

> which are under Consideration. But there are such general Complaints of the dearness of the raw Materials, that the affair has been much at a stand, and I have been obliged to write to Mr Pitt, who has given me reason to understand on his part, that he will make an abatement. When you consider that the Potters have now a Lease of good Materials, close to St Stephens, at only 12 gs.[1] p.year and when Carthew will also sell them good [china clay] nearly at the rate of common pipe-clay, you may easily suppose what Chance I shall have in carrying on a Manufactory, when it becomes general in Staffordshire, which is part of the Plan.
>
> It is impossible to oblige the Potters to use my materials. They will go where it is cheapest. I am induced therefore to consult you upon the occasion, to know the Sentiments of your Cousins, whether it would not be most for our mutual advantage, to come to some specific agreement for the term of the Patent, which expires in 1796.
>
> We should all undoubtedly make the most we can, but we ought not for our own sakes to uphold a false Glare of Advantage, whilst we are losing the real fruits. The present plan has a Clause in it giving liberty to every Potter to make the Porcelain in his own works, on payment of a certain fine to the Company. No power can obliged them to buy the Material, but [at] a Moderate Price, when it is likely they might be induced to purchase them by good Management.
>
> You are sensible that one consequence of the use of other clay must be, the old work will drop from its particular disadvantages, in which case the Lease will fall into Mr Pitt's hands, and your Cousin's claim will sink in course. It therefore becomes a mutual benefit to sell the clay as cheap as possible ... They know what has already been received £120 from the year 1774 to 1778. Since that time it has been much less nor is there a chance in the present circumstances of making it otherwise than a trifling object...

Mr. Charleston then quoted a draft of a letter dated 22 August 1781, which shows that the original agreement with Cookworthy still seriously affected Champion's plans and that Cookworthy's executors at least wished to know of Champion's plans. The rough draft 'full of corrections' reads:

> George Harrison will be obliged to his cousin James Fox to inform Richard Champion that the Executors of Mr Cookworthy are disposed to promote his views in introducing the China Manufactory among the People of Staffordshire and should be glad [if] R.C. would write him fully respecting the terms upon which he would propose to put the Business into their Hands as far as regards the claim upon the manufactory.

A further letter seemingly in reply to the just quoted request, written by Richard Champion from Bristol to George Harrison, is dated 3 September 1780, but the year is almost certainly an error for 1781. Again the main object of the letter is to obtain an abatement in the price of the raw materials – a vital consideration. In part the letter reads:

> ...When I first went into Staffordshire in the Spring my views were considerably more enlarged than they are at present. I intended to have established a large work and if Mr Wedgwood should have supported it, I might have done it. But this opposition prevented me and I have now entered into an agreement with ten Potters only, who if they like the Manufactory on its Establishment in the County are to give me a certain sum for liberty to use it in their own works, but I have also liberty to sell to any other I please on the original Plan for a Company, there was a clause designed to be inserted, that every Potter who belonged to it, should have on payment of a certain fine, liberty to make China in his Works.
>
> In this situation I naturally looked to some Advantages from the sale of Materials but the high price of them, compared with those of Trethewys (Twelve guineas a year) and Carthews equally cheap, made me have very little hopes of advantage.
>
> The Potters who knew the prices and your claim made this a capital objection to a Company, I therefore laid the case fairly before Mr Pitt, who was equally concerned with me, with respect to the use of his Materials. He wrote me that he would make any reasonable Abatement.
>
> The case stands thus with all of us, I have a lease from Mr Pitt for 99 years, you have the same Claim from me as he receives for the Materials, but I carry on the smallest work, the advantages you will either receive will be trifling. Again, if I carry on no work, the Lease falls into Mr Pitt's hands, he may make what Bargain he pleases with fresh leases, or sell his Materials, and your claim sinks in course, as it only exists with my Lease, which is Determinable on my carrying on the work or not.
>
> Mr Pitt is certainly in the worst Situation if I do, because the tax which I consented to lay on his Materials by my Agreement with Mr Cookworthy, makes the Materials cost so much (and being a perpetuity without a possibility of its ceasing) that in its present state it must naturally throw the sale of Materials into other hands to his great Injury.
>
> The Remidy comes next. I wish to reap Advantage naturally from the sale of Materials. I wish equally for you. Mr Pitt must do the same. But strong as all our Wishes are, I see no method than you consenting to retain you claim to a certain period or such a certain price per annum as we can agree on. But to settle this arises fresh Difficulties. Hitherto what has arisen to you has been very trifling. In future if I could render the Materials tolerably cheap, it may increase. But if this is not to be done, it must be a total loss to all you and me, as Mr Pitt may by my not being [able] to carry on the work, enter into fresh Agreements.
>
> At present he seems willing to agree to reasonable terms. You will please always to carry this in your View, that the Potters will buy where they please, and that there is no other way of engaging them than by selling cheap.

George Harrison's reply to the above was dated 19 September, thereby confirming the year of the previous letter, but the executors seemed to have been as much in the dark as to the precise details of Cookworthy's original arrangements as we are today. The reply to Champion read:

Respected Frd.
I am obliged to thee for the Information contained in thy Favour of the 3d. Inst, relative to the China Business and in case any determinate Plan of prosecuting it should be fix't on shall be very willing to promote thy views of Advantage, as far as I can consistant with the just Claim of those concerned as W.C.'s Representatives, to whose consideration I shall very cheerfully submit any terms though may propose either upon the Plan of retaining their claim to a certain Period or to a certain Price per annum which ever may be most compatable with thy views, and I doubt not their compliance with reasonable Terms.
I own I am not yet perfectly inform'd on what Ground their claim rests, but as it is for the Merit of Invention I shou'd presume that whilst any Advantage arises to thee from the Manufacture, whether by way of a Fine from the Potters, or from the sale of Materials, their claim will be valid in some proportion but on this subject I may probably be further inform'd ere anything more passes between us.'

It is interesting to note that in the August 1781 letter Richard Champion stated 'I have made Proposals which are under consideration ... but the affair has been much at a stand ...', which to me indicates that the Company was not as yet established or the potters in agreement to proceed.

However, in his letter of 3 September 1781, Richard Champion gave the impression that an agreement had been reached: '...I have now entered into an agreement with ten potters only'. But the following words rather complicate the situation and make one wonder what had been agreed, for he continued that the ten potters 'who if they like the Manufactory on its Establishment in the county are to give me a certain sum for liberty to use it in their own works'. Here I think Champion was referring to the potter's right to purchase china stone and china clay to produce their own chinawares. His letter continues to underline this point but the statement refers to 'the original agreement', not necessarily to the final agreement. This agreement may, however, have retained 'a clause ... that every Potter who belonged to it [the Company], should have on payment of a certain fine, liberty to make china in his Works'. We unfortunately, do not have any known surviving agreement or other like document. It is quite possible to read into these letters that Champion was only concerned to manufacture and supply the basic porcelain mix which he would sell to various Staffordshire potters.

We may, however, I believe, agree that the ten or so Staffordshire potters met and agreed together to form a new company to work Richard Champion's patent rights locally. The precise details of their collective or individual commitment (or investment in shares) is not now known but it is believed that shares were purchased by some of the leading potters or personalities. These we can be reasonably sure included Anthony Keeling, John Turner, Thomas Heath, Samuel Hollins, Jacob Warburton, Charles Bagnall, Joshua Heath and William Clowes. Brief details of these nine early partners, to whom we must add John Daniel, the factory manager, and John Hollins, are given on pages 148-157.

Mr. Roger Pomfret has, however, pointed out to me that, under the terms of the original patent granted to William Cookworthy and its extension to 1796, the new owner of the patent rights, Richard Champion, would have invalidated the patent had he sold shares to more than five persons.

I have reproduced the English patent (which did not relate to Scotland) in Appendix I, but here draw attention to the section which reads, in part:

> ...our Letters Patent are upon this express Condition, That if the said William Cookworthy, his Executors, Administrators, or assigns ... during the continuance of this grant shall make any transfer or assignment ... of the said liberty and privilege, or any share or shares of the benefit or profit thereof or shall declare any trust thereof to or for any number of persons exceeding the number of five; or shall open, or cause to be opened, any book or books for public subscriptions to be made by any number of persons exceeding the number of five or shall presume to act as a corporate body; or shall divide the benefit of these our Letters Patent, or the liberty and privileges hereby by us granted; into any number of Shares exceeding the number of five ... that then, and in any of the said cases, these our Letters Patent and all liberties and advantages whatsoever hereby granted, shall utterly cease, determine and became void...

It is not now known if this then standard and long-standing condition of the patent was known to Champion but he should surely have been advised of it by his numerous friends. It was certainly incorporated in the extension to the patent, which had been of the greatest interest to the Staffordshire potters who under Josiah Wedgwood's leadership had approved the granting of the extension. The patent was in the normal manner published and was available to all interested parties.

Was it Champion's act of trying to interest ten or more Staffordshire potters in the purchase of shares in a new company his undoing? Was this why the patent was not watertight and why other would-be manufacturers could make transparent porcelains using the Cornish china stone and china clay? Or had Champion found a way of selling the patent without breaching this condition? He might have sold out to two or three persons who might later have allowed in more interested parties. He may not have sold the patent at all; the Staffordshire partners seemingly never claimed that their products were patented. At this stage over two hundred years later we just do not know the original situation.

It certainly does seem to be the case that Champion had in fact sold his know-how or right to produce a type of true or hard-paste porcelain in the Plymouth and Bristol manner to a group of Staffordshire backers, possibly not all of whom were working potters. He obviously reserved or obtained for himself some form of remuneration. On the evidence of later dissolution of partnership notices such a Company or working partnership was established and with various changes continued in being for over fifty years.

It is recorded by Hugh Owen who had access to Champion family papers that Richard Champion and his large family left Bristol for Newcastle in Staffordshire on 5 November 1781. We can assume that by this period the various Staffordshire potters and backers had agreed at least in principle, to purchase shares in a new Company or to set up a new manufactory from which Richard Champion stood to gain.

Richard Champion had stated in September 1781 that he had come to an agreement with 'ten potters only', a form of wording suggesting that he was hoping for a larger number or that more had originally showed interest in the venture but in the event only ten had agreed to join the proposed new company.

We also do not know the name of all ten partners and it could be that some dropped out after Champion had written of ten. It could be that all ten were not willing to work together in partnership but that two or more agreed to pay a separate fee or 'fine' in order to produce porcelain using Champion's raw materials in their own works independently of the partnership. This would have included some form of financial payment to Champion. He was not in Staffordshire to give away his livelihood!

Apart from Anthony Keeling and John Turner, plus perhaps Samuel Hollins and Jacob Warburton, these shareholders are not all that well known and I would think that the 'list of names ... of substantial and enterprising potters' given to Richard Champion by Josiah Wedgwood would have included several more names. Studying the directories of the 1780s one would select William Adams, Ralph Baddeley, Hugh Booth, Josiah Spode, The Whiteheads, Wilson (with James Neale), Thomas Wolfe and Enoch Wood, to list the more important names known to us today, as suitable potters to have been approached by Champion. Some or all of these may not – like Wedgwood himself – have been interested in producing china ware; others may already have been conducting their own experiments to produce good marketable porcelain; others, no doubt, could not lay their hands on the ready cash needed by Champion in exchange for his franchise. It would seem likely that some of the partners were pure investors, supplying funds in exchange for shares in the new company; not all were necessarily practising potters.

It is, I think, probable that Richard Champion did not succeed in raising the full amount of £6,000 mentioned in Josiah Wedgwood's famous last letter to Thomas Bentley – 'He tells me he has sunk fifteen thousand pounds in the gulf; and his idea is now to sell the whole art, mystery and patent for six...' (dated 'Etruria, 12th November, 1780').

If we assume that he succeeded in raising only £5,000 from ten persons, then the individual commitment was obviously £500, providing the division or holding of shares was equal. If the number of partners was less, then the individual cost was higher – for eight persons over £600. If only five shares were in fact issued, to abide by the legal wording of the patent, the sum required would have been £1,000 a share.

Now one must remember that in the 1780s this was a very considerable amount, especially to find in ready money. Contemporary letters and records show that cash payments were rare; potters had to be content with forward-dated orders to pay and individuals were made bankrupt for absurdly small amounts which they seemingly could not raise.

There are several different methods of endeavouring to equate eighteenth century values with today's inflated (or deflated) currency. If one takes the average working man's wage then as £1 a week one can easily multiply this by two hundred to bring the sum up to today's equivalent. Our £500 or £600 of the 1780s, therefore, becomes a £100,000 or more in the early 2000s!

This sum, be it £500 or £100,000, was, of course, only the initial payment for the share or permission to produce china under Champion's patent rights – the key franchise. The earthenware potters now had to set up a factory, engage a manager and the new workforce, purchase raw materials and fuel and in general find the extra funds necessary to establish, produce and market a new commodity. There is, I believe, no evidence or suggestion that any of the potters closed their own potteries or ceased to produce their existing earthenwares. All work and costs connected with the new china-making adventure were extra involvements. These charges admittedly would have been shared between all the partners, but so would the income and also the profits would be depleted by the division, once the goods had been successfully produced, sold and belatedly paid for!

I think it clear that the partners would have incurred considerable initial costs, that they would have had a lengthy wait for any return on their investment and that the eventual dividends would have been very small, certainly in the first few years. The production of porcelain, even more than pottery, is fraught with difficulties and the rewards are extremely modest – as Richard Champion and others could have testified! The earliest porcelains attributable to this new Staffordshire partnership are quite mundane and their complete tea services would have been sold at £2, £3 or £4 only, to match in price the various other makes then available.

The earliest authority we have for the initial history of the new firm or combination is Simeon Shaw who gave the basic points in his 1829 privately printed book *History of the Staffordshire Potteries.* After writing of Cookworthy and Champion, Shaw stated (whilst the New Hall Company was still in being) that Champion sold his patent:

> to a Company in Staffordshire: Mr Samuel Hollins, Red china Potter of Shelton; Anthony Keeling, son-in-law of Enoch Booth, Tunstall; John Turner, Lane End; Jacob Warburton, son of Mrs Warburton of Hot Lane; William Clowes, Potter; and Charles Bagnall, Potter, Shelton. After this agreement Mr Champion directed the process of Manufacture, for the Company at the Manufactory of Mr Anthony Keeling, at Tunstall; but when that gentleman [Champion] removed to London in 1782, a disagreement ensued among the partners; Mr Keeling and Mr John Turner withdrew and they who continued together engaged as managing partner, Mr John Daniel ... and settled the manufactory at the New Hall, Shelton, only a short-time previously erected by Mr Whitehead, of the Old Hall, Hanley; on which account the Porcelain had the appellation of New Hall China; and during the life time of the several partners, the concern had been carried forward to their great profit. Mr Jacob Warburton was the principal Gentleman to whom the Potteries are indebted for his spirited introduction of the Porcelain manufacture; even at the present day [the late 1820s] a highly important branch of the Trade, greatly contributing to extend the celebrity, advance the interests and promote the prosperity of this very extensive and populous district.

On other pages Simeon Shaw mentioned points relating to the new Staffordshire partnership formed to work Champion's patent rights. On page 203 he stated:

> The company agreed to supply ground-stone from their mill for any manufacturers, not to be used in the glaze of a transparent body. Thus to the energetic enterprise of Mr Warburton and his colleagues, may be chiefly ascribed the introduction into our Pottery and Porcelain of these valuable materials, indispensible to the improved solidity, durability and texture of the ware and rendering it greatly superior to all previously manufactured.

This reference to a glazing material, or composition, for use on earthenwares probably relates to the 'China Glaze earthenwares' which are featured so much in Staffordshire directories of the 1780s. Typical directory entries read:

> William Adams & Co., Manufacturers of cream coloured Ware and China glazed Ware painted,
> Bourne & Malkin, Manufacturers of China glazed, blue, and cream coloured Ware,
> John & George Rogers, Manufacturers of China glazed Blue painted Wares and Cream coloured

to give only some of the Burslem potters listed in *Bailey's British Directory* for 1784 and repeated in Tunnicliffe's 1787 *Directory.*

There has also been much discussion on the subject of 'composition'. Was it a glaze or a special porcelain mix marketed by the New Hall partners? According to the early writers it was related to the New Hall Company and to their acquired rights in Cookworthy's original patent (see page 416). The 'composition' was seemingly available and used. For example, in October and November 1797 Valentine Close of Hanley supplied the Chamberlain factory at Worcester with over two tons of 'composition' at the basic cost of 6s. a hundredweight or £6 a ton. The Chamberlains were able to purchase the basic china stone from Cornwall at a quarter of this price. In May 1795 Wedgwood was able to supply Cornish china clay at £4.4s.0d. and china stone at £1.10s.0d. a ton.

Simeon Shaw further noted on his page 203:

> Mr Champion resided in the Potteries until the formation of the Rockingham Ministry in March 1782 when he removed to London on being appointed Deputy Paymaster of the Forces, under Mr Burke ... The enjoyment of the situation however, was of short continuance, owing to the dissolution of that short-lived Ministry [on 1 July 1782]; after which his extensive mercantile connections required his presence in America, he visited that Continent; and having successfully arranged his affairs, settled at Camden in South Carolina...

We might wonder how always hard-up Champion came to be able to emigrate and settle in America. Certainly, he had many influential and wealthy friends, but the sale of his rights to the new Staffordshire company no doubt supplied new funds. Indeed Dr. John Aikin in his *A Description of the country from Thirty to Forty miles round Manchester,* which was published in London in 1795, stated under Shelton: 'the porcelain or china manufactory carried on under the respectable firm of Hollins, Warburton & Co ... The ingenious Mr Champion of Bristol ... obtained a patent ... which he sold to the above gentlemen for such a sum of money as enabled him to retire to America'. This may not be accurate, but it represents a near contemporary view.

Shaw's account of the formation of the new partnership at Tunstall and the names of the six potters concerned, together with the fact that Anthony Keeling and John Turner soon disengaged themselves, was most probably based on information given by Jacob Warburton with whom he was obviously on friendly terms. Warburton was one of the original partners and Shaw's account should be authoritative. On pages 204 and 205 Shaw gives a glowing account of Jacob Warburton 'equally respectable for social virtues, great mental ability and extensive literary acquirements...', even quoting his final words uttered before his death on 19 September 1826, aged eighty-six. Whilst some faults can be found in Shaw's version of the facts, they are substantially correct and have formed the basis for all subsequent authors to work upon.

Yet this Warburton-cum-Shaw account offers but the bare bones, especially regarding the early years at Tunstall. We cannot now be certain when the new manufactory was set up or started production at Enoch Booth's former pottery, then owned by Anthony Keeling, or when the first partnership was dissolved[2] on account of the reported withdrawal of Anthony Keeling and John Turner (both important potters), and the re-establishment of the co-partnership at the New Hall at Shelton. Was there a time-lag between the cessation of the Tunstall works and the establishment of the new porcelain works on the New Hall estate? Almost certainly there was a void period. We do not know the trade name under which the original partners commenced to trade at Tunstall. It should be noted that Richard Champion had left Staffordshire before the new works were established at the 'New Hall'.

The pre-Shelton period, that is the duration of the enterprise at Tunstall, seems to have been very little researched. However, the Land Tax returns preserved in the Staffordshire County Record Office at Stafford shed a little light on the possible duration of the partners' occupancy of the Tunstall premises although, unfortunately, the entries are exceedingly brief and do not give the precise information we seek. The Land Tax records for Tunstall are headed:

> An Assessment made in pursuance of an Act of Parliament passed in the present year of his Majesty's Reign for granting an aid to His Majesty by a Land Tax at four shillings in the pound for the service of the year 1781.

The following entries are arranged in three columns, headed respectively 'Name of Proprietor', that is the owner of the Land or property, then 'Names of the Occupiers' and lastly the 'Sums of Assessment'. The full listing, most probably a fair copy taken from previous notes, is signed, sealed and dated 21 May 1781 (the 2 in the day number is unclear and poorly formed but the digit must be a 2 or 3). The day 21 or 31 May is only relevant in showing that the fair copy had been completed, agreed and signed by that date and the headings of other such returns show that the period covered was generally from 5 April of the previous year (in this case 1780) to 4 April of the next year, i.e., 1781.

The April 1781 entries which concern us are the properties or land then owned by:

a) Enoch Booth Trustees
b) Anthony Keeling

The occupiers are then given as:

a) Themselves and others (Assessment 9s.4d.)
b) Himself (Assessment 2s.6d).

The expressions 'Themselves' and 'Himself' are standard terms used when a group of persons or the individual owner is also occupying and working the property. The additional notation 'and others' was rarely used in these Land Tax Returns, but when it does occur it clearly shows that other (unnamed) persons were also involved in the occupancy, most probably in partnership with the first named.

We can therefore glean the information that Enoch Booth's (who died in March 1773) former premises at Tunstall were, on or before 4 April 1781, owned by his Trustees and that these Trustees (who no doubt included his son-in-law Anthony Keeling as well as Enoch Booth's son, also named Enoch and described as a 'potter' in an addition to the Will which was dated 6 May 1773) were occupying the premises in partnership with 'others'. At the same time, Keeling occupied smaller premises – perhaps his dwelling house assessed at 2s.6d. as opposed to the Enoch Booth premises assessed at 9s.4d. We therefore learn that a form of partnership was probably in being on (or before) 4 April 1781 at Enoch Booth's former pottery at Tunstall, the site always quoted as the first used by the new partnership formed to work the Cookworthy/Champion patent rights. What we cannot be sure of is whether this group of occupiers were those who came together to produce the new porcelain and if a new porcelain manufactory was then in production.

The next available Tunstall Land Tax Returns were signed and sealed on 15 May 1783 and show the position between April 1782 and April 1783. These evidence the fact that the premises formerly listed as owned by Enoch Booth's trustees had now passed to Anthony Keeling. However, they seemingly were still occupied by a partnership, the official description being 'Himself and others', with the same Land Tax assessment of 9s.4d.

I think these 1783 Land Tax returns suggest that the

original partnership was still in being and occupying the Tunstall manufactory in April 1783, also that Anthony Keeling and presumably John Turner were still in the partnership. If I am correct in my interpretation of the available brief records the duration of the original partnership working at Tunstall was longer than we had assumed from our reading of Simeon Shaw's brief statement.

The Tunstall period may well have been even longer than the period of April 1781 to April 1783 for unfortunately the next available Tunstall Land Tax return is for 1786. By this time the old Enoch Booth pottery which had passed to Anthony Keeling's ownership by April 1783 had seemingly been subdivided, presumably after the removal of the so-called New Hall partnership. In 1786 we find Anthony Keeling occupying part of the land himself. This portion was valued at 5s.6d. rather than the former 9s.4d. Another portion valued at 3s. was occupied by the little-known Joseph Smith and partners. Reginald Haggar has noted that Joseph Smith was 'potting in Tunstall in 1784', on the evidence of his inclusion in the Tunstall Land Tax returns of 1781, 1783, and 1786 as owning and occupying land or property valued at £1.14s.10d., a considerable sum.

It is interesting to note that Joseph Smith had been in partnership with Anthony Keeling in a 'Flint Mill concern' at Tunstall in the 1780s. This partnership was dissolved on 6 September 1790. Joseph Smith also potted at one period at least in partnership with Peter Swift, but the firm of Smith & Swift was dissolved on 12 February 1794. One of the Smith's potteries was advertised to be let or sold in 1802.

Returning to the important question of the new company's occupation of Anthony Keeling's Tunstall premises into 1783, it must be stated that the position is complicated when we investigate the Shelton Land Tax returns, for that to 5 April 1783 does show the occupier of James Neale's property, which we know now as New Hall, was 'Sam Hollins & Co', a hitherto unrecorded description (although Samuel Hollins is listed alone, not as a company, in Bailey's 1781 *Directory)* which could well relate to the new so-called New Hall partnership. The question of the Shelton records is detailed in the following chapter. Unfortunately, we do not have Land Tax Returns for Shelton or for Tunstall for the year to April 1782.

Before progressing to discuss the wares that may have been produced by the new porcelain producing partnership at Tunstall, I should like to give an all too brief resumé of Enoch Booth's potting career, for it was at his former pottery that the story of the New Hall porcelain commenced. It is brief simply because we lack details, but he was undoubtedly a very important 'Master Potter', one who is widely credited with far-reaching improvements in the industry.

I am indebted to Mrs. P.A. Halfpenny, the former Keeper of Ceramics at the City of Stoke-on-Trent City Museum and Art Gallery (now The Potteries Museum), for the following basic facts. Mrs. Halfpenny has been unable to locate any record of his date of birth, but we can work back from the 1717 Inland Revenue's list of apprentice agreements which show that Enoch Booth, son of Ephraim Booth of Astbury, Cheshire, was apprenticed to a Thomas Heath of Shelton, a potter. A fee of £7 was paid. It seems likely therefore that Enoch Booth was born before 1710 and possibly in about 1707.

The Wolstanton registers show that he married Anne (or Ann) Child in 1728. Anne was one of six daughters of Thomas Child of the Manor House, Tunstall, a rich and important personage who died in 1735. At this time Enoch Booth was potting at Hanley and, according to a document in the Potteries Museum, Enoch and Anne Booth released their sixth part of Thomas Child's estate and took in exchange lands at Tunstall. At some unknown period, about 1730, a son also named Enoch was born to Enoch and Anne Booth. A daughter, Anne, was born in 1735 but Anne Booth (Thomas Child's daughter) died in 1738.

Enoch Booth junior took an early interest in his father's trade for in February 1756 the insurance cover on the house and pottery was taken out by the son. The entry, discovered by Mrs. Elizabeth Adams in the Sun Insurance Company archives at the Guildhall Library, reads:

> Enoch Booth junr. of Tunstall in the Parish of Woolstanton, Co. Stafford, Earth Potter. £1,000 (dwellinghouse £300. Pottery Buildings £400, other properties £33).
> (Policy 150761 of 2 February 1756)

Enoch and Anne Booth's daughter Anne (b. 1735) married Anthony Keeling of Stoke in August 1760, when the marriage was witnessed by William Yates and Hugh Booth. I will return to Anthony Keeling shortly, but first I have to record the death of Enoch Booth in March 1773, when he would have been in his mid-sixties.

Mr. Rodney Hampson has traced Enoch Booth's will, dated 27 February 1773, at the Lichfield Record Office. The main details are that at this period just before his death he was seemingly still potting at Tunstall. The main estate including rents and profits was left to his son Enoch, and on his death in turn to his son William Booth. His grandson Enoch Keeling was to receive £100 on attaining the age of twenty-one or on an earlier marriage. Enoch Booth's 'Grand-daughter Yates' received £20. The signature was witnessed by Edward Sneyd, Charles Spooner and Moses Ridley. In a later note the appointed trustees, John Hales, potter of Cobridge, and Joseph Booth (Enoch's cousin), butcher of Hanley, passed this responsibility on to Enoch's only son Enoch Booth of Tunstall, potter. Enoch Booth in his 1773 will obviously intended that his Phoenix Pottery in Tunstall High Street should be continued by or for the benefit of his son and for his grandson. This seemingly came into being as his son-in-law Anthony Keeling continued this pottery. Enoch Booth junior is not recorded as potting under his own name.

As to Enoch Booth's ceramic career or achievements, Simeon Shaw's 1829 book *History of the Staffordshire Potteries* must again serve as our basic authority. Shaw noted 'Mr Enoch Booth first introduced that most important improvement in the manufacture of pottery the fluid Glaze…' and (on page 176):

> Mr Enoch Booth, of Tunstall, first united the clays of the neighbourhood carefully levigated, in union with those from the South of England, (Devon and Dorset) and a certain proportion of Flint … This body he first glazed with lead ore; next he mixed it with one of the clays, and then added a little dry calcined flint in powder; and finally, he used lead and flint in a liquid state, or Littler's method, but with this difference, Littler dipped the clay unfired ware into his liquid; but Mr Booth fired his once, and dipped the Bisquet ware…

Arnold R. Mountford (then Director of the City Museum & Art Gallery, Stoke-on-Trent) in his specialist book *The Illustrated Guide to Staffordshire Salt-Glazed Stoneware* (Barrie & Jenkins, London, 1971), writing a hundred and forty years after Shaw, noted:

> Enoch Booth of Tunstall is said to have been the first potter in Staffordshire to use a liquid glaze containing lead and flint on biscuit earthenware in about 1750. As mentioned above, a scratch-blue mug with a slightly spreading base and decorated with three grotesque birds, acorns and leaves bears his name and the date '1742'. A fine loving cup in the City Museum, Stoke-on-Trent, has 'EB 1754' incised, with floral decoration and a narrow band of rouletting below the lathe-turned rim – and this example is also attributed to Enoch Booth. Enoch Booth and his son Enoch were also makers of enamelled salt-glaze and had an established trade by contra with Thomas and John Wedgwood of the Big House, Burslem. Lack of contemporary documentation prevents a real assessment of Booth's standing in the pottery industry, but it is quite obvious from what is known that he was justly described as a master-potter.

Mr. Mountford illustrated as his Plate 166 the inscribed 'EB 1754' salt-glazed loving cup. A documentary salt-glaze mug in the Fitzwilliam Museum at Cambridge, is inscribed 'Enoch Booth 1742' – see my *An Illustrated Encyclopaedia of British Pottery and Porcelain* (Barrie & Jenkins, London, 1966), Plate 62 – but of course no name mark was used on Booth's salt-glaze wares or on his creamwares. Arnold Mountford also stated (his page 57) that Enoch Booth had a decorating-shop at his Tunstall factory. He then states:

> In the 1760s, he was supplying the Wedgwood brothers as follows:
>
> 1767 June 18 by 1 Doz.Enamel Teapots 7.0
> Sepr 2 by 22 Enamel Tpots 9.8½
> Novr 5 by 18 Enamel teapot and one Red Qt Coffee pot as Bill 9.0½
> NB one Teapot had one Broken spout
> 1768 Apr 14 by 35 Enamel Teapots as pr Bill 17.5½
> The above items cannot be confused with creamware, for on the same page we read:
> 1770 Sep. 17 by 4 Doz cream cups and saucers 6.0
> Elsewhere in the account book creamware is described as 'cream colour'. Thus, items sold to Aaron Wedgwood, viz:-
> 1767 May 29 by Enamel teapots he had of Mr E Booth as bill 7.0.
> Would most probably have been salt-glazed stoneware…

A superb early creamware punchbowl in the British Museum is widely cited as an example of Enoch Booth's use of liquid glaze. This example is painted with underglaze blue panels in the Chinese style and is inscribed under the base 'E.B. 1743'. This example is illustrated by Donald Towner in his book *Creamware* (Faber & Faber, London, 1978) and his Plate 1A and B. The figure subject interior is shown as Plate 63 in my *Illustrated Encyclopaedia of British Pottery and Porcelain*. The early creamware teapot inscribed under the base 'F. Morgan. Tunstall. Oct.20th 1743' and sold at Messrs. Bonhams' London auction rooms in November 1994 for £34,000 was also almost certainly produced at Enoch Booth's pottery.

We therefore have rare dated pieces of 1742, 1743 and 1754 attributed to this Tunstall potter. Shipments of earthenwares from the Potteries along the River Weaver are recorded in the Weaver Navigation Records kept in the Cheshire County Record Office. These include references in the 1740s to earthenwares belonging to Enoch Booth. It is quite clear that Enoch Booth of Tunstall was a leading Staffordshire potter and some eight years after his death (in 1773) this pottery was taken over (at least in part) for the production of the new Staffordshire porcelains in about 1781 or 1782.

Over forty years later Simeon Shaw, writing in 1829, noted that Tunstall in the eighteenth century was a very small township:

> Tunstall has risen, during the present century, from being a mere small street, of about twenty houses in the highroad and about forty more in the lanes leading to Chatterley and Red Street, into a town of moderate size...

The 1781 Land Tax Returns for Tunstall has only forty-four entries.

Returning to our main story of the establishment of the Staffordshire porcelain producing partnership, we have, I believe, shown that Richard Champion was in Staffordshire in 1781, then aged only about thirty-eight. By 3 September of that year he was able to write that he had 'now entered into an agreement with ten potters...'. This does not necessarily mean that they had agreed to establish their first works or that Enoch Booth's pottery had by then been amended or enlarged and that all the materials required to produce the new porcelains were available. But on the other hand we have shown that Enoch Booth's Tunstall premises were in or about April 1781 occupied by an unnamed partnership which probably included Anthony Keeling. Certainly by the time the 1782-3 accounts were written up in mid-May 1783, the premises were recorded as being worked by 'Anthony Keeling and others'.

It seems to me reasonable to suggest that the pottery at Tunstall would not have been producing porcelains on a commercial scale before 1782. If I am correct in this belief then Champion can have had little connection with the new venture for it is recorded that this former Bristol porcelain maker left Staffordshire on 6 April 1782 for London and subsequently for America, where he died in October 1791.

The traditional belief is that Anthony Keeling and John Turner, two of the leading original potters, left the partnership soon after Champion departed for London. Most authorities have taken this very literally, and assumed that these two potters left early in 1782 and that consequently the remaining partners were forced to move from the Booth-Keeling premises at Tunstall to Shelton Hall, later to be called the New Hall.

I do not think it necessarily follows that Keeling and Turner left the company in, or soon after, April 1782 but if the disagreement did take place at this period then the company's duration at Tunstall would have been extremely brief, a mere few months. I have already noted that the Tunstall Land Tax returns for the twelve months to 5 April 1783 and signed and sealed on 15 May 1783 show the former Booth pottery at Tunstall as being occupied by Anthony Keeling 'and others'. In other words, a partnership was working the pottery with Anthony Keeling. They were, however, not necessarily producing porcelain. Contrary to the general view I feel that the partnership was still in being and working together at the Tunstall premises at least into 1783. However, we must bear in mind that this Anthony Keeling partnership could have been an entirely different one, working the new Tunstall porcelain manufactory after the original remaining partners had moved to Shelton and commenced to trade at Shelton on New Hall.

Although Anthony Keeling and John Turner, two of the original partners; were not destined to play a leading part in the New Hall company, their initial support as leading and no doubt prosperous potters was of great importance. I need therefore to give details of their careers.

Anthony Keeling was probably the most important to the new partnership for he lent, or more probably rented, his own pottery to the new concern. I consider that he must have been the key figure in the initial partnership, being responsible for the day-by-day management of the factory – his own. He surely introduced the production of Champion's amended porcelains to Staffordshire. On his leaving the concern the partners employed John Daniel as the new manager. Anthony Keeling was born in 1738 and in 1760 married Anne, a daughter of the well-known Tunstall potter Enoch Booth. Keeling and his father-in-law traded together from at least 1759 and on the death of Enoch Booth in 1773, Anthony Keeling continued the business at the Booth family pottery.

The Tunstall Land Tax returns for the period to April 1781 (the first available) shows the Booth pottery as being owned by Enoch Booth's trustees, among whom Anthony Keeling and his wife Anne (one of Enoch Booth's daughters) were almost certainly included, with initially John Hales and Joseph Booth who passed their responsibilities on to young Enoch Booth. The pottery was then listed as being occupied by 'Themselves and others', in other words by a partnership. The next available Land Tax returns, those to April 1783, give the occupiers as 'Anthony Keeling and others'. However, by the time of the next available return (of 1786) he is listed as occupying a perhaps smaller pottery but probably now adapted to produce china on his own account. The former partners in the new venture had moved to Shelton and seemingly Joseph Smith had taken over part of the property where earthenwares were made – see page 95.

I am as yet unable to state when Anthony Keeling commenced to produce porcelain as well as earthenwares on his own account, but prior to 1792 he was involved in a large china producing partnership at Hanley. This little-known firm of Anthony Keeling & Co., which also traded as Keeling, Perry & Co., comprised six partners. In this company, which was dissolved on 11 November 1792, 'Mr Anthony Keeling of Tunstall' was authorised to receive payments of debts or pay monies owing. Keeling was obviously the leading light in Anthony Keeling & Co. 'china manufacturers'.[3]

It is not certain if Anthony Keeling continued to produce china at his Tunstall pottery but I think this was very probable. Within a few years his sons joined him and he traded as Anthony Keeling & Sons (c.1792-5) and from about 1795 as Anthony and Enoch Keeling. The last firm or partnership of the 1795-1814 period certainly produced china ware and I believe that Anthony Keeling produced New Hall type porcelains from about the period when he and John Turner left the original Staffordshire partnership, that is, in or about 1783. It is currently (c.2000) believed that Keeling and subsequent partnerships produced the porcelain loosely termed 'Factory X'.

The early writers state that Anthony Keeling retired in 1810 and moved to Liverpool where he died in January 1815. He certainly died in Liverpool but the local directories of the 1810-5 period do not include his name and the Tunstall Land Tax returns show him as owning two of the three separate Keeling properties in Staffordshire up to 1814.

While the New Hall company obviously continued and prospered at Shelton after Anthony Keeling and John Turner had left the partnership in the early 1780s, one wonders how it might have expanded still further and perhaps become the largest china producing firm in the history of late eighteenth and early nineteenth British ceramics, had these two important potters remained to play their full part in the venture. This had been Champion's dream.

Turning to John Turner (1738-1787), his standing (as a Master Potter at Lane End) was probably even higher than Anthony Keeling's. Certainly Turner's various types of earthenware approach in taste, neatness and general quality Josiah Wedgwood's renowned wares. Furthermore Turner, with Josiah Wedgwood, represented the Staffordshire potters in their earlier fight against the extension of the Cookworthy/Champion patents. Turner also went with Wedgwood to Cornwall in search of china clays.

The full story of John Turner's career and good examples of his earthenwares are told and shown in Bevis Hillier's standard book *The Turners of Lane End* (Cory, Adams & Mackay, London, 1965). While I do not know of any evidence to prove that John Turner was one of the original partners in the new china making enterprise, the tradition seems firmly established and was first planted by Simeon Shaw in his 1829 book. Unfortunately, no official dissolution of partnership notice seems to have been published in the 1780s and no other known early documents give the names of all the original partners.

I, however, accept the tradition, especially as the Land Tax returns substantiate the other part of Shaw's account, that Anthony Keeling was also concerned but soon left. What is not clear is why Anthony Keeling and John Turner left the first partnership. In neither case would it have been due to shortage of funds. John Turner would not have left if Keeling merely wished to use his pottery to produce his own earthenwares or the new type porcelains. It would seem that for some reason these two leading potters were dissatisfied with the arrangements or with the slow progress being made in introducing or re-introducing the porcelain industry to the Staffordshire Potteries. Most probably the expected profit was slow to materialise.

I believe that both Keeling and Turner were still interested in producing porcelain as well as their earthenwares. Some porcelains were produced by John Turner before his death in 1787 and his sons John and William later successfully produced well-potted china. In this regard the reader is referred to *Staffordshire Porcelain* (Granada Publishing, London, 1983), Chapter 6.

THE TUNSTALL PORCELAINS

Let us now proceed to consider what types of porcelain might initially have been produced by this Staffordshire partnership working the Cookworthy-Champion Patent before the Company moved to new premises at Shelton. If you favour the old view that Anthony Keeling and John Turner left soon after Champion moved to London in April 1782, then it follows that the Tunstall production was limited at the most to a six or seven month period between the 'potters' entering into an agreement in about September 1781 and April 1782 when Champion left Staffordshire. During this short period the production line had to be set up and any teething troubles overcome. Examples existing today, more than two hundred years later, would be very scarce.

As previously stated, I believe the Tunstall period was somewhat longer, perhaps a matter of eighteen months.

It was, I believe, that great, gentlemanly, New Hall collector, the late Geoffrey Grey, who first separated a group of porcelains, apparently of the correct period in the early 1780s, and suggested that they represented the earliest type of known 'New Hall' Tunstall period porcelain. These researches were included in the second part of his English Ceramic Circle paper, read on 26 October 1969. This was subsequently published under the title 'New Hall, Hard-Paste Porcelain' in *The Transactions of the English Ceramic Circle* Volume 8, Part 1 (1971). Mr. Grey noted that:

> Common to all pieces of the group is a form of reeding which differs from that used at New Hall almost from the start of the first period, in that the reeds (and flutes) are separated, not continuous.[4] The group also includes certain shapes, notably of tea caddies and handle forms, not yet recorded on authentic New Hall wares. Moreover, there is a considerable variation within the group in the colour and translucency of the pieces, and in the degrees of success achieved in the firing of the body and glaze … Qualitative analysis of some of the key pieces shows the body to be of the early New Hall hard-paste type. The glaze in most cases appears to be of the same general character as the New Hall glaze and in several cases is indistinguishable from it … Finally, there are some shapes and potting features which we have noted on New Hall wares…

Mr. Grey also wrote 'with the exception of the heavier tea-caddy, all pieces are decorated with well-known patterns from the earliest part of the New Hall pattern book ***(sic!),*** and painted in the New Hall manner…'. However, I do not fully agree with this statement having over the years discovered other specimens which do not seem to match accepted later New Hall patterns, so that some patterns found on this early class do not seem to appear in the accepted range of later New Hall porcelains. This is of little consequence to the basic theory.

Mr. Grey did not go as far as to suggest that this early group of porcelain was made in the first Tunstall period, but he did write that he accepted these porcelains 'as products of New Hall during this exploratory or prototype stage; and I would assume that the special reeding and other features, peculiar to the group, were discarded before my so-called "first period" got under way'. Mr. Grey probably did not refer to these 'reeded' or corrugated porcelains as being made at Tunstall for in his specialist New Hall chapter in the multi-authored book *English Porcelain 1745-1850* (edited by R.J. Charleston, Ernest Benn Ltd., London, 1965) he referred to the Tunstall period as being 'an abortive start'. I, however, believe that the corrugated surfaced porcelains of the types here shown in Plates 19-46 and Colour Plates 1-3 could have been made at Tunstall under Keeling's management, before the company transferred to Shelton. The examples cited by Geoffrey Grey are shown in Plates 9-11 of his E.C.C. paper.

Mr. David Holgate in his 1987 book *New Hall* did tend to the view that this group of porcelains was made during the initial Tunstall period, speculating that the pieces were 'either made with Champion at Keeling's works or after Champion, Turner and Keeling had left and the remainder moved to Shelton Hall. The first products were probably the group which has "corrugated" moulding over the surface … I am convinced that this is a group of early products of the factory…'. However, in the captions to the illustrations of this type of porcelain, Mr. Holgate uses the rather wide dating '1782-5', extending the group into his Shelton period. In his later E.C.C paper *(Transactions,* Vol. 14, Part 2, 1991) Mr. Holgate suggests that the range of these corrugated porcelains is too large for them to have been made at Tunstall, but he was assuming that the company was there only for a short period and this is not necessarily the case! He has more recently suggested to me that there could have been an overlap, some corrugated wares being made in the Tunstall period and other examples at Shelton.

No porcelains of this corrugated group were included in George Stringer's 1949 book *New Hall Porcelains* or indeed in any works published before Geoffrey Grey's E.C.C. paper read in 1969 and published two years later.

In general terms the so-far identified porcelains have a form of reeded or fluted outer surface which Mr. Holgate correctly terms 'corrugated' as there is a flat base between each undulation, a flat valley between each hill – see Plate 19. This flat valley is clearly seen on the larger objects, teapots, etc., but is of course less clear on the smaller items. Rather similar fluting can be found on some Bristol hard-paste porcelains of the late 1770s and on other earlier and later porcelains, but the corrugations differ from the class of Staffordshire porcelains of the early 1780s here under discussion. Most of the pieces here attributed to this Tunstall period have twenty-eight raised ribs in the corrugations, except the teapot which has thirty. It should, however, be noted that several other factories produced some shapes having twenty-eight ribs or corrugations – it is not an infallible guide to origin.

These Staffordshire relatively thinly potted corrugated forms were moulded, but plain hand-thrown components can be added to the main moulded form so that a corrugated creamer can have a thrown base luted on to the moulded body. Reeded or fluted forms are by no means unique to this class; some delightful Bristol teawares are so treated, as are some early Worcester teawares of the 1750s, but these shapes usually lack the pronounced flat valleys of these new Staffordshire porcelains. It is relatively expensive to produce such

Plate 19. *A rare corrugated, moulded, small mug with typical handle form. Painted with the 'mug spray and border' design rendered in a simple early style. Twenty-eight ribs. 3½in. (8.89cm) high. c.1782-83. See Colour Plate 1.* Godden collection

Plate 20. *The reverse side of a Bristol hard-paste porcelain plate showing the inner additional footrim to help keep the plate straight in the firing. This was not needed with the new Staffordshire hybrid hard-paste porcelains. c.1775-80.* Private collection

moulded shapes which necessitate master models and a series of working moulds which have to be replaced from time to time. The production of moulded corrugated forms probably increased the initial factory costs by about ten per cent and to some degree the undulating surface restricts the decoration and makes the burnishing of the gilding more difficult. It follows that the management must have had good reasons to introduce and so greatly favour such moulded corrugated surfaced porcelains rather than to concentrate on the less expensive, plain surfaced hand-thrown wares. It would, however, be difficult to believe that all the Tunstall period pieces were of the moulded corrugated type.

The basic reason for corrugating any material is to add strength without adding thickness of material. This is true of corrugated iron, of corrugated cardboard and equally of corrugated porcelain. The end result was that the new Staffordshire management (we do not yet have a trading name) were able to produce relatively thinly potted teawares of a pleasing light weight and delicate feel. More importantly, less porcelain body needed to be used than would have been needed for thicker walled hand-thrown articles. This in turn meant that less of the expensive West Country china clay and china stone was used and the management linked to Champion's agreement had to pay over the going rates for their raw materials. A saving of ten per cent in cost of the body used was of vital importance to a firm striving to sell their new porcelains in a market which was already well served with less expensive and often better decorated porcelains produced by well-known firms of long standing, such as those at Derby or Worcester. The saving in raw materials probably more than offset the added cost of forming the objects in moulds.

The corrugations also add strength, for this group of porcelains do not evidence the firing difficulties experienced earlier at Bristol. The new cups retain their shape, the handles are not twisted by the partial unwinding of hand-thrown shapes, for they are not thrown. The rare new Staffordshire plates do not show, or need, the added second supporting footrim found under most Bristol plates – see Plate 20.

Apart from the assistance of the corrugated forms, the porcelain body itself must have been slightly changed from that previously used by Champion at Bristol. It is also very probable that the firing sequence or the firing temperature was amended, as David Holgate originally suggested. I have had a typical example of the early corrugated class of porcelain professionally analysed by Messrs. Watts, Blake, Bearne & Co., Plc., of Newton

PLATE 21. *The corrugated moulded teapot from the 'Davis Festoon' service shown in Plates 22-7. This Tunstall period set, like all pieces of this early class, is unmarked. Thirty ribs. 9in. (22.86cm) long, 6¼in. (15.88cm) high. c. 1782-83. See Colour Plate 2.* GODDEN COLLECTION

Abbot, who conduct such services for the Department of Ceramic Technology and Geological Sciences at the North Staffordshire Polytechnic. The result shows that the corrugated wares were remarkably similar in chemical make-up to that of a Bristol specimen. Indeed, it is a far nearer match to Bristol than it is to a later New Hall body! It must be borne in mind, however, that differences will occur in the make-up of different pieces made by the same factory and that the management were still experimenting. One must be careful not to place too much reliance on the analysis of one or two specimens.

The visual appearance of the pre-1780 Bristol hard-paste porcelain and the post-1781 Staffordshire so-called hybrid hard-paste porcelains is, however, vastly different. The appearance was to change yet again when we come to consider the mainstream New Hall porcelains made at the Shelton works.

The porcelain body of the almost complete corrugated tea service of the early 1780s here shown in Plates 21-7 is not nearly as white as the earlier Bristol body, the Staffordshire body being distinctly creamy in surface tone. The Bristol body too has a good white translucency when held to the light; the new Staffordshire body is not so translucent and shows a quite green tone. For these reasons I believe the new Staffordshire mix of the 1781-2 period differed somewhat from that previously made by Richard Champion at Bristol. It must be stated, however, that the appearance of this class is variable; some pieces are greyer than the usual rather creamy tone.

None of the so far recorded examples of this corrugated surfaced porcelain of the early 1780s bears any kind of factory mark, pattern number or painter's tally marks. This is in contrast to Champion's practice earlier at Bristol, where most of his productions bore the painted cross device, usually with the painter's or gilder's tally number added under the mark or by the copy of the Dresden

Plate 22. *The corrugated covered sugar bowl from the Tunstall period tea service painted with 'Davis Festoon'. This set includes gilt edging and trim. Twenty-eight ribs. 5½in. (13.97cm) high. c.1782 83.*
Godden collection

crossed swords device. It is true also, that none of the standard Bristol patterns was exactly copied or used at the Staffordshire works, although some continuation of fashionable styles of the period can be noted. These included festoons of flowers, but this motif is by no means restricted to Bristol and to these Staffordshire porcelains or indeed to British ceramics.

These facts lead one to question how large a part Richard Champion played in the establishment of the venture. Seemingly the new Staffordshire partners had the larger say in the fresh Staffordshire shapes and added designs, although the new porcelains do not appear to mirror the partners' various earthenware forms or designs. It is worthy of note that Champion lived at Newcastle, not close by the works at Tunstall. The Sun Insurance cover on his properties, which is dated 18 March 1782, shows that he owned or occupied a brick-built and tiled house in Merrill (now Merrial) Street (valued at £200). His 'China therein' seems only to be household items, not a stock in trade, as the value placed on this china was 'not exceeding one hundred pounds', that is the same maximum as his books and his wearing apparel. Apart from his residence in Merrill Street, Newcastle, Richard Champion also insured a 'Laboratory' in a separate brick and tiled building covered for a maximum of £100, also his 'Utensils and Stock in trade consisting of Cobbalt and Blue colour, prepared therein only' to a value of £400. Underglaze blue decoration has not been noted on these early corrugated surfaced porcelains, but then Champion left for London on 6 April, a fortnight or so after having taken out this 1782 policy. The mention of 'Cobbalt' and 'Blue colour' in Champion's Staffordshire laboratory is interesting and suggests that he was still striving to master the technique of painting or printing in underglaze blue on the amended body. This is understandable, for the mass middle-class porcelain market was centred on the low priced blue and white designs, be they the large imports from China or the Worcester or Caughley essays in this style. The new partnership would have sought to rival these saleable porcelains.

The late Mrs. Kit Holgate, however, interestingly suggested in her paper published in the *Journal of the Northern Ceramic Society,* Vol. 6 (1987), that the blue printed porcelains with the lion crest mark (as shown on page 285) might have been produced in the earliest period of the company's existence. Further discussion on this point is given from page 288.

Some six years before the new partnership was established in 1781 Josiah Wedgwood attempted (without success) to set up his co-operative venture to produce porcelain in the Staffordshire Potteries. It was then (in 1775) their main aim 'to make a useful white porcelain body with a colourless glaze for the same, and a blue paint under the glaze...'. The necessity to produce such Chinese style blue patterned porcelains remained in the early 1780s and must have concerned Champion and the new partnership.

Turning to consider the corrugated porcelains known to me or illustrated in other works, we find these are restricted to tea and coffee services, or parts thereof, and to mugs, jugs and similar small articles such as a custard-cup and cover.

The 'full' tea and coffee services comprised the standard components of the period, that is:

Teapot and cover (Plate 21)
A sugar bowl and cover (Plate 22)
A milk (or cream) jug and cover (Plate 23)
A tea canister (or 'tea vase') and cover (Plate 25)
A waste bowl (Plate 39)
A spoon-tray (Plate 26)
Two bread and butter or cake plates, of slightly different sizes (Plate 27)
12 saucers (Plate 27)
12 teabowls (Plate 27)
12 coffee cups (Plate 37)

The teapot most probably would have been sold with a

Plate 23. *The covered milk jug from the Tunstall period corrugated tea service painted with 'Davis festoon'. Twenty-eight ribs. Note the rare but typical handle form and the slight bead at the base of the spout. 5¼in. (13.34cm). c.1782-83.*
GODDEN COLLECTION

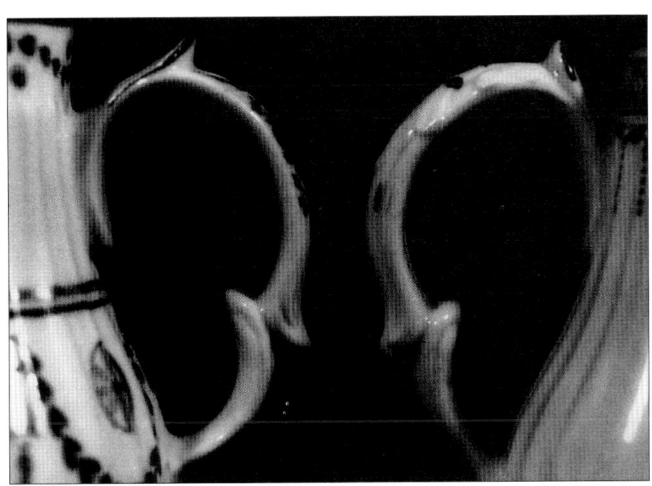

Plate 24. *Detail of typical Tunstall period moulded handles from the milk jugs shown in Plates 23 and 31. c.1782-83.*

Plate 25. *The tea canister and cover from the 'Davis Festoon' pattern corrugated tea service shown in Plates 21-7. Twenty-eight ribs. All such New Hall canisters are rare, early ones particularly so. 6½in. (16.51cm) high. c.1782-83.* GODDEN COLLECTION

stand but I do not know of a surviving corrugated example.

A matching coffee pot and cover (and perhaps also a coffee-pot stand) would also most probably have been available, as an extra, but no specimens of this early corrugated form[5] are known to me, although a rare spouted jug is shown in Plate 42. This stands 8¾in. (22.23cm) high and could have been used for coffee, although such jugs are not usually so designated.

The almost complete tea service now in my possession and illustrated in Plates 21-7, like other early corrugated wares, does not bear a pattern number. There is, however, a need to designate these early patterns because we are going to discuss some of these in future chapters as they occur on later true New Hall porcelains. The early partners, painters and clerks would also have needed to have identified each pattern. Originally names may have been used, before the numbers increased to such a degree that a pattern numbering system was employed.

I therefore will use simple names for patterns which have not as yet been found to bear a pattern number. This pattern I will call the 'Davis Festoon', as I purchased this set from another dedicated collector – Peter Davis. Several patterns may originally have been linked with a person, a retailer or other important customer who first ordered or suggested the pattern. Incidentally, the later New Hall underglaze blue designs did not have a pattern number (unless gilding was added) and these would have had a factory name such as 'Chinese Island' or 'Blue Floral'. When gilding was added to a blue printed design, the pattern number relates to that gilt edge, border or trim.

Obviously, the public could have chosen a 'short' rather than a 'full' service or indeed any make-up of components which suited personal needs or purse. A 'short' set would not have included the tea canister or the spoontray and the number of teabowls (or cups) and saucers might have been reduced to eight or six. It is also probable that on the less expensive designs the covered sugar bowl would have been replaced by an open bowl, smaller in size than the waste bowl.

With the exception of a teapot stand all the component pieces in a full tea service are happily represented in a service in the Godden collection. This 'Davis Festoon' service, neatly decorated in sepia and gold, is important in our study of these early Staffordshire porcelains in that it may well be the only corrugated set still complete with the original matching components, although several part services are known, most of which have now been split up between various collections.

If we examine my 'Davis Festoon' tea service with its moulded corrugated surface as illustrated in Plates 21-7, several features are noteworthy. First, this service,[6] which has every appearance of having been kept together ever since it was first sold (that is, it has not been 'made up' from several services, as can be the case with later sets of common patterns), includes components having different handle forms.

It is as if the management, when this service was made, had not agreed upon a standard handle form but were experimenting with several shapes, for we find differing handles on the teapot, on the milk jug and on the coffee cups. However, it could merely be that the manager, foreman, store-keeper or decorators were not as concerned about matching shapes as modern workmen and buyers would be. It must be remembered that the work people would have produced a range of moulded teapots which were fired, glazed and refired before being put away in the glost-ware store; similarly a supply of covered milk jugs would have been made, likewise all the other standard wares were made in batches and stored in their undecorated state. Only when orders were received for individual patterns would the component parts of a tea service be fetched from the whiteware store to be decorated and completed for sale.

A factory has to keep in stock and have readily available a selection of blanks – which cost relatively little to produce – but it does not or did not keep in stock quantities of expensive decorated porcelains which might never be required. As orders came in that ware was made ready to satisfy a firm request for a tea service of a specified design.

In this way it can happen that the 'wrong' form of teapot might be chosen from the store to be decorated or an odd shape of milk jug included. On balance I do not think that any errors were made in selecting the blanks before this tea service was decorated. I believe that the shapes were intended to be used together and that the difference in handle shape was not considered to be important.

Each of these three handle forms found included in this service occurs also on other porcelains of this early corrugated type. They may be considered to be standard forms, common, if that is the right word, to this rare group of porcelains. These early handle forms should be closely studied; they are a helpful guide to origin.

Plate 26. *The spoontray from the 'Davis Festoon' tea service. The basic shape occurs in Chinese export market porcelain, in Bristol (Plate 11), in Caughley and several other types of English porcelain. Glaze-free flat base. 5¾ x 3⅞in. (14.61 x 9.84cm). c.1782-83.* Godden collection

The moulded handles, particularly the milk jug handle and the cup handle, are extremely well designed and have been sharply moulded. Indeed quality and neatness of potting are characteristics of all pieces in this service and of all related early pieces. Great care was seemingly taken in their manufacture – far greater care than is usually seen on New Hall porcelains made after 1800. This care and the intricate handle forms may, however, show some general Bristol influence.

The moulded shapes have the initial appearance of being slip-cast, in that the walls are quite thin and a slight mirror image of the outside undulations may be seen on the inside of the object. However, on close examination I believe that the wares were press-moulded, the technique previously used at the Bristol factory. The two main reasons for this view are that the pieces do not show on the inside the slip-cast characteristic concave recession of the slip where the walls meet the base of the article. Also, the porcelain walls of these ribbed forms sometimes show the spiral wreathing marks which can only occur in a mix which has been worked on a revolving wheel or pressed into a spinning mould.

With slip-cast forms the porcelain mix is reduced to a liquid state and is then poured into dry plaster-of-Paris moulds, which absorb the water leaving, after a period, the porcelain walls of the object. With press-moulded forms a thin slab of still pliable porcelain mix or a thrown object of approximately the correct size and shape is pressed by hand firmly into the corrugated shaped mould which would be turned while the inside surface is trimmed and smoothed with special tools by the presser or his assistant. It is not always appreciated that a great deal of hand-finishing is required for moulded shapes. Even with teabowls or cups the inside has to be cleaned up, the top edge trimmed, the foot added or turned. With larger pieces made in two-piece moulds the mould marks or joints had to be rubbed down or 'fettled'. As I have already noted, some forms require both moulded parts and hand-turned components, such as the knobs of a moulded jug. The fettling – that is the cleaning up of the joints – on these pieces is very neatly accomplished on this early tea service. It is significant that the only New Hall workman (Charles Sheen) known to us by name stated (at a later period, in November 1790) that he did nothing else but 'throw and press' so underlining the point that the pieces were probably press-moulded.

Just as the potting of these early shapes is careful and neat, so is the glazing, particularly in the way that the unfired glaze was trimmed away from the footrims or bases and from the bottom edge of the covers. This needs to be cleaned off as the glaze – a glass-like mix – will in effect glue the object to the base of the saggar or shelf if it is left at the point where the object rests. To avoid such damage or blemishes the object needs to be raised from the firing surface by various methods or the glaze carefully cleaned away to stop it flowing on to the base. Different factories employed different systems to obviate losses in the glaze firing stage. The New Hall management always had the glaze neatly cleaned from the feet or base of their porcelains. They are dry, or glaze-free, at the bottom of the foot or base.

The early corrugated forms which I attribute to the Tunstall period show this careful trimming away of the glaze from the footrims to a remarkable degree. It must not be assumed, however, that a clean glaze-free footrim is unique to these porcelains. This is by no means the case. The Chinese hard-paste porcelains likewise show this characteristic, especially in the way the plates are trimmed, and many other types of porcelain have well wiped or lathe-turned glaze-free bases. However, if you have a piece with a glazed-over footrim or base, it is I believe unlikely to be New Hall of the earlier hybrid hard-paste period.

The extremely rare and important part tea service which I have discussed and illustrated in Plates 21-7 is neatly decorated in a simple, rather classical style in gold and sepia. The handles of the teapot, the milk jug and the coffee cups are painted with a neat floral spray in sepia with slight gilt embellishment. In my experience this handle decoration is unique to this 'Davis Festoon' service. The edges to my service are all gilt, but a presumably less expensive version has enamel painted brown on sepia rims rather than gold.

The various neatly moulded intricate handle forms are particularly worthy of study as these may well assist in the identification of other related porcelains. It is perhaps strange that in a service with these ornate handles on the milk jug and cups, the main piece – the teapot – should have a relatively plain handle, although the outside surface is slightly stepped. This simple but good handle with the thumb-rest pointing forwards and upwards is found on other corrugated teapots, notably on the fine teapot shown on the dust jacket of David Holgate's 1987 *New Hall*. This simple handle form also occurs on later mainstream New Hall porcelains made at Shelton rather than at Tunstall – see Plates 64 and 101. However, this basic early teapot shape was also made with a more intricate two membered handle more in keeping with the other moulded handles on my sepia and gold decorated service – see David Holgate's Plate 7. With these early corrugated surfaced teapots one should note the slight moulding under the spout at the

Plate 27. *One of two bread and butter (or cake) plates from the 'Davis Festoon' service shown in Plates 21-6. Here posed with one of the teabowls and saucers. Twenty-eight ribs Plate 8¼in. (20.96cm) in diameter. c.1782-83.* GODDEN COLLECTION

lower end, also the manner in which the trimly turned knob is mounted on a neat plinth.

Relatively short as the first experimental period may have been, several different forms of teapot are known. A very rare early corrugated teapot of slightly curved barrel shape was illustrated by the late Geoffrey Grey in his important paper 'New Hall, Hard-Paste Porcelain' *(Transactions of the English Ceramic Circle,* Vol. 8, Part 1, 1971), Plate 9A, and also by David Holgate as Plate 8 in his 1987 book. This has a pointed knob similar to that on the sepia and gilt 'Davis Festoon' teapot (Plate 21) and the inward pointing thumb-rest links the two pots.

A hitherto unrecorded straight-sided circular and corrugated walled teapot appeared in 1995. This is decorated with New Hall's later pattern 3[7] (see Colour Plate 4). It is of a shape seemingly unique to our new Staffordshire partnership of the early 1780s. This early popular pattern we can term flower spray, but it may be found with several border variations. This one early pattern illustrates the difficulties we are to encounter in our study of New Hall porcelains. Several versions (not necessarily all originally given the same name or number) are discussed by David Holgate under the title 'Variations on a theme of New Hall's Pattern 3' *(Northern Ceramic Society Journal,* Vol. 16, 1999). The same pattern was also produced by Factory X and at Liverpool. Other very similar floral designs were also produced at the New Hall works – see, for example, Plate 36.

PLATE 28A. *The plan view of the rare, oval, floral knob from the corrugated teapot shown in Plate 28.*

PLATE 28. *A very rare corrugated Tunstall period teapot, with oval floral knob (see detail). Painted with a version of the early pattern, later to be allocated the New Hall number 3. 6¾in. (17.15cm) high. c.1782-83. See Colour Plate 5 for reverse side.* GODDEN COLLECTION

PLATE 29. *Details of the moulded teapot handle from the corrugated Tunstall period teapot shown in Plate 28.*

The globular shaped corrugated surfaced teapot featured in Plates 28-9 is another extremely rare specimen seemingly made in the earliest days of the partnership when the output was particularly small and no standard shapes had been decided upon – the experimental period. The added simple flower spray pattern is, however, one which was to be adopted and used by the partnership at a slightly later period when it had been re-established at the New Hall works at Shelton. It was to become pattern 3 (found with various border designs), although the pattern was certainly not unique to this Staffordshire partnership. A most unusual feature of this teapot is the stylised floral knob which is oval in plan rather than circular as one would expect. The handle form, like that on the sepia and gilt teapot, is slightly ridged or stepped. This feature is not

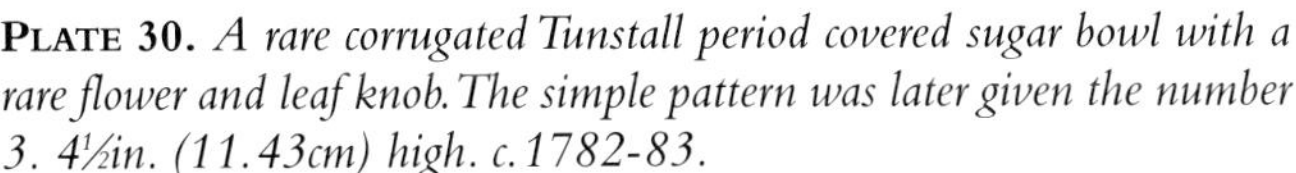

PLATE 30. *A rare corrugated Tunstall period covered sugar bowl with a rare flower and leaf knob. The simple pattern was later given the number 3. 4½in. (11.43cm) high. c.1782-83.*

CASTLE MUSEUM, NORWICH (NORFOLK MUSEUM SERVICE)

Plate 31. *A rare corrugated milk jug decorated with a simple 'puce wave' border design. The typical early moulded handle can be seen – see also Plate 32. 4⅛in. (10.41cm) high. c. 1782.* Godden collection

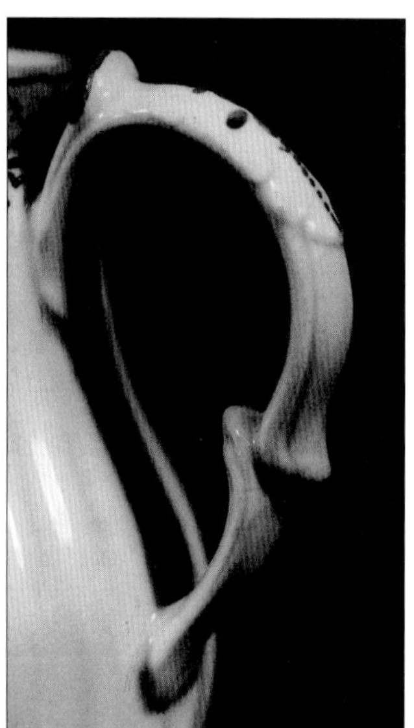

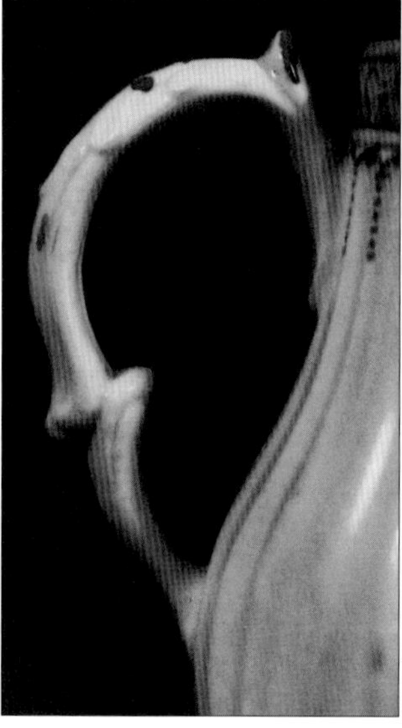

Plate 32. *Two views of the typical Tunstall period moulded handle found on the jug shown in Plate 31.*

unique to New Hall but is worthy of note. In this case it is picked out in puce with ermine-like markings, as shown in Plate 29.

A corrugated moulded circular covered sugar bowl (Plate 30) in the Castle Museum at Norwich is decorated with the same simple flower spray design and border motif. This, however, has a conventional type of more naturally formed flower knob. This feature, with its double-banked petals and long stem, is very similar to the knob found on the Baddeley-Littler class of porcelains of the same approximate period (see page 317). At least one other floral knob, corrugated sugar bowl is known.

The corrugated walled milk jug shown in Plates 31-2 (alas without a cover) is of a different form from that included in the sepia and gilt 'Davis Festoon' teaset (Plate 23) suggesting that at least two basic sets of teaware forms were in production. This 'puce wave' jug may have accompanied teapots and sugar basins of the types shown in Plates 28 and 30. The porcelain body too appears quite different from the sepia 'Davis Festoon' teawares; it is far whiter, not creamy in tone.

The moulded spout is much the same as the sepia and gilt creamer, with the characteristic little dimple at the base of the ribbed spout, a feature repeated on later New Hall forms and also found on some earlier Bristol specimens. The well-modelled moulded handle has the outward pointing thumb-rest, although in this case it is pointing upwards, but the main feature to note is the additional leaf-like reinforcement running down the handle for about an inch from the thumb-rest, as shown in Plate 32.

The simple but neatly painted border decoration is in puce and the painted handle decoration takes the following form.

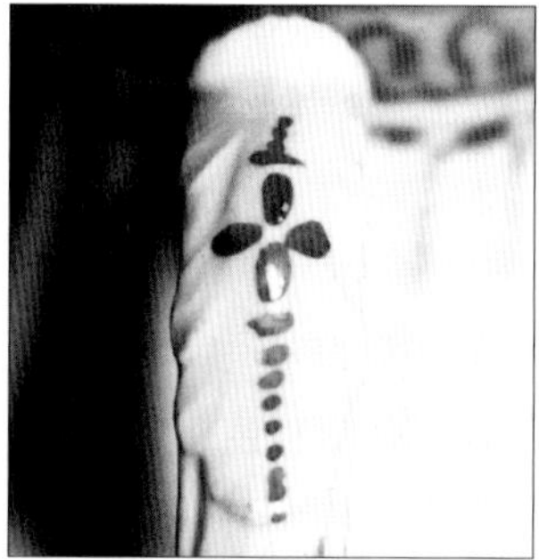

Another early type of corrugated moulded cream or milk jug is of the shape we term 'helmet' because it is somewhat similar to a guard's upturned helmet. The basic shape is, of course, well known in silver and the porcelain examples will have been inspired by the silversmiths. The example shown in Plate 33 is neatly enamelled with a pattern which was later to be numbered '67' when the New Hall pattern numbering system came into being. It proved to be a popular pattern over several years. This and similar specimens show both differences and similarities with the later accepted New Hall examples which are much less rare than the early type here shown.

Plate 33. *A Tunstall period corrugated helmet shape tea service jug with typical early moulded handle. This basic shape was continued into the true New Hall period. 4¼in. (10.8cm) high. c.1782-83.* Godden collection

Plate 33A. *The corrugated Tunstall period helmet shape jug shown in Plate 33, posed with a similar early example which has a slightly different moulded handle with leaf moulding running down from the thumb-rest. Patterns later given the number 3 (a variant) and, right, 67. 4¼in. (10.8cm) high. c.1782-83.* Godden collection

Plate 34. *A very rare corrugated, three-footed Tunstall period creamer, with typical moulded handle. Pattern later numbered 121. 4½in. (11.43cm) high. c.1782-83.* Photograph David Holgate

The points of difference between the two are that this corrugated example has the ribbing stopping short of the top edge, thereby creating a flat border for later decoration. This feature is reasonably constant. The later true New Hall jugs have their fluting continued up to the top edge. This early helmet jug also has the well-modelled two membered handle with a backward pointing thumb-rest. The handle decoration is of the same type as the creamer previously discussed – the four petalled formal floral motif with dots of graduating sizes above and below the main device. The thumb-rest is picked out on its upper surface with puce dashes in a standard manner. David Holgate in his 1987 book illustrates another small jug of this type as his Plate 35.

Other early corrugated class small jugs of this type are illustrated in the late Geoffrey Grey's E.C.C. paper,[8] his Plate 10A, B and C. This authority also illustrated as Plate 9F an extremely rare small barrel-shape creamer of this pattern 67. This also had the characteristic early double membered handle with a backward pointing thumb-rest. Slight variations of handle form can be expected. The fluting continues to the top shaped edge of the body. See also David Holgate's Plate 129. The rarity of such examples is underlined by the fact that I have as yet been

Plate 35. *A Tunstall period corrugated teabowl and saucer painted with the design later numbered 121. The corrugation on saucers of this type is usually very shallow and does not extend to the centre. Diameter of saucer 5¼in. (13.34cm). c.1782-83.*
Godden collection

PLATE 36. *A Tunstall period corrugated coffee cup and saucer, painted with a rare, unnumbered early design. Note the characteristic handle form. Cup 2½in. (6.35cm) high. c.1782-83.* GODDEN COLLECTION

unable to trace fresh examples to illustrate. Mr. Grey also illustrated as Plate 9A an early barrel shape teapot which could well be of an originally related form.

Mr. Grey was able to show yet another rare and early type of cream or milk jug, as his Plate 11E. This was of the basic helmet shape but without a thumb-rest or relief-moulding on the handle but with an outward kick approximately two-thirds of the way down, a rare handle form also seen on an early gilt coffee cup shown in Mr. Grey's Plate 11D.

Another extremely rare form of corrugated bodied open milk or cream jug is raised on three moulded feet (Plate 34). The handle form on this example is characteristically neat and well moulded. Similar early three-footed (with a plain surface) creamers were also issued with different handles. The added simple floral decoration in the style of the Chinese export market porcelains is one of those that occur on this early class of corrugated porcelain and also on the later mainstream New Hall porcelains, under the pattern number 121. In passing one might wonder why such an early and seemingly popular pattern (perhaps originally termed 'four sprays') was given this relatively late pattern number when the pattern book was prepared. One would have expected it to have been in the first dozen. The answer is probably that, when in about 1790 the pattern book was drawn up and numbers allocated to earlier, named, designs, the arrangement was haphazard rather than chronological.

A teabowl and saucer matching the enamelled jug of pattern 121 is illustrated in Plate 35. This illustration serves to show well the relatively shallow widely spaced corrugations on these early saucers, in comparison with the deep, close corrugations on the teabowls and cups. However, both the saucers and the cups have twenty-eight ribs, the standard early New Hall fluting.

As I have previously noted, the complete full tea service, with the more expensive decoration having some gilding, originally included both handleless teabowls and handled coffee cups (see Plate 27). The coffee cups can vary slightly. Those in the sepia and gilt 'Davis' pattern tea and coffee service are wider and slightly shorter than that shown in Plate 36. The handle forms are also slightly different, as can be seen in Plate 37, in that the sepia

Plate 37. *Two Tunstall period corrugated coffee cups. The left example which is rather wider and lower than that shown on the right is from the 'Davis Festoon' set (Plates 21-7). The moulded handles are slightly different, as are the basic shapes, 2¼ and 2⅜in. (5.72 and 6.03cm) high, c.1782-83.* Godden collection

examples show more modelling with a slight rib down the side where the two members join – as if they were two-ply. This feature is not apparent on the gilt taller cup, also seen in Plate 37. These differences must have been intentional as both the body form and the added handle were produced from moulds.

The cup shown in Plate 38 is perhaps even rarer than the coffee cup in that in its proportions it seems to be a handled teabowl or, more correctly, a teacup. The neatly formed moulded handle links with that on the coffee cup in the sepia and gold 'Davis Festoon' service. Other early rare handled teabowls are featured in Geoffrey Grey's paper 'New Hall Hard-Paste Porcelain', *Transactions of the English Ceramic Circle* Vol. 8, Part 1 (1971), Plate 10, D and E, and in David Holgate's Chapter 5 in *Staffordshire Porcelain*, Plate 93, middle. The handle decoration on my handled teabowl cup (Plate 38) comprises three dashes and seven dots in descending size from the top downwards.

Continuing the study of the corrugated type teawares, one finds at least two variations of the slop bowl form. One is of conventional bowl form with a continuous convex curve from the top of the footrim to the top edge (see Plate 39, left). This type was made in at least two sizes, one with a diameter of approximately 6in. (15.24cm), the other with a diameter of 4½in. (11.43cm). The smaller sized examples most probably served as the sugar bowl in the less expensive sets which did not include a covered sugar bowl. One other type of bowl has a more angular profile canting further inwards from a point approximately halfway down the body. Such a bowl from the sepia and gold 'Davis Festoon' service is shown in Plate 39, right. A similar bowl reappears rarely in New Hall porcelains of the 1790s.

Apart from the corrugated teaware forms there is an extremely rare additional class of moulded porcelain which I am sure is contemporary with these corrugated pieces and made at the same factory site. I refer to the half-fluted bell-shape cup. A good example is shown by David Holgate in *New Hall,* Colour Plate 4 and Plate 125. The basic shape of cup is well known in Chinese export porcelains and was much favoured at the Caughley factory and indeed at Bristol and at the Isleworth factory. I have a sweetly potted lightweight saucer (Plate 40) decorated with a simple design which matches that found on corrugated and plain teawares. The surface tone is slightly creamier than some corrugated pieces; indeed it matched in body-tone respects my sepia and gold 'Davis Festoon' tea service. As an example of neat trim potting it nears the perfection found with Chinese saucers. This success should have encouraged the Staffordshire potters striving successfully to introduce porcelains into the Potteries.

An extremely rare early teapot form shown by Mrs. Kit Holgate in her paper 'An Urn amongst the Flowerpots', published in the *Journal of the Northern Ceramic Society,* Vol. 6, 1987, Plate 31, may well have been produced for tea services of this very scarce type. This authority also illustrated as her Plate 32 a cup to match this shape.

Having just completed the typescript of this book, I happened to be sorting some old slides and came across two showing a remarkable teapot (Plate 39A).[9] These I had noted were sent to me by Dr. Bernard Watney in 1988, I assume as an unattributed puzzle. I, however, belatedly noticed two important characteristics which may well point to a New Hall origin within the period discussed in this chapter, although the basic surface decoration is quite different from that shown by any other English porcelain teapot of this period, in the early 1780s.

I then had not handled or even seen this startling teapot, but from the slides it was evident that this untypical fancy teapot was of a shaped oval form, with a raised prow to the neck. It bears relief moulded swags and other motifs, picked out in bright colours including overglaze blue, and has gilt spots on the body. It stands on four curled leaf motif feet. It is quite unlike any other Staffordshire porcelain of the 1780s but is similar in style to some Staffordshire 'dry-body' earthenwares. In this respect it may show the influence of the potters including Keeling or Turner who were involved in the new porcelain producing partnership. This ornate form was probably produced as a single teapot, or with a matching sugar box

Plate 38. *A rare Tunstall period corrugated handled teacup and saucer painted with a variant of pattern 3. Diameter of saucer 5¼in. (13.34cm). c.1782-83.* Godden collection

and creamer, not as part of a complete tea service. Such three piece sets were usually made in basalt and other ceramic bodies.

The early features suggesting a possible link with these Tunstall period porcelains of the approximate period c.1782-4 are:

A. The oval floral knob, which appears similar to the corrugated teapot shown in Plates 28 and 28A. This appears in conjunction with:
B. The handle form seen on the corrugated teapots in Plate 21 and later in Plate 64.

If I have now correctly attributed this teapot to the early part of the New Hall story, it poses the question – what other strange or untypical forms await discovery? Vases or perhaps even figures?!

I shall in Chapter VI illustrate and discuss the early New Hall porcelains made at Shelton after the transfer from Tunstall. I shall there show that some patterns found on these corrugated porcelains, which are here attributed to the early experimental period at Tunstall, continue to be used on the Shelton New Hall porcelains, as do some of the moulded and painted features.

The partnership produced mugs in this early period. Small sized examples of an attractive barrel shape form are recorded, but are extremely rare. The example in Plate 19, earlier in this chapter, shows the typical so-called corrugations to good effect. Details of the early moulded handle form are shown in Plate 41. Rare as these mugs undoubtedly are, they were made in various sizes and with different moulded handles.[10]

In addition to the conventional components of an English tea service, one also finds large jugs in this type of Staffordshire corrugated porcelain. One of these rare articles stands 8½in. (21.59cm) high and is shown in Plate 42. They have been called hot-water jugs and this may well have been their function – to hold hot water to recharge the teapot. However, if, as is possible, they originally had covers, these 'jugs' could have been the so far missing coffee pots. I write 'they', but in fact only one of these large jugs is known to me and this represents the largest article known in this early class of corrugated moulded Staffordshire porcelain.

Apart from the corrugated teaware shapes which I have listed, small custard cups are recorded – see Mr. Grey's E.C.C. paper, *Transactions,* Vol. 8, Part 1, 1971), Plate 10G.

It is accepted that the factory established at Shelton Hall produced good-looking moulded so called cabbage-leaf jugs which were popular items at most English factories of the period. In fact the New Hall factory produced at

Plate 39. *Two Tunstall period corrugated waste bowls of different forms. The right-hand example is from the 'Davis Festoon' set, shown in Plates 21-7. Diameter 6 and 6¼in. (15.24 and 15.88cm). c.1782-83.* Godden Collection

Plate 39A. *An oval relief-moulded teapot, with knob form linking with Plates 28 and 28A. The handle shape is similar to that in Plates 21 and 64. This brightly enamelled and gilt relief-moulded teapot is unlike any other acknowledged New Hall examples but it is submitted as a strong contender. 7½in. (19.05cm) long, 5in. (12.7cm) high. c.1783-5* Godden Collection

Plate 40. *A very neatly potted Tunstall period saucer with shaped edge and double convex profile. The matching teabowl is of a standard corrugated form as Plate 35. The teapot in Plate 87 may match this saucer in service shape. Diameter 5in. (12.7cm) high. c.1782-3.*

Godden collection

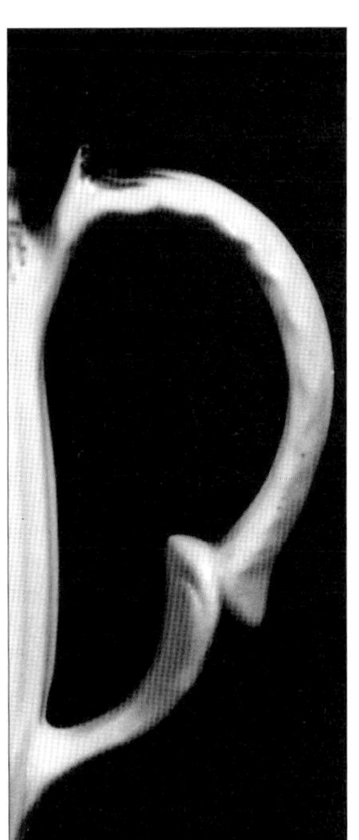

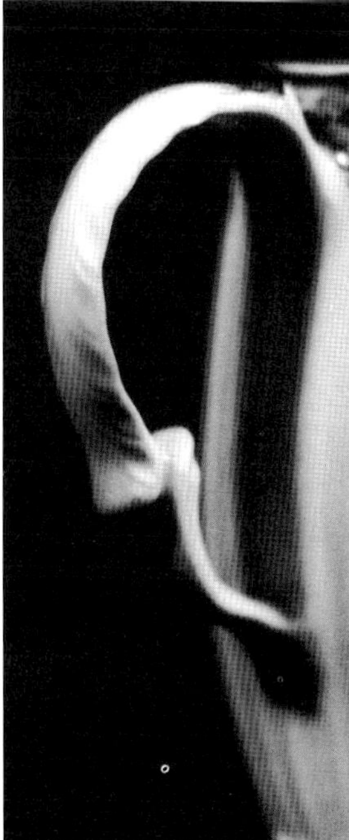

Plate 41. *Details of the early moulded handle found on the Tunstall period small mug illustrated in Plate 19. Later examples may have a simple handle form.*

PLATE 42. *A very rare large size Tunstall period corrugated jug, painted with a typical early floral pattern. The moulded handle is also a characteristic feature. 8¾in. (22.23cm) high. c.1782-3.* GODDEN COLLECTION

least two slightly different versions. I believe the earliest examples (as Plate 43) may belong to the Tunstall period and therefore link with the corrugated porcelains. The inside of this example, with its mirror image of the exterior moulding, appears to have been slip-cast.

The superb example in Plate 43 has the same well-moulded handle form as the corrugated jug in Plate 42. The foot and base also link extremely closely and the base is different from the base of slightly later Shelton period jugs known to me. If this thinly glazed leaf-moulded jug is of the earliest Tunstall period, then it would suggest that some of the rare leaf-moulded mugs, as Plate 44, were also made in this initial period. A probably slightly later cabbage-leaf jug form is shown in Plate 212. That has a different moulded handle shape.

Before leaving my account of these early articles I wish to point out that our researches to date have been confined to these characteristically moulded corrugated porcelains. It must be borne in mind that these moulded forms were more expensive to manufacture than simple

Plate 43. *A Tunstall period cabbage-leaf jug of the type made by most English porcelain manufacturers, but most examples have a mask-head spout. Note the typical moulded handle and compare with its near match in Plate 42. 8¾in. (22.23cm) high. c.1782-3.*

Godden collection

Plates 43A and B. *Details of the neck and spout moulding and of the foot moulding on the cabbage-leaf jug shown in Plate 43.*

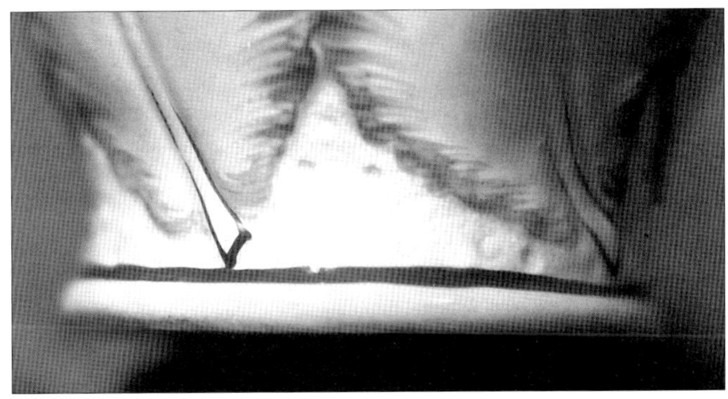

Plate 44. *A rare small size moulded cabbage-leaf mug, of similar type to the better known jugs (Plate 43). See also Plate 44A for detail of the moulding. Such mugs were made in various sizes and bear different added patterns (see Plate 82) or in this case gilt initials. 3¾in. (9.53cm) high. c.1782-3.* Godden collection

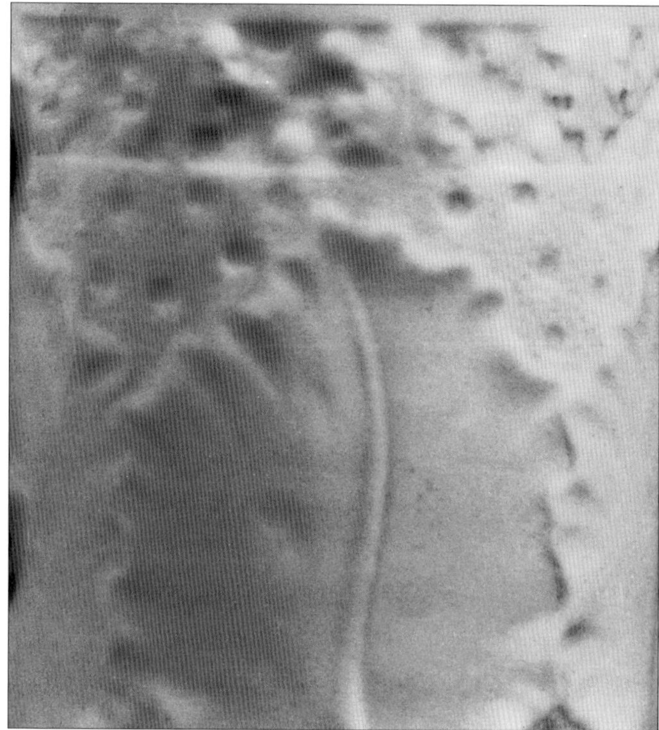

Plate 44A. *Detail, showing the moulded border and leaf design on the Tunstall period mug, shown in Plate 44. Later examples may have a simple handle form.*

hand-thrown shapes, but less body may have been used. Unless the new porcelain mix was quite incapable of standing up to being thrown and successfully fired, then there should be as yet unidentified thrown early teawares. Much of the early New Hall Shelton porcelain was thrown on the potter's wheel. I feel non-moulded Tunstall period porcelain produced by the earliest partnership c.1781-3, must exist.

Perhaps one example of the plain-surfaced, non-corrugated wares may be the little custard-cup now missing its cover shown in Plate 45. We could note the moulded handle form which is extremely close to the coffee cup handle on my sepia and gold 'Davis Festoon' tea service. However, it is rather thickly potted for this early class and is decorated with an underglaze blue print – a type of decoration not, as yet, recorded on other pieces of this Tunstall period.

Another example may be the milk jug bearing a version of pattern 3, which I have included as additional illustration Plate 45B. This rare specimen (which surfaced in December 1999) has an intricately moulded handle form, similar to a Bristol handle shape – see Plate 13.[11]

Before proceeding to discuss the main part of the history of New Hall porcelain, that produced at Shelton at the 'New Hall', I should mention a theory that the early porcelains were decorated outside the factory, by independent decorators, and that Anthony Keeling was responsible for the decoration of the first products. Over the years this idea has been rather amended in the telling. Leonard Whiter in his book *Spode* (Barrie & Jenkins, London 1970, revised edition 1978) stated:

> Shaw tells how Hollins, Warburton & Company employed outside enamellers when they first began making porcelain under Champion's patent but that this activity was soon transferred to the main factory.

But when we refer back to Shaw's 1829 *History of the Staffordshire Potteries* we find that, when writing of Enoch Booth and his Tunstall works, he stated:

> ...his son-in-law and successor Anthony Keeling, employed Enamellers, of the porcelain, then commenced making under Mr Champion's Patent, in copartnership with Samuel Hollins, J & P [*sic*] Warburton and William Clowes. But very soon afterwards this was transferred to Shelton, under the firm of Hollins, Warburton & Co.

I am unable to read into Shaw's statement that outside (that is non-factory employed) decorators were used and in several instances the same patterns and styles of painting are continued over from the early corrugated porcelains into the mainstream of New Hall porcelain which was certainly made and decorated at the works in Shelton. It is, however, possible that some true New Hall porcelain was sold in the white undecorated state to independent decorators or other firms. But remember the best profit margin (to be shared between several partners) would be obtained by selling finely decorated tea services and other wares.

It will have been noted that all these obviously early essays were rather sparsely decorated with simple, mainly floral designs. No ground colours or intricate borders are found. On the other hand, some gilding was used and at least three different (as yet unnumbered) entirely gilt patterns are known (Plate 46). Some of these also occur on Worcester teawares of the approximate period 1775-85. I can only illustrate cup, teabowls and saucers but complete early teasets must have been produced and await discovery. Gilders' numbers may occur on the inside of the footrims. Generally it is a number 1 or a dash, but I have one early plate with the number 43 on the inside of the foot. Such gilders' numbers can occur on Caughley, on Derby porcelain and on Chinese porcelains gilt here by independent decorators. I have not noted gilders' marks on post-1784 New Hall porcelains.

While I might be wrong in attributing the early corrugated wares to the first period at Tunstall, these pieces of the approximate period 1781-3 are extremely interesting; they are well potted and neatly decorated. Their modest success obviously led to greater things, to a factory that was to exist for over fifty years. They are rare but important pioneer pieces. There are several features which link this small class of porcelains to the slightly later New Hall. I acknowledge that for convenience and following tradition all the porcelains made by this partnership from c.1781/2 onwards will always be called simply 'New Hall', a name that arose from the situation of the second factory site, at Shelton.

It has been suggested by some that all porcelains produced by the various partnerships which acquired or worked the Cookworthy-Champion patent should be classed as New Hall. This may well be very convenient but it pays no homage to the all important initial period when the partners or shareholders were working Keeling's pottery at Tunstall. I have treated the true New Hall period, that is after the manufactory was established at Shelton Hall – the New Hall – separately in Chapter VI.

Finally, in this chapter, it is of interest to consider what the ten (or perhaps eight) original investors in the new

Plate 45. *A small handle pot (of custard cup type) decorated with underglaze blue prints (see also Plate 236). The moulded handle links this plain turned form with Tunstall period corrugated teawares – see Plate 45A. 2in. (5.08cm) high. c.1782 83.* Godden Collection

Plate 45A. *The blue printed pot shown in Plate 45, posed with a cup from the 'Davis Festoon' tea service shown in Plates 21-7, relating to the Tunstall period.*

Staffordshire porcelain factory might have expected, or rather received, for their then considerable investment. We have now no access to their accounts but we could briefly consider the situation as it related to the establishment of the Pinxton porcelain factory in Derbyshire in the mid-1790s, some twelve or so years after the Staffordshire potters and venturers were being invited to purchase from

Richard Champion his patent rights to produce true porcelains.

Whilst the Pinxton porcelain was technically quite different from the higher fired New Hall wares, the basic costs of setting up their porcelain factories and the production of the porcelains would have been much the same, but perhaps rather greater for New Hall. The selling prices for their products would, however, have been much the same. The prices of the standard lines – the teawares – were remarkably standard as the various porcelain manufacturers were in very keen competition with each other and none could be out of step, at least not on standard teaware prices.

Our informant on the costs and profits involved in

Plate 45B. *An extremely rare tall milk jug decorated with a version of pattern 3. The moulded handle form was earlier used at the Bristol factory – see Plate 13 (the jug and cup handles). A flat bridge is applied over the rear of the spout, a rare feature on English porcelains. 4½in. (11.43cm) high. c.1782-3.*

Godden collection

PLATE 46. *A group of Tunstall period corrugated teawares decorated with simple unnumbered gilt patterns. The gilt border design on the cup can also occur on other porcelains such as Worcester. Gilt 'I' or dash on inside of footrim on the right-hand teabowl and saucer a rare feature. Diameter of saucer 5in. (12.7cm). c.1782-3.*
GODDEN COLLECTION

establishing a late eighteenth century porcelain factory was William Billingsley, the Derby-trained ceramic artist and would-be porcelain manufacturer. In the summer of 1795 Billingsley was endeavouring to interest a local landowner, John Coke, in establishing a porcelain works at Pinxton, on the successful Derby plan. Billingsley was to be paid to manage the works, whilst Coke, the sleeping partner or investor, would enjoy the main share of the profits.

Billingsley's important first letter, dated 22 August 1795, outlining to Coke the envisaged costs and profits of establishing a porcelain factory in the 1790s, was published first by L.M. Booth in his article 'William Billingsley and the Pinxton China Factory and some unpublished original factory records' *(The Connoisseur* magazine, January 1963). In the same year Mr. C.L. Exley published his specialist book *The Pinxton China Factory* (Mr. and Mrs. R. Coke-Steel, Sutton-on-the-Hill, 1963). The reader will find full details of Billingsley's perhaps slightly optimistic figures in either of these early sources. The success of this Derbyshire enterprise is well shown in later specialist books. These include *The Patterns and Shapes of the Pinxton China Factory 1796-1813* by N.D. Gent (privately published, Pinxton, 1996) and *Pinxton Porcelain 1793-1813...* by C. Barry Sheppard (privately published, 1996).

In essence Billingsley estimated that to produce a kiln of white (undecorated) porcelain a week the manufactory would cost some £500 to build. This hopefully weekly kiln firing would comprise seventy teasets, of which sixty sets might be in a saleable condition,[12] with an expenditure of £34. These, as yet undecorated, teasets would sell for 19s. (95p) each, giving a total sale price of £57, resulting, it was estimated, in a profit of £23, or with extra costs or kiln losses a profit of £15 a week.

Turning to the decorated tea services, in the highest, the middling and the lowest style, William Billingsley estimated that to decorate twenty teasets a week in the middle and simplest style (which we might equate to early would-be New Hall Staffordshire porcelains of the early 1780s) would cost £1 resulting in a profit (if the sets were successfully sold) of 10s. (50p) a set, or £10 a week. A total mix of white and decorated tea services (or parts thereof) that could be produced per week would yield a profit of £25. This sum (which was probably never achieved) might well be very acceptable when divided only between Billingsley and John Coke but a similar amount shared between eight or ten Staffordshire partners who had each invested a sizeable amount in the venture would obviously not be all that attractive!

At Pinxton, however, Billingsley's letters were successful, for Coke agreed to provide the funds for a new porcelain manufactory to be managed by William Billingsley. The factory was built and completed in approximately six months between October 1795 and the end of April 1796, at a cost of slightly over £1,000.

Mr. Exley's book on Pinxton china gives much interesting information on the expenses of setting up that factory and on the workmen employed. These amounted to thirty-three by the summer of 1798. Leading artists, often from the Derby factory, were paid approximately 4s. (20p) a day, or £1 for a five day working week, providing always that work, in the form of orders, was available.

The partnership between John Coke and William Billingsley was dissolved by mutual agreement on 15 April 1799. Mr. Exley was of the opinion that in the first three years of the concern no profit was made and that Billingsley did not draw a salary. Porcelain manufacture has always been a risky business, the profit seldom as large as might be suggested by anyone seeking backers for such an adventure. In the mid-1790s, when the Minton pottery was being set up, the two owner-partners allowed themselves a guinea a week on which to live. Perhaps here lies the simple reason why Turner and Keeling left the early partnership. The initial claims for a likely profit from the large partnership were not forthcoming. They could do better for themselves by concentrating on their own earthenwares or perhaps themselves commencing to produce porcelain, without sharing the small profit with several other investors.

When viewing a case of these now rare Staffordshire porcelains of the early 1780s, here tentatively attributed to the early Tunstall period before the move to the 'New Hall', it is noteworthy that they appear to have a close-knit family likeness but that they are of an individual type. They cannot be mistaken for any other make. Taking the major known porcelain manufactories of the early 1780s, they are unlike Caughley, Derby, Flight-Worcester, Isleworth or Lowestoft. One might, however, in the case of at least one floral pattern,[13] find a slight linkage with a Pennington-Liverpool design. I prefer to think, however, that Pennington copied the design from these new Staffordshire porcelains. I regard these Staffordshire wares of the 1780s as noteworthy innovators. Later, of course, the New Hall type patterns loosely based on the popular Chinese export market porcelains were copied by all and sundry – because they were to prove so popular.

Before I leave discussion of the Tunstall period, it should be noted that Anthony Keeling and succeeding partnerships (such as A. & E. Keeling) continued their potting at the original Keeling manufactory. There, once the remaining partners moved to the New Hall at Shelton, Keeling produced both earthenwares and porcelains. The porcelains included what we could term 'New Hall look-alike' teawares. The Keelings at Tunstall (and for a period at Hanley) were almost certainly the makers of the large class sometimes termed 'Factory X' – see page 98.

---

1. Guineas (£12.12.0 or £12.60p).

2. I have been unable to trace an official dissolution of partnership notice relating to the Tunstall period.

3. Anthony Keeling's company and A. & E. Keeling were almost certainly responsible for the large group of New Hall type porcelains usually classified as 'Factory X' porcelains. See page 98.

4. Later collectors used the term corrugated for these early wares. David Holgate and I use this description in our writings.

5. A reeded coffee jug and cover with a lip rather than a long spout matching this Davis pattern was found in France and was sold by Messrs. Bonhams in December 2002. The body was reeded in a later style than the Tunstall corrugation. The knob and general body shape was as my Plate 302. I regard this coffee or hot-water jug as a later replacement, c.1787.

6. Purchased in post-war years from a cottage in Yorkshire – as a complete service.

7. We could perhaps now call this popular early pattern, number 3, the 'Holgate' pattern.

8. *Transactions of the English Ceramic Circle,* Vol. 8, Part 1 (1971).

9. This teapot surfaced in May 2000, as Lot 807 in the second section of Dr. Watney's sale – catalogued simply as 'Staffordshire'. It is now in my New Hall collection, a costly (£2,200) but a happy purchase.

10. One standing 4¼in. (10.8cm) high and hearing a similar enamelled pattern to my Plate 19 is illustrated as Lot 446 in the Watney Collection sale catalogue of 22 September 1999 (Messrs. Phillips, London). The moulded handle is similar to my jug, Plates 212 and 213, right.

11. Another very rare low cream jug (perhaps from a cabaret service) was included in the second section of the Watney sale held by Messrs. Phillips on 10 May 2000 (Lot 800).

12. The soft, Derby type Pinxton porcelain body might well have suffered larger firing losses than the harder new Staffordshire body and glaze.

13. See Plates 28, 30, 36 and particularly Plate 37.

CHAPTER III

The New Hall Marks, Markets and Prices

In my original draft of this book I placed this section on marks in the traditional position at the end of the main text – in fact it was to be added as an Appendix. On reflection, however, it seemed more helpful to place this key section at an early point, in order that the reader may quickly become aware of the fact that very few specimens bear a true trade or factory mark but that other guides to identification can be available in the form of pattern numbers and workmen's tally marks.

There are, admittedly, some disadvantages in treating the marks before the full story of the company's history has been explained or before a good range of its products have been illustrated and discussed, for readers will find themselves introduced to difficulties and to complex points before they are aware of the full background. However, on balance I think it is helpful to dispose of the question of the markings which will be found on the porcelains before I proceed to discuss the products in detail.

It is a matter of some surprise to find that the products of this great Staffordshire porcelain producing combination should not have employed self-explanatory factory trademarks, at least for most of the fifty years' duration.

Unfortunately, any form of mark is extremely rare, but the New Hall management was certainly not alone in this reticence to mark their products in a distinguishing manner. The various partners who potted under their own names in most cases also neglected to mark their earthenwares, as did many of the contemporary porcelain firms.

The early post-Bristol, Staffordshire porcelains discussed in the previous chapter were totally unmarked; indeed, with one unique exception, no New Hall porcelain bore a factory name mark before about 1812 or later. That is, for some thirty years no identifying device was used. The

PLATE 47. *Left, the blue and gilt silver shape New Hall teapot (of pattern 152) with the unique incised inscription on the base, 'Ralph Clewes. New Hall Fecit'. 4¾in. (12.07cm) high. c.1787-93. The teabowls of pattern 153 are discussed on page 126.*

VICTORIA AND ALBERT MUSEUM. CROWN COPYRIGHT

exception appears to be a unique presentation example inscribed by a workman or a person visiting the factory. This example is a teapot in the Victoria & Albert Museum (reference number C34.1918) decorated in underglaze blue and added gilding (of pattern 152 – see Plate 47). Under the base is the incised inscription 'Ralph Clewes. New Hall Fecit'. The cursive writing is not clear and the surname may be Clowes.[1] Various factories permitted visitors to help produce a piece and encouraged them to incise their name into the unfired body; the Wedgwood company even today still permits V.I.P. visitors to so inscribe a piece which is later presented to them as a memento of the occasion. Nevertheless, this teapot is a key piece of documentary 'New Hall' porcelain of the approximate period 1790-5 but, alas, it seems to be unique and the designation should be regarded as a personal inscription, not as a true factory mark. The place name 'New Hall' is, of course, the most significant part of the short inscription.

The blue printed crest mark here reproduced is a puzzling device which has occasioned much discussion over the years as to its origin and significance. This crest device occurs on some, but by no means all, examples of early underglaze blue printed New Hall type porcelain of the approximate period 1782-8. It is associated with two patterns in particular, the so-called 'Gazebo' pattern, as illustrated in Plates 235-49 and 252 and 'The Man on the Bridge' blue printed design, as shown in Plates 250 and 253-63. This device does not occur on other classes of decoration, only on two or three blue printed Oriental landscape type designs and then not necessarily on all pieces from a tea service. Formerly the crest marked blue printed porcelains of this type in the Victoria & Albert Museum collection were displayed in the Caughley section, but later the pieces were considered to be New Hall. There has in recent years been much discussion regarding this underglaze blue crest mark – see Chapter VII for the differing opinions.

Turning to accepted New Hall post-1784 Shelton porcelains, it should be noted that the enamelled and the gilt New Hall porcelains made before about 1800 certainly do not bear a maker's mark, nor do they bear painters' or gilders' numbers or other forms of tally mark by which individual work could be checked for quality or for payment purposes, but some rare examples do bear an overglaze cross mark. These very rare cross-marked examples could hark back to the Bristol system of marking or the pieces could be replacements to cross-marked Bristol services. It is also possible that such marks were added in the nineteenth century when it was fashionable to call some New Hall 'Cottage Bristol'. The addition of a cross mark would have enhanced the value and interest in an originally unmarked specimen. It would certainly be incorrect to treat a cross device as a true New Hall mark. Various cross marks appear on many types of porcelain; in the main these are workmen's marks.

A similar problem arises over some rare examples which have copies of the standard Sèvres factory mark. Two teabowls with this mark and the date 1782 are in the Victoria & Albert Museum and are here illustrated in Plate 47. They were purchased (as Worcester) by Lady Charlotte Schreiber in Bordeaux on 22 March 1875: 'we found two very curious Worcester cups, bearing a forged Sèvres mark and (in gold) the date 1782'. It is now generally believed that these marks were added at a later period; the style (pattern number 153) also is too late for the year 1782 as far as New Hall is concerned and the decoration hardly links with the Sèvres factory mark, but they could have been made for the French market as they were found in France.

Also, in a negative manner, I must mention that a cursive capital 'N' mark incised into the body does not in my experience occur on New Hall porcelains, although the early writers attributed this initial mark to New Hall. It is much more likely to appear on Derby porcelain, c.1770-90.

Although pattern numbers are not true factory trademarks and are in themselves unhelpful – in that every factory had a pattern 100 or 200 and so on – they still remain a very helpful guide to the origin of a piece and some general remarks are therefore not out of place in this section.

It must be noted that at first the New Hall management did not seem to have numbered its porcelain patterns. Perhaps initially names were used to designate different designs before the number of patterns in production made it necessary to draw up a pattern book and to allocate relevant numbers to designs probably already in production. New Hall porcelains made in the first two or three years certainly will not bear a pattern number and even when the numbered system was in being it is extremely rare to find specimens bearing numbered designs below about fifty. Seemingly many of the early patterns had been discontinued by the time the numbering system had been introduced or few of the early patterns were then being ordered.

Although collectors now use some early pattern numbers for reference (numbers such as 3, 12, 20, 22), these numbers in practice are almost never found on early specimens, the identification of these numbers being based on rather rare later specimens bearing the earlier designs. As a good general rule porcelains bearing pattern numbers below fifty will not be New Hall, although they may be in the accepted general style of such wares.

It is unfortunate that I and other writers have in the past reproduced an admittedly typical form of New Hall pattern number and this single specimen has been taken as the norm.

The example here shown appeared in my 1966 book *An Illustrated Encyclopaedia of British Pottery and Porcelain* (originally published by Herbert Jenkins). I mentioned in the caption that other variations occur – 'No 173', 'N 241', '195', but the point I was endeavouring to make in the space available seems to have been missed by some readers. The significance of my caption was that these and other New Hall pattern numbers can be prefixed 'No' or 'N' – both being standard abbreviations for the word 'Number'; also that the numbers can occur in an unprefixed state, merely the digits being painted. This point applies to most manufacturers; the numbers can vary in the form that they are rendered, the manner largely depending on the whim of the individual painter. In my experience it is extremely rare to find a 'No' or 'N' prefix on post-1815 bone china New Hall porcelains.[2] I show a few typical New Hall painted pattern numbers to illustrate the diversity of style. In fact the abbreviation 'No' is rarely found on New Hall porcelains.

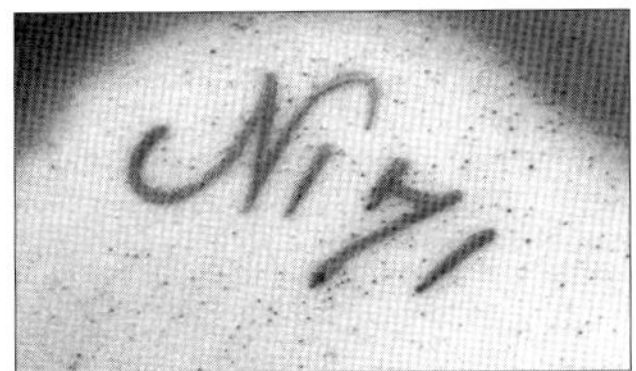

The style of painting the pattern number also varies greatly but as a general rule the more costly decorated pieces bear a neatly painted pattern number, whilst the cheaper designs painted by perhaps child labour tend to have pattern numbers painted in a seemingly hasty manner, with little care in the rendering.

In my experience New Hall pattern numbers are painted in enamel colours, extremely rarely in gold, even when the decoration is entirely composed of gilding. Also, they seem to have been painted without a full stop following the number, or indeed the 'N' or 'No', if these abbreviations occur. However, one of the several tally marks discussed on page 129 can accompany the number. It has been observed that the number should be read looking from the centre of the base. In other words the painter placed the plate or other object in front of him and usually added the number at a twelve o'clock position. However, few, if any, rules are watertight.

In writing of the way that the New Hall pattern numbers were rendered, it should not be assumed that all specimens bear such a number. This is far from the case. As a good general rule no New Hall cup, teabowl or saucer made before about 1820 will bear a pattern number; the numbers occur only on the major pieces in a tea service. This practice was, however, seemingly amended in later years. Very many examples, even of teapots, do not bear a number and this is especially true of the earlier period, prior to about 1790. In my chronological sequence of examples illustrated in the colour plates the first article to bear its pattern number is Colour Plate 33, although earlier specimens can be identified by association or tradition. The New Hall management was certainly not the first to have employed a pattern numbering system. The Derby management may have pioneered pattern numbers on porcelain well before New Hall.

The occurrence of the pattern number can be and often is the vital evidence that will prove or disprove a New Hall attribution. Illustrations or descriptions of the more commonly found patterns are readily available, in this and other books. Consequently, a numbered specimen can be checked with such published material and if the pattern agrees with the New Hall pattern number for that design then the attribution is all but assured. Only in one case has a duplication been noted; this is pattern 238. It is also possible that where another firm has been asked to supply replacement pieces to a given pattern, these extra and later pieces have had the pattern number of the original sample piece added, but the likelihood of such pieces being found is very small. It should be noted that in a few cases an

PLATE 48. *A group of English porcelains all bearing versions of the Chinese export market design often called the 'Knitting Wool' pattern (on account of the border motif). These bear various pattern numbers but only number 195 will indicate New Hall origin – as the coffee pot. Coffee pot inscribed 'N 195'. 9¾in. (24.77cm) high. c.1790s.* GODDEN REFERENCE COLLECTION

incorrect number has been painted on a piece – human failure being no doubt to blame – but again such errors are very rare.

Further notes on New Hall pattern numbers will be found on page 431 together with a check list of the New Hall numbered patterns illustrated in this book. The checking system can, and often does, work in reverse. For if the number does not compare exactly with the published New Hall version then the piece was almost certainly not made at the New Hall factory. This point is well made in regard to the popular and by no means rare New Hall pattern 195 shown here as Plate 48 and elsewhere in the book at Plates 163, 175, 302-4 and 310-1. Examples of this Chinese style formal floral pattern, often termed the 'Knitting Wool' pattern, can be found with the following pattern numbers: 2, 7, 109, 124-5, 135, 145, 189, 195 and 205 or 1205 (see also page 323).

Of these specimens bearing a pattern number, only those numbered 195 will be New Hall. None of the other specimens is likely to bear a true factory name mark but the sources for these different versions of the same pattern are 2 – Turner porcelain; 7 – Minton; 125 – 'Factory Z'; 145 – 'Factory X'; 189 – Herculaneum-Liverpool. I do not know the origin of the other numbers found on porcelains bearing this one pattern. The Grainger factory at Worcester also produced this design, as did Miles Mason and Pinxton in Derbyshire as well as various earthenware manufacturers.

Apart from the New Hall patterns illustrated in this book (see page 431) check lists will be found in both editions of David Holgate's books on New Hall. The reader is earnestly referred to Mrs. Pat Preller's 2003 book *A partial reconstruction of the New Hall Pattern Books.* A specialist book listing hundreds of traced New Hall patterns is A. de Saye Hutton's *A Guide to New Hall Porcelain Patterns* (Barrie & Jenkins, London, 1990). Unfortunately, none of the New Hall pattern books seems to have survived, probably as the works were not continued by another porcelain producing firm after the 1835 closure. We have still not traced over fifty per cent of the patterns that must have been produced!

A series of different hand-painted tally marks occur on both New Hall hard-paste and the later bone china articles. These are believed to relate to individual painters or teams of decorators or printers. These devices are very helpful in identifying examples within the approximate period 1805-20. The earliest pattern number I have with such an additional device is number 478, the latest 1162, but this range will no doubt be extended slightly as research progresses. However, I do not think they occur on post-1820 New Hall porcelains.

A selection of these tally marks are here reproduced. These can occur both in association with a pattern number or on their own. They occur on both hand-painted and on printed designs.

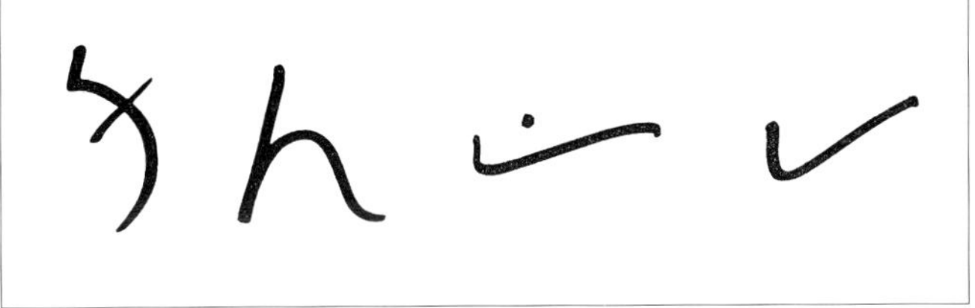

Commonly found tally marks on New Hall porcelains, c.1800-20.

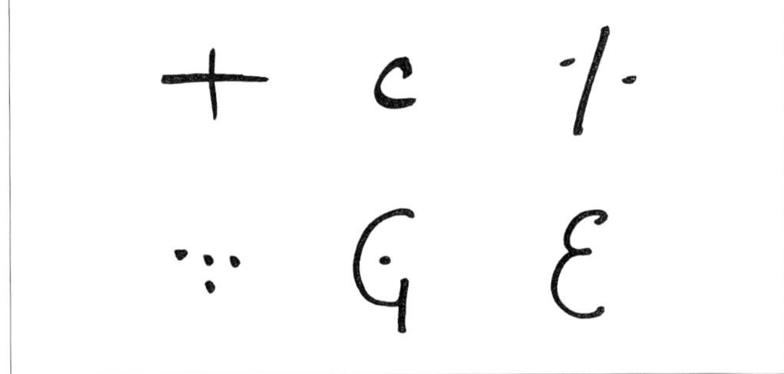

Less commonly found New Hall tally marks. The last two are given by other authorities but have not, as yet, occurred on examples which the author has handled.

It is noteworthy that the special hand-painted crowned 'Warburton's Patent' mark which is found on the major pieces of tea services decorated by Peter Warburton's patented process for bat printing in gold or platinum (as Plate 49)[3] does not include any mention of the source of the pieces – the New Hall manufactory. Indeed, G. Stringer, writing his specialist book *New Hall Porcelain* (Art Trade Press, London, 1949) was not aware that this mark appears only on New Hall porcelains. He records how he was offered a fine teaset by a dealer but that he turned down the opportunity to add this set to the works collection, as it was not, he thought, New Hall!

PLATE 49. *A selection of New Hall tablewares bat printed in gold under Warburton's 1810 Patent. The plate and waste bowl marked with crowned name mark – see page 129. Diameter of plate 8½in. (21.59cm). c.1810-2.*
GODDEN OF WORTHING

The 'Warburton's Patent' mark occurs only on New Hall hybrid hard-paste porcelain pieces of the approximate 1810-12 period. This process of printing in gold must have been expensive and seemingly it was only employed for about two years. This mark relates only to the pieces decorated by Peter Warburton's patented printing process.

The first true 'New Hall' printed trademark comprises this designation contained within a double lined circle, as the example here reproduced.

This name mark can occur printed in any colour. In the case of printed or printed outline patterns the mark will be in the colour used for that print; in the case of an underglaze blue print the mark will be in blue. It is often, as in this case, not clearly printed.

It is possible that this printed mark was adopted in 1814 when the firm's trading name was changed from the partnership to the 'New Hall Porcelain Company'. Even in this short period the mark was sparingly employed. It is found only on bone china examples – see Chapter X.

The name marks 'New Hall' or 'Newhall' painted or printed in a straight line very rarely occur, being variations on the more usual circular printed marks. The hand-painted 'Newhall' mark has been noted on teawares of pattern 1357.[4]

Some jugs and mugs of the approximate period 1820-30 which are decorated with blue or mauve moulded relief motifs (as Plate 456) bear under the base a coloured porcelain pad mark which incorporates the initials 'N H'. This rather rare New Hall mark in relief seems to be unique to these sprigged pattern jugs and mugs. One jug with this sprigged initial mark bears the date 1825. Factory 'wasters' found on the old factory site, later occupied by Dudson's, include parts of such jugs with the remains of this raised initial mark.

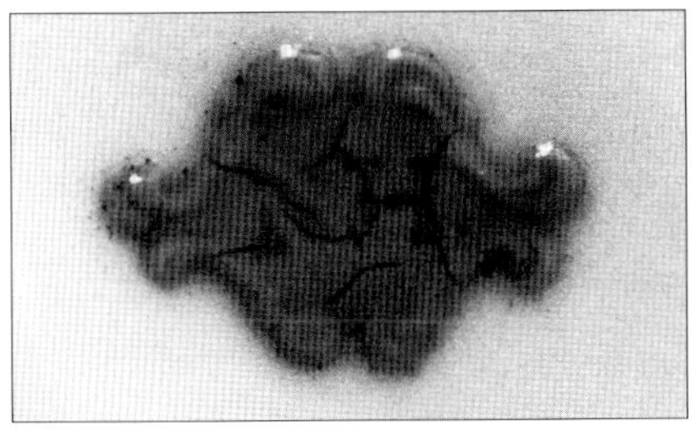

Several post-1835 printed or other marks incorporate the name 'New Hall'. In some cases this relates to the factory name, being used by later earthenware firms occupying the factory site, such as Thomas Booth (& Sons). In other cases the name refers to the pattern, style or shape. The New Hall Pottery Co. Ltd. of the 1899-1956 period also correctly used printed marks which incorporate the famous New Hall name – see Chapter XI.

THE MARKETING OF THE WARES

Having discussed the New Hall marks or rather having noted the lack of a uniform system of name marking, we can turn to consider how the wares were marketed and then endeavour to discover the prices charged for the articles.

It may seem surprising that the new firm should in a short space of time have established itself so firmly without using the name mark and seemingly without the help of advertising; it seems to have broken into the porcelain trade without effort. Previously Caughley, Derby, Liverpool, Lowestoft and Worcester were the factories or centres which supplied the bulk of the post-1780 English porcelain used in this country, although we must also remember the very popular importations from China. From the middle of the 1780s the new Staffordshire 'Real China' took much of the market for middle price range useful porcelain. Its success in turn prompted other manufacturers to produce similar porcelains.

First, I believe that the situation and make-up of the new company greatly helped its sales. Several of the partners in the enterprise were established Staffordshire potters who had built up their sales of earthenware and were surely in communication with retailers up and down the country, with wholesalers and perhaps with exporters. As shareholders in the porcelain manufactory it would have been in their interests to help to channel New Hall porcelain into these outlets, especially as in most cases the porcelains did not conflict with the sale of their own earthenwares. Relatively little blue painted or blue printed porcelain was produced to compete with their earthenwares. The main output was in teawares which everybody preferred in porcelain rather than earthenware. If the New Hall porcelains were cutting into the existing trade it was at the expense of the Chinese porcelains and the non-Staffordshire firms, not really at the expense of the Staffordshire earthenware potters.

This marketing assistance is particularly understandable in the case of the manufacturers who happened to have a financial interest in the new company as they were, in effect, shareholders in the concern. It is, however, also true of all the potters, for the New Hall porcelains were supplied within the trade at a generous twenty-five per cent discount. If other potters had their own outlets, their own retail shops or export markets, they could reap a profit, with no manufacturing risk to bear, by selling the new local Staffordshire porcelains. Even the great Wedgwood firm overlooked past differences with Richard Champion and purchased some New Hall porcelains, at twenty-five per cent discount. Wedgwood and other potters were dealing with their own kind, local potters whom they met frequently to discuss matters of mutual interest. The New Hall Company had the benefit of local goodwill.

This goodwill extended outside the Staffordshire potteries. It is revealing that the good reputation of the New Hall middle market wares enabled Joseph Lygo, the manager of William Duesbury's London showrooms for Derby porcelain, to recommend to a new Bath retailer, in November 1792, that he should stock New Hall porcelains.

Lygo suggested to the new 'chinaman', Richard Egan, that he should order the following goods, which presumably represented tried and trusted standard good selling lines. For Egan's opening in Bath Lygo suggested, or had purchased on his behalf, '6 boxes of Foreign China from Fleet Street'. It is not clear if this was Chinese porcelain or French porcelain. Most probably it was Chinese, purchased from Abbott & Mist's establishment in London's Fleet Street. There were also five crates 'full of Blue and White Staffordshire ware from Spodes' and nine boxes of Derby china. In a letter dated 6 November 1792, Joseph Lygo suggested that Richard Lygo in Bath ordered 'Black Tea pots' from Mr. Yates. These would have been the popular black basalt teapots as made by John Yates of Shelton and by nearly every other potter of the period. As to New Hall china, Lygo stated that this was to be ordered 'by the Waggon immediately'. The New Hall porcelains were presumably middle market tea services of rather cheaper types than Lygo could supply from the Derby factory. The Derby establishment obviously did not stock New Hall wares for Lygo stated 'I do not know the names of the People at the New Hall China works but if you direct a letter to the Proprietors it will be the same'. By 1792 the 'New Hall' name was firmly established, even if the names of the individual partners were not universally known, even within the trade. Incidentally, when considering the prices of porcelains or other goods it might be helpful to remember that Lygo engaged for Egan 'Mr Phillips' principal man' at a salary of 30gns. (£31.10s.0d.) a year or approximately 12s. (60p) a week, but this wage must have included board and lodging.

It can be taken, I feel sure, that the New Hall porcelains were widely distributed throughout the British Isles. They had quickly built up a reputation for a dependable body and for reasonable prices. These were important considerations when one remembers that most retailers carried a stock of several different types and makes of pottery and porcelain. The New Hall porcelains had to find their place in the market and attract the buyer. This the new Staffordshire porcelains obviously achieved and successfully continued for a period of over forty years.

Several examples of New Hall hard-paste porcelain have been seen bearing the name of a retailer. The most commonly found marks or inscription is 'Cotton. Edinbro' or 'Cotton.High Street, Edinburgh'; another is 'Abbott & Mist. Fleet Street' (London). Others such as 'Morris & Son, Ayr' are obviously rarer as small provincial dealers would have sold fewer examples. It must not be thought for one moment that these retailers' marks denote a certain New Hall origin for the piece. Elijah Cotton had an important china, earthenware and glass shop or 'warehouse' in the High Street from at least 1806-10. In the latter part of 1810 he was in great financial difficulties, if he was not actually bankrupt. There exist in the Wedgwood archives housed at Keele University several letters relating to meetings held at the Swan Inn, Hanley, to discuss what could be done by the various potters to cut their potential losses. This correspondence[5] shows that Elijah Cotton was purchasing earthenwares or porcelains from various Staffordshire firms, not only from the New Hall Company. Messrs. Wedgwood and the Ridgways were certainly also involved. One typical letter written on 12 December 1810 reads:

> Mr John Ridgway with compliments to Messrs. Wedgwood and Byerly requests their attendance at a meeting of the Creditors of Mr E Cotton (Edinburgh) to be held at the Swan Inn on Friday next at 10 o'clock, for the purpose of receiving his report on that Estate and for taking the general interests of the Creditors into consideration.

The basic point here is that retailers' marks are seldom unique to one manufacturer.

The situation concerning Messrs. Abbott & Mist (c.1806-9), the important London firm in Fleet Street, is also interesting. This partnership had traditional links with the Turners of Lane End, but Bevis Hillier's specialist book *Master Potters of the Industrial Revolution – The Turners of Lane End* (Cory, Adams & Mackay, London, 1965) includes a very lengthy list of potters who also supplied

this London firm with its stock. This partnership was dissolved on 25 March 1809, after which James Underhill Mist continued on his own account.

London, being the financial, commercial and fashionable capital of the nation (if not of the world!), boasted amongst its shops a surprisingly large number of china dealers or 'chinamen', as they were called. Some were very large concerns supplying royalty and the nobility, others catered for the mass market in lower priced wares. Some firms lasted for a hundred or more years, others were of short duration. One 'chinaman' who failed was Joseph Tansley who was declared bankrupt in 1801. His extensive 'Stock in Trade comprising a general assortment of porcelain, glass and earthenware' was sold by auction by Mr. Phillips in January 1802. Three lots comprised selections of named New Hall porcelain:

Lot 107 Four enamelled teapots, 12 sets of New Hall cups and saucers, 22 ditto milk pots, 18 coffee cups, 3 sugar boxes, 6 pint basons and 12 half-pint ditto. Sold for £2.2s.0d.

Lot 111 Five New Hall china teapots, 3 sugar boxes, 8 pint and 12 half-pint basons, 12 sets of tea cups and saucers, 10 half pint ditto, 14 milk pots and 17 coffee cups. Sold for £1.15s.0d.

Lot 112 Six New Hall china teapots, 2 sugar boxes, 5 pint and 5 half-pint basons, 11 basons and saucers, 6 sets of tea cups and saucers, 6 milks and 24 coffee cups. Sold for £1. 7s.0d.

It must not be thought that these odd assortments necessarily represented the dregs of a bankrupt's stock for on other evidence we learn that more often than not the smaller dealers ordered individual components of a tea service, not a complete service. The manufacturer's price list includes the individual units and their prices as well as the price for a complete service. There was also seemingly no reduction in price for the purchaser of a complete service!

The ability to order individual units did, however, enable the buyer to replace damaged pieces or to enlarge an existing standard service. One of the Hollins, Warburton, Daniel & Co. accounts with Josiah Wedgwood was for odd items almost certainly to enlarge an existing tea service. We find invoiced on 17 April 1812:

6 Tea cups and saucers, no 446	£1. 9s.4d.
12 Tea saucers, no 446	£1. 9s.4d.
2 Bread plates, no 446	17s.4d.
	£3.16s.0d.
Discount 25%	19s.0d.
	£2.17s.0d.

The twelve saucers were possibly for the original twelve coffee cans or coffee cups which would not originally have had their own saucers. The cup and saucers were charged at 4s.10d. each (24p), less 25% trade discount. I show a teapot of this blue enamelled and gilt pattern in Plate 50.

PRICES

We can gauge some of the New Hall prices from the Wyllie trade accounts to be discussed and from a few other sources such as the Wedgwood archives. Where we have only the cost of individual articles we can link these with an undated but, I assume, early nineteenth century list of teawares as issued by Hollins, Warburton, Daniel & Co. This chart is reproduced on page 141 and further discussed on page 142.

For example, the six cups and saucers of pattern 446 priced retail, that is before Wedgwood's trade discount of 25% was deducted, can be related with the list price of

£7.16s. for the complete, forty-five piece, tea service. This design is a known, reasonably popular, middle of the range pattern comprising a so-called Japan style pattern of underglaze blue trees with overglaze enamels and some gilding. It occurs in the pre-1812 hybrid hard-paste body on shapes popular from about 1800 – see Plates 50 and 187.

At an earlier period, in September 1789, Josiah Wedgwood ordered or received a selection of New Hall teacups and saucers all of different but unnumbered patterns. The prices are interesting. Six enamelled teacups and saucers of different patterns were invoiced at 6s., or 1s. each if the unit price was equal. This price equates to a complete service costing under 30s. (£1.50). This is under the lowest price quoted in the price list shown on page 141. The enamelled design must have been very simple.

Four blue and white cups (or teabowls) and saucers were invoiced at 10½d. each. These were presumably four different blue printed patterns in the Oriental style – see Chapter VIII – but the price of a matching set when multiplied up equates to approximately £1.8s.0d. (£1.40p). This price bracket of 10s.6d. a dozen cups and saucers is less than half the lowest price given in the c.1800 listings issued when handled cups rather than teabowls were the norm.

This suggested price of under 30s. or £1.50p for a New Hall blue printed tea service without a gilt border is very low and would seem to compare favourably with the main competition – the Chinese tea services. These admittedly would have varied in price, as they originally entered the trade retail chain via the East India Company's auction sales of their importations.

In the same month and year (September 1789) as Wedgwood ordered the four blue and white cups and saucers, the major London dealer, Robert Fogg, quoted a set of representative prices for his Chinese teasets to William Duesbury. The quotation reads:

> Sept 26th 1789.
>
> Sir,
>
> Patterns of Nankin China teasets.
>
> The prices of teasets of China are as follows. The quality is as your sets, with addition of tea jar and spoonboat.
> No 1, £6-10-0; 2, £6; 3, £5-10; 4, £5; 5, £4; 6, £3-13-6; 7 & 8, £3-3 each.
> The price I charge you is a whole-sale price.
>
> Robert Fogg, Jun.
> London.

To these wholesale prices one could add a further quarter to obtain a likely retail price. These trade prices, ranging from £3.3s.0d. to £6.10s.0d. per set, complete with spoontray and tea canister, were obviously related to numbered samples. We unfortunately cannot now tell the types of decoration on these Chinese or 'Nankin China' tea services. The likelihood is that in 1789 the more expensive sets would have been enamelled figure patterns, or simple floral designs, as I show in Plates 1-5, although the description 'Nankin' usually denotes blue painted Chinese porcelains. The cheaper sets were almost certainly the always popular Chinese hand-painted underglaze designs, as Plates 6-7. Possibly the samples 5 and 6 at £4 and £3.13s.6d. had some gilding added in London.

Returning to the New Hall blue printed tea services sold retail for little more than £1 or for less than £1 wholesale, the profit margin for the New Hall management must have been almost non-existent. It was presumably kept low by the even lower price of blue and white earthenware sets and by the cost of contemporary Caughley, Isleworth, Liverpool or Worcester blue printed porcelain services.

The 1789 Wedgwood-New Hall bill also includes a sample white and gold cup and saucer invoiced at 2s.5d. This unknown gilt pattern multiplies up to £1.9s.0d. (£1.45) a set of twelve cups (or possibly teabowls) and saucers, giving an approximate cost of £3.16s.0d. (£3.80) for a complete service when related to the slightly later table reproduced on page 141. Unfortunately no pattern numbers are quoted, but the relatively high price of the gilt example over the standard enamelled specimens is instructive.

These 1789 unnumbered white and gold decorated teawares were probably of a very simple design for a further Josiah Wedgwood order supplied by Hollins, Warburton & Co. just over a year later (in November 1790) helpfully includes the pattern number 64 and relates to teawares of a simple gilt pattern comprising only two gilt lines, one rather thicker than the other. The quoted prices, including a teapot (size 12) at 6s., its stand at 2s.9d., cream ewer at 3s.6d. and the sugar bowl with cover at 4s. equate to much the same basic price for the complete service of approximately £3.18s.0d. (£3.90) when related to the later teaware price list, as reproduced on page 141.[6]

It is of interest to note here that these prices may have been higher than those charged by Richard Champion for his rather earlier Bristol tea services. There is in the Bristol Museum a receipted account for a forty-three piece Bristol tea and coffee set sold to a private customer for a mere £2.2s.0d. and this included a coffee pot and stand. We unfortunately do not know the type of decoration on this set but it seems to have been at least a middle market set in that the sugar container had a cover,

PLATE 50. *New Hall hybrid hard-paste teapot bearing pattern 446 and so marked. This pattern was supplied to Wedgwoods in 1812, the cups and saucers being charged at 4s.10d. each less 25% trade discount. This pattern can occur on either teapot or teaware shapes. 7¼in. (18.42cm) high. c.1810-12.*

PRIVATE COLLECTION

as did the milk pot. In my experience the cheapest class of service would have had an open bowl for the sugar and an open jug, without the cover.

Our most interesting contemporary insight into the prices of the more ordinary types of New Hall porcelain in the nineteenth century is given in the surviving accounts of a London glass and china dealer, John Wyllie. These documents, housed in the Public Record Office, were first researched by Mrs. Ann Eatwell and Alex Werner, the results of their work being published in the *Journal of the Northern Ceramic Society,* Vol. 8 (1991) under the title 'A London Staffordshire Warehouse 1794-1825'. The more interesting records of ceramic interest were later photocopied for the use of researchers and are now available at the Guildhall Library and at the specialist Reference Library at Hanley, part of the Stoke-on-Trent Library service.

Wyllie was then to be one of several traders who were able to term their shops a 'Staffordshire Warehouse' meaning that they stocked the well-known and fashionable Staffordshire earthenwares. The records show that he placed orders with very many Staffordshire potters or firms ranging from such important potteries as Wood & Caldwell, Mintons and the New Hall concern down to small, now little-known or completely forgotten potters.

In the main the Wyllie shop, run successfully by John (d.1821) and then by his widow Ann Wyllie, stocked medium to low priced ceramics – mainly printed earthenwares, basalt teapots, lustre jugs and large quantities of blue printed 'Willow' pattern useful wares.

The surviving accounts (produced for a law action in 1856) may well not be complete, but relatively little porcelain was ordered or, rather, features in the available records – none from Spode or from Wedgwood, both of which firms had their own London showrooms, and relatively little from Mintons. Most porcelain was supplied by the New Hall partnership listed as Hollins, Warburton & Co. or as Hollins, Warburton, Daniel & Co. These New Hall porcelains, which were overwhelmingly teawares, comprised the less expensive designs and the standard components of teasets. For example, no coffee pots were ordered. However, the articles listed can, I believe, be taken to represent the partnership's best-selling lines, their 'bread and butter' goods – the type of porcelain carried by countless china dealers up and down the country and, indeed, the type of less expensive articles that would have comprised the main export lines of the partnership.

I list (with some comments) the more important entries from the copy document which I examined at the Reference Library at Hanley. I have used standard modern spellings and added descriptions etc. in brackets where necessary to help make the meaning clear to present-day readers.

The first entry for New Hall porcelains, dated 16 August 1805, makes the point that slightly sub-standard goods, termed 'seconds', were available at reduced prices – 'To overcharge on 12 sets tea (cups and saucers) no 425, only 2nds, £1.4s.0d.' The following contemporary prices which I have quoted were probably the standard retail prices, when relating to sales.

The New Hall partners allowed the Wyllies 25% trade discount on their accounts, the same percentage allowed to Wedgwood. This seems to have been a more generous discount than that given by other manufacturers. 10% was the normal amount and various trade agreements sought to control any undercutting of prices by way of a higher discount, although in 1796 an extra 5% was permitted for payment within six months. Perhaps the 25% discount was because the accounts were settled very quickly or perhaps this generosity explains the general popularity of the New Hall porcelains in the china trade.

New Hall's pattern 425 (Plate 51), a very popular, inexpensive, Chinese style figure pattern, was termed 'Image' or 'Imaged' in these accounts but is known to present-day collectors as the 'Window' pattern. A selection of this printed outline coloured in pattern was invoiced on 2 September 1809 and on numerous later dates. Complete tea services were seldom listed but rather the separate units were individually priced, commencing with 'Setts of teas'. These were presumably runs of twelve teabowls (or teacups) and their saucers, but the abbreviated entries merely read:

40 Setts teas, Imaged 425	at 6s. or
40 Setts, handled ditto	at 7s.

In this case the 425 pattern teabowls and saucers were 6d. each (2½ new pence) or 7d. each when they were handled teacups and saucers. The slightly faulty examples or 'seconds' were 4d. per teabowl and saucer. Remember that all New Hall prices were subject to 25% trade discount.

In 1809 other standard tea service units bearing pattern 425 were invoiced at

Teapots	4s.
Sugar bowls and covers	2s.3d.
Slop bowls	1s.9d.
Sugar bowls	1s.
Creamers (also described as Milks.)	1s.

In December 1809 the older pattern 171 was also ordered. By no means all orders were for the latest patterns but, rather surprisingly, the quite common and therefore originally popular simple floral patterns such as 186 or 195 (see Plates 305 and 163 etc.) do not appear on the surviving Wyllie records.

In December 1812 various teawares decorated with the black, bat-printed, landscape pattern, New Hall's new bone china pattern 1063, were invoiced. These sets bear various landscape and related printed designs. The prices charged were:

Teapots	3s.6d.
Sugar boxes	2s.
Slop bowls	1s.6d.
Sugar bowls	1s.
Cream ewers	1s.
Plates	1s.6d.

It will be observed that at least in the case of the less expensive patterns a bowl (smaller than the slop bowl) was available instead of the covered sugar box. In most cases the cost of such open bowls were approximately half the price of the oval (boat shape) covered sugar box.

Patterns ordered and therefore available in 1815 were 1040, 1045 (Plate 52), 1063, 1066, 1109 (Plate 53), 1153, 1266, but design 1109 was sold as early as August 1814, the teapots being at the standard charge of 3s.6d.

In addition, some teawares were described in words (not by a number) such as 'Black Landscapes' or 'Black Infants'. The latter are, I believe, the delightful bat-printed designs which we associate with Adam Buck – see Plate 53. Both types were priced the same, teapots at 3s.6d., the stands at 2s.6d., jugs at 1s.

In 1815 some sets were ordered complete; these tea services comprised forty-one pieces. Pattern 1153 was priced at £6.4s.10d. in April 1815. In July pattern 1266 was charged at £7.6s.3d. for the complete tea services. On 1 November 1815 a set of pattern 1055 was priced at £2.7s.0d or at £1.17s.0d. without the coffee cans. Pattern

1409 was £2.7s.10d. The highest number then ordered by Wyllie in or before November 1815 was a complete set of pattern 1597 at £2.12s.10d.

I have just written 'in or before' because it is not clear if the date given in the written-up accounts relates to the date when the order was placed or if it relates to the date when the goods and the New Hall invoice were received. This was most probably the case as the entries include the charge for casks or boxes. Therefore the goods were ordered some time before the dates here given.

In April 1817 the goods received from New Hall included five dozen coloured jugs supplied in five different sizes – from the largest size 6, in which there

PLATE 51. *New Hall hybrid hard-paste coffee pot and cover, decorated with the printed outline popular pattern number 425. This standard reasonably priced Oriental-looking design can be found on a large range of objects. 10¼in. (26.04cm) high. c.1795-1800.* PRIVATE COLLECTION

PLATE 52. *A New Hall bone china London shape teapot and cover painted with an inexpensive popular design, pattern 1045, available by at least 1815 and charged at 3s. in 1818 – see page 140. Like many other saleable designs, it was copied by other firms. 6¼in. (15.88cm) long. c.1813-7.* FORMERLY GODDEN COLLECTION

Plate 53. *New Hall bone china teawares. Decorated with the popular and inexpensive bat-printed series of designs used under the pattern number 1109. Note the enamelled, not gilt, simple edge. These were described as 'Black infants'. The teapots were charged at 3s.6d. (about 18p). c. 1815. Plate 8¼in. (20.96cm). c.1813-8.*
Formerly Godden collection

were six to the dozen at 3s.6d., i.e. £1.1s.0d. for the six down to the smallest size, in which thirty-six were counted to the dozen. There were another five dozen 'Blue Jugs' with the same assortment of sizes.

In the next selection, written up in June 1817, further coloured and blue jugs were entered in the account books. New Hall jugs with relief sprigged motifs are illustrated in Plates 439-43 and 452-6. Mugs in two sizes were received in August 1817. Many sizes were ordered in subsequent years. A complete teaset of pattern 1701 was entered in April 1817 at £2.12s.6d. Individual teawares of pattern 1724 were also included with teapots at 3s. For the first time we find a reference to a new shape described as 'Grecian' in relation to pattern 1266. In August 1817 we find an earlier pattern being issued with these cups – '12 sets handled Grecian teas, no 1045 £3.0s.0d.' This design was the popular rather cottagy 'shell' pattern, devoid of any gilding – see Plate 52.

In October 1817 a complete teaset of pattern 1655 was entered at £6.16s.6d., a much higher than average price. However, the next line relates to teacups and saucers described by words rather than a simple number. The words even now give trouble for in the *Journal of the Northern Ceramic Society* article they are quoted as 'bamboo sprig' whilst I regard the description as 'Barbeau Sprig', which is the name given to small French style formal cornflower sprays, a type of French style decoration popular at several English factories. These cornflower sprigs, often with gilding, occur scattered on the porcelain, painted in pink, blue and green. The Barbeau sprigs were also known in England as Angoulême sprigs as these small flower designs occurred on so many of the popular medium priced French imports from this Paris factory. The descriptions 'Angoulême sprigs' and 'Tournay sprigs' also occur in the original Chamberlain (Worcester) list of patterns, at £4.14s.0d. (£4.70) for a complete teaset. Such simple patterns were reproduced at most English porcelain factories within the approximate period 1785-1825. New Hall's pattern 1547, usually found on post-1812 London shape teawares, is of this type – see David Holgate's Plate 355.

Another description occurs on the October 1817 listing – 12 sets teas Blue Temple, fluted, at 5s.6d. The word 'fluted' is not clear,[7] but the main description undoubtedly relates to the underglaze blue printed 'Pagoda' pattern (Plate 383) which was so popular at many factories. It is surprising that the New Hall version had not been ordered by this retailer in earlier years. Blue printed designs were usually not allocated a pattern number, unless a special gilt border or other decoration was added.

In October 1818 other blue printed teawares were

ordered from Hollins, Warburton, Daniel & Co. These included '12 sets of blue Temple pattern handled tea cups scolloped, Grecian shape.' Other such tea services were apparently embellished with gilding for we find listed also '2 sets Blue Temple burnished china complete' and '2 sets Blue Temple do., no coffees.'

This 'Blue Temple' pattern may or may not have been different from the sets ordered in 1819 when the description 'Brosley'[8] was used. This is the popular printed Chinese landscape design copied from Chinese originals at the Caughley factory in the eighteenth century, a design that was to become extremely popular and copied by most early nineteenth century English factories. It can be regarded as the forerunner to the 'Willow' pattern. Typical entries in the 1819 accounts read: '4 sets Grecian (shape) Blue handled teas, Brosley' or '12 sets Grecian scolloped Brosley teas'. Typical New Hall 'Brosley' or 'Blue Temple' porcelains of this bone china period are shown in Plates 290-1 and 383. It is interesting to observe that in July 1813 the Wyllies also ordered '2 complete tea sets, except cans, Brosley gilt edge' from Thomas Minton. These were priced at £2 per set but in this case it is not clear if they were of porcelain or of earthenware – probably the latter. In 1824 a complete Brosley pattern tea service was entered in the accounts from Mrs. Ann Peover, the Hanley manufacturer. Other Brosley pattern teawares were ordered from J. & W. Ridgway. It was almost a universal English Oriental style design.

In March 1819 there is a reference to a 'new shape' of jug but no clue is given as to the precise form. The reader is referred to Chapter X for a discussion of bone china jug shapes – see page 396.

In July 1819 embossed shaped teawares of pattern 1930 were being ordered – '12 Sets Grecian handled china embossed, 1930'. This pattern number occurs on teawares with the moulded basket-weave design, as Plate 54. In March 1823 twelve sets of embossed teawares of pattern 2591 were ordered at £3.3s.0d. each, with odd teapots at 2s. In October 1824 embossed china teawares of patterns 41 and 49 were ordered from Mrs. Peover of Hanley. The teapots were 1s.6d. each, which probably would have undersold the New Hall examples. This entry reminds us that popular patterns and embossed (moulded) shapes were apt to be copied at various factories – there was no copyright law.

In December 1823 three sets of china 'ornaments' were invoiced from New Hall at £1.1s.0d. per set. These objects, probably those which we now call spill-vases, were decorated with a colourful Japan pattern. Very few New Hall examples of these popular and functional small vases have as yet been identified, but see Plate 404. At the

Plate 54. *New Hall's bone china teawares with moulded basket-weave design. Perhaps the 'embossed' teawares ordered in the early 1820s. This printed outline pattern is number 2383. See also Plate 375. Creamer 6in. (16.24cm). long. c.1825.* Godden of Worthing

same period there are two entries for 'Toy (?) jugs blue ground, flowers and gold'. The first word is indistinct but it appears to be 'Toy' (that is miniature pieces) and the price for these rather richly decorated objects was 2s.8d. each. No New Hall examples of this period have as yet been identified, but earlier miniature jugs decorated in an expensive manner have been seen.

A note at the bottom of a page dated 22 December refers merely to priced pattern numbers. These prices no doubt relate to complete bone china tea services. These were:

1411	£7.16s.0d.
1677	£6.16s.6d.
2384	£7. 6s.0d.
2506	£4.17s.6d.
2657	£5. 7s.3d.
2789	£7. 6s.3d.

The examples priced about £6 must have been very ornately decorated.

In the 1822-period the Wyllie orders for New Hall porcelain tailed off and then ceased. The highest pattern number noted is 2789 which occurs in the 1823-4 period, but it must be remembered that even in the early 1820s some former mainly inexpensive patterns were still being ordered, although these were sometimes written up by simple, presumably familiar, names – 'Shell' (pattern 1045? Plate 52) or 'Sprig' – rather than by the pattern number. The orders were tailing off at this period, not so much because the New Hall factory may have been losing its way in the market but in this case because Ann Wyllie's involvement in the pottery and porcelain side of her glass business was being wound down.

It must not be thought that all the ceramics or indeed all the porcelains had been ordered from the New Hall partnership. This was far from the case; Mintons, John and Richard Riley, Mrs. Peover, Thomas Wolfe and others supplied some china ware whilst others supplied earthenwares of various types to round off the stock held by this one London retailer. Much earthenware, including the popular 'Willow' pattern, was ordered from Peter Warburton's pottery at Cobridge, one of the New Hall partners who also owned his own earthenware manufactory.

Also, it must not be thought that the Wyllie entries represent the full picture of the New Hall production. They clearly only show a very small proportion of it, a very few of the more popular patterns and types, nearly all teawares. It should also be borne in mind that the factory continued for approximately another ten years and Anthony de Saye Hutton's book *A Guide to New Hall Porcelain Patterns* attributes pattern numbers up to at least 3903 to this long-lasting firm. The list may also have reached into the four thousands with some additional fractional numbers; however these unusual numbers, including '4', may relate to the required shape – see page 381.

I have abstracted a few prices charged for New Hall teapots in these Wyllie records. Other entries are given, but in many cases the pattern number is not quoted or is not now clear. The year of the priced entry is given in brackets; this is not necessarily the year in which the design was introduced.

171	3s.-	(1815)
188	5s. (some gilding)	(1813)
425 'Window' pattern	4s.-	(1809)
709 Black (printed) landscapes	3s.6d.	(1815)
1043	3s.	(1815)
1045 'Shell' pattern	3s.	(1818)
A design issued by several other factories.		
1063 Black (printed) landscape	3s.6d.	(1812)
See page 341 for other prices.		
1109 'Black (printed) Infants'	3s.	(1815)
1930 'embossed'	4s.9d. (including stand)	(1816)
2591	2s.	(1822)
2720	1s.8d.	(1823)

The last two patterns have not as yet been discovered or noted by collectors.

Whilst these prices relate only to the period indicated, it is probably the case that they would have remained very much the same over a longish period. Indeed it could be that they drifted downwards as the competition from other firms made itself felt. It is possible also that the post-1813 bone china teawares were rather less expensive than the same (or like) patterns when they were issued in the earlier hybrid hard-paste body. The cost of a 'Window' (425) pattern teapot at 4s. in 1809 seems rather high, considering that it is a coloured in printed outline design but, on the other hand, it is an 'all-over' type design with little unpainted porcelain showing – see Plate 51. It is also true that teapots of this design supplied in 1815 were priced at 3s.6d. each rather than the earlier 4s. This could have been because they were by 1815 bone china examples. As previously noted, this London dealer called this popular pattern 'Image' or 'Imaged'.

It is noteworthy how individual component units of a tea service were ordered, rather than the complete service. Even teapot stands were usually priced separately from the teapots. The stands too seem rather costly. Bat-printed landscape or Adam Buck type figure designs of pattern

PRICES OF COMPLETE TEA SERVICES OF CHINA,

45 *Pieces, each charged separate,*

AT THE MANUFACTORY OF HOLLINS, WARBURTON, DANIEL AND Co.

SHELTON, STAFFORDSHIRE.

	L. s. d.	L. s. d.	L. s. d.	L. s. d.	L. s. d.	L. s. d.	L. s. d.	L. s. d.	L. s. d.	L. s. d.	L. s. d.	L. s. d.	L. s. d.	L. s. d.	L. s. d.	L. s. d.	L. s. d.	L. s. d.	L. s. d.	L. s. d.
	2 18 6	3 8 3	3 18 0	4 7 9	4 17 6	5 7 3	5 17 0	6 6 9	6 16 6	7 6 3	7 16 0	8 5 9	8 15 6	9 5 3	9 15 0	10 4 9	10 14 6	11 4 3	11 14 0	12 3 9
12 Cups and 12 Saucers	1 2 0	1 5 6	1 9 4	1 13 0	1 16 8	2 0 4	2 4 0	2 7 8	2 11 4	2 15 0	2 18 8	3 2 4	3 6 0	3 9 8	3 13 4	3 17 0	4 0 8	4 4 4	4 8 0	4 11 8
12 Coffee Cups	0 15 0	0 17 6	1 0 0	1 2 6	1 5 0	1 7 6	1 10 0	1 12 6	1 5 0	1 17 6	2 0 0	2 2 6	2 5 0	2 7 6	2 10 0	2 12 6	2 15 0	2 17 6	3 0 0	3 2 6
Tea Pots, each..........	0 5 0	0 5 10	0 6 8	0 7 6	0 8 4	0 9 2	0 10 0	0 10 10	0 1 8	0 12 6	0 13 4	0 14 2	0 15 0	0 15 10	0 16 8	0 17 6	0 18 4	0 19 2	1 0 0	1 0 10
Slop Bowl, ditto..........	0 2 6	0 2 11	0 3 4	0 3 9	0 4 2	0 4 7	0 5 0	0 5 5	0 5 10	0 6 3	0 6 8	0 7 1	0 7 6	0 7 11	0 8 4	0 8 9	0 9 2	0 9 7	0 10 0	0 10 5
Sugar Box, ditto........	0 3 0	0 3 6	0 4 0	0 4 6	0 5 0	0 5 6	0 6 0	0 6 6	0 7 0	0 7 6	0 8 0	0 8 6	0 9 0	0 9 6	0 10 0	0 10 6	0 11 0	0 11 6	0 12 0	0 12 6
Cream Ewer, ditto......	0 2 6	0 2 11	0 3 4	0 3 9	0 4 2	0 4 7	0 5 0	0 5 5	0 5 10	0 6 3	0 6 8	0 7 1	0 7 6	0 7 11	0 8 4	0 8 9	0 9 2	0 9 7	0 10 0	0 10 5
Plate, Large, ditto	0 3 6	0 4 1	0 4 8	0 5 3	0 5 10	0 6 5	0 7 0	0 7 7	0 8 2	0 8 9	0 9 4	0 9 11	0 10 6	0 11 1	0 11 8	0 12 3	0 12 10	0 13 5	0 14 0	0 14 7
Ditto Small, ditto	0 3 0	0 3 6	0 4 0	0 4 6	0 5 0	0 5 6	0 6 0	0 6 6	0 7 0	0 7 6	0 8 0	0 8 6	0 9 0	0 9 6	0 10 0	0 10 6	0 11 0	0 11 6	0 12 0	0 12 6
Tea Pot Stand, ditto	0 2 0	0 2 4	0 2 8	0 3 0	0 3 4	0 3 8	0 4 0	0 4 4	0 4 8	0 5 0	0 5 4	0 5 8	0 6 0	0 6 4	0 6 8	0 7 0	0 7 4	0 7 8	0 8 0	0 8 4
The above 45 Pieces	2 18 6	3 8 3	3 18 0	4 7 9	4 17 6	5 7 3	5 17 0	6 6 9	6 16 6	7 6 3	7 16 0	8 5 9	8 15 6	9 5 3	9 15 0	10 4 9	10 14 6	11 4 3	11 14 0	12 3 9
Services as above with 8 Coffee Cups 41 Pieces	2 12 10	3 2 5	3 11 4	4 0 3	4 9 2	4 18 1	5 7 0	5 15 11	6 4 10	6 13 9	7 2 8	7 11 7	8 0 6	8 9 3	8 18 4	9 7 3	9 16 2	10 5 1	10 14 0	11 2 11

Allbut, Printer, Hanley.

PLATE 54A. *Early nineteenth century Hollins, Warburton, Daniel & Co. price list for New Hall teawares. Complete forty-five piece tea services ranged from £2.18s.6d. to £12.3s.9d., depending on the amount, or quality, of the decoration.* FLINTSHIRE RECORD OFFICE

709 or 1109 (Plate 53) were priced at 2s.6d. whereas the larger teapot and its cover was 3s.6d.

Most collectors will know that these standard bat-printed designs (see Chapter IX) were issued with various border designs and in different colours. The Wyllie firm seems always to have ordered the standard black onglaze prints in the cheapest version with black enamel simple line edges rather than the often intricately gilt embellished versions of the same basic prints. The gilt bordered versions would naturally be more expensive than the plain, but unfortunately we cannot gauge by how much.

It would seem, however, that the colour with which the bat-printed design was tinted did not affect the price – except for the costly gold printed 'Warburton's Patent' essays – but the gold printed pieces do not seem to have been ordered by this retailer. A very few references occur in the Wyllie accounts for purple printed landscape teawares in the 1814 period but these are the same price as the black landscape versions.

Turning for a moment from the Wyllie documents there is an undated list of 'Prices of Complete Tea Services of China' as issued by Hollins, Warburton, Daniel & Co., perhaps in about 1815.[9] Two types of complete London shape (?) tea services were listed. In the nineteenth century the 'Full' or forty-five[10] piece set comprised:

Teapot and cover
Teapot stand
Sugar box and cover
Cream ewer
Slop bowl
2 plates, of different sizes
12 teacups
12 coffee cups
12 saucers

There was also the forty-one piece set which included eight coffee cups, not twelve. Such sets were always a little less expensive than the 'full service'. Each unit was also priced separately. Unlike similar price lists from other factories there is no reference to coffee pots or to the extra items that made up a breakfast service. Most pre-1790 New Hall 'full' tea services would also have included a spoontray and a tea canister and cover, units that were not included in nineteenth century services.

The New Hall printed price list includes 'full' services ranging from £2.18s.6d. to £12.3s.9d. (or £2.12s.10d. to £11.2s.11d. for the shorter sets). The difference between the cheaper sets and the more expensive was due to the expense and intricacy of the decoration. There were twenty different prices for complete sets. The New Hall teapots on this undated list range from 5s. to £1.0s.10d.

It is a little surprising to find that a similar list issued by

Job Ridgway & Sons in January 1813 includes complete tea services at rather lower prices. The Ridgway sets range in twenty bands from £1.6s.5d. to £10.10s.0d. This firm also featured the shorter sets having only eight coffee cans (or cups). None of the Ridgway prices matches exactly with the New Hall range but approximately similar prices can be found. New Hall had a range at £3.8s.3d.; the nearest Ridgway price was £3.10s.0d., but such comparisons are meaningless as we do not know what type of decoration was added.

The same basic nineteenth century make-up of English porcelain tea service remained constant for many years. In the 1840s Samuel Alcock & Co. of Burslem was listing forty-five piece teasets from prices as low as 11s.6d. upwards in twenty-nine bands to £10.10s.0d. They also issued short sets with eight coffee cups and even cheaper sets without coffee cups. These pure teasets, as sold by Alcocks well after the New Hall factory closed, ranged from 9s. to £8.8s.0d.

Returning to the study of the Wyllie accounts, these do not upset our established picture of the New Hall porcelains but under the date 24 December 1812 there appears the entry '12 sets teas full imaged 1066. £3.12s.0d.'. Both the main New Hall specialist authors state that this 1066 pattern was the bone china version (with amended border) of the earlier hybrid hard-paste pattern 425. Can this be true? If so, it should follow that New Hall's bone china was available in (or slightly before) December 1812. The Wyllie or the New Hall clerk's amended description 'full imaged' rather than the earlier description 'imaged' may well provide the correct simple answer; they were two different patterns. It should, however, be noted that in the same December 1812 entry there appear various teawares of 'Black landscape china no. 1063', a pattern number usually associated with the bone china body.

To complicate the issue I must point out that teawares of pattern 425 (the earlier hybrid hard-paste version of the bone china design 1066) were supplied to the Wyllies in 1815 and 1816. Could these orders have comprised hybrid hard-paste porcelain at this period? It should be borne in mind that when the change in body took place the factory would have held large stocks of the former hybrid hard-paste undecorated blanks. These would certainly not have been thrown out; rather they would have been taken down and decorated with overglaze patterns for as long as the stock lasted or until the shapes were deemed to be too old-fashioned and unsaleable. However, price conscious dealers would probably have been quite happy to purchase the old shapes as long as the price was right! Taste or fashion in the country would also not have been so particular as in the cities.

The seemingly very brief Wyllie purchase entries have raised some interesting points. Perhaps other records will one day be found and researched. In recent years several long-lost factory pattern books have come to light. Could the New Hall records still be lurking somewhere?

In the meantime, for a brief insight into the products of the 1830s we have only the basic descriptions given in the announcement relating to the auction sale held in October 1835 comprising:

> All the very valuable stock of Burnished Gold and other china, which consists of complete rich burnished gold tea services, in a great variety of shapes and patterns; also breakfast services to correspond. A very choice assortment of dessert and toilet services, with numerous modern and fancy ornaments, &c, &c. A very general assortment of common, china, Hawkers' sets &c.
> This will be found a most advantageous opportunity for Merchants and China Dealers

I shall be discussing and illustrating some of these later New Hall porcelains in Chapter X, but first I have to set the New Hall scene at Shelton and mention the various partners.

---

1. A William Clowes was a partner in the New Hall Company. Ralph may have been a relation, accounting for this unique inscribed teapot, providing the incised name was Clowes or that the family used alternative spellings.

2. The abbreviations certainly occur on other nineteenth century porcelains. such as Minton.

3. See also Plates 323-4 and page 336.

4. Such rare non-standard marks may have been employed by firms such as Dudsons, which seemingly produced bone china wares for the New Hall Company at about this period.

5. See Jill Turnbull's paper 'Staffordshire Potters and Scottish Merchants' published in the *Journal of the Northern Ceramic Society*, Vol. 9 (1992).

6. This order (ref. Wedgwood Mosley 145,H. folder in the Wedgwood archives) includes '18 coffee cups white and gold No. 64 at 1/7d each', perhaps suggesting that an existing teaset did not include coffee cups.

7. London shape New Hall teawares occur with the blue printed Chinese style landscape design of 'Broseley' or 'Temple' type. Some of these have slight ribbing or moulded fluting with or without a wavy edge. These moulded surfaced wares may be the same as those described in 1818 as 'scolloped'.

8. English trade name for printed copies of Chinese designs. The original was introduced at the Caughley factory situated near Broseley, the largest nearby town, the post town.

9. Document D/HC/C./48 (Catherall papers) in Flintshire Record Office.

10. The count includes covers as separate pieces.

CHAPTER IV

The New Hall Works and the Partners

Correctly speaking we should not refer to the new Staffordshire porcelains as 'New Hall' until after the remaining partners moved from Tunstall in about 1784 and successfully established themselves in (or close by) Shelton Hall,[1] called in this case 'New Hall' (as opposed to the 'Old Hall'), also at Shelton. It is certainly very convenient to classify all products produced by the new Staffordshire partnership from c.1781 simply as 'New Hall', for the personal names under which the partners originally traded are not clear, nor were they generally known at the time. In later years the partnership changed several times, giving rise to additional difficulties over the trading style.

Josiah Wedgwood, giving evidence in London in February 1786, referred to the company merely as 'the proprietors of Mr Champion's patent' although he referred to other china manufacturers by their names. In 1792 Joseph Lygo, the manager of the Derby retail shop in London, wrote: 'I do not know the names of the People at the New Hall China Works but if you direct a letter to the proprietors it will be the same...'.

Furthermore, when I first visited the Staffordshire Record Office to study the Land Tax returns in order to sort out the various trade styles under which the company traded, I completely failed to trace the New Hall partnership. In fact I jokingly stated that I had discovered the reason for the company's success – it had failed to pay any taxes! The reason for my lack of success, I was later to discover, was that the names recorded were not those that I was expecting or searching for – see pages 146-7.

One of the difficulties encountered in researching Staffordshire potters of the 1780s is that the few directories of the period seem, in some respects, to be inaccurate or simply an exact copy of its out-of-date predecessor. These late eighteenth century small directories may not be complete and they are certainly abridged, thus not reflecting the whole population of the various towns listed. In regard to William Tunnicliffe's c.1787 directory or *Survey of the County of Stafford* one finds in the seven Potteries towns only the potters listed, no other traders or shopkeepers or 'Merchants and Manufacturers'. On a preceding page, where the town of Rugeley is featured, only five names are listed – all hat manufacturers. In regard to Newcastle-under-Lyme, this Staffordshire township also seemingly comprised only five traders, again all hat manufacturers! Tunnicliffe seems to have lifted all his entries concerning potters from Bailey's larger *British Directory* for 1784, when the entries were presumably correct, although they might not have been in 1787!

A further difficulty is that some directories do not seem to bear a printed date of publication – a very convenient omission for the printer and the booksellers of the time but unhelpful to present-day researchers. The difficulty in identifying the names of the New Hall partners and their changing trading style has continued to the present day, although few authorities make such a hash of the problem as the author (or his translators) of Ludwig Danckert's *Directory of European Porcelain* where it is stated that 'Champion sold his right finally in 1781 to the Society of the Staffordshire Potteries'! What a good idea. The new society could have termed their wares 'Society Porcelain' and their company 'The Society'. As it was they settled for the convenient address – 'New Hall'.

The factory site, the 'New Hall' itself, gives rise to difficulties. It was reputedly originally called Shelton Hall, although there were two other residences of this name – hence the change to the 'New Hall'. Simeon Shaw, writing before 1829, noted in his privately printed book, *History of the Staffordshire Potteries,* that the remaining partners 'settled the manufactory at the New Hall, Shelton [in the early 1780s] only a short time previously erected by Mr Whitehead'.[2]

How did this recently built residence come to become a porcelain manufactory in the 1780s? Existing documents quoted at length in previous books and specialist papers indicate that in July 1773 Alice Dalton had surrendered 'Shelton Hall to Humphrey Palmer of Hanley, Potter' who seemingly rented it to his son, Thomas. In December 1778 we read of 'Shelton Hall with little Croft adjoining … and all … Pot Ovens ... now in the holding of Thomas Palmer to the use of John Hollins, Ralph Baddeley and Thos. Smith'. Subsequently, but before the new partnership's move, the Shelton (or New) Hall passed to John Turner of Lane End[3] and then to James Neale, the London dealer in pottery and porcelain. A document I quote on page 406 mentions a Samuel Bolton as the first occupier of the New Hall.

The question is, was the New Hall really a residence, later adapted into a pottery or warehouse, or were the works in the grounds, forming merely part of the estate? I will return to this point later.

In discussing the partners in the true New Hall porcelain producing partnership once it settled at the New Hall at Shelton (Hanley), we can here disregard the earlier pioneer partners involved in the first manufactory at Tunstall – Anthony Keeling and John Turner. They have been discussed in Chapter III and there seems little or no doubt that the earlier writers correctly stated that a disagreement arose at Tunstall after which the senior potters Keeling and Turner left the co-partnership. The remaining owners of Champion's patent rights were then forced to leave Keeling's Tunstall premises. The partners re-established the porcelain works at, or near the 'New Hall' at Shelton – the rest is history or rather the subject of this book.

In seeking out personal names for the partners or their firm we find that the first printed reference to the so-called 'New Hall' firm even occurs under an incorrect town, 'Handley' or Hanley, rather than Shelton.[4] The partnership name 'Heath, Warburton & Co.' occurs in Bailey's *Western Directory* for 1784 (but the company does not occur in two listings attributed to 1783). The 1784 entry is repeated under Hanley in William Tunnicliffe's *A Survey of the County of Stafford,* my copy of which has the pencilled date 1787. It is interesting and noteworthy that the names Heath, Warburton & Co. have the description 'China Manufacturers' added. This is a unique trade description (relating only to china or porcelain manufacture) in these directories, having only a near match in the description given after the name Hugh Booth of Stoke 'Manufacturer of China, China glaze and Queen's ware in all its various Branches'. Other manufacturers were described simply as 'Potters' or list basic types of earthenwares, although I believe some may have made porcelain as well as various types of earthenware.

Apart from the title 'Heath, Warburton & Co. China Manufacturers' as given in the directories of the mid- to late 1780s, I do not know of any surviving letters, accounts or such documents relating to the partnership name used prior to the adoption of the well-known partnership name Hollins, Warburton & Co. in or before September 1789. Then this style appears on a printed billhead with the description 'Manufacturers of Real China, Shelton, Staffordshire'. Such a printed billhead occurs in the Wedgwood archives now housed at Keele University and this example is dated September 1789.

Very little is known about the early partners included in the trade style 'Heath, Warburton & Co.' and previous writers have assumed that the first named partner was Joshua Heath who was certainly mentioned in a 1793 document (see page 145) and signed the 1803 agreement relating to the purchase of the factory premises. The original main partner, however, may have been Thomas Heath, not Joshua, a point I will return to shortly.

But firstly, let me refer to the New Hall premises and their ownership. Apart from later (nineteenth century) earthenware models showing no kilns but inscribed 'New Hall China Manufactory Staffordshire. 1813' (see page 407) and at least one smaller model inscribed on a tablet 'New Hall Warehouse', we have to rely on three sources of contemporary information, the Salop Fire Office Records discovered by Mr. Roger Edmundson and various documents preserved in the William Salt Library at Stafford researched by David Holgate and reproduced as Appendix II in his book *New Hall.* We also have basic facts published by Mrs. Audrey M. Dudson and incorporated in her book *Dudson, a Family of Potters since 1800* (Dudson Publications, Hanley 1985).

Mrs. Dudson, drawing on a series of Duchy of Lancaster Manorial court records, notes that in 1773 the Shelton or New Hall Estate comprised the Hall, its gardens, yards, stables, outbuildings and various named parcels of land. The Hall was in 1773 purchased from Alice Dalton by

Humphrey Palmer, the originally successful Hanley potter, who converted at least the outbuildings into a pottery which was worked by himself or his son, Thomas. Part or all had, however, been let to other potters including John Turner – see page 98. After Humphrey Palmer's death the estate passed in 1789 to his daughter Mary but had by this time been let to the so-called New Hall partnership. The reader is also referred to my Chapter XI.

The helpful Salop Fire Office Policy, number 1562, dated 22 March 1792, was issued to Messrs. Hollins, Warburton & Co. and covered:

1. A stock of china in their potworks in one connected range near New Hall in Hanley aforesaid, not exceeding one thousand pounds.
2. Biscuit ware therein only, not exceeding two hundred pounds.
3. Stock of China in potworks in one connected range at Booden Brook in Hanley aforesaid not exceeding five hundred pounds.[5]
4. Working utensils in their pottery at New Hall aforesaid not exceeding one hundred pounds.

N B All brick and tiles

It is noteworthy that the first description is for the potworks 'near New Hall', not in or at New Hall, and that there was seemingly another potworks at nearby Booden Brook where a large stock of china was kept.

Slight amendments were made in the fire office records on 13 April 1793 when the stock of chinaware in paragraph 1 was removed to 'the new brick and tiled building in Hanley'. This seems strange as they were just over a year previously at the potworks near New Hall; now the stock was in a newly erected building. Secondly, the stock of china formerly at Booden Brook was now (in April 1793) removed to 'the New Hall' but was reduced in value from £500 to £400. A new entry '5' refers to a stock of plain china in the 'white warehouse and painting shops' not exceeding in value £200. It is interesting that in 1793 'new' brick and tiles buildings were brought into use. Could the New Hall manufactory have been rebuilt or enlarged in or before 1793?

The Court Rolls relating to land transactions within the manor of Newcastle painstakingly researched by David Holgate and Harold Blakey record the surrender by Maria Elliott (formerly Bagnall) of house with gardens in Shelton late in the holding of Esther Booth to 'the use of Samuel Hollins, Jacob Warburton, John Hollins, John Daniel, William Clowes, Charles Bagnall, and Joshua Heath, china manufacturers as tenants in common…'. This important reference (DL30.507/26) is dated 4 February 1793, but only lists seven partners.

Returning to Salop Fire Office insurance records, in September 1793 a further additional entry '6' was made to the March 1792 policy, relating to 'a dwelling house, barn and two stables' also built of brick and with a tiled roof. The value of these connected buildings was not to exceed £100. This policy was in the name of the company, not of an individual, although it is possible that it was for the use of the managing partner, John Daniel. The estate and stock was now in 1792 insured for £1,900, the annual premium being £4.11s.0d.

A further policy dated 7 November 1810, now in the name of Messrs. Hollins, Warburton, Daniel and Clowes, includes the manufactory plus 'their dwelling house called New Hall situate near the above manufactory' (insured for £300).[6] However, in a memorandum dated 15 August 1812 this last part was deleted as it was 'being taken down' but at the same period their warehouses, packing house and two counting houses under the same roof near '6' (the barn stable and small house situate near to the premises) was increased in value. Was this perhaps the large warehouse depicted in the pottery model, one example of which is clearly dated 1813?

Additional helpful information on the New Hall estate is given in an agreement made on 1 March 1803 between Mary Palmer and the New Hall partners. This agreement relates to 'all that building and tenement called the New Hall formerly used as a China warehouse together with the Hovels [i.e. kilns], Workshops, Manufactory and Buildings belonging thereto. And also all these seven several Closes pieces or parcels of land lying together and adjoining to the said buildings and premises – twenty nine acres … together with full and free liberty power and authority to and for the said Hollins, Warburton, Daniel and Company to get or use marl from the said premises for the use of the said China Manufactory To Hold the said Manufactory … during the term of fourteen years, pay … unto the said Mary Palmer … the yearly rent … of £210 and also further yearly rent – of eight pounds per cent for all money to be hereafter laid out and expended by the said Mary Palmer in erecting new buildings for the use of the Manufactory. And also that the said Mary Palmer … will pay unto the said John Hollins … sums of money (not exceeding … the sum of £300) which they shall require for the purpose of erecting new buildings to the said manufactory…'.

Following Mary Palmer's death the family estate was eventually sold in April 1810 to the New Hall partnership, then trading as Hollins, Warburton, Daniel & Co., the cost to the company being £6,800. It later passed to John Daniel in August 1814, then to his sister Alice and reputedly to William Clowes in February 1821; but in

1823, after the death of Clowes, the remaining estate passed to Hugh Henshall Williamson by whom it was sold in 1843 for £3,050. Details of the later owners of the divided property are listed by David Holgate on his *New Hall* page 234 and by Mrs. Dudson in Chapter 5 of her book. The ownership of the estate is extremely complicated as several persons seem to have held shares in it and these passed to different people on the death of each partner. My Chapter XI gives further details.

I think it is probable that the New Hall itself was not originally used as a porcelain works but that the manufactory was adjacent to it, possibly in the adapted outbuildings, although the 1803 agreement states that the house was used as a 'China warehouse', perhaps for the storage of the finished stock. This position is also I think underlined in a now mislaid document dated July 1779, quoted by Major Stringer in his 1949 book *New Hall Porcelain* (on his page 11), but this relates to a period before the new porcelain producing partnership took over the existing pottery. However, it is important and I refer to this document in the next column.

The early writers gave surprisingly little information on the New Hall premises. Simeon Shaw in his 1829 book noted only that the partners:

> ...settled the manufactory at the New Hall, Shelton only a short time previously erected by Mr Whitehead, of the Old Hall, Hanley; on which account the Porcelain had the appellation of New Hall China.

John Ward (using to some degree Shaw's material) in his much larger 1843 history did little better, noting in his Hanley-Shelton chapter:

> The New Hall in Shelton, at the junction of one of the branch-roads towards Burslem, has been long celebrated as a china manufactory and was the first established in Staffordshire at which the making of porcelain was carried on with success...

Some twenty years later the great Victorian ceramic historian Llewellynn Jewitt researched the subject in more depth when preparing his series of articles for *The Art Journal* magazine. The New Hall section was published in the January 1864 issue and contained the following account of the New Hall estate:

> ...they took a house at Shelton, known as 'Shelton Hall' afterwards the 'New Hall,' in contradistinction to the 'Old Hall,' celebrated as being the birthplace of Elijah Fenton, the poet. At this time Shelton Hall, which had been purchased in 1773 off Alice Dalton, widow, who had inherited it from her brother, Edward Burslem Sundell, by Humphrey Palmer, was occupied by his son, Thomas Palmer, as a pot-work. In 1777 Humphrey Palmer, intending a second marriage with Hannah Ashwin, of Stratford-on-Avon, gave a rent-charge of £30 on the Hall and pot-works, and a life interest in the rest of the estate, as a dower to that lady, reserving the right for his son, Thomas Palmer, the potter, to get clay and marl from any part of the estate for his own use. In 1789, Humphrey Palmer and his wife being both dead, the estate passed to their infant and only child Mary Palmer, of whose successor's executors, after some uninteresting changes, it was, as will be seen, ultimately purchased by the china manufacturers. At this time the works had been considerably increased, and they grew gradually larger, till, in 1802, they are described as three messuages, three pot-works, one garden, fifty acres of land, thirty acres of meadow, and forty acres of pasture, &c...

This interesting account was subsequently incorporated in the Shelton section of Jewitt's great work *The Ceramic Art of Great Britain* (Virtue & Co., London 1878, revised edition 1883). Jewitt had obviously consulted source material before penning the above paragraph, perhaps the documents now in the William Salt Library at Stafford (folio D 1798/536) and which were listed by David Holgate in his Appendix II.

In addition to Jewitt's review, Major G.E. Stringer in his 1949 *New Hall Porcelain* quotes a deed or surrender document of 7 July 1779 which substantiates some of Jewitt's information and at the same time adds to it. The main details of this document are:

> To this Court comes John Hollins of Newcastle, mercer, Ralph Baddely of Shelton, potter and Thomas Smith of Penkhill, Gent, and surrender – all that messuage called Shelton Hall with the little croft thereto adjoining and all potworks, barns, stables, gardens hereditaments and appurtenances to the same belonging ... late the estate of Alice Dalton and called the Hall Meadows, the Middle Field ... and all ways, watercourses and appurtenances to the same belonging, to the use and behoof of John Turner of Lane End ... Potter, for the term of 99 years if Humphrey Palmer, late of Hanley, potter, shall so long live.

After reading the above two accounts one would deduce that in the early 1780s, when the new partnership was moving from Anthony Keeling's Tunstall pottery to the new works at Shelton, the Shelton Hall estate was owned by Humphrey Palmer or occupied by his son Thomas or by John Turner. With this firmly in mind I, as previously mentioned, was on my first attempt unable to trace the so-called New Hall partners as occupying premises in Shelton in the 1783 to 1788 Land Tax returns. Neither Humphrey nor Thomas Palmer nor John Turner appeared in the Shelton records.

I solved the problem by working back from nineteenth century Land Tax returns when in the 1820s and 1830s the property was listed under the title 'New Hall Co.', recommencing at the first Shelton Land Tax return, that of 1781. I then found the entry 'James Neale for Palmers £1.19s.3½d.'

James Neale, the famous London china and glass dealer and the Hanley pottery owner, with his partner-cum-factory manager Robert Wilson, comes into our story because he had been Humphrey Palmer's business partner prior to Palmer's failure early in 1778. As Josiah Wedgwood wrote to Thomas Bentley on 14 March 1778, '...Mr Neale is come down to settle the affairs ... the other creditors hope he will take all and pay the debts'. Seemingly James Neale did take all Palmer's property and as a result of this Humphrey Palmer surrendered all his property on 23 March 1778 to 'James Neale of Saint Paul's Church Yard, London, Merchant'. The foreclosure document is now in the Hanley Reference Library, Stoke-on-Trent. The basic outcome of his foreclosure is that the Shelton Hall estate rested in James Neale's name until April 1810. However, it also seems that the New Hall estate had been left by Humphrey Palmer to his daughter Mary but she, on her father's death, was a minor and therefore Neale held it, perhaps as a trustee until she came of age.

Advancing the research on the Shelton Land Tax returns, we find the next available demand to 1781 was 1783. In this year covering the period to 5 April 1783 we discover that the same property owned by James Neale and valued at £1.19s.3½d. was now occupied by 'Sam Hollins & Co.'. This is a mystery description, not previously recorded, but it may record the earliest so-called New Hall partnership. This may not be a true trade name but rather the clerk's indication that the Shelton Hall estate was occupied by Samuel Hollins and others, working in partnership. This explanation would seem very likely, especially if it was repeated in subsequent annual returns, but this was not the case; 'Sam Hollins & Co' occurs only in 1783.

Further study of the original Land Tax Returns is complicated and for this reason I have transferred this aspect of the New Hall story to a separate section – Appendix II – so as not to unnecessarily complicate the history or delay the discussion of the New Hall porcelains.

It is strange that the partnership name 'Hollins, Warburton & Co.' as used on billheads from at least 1789 does not occur in the Shelton Land Tax returns which instead give the occupier (not the owner) as Thomas Heath. Other records are, however, imprecise or out of date, for example the style 'Hollins, Warburton & Co.' does not occur in directories until Chester & Mort's of 1796 when in the 'Sheldon' (Shelton) section we find the slightly incorrect name 'Hollings, Warburton & Co. china manufacturers'. However, we have at least one printed billhead which reads:

Bot. of Hollins, Warburton & Co.
Manufacturers of Real China, Shelton, Staffordshire

A copy in the Wedgwood archives at Keele University is dated September 1789. This account, made out to Josiah Wedgwood Esq., was receipted on 11 November 1789 and signed by John Daniel who was by then obviously well connected with the firm, and reputedly the day-to-day manager of the jointly owned works, but whose name had not yet been included in the company's trading style. This style 'Messrs. Hollins, Warburton & Co.' also occurs written as a heading in John Wedgwood's crate account books (in the Potteries Museum collection). The first entry under this heading is dated 23 May 1787, that is within the period when the directories were listing Heath, Warburton & Co. The trade style Hollins, Warburton & Co. was that used from at least 1787 to about 1799 or later, although I have previously stated the partnership and its china were familiarly referred to as 'New Hall'. A document of February 1793,[7] relating to a surrender of land in Shelton, mentions Samuel Hollins, Jacob Warburton, John Hollins, John Daniel, William Clowes, Charles Bagnall and Joshua Heath – China Manufacturers as tenants in common.

From about 1799 the revised, fuller title Hollins, Warburton, Daniel & Co. came into use, although occasionally the old style, without Daniel's name, occurs. In contrast the local rate records (not the Land Tax returns) tend to list John Daniel (& Co.) as the occupiers of the New Hall premises until the time of John Daniel's death early in 1821. From the rate dated 1812/1813 the ownership of the works changed from Miss Palmer to John Daniel. In 1822 the ownership of the pottery was written in as the New Hall Company. This description was continued for both the ownership and the occupiers until 1827 when the ownership was amended to Daniel & Co. and the occupiers as Hollins, Warburton & Co., the old style. This was quickly amended to show Hollins, Warburton & Co. as the owners of the property rather than Daniel & Co. In 1828 the ownership was listed as Hollins & Warburton but again reverted to Hollins, Warburton & Co. and to Hollins & Co. in March and May 1832. After this rate return the late Alfred Meigh did not transcribe the names of the factory owners from the now destroyed original records.

This list of owners and occupiers of the New Hall premises in Brook Street, Shelton, is admittedly confusing. It is as if nobody was sure of the trading style of the partnership or of the names and relative importance of the various partners, a situation which has remained ever since the company was first established at Tunstall! We are on safe ground if we refer to the Shelton period porcelains of the approximate period c.1783-1835 as 'New Hall', for after all when the firm did mark their wares with a standard printed mark it was the words 'New Hall' within a double lined circle. The initial mark 'N H' also occurs as a raised pad on some jugs – see Plate 456 and page 131.

It is clear that just before the move from Tunstall two of the principal partners, Anthony Keeling and John Turner, had disassociated themselves from the co-partnership. Indeed, according to tradition it was Keeling's departure that obliged the remaining potters to seek new premises in another part of the Potteries.

The loss of Keeling and Turner must have been a serious blow to the remaining partners as, not only would the financial backing of Keeling and Turner have been withdrawn (for they are not named in later documents or partnership details), but those remaining would probably have been forced to purchase additional shares in the company unless John Daniel, the new manager (if he was a new additional partner), was willing to buy Keeling's and Turner's holdings. Also, the wholesale and retail outlets of these two important earthenware potters might well have been lost to the new company. Even more serious would have been the situation if one or both of these potters had decided themselves to manufacture porcelain in competition with their former associates. If they had not sold their shares or demanded a repayment they might well have been fully entitled to produce their own porcelains, having originally paid for this right.

It is quite clear, however, that the remaining partners were able and happy to continue production under the Cookworthy-Champion patent even when this meant setting up a new porcelain producing factory with all the additional expense that this entailed. Perhaps they had little choice in the matter having purchased these rights for some thousands of pounds. If their venture had been seen to fail they could hardly expect to resell these rights to other potters. They had to make a success of the venture, or lose their investment. Having made this point, I think it probable that the early productions made at Tunstall before the departure of Keeling and Turner did give the remaining partners some encouragement. The porcelains which in Chapter Two I have attributed to the initial Tunstall period are visually devoid of manufacturing faults or shortcomings. They would form a sound if unexciting base on which to build up a larger manufactory.

Although I do not consider the identification of all the individual partners or indeed the trade style of the company over the various periods to be of great consequence, it is convenient to list the various partners connected with the New Hall company once it had been established at Shelton, that is after Anthony Keeling and John Turner had retired from the partnership and in effect returned to their respective potteries. It must not be thought, however, that the partners whom I am about to list spent their days at the New Hall works. All had their own potteries or other businesses and, with the exception of the manager, John Daniel, all should be regarded as shareholders or backers rather than having day-to-day control of the porcelain works. This too would have been the position with the various partners in the main Worcester factory – most were merely backers or 'sleeping-partners'. This situation possibly related to other great names, maybe to William Cookworthy himself at an earlier period.

Having made this basic point, I must give some details of the partners who are known to us by name. When one uses a firm's name, one tends to place first or to include the names of the most prominent persons concerned (the main backers), leaving others of less importance to be covered by the all-embracing abbreviation '& Co.' for 'and Company'. In the case of the New Hall Company we find only the names of Heath, Hollins, Warburton and Daniel included in the firm's official titles. Others are known to us through dissolution of partnership notices or other documents.

Of these named potters, or other persons, we know least about the first named – Heath – the prime name in the first known partnership of Heath, Warburton & Co. Previous writers have assumed this person to be Joshua Heath who was mentioned in a New Hall estate leasehold agreement of 1 March 1803. Earlier a 'Mr Joshua Heath' was included in the Shelton Land Tax returns, but when one refers to the return of 1784, covering the period from 6 April 1783 to 5 April 1784, we find that the New Hall property was occupied by Thomas Heath, not Joshua. This information was repeated in all the available Land Tax returns until that of 1795. The next, of 1797, lists John Daniel, the factory manager, as the occupier.

THOMAS HEATH (c.1737-1812?)

I have experienced great difficulty in tracing relevant details of Thomas Heath or even in deciding which person of this name was involved in the New Hall partnership. Mr. Rodney Hampson has informed me that the Mormon International Genealogical Index includes three hundred and forty Staffordshire entries under the name Thomas Heath. Mrs. Pat Halfpenny, the former

Keeper of Ceramics at the City Museum and Art Gallery, Stoke, has also supplied me with a three page list of documents relating to Staffordshire potters of this name! While I cannot trace any reference to a Thomas Heath in previous works on New Hall porcelain, we can, I believe, narrow the list of possible New Hall partners to a relatively few Thomas Heaths.

There is mention of an early eighteenth century potter of this name. Simeon Shaw, for example, noted:

> Mr Thomas Heath of Lane Delph in 1710 made a good kind of Pottery, by mixing with his other clay a species obtained from the coal mines, which by high firing became a light grey ... His three daughters were married to persons who afterwards became celebrated potters – Mr Neale, of London, Mr Palmer of Hanley – and Mr Pratt of Fenton... He also used the wash of Pipe Clay, first practised by Mr Astbury

I have already noted on page 95 that Enoch Booth was apprenticed to a Thomas Heath of Shelton in 1717. It is also recorded (in the *Victoria History of the County of Stafford* (Vol. VIII, page 153) that Thomas Heath sold his estate and Flint Mill at Hanley in 1738. Mr. Rodney Hampson informs me that this Thomas Heath, the son of James Heath, was christened at Newcastle-under-Lyme on 16 November 1699, and that he married Hannah Amison at Newcastle on 1 June 1732. One of their daughters married James Neale at Stoke on 31 August 1762. Humphrey Palmer (to be Neale's partner) married another daughter, Mary Heath, in October 1751. This Thomas Heath had interesting connections with persons who were to own the property at which the New Hall Company later traded, but it is not possible for this Thomas Heath (born 1699) to be that active in the 1790s.

Mrs. Halfpenny has sent me basic records relating to another Thomas Heath who certainly lived at the period here under discussion, that is the 1780s and 1790s. In this case we have records of the birth and death but not of the middle or working period. Working backwards, the *Staffordshire Advertiser* of 1 February 1812 records the death of Thomas Heath:

> On the 25th inst. after a lingering illness, Thomas Heath Esq. In the 74th year of his age, late of the Old Hall at Hanley in this county.

This surely links with a baptism recorded in the Burslem Parish Registers where on 6 March 1736 (old style or 1737 new style) is noted the baptism of Thomas, the son of John and Mary Heath. A marriage settlement evidences that Thomas Heath married Sarah Simpson in March 1763. At least one son, John, seems to have been born to Sarah Heath and possibly others, William and Thomas? David Holgate kindly informed me of court records in the 1780s relating to Thomas Heath and his wife Sarah and to their eldest son, John.

The date of death in 1812 fits in well with changes in the Land Tax returns for our Thomas Heath. The mention of a lingering illness is of interest as the 1796 *Staffordshire Pottery Directory* lists a Thomas Heath under 'Gentry' showing that he had retired from business by this period.

I am at present unable to comment on the description given in the 1812 obituary '...late of Old Hall at Hanley...' unless it could be a very erroneous reference to Thomas Heath as a partner in the New Hall China Company. I cannot trace any reference to a Thomas Heath being associated with the Old Hall or with the Old Hall Pottery. However, the Hanley Land Tax returns list Thomas Heath as owning land, taxed at the above average rate of 10s. from the early 1780s to 1809. There are no returns between that and 1812. The entry is not included after this date, that is when Thomas Heath died.

Another Thomas Heath (born c.1771), a brother-in-law to William Adams, was active at Hadderidge, Burslem. He purchased much of the Adams Estate in 1806, but he lived until 1839, long after the probable death of the early New Hall partner of the same name, and I merely include this reference for the sake of completeness.

The dearth of information on Thomas Heath in reference books is, however, made up for by the very basic references in the available Land Tax returns from the early 1780s onwards, which I quote in Appendix II. He was obviously an important person, his signature occurring as an Assessor on some returns, and in 1794 and 1795 he is described as a Gentleman, a rare distinction but one also given in the 1796 *Directory*.

It seems likely that the Heath in the firm of Heath, Warburton & Co. was the Thomas Heath who had important interests in the vital local coal mining industry, vital not only to the potters but also to the iron industry and other contemporary expanding industries involved in the Industrial Revolution.

There is a further interesting item of information on Thomas Heath, for a person of this name was involved with another china producing firm at Hanley contemporary with New Hall – Messrs. Anthony Keeling & Co. Another partner with Thomas Heath in this firm was Samuel Perry who also had mining interests. Could Thomas Heath have enjoyed interests in both, presumably rival, porcelain producing partnerships? Perhaps, if we are dealing with the same person, he had left the New Hall firm before joining with Anthony Keeling, Samuel Perry, Edward Keeling, John Shorthose and Thomas Shelley in their Hanley china works.

We just do not know and the answer is of little consequence to our understanding of the New Hall products.

JOSHUA HEATH

David Holgate, in his English Ceramic Circle paper 'New Hall, Some interesting Nuances' *(Transactions* Vol. 4, Part 2 of 1991), put forward a convincing claim for Joshua rather than Thomas Heath being an original partner. Mr. Holgate correctly stated that a 1790 lease agreement with Mary Palmer (the owner of the New Hall property) includes the names of the New Hall partners. These in the order originally given were S. Hollins, J. Warburton, John Hollins, C. Bagnall, J. Daniel, W. Clowes and Joshua Heath. Joshua Heath is also listed last in a surrender of property in February 1793. Another agreement dated 1 March 1803 also includes Joshua Heath, after William Clowes. Joshua Heath had died by 9 May 1805 when 'Elizabeth Heath, widow of Joshua (Gent) was admitted to the undivided seventh part of all that dwelling house ... etc now in the occupation of Samuel Hollins and other partners of the firm called the China Company ...', to quote from documents in the Public Record Office discovered by Mrs. Dudson.

It is clear and agreed that from 1790 Joshua Heath was one of the partners, but I consider that these relatively late references and, more importantly, the placing of the name towards the end of the list of partners and the dropping of the name Heath from its prime position in the early firm of Heath, Warburton & Co., do not link up with Joshua Heath being an original and leading partner, bearing in mind the fact that Thomas Heath was listed in the Land Tax returns as the occupier of the New Hall premises from 1784 to 1795. Certainly, however, Thomas Heath's name does not appear listed as a partner in any known New Hall leases or other documents. The importance to the company of Thomas Heath would have been his interest in coal mining. The company had the access to the Cornish raw materials but cheap good coal was even more important and was one of the main reasons given by Champion for moving from Bristol to Staffordshire.

Returning to consider Joshua Heath, a named partner in the New Hall company, a Joshua Heath is mentioned as a potter in a New Hall leasehold agreement of 1 March 1803. He, with Charles Bagnall, are there described together as 'gentlemen' rather than as potters, but there are many records of a potter of this name. One signed the 1770 agreement on uniform pricing. Jewitt mentioned in his 1878 *Ceramic Art of Great Britain* that Joshua Heath had worked in association with Charles Bagnall and I have discovered a dissolution of partnership notice relating to 'the copartnership between us Joshua Heath and Charles Bagnall of Shelton ... Potters and Copartners'. This notice was dated 'Shelton November 10th 1787'. Joshua Heath's name also occurs in the first available Shelton Land Tax return of 1781 and the 1789 Loyal Address signed by the Staffordshire Potters. Joshua Heath may also have continued his ceramic interests by involvement in the considerable firm of Shorthose & Heath or Heath & Shorthose as it was sometimes given. The Shelton Land Tax returns show him owning and occupying up to 1797 after which the occupiers are given as Robert (and later David) Wilson, William Mellor (or Miller) and Charles Bagnall. From 1809 the ownership changed to Charles Bagnall and David Wilson as the sole occupier.

However, although Joshua Heath must have been a very useful backer, supplying much needed capital to the concern, he seemingly had little involvement in its daily affairs. If I am correct regarding Thomas Heath, then Joshua Heath was never a named partner in the New Hall company's trade name. David Holgate has stated that he died in 1805, but the name continued to be included in the Shelton Land Tax returns until 1808 after which that of Charles Bagnall replaces Heath. Perhaps in this respect the official returns are incorrect unless Heath's estate continued payments in his name.

JOHN HOLLINS (d.1804)

The next named partner with the surname Hollins had succeeded one Heath in this prime position in the firm's trading style by at least September 1789. There were, however, several potters of this name in the Potteries and two of these were associated with the New Hall company. These two partners were John and Samuel Hollins.

Of these, Samuel is certainly the best known and John Hollins did not receive a mention in David Holgate's original 1971 book *New Hall and its Imitators,* although this omission was corrected in the updated 1987 *New Hall.* John Hollins' name occurs in a document dated 7 July 1779, relating to the surrender of Shelton Hall 'with the little croft hereto adjoining and all potworks, barns ... to the same ... belonging ... To the use and behoof of John Turner of Lane End ...Potter, for the term of 99 years, if Humphrey Palmer late of Hanley, potter, shall so long live'. This followed Humphrey Palmer's bankruptcy and his surrender of other potteries and land to James Neale, as detailed by Diana Edwards in her book *Neale Pottery and Porcelain* (Barrie & Jenkins, London, 1987). Humphrey Palmer seemingly left the Shelton Hall property and land to his young daughter for the rate records list a Miss Palmer as owning the pottery occupied by Messrs Hollins, Warburton, Daniel & Co. long after her father's death in 1787.

David Holgate in his 1987 *New Hall* lists the several documents now in the William Salt Library at Stafford which relate to the Palmer family's ownership of the New Hall (Shelton Hall) estate from 14 July 1773, when Humphrey Palmer acquired the land, into the 1840s at a time when the New Hall company had been disbanded. The most important document listed in Mr. Holgate's Appendix II is that dated 1 March 1803, drawn up between the landlord Mary Palmer (then living in Birmingham) and her tenants, the so-called New Hall partnership. The partners were here listed with 'John Hollins of Newcastle-under-Lyme ... Gentleman' leading the names followed by 'Samuel Hollins of Shelton ... Potter' and others 'Copartners together under the firm Hollins, Warburton, Daniel & Company'.

John Hollins, the shareholder in the china-producing partnership, was by trade a mercer and draper. His customers included Josiah Wedgwood and family and the Wedgwood archives include annual accounts for their purchases. The Newcastle Land Tax returns of the 1780s show that John Hollins owned his own premises. This partner died in March 1804, the notice in the *Staffordshire Advertiser* of 31 March 1804 correctly recording that he had been 'one of the persons in the New Hall Manufactory...'. It also noted that he was an Alderman of Newcastle. His estate, however, continued to have an interest in the New Hall company for over a further five years. This fact is made clear by the dissolution of partnership notice published in the *London Gazette* of 16 December 1809, which records the fact that as from 11 November 1809 Charles Bagnall, then in his sixties, retired as did Ephraim Chatterley who signed as executor of John Hollins. Chatterley's signature to this document shows that John Hollins' shares had not previously been sold and that any monies that he had put into the enterprise as a backer had not previously been fully repaid. The remaining partners had been reduced to four under the 1809 dissolution of partnership – Samuel Hollins, Peter Warburton, William Clowes and John Daniel.

It has always been presumed that Samuel Hollins, a well-known potter, was the leading partner and the first named in the company's trade style. However, it is possible that John Hollins (1736-1804), a well-established Newcastle shopkeeper and/or banker could have provided the much needed capital required by the original partners, several of whom were potters, probably lacking large ready funds. Potting know-how is vital but one cannot practise the craft without funds to purchase the raw materials and pay the rent and workforce.

David Holgate has underlined his description of John Hollins as a mercer (see his 1991 E.C.C. paper) but there seems a chance that he was also a banker. At least one John Hollins was so described in 1788. The *London Gazette* of 14 October 1788 (number 13034) carried a notice concerning the estate and effects of Thomas Astbury, potter. A meeting of the creditors was to be held at the Crown Inn, Newcastle under Lyme on 7 November and accounts were to be submitted to 'Mr John Hollins of Newcastle, Banker...'. Of course he may also have traded as a mercer for bankers in the eighteenth century could be quite small concerns. It is interesting to note, however, that John Hollins' house in 1804 was partly used as a bank:

> ...that capital Freehold messuage or Tenement ... in the principal street in Newcastle ... late in the possession of John Hollins Esq a ... spacious shop to the front, now used as a Banking house By Messrs. Horwood & Co...

Mercer or banker John Hollins was obviously a backer in the New Hall partnership, not a potter. David Holgate has given other helpful information on John Hollins and on the Hollins family. It is also interesting to note that John married (in 1762) Mary Baddeley, a well-known surname in Staffordshire pottery and one associated also with the manufacture of porcelain.

SAMUEL HOLLINS (1748-1820)

Turning to Samuel Hollins, we find that this Shelton potter was certainly a leading and early partner in the new Staffordshire partnership. I have already recorded that the first Land Tax return for the New Hall property in the April 1782-83 period was in the name of Sam Hollins or 'Sam Hollins & Co' and he again appears before John Hollins in the 1793 listing.

Samuel Hollins must have been a wealthy and a leading master potter in the community. In 1796 he was elected Mayor of the Mock (or Moot) Corporation of Hanley and Shelton. He also had shares in two coal mines and was a partner in the Hendra Company which supplied the vital Cornish raw materials to Staffordshire potters. Rodney Hampson has informed me that, on the death of Thomas Hollins in 1773, his brother Samuel was left the White House in Shelton, also a separate pottery of some size as it had three hovels (or kilns) with cottages and land. In 1777 he was supplying Josiah Wedgwood with dinnerwares which were almost certainly of creamware. No wonder he was on Wedgwood's list of 'the most substantial and enterprising potters amongst us' in 1780.

By 1787 he was able to follow his father's (Richard

Hollins) charitable acts by enabling another church to be built in Hanley. His father (b.1702) had died in 1780, having potted at Upper Hanley Green for some thirty years. Perhaps Samuel assisted his father there and inherited much of the family property. He seemingly lived during his working life in Shelton Hall for his son Thomas is recorded as having been born there. However, as there were three buildings called Shelton Hall, one cannot now be sure if the Hollins family lived at the one later called the New Hall.

Samuel Hollins' own post-1785 earthenwares, which sometimes bear the impressed name mark 'S.HOLLINS', are always extremely neatly formed. Typical examples of his dry-bodied earthenwares are shown in my *Illustrated Encyclopaedia of British Pottery and Porcelain* (Barrie & Jenkins, London, 1966, Plates 313-6). These pieces, of course, show no similarity to the New Hall porcelains and this was the case with the products of all the potting partners. A rare impressed marked 'HOLLINS' pearlware plate is illustrated in Dr. M. Holdaway's *Hollins Blue and White Printed Earthenware* (Morley College Ceramic Circle, London 2001).

On Samuel Hollins' death in 1820 his shares in the New Hall Company were valued at £5,975 at a period when the concern was being offered for sale. These shares were left to his son, Thomas Hollins, who thereby retained an interest in the company's affairs. One of his many daughters, Ann, married Herbert Minton and one of his grandsons, Michael Daintry[8] Hollins (b.1815), became a partner in the Minton firm. As previously noted by me, Samuel Hollins was always listed in the available documents after John Hollins, although the names are not given in alphabetical order. His executors, apart from his son, included the New Hall partners William Clowes and John Daniel.

JACOB WARBURTON (1741-1826)

The next name to consider in the firm of Hollins, Warburton & Co. is Warburton, but again we have two persons of this surname to consider, Jacob and his son Peter. First we have Jacob Warburton who was born in 1741,[9] the second son of John Warburton (1720-1761) and Ann Daniel. We also have Peter Warburton. Both are respected names in the annals of Staffordshire ceramics and both were practising potters, as were other members of the family.

Jacob Warburton was to be a major benefactor under Alice Daniel's 1823 will but did not survive to receive her gifts, which included part of the estate of Alice's brother John, the New Hall factory manager. Alice left to her cousin Jacob Warburton a third share in the Daniel estate plus a legacy of £1,000. This was, however, shared between his surviving son Benjamin Warburton and three daughters – Mary Moseley, Ann Pike and Katharine Voss.

Jacob Warburton potted at Cobridge. He retired on 11 November 1800, after which his sons initially continued the pottery. Peter and Francis Warburton also potted together up to March 1802. Jacob was seemingly the source of much of the information given to Simeon Shaw for his account of the New Hall Company as incorporated in Shaw's *History of the Staffordshire Potteries* published in 1828. Jacob Warburton's obituary, which appeared in *The Staffordshire Advertiser* of 30 September 1826, was probably penned by Simeon Shaw. It read:

> Forty years ago in conjunction with a few other spirited individuals, Jacob Warburton contracted with the late Richard Champion Esq., a respectable merchant in Bristol, for the purchase of his patent right to the exclusive use of Cornish clay and stone for the manufacture of porcelain. In the year 1782, after making some experiments at Tunstall under the direction of Mr Champion, they established a china manufactory at the New Hall in Shelton ... Mr Warburton had for many years withdrawn himself from the cares and fatigues of his commercial engagements and on his second marriage, the result of a long cemented friendship and mutual attachment, he retired to Ford Green House...

Jacob Warburton was certainly a leading shareholder in the New Hall enterprise and was almost certainly one of the original partners and one of the most important local potters suggested to Richard Champion by Josiah Wedgwood in November 1780. It will be his name that featured in the early trade style Heath, Warburton & Co. and in the later firms of Hollins, Warburton & Co. and Hollins, Warburton, Daniel & Co.

PETER WARBURTON (1773-1813)

Peter and Francis were two of the sons of Jacob and Mary Warburton. The brothers potted together at Bleak Hill, Cobridge, until the dissolution of partnership on 29 March 1802, after which Peter continued on his own account until about the time of his death in January 1813 at the early age of forty. His fourth-part share in the New Hall concern then reverted to his father Jacob and to John Daniel, as his trustees, acting for his wife Mary and their surviving children. In a codicil to his will, dated 24 January 1811, he stated that on 26 April 1810 he, with his then partners – Samuel Hollins, John Daniel and William Clowes – had purchased the New Hall potworks, pot ovens, barns, stables, yards, etc.

Apart from his own pottery business, Peter Warburton seems to have replaced his father as a partner in the New

Hall enterprise at a period prior to the 1 March 1803 agreement to which Peter's, not Jacob's, name is affixed. Of all the known partners, Peter Warburton literally made most mark on the New Hall porcelains for the boldly painted mark 'Warburton's Patent' directly relates to Peter's patented process for bat printing in gold or silver. This patent number 3304 of 1810 is discussed at greater length in Chapter IX, but it is interesting to note here that the specially painted mark features Warburton's name, not that of the manufacturing firm, New Hall. Peter Warburton was also one of the more important local potters who were partners in the Hendra Company, a co-operative style clay-supplying combination.

JOHN DANIEL (c.1756-1821)

John Daniel (born c.1756), the son of Ralph Daniel, was an extremely important figure in the New Hall story; indeed he was the key figure for most of the firm's history although he was the youngest of the known early partners. He was, according to Simeon Shaw, 'engaged as managing partner' when the company moved to Shelton and as such he was probably the only partner who would have been responsible for the day-to-day running of the china works. He was most probably also responsible for introducing the new shapes and the patterns used to enhance them.

The Shelton Land Tax returns list John Daniel as the occupier of the premises in succession to Thomas Heath from 1797, sometimes in his singular name, at other times as 'Daniel & Co.', which would have been a fair description of the company. Between 1809 and 1822 he or 'Daniel & Co.' are also described as owning the manufactory. John Daniel was reputedly the 'manager' of the New Hall works from its earliest Shelton days; this is perhaps unlikely, although a manager would have been required, but this is now impossible to confirm. He certainly signed the earliest known receipt, one for china cups and saucers supplied to Josiah Wedgwood in September 1789. It is difficult to know what experience John Daniel had acquired prior to gaining his position with the New Hall partners, but the fact that he was Jacob Warburton's cousin must have helped, although he was only in his twenties when he joined the New Hall company. The Land Tax returns of the 1780s list several John Daniels, as do other contemporary records. One, probably the New Hall manager, was also one of the shareholders in the Hendra (clay supplying) company. As an executor of William Mellor, he also found himself a partner in the china producing firm of Keeling, Toft & Co. of Hanley, early in the nineteenth century.

Frederick Rhead who claimed (probably incorrectly) to be a distant relation of John Daniel, writing in the *Connoisseur* of December 1916, gives us a little pleasing insight into Daniel's character:

> He was undoubtedly a humane and kindly personage, and seems to have managed his apprentices without the constant application of the rattan and the rope's end, which instruments of castigation occupied in those days an important position among the tools of the craft, being usually hung on a wall near the gates of each pottery as a warning and terror to possible delinquents. Each Martinmas, John Daniel gave every apprentice a new pair of clogs – an eloquent commentary on the state of the roads.

Frederick Rhead recorded also that his great-grandmother, Charlotte Woolliscroft, was apprenticed at the New Hall works under John Daniel, hence the family's knowledge of his concern for the well-being of the apprentices.

John Daniel died on 18 January 1821. *The Staffordshire Advertiser* described him as '...John Daniel, Gent. of Hanley aged 65 years, one of the proprietors of the long established concern the New Hall China Manufactory ...'. He seemingly did not marry but lived with his sister, Alice, who administered his affairs after John's death. Good details of the will are given by David Holgate in the *Journal of the Northern Ceramic Society,* Vol. 3 (1978-9).

I believe that John Daniel was a relatively wealthy man, who on his death owned several properties, although Alice stated that the estate was under the value of £3,000, then a large amount. In August 1814 the New Hall China Works was reportedly sold or perhaps merely transferred by the partnership to John Daniel and was further transferred on his death to William Clowes. John Daniel was not only the manager, responsible for the running of the china works, its shapes, designs and workforce, he was the most important of the partners, at least in the early part of the nineteenth century.

Various personal details have been recorded suggesting again that John Daniel was of standing and importance. John Ward, for example, recorded in or before 1843:

> This gentleman had a pious horror of parsons; and was buried by his express desire, without any religious ceremony, on a spot of ground in the village of Endon (between Shelton and Leek), belonging to an estate he possessed there. A monument is built over his grave.

The local *Staffordshire Advertiser* of 27 January 1821 provides the basis or confirmation of John Ward's statement. The contemporary account reads in part:

> ...his mortal remains were conveyed in a hearse – to Endon ... and interred in a piece of ground at the village belonging

> to him ... he was committed to the 'House appointed for all living' without the observance of the office in religion in any shape, conformable with the opinions of the Free Thinkers to which it is understood he had long been a disciple...

His sister shared his Free Thinkers beliefs and was later buried beside him under a tree at Endon, leaving funds for the maintenance of their last resting place, now part of a private garden.

John Daniel, the factory manager for over thirty-five years, must have engaged all the gilders and painters, including Fidelle Duvivier (see Chapter V). He seemingly died in harness for the various documents refer to him as a 'China Manufacturer'.

It is interesting to note, as did previously Mr. Holgate, that John Daniel's sister's will originally recorded that Sampson Daniel (her cousin) had acted as the 'Warehouseman or Book-keeper at the New Hall Manufactory'.[10] This information, with other facts relating to Alice Daniel's eleven page will, are recorded by David Holgate in his paper 'Unravelling a Staffordshire Knot...' published in the *Journal of the Northern Ceramic Society,* Vol. 3 of 1978-9. The original very detailed document is preserved at the Lichfield Record Office, Staffordshire.

ALICE DANIEL

Alice Daniel was the unmarried sister of John Daniel, the factory manager. On his death in January 1821 Alice was John Daniel's sole next of kin. As her brother died intestate, Alice inherited, by Letters of Administration, all John Daniel's possessions.

These included his share in the New Hall company, then termed Messrs. Hollins, Warburton, Daniel & Company, as well as various property owned or worked by the partnership. Alice Daniel was therefore a shareholding partner from at least January 1821 until her own death in June 1827. She may have been a partner from an earlier period if she had purchased or otherwise obtained shares from other retiring or deceased partners.

In her own will dated 29 November 1823 she left her property including the estate at Endon, also the land at Booden Brook, Shelton 'upon which a Fire Engine Mill and other buildings have been erected and in the occupation of Messeurs Hollins Warburton Daniel and Company'. Other Daniel property in Slacks Lane, Hanley was also designated, 'also all my share and interest in the New Hall China Manufactory and concern and the property thereof land all and singular my personal estate chattels and effects of every sort...'[11] were left for her joint executors, Job Meigh, potter of Shelton, and John Moseley of Cobridge, another well-known local potter who obviously was friendly with the Daniels and may have enjoyed connections with the New Hall Company.

It is interesting to see mentioned in Alice Daniel's will a legacy to Thomas Brocas, the leading china dealer in Shrewsbury. Brocas has previously been associated with selling local Shropshire porcelains made at the Coalport works but he obviously also had links with some of the partners in the Staffordshire New Hall company. Indeed in November 1804 he stated that he had been dealing with the leading Staffordshire manufacturers for sixteen years, that is since 1788.

WILLIAM CLOWES (b. c.1745-d. 1822)

William Clowes, another partner in the New Hall company, is a mysterious figure. He was described as a 'Gentleman' rather than a potter and David Holgate states 'I firmly believe that he gave only financial support to the firm'.

Our endeavours to unravel the story of William Clowes (sometimes spelt Clewes in contemporary documents) is confused by the fact that both father and son had the same name. It was the son who was born in about 1745 who was later to join the New Hall partnership. David Holgate has noted that the father was born in 1728 and died in 1782 and that he married Jane Henshall.

Notwithstanding previous statements that Clowes was not a potter, we have several references to a William Clowes as at least a partner in retailing and in earthenware producing partnerships. I believe these relate to our William Clowes, who by at least the early 1790s had joined the early partners in the New Hall partnership.

A William Clowes (& Co.), a London wholesaler of Staffordshire earthenwares, advertised in the *General Evening Post* in May 1778. This notice, first published by Nancy Valpy in *The Transactions of the English Ceramic Circle,* Vol. 12, Part 2 (1985), reads:

> STAFFORDSHIRE WARE.
>
> SOLD BY WILLIAM CLOWES & CO
>
> At 112 in the minories where Merchants and Dealers may be supplied with any quantity at the Shortest Notice and on the most reasonable Terms or at their manufactory, at Longport, near Burslem, Staffordshire.

His partners in this concern were William Walker, John Fry junior and Robert Williamson. This partnership was dissolved on 27 November 1780, at which period they also had a warehouse or depot at Brook's Wharf,

Queenhithe, on the Thames riverside. From the November 1780 dissolution the firm continued under the style Clowes & Williamson.

Although the 1778 London advertisement refers to the firm's manufactory at Longport, the directories of the 1780s list the earthenware firm of Clowes & Williamson at Fenton. However, by about 1790 the trade style was amended to Henshall, Williamson & Clowes, a firm which did use a Longport address. This partnership was dissolved on 11 November 1800. Apart from these connections with earthenware producing firms, a William Clowes was also a partner – with other leading potters – in the Hendra Company.

His connection with the New Hall company may arise from the fact that he had married first into the Hollins family, to Sarah Hollins, the granddaughter of Richard Hollins and I believe the daughter of Samuel Hollins. It is not known when William Clowes joined the New Hall partnership but he could have been one of the original ten. Hitherto, it has only been noted that his name is included as 'Gentleman' in the March 1803 articles of agreement concerning the purchase of the New Hall property and that he is also named in the 1804 and 1809 dissolution of partnership notices. However, he is listed with other New Hall partners as 'China manufacturers' in the Court Rolls dated 4 February 1793 (see page 145). This is of importance as it might have been supposed that William Clowes joined the firm after his inheritance from Josiah Brindley in or after 1795, as reported by David Holgate. David Holgate has also noted that in 1821, after the death of John Daniel, the New Hall estate was surrendered to William Clowes but he in turn died in the following year.

David Holgate in his 1987 book gives a good account of the domestic position regarding William Clowes and his relations. He makes the valid point that Clowes was a wealthy man. He was seemingly an important figure in the later history of the New Hall Company and Mr. Holgate further believes that Clowes 'had the real entrepreneurial spark'. It certainly was unfortunate that he died in 1822 at a period when the company needed such a figure at the helm.

CHARLES BAGNALL (c.1747-1814)

Charles Bagnall was a partner in the New Hall concern from its earliest days. He was related to Hugh Booth of Tunstall. Like other partners he had his own earthenware works to engage his main interests. From at least the early 1780s Charles Bagnall had been trading with another New Hall partner, Joshua Heath, in the Shelton firm of Heath & Bagnall. This partnership was dissolved on 10 November 1787. He is recorded potting on his own account at Booth's former pottery at Tunstall, from about 1777 into the 1790s. He further acted as a dealer in raw materials, principally white lead and zaffer. He was seemingly an important member of the New Hall concern, signing some of the surviving letters on behalf of the company 'for self, Hollins, Warburton & Co.'

Charles Bagnall was also a partner in the firm of Samuel Perry & Co. which worked the important New Hays and Sneyd Green Collieries. By 1798 he had interests in other collieries with John Turton, a partnership which was dissolved in January 1802. He was in addition a partner in the clay producing co-operative, the Hendra Company.

As is made clear in the official dissolution of partnership notice, Charles Bagnall retired from the New Hall partnership as from 11 November 1809. It should be noted that an undated but probably early Hollins, Warburton & Co. account or note (in the Wedgwood archives) is signed 'for Hollins, Warburton & Co. samp Bag...' – a part signature almost certainly of Sampson Bagnall who may have been related to Charles Bagnall. The porcelains mentioned are twelve gilt breakfast cups and saucers, of pattern 64. A Sampson Bagnall is listed in the Shelton Land Tax returns of the 1780's.[12] He may have preceded John Daniel as works manager or clerk. There were, however, at least two Sampson Bagnalls at or near New Hall. Sampson Bagnall 'the younger' was working in partnership with Thomas Fletcher. They separated in April 1796 after which 'the business at the manufactory near Booden Brook' was continued 'by the said Sampson Bagnall, the younger'. His former partner had been a leading engraver or printer of earthenwares. Sampson Bagnall was soon concerned with a further dissolution of partnership; that between Joseph Boon and himself, which ended in November 1796. Sampson Bagnall 'of Shelton' and Thomas Fletcher were with James Ross (the Worcester engraver) executors to the January 1801 will of William Smith, engraver, of Hanley.

The indistinct or incomplete signature in the New Hall company's receipt or invoice is therefore puzzling. Could the manufactory near Booden Brook have been part of the New Hall estate and could Sampson Bagnall or William Smith have been responsible for the superb printing found on New Hall porcelain?

JOHN TITTENSOR

Although I am not sure if John Tittensor joined the company as a shareholder and partner in the early 1820s, this could well be the case. It is known that he acted as the factory manager after John Daniel's death in 1821 and

Daniel was most certainly a leading partner. John Tittensor may well have purchased shares in the company and so held a financial interest in the success of the firm he was to overlook.

Little is known of John Tittensor. A potter of this name was in a short partnership with Charles Tittensor at Hanley, in succession to Messrs. Pipe & Tittensor as from 1 July 1803 to about 1807. Charles and then John Tittensor were later employed as travellers-cum-salesmen for the New Hall Company. Charles died on the road in 1815 and was succeeded as the firm's traveller by John; in this way he would have gained experience before he succeeded John Daniel as works manager in 1821. Subsequently his name appears in several sale notices relating to the New Hall premises. One of 1831 shows that John Tittensor was occupying the 'dwelling house adjoining' the manufactory. He seems also to have been concerned with the Cobridge firms of Blackwell and Dillons and with Francis & Nicholas Dillon. These partnerships were dissolved on 28 February 1828 and in November 1832 when John Tittensor was one of the signatories. The notice also requested that all outstanding accounts be delivered to 'Mr Tittensor at the New Hall Works, Shelton...'

HUGH HENSHALL WILLIAMSON

There is a case for considering Hugh H. Williamson (c.1785-1867) as being a partner in the New Hall company at least in its later years, perhaps in succession to William Clowes (his father-in-law) who had died in December 1822.

In the nineteenth century there must have been several changes in the partners or shareholders as the more elderly partners retired or died. Such events resulted in their holding of shares in the New Hall company being willed to others or being put on the market as estates were wound up. These later shareholders, such as Hugh Williamson, would not necessarily have been concerned with the day-to-day running of the factory.

My inclusion of Williamson's name in this section arises from the published details of the bankruptcy proceedings against the Edinburgh 'Chinaman' Elijah Cotton in 1827. Details of this together with a list of creditors is given in Jill Turnbull's paper 'Staffordshire Potters and Scottish Merchants' published in the *Journal of the Northern Ceramic Society,* Vol. 19 (1992). It would appear that Messrs. Hollins, Warburton, Daniel &.Co.'s claim of £158.4s.9d. was presented and presumably vouched for by Hugh H. Williamson, described as a partner in the New Hall Company.

Apart from this 1827 reference to Hugh Williamson as a partner, we have some other references that tend to lend weight to this description. He was related by marriage to William Clowes (a longstanding partner) having married his daughter Anne in March 1814. He was later one of the two trustees for William Clowes' estate. Hugh Williamson's name also appears on documents or notices concerning the New Hall estate, including the sale notice of October 1825, quoted at length by David Holgate. In that document he is described as H.H. Williamson Esq, Greenway Bank. David Holgate has also noted that in 1843 Hugh Williamson acted on behalf of the families of the original partners negotiating the sale of the factory and the remaining parts of the New Hall estate. Hugh Henshall Williamson and his wife Anne are also mentioned in Ann Booth's will in relation to the surrender of a share in the former New Hall estate, agreed in August 1837. On the evidence of the 1827 Elijah Cotton bankruptcy documents he was also one of the partners in the concern – perhaps only by marriage to Anne Clowes or by direct inheritance of William Clowes' shares.

Hugh Henshall Williamson was the son of Robert Williamson of Longport and of Anne Brindley (née Henshall). He was to have many interests apart from pottery. By 1828 he was operating the Scotia and Pinnox Collieries and later the Goldendale Ironworks. In 1834 he was appointed High Sheriff of Staffordshire. Robert Williamson had been engaged in the Henshall, Williamson & Clowes pottery partnership at Longport. Hugh Henshall bequeathed this home – Greenway Bank, a mansion – to the young Williamsons. Hugh Henshall Williamson, with his wife and brother, Robert, were partners in the Longton firm of Henshall & Williamson (c.1800-31), pottery manufacturers at Longport and retailers in Dublin. Robert initially retired in May 1826 at which period Hugh Henshall had died or retired. Anne and Hugh Williamson continued as joint partners for a short time until his mother Anne died. Hugh retired at the end of 1830 after which his brother Robert continued the firm. The pottery was later sold to Messrs. Davenport.

Hugh Henshall Williamson was obviously a wealthy man having coal mining and also canal and barge carrying interests as well as being a partner in the quite important earthenware firm of Henshall and Williamson. Their pottery worked six ovens. By 1827, and probably from the death of William Clowes in December 1822, he may well have been a partner in the New Hall company, either in his own right or acting for his wife, Anne, the daughter of William Clowes.[13] Hugh Williamson died on 3 December 1867, perhaps the last of the partners in the New Hall concern.

JAMES NEALE (c.1739-1814)

It has also been suggested, notably by David Holgate, that James Neale may have been one of the early partners. This is quite possible for he was a reasonably wealthy London 'chinaman', the former partner of Humphrey Palmer and later of Robert Wilson, potting as Neale & Co. in the approximate period c.1778-92. Both were clearly well known to Josiah Wedgwood and it is reasonable to assume that they would be on the list of potters given by Wedgwood to Champion when he was seeking to sell the patent rights. Also it is significant that Neale owned or acted as trustee in the Shelton Hall or New Hall estate.

We must, however, also bear in mind that James Neale's name does not appear in any of the known New Hall porcelain company's agreements, nor was he mentioned by any of the early writers in connection with the New Hall Company. His connection with the New Hall estate, however, lasted until April 1810, when Esther Palmer, Elizabeth Palmer and James Neale surrendered the New Hall to the New Hall partnership, then listed as comprising Peter Warburton, Samuel Hollins, John Daniel and William Clowes. The Derby factory archives and accounts also show that Neale traded with that company and even in 1787 requested that simple square candelabra porcelain bases were made for him at Derby rather than at the New Hall works. If James Neale was a partner in the New Hall concern I suggest it was for a very short period, not later than say 1786, but I feel that he was never involved, for such a partnership would have conflicted with his large and established interest in Wilson's Church Works at Hanley.

On the face of it the New Hall Company was extremely well placed to succeed. The company owned the patent rights to manufacture 'real china' or a translucent mix using china stone and china clay from Cornwall. It had existing rights in procuring such raw materials. It reputedly enjoyed a good trade in supplying other potters with the special glaze or 'composition' made under the patent rights.

Its partners were seemingly a well-balanced mix; at least three early partners were practising potters. I like the term 'master potters' for such folk as Samuel Hollins and Jacob Warburton, if not for John Daniel.

At least two, Thomas Heath and Charles Bagnall, had colliery interests and were therefore in a position to supply the company with the vital fuel at, I assume, a favourable rate. Always remember that it takes approximately eight to ten tons of coal to fire one ton of earthenware or china, perhaps even more for the high-fired New Hall porcelain. Therefore, the cost of coal was more important than the cost of clays.

Thomas Heath and Charles Bagnall with their colliery interests were also probably able to supply finance, as were the potters; at least they would have been in a position to purchase their shares in the concern, although the main funds for the setting up of the new porcelain producing enterprise and its day-to-day running would have been supplied by John Hollins, the mercer or banker from Newcastle who had no ceramic knowledge, and by William Clowes, the one-time London retailer and Staffordshire potter who by tradition is also regarded as one of the company's backers. Joshua Heath is regarded as another potter who supplied the partnership with capital. I am not sure if the fact that James Neale, the important London china, earthenware and glass dealer, was the effective land-lord of the New Hall estate prior to about 1801 would have benefited the sales of the company's china in the capital. Probably not, or to only a small extent, as Neale and his partner Wilson did at least for a period in the 1790s produce their own very good quality porcelains, examples of which are shown in *Staffordshire Porcelain* (Plates 61-82). However, it is clear that the Neale establishment in London also stocked various types of pottery and porcelain.

One should note that some of the persons which I, and others, have confidently listed as one-time partners in the New Hall venture were not known as practising potters. Yet Wedgwood in his 1780 letter wrote of 'the most substantial and enterprising potters amongst us' (page 89).

Richard Champion also wrote in various letters of 'potters', not other backers. Perhaps other names merely paid the required 'fee' to make their own porcelain in their own works, without being a named partner in the new enterprise. Seemingly the New Hall partnership, even before the patent ran out in 1796, did not claim to produce a unique type of porcelain although they used the term 'Real China'.

Our views on the merits of New Hall porcelain have certainly changed over the last hundred years. John Sparkes of the Royal College of Art at South Kensington writing in the 1890s remarked:

> Champion's recipes and patent were disposed of in 1781 to a Staffordshire company working at New Hall and hard paste porcelain was thus introduced into Staffordshire. But the few pieces of their work that are known are quite devoid of taste and it is evident that none of Champion's skilled men could have followed their master's patent...[14]

John Sparkes may have been following the earlier views of William Chaffers, the influential author of *Marks & Monograms* (the then standard book on ceramic marks) and the author of *The Keramic Gallery.* In this last work the New Hall products are quickly dismissed:

> The New Hall China Works ... The ware made here was not of a fine character; inferior artists were employed in its production, and it was never held in any great esteem. The manufacture consequently soon fell to decay, after many changes...

In fact it lasted from c.1781-2 to c.1835, that is for over fifty years!

W.B. Honey, a former Keeper of Ceramics at the Victoria & Albert Museum, was not much kinder when writing in his standard guide *Old English Porcelain. A Handbook for Collectors,* first published in 1928 with a revised and expanded third edition published in 1977 by Faber & Faber. This authority, however, took a contrary view concerning a visual link with the earlier Bristol porcelains:

> The hard-paste of New Hall is sometimes not easily distinguishable from the Bristol 'cottage china' ... The slight patterns are often very charming, though the material itself is seldom free from imperfections and was often cold or grey in tone ... Sprigs and festoons were much in favour as before at Bristol; black, red and pink enamels predominate...

As most readers will know, the New Hall management did indeed produce in large quantities a range of such simple floral designs in the general style of the Chinese export market porcelains (see Chapter VIII). They were popular because such teawares (painted by cheap labour and without gilding) were very inexpensive. Similar simple designs were produced by most English porcelain manufacturers of the 1785-1815 period. However, popular as were these inexpensive wares, they do not by any means represent the whole range of New Hall patterns.

Unfortunately these simple designs were taken by early writers to represent the whole of the factory's output and to compound the problem similar patterns produced by other contemporary makers tended to be classed incorrectly as New Hall. It was a generally believed rule that the New Hall porcelain was never gilt. This is nonsense.

When I started collecting some very finely decorated New Hall porcelain was not recognised as such. It is therefore not all that surprising to find that in 1946 George Eyre Stringer, who was building up the then New Hall company's works collection (an assembly later divided and sold to the Hanley Museum – now 'The Potteries Museum' – the Hove Museum and to an American store, Marshall Fields of Chicago), he did not recognise as New Hall a clearly marked 'Warburton's Patent' gold printed tea service of pattern 888. Major Stringer quoted in his 1949 book the letter of rejection he wrote to the dealer seeking to sell the complete New Hall service for under £100:

> I suggest your set was made by one of the well-known porcelain makers of the early nineteenth century using Peter Warburton's patented process under License ... it seems to me that Derby, Davenport, Coalport or Chamberlain-Worcester, would have to be considered as possible makers.

That author was not alone in failing to appreciate that this mark only occurs on New Hall porcelain. Today we regard such gold printed New Hall 'real china' teawares as being one of the most typical, key types!

In regard to the gilt designs we are now quite aware of the fact that good quality gilding was produced from the earliest days; indeed that some quite early patterns comprise solely gilt enrichments – see for example Plates 89, 93-4, 96, 100-1 and 125. As we shall see in the next chapter, New Hall porcelain can be superb and very finely decorated. A new light is being shone on these Staffordshire porcelains; we are discovering articles and styles unknown to earlier writers who formed their opinions without knowing the full story – not that we shall ever be able to view all the objects made at this important Staffordshire factory from the 1780s onwards, nor of course know the complete story!

To help us see some of its delights I will introduce you to the work of its leading artist, Fidelle Duvivier, who enjoyed an international reputation.

---

1. Three residences shared the name Shelton Hall.

2. I have some doubts about the later part of Shaw's statement, but the date of the building or of Mr. Whitehead's connection with it does not affect the post-1780 story of the porcelains.

3. Manorial Rolls for 7 July 1779, see David Holgate's paper 'New Hall, Some Interesting Nuances' published in the *Transactions of the English Ceramic Circle,* Vol. 14, Part 9 (1991).

4. In fact several contemporary references give Hanley rather than Shelton as the place name but before 1812 they were two distinct townships.

5. Although a 'potworks' is mentioned no working materials are insured.

6. This wording suggests that the porcelain works were not actually at or part of the 'New Hall'. In the same way, at an earlier period the Longton Hall works were outside the Hall, not in the main building.

7. Newcastle under Lyme Manor Court Rolls (P.R.O. Ref. DL30/507/26), a document kindly brought to my attention by Mr. Harold Blakey.

8. Daintry was the maiden name of his wife Nancy, on whom Samuel settled his late brother's Shelton pottery in 1780.

9. Some authorities give Jacob's year of birth as 1740.

10. The reference to Sampson Daniel and his £200 legacy has been crossed through, an apparently contemporary but not initialled deletion, in the will deposited at Lichfield.

11. This being a legally drawn up will, no punctuation is included.

12. One Sampson Bagnall (b.1720) potted at Hartley from at least the 1780s. He died in 1803.

13. William Clowes' will reported upon by David Holgate in the Northern Ceramic Society *Journal* (Vol. 2, 1978-9) does not seem to mention Clowes' shares or interest in the New Hall partnership. He may have parted with them before his death, if indeed the company issued shares.

14. *Potters: Their Arts and Crafts* by John Sparkes and Walter Gandy (S.W. Partridge & Co., London, n.d., c.1890).

Detail of Fidelle Duvivier's landscape painting, note the kilns, from a dessert service as shown in Plate 201.

CHAPTER V

Fidelle Duvivier and other Decorators

Having in the previous chapter listed the known New Hall partners, most of whom would have been only financial backers or shareholders in the company, not exercising day-to-day control over the manufactory or influencing greatly its products, it seems right to mention the artists who obviously influenced the finished porcelains.

This would have been relatively simple if I was writing of other large factories – Derby, for example, or Chamberlains of Worcester – factories with surviving records. Yet when we come to consider the New Hall decorators we have almost a complete blank. Really we only know one name that we could call a ceramic artist of note, but a study of his life and work serves to underline several points. These include the international aspect and migratory nature of some ceramic artists and in this case how even signed examples have been misattributed, mainly because of the old idea of New Hall producing only mundane porcelain patterns clouding our judgement of the better class, more expensive, designs.

The artist about whom we have the most information, is Fidelle Duvivier, who was born at Doornik (Tournai) on 6 August 1740. This Continental artist has been referred to by recent researchers as 'the prototype of the cosmopolitan, highly mobile painter' and one of the 'international porcelain circuit'. Let us first consider the evidence for this artist's work at the New Hall factory, a middle-market English concern hardly internationally renowned in the latter part of the eighteenth century. Fidelle Duvivier's employment at New Hall after a successful career at Chelsea, Derby and at various Continental porcelain factories makes the point that in the mid-1780s the New Hall partners intended to produce at least some high class expensive wares, perhaps to rival Derby. Such goods were probably mainly aimed at the London market.

We owe much of our knowledge of Duvivier's progress in this country to Llewellynn Jewitt who seemingly, in or before the 1860s, had access to various documents and was even able to locate, identify and sometimes buy examples of Duvivier's work from the original owner's relations and so associate a style of painting to a known painter before later collectors had discovered or recorded signed examples of Fidelle Duvivier's painting on English porcelains.

Fidelle Duvivier, it must be stated, was but one of several ceramic artists with this surname, one of whom, his cousin Henri-Joseph (1740-1771), was employed at the Chelsea factory before 1763. Fidelle, however, seems to have worked at Jean Peterinck's important Belgian factory at Tournai in the early 1760s (with his cousin) when he was in his early twenties. Mlle. M. Jottrand in her paper 'Tournai Porcelain and English Ceramics' *(Transactions of the English Ceramic Circle,* Vol. 10, Part 2, 1977), quoted an account dated 26 September 1764 from Peterinck at the Tournai factory for porcelains supplied to a Brussels china dealer. The three cabaret services quoted are described as by 'Duvivier', by 'Duvivier L'anglois' (perhaps Henri-Joseph) and lastly by 'Fidel Duvivier'. These are all richly decorated sets (cabaret services are normally superbly painted products). The rich decoration and the mention of Duvivier's name does not point to an apprentice, although it has been stated that Fidelle Duvivier was apprenticed under Jean Peterinck at Tournai.

Sadly any once available Tournai archives were destroyed early in the last war. We do not therefore know when Fidelle first worked at Tournai or how long he stayed with Peterinck. I do not believe that he stayed there for long after 1764. There is also the point that the cabaret tea service sold in September 1764 may have been decorated well before that date. It was not necessarily a new production.

I believe, no more at this point, that Fidelle Duvivier worked at the Chelsea factory up to the period of its sale to William Duesbury in 1769. We are certainly on firm ground in stating that he engaged to work for Duesbury at Derby on 31 October 1769.

The now tattered incomplete document (see page 181) quoted, in part, by Jewitt shows that by this period Fidelle Duvivier 'of the Borough of Derby' was earning the very reasonable adult wage of 24s. a week, plus £5 at the end of the four year term 'in case he shall merit the same'. We do not know if Fidelle completed the agreed four year term bringing us up to October 1773, but he certainly seems to have left Duesbury's employment on good terms for importantly he wrote to William Duesbury's son in 1790, seeking work. Fidelle's family were certainly still at Derby in March 1771, when young Peter Joseph Duvivier was baptised as the son of Fidelle and Elizabeth Duvivier. Still it would seem that the agreed four year agreement was for an unusually long period, perhaps showing how anxious Duesbury was to engage and hold Duvivier.

With this or any other agreement it should be remembered that it could be terminated at any period by mutual agreement. Although there was in this case a high penalty of £50 if the contract was broken, this could of course be waived (or simply paid) if good enough reason arose. Duvivier may even have asked to be allowed to paint non-Derby porcelains within the period of the agreement with Duesbury for it was part of the signed agreement that 'William Duesbury – shall and will only pay the said Fidelle Duvivier in proportion and after the rate aforesaid for such part and so much of every week as he shall actually paint for the said William Duesbury'. He could seemingly paint for half the agreed working week, for half pay!

We then lose sight of Fidelle Duvivier's movements, but in the early 1780s he was working in Holland at the Loosdrecht (Oude Loosdrecht) factory. The Dutch authorities have unearthed interesting new material relating to Duvivier.[1] He was seemingly a Roman Catholic, not a Huguenot as was once believed. He was also a member of the Mason's Brotherhood and as such I assume he was considered a person of some standing. Fidelle's signature often includes three dots '∴' which is stated to be a Masonic sign or identification device.

Whilst records relating to the Loosdrecht workpeople do not now exist, the baptism of a daughter (Maria Susanna Frederica) took place at the local Slootdijk[2] church on 24 October 1783. The parents were our Fidelle (or Fidelis) Duvivier and his wife Elisabeth (née Thomas). The factory manager, Daeuber, acted as godfather.

The mention in these Dutch records of Elizabeth Duvivier's maiden name, Thomas, is of interest. It is possible that she was the daughter of Francis and Elizabeth Thomas. Francis Thomas (d.1770) was the manager of the Chelsea porcelain factory under Sprimont and was engaged to run the works after it was purchased by James Cox in 1769. Thomas also dealt in Chelsea porcelains. Both Fidelle and his cousin Henri-Joseph Duvivier worked at Chelsea. Perhaps it is not too late to discover details of Fidelle's marriage to Elizabeth Thomas at Chelsea in the 1760s.

Fidelle would have been of marriageable age at this period, twenty-five in 1765. In 1769, when the Chelsea factory was sold, first to James Cox and then sold on to William Duesbury of the Derby factory, Duvivier was twenty-nine. It seems that Fidelle Duvivier could have been taken over by Duesbury when he acquired the Chelsea factory. He then entered into a new agreement dated 31 October 1769 when he had moved to Derby. We do not know how long Fidelle remained in Holland, working at the Loosdrecht factory[3] after the birth of his daughter in 1783, or if he worked at other Continental factories before returning to England and Staffordshire. By this period he had established an international reputation as a ceramic artist and his work might appear on several makes of eighteenth century porcelain.

We are again on firm ground in stating that Duvivier was working for the New Hall partnership in, and probably before, 1790. We have his much quoted, now highly important self-explanatory letter establishing the fact that he worked at the New Hall factory for an unknown period up to about November 1790. This was quoted by Jewitt over a hundred years ago, as reading:

> Hanley green, the 1 novebr. 1790
> Mr Dousbery, sir, [I?] take the liberty Adressing you with a few lines, as mine Engagement in the New Hal Porcelaine manufactory is Expired, and the proprietors do not intend to do much in the fine line of Painting, therefor think of Settling in new Castle under lime Being engag'd to teach Drowing in the Boarding School at that place, one School I have at Stone, so as to have only three days Spare in the week for Painting which time Could wish to be emply'd by you preferable to eany other fabrique, because you like and understand good work, as am inform'd my painting now to watt I did for your father is quit different but without flatering my Self Hope to give you Satisfaction, in Case you Schould Like to imply me Sir your anser will much oblige your
> Humble Servant.
>
> Duvivier.
>
> P S the Conveyance would be much in fevoir for to Send the ware to and from ther is a waggon Every Week from darby to new Castle.'

We do not know when his expired engagement at the New Hall works was entered into but if, like the earlier Derby agreement, it was originally for a four year period, he joined the New Hall Company in Staffordshire in or about November 1786. This dating 1786-90 seems to agree neatly with my dating of the New Hall forms which were decorated by this artist.

He may, however, have joined New Hall in 1787 rather than in 1786 for there is the non-New Hall Duvivier signed beaker which has traditionally been attributed to the Turner factory. This is dated 'Lane End, June 1787.'[4] There is also the problematic stained and crazed bowl in the British Museum which is inscribed 'Lane End, July 1787.' I say problematic because we are not sure if it is of Turner's or of New Hall manufacture. David Holgate considered it to be New Hall and I tend to agree. It certainly, in its style of monochrome figures in landscape, accords with Duvivier's painting on New Hall teawares.

Returning to the 1790 letter, it seems most unlikely that William Duesbury II would have been interested in sending Derby blanks to Staffordshire for Duvivier to decorate and return, as suggested in Fidelle's letter. No mention is made of the firing of the painted pieces. Duvivier's painting would almost certainly have required several firings in at least a muffle kiln. Intricate overglaze decoration could hardly have been packed and transported to Derby without being fixed by firing. The letter stated that he was engaged to teach drawing in a boarding school and that he was or had been similarly engaged at Stone. His ceramic painting on New Hall porcelain perhaps never represented full-time employment. Certainly his work is today extremely rare and must always have been restricted to the more costly tea or much rarer dessert services and to other expensive objects such as the known mugs and jugs – Plates 55-61.

As to the New Hall pieces which bear Fidelle Duvivier's name, these are extremely few in number and they may even represent freelance work carried out on New Hall blanks for his own commercial profit, although he was, I assume, still in Staffordshire when all the New Hall porcelains were decorated. However, some of the signed pieces may slightly post-date the November 1790 letter to Duesbury which at least proves that Duvivier was still seeking to decorate some porcelains in his own time. He may well have carried out a few special commissions for the New Hall company or for private individuals provided he was still able to have his work fired. My theory that the signed pieces were non-factory decorated products is simply based on the point that at this period (prior to 1790) factory employed artists were seemingly not permitted to add their own signatures. Yet two of the known Duvivier examples are signed twice over. Perhaps he was merely vain!

The known signed examples of Fidelle Duvivier's painting on New Hall porcelain comprise the following pieces:

A) A figure subject mug, now in the Victoria & Albert Museum,[5] Plates 55-8, with double signature (C.128.1977, purchased from Messrs. Klaber & Klaber).

B) The figure and inn subject mug,[6] formerly in Dr. Margaret Vivian's collection, Plates 59-61, also with double signature. (Godden collection, ex S. Spero, ex Sotheby's New York.)

PLATE 55. *The left side of the New Hall mug shown also in Plates 56 and 57. Signed, lower left, 'Duvivier pinx' – see Plate 58. 3⅝in. (9.14cm) high. c.1785-90.* VICTORIA AND ALBERT MUSEUM. CROWN COPYRIGHT

PLATE 56. *The central position of the twice signed New Hall mug, painted in overglaze enamels in a typical manner. Gilt line borders 3⅝in. (9.14cm) high. c.1785-90.* VICTORIA AND ALBERT MUSEUM. CROWN COPYRIGHT

PLATE 57. *The right side of the New Hall mug shown also in Plates 55 and 56. Note the strong foreground and faint distance, also the outlined leaves to the right of the central figure. Signed 'Duvivier'. 3⅝in. (9.14cm) high. c.1785-90.* VICTORIA AND ALBERT MUSEUM. CROWN COPYRIGHT

PLATE 58. *Detail from Plate 55 showing the faint signature 'Duvivier pinx' to the left of the dog. Note the different techniques employed in painting the trees – stipple effect for the higher tree and a wash painted over for the lower bush above the dog.*

Plate 59. *A superb New Hall mug painted with a 'Good Woman' inn scene, taken from Hogarth's print 'Noon'. Signed by Duvivier, at both sides – see Plates 60 and 61. 5⅝in. (14.29cm). c.1785-90. See Colour Plates 9-11.* Sotheby's, New York

Plate 60. *The left side of the Duvivier signed New Hall mug, painted with a Hogarth inn scene – the 'Good (headless) Woman'. See also Plates 59 and 61. 5⅝in. (14.29cm). c.1785-90.* Godden collection

C) A typical New Hall clip-handled coffee cup painted with animal fable subject in landscape. This cup is signed under the base 'F. Duvivier, fecit'. It is at the Luton Museum. It was with related pieces illustrated by Major W.H. Tapp (as Worcester) in *Apollo* magazine of March 1941 and correctly attributed by David Holgate in his book *New Hall* (Faber & Faber, London, 1987), Plate 110 and various papers.

To this all too short list of New Hall signed examples we can add the beautifully painted, twice signed and dated 1772, Worcester porcelain teapot in the Marshall Collection at the Ashmolean, Oxford and the mysterious (non-New Hall) and now much damaged so-called Gerverot beaker of 1787. These five rare signed examples enable us to form a good idea of Duvivier's style of painting within the approximate period 1775-90. Fidelle Duvivier can be considered to be one of the earliest ceramic artists to have signed his work on English porcelain.

There is also to consider the monochrome painted bowl in the British Museum. This piece bears a typical Duvivier

Plate 61. *The right side of the New Hall mug shown in Plates 59 and 60. The signature, clear of the painting, reads 'F Duvivier pinx.' 5⅝in. (14.29cm). c.1785-90.* Godden collection

Plate 62. *The New Hall jug decorated by Duvivier and made for Sampson Daniel, the factory's book-keeper. It was still in the Daniel family and attributed to Duvivier, when L. Jewitt engraved and wrote of the New Hall products in 1864. 5¾in.(14.61cm). c.1790 or later.* The Potteries Museum, Hanley

style composition of figures in landscape. Contrary to some beliefs this is not signed but it does bear the inscription 'Lane End July 1787' in the manner of the non-New Hall Gerverot beaker which is signed by Duvivier. Indeed it has been stated that the similar calligraphy leaves 'no doubt' that both inscriptions were painted by the same hand. This badly crazed and stained bowl can be considered as an unsigned but key example of Fidelle Duvivier's work. Both the signed beaker and the bowl are illustrated and discussed by Bevis Hillier in his 1965 book *Master Potters of the Industrial Revolution, the Turners of Lane End* (Cory Adams & Mackay, London).

I must also mention the initialled large jug which is featured as an engraving in Llewellynn Jewitt's 1864 pioneer *Art Journal* article and in his later book *The Ceramic Art of Great Britain* first published in 1878. This piece is now in The Potteries Museum at Hanley. Of this piece Jewitt wrote: '...a jug carefully painted with birds and bearing in front the initials "S.D.". This jug was made at New Hall for Sampson Daniel, a cousin of John Daniel, one of the partners, and still in the possession of his grandson Mr Daniel of Hanley'. This very well painted jug showing kilns in the background is generally considered to have been painted by Fidelle Duvivier.

Plate 63. *The right-hand side of the New Hall jug shown in Plate 62, showing typical Duvivier kilns faintly depicted in the background. Note also the dropping branches in the foreground. 5¾in. (14.61cm). c.1790 or later.* THE POTTERIES MUSEUM, HANLEY

Indeed I have even heard it referred to as being a personal present to himself, the initials being incorrectly quoted as 'F.D.'.

This New Hall jug remained in the Daniel family until it was purchased by Geoffrey Bemrose, the then Keeper of the Stoke-on-Trent City Museum, in the late 1930s. It was illustrated as Fidelle Duvivier's painting by Major Tapp in the *Apollo* magazine of March 1941, although Major Tapp and apparently W.B. Honey of the Victoria & Albert Museum did not believe that it was of New Hall porcelain.

This jug, which is illustrated in Plates 62-3, is now accepted as a standard New Hall jug form. They were seemingly much favoured as presentation pieces, for so many bear initials under the spout. Plates 220-6 show other New Hall jugs of this shape but, as with other basic forms, they were made in various sizes or other capacities. If we accept that the 'S.D.' example mentioned by Jewitt in 1864 was painted by Fidelle Duvivier, then this jug shape may have been in production from 1790 into the early 1800s. This is not an unreasonable suggestion as it is a very good, attractive shape, well fitted for its basic purpose and giving a good area for various decorative motifs. We must also consider the possibility that Duvivier

The c.1863-4 Art Journal *engraving of Llewellynn Jewitt's New Hall teapot which he recorded had been painted by Duvivier for Charles Bagnall, one of the partners in the New Hall concern. See also Plate 64.*

THE ART JOURNAL, JANUARY 1864

decorated at least some New Hall porcelain after November 1790, when he wrote to William Duesbury to state that his employment was coming to an end.

Returning to Sampson Daniel, for whom this jug was made, John Daniel's sister Alice in her will mentioned her cousin Sampson Daniel as being the New Hall company's bookkeeper or warehouseman. This jug is not the only well painted example painted for the Daniel family.

In addition to the signed examples we must consider two further pieces mentioned by Llewellynn Jewitt in the 1860s and 1870s when this authority published engravings of two unsigned pieces which he then knew to represent Duvivier's work for the New Hall management. These two examples happen to typify Duvivier's so popular painting on New Hall porcelains.

Of the early (c.1786-8) New Hall teapot which I show in its engraved original *Art Journal*[7] form, Jewitt wrote in the *Art Journal* of January 1864:

> The first engraving exhibits a remarkably fine beautifully painted teapot in my own collection, which is worthy of very careful attention. One side (shown in the woodcut) is an exquisitely painted group of children playing at blind mans buff[8] ... In the background is a view of a pot work, with a kiln... On the opposite side of this teapot is an equally well painted group of a boy riding on a dog, and on the lid are also two little figure vignettes.
>
> This piece which it is fair to presume was the best the works could produce, was made for and belonged to one of the partners, Charles Bagnall, from whose family it passed more than half a century ago, by marriage to a Mr Sutton, from whose own octogenarian hands it has passed into my own. The tea-pot was painted by Duvivier, a French [*sic*] artist of celebrity who ... was employed at these works.

This teapot appeared again engraved in Jewitt's *The Ceramic Art of Great Britain,* which was first published by Virtue & Co. Ltd. in 1878, and the pot was later sold as part of Jewitt's varied personal collection. Its present whereabouts is, alas, unknown to me although it has surfaced once or twice since it was sold with part of Jewitt's collection. Through the kindness of David Holgate I have been able in Plate 64 to show one side of this splendid and early Duvivier-decorated teapot (compare the rare early form with Plates 21 and 101) as it appeared in Sotheby & Co.'s advertisement in *The Connoisseur* of February 1925 where it was described as Bristol. It may still be resting in a collection as Bristol rather than New Hall.

Plate 64A illustrates a coffee cup (one of several Duvivier decorated examples in the Luton Museum collection) which may well link with Jewitt's teapot. The

Plate 64. *The New Hall teapot painted by Fidelle Duvivier and mentioned by Jewitt in 1864 as being made for Charles Bagnall, one of the New Hall partners. Passing from Bagnall to a Mr. Sutton from whom Jewitt purchased this 'remarkably fine beautifully painted teapot'. Assumed height (see Plate 101) 6¼in. (15.88cm). c.1785.* Present ownership unknown to the author

simple border design appears to match. See David Holgate's Plate 112 for three others from his set.

Jewitt also illustrated well over a hundred years ago[9] a single dish from a dessert service painted with a typical Duvivier landscape design featuring a windmill on the left (see Plate 65). Of this Jewitt wrote in, or rather before, 1864:

> ...In the centre of the [engraved] group I have given one piece of a dessert service belonging to Mr Gray, which was made for Mr Daniel, one of the partners, and purchased at the sale of his effects, now many years ago, by its present owner. The form, it will be seen, is remarkably good, and the ornamentation striking. Each piece bears a landscape, beautifully and softly painted by Duvivier. These examples will be sufficient to guide collectors in correctly appropriating the productions of these interesting works.

Originally I wrote:

> How one would like to know what other goodies were sold from John Daniel's effects for he was for so long the Manager at the New Hall factory but here we have an old engraving of one dish from a Duvivier-decorated dessert service, with a memorable pedigree and an association with New Hall's most talented Continental decorator, traced back into the middle of the nineteenth century.'

Plate 64A. *Some New Hall coffee cups (with grooved handles) in the Luton Museum match the Jewitt teapot (Plate 64) in border and in the general style of child subject. These may have been part of the same set, or from another similar service. I show one of these cups. See also* Apollo *magazine, March 1941. 2¾in. (6.99cm) high. c.1785.*

Luton Museum

Centre, the dessert dish shown by Jewitt in 1864, as being made for John Daniel (the New Hall factory manager) 'beautifully and softly painted by Duvivier' – see Plate 65. Various pieces from this service are here illustrated, see Plates 65-7 and 195-201. The Jewitt engraved jug (left) is shown in Plate 62.

THE *ART JOURNAL*, JANUARY 1864

This really splendid scenic-painted dessert service has recently re-appeared and representative pieces can now be shown – see Plates 65-7, 195-201 and 207. I have also included a few detail illustrations showing the centre paintings from various pieces included in this service. They show well Fidelle Duvivier's style and technique. It is hard to overstate the importance of this part dessert service for most of these New Hall dessert shapes have not previously been recorded. The service made for John Daniel, the factory manager, shows what high standards the factory rose to achieve in its first ten years, that is before Fidelle Duvivier stated in a letter dated 1 November 1790 that he was leaving and that the management did 'not intend to do much in the fine line of painting' – see page 161. This wording suggests that they had previously carried out at least some high class and therefore relatively expensive decoration as is truly witnessed by this dessert service.

I propose to take Llewellynn Jewitt's statements as factual, for I believe that he spoke with the then owner, a Mr. Gray who had purchased the set at the sale of John Daniel's effects. Certainly there can be no dispute that the landscapes were painted by Duvivier – these shout his name! Seemingly, Jewitt, whilst in the Potteries in 1863, selected this one (now damaged) dish and drew it so that it could be engraved by a specialist engraver employed by the *Art Journal* management to illustrate Jewitt's article published in the issue of January 1864. While the engraving is clearly taken from the dish shown in Plate 65, there are minor differences which arose from the engraving being taken from Jewitt's own drawing, not from the dish. There are in fact errors in the representations of all three pieces engraved in Jewitt's article (page 164), the Sampson Daniel jug (Plate 62) – now in The Potteries Museum at Hanley – and in the proportion of the engraved cup and saucer.

John Daniel died intestate in January 1821. He was unmarried and had lived with his spinster sister, Alice, and the service therefore formed part of their joint residence or home. All John Daniel's possessions legally passed to his

Plate 65. *The New Hall dessert dish painted by Fidelle Duvivier and believed to be the same example drawn and engraved for Jewitt's 1864* Art Journal *article. 10 x 9in. (25.4 x 22.86cm). c.1785-90.*

Godden collection

One of the typical Duvivier scenes as painted on the New Hall dessert service shown in Plates 65-7 and 195-201.

A Duvivier painted scene, perhaps depicting a riverside factory, from the New Hall dessert service shown in Plates 65-7 and 195-201.

A Duvivier painted racing scene from the dessert service shown in Plates 65-7 and 195-201. There was a racecourse at Newcastle-under-Lyme, near Hanley. See Plate 67 for the complete dish.

One of the typical Duvivier scenes as painted on the New Hall dessert service shown in Plates 65-7 and 195-201.

A typical Duvivier landscape scene, with kilns in the background, a figure on horseback and a dog.

A detail from the dessert centrepiece shown in Plate 66, perhaps showing John Daniel and his sister, with a typical Duvivier dog.

sister who in turn died on 9 June 1827. We do not now know if Alice sold any of the household effects after her brother's death but, as she continued to live in their joint home, a sale of the effects seems unlikely.

Under Alice Daniel's will drawn up on 29 November 1823, that is after she had inherited her brother's property and effects, she instructed her servant George Bradshaw to 'have sole care of all my goods and effects' 'and he shall be employed in looking after my real estate'.

The effects could be sold at auction or privately as and when the executors thought fit. After Alice's death in June 1827 her property at Shelton, Hanley and Endon was sold by auction, the Daniel residence not being sold until January 1830. Unfortunately, Rodney Hampson has been unable to trace any announcement of the sale of the contents of John and Alice Daniel's house, but any sale should have taken place in or before January 1830.

Llewellynn Jewitt, in his January 1864 *Art Journal* article, stated that Mr. Gray purchased this dessert service at the sale of Mr. Daniel's effects and it would appear that the then owner was knowledgeable about its history – that it was New Hall porcelain, that it had been painted by Duvivier for John Daniel.

It would seem that Mr. Gray, the buyer, was discriminating, had funds to purchase the secondhand service and liked it well enough to keep it for thirty or so years before drawing it to the attention of Llewellynn Jewitt as being worthy of being featured in an article in the *Art Journal* magazine. The factory had been closed for less than thirty years when Jewitt chose to single it out for such treatment.

PLATE 66. *The footed centrepiece from the Duvivier painted scenic dessert service made for John Daniel. Note the unusual and difficult to render rainbow effect. 11¾in. (29.85cm) long, 3¼in. (8.26cm) high. c.1785-90.* GODDEN COLLECTION

Jewitt did not give any forename or initial for his Mr. Gray but Rodney Hampson and I believe the proud owner would have been Thomas Cartlidge Gray of Hanley. I have been unable to trace very much about Thomas Gray. He was born at Hanley, in about 1800, and was working in a china producing partnership there in the 1830-36 period. He married Miss Bagnall[10] in March 1831 and the couple presumably jointly shared the pleasure of the New Hall porcelain dessert service painted by Duvivier and here pictured in Plates 65-7, 195-201 and 207. He is listed as a traveller in William White's 1851 *Directory of Staffordshire*. On account of his earlier calling as a china manufacturer he was later a traveller or salesman in pottery and porcelain and was still employed as a commercial traveller in 1867 when in his late sixties and sufficiently well known locally to have been introduced to Jewitt when that Derby-based writer visited the Potteries to research the history of the leading firms.

It is interesting to note that Thomas Gray survived a train crash in November 1855 and, as a result of assistance given to him and his fellow passengers by the landlord of the Kings Arms Hotel at Lancaster, Thomas Gray presented a well-decorated and suitably inscribed marked Samuel Alcock porcelain comport or centrepiece to Mrs. Pritt.[11] The fact that this presentation piece was clearly made at Alcock's Hill Pottery at Burslem suggests that Thomas Gray was then the traveller for this large and important firm.[12]

It can I believe be reasonably expected that such an experienced ceramic artist and a drawing master as Fidelle

PLATE 67. *A shaped edge New Hall dish from the Duvivier painted dessert service made for John Daniel. This unique racing scene may well be local, well known to Daniel and to Duvivier. 9¾ x 7¼in. (24.77 x 18.42cm). c.1785-90.* GODDEN COLLECTION

Duvivier would have accurately rendered contemporary views known to both himself and to the local potter cum factory manager for whom the service was being made. If the same exercise was being attempted today I am sure that at least some of the views or scenes would be factual and meaningful.

Alas, I as yet cannot prove the point for there seems a total lack of views of the Potteries as they were in the latter part of the eighteenth century. The different quite small townships were, however, in a very rural setting and many of the individual potteries were surrounded by fields or open country. Many of the potters owned large tracks of land which were cultivated, grew hay (for packing) or were grazing fields for cattle or the all important horses. The county was also well provided with streams and mill pools.

Perhaps this special dessert service, with its relatively large areas for painting, represents a unique multi-part view of rural Staffordshire as it was around 1790. Certainly the view of a horse-drawn barge crossing an aqueduct (Plate 207) gives the flavour of the period and of course canals and aqueducts were vital to the potters seeking to distribute their wares as cheaply as possible. The horse-racing scene (Plate 67) may well have been chosen to represent an interest of Fidelle Duvivier or of the recipient, John Daniel.There was at this period a racecourse at nearby Newcastle, one supported by the Potteries.

It would be out of place here to discuss further the individual scenes on this service which would when complete have included over thirty separate views. Some of these scenes which typify Duvivier's style so well are

PLATE 68. *A New Hall dessert plate of the same moulded shape as those in the John Daniel service (see Plate 201). This example was also painted by Fidelle Duvivier but was originally part of another splendid service. Diameter 8¼in. (20.96cm). c.1785-90.* FORMERLY GODDEN COLLECTION

shown in Plates 65-7, 196-201 and 207. Apart from the charm of the decoration, this service is of the greatest interest as it includes a very good range of dessert ware shapes, most of which have not previously been illustrated in books on New Hall porcelain.[13] The Duvivier-Daniel service shows New Hall in a new light.

Most established New Hall collectors can recognise Fidelle Duvivier's work without difficulty. Confining our attention to pre-1800 New Hall porcelain, the quality and style alone single out this artist's work. He was after all the only figure painter employed there in the eighteenth century. His large-headed figures, often of children, are quite characteristic, usually with black painted eyes and shoes. A smoking kiln or kilns are very often introduced into the composition. Duvivier was also fond of depicting windmills in the background or to one side to help the general decorative composition. A cropped tail to his horses and a familiar dog – perhaps his own – have also been noted as recurring features. The Duvvier breed of low-slung lean dogs, like his other animals, tends to sag amidships!

The background itself usually gently fades away into a misty distance and some cloud effects too are only seen if the piece is tilted to catch the light, so faintly painted or purposely fired out are they. The more detailed full colour Duvivier compositions were painted with great care and the work would have necessitated several firings to mature the different colours and to achieve the faded far distant effects.

The Duvivier scenes or other motifs tend to be rendered in the Continental style, without a formal frame. They are not fenced in as are so many scenes painted, for

Plate 69. *A small New Hall covered sugar bowl (probably from a matching complete tea service) painted by Duvivier with Sèvres-style child angels on clouds. Both sides are shown. 4⅛in. (10.48cm) high. c.1785-90.* Formerly Godden collection, photographs Peter Davis and Messrs. Phillips

example, by the Derby painters. Indeed, both David Holgate and I have noted several Continental aspects in Duvivier's painting on New Hall porcelain. One's style does not change as one travels.

Duvivier's open style of painting does call for a form of natural edging and a broken foreground to give a three-dimensional effect. A darkish tree was usually placed at the left, counterbalanced by buildings at the right. The rather colourful foreground normally included some red rock-like features, liberally surrounded by foliage, branches and twigs to attractively break up the foreground.

Few, if any, of these features are unique to Duvivier' s painting on New Hall porcelain, but in combination they are highly typical and are easily recognisable by those who are fortunate enough to have seen this artist's work.

The landscape tea services were sometimes painted in sepia. Whilst often rather naïvely painted, they have great charm and the hand of the master is very apparent. Superbly painted mugs (and probably jugs too) were also painted in monochrome. One such example now in the Victoria & Albert Museum is here shown in Plates 70-1.

Although the New Hall porcelain at this period is of the hybrid hard-paste type, the rather thick lead-based glaze seems to suit Duvivier's style or technique particularly well. His very rare work on Worcester, Caughley and Neale porcelain lacks the mellow depth of colour as seen on New Hall porcelains; the pigments do not fade away into the distance in such a realistic manner. New Hall and Duvivier seem to have suited each other very well. The carmine monochrome painted New Hall mug shown in Plate 70 was even attributed to Derby by a very competent judge – praise indeed. This example in the National Collection was presented to the Victoria & Albert Museum by Mrs. Winifred Williams, a generous dealer.

Rare as Duvivier's work at New Hall is, he painted in several styles. These have been summarised by David Holgate, as:

1) Full sized (!) figures of people, Plates 55-7, 68, 70-2, 76
2) Cupids, Plate 69
3) Revellers in front of an inn, Plate 59-61
4) Children, Plates 64, 70-2
5) Boat-scenes: i.e. Continental style river scenes, Plate 74
6) Birds on rocks (or in Continental style landscapes) Plates 75 and 81[14]
7) Outline figures in rural landscapes, Plates 78-80. (The attractive scenes with figures, as painted on John Daniel's dessert service, fall I assume into this category.)

This latter grouping of figures in rural landscapes is certainly the most often met with, perhaps because the description covers a very wide range of subjects. Most landscape designs include in the composition some figures, either in outline or painted in more detail. They

PLATE 70. *A New Hall mug painted in carmine monochrome with scene of children playing cards. See also Plate 71. 4½in. (11.43cm) high. c.1785-90.* VICTORIA AND ALBERT MUSEUM (C 151.1977). CROWN COPYRIGHT

PLATE 71. *The right-hand side of the splendid Duvivier painted monochrome mug, shown in Plate 70. 4½in. (11.43cm) high c.1785-90.* VICTORIA AND ALBERT MUSEUM (C 151.1977). CROWN COPYRIGHT

PLATE 72. *A New Hall cream or milk jug and cover painted by Fidelle Duvivier in a typical style, with kilns in the background. See also Plate 73. 5¼in. (13.34cm) high. c.1785-90.* GODDEN COLLECTION

PLATE 73. *The side view of the Duvivier painted monochrome tea service jug shown in Plate 72. Note the strong foreground, the stippled trees and the smoking kiln. 5¼in. (13.34cm) high. c.1785-90. See Colour Plate 15.* GODDEN COLLECTION

Plate 74. *A superbly painted New Hall coffee cup (note the clip handle form) and saucer. Painted by Fidelle Duvivier very much in the Continental manner. Cup 2½in. (6.35cm) high. c.1785-90. A similar cup is in the Victoria & Albert Museum.*

The Smithsonian Institution

Plate 75. *A rare and early New Hall bread and butter plate painted by Fidelle Duvivier showing his typical three-dimensional effect. Underglaze blue (and gilt) border. Painted 'No.7' on underside. A matching milk jug is recorded. Diameter 7¾in. (19.69cm). c.1785.*

Formerly Godden and Holgate collections

Plate 76. *A superbly decorated New Hall teapot painted by Fidelle Duvivier. The carriage and couple are very similar to those depicted on the dessert centrepiece shown in Plate 66. 6½in. (16.51cm) high. c.1785-90. See Colour Plate 16.*

Formerly Godden collection

Plate 77. *The reverse side of the New Hall, Duvivier decorated teapot shown in Plate 76. Again the good three-dimensional effect can be seen. The choice of subject underlines Duvivier's unconventional approach. 6½in. (16.51cm) high. c.1785-90. See Colour Plate 17.*

Formerly Godden collection

Plate 78. *A typical Duvivier painted New Hall teabowl and saucer painted in monochrome, with faceless figures. The faint background includes a windmill and smoking kilns. The matching jug is shown in Plate 80. Diameter of saucer 5in. (12.7cm). c.1785-90.*

Formerly Godden Collection

Plate 79. *A New Hall coffee cup (with clip handle form) and saucer, painted by Duvivier in monochrome. This example and the matching teabowl and saucer (Plate 78) are painted largely in a pronounced stipple effect. Cup 2¼in. (5.72cm) high. c.1785-90.*

Formerly Godden Collection

Plate 80. *The New Hall helmet-shaped (silver form) cream or milk jug matching the cup and saucers shown in Plates 78-9. The thumb-rest at the top of the handle is a rare feature for New Hall jugs. 5in. (12.7cm). high. c.1785-90.*

Godden collection

Plate 81. *Representative pieces from a superbly decorated New Hall tea service, painted by Fidelle Duvivier in the Continental manner. The jug handle matches that on the teapot and is similar to that shown in Plate 99. Painted pattern reference (?) 'NT 11'. 'No. 11' or 'N —11' is shown on some pieces. Diameter of plate 8½in. (21.59cm). c.1785-6.*

Messrs. Christie's

PLATE 82. *A rare relief-moulded early New Hall mug (see also Plate 44), well painted with sprays of flowers, perhaps by Fidelle Duvivier. 4in. (10.16cm) high. c.1784-8.* GODDEN COLLECTION

PLATE 83. *A very neatly potted and rare New Hall mug, well painted with flowers and gilt initial – possibly by Fidelle Duvivier. 3½in. (8.89cm) high. c.1785-90.* GODDEN COLLECTION

add interest to the composition.[15] Conversely, the cupid and bird subjects are extremely rare and may be limited to only one or two services. The Continental style river scenes (Plate 74) are likewise now very rarely found.

To the above list we can, I think, add two other subjects:

8) Well painted birds in trees, of the type seen in the Sampson Daniel jug shown in Plates 62-3. Exotic rather than natural birds.
9) Floral compositions. Whilst most New Hall flower painting is nondescript some few rather special pieces seem to be painted by a very delicate accomplished hand. A painter of Fidelle Duvivier's obvious wide experience and skill would almost certainly have been able to paint flowers and I believe that he would have been employed on such work as the occasion demanded. In the nature of the trade, particularly in Staffordshire at this period, there would probably have been more demand for floral patterns than for figure designs.

I feel that the delicate flower painting shown in the pieces shown in Plates 82-4 and 229 could well have been painted by Fidelle Duvivier. At this period, c.1785-90, it is possible that the New Hall management did not employ

PLATE 84. *A rare New Hall tumbler well painted with flower sprays and cursive initials – possibly by Duvivier. 3¾in. (9.53cm) high. c.1785-90.* FORMERLY GODDEN COLLECTION

any other highly trained and accomplished ceramic artists, although flower painting was required. It is, I feel, probable that Fidelle painted the border design on the jug shown in Plates 62-3, as well as the two panels which are clearly from his hand. The cursive initials and leafage ornaments also seem remarkably similar to those on the tumbler in Plate 84, which I consider was decorated by Duvivier.

I also feel that Fidelle may well have turned his hand to gilding. Some intricate gilding displays a flair that could well point to our most accomplished New Hall decorator – see Plates 137 or 156-8.

Duvivier certainly enjoyed a very high reputation – one unlike any other ceramic painter of the period. On Saturday 5 April 1786 Mr. Christie sold in his London room 'the elegant and rich household furniture, jewels, china, etc.' of a deceased Gentleman. This included as lot 56:

> A most capital and complete tea and coffee equipage of rich crimson and gold curiously painted in figures by the ingenious Mr Devivi, no other set of this colour was ever made, and the art is entirely lost since Mr Sprimont's decease. Contains 12 handled tea cups and saucers, 6 coffee cups and saucers, tea pot, sugar dish and cover, slop bason and cream ewer.

You would have the greatest difficulty finding any other artist named in eighteenth century Christie's catalogues as practising his craft in England. The 'ingenious Mr Devivi', so named, was almost certainly Fidelle Duvivier.[16] This surname occurs in various phonetic renderings in English records. This Chelsea teaset is almost certainly represented by that gold anchor marked teapot in the Victoria & Albert Museum which bears a minutely painted landscape and figures design, in monochrome (museum reference number C.204-1985).

Although as early as 1864 Llewellynn Jewitt had shown engravings of Duvivier's works on New Hall porcelain, later researchers such as Major Tapp mistakenly attributed the rare signed examples of Duvivier's work to Caughley or to Worcester. Seemingly at this period in the early 1940s it did not seem conceivable that such fine work could be on New Hall porcelain!

This mis-attribution to Caughley and Worcester led to the belief that Fidelle Duvivier had worked for Thomas Turner at Caughley and at the Worcester factory. I and other modern authorities do not believe that this was so. It may therefore be helpful to state the believed movements of this international ceramic artist, who worked for the New Hall partnership in their 'fine line of Painting' for a period prior to his letter of November 1790.

Few dates in this summary are certain but I will explain some of the key references later.

August 1740	Born at Tournai in Belgium,[17] the son of Jacob Franciscus Duvivier.
c.1755+	Believed to have been apprenticed at the local Tournai factory in the ownership of François-Joseph Peterinck. However, he could like Henri-Joseph Duvivier have learnt his trade in this country.
c.1760	May have come to England with his cousin Joseph (Henri-Joseph). Fidelle may have been employed at the Chelsea works or alternatively at the Giles decorating studio in London during the 1760s.[18] However, it must be borne in mind that he was working at the Tournai factory in Belgium in or about 1764.
1764	Mlle. M. Jottrand's paper 'Tournai Porcelain and English Ceramics' published in the *Transactions of the English Ceramic Circle,* Vol. 10, Part 2 (1977), includes quotation from a bill dated 26 September 1764 relating to richly decorated cabaret services. The basic descriptions from this Belgian archive read: Cabaret G en figures Chinoises dorées de Duvivier. Cabaret J Paysage en couleur de Duvivier L'anglois, bord doré Cabaret R en paysage de fidel Duvivier. Clearly the last service was painted by Fidelle Duvivier, as were probably the middle set by the English Duvivier and possibly the first set also which was decorated with Chinese style figure subjects in gold. There is a good collection of Tournai porcelain at the Musée Royal de Mariemont, where one may see the close connection in ceramic styles between Tournai and Chelsea and Chelsea-Derby or Derby porcelains.
Late 1760s	I believe that Fidelle Duvivier was working at Chelsea and at a period before 1769 he married the daughter of the factory manager, Elizabeth Thomas, who was later recorded as the mother of his daughter, Elizabeth.
October 1769	Fidelle Duvivier's 'of the Borough of Derby' agreement to paint for William Duesbury of Derby for a four year period at 24s. a week shows his move to Derby. A son, Peter Joseph Duvivier, was born to Elizabeth and Fidelle Duvivier, at Derby in March 1771.

December 1770 A complication arises at this point for Thomas Morgan wrote from London to William Duesbury stating:

'Mr De Vivest [?] of Tournay informed me of one Mr Garon who he says is a very ingenious modeller, who he says has infinite more merit than Ste... [?] gave me his direction at Brusseles and when there I sent for him and find that if you can find him employ he is willing to come to England...

There is also at Tournay one Robert Phenix an Englishman who says he can turn, throw, mould make the body and glaise [*sic*] the same as at Chelsea & Tournay. He is willing to come to England if you will employ him...'.

This letter at least shows the interaction between workmen on the Continent and in this country; they were seemingly pleased to move from country to country. The first unclear name almost certainly relates to one Duvivier who was seemingly known to Thomas Morgan, the London dealer, and to Duesbury, as no added information was given on his calling etc.

The Tournay modeller 'Garon' or Gauron seemingly came over to England, as Nicholas Gauron was employed at Chelsea in at least 1773 and perhaps later at Derby. The indistinct modeller's name 'Ste...' almost certainly relates to Pierre Stephan. The most puzzling aspect of Morgan's letter, however, is that he seems to have met a Duvivier at or near Tournay in 1770, unless Duvivier merely gave him the introduction to Gauron in London before Morgan left for the Continent. Also, we cannot be certain that the reference is to Fidelle Duvivier.

1772 At this period Fidelle Duvivier should have been still employed by William Duesbury under the October 1769 agreement but we have the twice signed (and dated 1772) Worcester teapot in the Marshall collection at the Ashmolean, Oxford.

This is the only known example of his signed painting on Worcester and it cannot be considered to have been decorated within the factory.

It may have been decorated at Giles'[19] or another London decorating studio, but no other such artist signed work is known. It seems that this was a special one-off piece painted by Duvivier possibly for a present or as a sample of the quality of his ceramic painting when seeking other employment.

c.1775 According to an old French authority Duvivier was working at Sceaux in France in the mid-1770s. This belief is open to some question.

1783+ Fidelle Duvivier was seemingly in Holland, working at the Loosdrecht porcelain factory at this period, before it was transferred to Amstel in 1784. The local records at Slootdijk record the christening of a daughter to Elizabeth Duvivier in October 1783.[20]

The two Duvivier decorated New Hall mugs in the Victoria & Albert Museum illustrated here in Plates 55-8 and 70-1 are illustrated in colour with an unsigned but typically Duvivier decorated coffee cup in Hilary Young's *English Porcelain 1743-93* (V. & A. Publications, 1999) with the dating 'about 1782-7'. This I am sure is too early and, one being signed, this example could even post-date his leaving the partnership's full-time employment (in 1790) – if it was ever full time. I have given all my illustrations a post-1785 dating.

1787 By at least this period Fidelle Duvivier was in the Staffordshire Potteries. We have two dated examples, inscribed 'Lane End. 1787', one being the problematic non-New Hall Gerverot beaker or small vase mentioned earlier in this chapter. The other 1787 piece is a monochrome decorated Duvivier style bowl in the British Museum. The piece has suffered over the years but is believed to be of New Hall porcelain. Certainly, they prove Duvivier's presence in Staffordshire in 1787.

November 1790 At this period we have Fidelle Duvivier's important letter to William Duesbury II, stating that his engagement at New Hall has expired and that the partners do not intend to continue the finer, expensive, styles of decoration, in which Fidelle specialised. Fidelle had reached the age of fifty by this time and was contemplating teaching drawing in Staffordshire.

c.1791 At an unknown period, but presumably soon after 1790, Fidelle Duvivier seems to have painted in his monochrome style at least one tea and coffee service for James Neale or, rather, for David Wilson, the manager-owner of the former Neale manufactory at the Church Works at Hanley – see *Staffordshire Porcelain* Plate 69 for representative pieces from a Neale-Wilson porcelain service almost certainly decorated by Fidelle Duvivier.

October 1792 The name 'M.Devia' appears for one fortnight's wage in the Chamberlain wages book at Worcester. This seemingly relates to Fidelle as one Worcester decorated Caughley tea service is recorded bearing figure subject panels that are undoubtedly by this painter. The Chamberlain records show that this then decorating establishment was purchasing white blanks from Caughley at this period.[21]

c.1793+ As I have previously mentioned, Duvivier's hand does seem to appear on some post-1790 New Hall porcelains, notably on the splendid jug in the Usher Gallery in Lincoln. This piece is illustrated by David Holgate as his Plate 114 and there dated to c.1800-10. There are also the sheep in landscape teawares which incorporate the year date '1796'. I show in Plate 85 the teapot from this New Hall tea service which was almost certainly painted by Duvivier. These pieces suggest that the painter either carried out some private commissions using New Hall blanks or that he continued to paint some special high class orders for the partnership after 1790. It has been suggested that Duvivier's painting also occurs on Pinxton porcelain of the mid-1790s. This belief arises from the mis-identification of the 1796 tea service (as Plates 85 and 86) as being Pinxton.

Apart from New Hall and other Duvivier decorated porcelains, various pieces of creamware produced by Ralph Wedgwood (& Co.) of Burslem bear charming Duvivier type figure and landscape designs. These should date from the 1790s and suggest that he carried out occasional work for various firms.

It is not known how he made his main living after 1790. He was a drawing master, as is shown by his 1790 letter, and this activity may well have been more remunerative and reliable than ceramic painting!

c. 1796 It is possible that Fidelle Duvivier emigrated to America in the mid-1790s. This statement is prompted by the discovery of references to a Duvivier and son practising as drawing masters in Philadelphia in local newspapers of 1796 and 1797

The references appear in Alfred Prime's publication *The Arts and Crafts in Philadelphia, Maryland and South Carolina, 1786-1800* (The Walpole Society, 1932) and were kindly bought to my attention by Mrs. Pat Halfpenny and Jonathan Gray. One announcement of March 1796 refers to an 'academy for Drawing and Painting, opened by M Duvivier, member of the Royal Academy at Paris ... Mr D teaches only by his own drawings...'. By May 1797 'Duvivier and Son had moved to a new address 'where they continue teaching drawing ... specimens of their abilities, consisting of views, landscapes, sea ports, historical pieces, fruit, & are to be seen and sold at their academy.'

However, several artists with this surname are listed in standard works on high art. E. Bénézit's international dictionary of painters lists twenty-five different Duviviers but not our ceramic artist Fidelle Duvivier. One would have thought that if our artist was advertising himself in America, he would make more reference to his skills in ceramic decoration.

As to the death of Fidelle Duvivier, authors have tended to accept Major Tapp's tentative date of October 1817, which would have given Duvivier's age at death as seventy-seven. We should bear in mind that Major Tapp, writing in *Apollo* magazine of March 1941, having searched without success for records of his burial at Derby, Madeley, Broseley, Kemberton, Worcester, Pinxton, Mansfield and 'every church within a five mile radius of Stoke-on-Trent', could only comment 'there is one significant entry in the Hanley Green registers dated October 12, 1817 which may well record the demise of Fidelle, but as the original registers were destroyed in the Chartists Riots and those that are preserved are evidently hastily made transcripts, there is obviously much margin for error, both in the spelling and in the placing of the names'.

It would seem that the Major was admitting that the 1817 entry did not really fit the facts! In an endeavour to check the entry discovered but not quoted by Major Tapp in 1941 I asked Mrs. P.A. Halfpenny, then of the City Museum, if she could spare a moment to check the

Plate 85. *A New Hall teapot of a post-1790 silver shape. This set was almost certainly painted by Duvivier, although the date 1796 (see Plate 85A) is after the period when his full time employment at New Hall had ceased. 6½in. (16.51cm) high. 1796.* Roderick Jellicoe

Hanley Green archives. Both she and Roger Pomfret, the then Chairman of the Northern Ceramic Society, could not find any relevant entry in the Registers. I therefore regard Fidelle Duvivier's date of death as being unknown, or at least unproven. I further do not believe that he decorated any British ceramics after 1800, although several optimistic attempts have been made to see his hand in various types of landscape and figure compositions or in exotic bird patterns. These were now in the nineteenth century standard forms of decoration, practised at most porcelain manufactories by a variety of painters.

It is all too easy to see Duvivier's hand in many finely painted bird and landscape subjects and there are admittedly many tantalising gaps in our chronological summary of his movements. I, for example, have played with the idea that he worked for Champion at Bristol prior to 1770-81, painting the rare Continental style riverside views and colourful birds in landscapes. Even the background landscapes and the foreground decoration on the magnificent armorial tea service made for Bristol's Member of Parliament in 1774 show Duvivier's style and technique. After the closure of Champion's Bristol factory Duvivier could have followed his employer to Staffordshire and the succeeding New Hall company. Alas, we have no proof, but it might help to explain why this famous highly trained and much travelled Continental artist came to decorate for the New Hall factory rather than for Derby or Worcester where the managements were more concerned with costly products largely aimed at the fashionable London market.

In this summary of the work of one quality New Hall artist working in Staffordshire in the approximate period 1787-90 (or later), it is remarkable how rare are the New Hall forms he decorated. The two twice-signed mugs (Plates 55-61) and the similar unsigned mug in the Victoria & Albert Museum with their simple loop handles

PLATE 85A. *The reverse side of the neatly decorated New Hall teapot shown in Plate 85. The motif is the crest of the Thomson family of Cornwall.* RODERICK JELLICOE

are of a practically unknown New Hall shape, although there is no doubt of their origin.

Likewise the now lost New Hall teapot engraved for Jewitt in 1864 is extremely rare in its basic shape. The dessert centrepiece shown in Plate 66 is the only example known to me and the related dessert dish forms are excessively rare, the New Hall dessert plates rather less so (Plate 68). I do not know of any Duvivier decorated New Hall coffee pot and only one spoontray – that to the set shown in Plate 81.

Only the cups and saucers or teabowls are standard. I cannot write of all the teawares being common for the teapot and the covered milk jug shown in Plates 64 and 72-3 are again of great rarity. The same could be said of the floral painted mug and beaker shown in Plates 83-4, if you accept these as being painted by Duvivier, but we know of a very small proportion of the output of this or any other eighteenth century porcelain factory.

One must consider the question, did the New Hall partners in the 1780s have a market for what Duvivier termed 'the fine line of painting'? Almost certainly not and that is why Duvivier was dismissed and his costly style of decoration was discontinued. Henceforth the management concentrated on attractive, often neat, serviceable teawares for the middle-class masses. In this it was most successful, but it rightly did not seek to rival the giants of the trade. It knew its place in the market, a very important place which for years it all but dominated.

The rare Duvivier decorated examples serve to show the heights which it could reach. In concluding this section on Fidelle Duvivier's work, I cannot resist quoting briefly from the late Reginald Haggar's review of examples included in the splendid 1981 exhibition of New Hall Porcelain held at the Stoke-on-Trent City Museum at Hanley. The review or 'assessment' included this modern artist's opinion of a case of Duvivier

PLATE 86. *A coffee cup from the 1796 tea and coffee service, a special order painted by Fidelle Duvivier. Pieces from this service have been attributed to different factories over the years. 2¾in. (6.99cm) high. 1796.*

MESSRS. PHILLIPS

decorated porcelains assembled for this display by David Holgate and the then Keeper of Ceramics, Mrs. Pat Halfpenny:

> Duvivier's atmospheric landscapes with windmills, bottle shaped ovens and buildings were always enlivened with figures and animals in the centre foreground while the powerful earth masses clumps of foliage and trailing branches near the baseline serve not only to loosen the vignettes into the surrounding white china, but also as a repoussoir, to give distance to the vistas...

Here we have a twentieth century local scenic painter paying deserved tribute to an eighteenth century ceramic artist. What an impact the local view New Hall dessert service would have made if it had been included in the 1981 exhibition. Even Mr. Haggar may have found it difficult to describe its charm and importance!

We certainly do not have signed examples of other decorators' work on New Hall porcelain and in the absence of factory records or other helpful material we have no guidelines. I do not, however, agree with David Holgate's opinion that apart from Fidelle Duvivier there was seemingly 'no room for them'! If we can assume that the New Hall porcelains were decorated within the factory, as seems the probability, then many other decorators must have been employed both within the Duvivier period (c.1787-90) and in the forty-five years after his employment there officially ceased in 1790.

It may well be that very few top ranking, highly paid artists were employed compared with the Derby or Worcester factories, but a good team of gilders and flower painters must have been employed over a long period. Interesting figure and landscape patterns occur on nineteenth century examples and high quality flower painting also appears. Admittedly, these richer designs are in a minority, because the factory seemingly concentrated on the large middle-class demand for reasonably priced teawares. Low prices necessitate simple designs.

Earlier authors, notably Frederick Rhead writing of 'New Hall China' in *The Connoisseur* in December 1916, mentioned four artists who later authorities have been inclined to discount, perhaps correctly. I will briefly mention these as Frederick Rhead was related to a New Hall apprentice, Charlotte Woolliscroft. It must be remembered, however, that we have no supporting evidence to link these painters with the New Hall works.

HENRY BONE

Rhead, like other early writers, mentioned Henry Bone, the famous enamel painter. In fact a local account of trading and manufacturing in Plymouth published in 1814 stated that 'Mr Bone, the celebrated enamel painter in London, learnt his art and was brought up in this manufactory.'

Henry Bone was born at Truro in February 1755 and was reputedly apprenticed to William Cookworthy of the Plymouth factory in 1771 and in January 1772 to Richard Champion of Bristol for a period of seven years. He may have been responsible for some good Continental style landscape with figure compositions found on Bristol porcelain. I do not, however, know of any early New Hall type porcelain that would be of the quality to suggest that

Henry Bone moved to the Staffordshire Potteries. Certainly by the time the new partners had established the porcelain venture, Bone had seemingly turned his attention to enamelling on copper, his first Royal Academy exhibit in this style being shown in 1781. I consider it extremely unlikely that Henry Bone decorated New Hall or indeed any other type of porcelain. He died in 1834, as the New Hall works was in its closing stages.

JOSHUA CRISTALL

Another fine art painter once associated with the New Hall works was Joshua Cristall. Cristall was born in 1767 or 1768. It has been stated that he was apprenticed to William Hewson, a leading London china dealer at 86 Aldgate. This seemingly led him to a period working for Thomas Turner at the Caughley porcelain factory in Shropshire. Here he certainly entertained hopes of earning a living by fine art painting but in a letter of c.1793 he was being advised not to leave steady employment for the risky Arts:

> ...I only wish to caution you against the headstrong ardour of youth. Persue your studies. Practice as much as you can; but do not think of depending on painting for a subsistence before you know the first rudiments of the art ... I find Mr Turner intends to send you to travel for him very soon. This will in every respect be a great advantage to you ... if you determine to leave Mr Turner when your times expires, I hope you will be careful not to quarrel with him...

That letter was written by Mary Woolstonecraft in March (the year is not given). A second letter dated 9 December was likewise addressed to 'Mr Cristall' at Caughley. It is written in the same vein but indicates that the artist was still at Caughley and had still not determined his future: 'I am sorry to hear that you are yet unsettled, halting between two opinions ... Determine like a man whether Drawing is to be the business or amusement of your future life...'. The remark 'I have seldom seen your sister since you left town' lends credence to the thoughts that Cristall had earlier been apprenticed to William Hewson of Aldgate.

He may well have acted as traveller for Turner and the Caughley works but his interest in painting won the day and he was to become a founder member of the Royal Society of Painters in Water Colours and later its President. He died in London in October 1847, aged eighty. Although Joshua Cristall's name is traditionally linked with the Davenport factory, I think it unlikely that he was engaged as a factory artist in the nineteenth century, after leaving Turner in the late 1790s. As a landscape and figure artist it is difficult to link his style to New Hall porcelains, with the possible exception of the Kent view tea service, as Plate 157. The post 1812 bone-china tea service shown in Plate 378 has been associated with Cristall (also with Henry Bone), but I think that at that period he was fully involved in London and with higher art. It is nevertheless just possible that he supplied drawings of landscapes which were used as the basis of the very popular New Hall overglaze printed designs. The magnificent forty-five piece teaset of 2215 shown in Plates 378-9 is featured in the Rheads' joint work *Staffordshire Pots & Potters* (Hutchinson & Co., 1906) and in F.A. Rhead's article on 'New Hall China' in *The Connoisseur* of December 1916. Some pieces have apparently Henry Bone's name but this was, I believe, added in the present century to enhance the value or interest.

Various standard books on British painters will give details of Cristall and other fine art personages. In this case I consulted Martin Hardie's *Water Colour Painting in Britain* Vol. II (B.T. Batsford Ltd., 1967). This authority suggested that Joshua Cristall entered the Academy Schools about 1795. He was sketching in the Lake District in the 1802-3 period and pencilled landscapes of the 1805 period are in the British Museum. Lord St Leven owns six watercolours of Cornish subjects which are signed and dated 1794. Martin Hardie states that Cristall was 'essentially a figure painter, though he excelled in the combination of figures with landscapes'. On balance it seems unlikely that Joshua painted at the New Hall works, although he could have painted blanks for Hewson in London about 1785 and slightly later for Thomas Turner at Caughley.

JOSEPH WAREHAM

Both Frederick Rhead (in *The Connoisseur,* 1916) and G. Woolliscroft Rhead in his *British Pottery Marks* (1910) state that Wareham was a New Hall artist before joining Mintons and G. Woolliscroft Rhead seems to have good knowledge of Wareham's ceramic career, giving him a personal entry in his 1910 book of marks:

> Joseph Wareham. An extremely able painter of flowers, birds, etc. in the Dresden and Sèvres style. Served his apprenticeship at the New Hall Works, afterwards worked at the Don Pottery. Migrated to London where he worked for Mortlock. Engaged by Herbert Minton at some date between 1846 and 1849. Made journey from London to the Potteries with his family and furniture in a canal boat; landed at Ebberns Wharf, Stoke on Trent. He boasted that he had worked for all the crowned heads of Europe. He did not sign his work.

The Census returns indicate that Wareham was born in Stoke in about 1783, being given as aged seventy-eight in

1861. His son James was born in London in about 1815, presumably when he was employed there by Mortlocks, the important retailer and decorating establishment which specialised in Sèvres style decorations.

His name appears in the Minton records from the late 1830s onwards in association with flower painting or Sèvres style exotic birds in landscapes. Minton porcelains made for Queen Victoria are certainly decorated by this accomplished ceramic painter – examples are illustrated in my specialist book *Minton Pottery & Porcelain of the First Period 1793-1830* (Herbert Jenkins, 1968).

If Joseph Wareham was apprenticed at the New Hall works, the likely period would be c.1798-1803. He had moved to London by at least 1815 and had presumably won a good reputation for his ceramic painting, otherwise he would not have been head-hunted or taken on by Mortlock, a leading decorator who would only be interested in high class work. It is possible that, having completed his apprenticeship at the New Hall Works, he remained there, almost certainly as a flower painter, until 1810 or a little later; that is, really up to the end of the hybrid hard-paste period. The splendid flower painted jugs – as Plates 224-6 – and the superb quality floral painted teawares and rare bold dessert services could well have been painted by Joseph Wareham. We do not know of other contenders at this 1800-12 period, although the large flower compositions are different from his later Sèvres style smaller floral groupings in compartments, reserved into coloured grounds. But New Hall at this period, if at all, did not produce such rich Sèvres style decoration. Joseph Wareham reputedly remained at Minton's to an advanced age and was seventy-eight at the time of the 1861 census.

FRANCIS EMERY

William Scarratt, writing in 1906, noted in his *Old Times in the Potteries* (privately published, Stoke, 1906): 'From a relative I learned that Mr Francis Emery of Cobridge, managed the decorative department [at the New Hall works] till about 1830...'. Elsewhere it is stated that Emery's daughter married Peter Warburton, one of the partners in the concern. I have been unable to substantiate these claims but if Francis Emery was the decorating manager in the closing stages of the concern he must have been a painter of some standing and possibly would have worked there for a considerable period.

I have been unable to discover much about Francis Joseph Emery who possibly also had a son of the same name. In the 1860s and 1870s we find listed Francis Emery & Son of Cobridge as 'colour manufacturers for china, earthenware and glass', a trade that would link well with a former manager of a porcelain decorating department.

A Francis Joseph Emery took out ceramic patents in 1859 and 1865. He or another person of this name was potting at the Black Hill works, Burslem up to the early 1890s. Jewitt stated that Emery joined Edward Clarke in partnership in 1877. At the end of the day we seem only to have family tradition for Francis Emery's association with decorating New Hall porcelains. A small notebook reputedly belonging to Francis Emery contains, with other notes, two receipts for New Hall bone china, helping to confirm family belief that Emery worked for the New Hall company.

WANTLING OR WILDIN

We have even less evidence for another New Hall painter mentioned by William Scarratt. After writing of Emery, this local authority noted 'also that Wantling of Derby, the celebrated runner worked as a painter and decorator for some years for this firm'.

I have no records for a china painter of this name. However, a note book, recorded by the late Reginald Haggar *(Northern Ceramic Society Newsletter* No. 26 of June 1977) contains recipes for New Hall bone china and glazes inscribed 'given by Ias (Jas?) Wildin, 18th October 1824'. It is at least possible that James Wildin was connected with the New Hall works in the 1820s enabling him to know the composition of the porcelain body and glaze – see page 364. Other recipe books, however, give details of many ceramic bodies; that knowledge was not necessarily restricted to workers within a given factory.

GILDERS

The New Hall partnership certainly employed some good gilders and perhaps Fidelle Duvivier turned his practised hand to gilding when required, but we have no record of the names of the New Hall gilders. It is possible, however, that a John Keeling was so employed. His will (of 1811) described him as a gilder and, apart from his wife, the other executor was John Daniel. The witnesses to the will, apart from the attorney, were Sampson Bagnall and John Tittensor, names closely associated with the New Hall Company. However, at this late period in his life he seems to have been carrying on a gilding or decorating business at his workshops and warehouse at Shelton. He also owned eight houses let to various folk – George Wood, Samuel Bourne, Samuel Percival etc. – whom he may have employed.

NON-FACTORY DECORATION

The early writers on New Hall often stated that the proprietors sold much of their output in the white, undecorated, state. I do not think that this was the case, but rather that these authorities had in mind the fact that the management were happy to sell their 'composition' to other firms.

The decoration all seems to be of a family! When we come to the introduction of pattern numbers from the 1790s onwards, the sequence fits in well with the period and forms and there are seemingly no examples of new lower numbers appearing out of place, as would happen if independent decorators or other firms had painted New Hall blanks with their own designs. I am of the opinion that all known or recorded New Hall painted patterns were added within the New Hall works, by their own workpeople. Unfortunately we know the names of so few of these hands.

We must remember, however, that several London china dealers employed ceramic painters and also there were several specialist decorating studios. All these purchased blanks from various sources but it seems that at the end of the eighteenth century Caughley and Chamberlains of Worcester supplied most of these white blanks. At a later period the Coalport factory were the leading suppliers.

There is, however, at least one New Hall mug which could have been decorated by an independent printer. I refer to a large mug in The Potteries Museum at Hanley (ref. no. 1992C 264). This example bears two well-engraved prints representing 'Spring' and 'Summer' and the back of these panels is signed 'T Fletcher. Shelton'. Thomas Fletcher worked as an independent engraver and printer at Booden Brook, Shelton, very near the New Hall factory from c.1796 into the nineteenth century. He could have purchased New Hall blanks to print, or he could have supplied engraved copper plates to the New Hall Company. The example cited has gilt initials and New Hall style gilt trim.

---

1. The reader is referred to the Dutch specialist book cum catalogue *Loosdrechts Porcelain 1774-1784* written by four contributors and published by the Uitgeverij Waanders, Zwolle in 1988.

2. Slootdijk is present-day Loenen, across the water from Nieuw-Loosdrecht.

3. A very interesting plate painted with seated figures under a tree is illustrated in the 1988 Loosdrecht exhibition catalogue as item 148. This colour trial piece with colour names in French is almost certainly an example of Fidelle Duvivier's work. There are several attractive monochrome painted teawares in the National Museum of Wales that are very much in the Duvivier style – see Loosdrecht examples D.W. 2191, 2524, 2526 or 2527.

4. This is illustrated by Bevis Hillier in his *Master Potters of the Industrial Revolution – The Turners of Lane End* (Cory, Adams & Mackay, London, 1965).

5. This example with that shown in Plates 70-1 is illustrated in colour in Hilary Young's *English Porcelain 1745-95* (V. & A. Publications) but with, I believe, too early a dating. See page 182.

6. This (headless) 'Good Woman' inn scene occurs as a print on a creamware jug in the Liverpool Museum illustrated as Plates 201-2 in David Drakard's book *Printed English Pottery* (Jonathan Horne, London 1992). The basic jest also appears in Hogarth's print 'Noon'.

7. The same engraving was also incorporated in Jewitt's *The Wedgwoods: being a life of Josiah Wedgwood* published by Virtue Brothers & Co. in or before April 1865.

8. The playing children painted by Duvivier on this teaset, and perhaps varied on other pieces from a complete tea service, are mirrored in subject at least in a Dutch (Amstel) porcelain tea and coffee service in the Amsterdam Historical Museum. See the *Northern Ceramic Society's Newsletter,*. No. 27 of September 1977. The contributor stated 'each item had a different picture in a wide range of colours of charming little children playing games such as battledore and shuttlecock, blind man's buff, leap frog, spinning tops...'. Duvivier, who painted in Holland, seemingly adopted some of his Continental subjects when painting in Staffordshire.

9. First in *The Art Journal* of January 1864 and again in his *Life of Josiah Wedgwood* published early in 1805.

10. His wife had died before the April 1861 Census at which period one unmarried daughter lived at their Edmund Street home.

11. The comport now in the Lancaster Museum was written of and researched by Derek Chitty – see the *Northern Ceramic Society's Newsletter,* No. 84 of December 1991.

12. This is confirmed in an account published in the trade magazine *The Pottery Gazette* of November 1878, which states that Thomas Gray, 'as canny as a Scot', was Messrs. Samuel Alcock's northern representative or traveller. See Dr. and Mrs. Geoffrey Barnes' contribution to *Northern Ceramic Society's Newsletter* No. 60 of December 1985.

13. This service has, however. been discussed and illustrated by David Holgate in his contribution 'A New Hall Dessert Service' published in *The Northern Ceramic Society Journal,* Vol. 15 (1998).

14. See also *Transactions of the English Ceramic Circle,* Vol. 14, Part 2 (1991), page 163.

15. In a like manner dogs or other animals were usually added to landscape compositions.

16. His cousin Joseph is believed to have returned to Tournai in 1763.

17. The Dutch authorities give the place of birth as Doornik and the exact date of birth as 6 August 1740.

18. Some mid-eighteenth century white Chinese porcelains seem to have been finely painted by Duvivier, very much in the Continental style. Examples are recorded with the initial 'D' incorporated in a mock-Sèvres mark.

19. Dr. Bernard Watney has suggested that Duvivier worked at Giles' Studio in London and there decorated some Chinese porcelains in the European manner. See his illustrated paper on this subject published in the *Transactions of the English Ceramic Circle.* Vol. 14, Part 3 (1992).

20. The reference to Duvivier working at Loosdrecht is given in *Loosdrechts Porcelain 1774-1784,* a multi-author catalogue of an important exhibition held in 1988 (Uitgeverij Waanders, Zwolle). The main text is in Dutch, but the illustrations include several landscape and figure compositions in the Duvivier manner.

21. For illustrations of this service and the documentation the reader is referred to my specialist book *Chamberlain-Worcester Porcelain 1788-1852* (Barrie & Jenkins, London, 1982), Plates 30, 238-41. Also to my *Eighteenth Century English Porcelain* Plates 244-5. See also *Caughley & Worcester Porcelain 1775-1800* (Antique Collectors' Club 1981), introduction to this revised edition.

PLATE 87. *An extremely rare form of early New Hall teapot, perhaps even relating to the Tunstall period and to the saucer form shown in Plate 40. 6½in. (16.51cm) high. c.1782-5.* PRIVATE COLLECTION

PLATE 88. *A simple standard form New Hall teabowl and saucer painted with an early design, perhaps linking with the first Tunstall period productions. The design also occurs on corrugated forms. Diameter of saucer 5in. (12.7cm). c.1782-5.* GODDEN COLLECTION

CHAPTER VI

The New Hall Porcelains, c.1784-1812

I have here commenced my New Hall story in 1784 because, as previously stated, I believe the first Tunstall period was of longer duration and commenced rather later than previously thought and because the new specialist porcelain works on or near the New Hall site at Shelton may have taken some time to be prepared and brought into production.

At this period in the early 1780s Chinese true (hard-paste) porcelain was still flooding into this country in the many vessels chartered to the East India Company. Our own very serviceable Caughley, Derby and Worcester English porcelain factories were in full swing and other smaller concerns, such as Isleworth, the various Liverpool factories and Lowestoft, were also taking some of the available market. But none of these competitors was situated in Staffordshire.

Importantly, the market was growing, as was the population of the British Isles. Towards the end of 1783 the Peace of Paris ended conflict with the major nations of France, Spain, Holland and the new United States of America. Overseas markets were again open to our trade.

At home as the population grew so did the fashion for drinking tea and to some degree making a meal of it! Complete tea services were highly saleable. As more and more East Indiamen brought home even larger quantities of tea, so the price tended to drop and the leaf became more affordable.

Importantly, also, the duty or government tax on tea had been drastically cut under William Pitt's 1784 Commutation Act (24 George III, Cap. 28). The old duty of 119% obviously encouraged large scale smuggling, whereas the new duty of 12.5% was bearable, only 5% of this being paid to the Customs by the importer.

The English East India Company, enjoying its state monopoly on importations of goods from the East, consequently increased its importations of tea, resolving:

> That in consequence of an Act of Parliament passed in 1784 for altering the Duties on tea, it will be expedient to send ships to China in the ensuing season to bring home at least eighteen million pounds of tea.

At least eighteen million pounds – and that was only the official Company's bulk order, taking no account of the profitable private importations undertaken by the ships' officers and crew. All this tea needed ceramic vessels in which it could be brewed and drunk – fashionable porcelain, for preference.

At the same period as the duty on the tea-leaf[1] was greatly reduced and tea became more affordable, the English porcelain manufacturers were also being helped by the reintroduction of a tax on silver. From 1 December 1784 6d. duty was imposed on each troy ounce of silver used in the manufacture of teapots, coffee pots, sugar bowls and cream jugs, to mention only the articles that related to the tea table. This tax on silver increased the cost of the raw material by some 10%. It was doubled in the 1797-8 period and increased again in 1815. The British ceramic industry narrowly escaped any taxation on its products and was indeed assisted by taxes on its fashionable rivals, the imported Chinese and Continental porcelains.

The post-1783 Staffordshire porcelains to be discussed in this chapter comprise the true New Hall 'real China' wares. These are the hybrid hard-paste type porcelains made at the 'New Hall' premises in Shelton after the first tentative establishment of the new partnership at Keeling's pottery at Tunstall had been abandoned and after Anthony Keeling and John Turner had left the original partnership, as outlined in Chapter II.

In that chapter I also detailed and illustrated a type of porcelain with its characteristic moulded corrugated surface which I attributed to that early pre-New Hall period. This belief may not stand the test of time but, as the body colour and the glaze can appear different from the accepted mainstream New Hall productions, I will retain this admittedly arbitrary division.

It must be understood, however, that the true New Hall Shelton porcelains include some reeded forms and obviously some patterns made earlier at Tunstall were continued by the new reduced Shelton partnership, because these patterns were in demand. It can be hard, perhaps impossible, to tell the 1782-3 Tunstall pieces from the early Shelton examples made in 1784 or 1785 in much the same way that if a car or furniture manufacturer moved his factory the products might not evidence any outward change in appearance.

The superb and extremely rare teapot form shown in Plate 87 is a case in point. Its profile may belong to teawares of the type illustrated by the rare saucer shown as Plate 40. It is perhaps best to call it transitional, c.1783-6, and not worry further – merely rejoice in the new Staffordshire porcelains! My later thoughts lead me to believe that this teapot does indeed relate to the early style pieces discussed in Chapter II. The moulded handle form appears to match those on the jugs shown in Plates 42-3. The enamelled design also occurs on early pieces such as the large jug (Plate 42). This unnumbered pattern seems to occur only on very early examples. It is not known to me on post-1785 New Hall porcelains. I have, however, left this problematic example in its original position in this chapter to illustrate the difficulty of exactly dating examples of the 1780s. Perhaps it is a foolhardy exercise!

Certainly the new porcelains will not, at first, include any marks or pattern numbers and the Shelton shapes and added patterns can appear very similar to those made earlier. We could indeed be over particular in endeavouring to separate the two classes or over optimistic in endeavouring to prove that saleable

Plate 89. *A tastefully restrained early New Hall gilt teabowl and saucer, linking with a later pattern numbered 64. Diameter of saucer, 5in. (12.7cm). c.1784-7 or later – a 1790 account relates to this pattern – see page 225.*
P.A. Glass collection

Plate 90. *A tastefully decorated New Hall teabowl and saucer of a rare enamelled and gilt pattern. Pattern number as yet unrecorded. Diameter of saucer 5in. (12.7cm). c.1784-7.* Private Collection

porcelains were made in the short period when the newly established partnership was centred at Keeling's pottery at Tunstall, in about 1782-3.

The partners (less Keeling and Turner), having then decided to continue with their adventure into the manufacture of porcelain in order to rescue their investment (that is, the money they had paid to Richard Champion in 1781 – see Chapter II), obviously chose the New Hall site. I write 'obviously' because we now know this as a fact. The choice may not have been obvious at the time, it may not have been the largest site or manufactory available or the best suited to produce porcelain. However, they avoided the earlier error of using one of the partners' existing potteries and therefore the adoption of the pottery and its subsequent production of porcelain did not adversely affect any one partner's own activities.

It is possible that workmen employed in the earlier Tunstall period were retained,[2] but certainly additional expense would have been involved in preparing the New Hall site and for an initial period the output of the new true New Hall porcelain would have been very small. We may have two initially experimental periods, not one.

The New Hall output may originally have been restricted in quantity but the variety of shapes is remarkably large, especially when we consider that the new porcelains were practically restricted to teawares.

It would be almost impossible to illustrate and discuss all the New Hall forms produced even in the decade 1785-95. Others have tended to concentrate on the highly collectable teapots, but I favour the cream or milk jug forms to show the diversity of the late eighteenth century New Hall porcelains. Most jugs will have been part of a complete tea and coffee service and their form, and certainly their decoration, will be mirrored in the whole service.

Nevertheless, I will need to illustrate some teapots and some other necessary components from eighteenth century porcelain tea services to complete my coverage of the factory's products.

The components of a standard eighteenth century tea service have already been explained – see page 141. The full or forty-three piece service (or forty-five pieces counting the teapot and sugar basin covers) includes a spoontray and a tea canister but not normally a coffee pot, although twelve handled coffee cups were supplied.

The make-up of a service could, however, be greatly varied. The retailer might order smaller sets (perhaps without the spoontray or tea canister) to reduce the basic cost or because his market was of a lower order. Likewise the buyer could purchase as much or as little as he or she desired. The existing nineteenth century price lists all make it clear that the different units were priced separately and presumably they were also available as individual pieces. It would also appear from these printed lists that there was no reduction in price if a complete tea service was purchased.

Tea service jugs present several problems. They were produced in various sizes and shapes, with or without covers, and it is hard to determine if one was intended for milk or for cream. They could, however, have been interchangeable. After all, a standard teaset had one set of saucers for a set of teacups and for the coffee cups, it being thought that both liquids would not be drunk at the same time. Yet in such a tea and coffee service there was only one small jug. It could surely have been used to hold either milk or cream – that is if cream was required with coffee. Likewise the handled coffee cup, holding a little more liquid than the handleless teabowl, could equally be used to hold tea. Yet if we refer to the only known printed price list for New Hall tea services, a list which may date from c.1790 or later, we find listed not milk jugs but a 'cream ewer', even although the list is headed 'complete tea services' and the list did not include a coffee pot. Incidentally, Ridgway's price list for teawares, dated 1813, also uses the term 'cream' for the jug. However, I think milk was the usual (but not the universal) additive for tea and some at least of these tea service jugs were used for milk rather than cream. I tend to refer to the larger capacity and the taller shapes as milk jugs, reserving the term 'creamer' for the smaller, lower vessels.

It should be mentioned that the top class factories such as Chelsea and Derby tended to favour the description 'cream ewer'. However, when we study the sale records of Worcester or indeed Bristol porcelains, as sold by Mr. Christie in London, we find the description 'milk pot' being used.

It could well be that the class of market and the quality and cost of the article affected the terminology! Just before the hard-paste porcelain patent came to Staffordshire, Mr. Christie held a sale of Champion's Bristol porcelain. This three day sale held in February 1780 included both 'cream ewers' and 'milk pots', both descriptions being employed in the same catalogues but for very different classes of wares:

A very rich cream ewer	(sold for 9s.)
A ditto	(sold for 8s.6d.)
A white and gold teapot, slop basin, sugar dish and milk pot	(sold for 9s.)
Ditto	(sold for 8s.)

If we have to differentiate between the two vessels and

PLATE 91. *A rare early New Hall 'high Chelsea ewer' with early well-moulded handle. This enamelled (non-gilt) Oriental figure design was extremely popular but is not confined to New Hall. Several different variations and styles of painting occur. This pattern was later numbered 20. 3¾in. (9.53cm) high. c.1783-6.*

GODDEN COLLECTION

PLATE 92. *A New Hall 'low Chelsea ewer' decorated with blue enamel border and enamelled flower groups. This popular pattern was numbered 22 but early examples are seldom so marked. 2¼in. (5.72cm) high. c.1783-6.*
MESSRS. SOTHEBY'S

their contents I shall retain my original views: a tall jug is a milk jug; the lower, smaller capacity vessel is a creamer or 'cream ewer', to use an eighteenth century term.

The taller form of jug could in the early period have a cover with a neatly turned knob.[3] The lower jugs – the creamers – were not made to have a cover. If a jug was intended to have a cover the border decoration tends to be on the outside of the top edge. With open jugs the decoration is usually on the inside, where it would be covered up or perhaps rubbed by a cover and its flange – see Plate 99. This rule is, however, certainly not watertight.

The early New Hall porcelains of the mid- to late 1780s are scarce. Today we can only trace one or two examples of some basic New Hall shapes; others may therefore still be unknown to us. Certainly this must be true of some early added patterns. Taking as an example the first fifty New Hall patterns, various authors and researchers have access to most major collections but can only cite the numbers of seven or eight known New Hall patterns, leaving over forty (over 80%) unrecorded or untraced by specialist collectors.

It follows that the early productions are very scarce and hitherto unrecorded shapes or unknown patterns will be costly – but not necessarily expensive!

No dated New Hall teawares of the 1780s are known to me and consequently it is difficult to decide the order in which the various shapes were introduced. Not all authorities will necessarily agree with my views, but it is important to bear in mind that at any one period the New Hall management would be producing more than one shape of teapot or of any other article. The all important china dealers and the buying public would have expected and obtained a choice of shapes, as they would of added patterns.

To some degree the different markets would also influence the shape. The upper end of the market would demand quality decoration and gilding on new fashion forms. Conversely, the less demanding end of the market, being very price conscious, would settle for standard patterns – apprentice designs without gilding on simpler standard forms. The early teabowl and saucer shown in Plate 88 is of this mass market type.

This rule, while true in principle, is not inflexible. Progressively more costly designs are shown in Plates 89-90, but all are on simple, standard teabowls and saucers. However, the popular so-called 'Chelsea ewers', as shown in Plates 91-2, are usually decorated with early simple designs devoid of gilding. Yet the form is complicated, being formed from plaster of Paris moulds with the handle being separately moulded and affixed to the body.

These Chelsea ewers were made at several British porcelain factories[4] and come in two sizes or amended forms – the high (Plate 91) and the lower (Plate 92) Chelsea ewer. The taller or high Chelsea ewer is the rarer in all factories. With New Hall examples it links, at least in regard to the ornate moulded handle, with the earlier corrugated surface porcelains shown in Plates 19, 23-4

Plate 93. *A rare faceted early New Hall teapot and stand, decorated with a simple gilt border design. Pattern number not recorded or perhaps allocated. Teapot 5½in. (13.97cm) high. c.1785.* Godden collection

and 31-4. The floral painted low Chelsea ewer with its simplified handle (Plate 92) is the rather more usual example, but it is still rarely found today. Both these related cream ewer forms could be painted with various patterns or decorated with underglaze blue designs, but the examples here depicted (later numbered pattern 20 and 22 respectively) are those most often found and therefore we can assume the designs most popular in their time. They were, however, not restricted to production by the New Hall partnership. Indeed, it is as well not to regard any New Hall pattern as unique.

It is convenient to discuss here other early forms of small capacity creamers or ewers. It is now difficult to decide if these (and the Chelsea ewers) were originally part of tea services or if they were sold individually. Several rare forms occur, such as a plain form of low Chelsea type ewer with a plain loop handle. Certainly, the patterns they bear are standard New Hall teaware designs of the 1780s.

Unfortunately very few early New Hall tea services now remain in a complete state to show us which forms were issued together. The corrugated set shown in Plates 21-7 represents a rare exception and serves to illustrate that the shapes and handle forms included in services were not necessarily an exact match. Another part service of the mid-1780s, which is seemingly as it was originally sold, is the charming wide faceted gilt tea service shown in Plates 93-4. This part service has a very rare form of rather squat jug linking in its general proportions with a low Chelsea ewer (Plate 94). In this case the low jug matches perfectly the other faceted shapes and a leaf-moulded Chelsea ewer type jug would have appeared completely wrong in such a restrained neat service. Yet, this apparent cream jug was included in a teaset, just as handled coffee cups were included. It can also be stated that similar low creamers made by other factories, such as Turner, are also found in complete services. A further rare New Hall example (bearing an unknown pattern number) is shown in Plate 95, a real delight.

If the slightly gilt faceted teaset (Plates 93-4) had been issued with a larger capacity milk jug, one would have thought that the correct form would have been that shown in Plate 96. The solid gilt pointed knob also matches the teapot and the tea canister covers. The moulded design at the base of the spout is typical of early New Hall and shows the quality of the design and workmanship in the mid- to late 1780s. A similar spout form also occurs on earlier Bristol jugs – see Plate 15.

Plate 94. *Tea service shapes matching the teapot and stand shown in Plate 93. The tea canister and faceted creamer shapes are particularly rare. Unnumbered gilt pattern. Tea canister 5¼in. (13.34cm) high. c.1785.*

Godden collection

PLATE 95. *A rare early New Hall faceted creamer with well-painted floral border design and gilt trim. Unnumbered pattern. 3¾in. (9.53cm) high. c.1785-6.* THE LATE A. DE SAYE HUTTON

PLATE 96. *An elegant and rare New Hall faceted lidded milk jug. Note moulding on lower part of spout. The pattern number in this gilt design is not recorded – along with many other early designs. 6¼in. (15.88cm) high. c.1785-7.* GODDEN COLLECTION

PLATE 97. *Three small 'Robin' cream (?) jugs, showing two different handle forms. Left to right: unnumbered early pattern, linking to that on the large early, corrugated, jug shown in Plate 42; a version of pattern 3; pattern 22. All unmarked, as one would expect at this period. See Colour Plate 25. 2½ and 2¾in. (6.35 and 6.99cm) high. c.1785-8.* GODDEN COLLECTION

The low 'Robin' creamers (so named by David Holgate) may be found in slightly different sizes and with a plain handle or the typical so-called New Hall clip handle. This handle shape, having the appearance of two pieces clipped or interlinked together, will be found also on standard teapot and other New Hall shapes (Plates 113-5 and 119-123). The three hand-turned Robin creamers shown together in Plate 97 are typical examples of this early shape. They were not intended to have covers. A typical Robin creamer is seen with related shapes in *Staffordshire Porcelain* (Plate 96).

The rare object shown in Plate 98, looking similar to a miniature sauceboat, has been called a creamer. Similar vessels more commonly found in Caughley porcelain were listed in the Caughley-Chamberlain records simply as 'Gadroon boats', as the Shropshire examples have silver-like gadrooning at the base. Worcester examples also occur.[5]

As the purpose of these little boats has always been subject to doubt, I would mention that '1 pair of butter

Plate 98. *A very rare form of early New Hall cream or melted butter boat, bearing a version of enamelled pattern 3. Note the New Hall clip form handle. 4¼in. (10.8cm) long. c.1785-8.* Messrs. Phillips

Plate 99. *Two rare and early New Hall milk jugs bearing enamelled, non-gilt, patterns. Note the slight ribbed, moulded handle form. Left pattern numbered 12. Right, unrecorded early pattern, as Plates 42 and 97 left. See Colour Plate 26. 4¼in. and 5½in. (10.8 and 13.97cm) high. c.1784-8.* Godden collection

PLATE 100. *A simple early New Hall covered milk jug, decorated with tasteful gilt border design. Pattern number not recorded. 5¾in. (14.61cm) high. c.1784-8.* GODDEN COLLECTION

boats,' priced at 2s.6d., was included with a tea service in an April 1775 invoice issued by the Bristol manufactory. This document is in the Bristol Museum. Presumably 'butter boats' held melted or liquidised butter. It is of interest to note that, whilst eighteenth century English porcelain tea services included two bread and butter plates, no butter pots were included. Liquid butter could have been added at the table from the 'butter boats'.

The small sauceboat-like boat here shown in Plate 98 could have fulfilled this purpose, as could the popular Chelsea ewers (Plate 92). These were also produced at Bristol (Plate 10) and at most other English factories, but were seemingly not always part of standard tea services.

Remaining with tea service jugs, one finds (dating to the mid-1780s) various hand-turned tall traditional 'sparrow-beak' milk jugs of the general shape found in the imported Chinese export market teasets and emulated at all eighteenth century English porcelain factories. The New Hall examples, however, as shown in Plate 99, are usually rather larger than those from other factories. The moulded slightly ribbed handle form with its thumb-rest may vary slightly and these jugs are to be found with or without covers. Note the painted border on the covered example is on the exterior, so that this feature is not hidden by the cover.

As with all hand-thrown shapes, the proportions of the sparrow-beak jugs can vary slightly. The tastefully gilt covered milk jug in Plate 100 is of the same basic shape as the two shown in the previous illustration, but the gilt example is rather taller and more slender. The spout also is rather larger and more pointed. The moulded handle has slight ribbing, as on the previous two. The knob is also attractively shaped and is affixed to a typical New Hall turned plinth. The knob form will be repeated on the globular teapot and the covered sugar bowl (Plates 101-2). The pattern number for this attractive gilt design is not recorded, but it will have been an early design.

This tall elegant milk jug form is shown again in Plate 101 with a matching teapot. This has an early form of handle which was used on the Tunstall period corrugated teapot shown in Plate 21. This handle shape is perhaps unique to New Hall and can occur on various slightly different but basically globular New Hall teapots of the mid-1780s. In this case the finely painted underglaze blue and gilt design is of an unrecorded number, but a similar pattern was employed at the contemporary Caughley factory.[6] The Caughley and Worcester factories also did not employ a pattern numbering system; New Hall was not alone in this regard in the 1780s.

The simple but attractive handle seen on these large sparrow-beak jugs is also found on other New Hall porcelains of the 1780s. Note the upward and backward facing thumb-rest. It must not be assumed, however, that this basic simple handle form is restricted to New Hall; variations will occur on other makes. Nevertheless, the New Hall version can occur on well-potted bell-shaped mugs (Plate 83) and on other shapes of pedestal-footed milk or cream jugs.

Complications arise with sparrow-beak handled milk jugs when we come (in the next chapter) to discuss the blue printed designs. Some, again very rare, examples with a blue printed lion crest mark have simple loop handles without any thumb-rest or moulding, as Plate 253. Others have a slightly indented handle form. Such simple New Hall sparrow-beak jugs are rarely found with enamelled patterns. There is also a very rare bulbous shaped blue printed milk jug in the National Museum of Wales' collection. This, with the matching globular teapot and covered sugar bowl, is

PLATE 101. *A rare early New Hall teapot with underglaze-blue and gilt design (also used at the Caughley factory). The basic shape links with the early pot shown in Plate 21 and with the Duvivier painted example, Plate 64. The jug is of the same form as Plate 100. Teapot 6¼in. (15.88cm) high. c.1783-7.*

FORMERLY GODDEN COLLECTION

illustrated by David Holgate in his 1987 specialist book *New Hall* (Faber & Faber), Colour Plate G.

A rare tall footed jug with an imp's ear like handle was made to match the rare early New Hall teawares with looped moulded motifs near the base. Such a jug (of pattern 121) is illustrated in Plate 109. A now lidless teapot of the matching shape is shown in Plates 103-4 with related wares in Plates 105-6. These teaware forms are very scarce and must date to the mid- or late 1780s. The blue and gold festoon pattern associated with these moulded teawares is as yet unknown with a pattern number. A slight variation on this design is shown by A. de Saye Hutton in his *Guide to New Hall Porcelain Patterns,* Plate 319. The large bread and butter plate of this design (Plate 106) is quite deep and has a diameter of 8½in. (21.59cm). A similar 'pixie ear' handle to the cup is also found on 'Factory X' (Keeling) porcelains of the 1790s. Similar spiral moulded teawares were made at the Derby factory. The teapot handle form is also similar to some Derby and Pinxton shapes. The New Hall management seem to have been well aware of what new forms were being produced at Derby, as these high quality porcelains were market leaders.

PLATE 102. *A rare form of moulded covered sugar decorated with the blue and gilt design usually found on these rare and early teaware shapes. See also Plates 103-6. 4½in. (11.43cm) high. c.1784-8.*

RODERICK JELLICOE

Plate 103. *The very rare form of spiral-moulded teapot. The blue and gold pattern associated with this Derby style moulding is shown also in Plates 102 and 104-6. Cover missing. 4¼in. (10.8cm) high. c.1784-8.*
Roderick Jellicoe

Plate 104. *The front view of the rare New Hall teapot shown in Plate 103. c.1784-8.* Roderick Jellicoe

Plate 105. *The rare early form, Derby style moulded waste bowl matching Plates 102-6. 3½in. high. c.1784-8.* Roderick Jellicoe

This class of teaware is discussed by Roger Pomfret under the title 'New Hall – the Enigma Variation' *(Northern Ceramic Society Journal,* Vol. 16, 1999). Mr. Pomfret, a knowledgeable authority, slightly questions the attribution of this class of moulded teaware to New Hall. It is certainly unusual but I am reasonably happy that these wares are New Hall, as was originally suggested by Geoffrey Grey.

Like other ceramic shapes, the pedestal form of porcelain jug copied fashionable silver designs. A particularly rare and early (c.1785-6) example is shown in Plate 107 (left); this has the early ribbed (or slightly stepped in cross section) moulded handle with a slightly later example on its right. Both bear versions of the same floral pattern (later numbered 3 which occurs with several edgings), but here the different placing of the border shows well the contrasting effect of such small changes. The thumb-rest also has been reversed on the later example.

The early outward pointing thumb-rest can also be seen on the rare three-footed form of silver shape New Hall milk jug. An underglaze blue hand-painted example is

Plate 106. *The large deep, plate, saucer, teabowl and coffee cup matching teawares shown in Plates 102-5. Diameter of plate 8½in (21.59cm). Smaller examples of 7¾in. (19.7cm) also occur. c.1784-8. See Colour Plate 27.* GODDEN COLLECTION

Plate 107. *Two rare early New Hall creamers, both enamelled with versions of later pattern 3. Note different 'tomato ketchup' coloured borders and their placing. 3¾in. (9.53cm) high. c.1784-8.* GODDEN COLLECTION

Plate 108. *A very rare, three legged, New Hall milk jug, similar in general form to an earlier Bristol shape. Decorated with hand-painted underglaze blue Oriental design. 4¾in. (12.07cm) high. c.1784-8.*
Godden collection

Plate 109. *A rare early New Hall moulded jug, matching in form the teawares shown in Plates 102-6 but with standard enamelled pattern, later numbered 121.4in. (10.16cm) high. c.1784-8.*
Charnwood Antiques

shown in Plate 108, but again this basic shape can be found with different moulded handle shapes. In general form this three-footed jug relates to an earlier Bristol shape.

The pedestal or upturned helmet shape milk jug with the upward and inward facing thumb-rest (Plate 107, right) is also seen on the larger example painted by Fidelle Duvivier with one of his typical monochrome landscape designs – see Plate 80.

As with most shapes, once the plain version has been accepted in the marketplace slight variations can be made. The pedestal form of jug (and any other later shape) can be enhanced with fluting or reeding or with spiral fluting or wreathing. In these cases the main body will have been formed in a mould, although this was usually affixed to a hand-turned plain base or foot. One particularly rare form of New Hall pedestal helmet jug has a handle form matching the gilt coffee cup shown in Plate 111.

The pedestal or inverted helmet shape of tea service jug (a basic form by no means restricted to this Staffordshire partnership) may be found with a plain loop handle or with a rather simplified version of the clip handle. The two types are shown together in Plate 112. The two versions were probably contemporary, the choice of handle being no more than following the teapot handle.

The clip handled examples are generally associated with the globular teapots with this handle shape – see Plate 113. The typical New Hall clip handle is certainly not the earliest form of handle to have been used, nor is it entirely confined to this partnership. Rather similar handle shapes can be found, for example, on Caughley cups The simple loop handle examples are usually associated with the so-called silver shape teapots to be discussed on page 221 (see Plate 154) and with teawares having fluted or ribbed body moulding.

Like all, or most, basic forms, these jugs can occur without body moulding or with faceting or fluting, as Plate 112. They were also made in various sizes. The vast majority will not bear a pattern number, as the practice of adding the number was not in general use at this period.[7] The basic shape can also vary. The elegant elongated examples, as Plate 114, are rather rarer than the perhaps earlier squat examples. It is surprising how many New

Plate 110. *A rare early 'U' shape New Hall helmet jug, with unusual forward-pointing thumb-rest at the top of the handle. Blue enamel dentil edge to unnumbered pattern also found on earlier pieces – see Plates 39 (left) and 40. 3½in. (8.89cm) high. c.1784-8.* The Potteries Museum, Stoke

Plate 111. *A very rare form of ribbed coffee cup with an unusual handle form. Early gilt, unnumbered, pattern. 2¼in. (5.72cm) high. c.1784-8.* Private collection

Plate 112. *Two New Hall helmet shape creamers with different handle forms. Neatly enamelled with Chinese export market type patterns – later numbered 78 (left) and 67 (right). 3¾ and 3⅞in. (9.53 and 9.84cm) high. c.1785-8.* Godden collection

Plate 113. *An assembled group of New Hall teawares with typical 'clip' handles. Enamelled standard and popular pattern, later numbered 20, but not exclusive to New Hall. Teapot 6½in. (16.51cm) high. c.1785-8.*
Private collection

Plate 114. *The side view of a New Hall covered milk jug painted by Fidelle Duvivier. Note the characteristic 'clip' handle form – see also Plates 72-3 and Colour Plate 15. 5¼in. (13.34cm) high. c.1786-90.*
Godden collection

Hall cream or milk jugs of the 1785-1810 period have survived. Does each represent a complete tea service, or were some sold separately?

We can now consider some of the characteristic New Hall jugs (and the related teapots) which have the so-called clip handle. This feature can be well seen in the tall lidded milk jug in Plate 114. The 'clip' could be likened to the interlocking of two sets of half-curled fingers. This rather rare tall milk jug is decorated in Fidelle Duvivier's typical style and consequently it is likely to have been produced and decorated before the end of 1790, when Duvivier's direct employment was terminated – see page 161.

This clip style handle can also be found on some rare large size jugs and on coffee pots, as well as the more commonly found teapots (see Plates 128 and 216). It naturally also links well with the clip handled coffee cups of the late 1780s, a form so popular with Fidelle Duvivier – see Plates 74 and 79. I regard the clip handle to have been fashionable in the approximate period 1786-94. It, however, seems confined in use to plain, non-fluted or non-faceted shapes.

All the milk or cream jugs so far featured in this chapter would have been originally issued with basically globular form teapots, that is, circular in plan. The teapots and the jugs vary greatly, in size, in handle or knob form, and they can occur with various fluting or body ornamentation, although this is rare with pre-1790 examples.

Plate 115. *An early 'clip' handled milk jug, painted with the popular pattern 20, shown with a rare large size jug, perhaps for hot water. c.1786-90. 4 and 7½in. (10.16 and 19.05cm) high.* GODDEN COLLECTION

Plate 116. *An attractive ribbed creamer with simple looped handle. Underglaze blue and gilt pattern number 154. 4¾in. (12.07cm) high. c.1790-4.* PRIVATE COLLECTION

Plate 117. *A surprisingly rare simple globular form teapot, as made by most eighteenth century firms, emulating Chinese imports. Slightly ribbed moulded handle with thumb-rest. Enamelled pattern later numbered 3, also found on earlier corrugated forms, see Plate 38. This design and slight variations are not exclusive to New Hall. 6½in. (16.51cm) high. (Old repair to tip of spout.) c.1784-8.*

Godden collection

Plate 119. *A rare early New Hall globular teapot with unusual flower knob but characteristic 'clip' handle. Painted in pink with design, later numbered '12'. 5in. (112.7cm) high. c.1784-8.* Norfolk Museum Service

PLATE 118. *A large size New Hall globular teapot and cover decorated with underglaze blue borders and tasteful gilding – in the style of contemporary Worcester and Caughley porcelains. 7in. (17.78cm) high. c.1785-8.* GODDEN COLLECTION

Turning from milk or cream jugs, we progress to the teapots which were produced in various sizes to cater for the customer's demand. Plates 117-22 show a representative selection of early New Hall globular teapots bearing different early patterns. All will be unmarked and all examples are of the standard New Hall hybrid hard-paste body.

However, an earlier version might have been very similar to the standard imported Chinese export market examples with a quite simple loop handle rather than the moulded handles shown in Plates 117-8. The handle associated with early New Hall globular teapots has a backward pointing thumb-rest at the top. The handle is slightly ribbed, as the jugs shown in Plate 99. This early form is rare, but a very large example is recorded, perhaps for punch rather than tea.[8] Whilst all New Hall teapots originally were sold with a stand, very few circular stands seem to have survived with their globular pots of the 1785-90 period.

The example with a particularly early handle form (Plate 117) is of an extremely rare type. With this and a few other teapots of the approximate period 1785-87, only one or two of each type are at present recorded or known to specialist collectors. The globular teapots with open flower knobs are also extremely rare, but are certainly not unique to the New Hall factory. The small example in Plate 119 is in the Castle Museum at Norwich with a large and interesting collection of other teapots. This and many other examples included in this magnificent gathering are illustrated in Robin Emmerson's specialist book *British Teapots & Tea Drinking* (H.M.S.O., 1992).

PLATE 120. *A small size New Hall 'clip' handled globular teapot, enamelled with a version of the pattern later numbered 3. 5¾in. (14.61cm). c.1784-8.* GODDEN COLLECTION

PLATE 121. *A New Hall 'clip' handled globular teapot, enamelled (in a typically naïve manner) with the Chinese figure pattern later numbered 20. 6in. (15.24cm) high. c.1784-8.* GODDEN COLLECTION

PLATE 122. *A typical New Hall 'clip' handled globular teapot, enamelled with a simple Chinese export market style pattern. Later allocated the number 78. 6¼in. (15.88cm) high. c.1784-8.* GODDEN COLLECTION

Apart from the basic globular pots, other rather rare examples are of a barrel shape – see Plate 123. Again, different versions can occur with varying handles, spout shapes, knobs or neck formation. Most of the rare New Hall barrel-shape teapots are of a plain shape; mould ribbed versions are known. Most or all of the globular or barrel shape teapots would have had matching stands, similar to a thickly potted saucer.

Another very rare form of teapot usually having a clip handle is of the low urn or vase shape of the general type illustrated by Jewitt – see page 166. Such an example is illustrated in the 1981 catalogue to the *New Hall Porcelain Bicentenary Exhibition* (Stoke-on-Trent Museum), Plate 11, item 19. This is seemingly related to (but rather later than) the corrugated example shown in Plate 21.

Blue printed patterns tend to have been applied to some shapes that are almost unknown with enamelled New Hall patterns; such an example is shown in Plate 255. This, with its ring knob, is very close to Derby and Neale porcelain examples but the silversmiths may again have inspired the basic design.

It is extremely difficult to give advice on identifying early and unmarked New Hall teapots. Correct points to note can often be misleading. Not only were several of the more popular New Hall patterns also produced by other manufacturers, but other features such as the deep base to the cover can be found on other makes. The strainer holes inside the teapot at the base of the spout were usually pierced in the following manner:

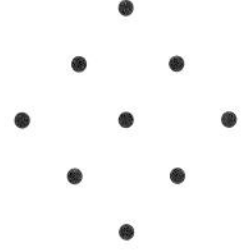

This is a helpful pointer, except that it is also standard to several other factories and is found on the contemporary globular teapots made at 'Factory X'. Yet if one does have a clip handle of the type shown in Plates 119-23, one can be almost certain that it is from the New Hall factory, the clip handle being the key feature.

The teacups issued with tea services of the 1780s and 1790s were of the handleless Chinese type – in other words they were teabowls. There are very, very few exceptions to this rule as far as the middle-class wares are concerned. The

Plate 123. *A New Hall barrel shape teapot with 'clip' handle and enamelled with the floral design numbered 140. These barrel shaped pots are quite rare. 5¾in. (14.61cm) high. c.1784-8.* Godden collection

taller coffee cups were always issued with the much more convenient handle. Of course there was nothing to stop one from using the handled coffee cup for the tea. A rare early cup handle shape has been shown in Plate 111.

The standard early form of New Hall coffee cup had a simple loop handle with a central groove (Plate 124). Taking a cross-section, it could be likened to a kidney-bean. In this respect it is similar to Caughley or Worcester handles of approximately the same period. It is the harder New Hall body and glaze which are the important features. Some Duvivier decorated coffee cups of the late 1780s, such as those in the Luton Museum (Plate 64A), have this grooved handle.

The example shown in Plate 124 bears one of several patterns of the 1780s which combine underglaze blue with overglaze gilding. This style of decoration is by no means confined to New Hall. Most of the leading late eighteenth century English porcelain manufacturers produced similar designs, notably Caughley and Flight period Worcester. In the case of the Caughley examples, some laid with the underglaze blue areas were supplied to specialist decorators or gilders to be completed. It is not known if the New Hall management did likewise, but some examples bear gilders' tally marks or numbers on the inside edge of the footrim. This is the case with the example shown, but such gilders' numbers seem to be unique to some early designs that could well have been gilt elsewhere – see also Plate 118. As a general rule New Hall gilders did not use personal tally marks.

Another form of simple elegant loop handle occurs mainly in faceted New Hall tea services of the type shown in Plate 125. Another example is shown in Plate 94, but this basic handle form is certainly not unique to this Staffordshire partnership.

The best known New Hall cup handle form is the so-called clip handle (Plates 126, 128 and 154-5) already discussed when writing of jugs. Obviously this moulded handle form occurs also on teapots, typically on those decorated by Fidelle Duvivier. This typical New Hall handle was probably in use within the approximate period 1787-95 but, as always, there would have been an overlap when two or more handle shapes were in general use.

PLATE 124. *An early New Hall coffee cup (with ribbed handle) and saucer decorated in underglaze blue and gilding. See also Plate 118. Cup 2½in. (6.35cm) high. c.1784-8.* GODDEN COLLECTION

PLATE 125. *Two cups (of differing sizes) and a saucer neatly gilt with an unnumbered pattern. In this case the set may have had handled teacups as well as handled coffee cups. For the covered milk jug see Plate 96. Cups 2¾ and 2½in. (6.99 and 6.35cm) high. c.1785-7.* FORMERLY GODDEN COLLECTION

Plate 126. *Two handled coffee cups from a New Hall tea service of pattern 167. The 'clip' handle (right) is rather more usual than the simple loop handle. 2¾in. (6.99cm) high. c.1785-90.*

Godden collection

Plate 127. *A ribbed New Hall coffee pot, enamelled with the Chinese figure pattern numbered 20. Note the relief-moulded floral ring on the spout. 9¾in. (24.77cm) high. c.1785-90.*

Private collection

PLATE 128. *A standard New Hall coffee pot form, with 'clip' handle and pierced knob. Decorated with the popular enamelled pattern 172 – much copied by contemporary competitors. The coffee cup is decorated with New Hall's pattern 186. Coffee pot 10½in. (26.67cm) high. c.1785-90.* MESSRS. SOTHEBY'S

Whilst all sets were equipped with coffee cups, early coffee pots are very rarely found. They were seemingly not part of the standard tea service, but they may have been part of the rare breakfast services or purchased for the morning meal. The coffee pot in Plate 127 may well have slightly preceded the clip handled examples (Plate 128). It is, however, possible that both forms were contemporary, the clip handled variety being reserved for the plain surfaced sets, the simple handle being applied to faceted or reeded wares. These moulded variants usually have a ring or chain of husks in slight relief around the lower part of the long spout. Others have a plain long curving spout. A particularly rare but post-1800 coffee pot is shown in Plate 329. Here the damage prone long spout has in effect been pushed back into the body to form a jug like lip.

New Hall coffee pots were sometimes issued with stands. These are rare and rather like a thickly potted flat saucer, the outline shape being related to the body of the coffee pot – faceted, ribbed or plain. They are rather like a teapot stand but with a smaller diameter. A good and rare example is shown in Plate 129. This is from a tea and coffee service with a silver shape teapot – see Plate 149.

Most of the early New Hall tea services that we have been discussing would also have been issued with small tea canisters and covers which held a supply of the dry

PLATE 129. *A shallow stand with ribbed edging and flat centre. These dishes, which are thicker in the potting than a saucer, are believed to be coffee pot stands. Others are faceted and some plain without moulding. This is certainly not a teapot stand as it was in the service with the silver shape teapot illustrated in Plate 149. Diameter 5¾in. (14.61cm). c.1790-95.* GODDEN COLLECTION

tea-leaves, so that the tea could be freshly prepared at the table. The tea canisters, or tea vases, but not please a tea caddy (which is a larger device usually made of wood), were made in several shapes. The blue printed examples and those decorated by Fidelle Duvivier were usually of a plain turned, shape. Examples painted with simple stock patterns might be faceted (Plate 130) or ribbed, to match the rest of the teaset.

All tea canisters originally had covers but these were small and were very often broken or lost. Complete canisters are rare and highly collectable. Consequently they tend to be costly! Their use seems to have been discontinued by or in the 1790s. One finds very few canisters to match in form the silver shape teapots, although David Holgate in his 1987 *New Hall* book does illustrate a rare concave shaped example, decorated with pattern 253. I do not think that tea canisters were issued with the waisted ogee oval teawares of the mid-1790s. A representative range of New Hall tea canisters is shown in Plates 81 and 130-2. A very good selection of five canister shapes was shown by Geoffrey Grey in 'New Hall, Hard-Paste Porcelain' published in the *Transactions of the English Ceramic Circle,* Vol. 8, Part 1, 1971. New Hall and other types of tea canister are featured in the 2002 exhibition catalogue *Tea, Trade and Tea Canisters* written by A. Agnew., D. Doxy and F. Marno, published by Stockspring Antiques of London – a fine study.

Another purely eighteenth century ceramic delight

PLATE 130. *A faceted New Hall tea canister with rather speckled glaze, decorated with pattern 83. Rare Bristol type mark in blue 'X'/12, perhaps added later. 4½in. (11.43cm) high. c.1785-90.* MESSRS. PHILLIPS

PLATE 131. *A neat green and gold New Hall tea canister and cover of pattern 84. These canisters have often lost their covers. 5¾in. (14.61cm) high. c.1785-90.* MESSRS. SOTHEBY'S

PLATE 132. *A ribbed and a faceted New Hall tea canister. The enamelled example of pattern 139 (left) has lost its cover. Gilt canister 5¼in. high. c.1784-87.* GODDEN COLLECTION

PLATE 133. *A very rare early form of New Hall spoontray enamelled with a simple pattern of an as yet unknown number, but see also Plates 42, 97 and 99. 6in. (15.24cm) long. c.1784-8.* PRIVATE COLLECTION

included in at least the more expensive tea services was the spoontray. As the name suggests, this was intended to hold the silver teaspoons. I show in Plate 133 a very rare, early, form of New Hall spoontray. This, like later examples, has a flat unglazed base.

The standard New Hall shape is as shown in Plate 134. The form alone is unhelpful as the Chinese imports were of this approximate shape, as were the Worcester and Caughley examples and at an earlier date the Bristol examples – see Plate 11. It is interesting to note that my early corrugated teaset of a pre-1784 period included this standard spoontray shape (Plate 26). It was the standard form. The New Hall examples are not alone in having a flat unglazed base A very rare and early form is also shown in Plates 133 and 263. Another very rare and early simple oval shape is shown in Plate 247. This can occur with enamelled designs or, as in this case, decorated in underglaze blue. All New Hall spoontrays are rare and very collectable.

All complete tea services would have been sold with a waste bowl. These were generally larger than those in use today and mirrored in surface decoration the teapot or other component parts of the set. They could have a plain, turned exterior or be faceted, ribbed or otherwise moulded. A selection of pre-1795 examples is shown in Plates 94, 105, 135, 154 and 156.

All but the most inexpensive New Hall tea services were originally equipped with a covered sugar bowl, or 'sugar box' as they were often called. Again in surface ornamentation they followed the teapot or creamer – plain, faceted, ribbed, etc. The knob form should match that on the teapot. The very cottagy, inexpensive sets might, as was the practice elsewhere, have an open bowl for the sugar, rather smaller than the waste bowl. The covered sugar bowls, circular in plan before about 1800, are quite rare as only one graced each complete service. Typical examples are shown in Plates 136, 140, 155 and 159.

I should mention (although I cannot illustrate a complete example) that some services of the mid-1780s and early 1790s were issued with Chinese-style rice-bowl type sugar bowls, that is, the cover has a circular raised rim, like an inverted saucer.[9] These are very rare, but again the form is not unique to New Hall, 'Factory X' (Anthony Keeling) being one contemporary which produced this now rare form of covered sugar bowl. The covers are often missing, as is the case with the example of pattern 119 shown with its silver shape teapot in Plate 149.

Plate 134. *A New Hall spoontray decorated with pattern number 83. Unglazed, smooth, underside but the shape is common to several factories. 5¾ x 3¾in. (14.61 x 9.53cm). c.1785-90.* P. PAGE COLLECTION

PLATE 135. *One of two bread and butter (or cake) plates and the large faceted waste bowl matching the gilt teawares shown in Plates 96 and 125. Diameter of plate 8in. (20.32cm). c.1785-90.*
FORMERLY GODDEN COLLECTION

It has been stated elsewhere that early New Hall tea services only had one bread and butter or cake plate (such plates are variously described). I believe, however, that our partnership followed the standard British fashion and their sets were sold with two plates.[10] These were in the eighteenth century of usually slightly different sizes and naturally one or both may not have been used if cake or other food was not being served. Once again the plate would mirror the style of the rest of the service, being a plain turned shape, relief moulded as Plate 106 or faceted as Plate 135. Although perhaps not the most interesting of teaware objects, they do show the pattern to advantage – see Plate 137.

It is perhaps worthy of note that none of the main teaware forms shown up to this point is featured in Major George Eyre Stringer's pioneer specialist book *New Hall Porcelains* (Art Trade Press, London, 1949). That work does not even feature the so typical New Hall clip handle which we now take to be a key feature of the 1785-95 New Hall porcelains. This fact illustrates how much our knowledge and research has increased in the post-war

Plate 136. *A typically small size New Hall covered sugar bowl bearing a simple gilt border motif. Like several early gilt designs, the pattern number is not given or recorded. 4in. (10.16cm) high. c.1784-8.*

Private collection

Plate 137. *A most attractive fluted bread and butter plate, bearing the enamelled and gilt New Hall pattern 160. Painted pattern number 'Nl60'. Diameter 7¼in. (18.42cm). c.1785-90.*

Formerly Godden collection

PLATE 138. *A New Hall ribbed so-called silver shape teapot, tilted to show the applied floret feet and the lines in the glaze as if fingers had been run over to wipe away surplus glaze. Note also the leaf-moulding on the underside of the spout. Unmarked pattern 20. Base 4¾ x 4⅛in. (12.07 x 10.48cm) – other sizes occur. c.1784-8.* GODDEN COLLECTION

years. The interesting early wares were almost unknown or unrecognised as New Hall specimens at that period.

Remaining with teawares we can now progress to the best known New Hall teapot shape of all, that usually referred to as the 'silver shape' but also designated the 'commode' shape or occasionally 'turreted'. The last description can, however, be applied to circular or oval teapots. This very popular form gives rise to many difficulties because even within the New Hall factory there were several different versions and the form proved so popular that many other manufacturers produced their close copies.

The original collectors' name, 'silver shape' (almost certainly not the description used by the manufacturers), is apt as most silversmiths within the approximate period 1785-95 were producing this shape of teapot, as were the various makers of Sheffield silver-plated pots. The vertical sides enabled such makers to produce the main body form from strips of silver, or silver-coated copper, which could be pressed into shape from dies, before other units or embellishment were added. It added to the ease of manufacture and consequently to a lowering of cost.

It must be understood that up to about 1790 the earlier types of porcelain globular teapot would still have been available for those who wished to purchase the older style. The globular teapots may also have been slightly cheaper than the rather larger new form, with its greater surface area to be painted and gilt. Still, by about 1795 the new silver shape of teapot had all but superseded other forms. The new pots were silver shape or oval in plan.

Whilst teapots were always available in different sizes, it is still a good general point that the earliest examples were of small size. These may date from c.1785.

The earliest New Hall silver shape teapots were raised on four applied flower or rosette like feet – see Plates 138, 141 and 145. While this feature may have been in use for a short period, at least four different moulds were employed in the production of these feet. The rosette feet, whilst lifting the pot slightly from its stand and following the silversmith's style, also raised the flat glazed teapot base from the base of the saggar in which they were fired. In effect they can be considered an ornamental form of Derby's pad mark or Chelsea's spur mark, yet they are only found on early New Hall teapots.

The rosette-footed New Hall teapots may be found in a surprising range of variations with different spouts, knobs, handles and body mouldings. A small range is shown in Plates 138-9 and 141-6.

The basic body form, with its vertical pillars, two each side, is shown in Plate 143. This is similar to the rather later example in the Victoria and Albert Museum which is the key inscribed 'New Hall' example (see Plate 47), the unique incised wording being 'Ralph Clewes. – New Hall fecit'. The place name 'New Hall' is clear and all important.

Having introduced this basic pillared shaped oval form, one can introduce facets (Plates 139 and 142) or ribbing (Plates 141 and 151) or later spiral fluting (Plate 152) within each type; variations of spout form, handle or knob can also occur.

Another early feature of some silver shape teapots is that the underside of the spout bears relief-moulded leafage or oak-leaf decoration. This often indistinct feature is sometimes picked out in colour, as the examples shown in Plates 141 and 143. The outlines can also be accentuated in gold.

The most usual form of knob on these moulded four-footed teapots is a rather small, pointed pine cone of leaf-moulded design. This feature is found on other items in a teaset, such as the tea canisters – see Plate 130. This solid (not pierced) knob form, but of a rather larger size, was also used on some globular shaped New Hall teapots. It is not unique to New Hall, although it rarely occurs on other makes.

It has always been considered that the earliest moulded form of silver shape teapot handle had herring-bone type moulding (to assist the grip), ending at top and bottom with a relief-moulded joint or bar as one might find with a silver or plated teapot where the wood or wicker covered handle joins the silver socket with its turned over reinforced edge.[11] These bars are sometimes picked out in gold on gilt examples (Plate 139). However, the narrow teapot shown in Plate 142 has a simple handle, devoid of the herring-bone moulding. I regard this too as an early example. The standard moulded herring-bone type handle noticeably tapers at each end. Again this mirrors the silver or plated examples where the shaped wooden or wicker covered insulated handle tapers to fit into the metal sockets affixed to the main body. The terminal where the handle joins the body at each end are usually neatly trimmed to a point, but they can be shaped in a U-like fashion. This form of moulded handle can occur on very rare low creamers following the general form of the main body of the teapot.

Plate 139 shows a rosette footed New Hall faceted silver shape teapot with its stand. The rather pointed ends to the stand match the faceted form of the pot. The body is rather wider than the probably earlier narrow example shown in Plate 142. Plate 140 illustrates the covered sugar bowl, the tea canister and the spoontray from the same service, painted (and neat gilt) with pattern 90. The main pieces always match the body moulding – faceted, ribbed etc. – of the teapot, although the spoontray is usually of this conventional shape.

The bases of the silver shape teapots usually show a surplus of glaze, often with bubbling and speckles. This surplus of glaze was seemingly semi-wiped by passing the hand across the glazed base before firing – at least that is the impression that is given by the ripples or lines that are often to be seen under these bases. This feature can be observed in Plates 138, 141 and 145. It can also occur on the rather later silver shape teapots which have a footrim rather than the moulded rosette feet – see Plate 151.

The early types of New Hall silver shape teapot often have straight tapered spouts. These were probably copied from the contemporary or slightly earlier silver or silver plated teapots. A silversmith or any metal worker can obviously produce a straight tapered unit from a pre-prepared sheet of metal far more easily than he can a shaped or curved spout. A child can do it with paper or cardboard!

I have used the description narrow, for some early footed teapots are very much narrower than others. Again I regard these narrower examples as early. Indeed, even within this rare, small group of early silver shape teapots there seems little or no conformity. It is nevertheless noteworthy that I do not know of any examples with the rosette feet that bear a pattern number.

We might at this point consider the question of pattern numbers. It has been suggested elsewhere that New Hall pioneered the use of pattern numbers. I do not consider this to be the case. The Derby factory seems to have introduced the use of pattern numbers before the New Hall factory was established. Certainly the system was in use at Derby by 1785, probably by 1780.

As yet few of the New Hall pieces I have illustrated or discussed have borne a pattern number. The earliest datable reference to their use in Staffordshire occurs in a

Plate 139. *A faceted New Hall silver shape teapot, shown with its stand. The form of stand varies according to the teapot form – see Plates 150 and 156. Floret feet. Enamelled and gilt pattern 90 – see also Plate 140. Stand 7 x 6in. (17.78 x 15.24cm). c.1785-90.* FORMERLY GODDEN COLLECTION

PLATE 140. *The faceted covered sugar bowl, tea canister and spoontray matching the teapot and stand illustrated in Plate 139. Pattern 90, but unnumbered on these pieces. Canister 5¼in. (13.34cm) high. c.1785-90.* FORMERLY GODDEN COLLECTION

Plate 141. *A ribbed New Hall silver shape teapot with floret feet. Note the moulded handle form and leafage on the spout. Enamelled pattern 121, but unnumbered. 8in. (20.32cm) long. c.1784-8.*

Formerly Godden collection

Plate 142. *A faceted New Hall silver shape teapot enamelled with pattern 121. This, perhaps early, faceted example has different spout and handle forms from the ribbed example shown in Plate 141. Four floret feet. 9in. (22.86cm) long. c.1784-8.*

Godden collection

'Hollins, Warburton & Co.' account dated November 1790. This relates to white and gold teawares of pattern 64. As the number was quoted on the invoice, the numbering system was obviously in being in 1790 and the major pieces of such a service would, for record purposes, most probably have carried that number.

The 1790 New Hall-Wedgwood invoice does not in itself prove that pattern numbers were introduced at the factory in that year. The system could have been introduced slightly earlier, but it does suggest that at least from 1790 onwards numbering was employed to coincide with pattern books. The old system of using names or descriptions had been superseded as would have been dictated by the growth of the number of patterns in production. A schoolmaster remembers the names of the scholars in his class or classes but not those of the whole school.

It has been considered that this type of small sized silver shape teapot was the product of the first period of New Hall manufacture, the date range 1781-7 being cited. I do not consider that they are as early as 1781-5, although examples do usually bear early (unnumbered) patterns, such as those later numbered 22, 78 or 121. It might be significant that the factory's leading decorator, Fidelle Duvivier, favoured globular shape teapots to paint before 1790, rather than the new fashion silver shape, if they were in general production in the 1780s.

The silver shape teapot of pattern 78 shown in Plates 144-5 has a short curved spout, differing from the perhaps earlier straight spouts. It has a reeded spout with leaf-like moulding near its base – compare Plate 143 with 144.[12] It has the early type four floret feet and pointed terminals to the handle joints. Some pots, however, have rounded ends where the handle joins the body. This is an attractive example of the type on which the factory based its commercial success.

The plain (non-fluted) silver shape teapot of pattern 122 shown in Plate 143 has an elegantly turned vase shape knob which is pierced to form the air vent. This is the first example of such a pierced knob that I have shown, yet it is widely regarded as a characteristic New Hall feature. Another perhaps slightly later example enamelled with pattern 78 is shown in Plate 144. The same form of pierced knob is also seen on the attractive globular teapot in Plate 147. This bears the same popular, inexpensive,

Plate 143. *A plain New Hall silver shape teapot, without ribbing or faceting and with pierced flask or flame-like knob. The knobs, being hand turned, can vary in proportion. Enamelled pattern 122 (not unique to New Hall). 8½in. (21.59cm) long. c.1785-90.* NEAL FRENCH COLLECTION

Plate 144. *A further New Hall silver shape teapot with pierced knob. The short, moulded spout, however, differs from others previously illustrated (see also Plate 145). Enamelled, unnumbered, pattern 78. 8½in. (21.59cm) long. c.1785-90.* GODDEN COLLECTION

Plate 145. *The underside of the pattern 78 New Hall silver shape teapot illustrated in Plate 144. The moulded Bristol style short spout form can be seen, also the floret feet and wiped appearance of the base. 8½in. (21.59cm) long. c.1785-90.* GODDEN COLLECTION

Plate 146. *A further 121 patterned New Hall silver shape teapot standing on four floret feet. The handle and spout combination differs from those shown in Plates 141-2. 8½in. (21.59cm) long. c.1784-8.*
FORMERLY GODDEN COLLECTION

enamelled pattern as the silver shape teapot pattern later numbered 121 in the New Hall pattern books. Probably several knob forms were available in china shops at the same period. There is always an overlap of shapes, several probably being available at any one time.

The New Hall globular shaped teapots have several Derby-like features which separate them from the general style of New Hall pots. There is the relief-moulded garland of leaves around the lower part of the spout, the indented foot and the overlapping lid, plus the handle form. All these features are reminiscent of popular Derby teapots of the early 1790s but some were also copied at James Neale's Church works at Hanley. In this case I believe Derby, not New Hall, introduced this shape, it being very rarely found in New Hall porcelain.

Here in Plates 146-7 we have two New Hall teapots of much the same period decorated with the same pattern (number 121). It was always a matter of choice which one was purchased. Personally I favour the globular pot. Both pour well, but the silver shape has the advantage of the enclosed front preventing spillage when an over full pot is tipped over the cup. The globular pot holds slightly more liquid, one pint seven fluid ounces against one pint four ounces. The latter is the average capacity of the early rather small New Hall silver shape teapot, mounted on their four floret feet. This same globular form also occurs adorned with underglaze blue printed designs (Plate 269).

Plate 148 illustrates yet another elegant teapot of this globular form but bearing the Chinese figure pattern later to be given the number 20. This was extremely popular and may be found on a wide range of New Hall shapes. A globular teapot with a clip handle and plain spout is shown in Plate 121. Some will worry as to which shape was the earlier. I fancy the Derby-like version with the loop handle was deemed a later improvement over the earlier clip handled version, but both may have been available at the same period. Again, variations can occur; the basic trimly turned body form can have different spout shapes, or different knob forms. All are pleasingly elegant. As to pieces of these simple enamelled patterns devoid of gilding and capable of being painted by inexpensive child labour, the Chamberlain Company at Worcester was selling similar complete teasets for less than £2 on plain (unfluted) shapes.

Plate 147. *A New Hall globular teapot with recessed foot and moulded spout in the Derby manner. Pierced knob as some silver shape pots. Enamelled unnumbered, pattern 121. See Colour Plate 31. 6½in. (16.51cm) high. c.1785-90.* GODDEN COLLECTION

PLATE 148. *A similar New Hall globular teapot, with pierced knob and moulded spout. Enamelled unnumbered pattern 20. 6½in. (16.51cm) high. c.1785-90.* GODDEN COLLECTION

Plate 149. *A ribbed New Hall silver shape teapot decorated with underglaze blue and gold, pattern 119. The handle does not have the earlier herring-bone type moulded handle. Painted pattern number 119, on teapot. 6¼in. (15.88cm) high. c.1790-5.* Private collection

Plate 150. *A New Hall silver shape teapot stand, the outline (for a ribbed teapot) differing from the faceted example shown in Plate 139. Others had a simpler outline matching non-moulded pots. Pattern 83. 7½ x 6in. (19.05 x 15.24cm). c.1785-90.* Godden collection

PLATE 151. *A ribbed silver shape teapot reversed to show later base with conventional footrim (not floret feet) and typical wiping away of the surplus glaze. Underglaze blue and gilt pattern 154. Base 5⅝ x 4⅝in. (14.22 x 11.68cm). c.1787-92.* S.A. PEMROSE

PLATE 152. *A spiral fluted silver shape New Hall teapot. Note the main pillars remain vertical and do not follow the fluting. Gilt pattern 198. 6¼in. (15.88cm) high. c.1787-92.* PRIVATE COLLECTION

PLATE 153. *A faceted New Hall silver shape teapot of pattern 89 shown with its matching faceted milk jug. Teapot 6in. (15.24cm) high. c.1787-92.* T. KIRKBY

Moving on from the early silver shape teapots, those which usually had the four moulded rosette feet, we come to rather larger pots nesting on a normal footrim. Of course at all periods different size teapots were made but from c.1790 the size was, in general, increased. Other earlier features, such as the moulded herring-bone grip on the handle, were retained for a period, as was the solid pine cone like knob, on reeded or faceted teapots – see Plates 149 and 151-3. However, the ends of the later handles tend to be curved like a 'U' (Plates 151-2), not trimmed to a 'V'. The handle also tends to be less tapered at the top and bottom. Pattern numbers can now appear added under the base.

With the larger silver shape teapots variations in spout form and the placing and form of the spout can also occur. The main body can be moulded into ribbing or other ornamentation. Also with this larger silver shape teapot of the 1790s we have the introduction of spiral fluting. This form of moulded decoration, of course, occurs on other makes of porcelain and it was especially favoured at the Flight factory at Worcester and also at Derby. With the New Hall spiral fluted teapots the two main pillars in the basic form remain vertical (see Plate 152). They do not follow the curved fluting as they do on some other makes.

I used to use the old term 'shankered' or 'shanked' for this popular spiral fluting or 'ogee curved fluted', to use

Plate 154. *A standard form of New Hall teapot, with pierced knob to the cover. Shown with matching teawares of pattern 142, a design not unique to New Hall. Teapot marked 'N.142'. 6¼in. (15.88cm) high c.1787-92.*
FORMERLY GODDEN COLLECTION

David Holgate's technical description. I have now discontinued the use of 'shanked' as it could have been used to describe the concave or waisted form sometimes associated with the spiral fluted forms.

The surface moulded ornamentation, as well as the added pattern, was naturally repeated on all the component parts of the service. Plates 153-6 show a few groups illustrating the various milk jugs (all rather tall) and other units that were made to match the silver shape teapots and their stands.

Plate 155. *A group of New Hall teawares decorated with a neatly rendered underglaze blue and gold design (number unknown). Teapot 6¼in. (15.88cm) high. c.1787-92.* MESSRS. SOTHEBY'S, NEW YORK

PLATE 156. *An attractive group of pattern 160 tea and coffee wares, of ribbed form. The coffee pot is rare and was seemingly not part of the services when sold, unless ordered as a separate item. See Colour Plate 33 for this pattern. Teapot 6¼in. (15.88cm) high. c.1787-92.* MESSRS. PHILLIPS, KNOWLE

PLATE 157. *The New Hall silver shape teapot from a service painted with views in Kent, copied from a 1793 book. See also Plate 158 and Colour Plate 32. 6¼in. (15.88cm) high. c.1793-6.* GODDEN COLLECTION

PLATE 158. *A detail of the elaborate gilding embellishing the spout of the teapot shown in Plate 157. The spouts on the finer quality New Hall teapots are often decorated in an ornate manner with gilt designs.*

All forms of added decoration occur ranging from blue printed designs and simple formal floral patterns that could be painted by young apprentices to sumptuous designs with intricate gilding. Such complete services might have ranged from under £2 to over £10, the style and quality of the decoration accounting for the difference in price.

As will always be the case, the cheaper sets sold in larger quantities than the more expensive and so today we find far more of the simple floral patterns, without gilding. These patterns, still in the 1790s and later, reflected the popularity of the imported Chinese porcelain teawares which were decorated in a similar style.

As stated, the very richly decorated tea services are rarely found as so few were sold. Some of the finest were possibly made to special order. This would almost certainly have been the case with the dated 1796 tea service here represented by the silver shape teapot in Plate 85. Pieces from this service have been known for many years. A teabowl and saucer in the Victoria & Albert Museum formerly lived in the Pinxton display case! The decoration of sheep in a landscape has the appearance and quality of Fidelle Duvivier's hand although the date on the pot is six years after he wrote that his engagement at New Hall had expired. This teaset (with other examples) suggests that he may have been available locally to undertake special orders. Apart from its charm, it is valuable in giving a date for this middle period of New Hall's silver shape teapot. It is also noteworthy that, although the commission would have been an expensive one, the teacups were still in the form of handleless teabowls.

Another superbly decorated New Hall tea service of the 1790s is painted in great detail with views in Kent. These views have obviously been copied down to the smallest detail and placing of the figures from Samuel Ireland's 1793 book *Picturesque Views on the River Medway.* The complete service was sold at auction in the early 1970s and was purchased by a then leading London dealer. It was then divided to please a number of collectors, few or none of whom at that period could afford the complete service.[13] The teapot is now on loan to The Potteries Museum at Hanley and shown in Colour Plate 32 and Plates 157-8. This may not have been the only teaset or other article decorated with scenes taken from this 1793 book with its engraved views in Kent, but it could have been a special order, perhaps placed by a retailer in Kent or by a wealthy resident in that county. The teapot obviously cannot predate the publication of this 1793 source book. None of the pieces bears a pattern number.

By this period, in the mid-1790s the New Hall silver shape teapot had settled down into a standard form and is usually only found in one size, the base measuring 5¾ x 4¾in. (14.61 x 12.07cm). However, at least one almost toy size example is known.

The covered sugar bowls, or 'sugar boxes' as they were then called, do not follow the shaped body form of the teapot. They are almost always of circular form, as were earlier examples. They were, however, usually linked to the teapot by having the same form of vase or flame-like knob – see Plate 159 for a typical example. This was solid, not pierced as were the teapot knobs; no air vent was needed for a sugar box. The various creamer shapes are discussed separately.

At this point I should remind readers that the extended (in period) original Cookworthy patent ran out in 1796. The New Hall partners no longer held any special rights over the use of Cornish china stone and china clays in a translucent body. Also, the bulk import of Chinese porcelain by the East India Company was coming to a halt. Several new English porcelain manufacturers were

Plate 159. *A simple New Hall covered sugar bowl with unpierced, teapot type knob. Blue sprigs with gilt leafage. Painted pattern number 'N.213'. 5¼in. (13.34cm) high. c.1790-5.* J.M. Standing

Plate 160. *A very rare form of New Hall silver shape teapot with unusual handle and spout, enamelled pattern 353. Painted pattern number 'No. 353', 5¾in. high. c.1800-5.* Private collection

Plate 161. *A standard, late, form of New Hall silver shape teapot, enamelled with Chinese export market design, number 354. Dated 1803. 6in. (15.24cm) high. 1803.*

Victoria & Albert Museum. Crown Copyright

established at this 1796-1800 period. Competition for the New Hall Company was increasing.

I have shown standard teapots, datable to 1793 or later, one being dated 1796. A similar pot inscribed 'Thomas and Betty Hanson' is dated 1798. These and some later dated examples made in the early 1800s show several salient differences from the earlier pots which may be dated about 1790-2, being what I term the middle period silver shape pots.

The earlier herring-bone moulded handle has now been replaced by a simple plain handle, devoid even of a thumb-rest. The affixing points end in a curved 'U' fashion. The knob form is almost always the pierced vase shape. Most silver shape teapots are now of the plain form, without additional fluting, reeding or spiral fluting. The junction of the sides with the base and the flat top have grown more pronounced, the upper junction reinforcement being entirely missing on the earlier four rosette footed examples.

The spout has settled down to a gentle curved elongated 'S' shape, formed from eight facets, the two side faces being parallel. It has been noted by others that the New Hall spouts on silver shape teapots have in profile a strong curve on the underside and a gentle curve at the top. However, this applies to almost all curved and tapered teapot spouts. It must not be taken as a sure sign of a New Hall origin. The later c.1798-1804 New Hall teapots are noticeably thicker in the potting and are consequently heavier than the earlier examples. This is again an observation that applies to other types.

Importantly, these middle and later period pots can bear pattern numbers. In fact those decorated with standard, popular, patterns nearly always bear the relevant pattern number painted under the base.

By the mid-1790s the, shall we say, standard New Hall silver shape teapot was being emulated by many other manufacturers, certainly by the partnership's several rivals in the Staffordshire Potteries. Versions were also made at Lowestoft and by Chamberlains at Worcester and probably by the later manufacturers in Liverpool. The earthenware potters also sought to undersell the porcelain makers, so that earthenware or black basalt examples may be found.

Many of the contemporary porcelain examples often bear close or even exact copies of New Hall patterns. The reader is also warned that some of the previously noted New Hall features may be found on teapots made by other manufacturers and that some of the silver shaped teapots illustrated in the older pre-Holgate (!) books are

PLATE 162. *An enamelled New Hall late silver shape teapot, seemingly of pattern 660, with black trim. Inscribed around the top 'Ester Rivett. Greendon. Northamptonshire 1804'. 6¼in. (15/88cm) high. 1804. See Colour Plate 35.* GODDEN COLLECTION

PLATE 163. *A globular New Hall teapot with pierced knob. The reverse painted with the popular and inexpensive pattern 195. The front adapted to take inscription and date 1798. Painted pattern number 'N 195'. See Colour Plate 34. 5¾in. (14.61cm) high. 1798.* GODDEN COLLECTION

not necessarily now considered to be from this Staffordshire factory.

If one is not very familiar with the New Hall body and glaze and the various tell-tale pointers then the added pattern is the most reliable guide, provided that the pot also bears the correct New Hall pattern number. In this way the teapot, with its unorthodox handle and spout shape shown in Plate 160, can be identified as a very rare New Hall version because it bears the correct, if rather high, pattern number '353'.

The standard New Hall silver shape teapot in Plate 162 is inscribed around the neck 'Ester Rivett. Greendon. Northamptonshire 1804'. It is the latest dated New Hall silver shape teapot known to me. It does not bear a pattern number, perhaps because it was a special one-off order, but the enamelled design is that recorded as 660. Popular as the silver shape teapot undoubtedly was at New Hall and other middle market manufactories (but not seemingly at Flights of Worcester, or at Derby, Pinxton, Spodes or Mintons), it was not the only basic form being made by our Staffordshire partnership in the mid- or late 1790s.

The neatly turned globular teapot[14] with the thumb-rest to the handle, as shown in Colour Plate 34 and Plate 163, bears a contemporary inscription with the names Jonathan and Betty Wood, and date 1798. It bears, where the inscription permits, the popular New Hall pattern 195 and the base bears the correct painted number. This pattern was produced by more than ten English porcelain manufacturers but each had its own individual pattern number for this one Chinese export market design – see page 129 and Plate 48.

To underline the point that New Hall or any other factory was producing a choice of different basic forms at one time, this same '195' pattern is applied to a New Hall silver shape teapot which also bears the date 1798. Such a silver shape example is illustrated by George Stringer in Plate XXVI of *New Hall Porcelain*. Another inscribed and dated 1798 example of the same popular pattern is illustrated by Robin Emmerson in his *British Teapots and Tea Drinking*.

I have at this point taken my chronological survey of New Hall teapots up to about 1800 or to 1804 in the case of one very late silver shape example. All these teapot shapes have been circular or have the shaped outline associated with the silver shape teapots.

We can now consider the oval plan teapots or at least the first of these. They are often called 'Ogee-oval' teapots but David Holgate described the basic shape well: 'an oval base and a waisted profile on which is superimposed curved fluting'. This New Hall teapot form is illustrated in Plates 164 and 166-9. The basic form is by no means unique to our Staffordshire factory and not all examples are fluted.

I think that it was in production at the same period as the later New Hall silver shape teapots, examples of which bear dates up to 1804. I do not know of dated examples of the New Hall waisted ogee shape but I do have a very similar Chamberlain-Worcester example which bears the date '1796'.[15] Bat-printed designs do not appear on this shape but the spiral fluted examples would not lend themselves to this form of post-1803 decoration, which is discussed in Chapter IX. I regard the New Hall ogee moulded teapots, which can be plain, faceted, ribbed or spiral fluted, to span the approximate period 1797-1803. The specialist teapot books will include a selection of similar shapes made at rival contemporary factories.

The waisted oval teapot shown in Plate 170 is a very rare form – the only one known to me – but it bears a popular pattern and the correct pattern number '171'. The handle and knob form are, however, very unusual for New Hall. Other matching teaware forms may well occur.

Some of my group photographs are helpful in that they show the form of the other component units found with the ogee teapots. The pattern numbers, of course, can have been introduced before the teawares were conceived. It is just a matter of a popular still saleable pattern being applied to a new fashion shape. It is, however, of interest to note the latest or highest number found on a given shape. This could give an approximate indication of the point when that shape was replaced by the next, or the point where the pattern numbers had reached, but extreme caution is required! In the case of the waisted ogee teawares, the latest New Hall number I have noted is 425.

I now come to discuss the milk (?) jugs which accompanied the silver shape teapots. Just as we encountered several variations in the teapots, so we also have complications with the jugs. The earlier small silver shape teapots with their four moulded rosette feet were normally accompanied by rather large inverted helmet shape jugs of the type illustrated in Plate 173. These may have been produced up to about 1789 or 1790.

About that time the teapots and the other items were embellished with spiral fluting. This necessitated a new jug form. The first version is believed to be the rare type shown in Plate 174, left. It is circular in plan and not an altogether pleasing shape. A strange feature of this example is that the spiral moulding changes direction at the front and back joints of the mould. The spiral direction is not

PLATE 164. *Representative pieces from a spiral fluted 'ogee' New Hall gilt tea service, with oval teapot and (handleless) sugar box forms. Pattern number 198. Teapot 7½in. (19.05cm) high. c.1797-1803.*
GODDEN OF WORTHING LTD

PLATE 165. *A neatly potted and attractive ribbed trio of saucer, teabowl and coffee cup. Pattern number 148 but not written on these pieces. Diameter of saucer 5½in. (13.97cm). c.1797-1803.* W. RIDGWAY

PLATE 166. *An oval 'ogee' teapot, cover and stand of pattern 233. Shown with a trio and pillared (silver form) jug. Pattern number on teapot and stand. 6¾in. (17.15cm) high. c.1797-1803.* GODDEN OF WORTHING

PLATE 167. *New Hall 'ogee' shape, spiral fluted, teapot, sugar box (with ring handles) and jug. Gilt pattern 270 (on creamer). Teapot 7½in. (19.05cm) high. c.1797-1803.* GODDEN OF WORTHING

Plate 168. *An unfluted 'ogee' shape oval teapot with matching shapes including pillared jug and coffee can, rather than the earlier shaped sided cup. Blue printed enamelled and gilt pattern 274, often termed 'Tobacco leaf' or 'Tobacco' pattern, after a Chinese original. Variations occur within different numbers. Teapot 7in. (17.78cm) high. c.1797-1803.* Godden of Worthing

PLATE 169. *A plain (not relief-moulded) part tea and coffee set of 'ogee' shape. Decorated with black and gold pattern 280. Pattern number on larger pieces. Teapot 10½in. (26.67cm) long. c.1797-1803.* MESSRS. SOTHEBY'S

PLATE 170. *A very rare oval New Hall teapot with an unusual moulded handle and knob shape. The enamelled pattern is the popular '171' design, as found on several makes. 9½in. (24.13cm) long. c.1797-1803.* GODDEN COLLECTION

Plate 171. *An unfinished New Hall spiral fluted 'ogee' shape covered sugar bowl. The design is laid only with the underglaze blue parts The pattern would be completed with gilding, as Plate 172. Pattern number not known. 5¾in. (14.61cm) high. c.1797-1803.* Private collection

Plate 172. *An oval 'ogee' shape New Hall covered sugar bowl. Underglaze blue border completed and enhanced by the gilder. Unrecorded variation on pattern 153, with additional blue and gold sprays. 5¾in. (14.61cm) high. c.1797-1803.* H. Wilson

Plate 173. *A faceted New Hall creamer (see Plate 153) of pattern 89 and a larger plain jug, marked '81'. 4¼ and 5in. (10.8 and 12.7cm) high. c.1797-1803.* Godden collection

Plate 174. *Two spiral fluted New Hall creamers. The fluting on the rare form shown on the left (pattern 180) runs in opposite directions on each side. The standard shape on the right (pattern 241) runs continuously in the same direction. 5 and 5¼in. (12.7 and 13.34cm) high. c.1797-1803.* Godden Collection

constant as it is on later jugs. The covered sugar bowl is also circular.

This scarce shape was soon replaced by one of oval plan, standing rather taller and with the spiral fluting stopping at what we could call the bust-line, below the neck – see Plate 174, right.

This shape can be found with quite low pattern numbers, showing only that some early patterns were still finding a market. I do not think this shape of New Hall milk jug was in production before 1800. These views differ from those expressed elsewhere and in general my dating of New Hall shapes tends to be rather later than those suggested by other authorities. The earlier circular plan jug and the improved oval version are shown together in Plate 174.

Just as not all the silver shape teapots were enhanced with spiral fluting (more usually found examples were reeded or faceted), so the matching jugs were issued with plain or faceted bodies. I show in Plate 175 a standard shape New Hall so-called 'obconical' jug. The basic shape can be likened to an inverted ice-cream cone. A jug of this form accompanied the teaset painted with panels of views in Kent, copied from a 1793 book. Do note that a dated source only indicates the earliest possible period of a copy.

This shape proved exceedingly popular and was probably produced for five or more years.[16] The size of these moulded jugs can vary slightly but most stand some 4½in. (11.43cm) high. They were also widely copied by rival firms who produced slight variations of handle form or of foot shape. Fortunately most New Hall examples will bear a pattern number, usually of a popular, recorded number. The New Hall origin can therefore be checked. Note that the New Hall obconical creamers have a simple loop handle, without a thumb-rest.

It would seem that when, in the 1790s, the new form waisted oval teapots were introduced, the obconical creamers also served these teasets. This was certainly the case with the early spiral fluted services similar to that of pattern 198, shown in Plate 164.

However, other oval waisted teapots without the spiral fluting were accompanied by jugs that seem better suited to the silver shape teapots in that they have two vertical pillars moulded as part of the body. Typical examples are shown in Plates 166-9.

Plate 175. *A standard shape so-called 'obconical' milk jug. The basic shape can occur with facets, ribs or spiral fluting. Pattern number 195. 4½in. (11.43cm) high. c.1800.* Godden collection

The spiral fluted examples, however, do not usually show these silver like pillars (which are such a feature of contemporary silver teapots) – see Plate 167. A rather rare convex fluted or ribbed creamer of this shape (without pillars) is shown in Plate 176. This bears pattern 449 and would be an example of the early 1800s.

The covered sugar bowls issued with the ogee-waisted teapots were oval in form, and in body moulding matched the teapots. Some rare, perhaps early examples did not have moulded ring-handles, although mock handles may be painted. The example shown in Plate 167 has gilt mock handles. As always, however, some services seem to have a non-standard mix of shapes.

Most oval New Hall ring handles were made separately and applied without thought to the curvature of the body, hence they stand slightly away from the body – see Plates 169 and 171-2. Other makes of similar sugar boxes tend to have moulded handles flush with the surface.

As the ogee waisted oval teawares were popular over a longish period from the late 1790s, perhaps into the early 1800s, different shape cups can occur. The teacups were usually handless teabowls – even on patterns 148 and 233 (Plates 165-6) – but some Bute shape handled cups are found. The coffee cup is of an ogee waisted form (Plates 145 and 167). Some coffee cups are almost straight sided with a plain loop handle – such an example is illustrated in Plate 166. The dated 1796 sheep pattern silver shape teapot (Plate 85) had coffee cups of this shape – see Plate 86. These gave way to the straight-sided coffee can (Plate 168).

New Hall teawares of the 1800 period include shapes which were later called 'Old Oval' at the Spode factory. This term is now widely accepted and relates to oval form teapots, covered sugar boxes and creamers with straight sides. These basic shapes were popular at several factories including Coalport, Masons, Minton and Spode, to name only the best known manufacturers. New Hall examples are here shown in Plates 177-8. The simple (not indented) handle form is noteworthy on New Hall examples. Early New Hall bat-printed designs of about 1803-4 first occur on the 'Old Oval' teawares (see Chapter IX) showing a continuation of its popularity into the early nineteenth century.

These 'Old Oval' teapots are rarely fluted but such a rare example is shown in Plate 179. The teasets of this form are

Plate 176. *A rather rare form of New Hall tea service jug, loosely based on a silver shape. Painted pattern number 449. 4¼in. (10.8cm) high. c.1800-5.* Private collection

Plate 177. *A part New Hall tea service decorated in underglaze blue and gold. Note the 'Old Oval' shaped teapot and covered sugar box and the Bute shape cup with loop handles. Painted pattern number 540. Teapot 6½in. (16.51cm) high. c.1800-5.* Sotheby's Sussex

mostly well decorated with added gilt decoration. The teacups will usually be handled, of the standard 'Bute' shape, as seen in Plate 177.[17] The coffee cups tend to be the straight-sided fashionable and perhaps French inspired can shape. See Plates 177-8. Coffee pots do not lend themselves to the oval straight-sided new forms so when these accompany such teasets they are of the former circular plan. They are of the shape that was issued with the silver shape teapot – see Plate 178. These shaped teapots were still available at the time when the oval waisted teapots were also available in the early 1800s.

The rather rare oval teapots with a slightly curved body and oval ball-like knob seemingly also date from about 1800. Plate 180 illustrates a typical example with the matching oval sugar box and jug in Plate 181. This smart design is number 472. This basic shape can also occur with surface moulding as shown in Plates 182-3. The part teaset, being of a rather sparse pattern, still has the old handle-less teabowl, although it has the more up-market coffee can replacing the earlier shaped cup.

The so-called 'New Oval' teapot which was also so popular at Spodes, Masons, Mintons and other factories, was also produced for a limited period at New Hall – see Plate 184. The name is taken from Spode's shape book and by its name obviously follows the straight-sided 'Old Oval' forms of c.1800-5, although, as always, there was probably an overlapping period when both shapes were being made. Plate 184 shows a New Hall New Oval

Plate 178. *Representative pieces from an 'Old Oval' shaped teaset decorated with a fanciful Chinese style landscape incorporating underglaze blue. The coffee pot was not part of standard forty-five piece teasets. Painted pattern number 570. Coffee pot 10in. (25.4cm) high. c.1800-5.* Messrs. Christie's

Plate 179. *A rare version of the 'Old Oval' New Hall teapot, with additional moulded indentations. Painted pattern number 839. 6¼in. (15.88cm) high. c.1800-5.* Brighton Museum & Art Gallery

PLATE 180. *A rare slightly rounded version of the usually straight sided 'Old Oval' New Hall teapot. Pattern number 472. 6$\frac{3}{4}$in. (17.15cm) high. c.1805.* PRIVATE COLLECTION

PLATE 181. *The oval covered sugar box and cream jug to the pattern 472 teapot shown in Plate 180. The ring handles stand slightly proud of the body. Painted pattern number 472. Creamer 4$\frac{1}{2}$in. (11.43cm) high. c.1805.* PRIVATE COLLECTION

Plate 182. *Representative pieces of a spiral fluted teaset, the basic shapes relating to those shown in Plates 180-1. Unrecorded (unmarked) pattern number. Coffee pot (not fluted) 10in. (25.4cm) high. c.1805.* Henry Spencer & Sons

Plate 183. *A spiral fluted covered sugar box of the shape shown in Plate 182. Gilt pattern 568 with red enamel fern motifs. Painted pattern number with painter's tally mark. 5in. (12.7cm) high. c.1805.* Private collection

Plate 184. *A New Hall 'New Oval' teapot with stand. This basic shape was produced by most English porcelain manufacturers. Painted pattern number 478. 10¾in. (27.31cm) long. c.1805-10.* Private collection

Plate 185. *A 'New Oval' type teapot but with high 'prow' at the front. This was a very popular shape. Blue and gilt pattern. Painted pattern number '638'. 10½in. (26.67cm) long. c.1810.* Godden of Worthing Ltd.

teapot of pattern 478. The same shape can also be found with bat-printed landscape designs of about 1805.

Another post-1800 teapot shape found only in the pre-1813 hybrid hard-paste porcelain has a rather rounded oval body with a high prow at the front end of the top section. These were called 'parapet' teapots, the Wedgwood shape book for c.1815 showing, for example, 'New Parapet', 'Old Parapet' and 'low parapet oval' shapes. The examples shown in Plates 185 and 187-9 are typical. The covered sugar bowls are oval or canoe shape with a loop handle at each end, as illustrated in Plates 187 and 189-90. Again I must emphasise that similar forms were produced

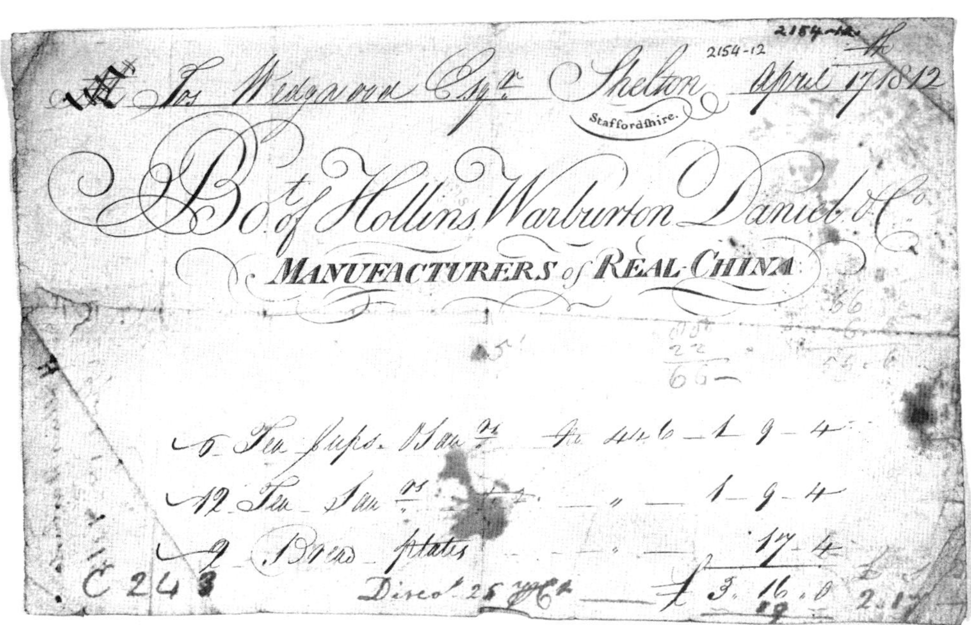

Jos Wedgwood Esqr. Shelton April 17 1812

Staffordshire.

Bot. of Hollins Warburton Daniel & Co.

MANUFACTURERS of REAL CHINA

6 Tea Cups ... No 446 1 9 4

12 Tea Saucers ... 1 9 4

9 Bread plates 17 4

Direct 25 ... £3 16 0

C 243

PLATE 186. *A New Hall (Hollins, Warburton, Daniel & Co.) account for teawares of pattern 446 dated April 1812. See Plate 187.*
UNIVERSITY LIBRARY, KEELE (JOSIAH WEDGWOOD & SONS' ARCHIVES)

PLATE 187. *Representative pieces from a New Hall tea service of pattern 446 (as ordered by Wedgwood in 1812). Note the cup and coffee can handles are of the number 9 shape, not the earlier simple loop handle as shown in Colour Plate 36. This pattern can occur with slightly different gilt trim or (see Colour Plate 36) with platinum (silver-like) trim rather than gold. Teapot 10½in. (26.67cm) long. c.1810-15.* MESSRS. PHILLIPS

at most English porcelain factories in about the 1805-12 period.

Plate 187 illustrates a part teaset decorated with pattern 446. This links with the New Hall invoice to Wedgwoods, dated 17 April 1812 (Plate 186). The cup and saucers, at £2.18s.8d. a dozen, link with the complete tea services priced at £8.5s.9d. This is slightly above the average price – see the price list reproduced on page 141. A slight variation of this design has the gilding replaced with silver, or rather platinum. These lustred designs do not carry a pattern number.

The jugs with New Oval type teapots, as shown in

PLATE 188. *Representative pieces from a New Hall tea service of pattern 484. The handleless sugar box is of a slightly unusual form and the cup handles are earlier than the number 9 type shown in Plate 187. Teapot 10½in. (26.67cm) long. c.1810-5.* MESSRS. SOTHEBY'S

Plates 187 and 189, follow the general body form of the teapot, although some are of a larger size and are deeper. These usually have a loop handle. Rather rarer examples have a forward pointing thumb-rest at the top.

This shape of teapot and other teawares are sometimes decorated in silver lustre or, more correctly, platinum lustre.[18] These lustred patterns do not seem to bear a pattern number and they may have been decorated outside the New Hall factory. There were in the Staffordshire Potteries several specialist decorators or lusterers. A good platinum lustre New Hall teapot is illustrated in Plate 191.

Bat-printed designs, which I believe were first used by the New Hall partnership from about 1803, occur on this shape of prow teapot and on the related teaware forms – see Chapter IX and Plates 320-2 and 325. The gold printed designs produced under 'Warburton's Patent' of 1810 were usually applied to this shape. New Hall's pattern 446 (as Plate 187) occurs on these prow shaped teawares. This design was invoiced to Wedgwood in April 1812.

New Hall's pattern 484, as shown in Plate 188, occurs on very rare teaware forms. An oval covered sugar box is shown by Mr. Ratheram in his contribution to the *Northern Ceramic Society's Newsletter* number 119 of September 2000, page 31. A bat-printed teapot, perhaps matching this form, is shown in Plate 1344 of *An Anthology of British Teapots.*

A very rare variation on the standard early nineteenth century prow teapot has a fleur-de-lis shape knob (Plate 192). The sugar box was also redesigned with upturned ends but no added handles to the body. The covers bear the fleur-de-lis knob form (Plate 193).

These rare tea service forms usually bear patterns in the mid-400s. The prow-shaped teapot and the matching units rarely have spiral fluting, but most examples have a

Plate 189. *A good quality New Hall tea service with underglaze blue bands, enhanced with intricate gilding and with flower painted panels. Painted pattern number 571. See Colour Plate 38. Teapot 10½in. (26.67cm) long. c.1810-5.*

Godden of Worthing Ltd.

Plate 190. *A graceful, standard shape New Hall covered sugar box decorated in red and gold with a hitherto unrecorded pattern. Painted pattern number 917. 7¼in. (18.42cm) long. c.1810-5.*

Private collection

Plate 191. *A New Hall prow shape teapot decorated with an unnumbered design, incorporating platinum lustre with red and blue enamel. 5¼in. (13.34cm) high. c.1810-5.* Private collection

Plate 192. *A rare prow shape New Hall teapot with fleur-de-lis type knob, decorated in black enamel with pattern 461. Painted pattern number. 5¾in. (14.61cm) high. c.1810-5.* Private collection

PLATE 193. *Rare New Hall teawares hand painted in green monochrome with landscapes. Similar views are more usually bat printed, as pattern numbers 462, 466, 511 or 709. Gilt borders. No pattern number. Teapot 10in. (25.4cm) long. c.1805-10.* GODDEN OF WORTHING LTD

smooth surface to receive the various patterns. These shapes more often occur with a conventional knob form, as Plates 321 and 322.

I originally included the teaware shapes shown in Plates 359-61 at the very end of the hybrid hard-paste period, linking the forms to the post-1812 bone china period. I have moved these forms to the bone china chapter, as all the examples I have seen have been of that period – see page 365. As you will learn from Chapter X, I believe that the bone china body was being produced by the New Hall management by at least December 1812. This dating has given rise to perhaps slightly confusing descriptions, such as 'in the pre-1813 hybrid hard-paste period' and also 'in the post-1812 bone china period'. The changeover took place in 1812 but old stocks of hybrid hard-paste blanks would have been still available and would have been decorated and sold for a short period.

BREAKFAST SERVICES

Apart from standard tea services of the well-known types and make-up, the New Hall partnership also made breakfast services. These were mainly made in the later bone china period but some were certainly produced in the hybrid hard-paste period, c.1795-1812.

Breakfast services or components were made in relatively small quantities, consequently breakfast articles

PLATE 194. *A rare New Hall spiral fluted posset-pot type double-handled bowl. An unfluted example is recorded complete with cover. Pattern number 353. 3½in. (8.89cm) high c.1790-800.*

MRS. A. DE SAYE HUTTON

are rare. The cups and saucers are usually of a larger size than the standard teacups. Large bowls can also occur, as can milk jugs of half-pint or pint size. Individual plates were made for breakfast services but were not included in tea services.

The real joys from the collector's point of view, however, are the other breakfast articles which include honey-pots, jam or preserve pots, muffin dishes with covers, eggcups, eggcup stands and butter pots. New Hall breakfast sets also included oval (slightly lobed edged) dishes of the type more usually associated with meat platters in dinner services. The early nineteenth century breakfast would often have included cold meats or similar food requiring such large dishes (in at least three different sizes) and, of course, the individual plates. As a general rule the New Hall breakfast sets were not decorated with the most expensive fancy patterns but are more likely to bear the simple bat-printed patterns including a range of landscape designs.

It is convenient to fit in at this point the spiral-fluted bowl of pattern 353 shown in Plate 194. David Holgate illustrates (as his Plate 83) a plain example without fluting but with its cover. He called this vessel a posset-pot – a very rare article in New Hall porcelain. The entwined twig handles with leafage terminals also occur on rare covered (chocolate?) cups – see Plate 232.

DESSERT SERVICES

We have up to this point been concerned with tea or breakfast wares, but the New Hall partnership also produced some unusual dessert wares. Indeed, Richard Champion at his Bristol hard-paste factory produced high quality and very decorative services for the all-important dessert course and it would have been surprising if his successors in Staffordshire had not attempted to emulate his success in this high class market, to rival Worcester or Derby dessert services.

Llewellynn Jewitt in his 1864 *Art Journal* article, 'New Hall China', stated that the factory produced 'tea, dinner, and dessert services of various designs'. I do not know of any New Hall dinner services which would have been expensive and probably consequently outside the factory's basic market level.

Importantly, however, Jewitt in that pioneer article did include a line engraving (taken from his previous drawing) of a single dessert dish (see page 168) from a scenic painted dessert service made, he stated, 'for Mr

Daniel, one of the partners, and purchased at the sale of his effects, now many years ago, by its present owner'. On his 1863 visit to 'The Potteries' Jewitt had evidently visited the owner (Mr Gray) and had seen the complete service. He noted 'Each piece bears a landscape, beautifully and softly painted, by Duvivier'.

I have previously discussed Fidelle Duvivier, the artist and his work and illustrated in the previous chapter some of the remaining pieces from what I believe was the service seen by Jewitt in 1863 and commented upon by him in the *Art Journal* article. It is now, however, time to discuss the service itself for this highly important set, or the major part of it, re-surfaced early in 1998. Quite apart from the landscape views painted by Duvivier, some of which I believe show Staffordshire real life scenes known to the artist and to John Daniel, the New Hall manager and partner for whom it was made, this set is highly important as it is the only known New Hall dessert service to have been preserved in a near complete state. It therefore shows us a good range of New Hall dessert ware forms of a quite early period. I judge it to have been produced in the short period when Duvivier was employed as a factory artist (c.1787-90) as the style links well with the majority of his landscape painted teawares featured in the previous chapter.

This service, when sold in April 1998, comprised:

A footed, oval shaped edged centrepiece (Plate 66)
Four shell-shaped dishes (Plate 196)
Pair long shaped edged dishes (Plates 197-8)
Pair long kidney shaped dishes (Plate 67 and 207)
One star or hexagonal shaped dish (Plate 65)
Two covered tureens[19] (as Plate 199)
One tureen stand (Plate 200)
Twelve plates (as Plate 201)

It is quite possible, indeed probable, that other units were originally made to complete the set. The centrepiece could have had a stand. As we have four shell-shaped side dishes (see Plate 195), the other shapes could well have

PLATE 195. *Part of the New Hall dessert service painted by Fidelle Duvivier for, it is believed, John Daniel, the factory manager. See also Plates 65-7, 196-201 and 207. Diameter of plates 8¼in. (20.96cm). c.1785-90.* FINAN, WATKINS & CO.

Plate 196. *One of four handled side dishes from the Duvivier decorated dessert service shown in Plate 195. See Colour Plate 41. 8¾ x 8½in. (22.23 x 21.59cm). c.1785-90.* Private collection

been issued in sets of four. The two tureens (for sugar and cream) are of different sizes,[20] looking rather odd together on the table. The set might have been issued with a pair of each size. Each would have had a stand with pierced edge. Only one (damaged) stand has survived. The tureens would almost certainly have been equipped with porcelain ladles with shaped, moulded handles.

This or other early New Hall dessert services may also have been issued with pierced edged fruit baskets. These rare pieces have twig and leaf moulded handles and moulded feet. They may occur in different sizes. Known examples bear typical Fidelle Duvivier landscapes and relate to the late 1780s – see Plate 202.

It is noteworthy that the New Hall dessert shapes do not closely copy fashionable Worcester or Derby forms. They were novel, except for the Sèvres like shell shape dish (Plate 196). Even these are superior to other examples of this internationally fashionable shape. They are deeper than most, with a neatly designed moulded handle. This design includes attractive scrolls unique, I believe, to New Hall. The wings to the handles are not symmetrical, one side being more curved than the other.

Plate 197. *One of the lobed oval side dishes (of slightly different sizes, see Plate 198) from the Duvivier decorated dessert service shown in Plate 195. 11¼ x 8½in. (28.58 x 21.59cm). c.1785-90.*
Private collection

Plate 198. *A lobed edged oval side dish from the Duvivier decorated dessert service shown in Plate 195. A similar shape dish is illustrated in Plate 197. See Colour Plate 42. 11½ x 8½in. (29.21 x 21.59cm). c.1785-90.* Private collection

Plate 199. *The smaller size tureen and cover from the Duvivier decorated New Hall dessert service shown in Plate 195 and Colour Plate 39, also Frontispiece. 6¼in. (15.88cm) high. c.1785-90.* Private collection

Plate 200. *The openwork edged lobed stand to the larger New Hall tureen shown in Plate 195. Old damage to edge. See Colour Plate 40. 9¼ x 7¾in. c.1785-90.*

PRIVATE COLLECTION

Plate 201. *One of the twelve Duvivier decorated plates from the New Hall dessert service shown in Plate 195. See Colour Plate 44. Diameter 8¼in. (20.96cm). c.1785-90.*

PRIVATE COLLECTION

Plate 202. *A fine openwork edged footed dessert entrée dish painted by Fidelle Duvivier in the same manner as the service shown in Plate 195. See Colour Plate 45. 4in. (10.16cm) high. c.1785-90.*
Private collection

These dishes in particular show well the very high quality of the New Hall porcelain body and glaze at this period. Any porcelain factory, English or Continental, would have been proud of this service. On the evidence of the quality of potting, the New Hall partnership could even have produced elegant wine or fruit coolers to grace their most expensive dessert services. Richard Champion had earlier produced such large pieces in his hard-paste Bristol porcelain.

All the shapes included in this service are extremely rare. Few such New Hall dessert services were apparently made. No forms matching this set have been featured in previous books on New Hall, apart from the characteristic moulded plates. Obviously, as twelve or more plates would have been issued with each service, such items outnumber any other New Hall dessert shapes that may occur.

It was, I believe, the illustration of such a dessert plate that led to the correct identification of the service just discussed, which had previously been described by an auctioneer as Continental. This plate, which I featured in my *Staffordshire Porcelain* (as Plate 110) and in the *Encylopaedia of British Porcelain Manufacturers* (Plate 298) and is again included in this book (Plate 68) illustrates the point that other dessert services were painted by Fidelle Duvivier with children and animals posed in front of typical Duvivier background scenery including his kilns and windmills. A superb dessert centre dish painted with birds in landscape within an elaborate green and gilt border is in the Nottingham Museum – perhaps another Duvivier decorated service.

With regard to these early New Hall dessert plates, it is not the twenty-four lobed edge which is the key feature – plates with a similar edge form were standard at the Caughley factory and at Worcester – but it is the way that the convex ribs are mirrored on the underside (as if the pieces were slip-cast) and the clear edging to the ribbing which leaves the centre of the plate flat and suitable to receive the decoration. The slip-cast appearance of the reverse side also applies to the moulding on the side dishes and the centrepiece.

Plate 203. *A New Hall dessert dish similar to those shown in Plates 197-8 but rather larger in size. Decorated with simple edge design and small sprays of fruit. 12 x 8¾in. (30.48 x 22.23cm). c.1788-92.*
Private collection

Whilst the sets painted by Duvivier during his short period at New Hall represent the highest level of its ceramic painting, other dessert services were made to sell at lower prices. Some sets were seemingly made painted rather naïvely with a mock Oriental scene in underglaze blue. Such sets would not have been gilt and might have competed in price with contemporary Caughley porcelain services or even with earthenware dessert sets. At the moment I only know of plates and a shaped edged dish from one such set and it is a matter of doubt if the full range of dessert shapes would have been used for relatively inexpensive blue painted services. Probably the openwork bordered tureens and stands would not have been included. A plate is illustrated in Chapter VII, Plate 295.

Other New Hall dessert services with plates of this shape must have been made but at the moment I only know of sets with two styles of overglaze enamel decoration. Representative pieces were illustrated by David Holgate in his paper 'New Hall – some interesting nuances' *(Transactions of the English Ceramic Circle,* Vol. 14, Part 2, 1991). One pattern matches pieces which have passed through my hands. Examples are here shown in Plates 203-4 and 206. The decoration is of good quality but is unlike any found on New Hall teawares of the 1780s. The border design is, however, of the same general style as that found on the key Duvivier scenic service. The New Hall factory also produced dessert services decorated with gilt designs rather like contemporary Caughley examples. These in general restrained style are rather like the early teawares illustrated in Plate 46. These gilt dessert wares are very rare. Gilders' numbers can occur on the inside of the footrim.

David Holgate also illustrated in his 1991 E.C.C. paper two pieces from a dessert service painted with a rather small size floral spray, within a floral border. I show in Plate 205 the star shape or six-sided shaped edged dish. This seems to match in form that from the Duvivier-Daniel scenic service, which is that originally engraved for Jewitt's 1864 *Art Journal* article – see page 168. The floral spray, however, does not seem to match conventional New Hall teawares.

Several years ago I had some covered dessert service tureens of similar shape to those found in the Duvivier-Daniel scenic service but the decoration was again unconventional and did not indicate a New Hall origin – at that time. These oval footed covered tureens were made in various sizes. Some examples have bunches of grapes moulded in porcelain and applied to the twig and leaf finial – rare and superb pieces. Such examples with the tureen and stand to match the dish shown in Plate 205 are illustrated by Miss Gaye Blake Roberts in her paper 'Wirksworth – The Elusive Manufactory', in 'Recent Research on Ceramics of Derbyshire' published by the *Derby Porcelain International Society Journal* II, 1991. Although the New Hall edge moulding is similar to Wirksworth factory wasters they do not exactly match and there can be no doubt that the Duvivier decorated dessert service is New Hall and post-dates the Wirksworth period (c.1772-77) by several years, the New Hall dessert porcelains under discussion being of the approximate period 1785-90.

I have tried not to further complicate the discussion of New Hall porcelains by introducing the several contemporary types which are very close in form or decoration to the New Hall examples, but in regard to the early dessert wares I should illustrate a near match kidney shape dish – compare Plate 206 with Plate 207. The fruit painted example (similar in decoration to Plates 203-4) is of a rather softer body and glaze than the more rounded shape used in the Duvivier-Daniel scenic painted set and is not as well decorated.

This non-New Hall example does link with some well-potted deep fluted shell shape dishes. The manufacturer appears to have produced earthenware as well as porcelain as a blue printed kidney shape dish of this form is in the Alton Museum in Hampshire. This (or a similar dish) is shown in Renard Broughton's paper on 'Early Chinoiserie Printed Pottery' published in *Newsletter* no. 100 of The Northern Ceramic Society (December 1995). The print is a version of that known to pottery collectors as 'Conversation' with an unusual floral border. The pearlware printed pieces may help us to identify the maker of the porcelain examples, but in the meantime the point is that at least one other manufacturer of the 1780s or early 1790s was producing dessert services similar to the earliest known New Hall shapes. The probable or possible maker of this porcelain dessert dish was Anthony Keeling. If this is the case it was made at the Tunstall factory where the original partners set up their first manufactory to produce Richard Champion's patented porcelains – see Chapter II.

Returning to true New Hall dessert services, several

Plate 204. *A New Hall dessert plate of the same form as the Duvivier decorated examples shown in Plates 195 and 201. The decoration matches the dish illustrated in Plate 203. Diameter 8¾in. (22.23cm). c.1788-92.* Private collection

Plate 205. *A floral painted dessert dish of an unusual form but matching in shape one in the Duvivier decorated service (see Plate 65 and page 168). Diameter 10in. (25.4cm). c.1788-92.* Roger Pomfret

PLATE 206. *A non-New Hall dessert dish similar in form to the New Hall Duvivier decorated example shown in Plate 207. The body and glaze is softer than the New Hall examples. 10¾ x 8in. (27.31 x 20.32cm). c.1790-5.* PRIVATE COLLECTION

PLATE 207. *A New Hall dessert dish from the Duvivier decorated service shown in Plate 195. The shape differs from the non-New Hall example shown in Plate 206. See also Plate 67 and Colour Plate 43. 9¾ x 7¼in. (24.7 x 18.42cm). c.1785-90.* PRIVATE COLLECTION

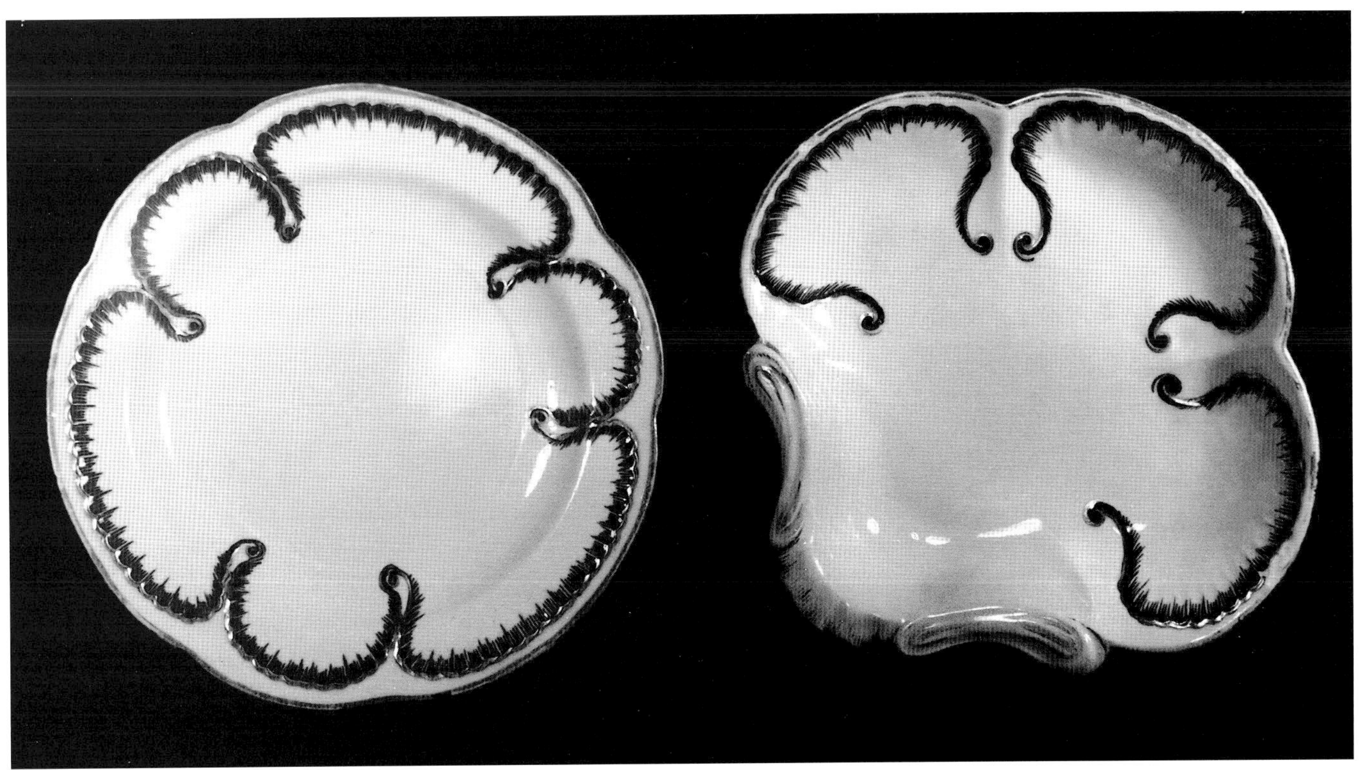

Plate 208. *Two shell-moulded New Hall dessert dishes and a plate, decorated in underglaze blue, with gilding. Diameter of plate 8¼in. (20.96cm). c.1790-5.* PRIVATE COLLECTION

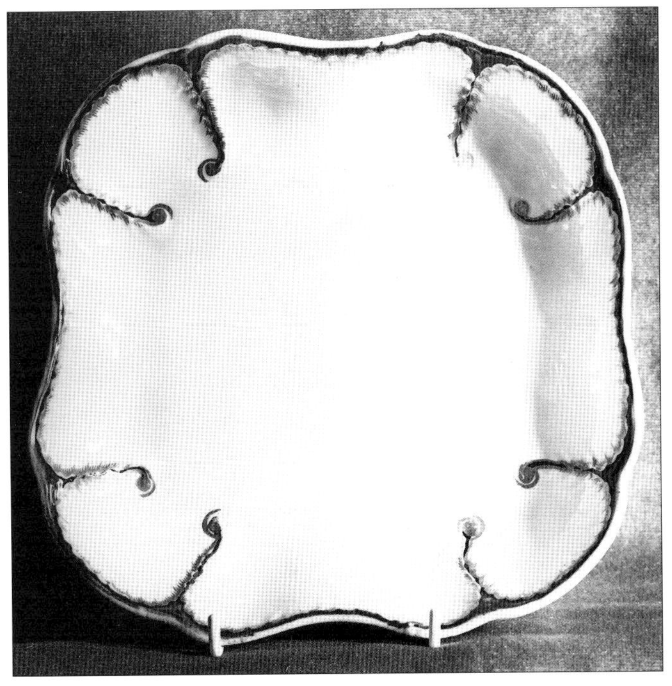

examples from perhaps just two services are known and have been illustrated by David Holgate.[21] Two further shaped dessert service dishes are shown in Plate 208 with a plate with its characteristic shell like moulding picked out in blue with gilt high-lights. This design was probably influenced by popular Sèvres shapes. The handled, again Sèvres shape, dish illustrated by David Holgate has a different handle moulding from that found on the Duvivier-Daniel service (Plate 196).

At least one dessert service of this moulded type has survived. David Holgate kindly showed me snaps of the main shapes but unfortunately the standard does not permit me to reproduce the forms. The set, as recorded some years ago, comprised:

- A footed centrepiece with basketwork edge and twig handles. Similar in general form to the Duvivier example shown in Plate 202.
- A basketwork edged stand, 10¼in. (26.04cm) long, perhaps for the centre dish. This is similar to the Duvivier decorated example, Plate 200.
- Oval tureens with a twig handle at each end (the covers were missing).
- Shell shape side dishes as Plate 208, above right.
- Square dishes, as Plate 208, left.
- Oval dishes, outline shape as Plate 209 but without the flower painting.
- Lobed-edged plates, as Plate 208, above left.

In addition this Sèvres style New Hall pattern is found on the lobed edged dish shown in Plate 297. David Holgate

Plate 209. *One of a pair of finely decorated New Hall moulded oval dishes matching in shape a blue and gilt example, as Plate 208. 11¼in. (28.58cm) long. c.1785-95.* Private collection

was able to illustrate two attractively moulded ladles from this service, one pierced (for sugar) and one with a solid bowl (for the cream). Other such sets must have been made as the shapes are moulded and expense was incurred in tooling-up to produce such dessert services.

Some years ago a splendid pair of oval dishes was sold at Christie's South Kensington galleries. These had a deep blue edge and moulding as the Sèvres style set just discussed, but were well painted with a central spray of flowers and with four small groups of flowers around the edge. These dishes were so good looking and unusual that they were not catalogued as New Hall. I show one of them in Plate 209. Other similar examples must await discovery; indeed, complete services must have been produced. A dessert plate of this moulded shape has been reported completely overdecorated with the Chinese figure subject design New Hall's pattern number 621.[22]

The tastefully restrained, slightly gilt, fluted plate shown in Plate 210 is I believe a New Hall example of about 1790-5. I also believe that it is from a dessert service but I am unable at present to show any other matching dessert service forms that would confirm my belief. However, very, very few New Hall dessert services of this period are known to collectors. All examples are unmarked and do not at this period bear even a pattern number. I cannot cite any examples of New Hall dessert wares of the 1795-1810 period, although some must have been produced in the hybrid hard-paste body within this period.

At a later period the New Hall partnership produced a wide range of decorative bone china dessert services. Many of these early nineteenth century examples have relief-moulded borders (Plates 354-8, 407-18). Many printed designs were adapted to fit dessert services so that tea and dessert wares could match each other. Pattern numbers also tend to appear on the nineteenth century New Hall dessert services.

Post 1812 New Hall sets produced in the revised bone china body can also bear the standard printed 'New Hall' circular printed name mark. These later wares are featured in subsequent chapters.

I have in this chapter on pre-1813 New Hall hybrid hard-paste porcelain concentrated on the tea and coffee utensils and on the much rarer dessert wares. These obviously form the bulk of the partnership's production but there are other articles that were produced because they filled a commercial need.

There are a few rarely found articles which seem to be restricted to blue and white decoration. The New Hall factory made some knife and fork handles of conventional

Plate 210. *A fluted New Hall dessert dish or deep plate decorated with simple gilt design. Diameter 8½in. (21.59cm), depth 1¾in. (4.45cm). c.1790-5.* Private collection

form; also asparagus servers, those wedge shape small trays with upright sides – see Plate 257. Such articles were produced by several porcelain manufacturers. They also occur in various makes of earthenware but, like the knife handles, they could not have shown much profit margin. They are discussed with the underglaze blue designs in the following chapter.

Other rare objects found with underglaze blue printed decoration include small leaf-shape dishes (Plate 248), a standard line with several factories. Small cups, like custard cups (Plate 265), are rarely found at an early period. All these items are quite small and, as far as the collector is concerned, small is beautiful, or at least desirable.

Other rare New Hall treasures include flasks, in form rather like two saucers affixed rim to rim with the footrims trimmed away, a neck of varying length being added at the top. These are known decorated with underglaze blue prints or with overglaze coloured designs.[23] That shown in Plate 211 is particularly rare, being perhaps a one-off design. Others can be of standard designs, such as pattern 984.

David Holgate also illustrates a very rare pair of casters or sifters decorated with the tasteful pattern 206, which includes gilding. This is the only pair known to me and illustrates well the rarities that may await the observant or lucky collector. They may have been intended for a breakfast service, when eggs or other food were

Plate 211. *A very rare New Hall porcelain flask. Blue printed examples also occur. 3¾in. (9.53cm). c.1795-1800.*
Private collection

Plate 212. *A typical New Hall moulded jug of a popular type. These were made in various sizes – see Plate 235 and Colour Plate 46. 8¾in. (22.23cm) high. c.1784-8.*
Godden collection

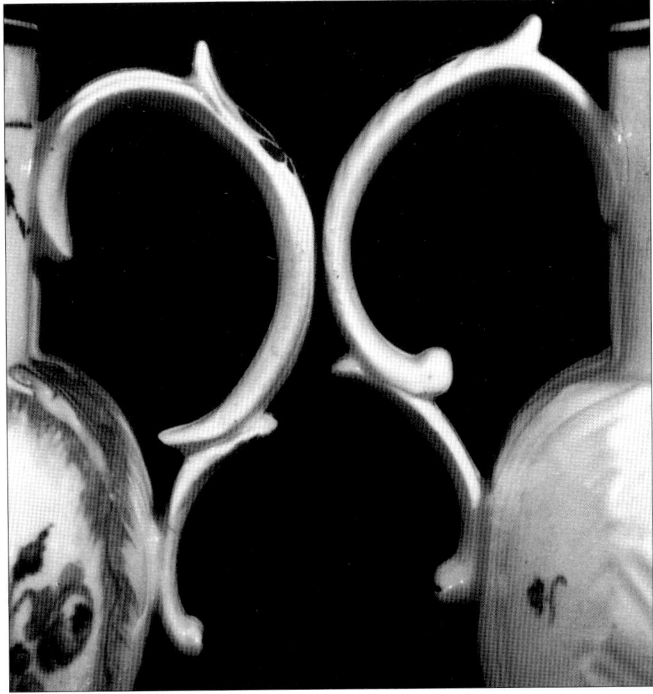

Plate 213. *Detail (right) of the moulded handle on the New Hall jug illustrated in Plate 212. Compare with the handle on the earlier jug shown in Plate 43.*

consumed, or perhaps served as muffineers to sprinkle cinnamon on hot buttered muffins, rather than for use at the tea table, although they bear a tea service pattern and its number in gold. Moulded and so rare spoons and ladles are other delights awaiting the blessed!

Large objects such as jugs are very much more obtainable. These are interesting examples as they were often especially decorated and inscribed, as gifts. Names or more often initials (or monograms) occur, but very seldom dates. The personal aspect of such jugs has meant that they tend to be preserved even when damaged, rather than be disregarded as might be a broken asparagus server.

The earliest type of New Hall jug probably dates back to the Tunstall period. I have shown such an early example in Plate 43. In general form these follow the earlier, almost standard cabbage-leaf jug as made at most eighteenth century English factories. However, the New Hall examples of the 1780s have a leaf-moulded spout which replaces the mask-head spout common to Caughley, Liverpool, Worcester and other manufacturers.

The example of this cabbage-leaf type shown in Plate 212 is, I believe, slightly later than that illustrated in Plate 43 and is of the true New Hall period. The body shape is slightly more bulbous than the Tunstall example and is rather thicker in the potting.[24] The handle form is also different, the earlier ribbing having been replaced by herring-bone type moulding giving the palm of the hand a good grip. This feature is, you will remember, also found with the early type of silver shape teapot. These rare jugs were made in several sizes, one as small as 5½in. (13.97cm) in height. They are excessively rare.

This type of slip-cast cabbage-leaf jug was made probably from the early to mid-1780s into at least the early 1790s, as is shown by the dated 1793 example shown in Plate 214. It should be noted that other factories produced close copies of this New Hall jug form.

All the New Hall enamelled cabbage-leaf jugs known to me are decorated with sprays of flowers.[25] The relief-moulded body does not really lend itself to complicated forms of decoration such as figure or landscape subjects,

Plate 214. *The front view of a New Hall leaf-moulded jug (Plate 215), inscribed and dated 1793. See also Plate 215. 6⅞in. (17.46cm) high. 1793.* The Potteries Museum, Hanley

Plate 215. *The side view of the inscribed and dated New Hall cabbage-leaf jug of the type shown in Plate 214. 6⅞in. (17.46cm) high. 1793.* The Potteries Museum, Hanley

Plate 216. *Two New Hall large jugs with characteristic clip handles. Left example enamelled with pattern later numbered 20. See Colour Plate 47 and Plate 217. The covered hot water (?) jug bears gilt pattern 52. 7¾ and 9½in. (19.69 and 24.13cm) high. c.1790-5.* Sotheby's New York

although at least one blue printed example is known – see Plates 235-6. We therefore find that other smooth surfaced jugs were produced. These also have the advantage that they can be hand thrown on the potter's wheel. No moulds have to be made or dried after each use, there are no seams to be 'fettled' or trimmed. The intricate handles, however, have to be moulded and applied to the turned object.

A rare and attractive plain (not leaf-moulded) jug with the moulded handle and leaf spout as found on the leaf-moulded examples (Plate 212) was sold by Messrs. Phillips in December 2001. I show it as Colour Plate 48. This example neatly painted in the Duvivier manner with panels of landscapes obviously preceded the clip handled ones shown in Plates 219-26.

Another elegant (spiral fluted) jug has been reported by Mr. Terry Ratheram.[26] This, having a spiral-fluted body, lacks the leaf-moulding seen on the more usual types illustrated in Plates 212-5 but has the leaf-moulded spout and tall form associated with those forms. It, however, has the clip type handle associated with the lower jugs shown in Plates 219-26. It can be considered to be a transitional shape, linking the two basic jug forms in the illustrations just cited.

Plate 217. *The front view of the large New Hall clip handled jug shown in Plate 216. Enamelled early pattern later numbered 20. 7¾ in. (19.69cm) high. c.1790-5.* Godden collection

Plate 218. *A rare form of New Hall large size jug, enamelled with a continuous scene. Gilt trim. 7¾ in. (19.69cm) high. c.1795.*
PRIVATE COLLECTION

Plate 219. *A fine New Hall jug of typical form, but tall with characteristic moulded handle shape. These jugs were made in various sizes and were decorated in many styles – see Plates 220-6. 8in. (20.32cm) high. c.1790-1800.*
MESSRS. SOTHEBY'S

Plate 220. *A good New Hall squat jug with clip handle. Personalised with initials. See Colour Plate 49. 7½in. (19.05cm) high. c.1795-1800.*
PRIVATE COLLECTION

Some rare jugs take the form of enlarged milk jugs or spoutless coffee pots. These may have been produced as extra components for tea, being used for hot water or for coffee. Plate 42 shows a very rare early (Tunstall period?) corrugated surfaced example, painted with floral sprays. A later form is illustrated in Plates 216-7. The naïvely rendered Chinese figure design became New Hall's pattern 20. The clip handle repeats that found on New Hall globular teawares of the mid- to late 1780s. The fluting at the base of the moulded spout and the bead at its base are noteworthy New Hall features seen also on earlier corrugated examples, as Plate 31. The gilt jug, of pattern 52, has a cover but that is not to say that all such jugs were originally covered. David Holgate illustrated this example with a conventional coffee pot (his *New Hall* Plate 29) illustrating that the body and handle form were identical, only the spout or lip being different. He terms this a hot water jug but it could have held hot milk, coffee or even chocolate, being much more hygienic than the long-spouted conventional coffee pot.

The neatly potted attractive jug shown in Colour Plate 48 is excessively rare. It is perhaps a transitional shape – as the spout is moulded – and in this respect with the handle form links with the larger cabbage-leaf jugs shown in

Plate 221. *A typical New Hall clip handled jug decorated with the printed based enamelled over Chinese style window pattern, number 425. 7¾in. (19.69cm) high. c.1800.* Godden of Worthing Ltd.

Plate 222. *A typical New Hall clip handled jug decorated with the printed based enamelled over Chinese style design, number 621. Gilt initials under the spout. 7½in. (19.05cm) high. c.1800.* Godden of Worthing Ltd.

Plates 43 and 212-5. This new version is difficult to date, especially if one were to attribute the painted panels to Duvivier, but it is perhaps 1790-5.

The tall purposeful-looking New Hall jug form shown in Plate 218 is also rare and difficult to date. The simple handle form is unusual and was replaced on the same body form by a standard New Hall clip handle. Such a clip handled example is in the Usher Gallery at the Lincoln Museum. That example is illustrated in David Holgate's 1987 book *New Hall* as his Plate 114. The main painted decoration of two horsemen in a landscape is attributed to Fidelle Duvivier, again complicating the dating of the Lincoln jug if this artist ceased to decorate for the partnership in 1790. We can now progress from these very rare jug shapes to one which was to become the standard form over several years.

By far the most popular shape of large New Hall jug of individual type was the hand-thrown bulbous body form represented by my Plates 219-26. The main characteristic is the three unit handle with the simplified clip joint at the highest point. These were, I think, produced over a longish period in the hybrid hard-paste body. Dated examples have proved very scarce but I would think most examples were produced between about 1790 and 1810.

Plate 223. *The side view of an initialled New Hall clip handled jug. The border design is New Hall's pattern 436, in this case also enamelled with a typical flower group. See Colour Plate 50. 7½in. (19.05cm) high. c.1795-1800.* Godden of Worthing

Plate 224. *A good and typical New Hall floral painted presentation jug, with characteristic handle form. 7½in. (19.05cm) high. c.1800-10.* J.A. Ward

Plate 225. *A very richly decorated New Hall presentation jug with gilt initial and superb flower painting. See Colour Plate 52. 7½in. (19.05cm) high. c.1800-10.* Private collection

A relative few bear standard numbered factory designs; most have rather expensive, special, overglaze decoration. I do not know of any with underglaze blue decoration. Being hand thrown, the general profile of the jug can vary, as can the depth of the collar. The example in Plate 219, perhaps an early piece, is taller than the more standard form in Plates 221-6. The size and capacity also vary. Most examples measure about 7½in. (19.05cm) high and hold two and a half pints of liquid. The smaller examples, standing about 6in. (15.24cm) high are much rarer.

The dating of this jug form is difficult. They are usually considered to be post-1800 but the initialled example now in the Potteries Museum at Hanley (Plate 62) could well have been painted by Fidelle Duvivier, as was claimed by Llewellynn Jewitt in 1864 – see page 168. This would suggest a date in the 1790s, if not the late 1780s. Another example in the Potteries Museum (illustrated by David Holgate as his original Plate 16) also appears to have been decorated by Duvivier. This example, like that shown in Plate 219, has leaf moulding on the spout. This may suggest an early version of this jug shape. A clip handled jug in the Usher Gallery at Lincoln is certainly decorated by Duvivier, but the body does not have a turned foot. It is perhaps an early version of this later popular shape.[27]

The two examples bearing standard printed outline Oriental figure designs shown in Plates 221-2 are of New Hall patterns 425 and 621. The border design of the initialled example illustrated in Plate 223 relates to teaware pattern 436. These may be considered to be early nineteenth century patterns, rather than earlier designs.

Most examples are well painted with flowers by a competent artist whose hand is also observed on New Hall teawares. The border designs vary widely, as does the surround to the monogram of initials. The gilding is also of a very high standard.

The floral sprays on these jugs very often include a kidney bean like petal as part of one of the roses or other flowers. Once seen – as I have arrowed in Plate 226 – one's eye is drawn to this personal characteristic of one New Hall painter. These jugs are handsome objects, typical of the high grade New Hall productions which span the approximate period 1790-1812. The latest example I have noted of this standard shape in the hybrid hard-paste body is dated 1812 and bears a rare overglaze printed subject and some platinum lustre trim.

A very unusual jug shape is shown in Plate 227. It is, of

course, unmarked but in body and glaze it appears to be New Hall and serves to show that other non-conventional shapes may occur. The squat jug form shown in Plate 228 is surprisingly rare in New Hall porcelain but the general shape and handle form is quite commonly found in earthenwares. This New Hall example is inscribed in gold and is dated 1811. It is a late example of the partnership's hybrid hard-paste body, soon to be superseded by bone china – see Chapter X.

Mugs are always rarer than jugs and certainly this is the case with New Hall examples. The barrel shaped mugs with corrugated sides, as shown in Plate 19, are of the earliest Tunstall period, made prior to 1785. Some cylindrical examples, which are usually of small size, bear leaf-moulding to match the large cabbage-leaf jugs. The handles on early examples are of an intricate early form. I show a neatly gilt initialled example in Plate 44. Others bear early pre-1787 enamelled patterns, usually floral sprays. An example enamelled with the floral sprig pattern later numbered 139 is illustrated by David Holgate as Plate 77 in his *New Hall*. These moulded mugs were made in at least two different sizes and at least two handle forms were employed.

An even rarer New Hall mug shape is shown in Plate 229. This is a really beautiful small object, neatly turned to a graceful shape and tastefully painted with trim gilding. It bears a gilt monogram so it was a presentation piece, made for some lucky owner. The simple handle form is duplicated in some milk jugs of the mid- to late 1780s.

Simple cylindrical mugs with a loop handle (without a thumb-rest) were obviously favoured by the partnership's leading ceramic artist, Fidelle Duvivier. I show in Plates 55-61 examples decorated by this artist. If they were painted within Duvivier's known period working at the New Hall manufactory, they should pre-date November 1790. They may, however, have been decorated by the artist as personal work at a slightly later date, as they can bear Duvivier's signature; in general eighteenth century ceramic artists were not permitted to sign their factory work – see Chapter V. This same shape of mug can also bear underglaze blue decoration and such examples would appear to date to about 1785-6. Like most ceramic forms, these cylindrical mugs were made in different sizes. Being New Hall they are unmarked! It could be considered that the New Hall mugs so well decorated by Duvivier were made for show rather than for everyday use. However, some bear drinking-related scenes. Perhaps the answer is that they were high class expensive presentation pieces.

Plate 226. *A rather squat but typical New Hall initialled presentation jug. The kidney-bean shape flower (arrowed) is noteworthy. 6¼in. (15.88cm) high. c.1800-10.* W.S. Hills

Plate 227. *An extremely rare jug form which on the appearance of the body and glaze appears to be New Hall but it is unrecorded with a conventional, identifiable factory pattern. 6¾in. (17.15cm) high. c.1800-5.* Private collection

PLATE 228. *A rare New Hall inscribed and dated ale or beer jug. The handle form is more usually found on earthenware jugs and is not unique to New Hall. 5¼in. (13.34cm) high. Dated 1811.*
GODDEN COLLECTION

PLATE 229. *A very rare and attractive New Hall mug, neatly painted with flower sprays (perhaps by Fidelle Duvivier). Gilt initial to front. 3½in. (8.89cm) high. c.1785-90.*
GODDEN COLLECTION

PLATE 230. *A good New Hall cylindrical mug with neatly painted design. Various sizes of this shape occur. 5¼in. (13.34cm) high. c.1790-1800.*
J.S. SULLIVAN

A great rarity, I think, of the late 1780s is the simply turned, initialled, tumbler or handleless mug shown in Plate 84.

Another rare class of New Hall mug is cylindrical with a simple flattened handle and a backward facing thumb-rest. A rare enamelled specimen is shown in Plate 230. This shape also occurs with underglaze blue printed designs of the mid-1780s. A similar handle is found on rather wider, squat mugs having a concave lip. This feature[28] is not unique to New Hall but most examples will span 1800 by a few years. The example illustrated in Plate 231 bears the boy in the window printed outline design, New Hall's pattern 425.

The New Hall partnership produced a few upmarket covered cups with rather deep, sometimes recessed, stands. These were made in at least two different sizes and also occur in a spiral fluted form. These two handled covered cups are often termed chocolate cups but their use was not necessarily restricted to this popular beverage. Plate 232 shows a very well potted example, alas without its stand. The twisted handles and leaf terminals[29] may have been inspired by fashionable Continental examples, although the basic shape was also emulated by other English porcelain manufacturers, from the 1790s. This rare New Hall example decorated with pattern 213 would not shame any factory! It is probably of the early 1800s. One example has been reported with silver (platinum) lustre decoration. Covered cups with ring handles seem to have been confined to the post-1812 bone china period.

Before closing this review of the New Hall hybrid hard-paste porcelains produced up to about 1812, we could look outside the factory boundaries and take a brief overall glance at the industry.

The greatest difficulty facing the New Hall management seems to have been taken in its stride. I refer to the loss of its patent rights to produce porcelain using Cornish raw materials, under William Cookworthy's original 1768 patent. This patent, assigned to Richard Champion, was extended (with limitations) to run until 1796. After that the process was open to all. It seems clear, however, that several factories in or outside Staffordshire had been producing similar types of hybrid hard-paste porcelain before 1796. This may have been under licence from the New Hall partnership or perhaps the recipes were so amended that they were deemed not to conflict with the patent.

I do not wish to complicate the story but, by the late 1790s, the following firms were amongst those producing porcelains which may be considered to have been in commercial competition with the New Hall products:

Plate 231. *A wide, low, version of the standard shape mug shown in Plate 230 but with indented lip not unique to New Hall. Printed and enamelled-over pattern 425. 5in. (12.7cm) high. c.1795-1805.*

Private Collection

Plate 232. *A very rare double-handled chocolate or caudle cup and saucer (missing its stand). Decorated with blue enamel and gilt French style design, pattern 213. 5in. (12.7cm) high. c.1800-10.*

Private Collection

Caughley, Chamberlain (of Worcester), Coalport, Neale, Pennington (of Liverpool), Whitehead, Thomas Wolfe and those which we at present term 'X', 'Y' and 'Z' plus the mystery maker of the 'W$^{(xxx)}$' marked porcelains.[30] Of course the makers of the 'X', 'Y' and 'Z' group may be included in those previously named. As I write (in 2002), the Keelings are considered to have produced the 'X' class porcelains. This large group could therefore have been made at the original (pre-New Hall) site – see Chapter II.

Competition also came from the earthenware manufacturers who were always able to undersell the more expensive porcelains. The makers of earthenware, with their 'china glaze' and 'pearl ware' useful wares, often decorated with underglaze-blue printed designs, engaged a very large slice of the market, as is evidenced by the number of pieces still surviving.

Some of the older firms producing traditional porcelains, not necessarily of New Hall's durable semi-hard body, had gone (or were about to go) out of business. The Lowestoft factory (established in the late 1750s) closed, we believe, in 1797. Isleworth had all but ceased the production of porcelain by 1800, as had most of the Liverpool manufactories.

The New Hall partnership, however, seems to have gone from strength to strength, although the partners kept to their main strength – the production of good quality, well-decorated, trimly made porcelain tablewares. In the late 1790s these were almost entirely tea services, catering for an ever widening market. Even though Great Britain was at war for most of this period, keeping down the export trade, the home trade expanded. The population was increasing at a high rate and more and more families would want to show off, if not use (on an everyday basis), their new style tea service.

New Hall porcelain was in fashion and in quality and price it could rival old and new competition, yet still their porcelains did not bear a name mark. However, they were certainly not alone in this lack of self-publicity.

---

1. In the eighteenth century and early part of the nineteenth century all tea was imported into the British Isles from China. There was no other original source.

2. The position would have been complicated if some of the original workforce had originally been employed by Keeling and were retained by him after the separation in order that he could continue his own pottery, making, we believe, the 'X' class porcelains.

3. Covered jugs may indicate that the jug was for hot milk, the cover helping to keep the liquid hot.

4. The English factories at Caughley, Liverpool, Lowestoft and Worcester, plus some smaller Staffordshire firms, produced versions of the original Chelsea ewer. Some earthenware manufacturers also undersold the porcelain examples.

5. See *Caughley & Worcester Porcelains 1775-1800* by G.A. Godden (Antique Collectors' Club, 1981), Plates 108-9 and 169-170.

6. Ibid., Plates 190 and 266.

7. Helmet shape cream or milk jugs bearing pattern numbers are more likely to be from 'Factory X' than from the New Hall factory.

8. This rare form also occurs with Duvivier's bird painting. See Plate 82 and David Holgate's 'New Hall – Some Interesting Nuances', *Transactions of the English Ceramic Circle,* Vol. 14, Part 2, 1991.

9. See David Holgate's *New Hall* (Faber & Faber, 1987), Plates 52-3.

10. A 1775 invoice for a 'complete sett' of Bristol porcelain does, however, include in the list of pieces only one 'Bread and butter' plate.

11. Philip Miller and Michael Berthoud, in their in *Anthology of British Teapots* (Micawber Publications, 1985), include illustrations of silver-plated teapots which illustrate these points – see their page 128. However, it should be noted that the moulded bars or mock joints are not unique to New Hall, nor do they occur on all New Hall examples.

12. Similar moulding was used at Bristol – see Plate 14.

13. The story of this service is briefly told in my *Eighteenth Century English Porcelain. A selection from the Godden Reference Collection* (Granada Publishing Ltd., London, 1985), Item 69. The matching covered sugar bowl and creamer are shown in Plate 206 of that work.

14. This teapot differs considerably from the earlier version shown in Plate 147. The 1798 pot has an insert rather than an overhanging lid.

15. See my *Chamberlain-Worcester Porcelain 1788-1852* (Barrie & Jenkins, London, 1982), Plates 42-3.

16. Patterns into the early three hundreds have been noted on obconical jugs.

17. Some Bute teacups have an indented Spode type handle – see *A Compendium of British Cups* by M. Berthoud (Micawber Publications, 1990), Plate 259. Some rare handleless cups occur of the basic Bute shape. These are larger and much deeper than the earlier teabowls. They may have been issued with breakfast services or have been intended for non-tea liquid drinks.

18. See *Collecting Lustreware* by G.A. Godden and M. Gibson (Barrie & Jenkins Ltd., London 1991).

19 A similar lobed oval form of dessert service tureen was also made (in a softer body) by the Baddeley-Littler firm, also situated at Shelton in the approximate period 1777-90.

20. For further details of this service see 'A New Hall Dessert Service' by David Holgate *(Northern Ceramic Society Journal,* Vol. 15, 1998). Both tureens are shown as Fig. 5.

21. See *New Hall* (Faber & Faber, London, 1987), Plates 75-6.

22. See *Northern Ceramic Society Newsletter* No. 119 of September 2000, page 29.

23. The Lowestoft factory also produced a range of flasks in a softer body. These Suffolk examples usually date from the 1780s up to at least 1798. Caughley examples in a soapstone body are also recorded. Examples of both types are illustrated in Godden specialist books on these factories.

24. The thickness of the walls and therefore the weight of the object can vary from piece to piece, especially with slip-cast articles. All depends on how long the slip is left in the mould and on the dryness of the plaster mould.

25. David Holgate has reported one with Chinese figure subject pattern number 20 as Plate 128.

26. See *Northern Ceramic Society Newsletter* No. 119, September 2000, page 31.

27. David Holgate illustrates this neat, smallish. jug in his 1987 book as Plate 114. He suggests it was decorated by Duvivier after the termination of his 1790 agreement – see page 161.

28. This concave lip is more usually found on good quality earthenware mugs, in various dry bodies such as caneware or basalt.

29. Similar moulded twig and leaf handles occur on the Duvivier decorated dessert service tureen shown in Plate 199. They also occur on the posset pot in Plate 194.

30. See *Staffordshire Porcelain* edited by G. Godden (Granada Publishing Ltd., 1983). David Holgate's *New Hall* also illustrates typical 'X', 'Y' and 'Z' class porcelains.

CHAPTER VII

The Blue Printed Designs and Blue Painted Patterns

I have already in Chapter I explained that Richard Champion at Bristol in the late 1770s had mastered the underglaze blue printing technique. The Bristol blue printed pieces are admittedly rare, as is most Bristol porcelain, but blue printed items certainly exist. Simple examples are shown in Plates 16, 18 and 233. Other specimens including plates and mugs are featured in Figures 6-8 of F. Severne MacKenna's book *Champion's Bristol Porcelain* (F. Lewis, Leigh-on-Sea, 1947). Seemingly, however, William Cookworthy earlier at Plymouth had not attempted or succeeded in printing in underglaze blue.

Richard Champion himself, writing in the third person in 1775, noted the importance of blue and white patterns at that time and the difficulties which he had experienced in producing saleable blue and white:

> There is one branch of the manufacture, the blue and white, upon which he has just entered, this branch is likely to be the most generally useful of any, but the giving of a blue colour under the glaze, on so hard a material as he uses, has been found full of difficulty. This object he has pursued at a great expense by means of a foreign artificer; and he can now venture to assert that he shall bring that to perfection which has been found so difficult in Europe in native clay...

The vast majority of such Bristol blue patterns, both hand painted and printed, are of Chinese style landscape compositions with or without figures. Remember that in the early 1780s masses of Chinese porcelains were being imported from the East by the Honourable East India Company and the majority of such popular Chinese porcelain was decorated in blue – see my *Oriental Export Market Porcelain and its influence on European Wares* (Granada Publishing, London, 1979) and Plates 6-7 of the present work.

Plate 233. *A Bristol hard-paste teabowl and saucer of slightly ribbed shape, printed in underglaze blue with floral design. Note the Chinese style border, of a type which occurs on some blue New Hall prints. See Plates 246 and 252. Diameter of saucer 4¾in. (12.07cm). c.1778-80.* Private collection

The English endeavours to match these Chinese porcelains closely followed their styles and, in an effort to match the low price of the Chinese originals, transfer-printing in underglaze blue was resorted to by most of our manufacturers, including the large scale works at Worcester and the Caughley factory in Shropshire. Blue printed Oriental style porcelains from these two factories are featured in my specialist book *Caughley and Worcester Porcelains 1773-1800* (Barrie & Jenkins, London, 1969, revised edition Antique Collectors' Club, Woodbridge, 1981). The New Hall company obviously sought to capture some of this market for low priced Oriental style useful wares. It was modestly priced not only because it was printed – a form of mass-production – but because the number of firings were kept down to two (or two and a half) rather than the three or more needed for overglaze enamel decoration and gilding. The blue printed designs were also applied by a small team of relatively low paid workers, not by the enamel painters and gilders. Low prices, of course, helped to make the wares saleable.

There is of course, an expense in producing printed designs, for the sets of all important copper plates have to be hand engraved by trained and competent draughtsmen or engravers. I write 'sets' because with, for example, a tea service decorated with a standard pattern of the same design, one needs engraved copper plates of various sizes and shapes so that the transferred designs fit all shapes. The saucer print will not fit around the upright coffee cup and the teabowls will need a longer but narrower version of the same basic design. Likewise the milk jug design will not fit the fuller bodied teapot. The two bread and butter plates will need a much larger engraving than the spoontray, and so on.

There is also the very important point that a busy factory would need several engraved copper plates to fit objects such as cups or teabowls and saucers. After all, each complete teaset needed twelve of each of these articles. Production would be considerably slowed if only one cup or saucer copper plate was available. A largish factory producing underglaze blue printed designs would have multiple or duplicate copper plates. Being hand engraved, each copper plate might well have slight differences in the detail. It can therefore happen that the saucers in a tea service show different versions of the same basic print. This can be very difficult for present-day students who wrongly expect all pieces to be identical! This was not necessarily the case.

In regard to the preparation or engraving of the copper plates used for the blue printed designs, we do not know if they were engraved 'in house'. I think that it is likely that the partnership employed their own engraver, as in general the designs are unique to New Hall and they fit well the New Hall shapes. The number of designs and the output of the blue printed porcelains would have given employment to a full time engraver or team within the 1785-1810 period. Certainly the very many overglaze bat-printed designs produced from about 1803 would have given employment to several experienced engravers.

'Tooling-up' for a printed design is costly, but once these sets of engraved plates are available the design can be applied to a multitude of articles before the copper plates need to be 'repaired', that is touched-up by the engraver, before acceptable prints can again be produced.

The method of transferring the image from the engraved copper plates to the porcelain (or earthenware) is rather complicated, especially when the 'hot' method is employed, as is the case with underglaze blue designs. First the engraving has to be deeper than that necessary for overglaze printing. Once available, the engraved copper slabs have to be heated and then, while hot, charged with a thick, stiff, oily mix containing the cobalt. This is accomplished by spreading the mix on the copper plate and forcing it into the engraved recesses with a special implement. Next the surplus is scraped from the surface, which is then bossed clean so that the colour medium is only in the recessed parts.

A special type of thin but strong paper is then carefully applied (without creases, etc.) and the sandwich of hot copper plate and paper is pressed together in a mangle-like press. Once this has gone under or through the press the pigment should have been transferred on to the paper as this was pressed into the cobalt charged recesses. The engraved inked copper then has to be reheated and the paper carefully eased off the copper plate and hung to dry before the surplus paper is trimmed away and the borders or mark cut out. This trimming is carried out by female labour or apprentices.

A supply of the once-fired but as yet unglazed porcelain has to be to hand and the approximate size piece of inked paper can now be carefully positioned on to the semi-porous porcelain (which, in some cases, has to be 'sized' before the inked paper is applied), without any creases or bubbles being left. This paper is then very firmly pressed and rubbed on to the body of the object so that the cobalt impregnated medium is transferred on to the object. The paper may then be soaked off leaving the impression – in the same positive manner as the copper plate was engraved, not as a mirror image. Again this operation is traditionally a mainly female trade and the printers work as a team, usually of three – one man, the presser and two

PLATE 234. *A New Hall blue printed covered sugar with added gilt border design. This gilt enrichment relates to pattern 473 – see also Plate 289. Painted pattern number. 7½in. (19.05cm) long. c.1810-15.*
GODDEN OF WORTHING LTD.

or three female assistants, one of whom cuts the transfer paper to convenient size and shape.

Once the design is on the piece it was found expedient to subject it to a light firing process to burn away the surplus oils so that the glaze would 'take' to the decoration and not run off the oily pigment. After this light firing (the 'half' previously referred to) the piece could be glazed and refired in the glost kiln in the normal way. It is the glost firing, or the action of both the glaze and the high firing temperature, which turns the cobalt from matt black to the beautiful blue colour we associate with porcelains. Various factors, however, can affect the tone of blue – the quality of the cobalt, the way it is prepared and mixed, the firing temperature, the atmosphere within the kiln and the make-up of the glaze. David Holgate was of the opinion that it is the chemical reaction between the black cobalt oxide and the glaze which produces the blue cobalt silicate and, of course, the glazes can vary. Most printed patterns on English porcelain are of a darker blue than that used for hand-painted patterns where the mix is much more liquid.

As a general rule printing is employed only where relatively long runs of the same pattern are required. In the case of tea services it would be more convenient and cheaper per unit to produce, say, sixty sets than one. In this way you would decorate sixty teapots using the same size engraving rather than dancing about printing one teapot, one creamer and one bowl etc. from different size copper plates. In the case of underglaze blue printing, where pressure is needed to press the inked paper firmly on to the ware, it is necessary to have well-fired biscuit wares produced by the conventional British method of firing the unglazed porcelain at its highest temperature, well over 1000°C. This contrasts with the Continental method (originally used also by William Cookworthy at Plymouth) of lightly firing the biscuit and then raising the temperature once the piece is glazed. This results in relatively fragile unglazed (biscuit) porcelain that may not stand up to the pressure needed to apply the inked paper.

This rather tedious method of hot-printing, so called because of the need to heat the copper plates on a stove-top, was not used in the overglaze bat-printing technique which I shall be discussing in Chapter IX.

While the earliest as yet recorded type of pre-New Hall period porcelain, the corrugated shapes featured in Plates 19-39, do not appear to have been transfer-printed in blue (probably as the undulating surface did not lend itself to this technique), this style of decoration does occur on quite early New Hall specimens, pieces of the approximate period 1784-5. These early underglaze blue prints can

PLATE 235. *Two views of a rare early New Hall blue printed cabbage-leaf jug bearing the popular 'Gazebo' design. See Colour Plates 53-5. The floral sprays are shown in Plates 236-9. 5½in. (13.97cm) high. c.1784-8.*

GODDEN COLLECTION

comprise small floral sprays, as Plates 236-9 and 265, or more commonly mock Chinese landscapes, often within intricate border designs which are close copies of those found on the contemporary imports from China, the Staffordshire company's chief competition in its early days. Of course other English porcelain manufacturers were also making similar Oriental style blue and white patterned porcelains, yet the New Hall subjects are in the main restricted to this porcelain producing partnership and few other popular patterns, such as the 'Fence' or the 'Fisherman' blue printed designs, were copied at New Hall.

The early blue printed New Hall porcelains do not bear a pattern number. This is true up to about 1795 but some later blue printed designs can have a pattern number added. This relates to the added gilt border, edging or trim, not to the basic blue print. I show in Plates 234, 289 and 291 examples of some typical New Hall gilt-enhanced blue printed designs. Do note that I am here writing of Chinese

PLATE 236. *The front of the moulded cabbage-leaf jug illustrated in Plate 235 showing the floral prints which can occur on other New Hall porcelains – see Plate 45. 5½in. (13.97cm) high. c.1784-8.*

GODDEN COLLECTION

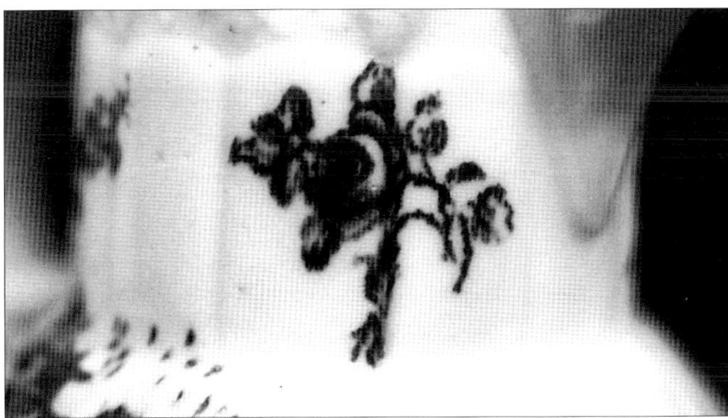

Plate 237. *Two of the floral prints which occur on the blue printed 'Gazebo' pattern jug shown in Plate 235.*

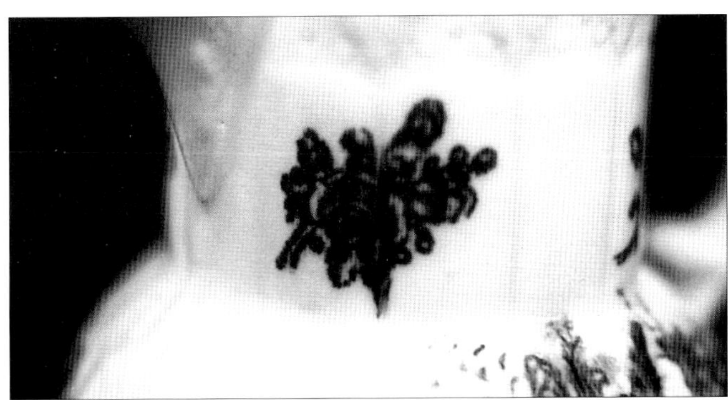

Plate 238. *Two further flower spray designs found on the early New Hall jug shown in Plate 235.*

Plate 239. *Two of the blue printed flower sprays which appear on the body of the jug shown in Plate 235.*

Plate 240. *Detail of the blue printed trim which occurs on the handle of the jug shown in Plate 235.*

style underglaze blue patterns, not of the many designs that incorporate some blue portions and are finished with gilding to complete the design. The blue printed Oriental style designs are complete in their own right. They can occur as an unenhanced blue print or with a Chinese style coloured line edging or with different gilt edgings or inner borders. The additional gilding is not necessarily an improvement, but the original buyers would certainly have had to pay a premium for the added gilt decoration.

When a pattern number does occur on the later post-1795 blue printed designs it can be expected to follow the factory practice of appearing only on the major pieces in a tea service, not on the teabowls, cups or saucers. As the pattern number (such as 473) relates to the gilding, it can occur on different printed designs, although all will be the popular Chinese landscape designs – see Plates 234 and 289. A much later gilt pattern 2483 (Plate 291) which occurs on bone china wares picks out or outlines the 'Willow' pattern style design in a manner which I and seemingly buyers of the period found distracting or unpleasant, for it is now rarely found. There is also the point that gilding is prone to wear, so giving much used pieces a shabby appearance.

Remaining with pattern numbers for a moment, one would not expect the earliest New Hall blue-printed pieces to bear a pattern number because before the 1790s few pieces of any style were so numbered. The first numbered example incorporating underglaze blue printing I have noted is pattern 272. This, however, is not the type of blue print which I am discussing, as the Oriental style formal floral pattern really serves only as a base for various enamelled over patterns numbered 272, 274, 360, 490 and 856 (see Plates 168 and 293). The first of the gilt border recorded designs added to standard underglaze blue printed pieces is pattern number 465 of the approximate period 1795-1800. Number 473 is of a similar type – see Plate 234. Plate 289 shows the same gilt border, pattern 473, but on a different blue printed design. I have not seen gilders' personal tally marks or numbers on later pieces bearing factory added gilt borders, but such gilders' marks can occur on other makes of blue printed patterns enriched with gilding.

Some early New Hall blue printed Oriental style landscape designs do, however, bear simple gilt edging or border motifs. This gilding of the 1780s is not as intrusive as the later designs and there is a possibility that this gilding was – in some cases – added elsewhere. Some such border designs also occur on Chinese blue and white or on Caughley porcelain of the same period. This duplication can simply be a case of copying, but on the other hand specialist gilders or decorating establishments in London could have been using blue printed wares from several sources, including New Hall, for their gilding. Such gilt blue and white sets would then be sold on at an enhanced price. This is not to say that all gilt New Hall blue printed teawares were decorated in London or elsewhere. I am merely observing that the same added border designs appear on other makes of porcelain and the possibility exists that the gilding was not carried out at the New Hall factory.

It is interesting to note that by September 1789 the New Hall management had issued and had available at least four different blue and white teaware designs. This fact is evidenced by a bill of that period covering, perhaps, samples supplied to 'Josiah Wedgwood Esq'. There were invoiced four cups and saucers blue and white of four different patterns at 10½ old pence each as opposed to six enamelled teacups and saucers at 1s. (5p) or a gilt design at 2s.5d. (12½p). Josiah Wedgwood enjoyed a trade discount of 25% on these retail prices. The blue and white examples were obviously the cheapest of the basic types of decoration and they almost certainly lacked the added gilding with which some blue patterns were further embellished. It should be added that although the items are described as cups and saucers they were probably handleless teabowls and saucers, as in the eighteenth century the teabowl was usually described as a cup. The additional description 'handled' was often added when this was the case.

This invoice of 7 September 1789 does not state that the four blue and white cups (or teabowls) and saucers were printed in underglaze blue but this was almost certainly the case and was perhaps so obvious to both parties that it was not stated. I know of only very few hand-painted New Hall blue and white designs (Plates 294-8) and specimens of these patterns are extremely rare, no cups and saucers being as yet reported. In comparison, the blue printed teawares are relatively common and by 1789 printing in underglaze blue was obviously the standard mode of producing the less expensive blue patterns at the New Hall manufactory.

Whilst most New Hall blue printed designs were applied to plain, non-relief-moulded, shapes, the process could be used to embellish undulating surfaces – although the cobalt blue had a tendency to run down the valleys. An interesting and extremely rare example is shown in Plate 235. This bears the two related 'Gazebo' prints to be discussed in more detail later.

Of course most other English manufacturers of the 1760-96 period produced similar so-called cabbage-leaf moulded jugs with other blue-printed designs, Caughley, Lowestoft, Worcester and the Liverpool factories being well-known examples. But these New Hall 'Gazebo' prints (seen also in Plates 241-9) are unique to this Staffordshire factory which did not favour a mask-head spout.

This small jug (more usual, larger, enamelled examples are shown in Plates 212-5) also bears seven small floral sprays. Two of these also appear on the rare perhaps custard cup shown in Plate 265. Others can occur on the New Hall asparagus servers[1] and these or other of these sprays may help to identify further New Hall blue-printed rarities. The top edge of this jug is finished with an overglaze green enamel line, emulating some Chinese blue and white importations. This jug which 'turned up' as I was completing this book serves to show how rare unrecorded shapes and new prints can still be found.

One of the earliest and the most characteristic of the New Hall underglaze prints is that called by present-day collectors the 'Gazebo' pattern or, as I term it, the overhanging rock pattern. A large version of this design is shown in Plate 241. Several slightly different variants occur depending on the size and shape of the object to be decorated. The tea canister shown in Plates 242-3 shows both sides of the related design.

Plate 241. *A shallow New Hall saucer shape plate decorated with the 'Gazebo' or overhanging rock design printed in underglaze blue. Two different borders occur, also several minor differences in the landscape. Diameter 8½in. (21.59cm). c.1783-8.* Godden collection

Plate 242. *The front view of a New Hall tea canister bearing the 'Gazebo' blue print but with a different border design from that shown in Plate 241. 4½in. (11.43cm) high. c.1783-8.* Godden collection

Plate 243. *The reverse side of the rare tea canister shown in Plate 242. Variations occur in this print due to different copper plates being employed. 4½in. (11.43cm) high. c.1783-8.* Godden collection

Plate 244. *A rare large New Hall bowl bearing stretched versions of the 'Gazebo' or overhanging rock print. Gilt line borders, border as Plate 241. Diameter 9½in. (24.13cm). c.1783-8.* Godden of Worthing

Plate 245. *A teabowl and saucer bearing a version of the 'Gazebo' pattern painted in underglaze blue. Note unshaded area over hanging rock. Lion crest mark (see pages 285-291). Diameter of saucer 5in. (12.7cm). c.1783-8.* National Museum of Wales

This New Hall blue printed design can be found in two distinctly different versions. One has a leaf-like border design, the leaves pointing into the centre of the piece (see Plates 241-5). This type of border also has two or more slight variations. Such differences may merely be due to the necessity of engraving separate copper plates so that the prints fitted the various sizes and shapes of object. The differences may, however, prove to be more significant. The other, rarer, version has a floral border (Plates 246 and 252). Also, on most examples the overhanging rock is shaded (Plates 241-2 and 244) but on some pieces it is mainly left unshaded (Plate 245). As with all these prints, several other slight differences can occur. Some are quite different, as is illustrated by the two rare leaf-shaped dishes of slightly different shapes[2] shown in Plate 248. On some small pieces only part of the design was used (Plate 247) and some examples have slight gilt enrichments or only a simple gilt line trim as occurs on the rare bowl shown in Plate 244. This bowl illustrates one of the characteristic faults found with many pieces of early blue printed New Hall porcelains – the glaze is often extremely 'peppered' with small black spots. The description 'peppered' should be self-explanatory; the surface of the glaze has the appearance of having been liberally sprinkled with black pepper. Some at least of these spots are burst bubbles. This defect can occur on other makes of porcelain but seldom to the extent found on these blue printed New Hall pieces. Strangely the defect does not occur on the earlier corrugated wares but seems mainly confined to the blue printed specimens of the approximate period 1784-8.

This blue printed 'Gazebo' pattern occurs on early teawares in conjunction with globular (Chinese style) teapots, which are particularly early and rare. A part teaset[3] of this type is shown with related pieces in David Holgate's 1971 book *New Hall and its Imitators,* Plate 185. This selection is interesting as the teapot (my Plate 249) and the creamer bear the rampant lion mark which is shown below and discussed further on page 288. It should be noted, however, that this crest mark does not necessarily appear on all pieces from this group. A saucer may have the mark but not the teabowl. It was not, seemingly, used consistently.

PLATE 246. *A New Hall teabowl and saucer decorated with the blue printed 'Gazebo' pattern (in a light blue) but with unusual floral type border, rather similar to the Bristol border shown in Plate 233. See also Plate 252. Diameter of saucer 5in. (12.7cm). c.1785-90.* GODDEN COLLECTION

I briefly noted in Chapter III that the attribution of this mark is open to some doubt, at least by some authorities. At the risk of being or appearing tedious, I should set out some of the difficulties concerning this crest mark (a most unusual feature on eighteenth century English porcelain) and the pieces on which it appears.

The authoritative Dr. Bernard Watney, in his specialist book *English Blue and White Porcelain of the Eighteenth Century* (Faber & Faber, London, 1963) wrote of the blue printed porcelains which bore this device:

> An interesting feature of some examples is that they bear the crowned, rampant lion mark of Frankenthal in underglaze-blue. At first sight it seems strange that New Hall should choose this somewhat unusual mark, but it may be recalled that Nicholas Berthevin, the French arcanist, had successfully decorated a few specimens of Frankenthal hard-paste porcelain by his highly secret method of transfer printing in underglaze blue about 1770-1772. We now find New Hall adopting this Frankenthal mark to commemorate the fact that they were the only other European hard-paste factory to succeed in printing underglaze blue decorations.

I subsequently had the temerity to question this statement on two counts. First I wondered if the mark on the English pieces was in fact a copy of the Frankenthal factory device. It differs considerably from the Frankenthal lion mark reproduced in the standard reference books. Secondly, it is also a fact that Champion,

PLATE 247. *A rare form of oval New Hall spoontray bearing a condensed version of the 'Gazebo' pattern. 6in. (15.24cm) long. c.1783-8.* PRIVATE COLLECTION

whilst at Bristol, was producing at least some underglaze blue printing on English hard-paste porcelain (see Plate 16). It was not first introduced at the New Hall factory.

I introduced a note of caution when illustrating the mark as it appeared on a blue printed 'Gazebo' pattern teabowl and saucer (in the National Museum of Wales ref. no. 2163) shown as Plate 674 in my 1966 book *An Illustrated Encyclopaedia of British Pottery and Porcelain* (Barrie & Jenkins, London). My caption reads 'New Hall-type blue printed porcelain teabowl and saucer, with very rare crowned lion mark (c.1790). Attribution open to some doubt'.

The late Dr. Watney and most other authorities seem not to have agreed with my uncertainty over the New Hall attribution for this mark. In Dr. Watney's revised 1973 edition he added a footnote to his original paragraph, which I have previously quoted. The new note reads:

> A 'lion-marked' teabowl has been tested by spectrographic analysis and found to be hard paste. It is amusing to note that one was taken to task for suggesting that 'lion marked' pieces were New Hall when the first edition of this book was published, but this has now been generally accepted.

David Holgate in his 1987 book *New Hall* certainly seems to accept Dr. Watney's diagnosis, as he states: 'A few of the early blue and white pieces were marked with a crowned Frankenthal lion under the glaze, but this mark was not used regularly'. He also very fairly added a footnote drawing attention to Mr. Pomfret's published views which agreed with my doubt that the pieces and mark were necessarily New Hall. He also made reference to a new theory held by Mrs. Kit Holgate. I shall refer again to this footnote shortly. I still have nagging doubts on the linkage of these English pieces to the Frankenthal factory in Germany[4] and in this book, in which I have not been afraid to rethink old problems, I might be forgiven for making further points regarding this puzzling mark.

It should be borne in mind that the lion crest mark could have other meanings. Mr. Roger Pomfret, in his researches on these blue printed porcelains, has pointed out that Louis-Victor Gerverot worked with (or carried out experiments for) John Turner. Gerverot reputedly made four firings of his experimental hard-paste porcelain before John Turner died in 1787. This period fits well with the likely date of the pieces under discussion and a nineteenth century authority (Heinrich Stegman) on this much travelled arcanist and ceramic painter noted that the trademark used by Gerverot was a lion.

Mr. Bevis Hillier in his book *Master Potters of the Industrial Revolution – the Turners of Lane End* (Cory Adams & Mackay, London, 1965) gives a good account of Gerverot's career. Further thoughts on this possible con-

Plate 248. *Two rare New Hall small leaf shaped dishes printed with different versions of the popular and early 'Gazebo' pattern. Note foreground and right-hand sides, different copper plates having been employed. Upper example 4 x 3¾in. (10.16 x 9.53cm). Four or more different sizes were made. c.1783-8.* Private collection

PLATE 249. *A rare and early globular teapot bearing a version of the 'Gazebo' design with gilt border and trim. Lion crest mark – see pages 285-291. 6¾in. (17.15cm) high. c.1783-8.* DAVID HOLGATE COLLECTION

nection are given by Roger Pomfret in his paper 'The Lion of Lane End' published in the *Journal of the Northern Ceramic Society*, Vol. 6 (1987). Roger Pomfret has also observed differences between this crest marked porcelain and its glazing and typical examples of New Hall's porcelains and made interesting comments on the forms used. However, the body and glaze of early New Hall porcelain does vary considerably. Roger Pomfret returned to discuss this problem mark in the *Journal of the Northern Ceramic Society* Vol. 12 (1995), where he again pointed out that this mark has not as yet been observed on mainstream or standard New Hall forms.

I believe that the significance of the lion crest is rather simpler and more localised that the previously claimed association with the German Frankenthal factory or with Louis-Victor Gerverot working with John Turner and re-using his former lion mark. The first point to note is that the device over the rampant heraldic lion is not a crown but rather an earl's coronet. Secondly, if one refers to local Staffordshire directories of the 1780s – that is the period of these marked porcelains – one finds engraved a page of crests with the general heading 'Nobility of Staffordshire'. That given in a shield shape device above the name Earl Talbot is our rampant lion, with a coronet above. I here reproduce the engravings from William Tunnicliffe's *A Survey of the County of Stafford* of 1787.

I suggest that it is possible that the crest mark relates to the Right Honourable Earl Talbot, the Earl of Shrewsbury, whose ancient family owned much land in Staffordshire and who resided at Ingestre Hall. The local Alton Towers was also at a later period a seat of the Talbot family. In the nineteenth century the then Earl of Shrewsbury certainly supported the local ceramic industry. The magnificent Daniel porcelain services made in 1827 for the Earl of Shrewsbury were described by Simeon Shaw as the 'most brilliant and costly kind ever manufactured in the district…' It is possible that in the 1780s Earl Talbot was connected with, or gave support to, the New Hall partnership or to another manufacturer who sought to show the Earl's crest as a factory mark.[5]

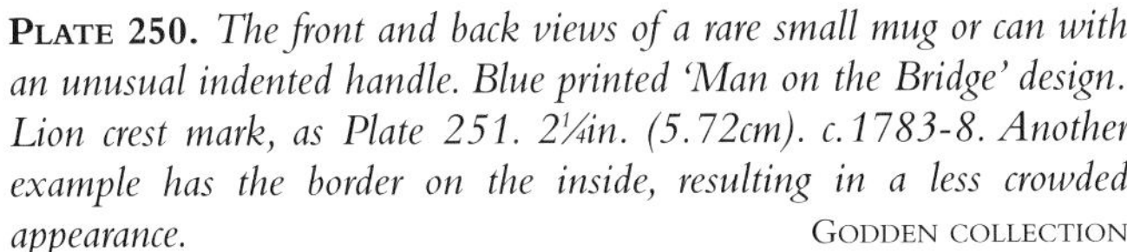

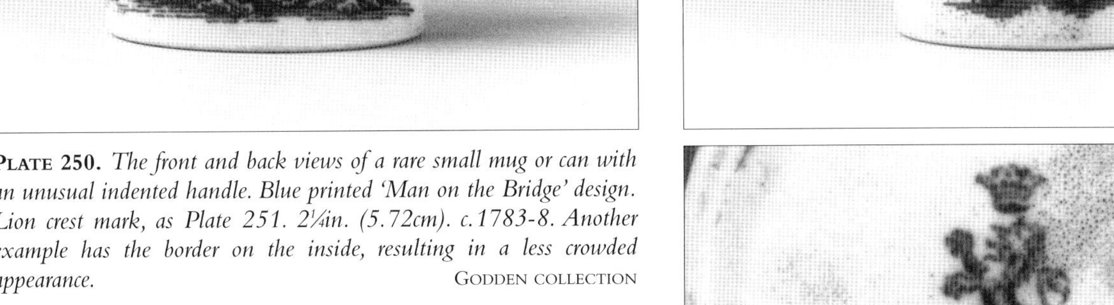

PLATE 250. *The front and back views of a rare small mug or can with an unusual indented handle. Blue printed 'Man on the Bridge' design. Lion crest mark, as Plate 251. 2¼in. (5.72cm). c.1783-8. Another example has the border on the inside, resulting in a less crowded appearance.* GODDEN COLLECTION

PLATE 251. *The base of the small mug shown in Plate 250, featuring the crest mark discussed on pages 285-291. Diameter of base 2⅛in. (5.4cm). c.1783-8.* GODDEN COLLECTION

PLATE 252. *A New Hall coffee cup (with clip handle) and saucer bearing the shaded rock version of the 'Gazebo' pattern with floral border – see also Plate 246. Cup 2¼in. (5.72cm) high. c.1785-90.*

B.W. WEST

Plate 253. *A rare group of early blue printed 'Man on the Bridge' designs. Note the simple loop handles. Lion crest marks. Teapot 6in. (15.24cm) high. c.1783-8.* Messrs. Phillips

Plate 254. *A plan view of the sugar bowl cover to the part teaset shown in Plate 253. These floral sprays differ from those on the jug shown in Plates 235-6.* Private collection

If, however, it is accepted that the lion mark relates to the local Talbot family crest, then some of the reasoning behind the attribution of this mark to Louis-Victor Gerverot, working for John Turner, has lost much of its weight.

In discussing further this mark one must not lose sight of the fact that Dr. Bernard Watney's footnote states that a marked teabowl and saucer has been 'tested by spectrographic analysis and found to be hard-paste'. However, I do not consider that it necessarily follows that this specimen and related pieces must be of New Hall manufacture just because they have been shown to be 'hard-paste' porcelain. Our comparative recent research has shown that many firms were producing similar types of (hybrid) hard-paste porcelains. It is quite possible that Keeling, Turner and the other so-called early New Hall partners were independently experimenting in porcelain manufacture. To be convincing one would like a series of tests to be carried out using the same apparatus under the same conditions, with specimens of other New Hall type porcelains, of 'Factory X' type, and including the porcelain beaker traditionally associated with Gerverot's name. This specimen which I have handled certainly seems to be formed of a very hard Continental type porcelain. I would

Plate 255. *A very rare New Hall teapot shape, rather in the style of some Derby examples – note the ring knob with mock strap fixture. Underglaze blue printed 'Man on the Bridge' pattern, with slight gilding. 6¾in. high (17.15cm). c.1785-90.* GODDEN COLLECTION

think that all these bodies, and others, would be shown to be of the hard-paste type.

A further suggestion regarding the origin or significance of this Talbot lion crest mark was put forward by the late Mrs. Kit Holgate in her paper 'An Urn amongst the Flowerpots' published in the *Journal of the Northern Ceramic Society* Vol. 6 (1987). In essence Mrs. Holgate's suggestion is that these blue printed pieces could have been produced by the original partnership at Keeling's factory at Tunstall, before Anthony Keeling and John Turner left the partnership. These crest marked specimens are certainly relatively early in date but if we accept this idea we are in difficulty over the larger group of so-called corrugated formed wares which I have tentatively attributed to the Tunstall period. These pieces discussed in Chapter II do not seem to match the lion marked blue printed porcelains.

We badly need to find a dated example bearing this mark. Two pieces in my collection, however, the small mug shown in Plate 250[6] and the tea canister (Plate 262), plus other recorded examples (Plate 261) are of forms not yet recorded in conventionally decorated New Hall porcelains. The slightly later New Hall blue printed porcelains that are indisputably of New Hall origin do not bear this crest mark, which occurs only on a relatively small number of early examples. If the mark was used at New Hall why was it discontinued and why does it appear on only some specimens and only in association with two or three patterns? I am not dogmatically stating that these porcelains are not New Hall. I am merely putting forward different points of view and underlining the fact that the attribution is by no means certain. I have always regarded the lion marked examples as not being New Hall, but I have just (February 2002) belatedly noticed that the marked tea canister shown in Plate 261 was seemingly printed from the same copper plate as was used for the unmarked and apparently true New Hall spoontray shown in Plate 263. We have a match between the two types![7]

Returning to the 'Gazebo' blue printed designs that led to the discussion on the lion crest marks, it could well be that two or more factories produced versions of the 'Gazebo' pattern. Certainly several different versions of the basic design occur and, as I have noted, the border design can also vary. This design is also known on unmarked non-New Hall earthenwares. Yet the non-crest marked cup and saucer shown in Plate 252 can certainly be regarded as New Hall on account of the handle form.

PLATE 256. *Two sides of a blue printed New Hall mug. For an enamelled example see Plate 230. 5⅜in. (13.46cm) high. c.1785-90.* GODDEN COLLECTION

Another interesting early New Hall blue printed Oriental style design is of willow pattern type, although it precedes the standard 'Willow' pattern. In this design a single rather over large man stands on the very angular bridge to the left of the main island and the pagoda-like structure. I will call this pattern the 'Man on the Bridge' pattern,[8] although it has been called the 'Ice Floe' pattern by some authorities. Versions of this design also occur on the softer bodied Isleworth porcelains and on Liverpool porcelains perhaps of the late 1780s or early 1790s.[9]

The main part of this design can be seen on the unusual teapot illustrated in Plate 255 and the whole rather expanded version on the rare mug shown in Plate 256 or on the plate featured in Plate 259. Again, some small articles bear only part of this design, such as the pagoda with its long low windows. The two rare asparagus servers shown in Plate 257 are cases in point. Some examples, such as the splendid teapot (Plate 255), have gilt enrichments, while originally less expensive pieces bear only the underglaze blue print. Several slight or even major variations of this pattern occur, mainly depending on the size of object bearing the print. Again the border design can vary. Large size objects such as plates bear an expanded version of the main, central, design with two figures in the foreground (Plate 259). Mr. Roger Pomfret in his 1987 paper *(Journal of the Northern Ceramic Society,* Vol. 6) regards this version as a separate design which he termed the 'Ice Floe' pattern. However, these figures occur on pieces that seem to have been sold with matching teawares missing these figures in the foreground – see Plate 253. I therefore regard this printed pattern as a single design, cut or adapted to fit various sizes or shapes.

The 'Man on the Bridge' pattern sometimes bears the intriguing lion crest like mark printed in underglaze blue; indeed all the teawares shown in Plate 253 are so marked. The cover to the sugar bowl (Plate 254) has small floral sprays which do not seem to link with those on the jug shown in Plates 235-9. Another lion crest marked example of an unconventional New Hall form is the covered jug with indented handle shown by Dr. Bernard Watney in his 1973 *English Blue and White Porcelain of the 18th Century*, Plate 96D. That example is in the Truro Museum.

These early New Hall or New Hall associated underglaze blue prints occur, very rarely, on unusual shapes such as the two lion crest marked tea canisters shown in Plates 261-2 or on the curved edged, unmarked spoontray seen in Plate 263. One hesitates to use the term unique for, being printed, several or many such objects must originally have been produced. Other as yet unrecorded shapes may await discovery. One or more may help to solve the puzzle as to the true origin of the crest marked examples.

Plate 257. *Two New Hall asparagus servers decorated with part of the 'Man on the Bridge' printed design. 3in. long. c.1785-90.* Peter Davis collection

Plate 258. *A blue printed teabowl and saucer bearing a version of the 'Man on the Bridge' print, with gilt edge. Lion crest mark – see pages 285-291. Diameter of saucer 5in. (12.7cm). c.1785-90.* Godden collection

PLATE 259. *A New Hall saucer dish or plate printed in underglaze blue with a version of the 'Man on the Bridge' design. This has several differences from the version shown on the crest marked saucer shown in Plate 258. Diameter 7¾in. (19.69cm). c.1785-90.*

GODDEN COLLECTION

It should be noted that several versions of this printed design occur, although all examples are scarce. On some examples the man on the bridge has been cut from the main design when the transfer paper was applied. This deletion was merely to enable the main feature to fit the object – an asparagus server or tea canister – see Plates 257 and 262. Two engravings of a saucer size print are shown in Plate 260 and once again it is possible that more than one factory was responsible.

The majority of the 'Man on the Bridge' blue printed wares are not marked. This design was seemingly a popular one and the print can be found on a wide variety of New Hall shapes, mostly prior to 1790. Some of these items are, as I have already noted, very rare, the Derby style teapot with its silver like ring handle being particularly so.

Another rare teapot form, a barrel shape pot with clip handle, is in the Castle Museum, Norwich and is illustrated by Robin Emmerson in his book *British Teapots and Tea Drinking* (H.M.S.O., 1992) Plate III, item 342.

A possible third New Hall Oriental style landscape print is very similar to the 'Man on the Bridge' design except that two figures are on the bridge and the buildings on the island are taller and lack the long low windows which are such a feature of the single man on a bridge print. This two-man version appears to be extremely rare and is only known to me via a covered milk jug (with a very rare indented handle form of the general type shown also in Plate 250) formerly in Geoffrey Grey' s collection and illustrated as Plate 191 in David Holgate's 1971 book. It is also illustrated as Plate 37 in Mrs. Holgate's paper published in the *Journal of the Northern Ceramic Society,* Vol. 6 (1987). Other English porcelain manufacturers produced rather similar blue prints in this popular Chinese style and this two figures on a bridge version can occur on Pennington's Liverpool porcelain[10] and on unmarked earthenwares of Turner type.[11]

Yet a fourth early New Hall blue printed Chinese style landscape design is also extremely rare and has only recently been recorded.. In essence it is like the popular Caughley 'Temple' or 'Pagoda' pattern, with an elaborate temple on the left with a man on a bridge lower right. The main distinguishing feature is a bird perched near the top of the centrally placed tree. I show a saucer in Plate 264 and would call this print 'Bird in a Tree'. I have not seen this print on main teaware forms, but the matching teabowl does not have or need the attractive inner border. This design has the painted Chinese style edging – a light manganese wash around the rim. I have been informed that the matching coffee cup has a simple loop handle which may indicate a date in the mid-1790s, but the overall appearance of the design on the saucer suggests a rather earlier date for at least the introduction of this scarce design. David Holgate has rightly pointed out that the saucers and plates of some other designs and factories have the added inner border to tidy up the design – see also Plates 281-2.

Some seemingly very early and rare New Hall porcelains bear underglaze blue prints of simple floral sprays. Plate 265 shows a small handled pot with a Tunstall period handle form. David Holgate illustrates as his Plate 107 an asparagus server with similar printed sprays. These sprays also occur on the unmarked blue printed 'Gazebo' pattern jug in Plates 235-9. The early rarities bearing these New Hall underglaze blue printed designs – the leaf dishes (Plate 248), the asparagus servers (Plate 257), small creamers and such objects are amongst the most desirable of all New Hall porcelains. Rare knife and fork handles in more than one size also occur with Continental style rococo blue printed motifs – see Plate 266. A small but deep, handled leaf shape may also have been issued with blue printed designs. A very rare blue printed design occurs on a small mug with simple loop handle in the Watney collection.[12]

I consider the deep plate or dish with a moulded edge

PLATE 260. *Two saucers bearing different versions of the 'Man on the Bridge' design. The example on the left bears the lion crest mark – see pages 285-291. Variations occur in all printed designs, however, as different copper plates were employed, usually on different size forms. Diameter 5in. (12.7cm). c.1783-8.* GODDEN COLLECTION

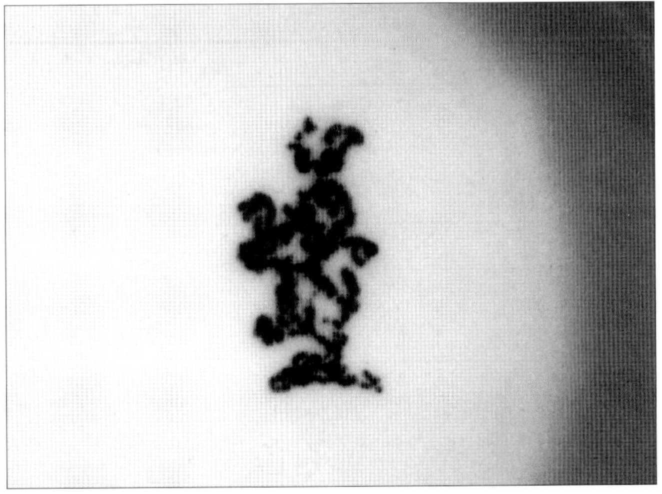

PLATE 260A. *Lion crest mark.*

PLATE 261. *A rare form of tea canister (not as yet recorded with a known New Hall enamelled pattern) bearing a version of the 'Man on the Bridge' design. Lion crest mark. 4½in. (11.43cm) high. c.1783-8.*
MESSRS. PHILLIPS

PLATE 262. *Two sides of a rare form of tea canister (not as yet recorded with a known New Hall enamelled pattern) bearing reduced versions of the 'Man on the Bridge' design. Lion crest mark. 3¾in. (9.53cm) high. c.1783-8.* GODDEN COLLECTION

PLATE 263. *A rare form New Hall spoontray bearing a version of the 'Man on the Bridge' design. 6⅛ x 4in. (15.56 x 10.16cm). c.1783-8.* GODDEN COLLECTION

Plate 264. *A rare blue printed design of conventional Chinese style but with a bird perched on the central tree. Diameter 5⅛in. (13.02cm). c.1788-93.* GODDEN COLLECTION

Plate 265. *Three views of a rare small handled pot bearing blue printed flower sprays. Two of these link with the cabbage-leaf jug shown in Plate 135. See Plates 236 and 238. 2in. (5.08cm) high. c.1788-93.* GODDEN COLLECTION

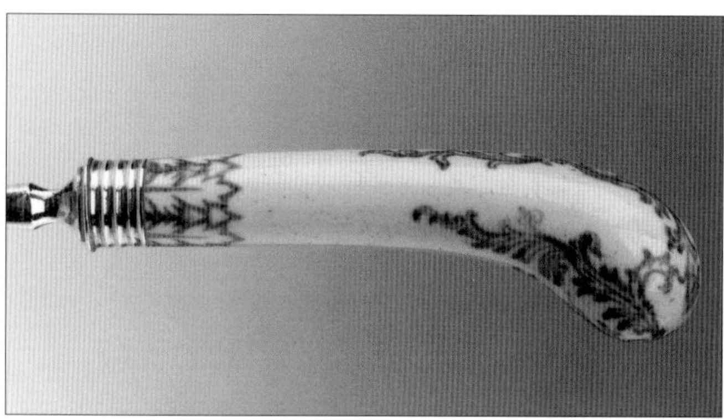

Plate 266. *A rare New Hall porcelain fork handle, decorated rather in the Continental style in underglaze blue. Handle 3in. (7.62cm) long (other sizes can occur). c.1785-90.* Godden collection

Plate 267. *A moulded edge plate of unrecorded form, decorated with underglaze blue prints. Diameter 8½in. (21.59cm). c.1785-95.* Godden collection

Plate 268. *An attractive New Hall teabowl and saucer printed with printed Chinese figure design in underglaze blue. Believed to be unique to New Hall. Diameter of saucer 5in. (12.7cm). c.1785-90.* J. Spooner collection

Plate 269. *A New Hall teapot decorated with the rare blue printed Chinese figure design, as Plate 268. See Colour Plate 56. The reverse side is shown in Plate 270. 6½in. (16.51cm) high. c.1785-90.*
The late A. de Saye Hutton

Plate 270. *The reverse side of the blue printed New Hall teapot shown in Plate 269. The same basic shape is shown in Plate 147. 6½in. (16.51cm) high. c.1785-90.* The late A. de Saye Hutton

Plate 271. *A waste bowl and saucer decorated with rare, related underglaze blue prints of bushes and birds, the 'Doves' pattern. Both specimens bear contemporary gilt edge and inner border. Diameter of saucer 5¼in. (13.34cm). c.1785-90.* Private collection

Plate 272. *A rare blue printed covered sugar bowl, with flower knob bearing the unique New Hall underglaze blue 'Doves' design, shown in Plate 271. 4in. (10.16cm) high. c.1785 -90.* Private collection

shown in Plate 267 to be New Hall. It is of an extremely rare form previously unrecorded from any factory. The main carnation (or gillyflower) motif occurs on Worcester, Caughley and Isleworth porcelains of the approximate period 1775-90 and may well have been inspired by the popular French blue and white porcelains. The moulded edge, however, probably owes its inspiration to Staffordshire earthenwares. It would be interesting to discover other plates and dishes of this basic form for this plate may well have been part of a dessert service. The attribution of this plate, its shape and the underglaze blue prints are, however, at the moment tentative.

One of the rarest and most attractive of the New Hall blue printed designs comprises two related prints depicting Chinese style children in a garden type setting within an attractive floral border. Dr. Bernard Watney, in his standard book *English Blue and White Porcelain of the 18th Century* (1973) shows, as Plate 96A, a New Hall coffee cup and saucer, similar to my teabowl and saucer shown in Plate 268. David Holgate illustrated as his Plate 97 a very rare New Hall flask in the Castle Museum at Norwich which has the same attractive blue print on both sides. A helmet shaped creamer with this pattern is in the

Plate 273. *Two New Hall clip-handled coffee cups bearing different versions of the underglaze blue 'Doves' print shown in Plates 271-2. The left-hand example has gilt trim, the less expensive version on the right has an enamelled line edge. 2½in. (6.35cm) high. c.1785-90.* Godden collection

Plate 274. *The reverse side of the two coffee cups shown in Plate 273. Slightly different versions are shown from different copper plates. The moulded handles also show some slight differences, although both examples seem to have been produced at the New Hall factory. 2½in. (6.35cm) high. c.1785 -90.* Godden collection

Plate 275. *A New Hall spoontray printed in underglaze blue with the so-called 'Trench Mortar' or 'Malayan Village' design, with gilt edging. 5¾ x 3¾in. (14.61 x 9.53cm). c.1790-5.* GODDEN COLLECTION

PLATE 276. *A New Hall teapot stand printed with the 'Trench Mortar' or 'Malayan Village' design. This example, when compared with the spoontray in Plate 275, illustrates how a standard design has to be re-engraved and amended to fit another shape or size of object. 7½ x 6¼in. (19.05 x 15.88cm). c.1790-5.* GODDEN COLLECTION

PLATE 277. *A New Hall saucer shape plate showing the full version of the 'Trench Mortar' or 'Malayan Village' blue painted design. This and many other printed designs show shading and the water washed in by hand in a pale blue. Diameter 8¼in. (20.96cm). c.1790-5.* THE LATE A. DE SAYE HUTTON

Victoria & Albert Museum collection.

A superb teapot formerly in the de Saye Hutton collection is illustrated in Plates 269-70. The print on the reverse of most articles shows a very strange vase motif which, like the main Chinese style figure subject, seems unique to the New Hall factory. These subjects are shown to good effect on the rare waste or slop bowls. I have not found a plate with this design but they must have been made, two to a tea service. As with other New Hall prints, several slight variations occur. Note, for example, the fence on the right on the teapot and that on the saucer. These attractive blue printed Chinese figure prints seem unique to New Hall as far as porcelains are concerned, but the subjects can also occur on earthenwares, perhaps of Swansea make.[13]

An unusual and rare New Hall exclusive pattern is shown in Plate 271. This is known to present-day collectors as the 'Doves' pattern. One side, presumably the main feature as it appears on the facing side of cups (see Plate 273), includes two dove like birds flying each side of a flowering bush or shrub (of prunus or tea-plant type). The associated print features a broken, willow (?) tree trunk with a living branch growing out of the right side – see Plates 271-3. A leaf border is associated with these prints. The National Museum of Wales (Cardiff) has a very rare small globular teapot with this print, also an en suite covered sugar bowl (as Plate 272) and a most unusually shaped large milk jug.[14] These rarities are shown by David Holgate as Colour Plate E in his 1971 book The pieces in the National Museum of Wales are of particularly rare shapes, with well-modelled floral knobs to the small teapot and sugar bowl covers.[15] Again the basic design was re-engraved with variations and some examples bear additional gilt borders – see Plates 273-4.

Plate 278. *A New Hall trio of saucer, teabowl and coffee cup bearing the underglaze blue painted 'Trench Mortar' design with added hand-applied washes and gilt trim. Diameter of saucer 5⅛in. (13.02cm). c.1790-5.*
A. Taylor collection

Plate 279. *A spiral fluted handleless oval covered sugar bowl bearing the 'Trench Mortar' print with hand-applied washes and gilt trim. 5½in. (13.97cm) high. c.1795-1800.* B.W. East collection

These previously mentioned New Hall blue printed designs are the earliest and I believe that they occur only on pieces made before about 1790, that is they are patterns of the 1780s. However, a second batch of blue printed patterns was introduced for the 1790s and used into the early years of the nineteenth century.

A quite common blue printed pattern depicts a more European style house on an island with a row of bamboo posts forming a barricade, or sun-shade type fence. Dr. Watney once called this design the 'Trench Mortar' pattern and this strange designation will probably remain with collectors! However, earthenware collectors may know this same Chinese-inspired pattern as 'Malay House', 'Malayan Village' or 'Pearl River House' pattern. Plates 275-6 illustrate a teapot stand and a rarer spoontray. These two objects serve to show how a basic design had to be amended to fill different shapes or sizes of object. The spoontray carries a wider but shorter abbreviated version of the same motif. The plate in Plate 277 even differs from the teapot stand where the design has been slightly abridged to fit the shape. It should be noted that this pattern occurs hand painted on Chinese hard-paste export market porcelain (Plate 7) and printed on at least

PLATE 280. *A Chinese hard-paste porcelain teabowl and saucer hand painted with the 'Emerging Boat' pattern. This, like other Chinese designs, was copied (in printed versions) at New Hall. In this case the gilt borders were added in England. Diameter of saucer 5in. (12.7cm). c.1785-90.* MISS B.E. MAGNESS

one other non-New Hall English make of porcelain. It should also be noted that this blue printed design also occurs quite frequently on English earthenwares. Examples are featured in Robert Copeland's book *Spode's Willow Pattern and other Designs after the Chinese* (Studio Vista, London, 1980), Plates 22-7. The earthenware examples are not New Hall. It is a surprise to find that some tea or breakfast services bearing this pattern include handled teacups, rather than handleless teabowls.

Another very popular New Hall blue printed design is that which I shall term 'The Emerging Boat' pattern because in this general 'Willow' pattern type design this version has a Chinese style boat pulling away from the main island with its very prominent willow tree. Indeed, the 'Crossed Willow Tree' motif may be the best description for this pattern, except that some other designs include a less prominent tree with crossed-over trunks. The hand-painted Chinese design occurs on Chinese export market dinner services and other forms and is shown here in Plate 280. It is shown on both porcelain and on earthenwares in Robert Copeland's *Spode's Willow Pattern*..., there termed the 'Rock' pattern. It is also a standard blue printed design found on Caughley porcelain, usually at a period slightly before the New Hall porcelains were made. This 'Emerging Boat' print occurs on various forms of New Hall teawares fashionable around the 1800 period, although it may have been introduced in the 1790s. The early versions (as Plate 281) show rather spiky leaves to the crossed willows. Later versions are more regular (Plates 282-3). Like other blue printed designs, it can occur without gilding, with simple gilt line embellishments or with quite intricate gilt borders. When intricate borders occur one can find pattern numbers added to the major pieces in a service. The covered sugar basin shown in Plate 234 has the pattern number '473' which relates to this border. The same gilding and pattern number can occur on other blue patterns – see Plate 289.

The secondary print found on the reverse of some pieces is shown on the slightly gilt, so-called silver shape teapot in Plate 284. The form of this teapot and that shown by Dr. Watney in his Plate 96B suggests a date in the 1790s at least for these pieces, but most specimens bearing this print relate to the early 1800s.

As with other printed patterns, several different versions can be found, depending on the shape of the article and

PLATE 281. *A New Hall coffee cup and saucer printed in underglaze blue with a close copy of a Chinese hand-painted design – see Plate 280. The foreground and water has been shaded in by hand brushwork. Diameter of saucer 5in. (12.7cm). c.1790-5.* W.A. VYSE COLLECTION

PLATE 282. *A blue printed New Hall saucer shaped plate from a tea service showing a slightly different version of the 'Emerging Boat' pattern. Compare Plate 281 with this plate. Diameter 8½in. (21.59cm). c.1790-5.* GODDEN COLLECTION

PLATE 283. *A New Hall oval, handled covered sugar bowl bearing an elongated, shallow version of the 'Emerging Boat' design. Compare this with Plate 282. Each tea service would have required many different copper plates to fit the various shapes and sizes of pieces. 5½in. (13.97cm) high. c.1795-1800.* THE LATE A. DE SAYE HUTTON

Plate 284. *The reverse or auxiliary print to the basic 'Emerging Boat' print (as also seen on the cover to the sugar bowl in Plate 283). The spout on this teapot is particularly well gilt. 6in. (15.24cm) high. c.1795-1800.* G. Page collection

Plate 285. *A New Hall covered sugar bowl bearing a revised version of the 'Emerging Boat' print, now including two boats and a different tree. This is sometimes referred to as the 'Ducks' pattern. 7½in. (19.05cm) long. c.1805-15.* J.A. Chamberlain collection

PLATE 286. *A New Hall saucer shape plate from a tea service showing the full version of the revised, or second, 'Emerging Boats' (or 'Ducks') blue print. Gold line edge. Diameter 7¾in. (19.69cm). c.1805-15.* GODDEN COLLECTION

possibly on the period of manufacture. The earlier, pre-1800 examples of this pattern seem to be printed in a particular deep bright tone of blue. In some versions the sunshade like covering to the emerging boat has seemingly been divorced from it and appears more as a separate rock.

One rather rare 'ducks version' of the emerging boat design may, I believe, be considered as a separate pattern. The covered sugar basin in Plate 285 bears this probably post-1800 design and the full version is seen in Plate 286. The differences between this and the standard versions are many but the main point is that the former very prominent crossed-over willow branches now appear more as an apple tree and another Chinese style border is used. The boat has also been redrawn and another comes to join it from an opposite small island. If you are seeking a separate name for this pattern I suggest 'The Emerging Boats' – note the plural form. It has also been referred to as the 'Ducks' pattern, as various waterfowl are active in the design. The engraving technique has also changed to the later stipple effect, dots rather than straight lines or cross-hatching.

Another very elaborate Chinese style 'Willow' pattern

PLATE 287. *A New Hall teapot stand decorated with yet another Chinese landscape design with two moths or butterflies above the temple. Oriental style green line edge. See Colour Plate 57. 7¾ x. 6½in. (19.69 x 16.51cm). c.1795-1805.* GODDEN COLLECTION

PLATE 288. *A New Hall coffee pot, of standard shape, bearing the two moth 'Willow' pattern type blue print, as Plate 287. Oriental style green line edge. 10¼in. (26.04cm) high. c.1795-1805.*

GODDEN COLLECTION

type design found on New Hall porcelains can be distinguished by the two moths or butterflies occupying the air space in the top middle of the picture. I show the teapot stand and coffee pot versions of this, probably post-1800 design in Plates 287-8. Again, some versions have added, factory, gilding. The gilt star and the gold inner border added to the saucer shown in Plate 289 quite spoil the blue printed design, but such additions would materially have increased the cost of the set. The pattern number for this gilt version is again 473, as this number relates to the gilt decoration. This gilt border was used also on the different print shown in Plate 234. Some of the New Hall blue printed designs of the post-1795 period can bear Chinese style green or brown enamel edges instead of a more expensive gilt line. Such painted edges are certainly not confined to New Hall examples.

Possibly, as research continues, other underglaze blue prints will be found on pre-1813 New Hall hybrid hard-

Plate 289. *A New Hall saucer bearing the two moth blue print (as Plates 287-8) but enhanced (or spoilt!) by the added gilding, as Plate 234. Gilder's sign and pattern number 473 which relates only to the gilt border design. Diameter 5¼in. (13.34cm). c.1805-13.*

Dr. A. Kirkby collection

Plate 290. *A post-1813 New Hall bone china saucer shape plate from a tea service bearing a typically light toned version of the popular 'Pagoda' or 'Broseley' pattern. This design is by no means restricted to New Hall. Blue printed 'New Hall' mark in double circle. Diameter 8½in. (21.59cm). c.1813-18.*

D. Greenfield collection

paste porcelain. It is certainly surprising that I have not as yet noted the most popular of all Chinese style landscape designs on the earlier New Hall porcelains. I refer here to the so popular variously called 'Pagoda', 'Broseley' or 'Two Temple' pattern, as Robert Copeland described this pattern. Typically this design is very similar in general content to the 'Willow' pattern but with the bridge usually on the right rather than the left of the main island. A zig-zag type wall appears between the pagoda or temple and the centrally placed tree. Various windows are let into this wall. A fence or bridge crosses the lower right-hand corner of the design. It is, however, found on post-1813 New Hall bone china teawares.

This blue printed design is shown on a New Hall bone china saucer shape plate (Plate 290). This example bears the post-1813 printed 'New Hall' circular mark in underglaze blue. This plate was printed from a delicately engraved copper plate. The shading is in the form of small dots rather than engraved lines or cross-hatching, a technique associated with the earlier prints. The blue is a pleasing bright but light blue, a tone associated with the bone china and its related glaze rather than with the earlier body with its greater firing temperature.

This 'Pagoda' or 'Broseley' pattern appears on other New Hall bone china teawares, sometimes with various gilt enrichments. In one case all the main outlines are picked out with gilt lines to its disadvantage! This over-gilt version (Plate 291) is believed to be New Hall's pattern number 2488 and as such probably dates to the 1820s. This pattern was introduced at a surprisingly late period at the New Hall factory. It occurs in its original hand-painted version on Chinese porcelains and was then much copied in printed versions at the Caughley factory in the 1780s and 1790s. It is to be found on most early nineteenth century English porcelains and on many makes of earthenware.

Other blue printed designs were used as a base for various patterns that varied according to the added ground or enamelled over-printing, sometimes with gilding. The coffee cup[16] on the right of Plate 293 shows the most common of these blue base prints. The coffee can on the left shows one of the coloured over designs. New Hall's patterns 272, 274, 360, 490 and 856 represent recorded versions of this basic blue printed design. At least three other versions occur but their numbers have not as yet been recorded.

Plate 291. *A New Hall bone china London shape teacup and saucer bearing a version of the 'Pagoda' or 'Broseley' pattern, with outlines picked out in gold. Pattern number 2483 (referring to the gilt version) on the cup. Diameter of saucer 5½in. (13.97cm). c.1820-5.* Godden collection

Before leaving the subject of underglaze blue printed designs transferred from heated copper plates by way of transfer paper, some rare blue designs were transferred by the bat-printing process – to be discussed in Chapter IX. These blue designs were in fact applied on to the glaze, but the cobalt readily sinks into the glaze giving the effect of an underglaze blue print or painting. The bat-printed designs, being made up of small dots rather than engraved lines, have a finer effect than the earlier type. Indeed the bone china examples shown in Plates 290-91 may have been bat printed on (rather than under) the glaze.

It is convenient in this chapter to discuss also the few rare New Hall designs that were hand painted in underglaze blue. These designs tend to be early, prior to 1795, and they are mainly known on unusual shapes, not on standard teawares. These blue designs do not bear a pattern number or any other form of mark.

The 'House, Rocks and Tree' pattern is here shown on an early three-footed jug (Plate 108) and reversed on a simple mug form (Plate 294). I consider both these to be versions of the same pattern, for with hand-painted designs individual interpretation takes a hand. Also, of course, the basic pattern is adapted to suit different shapes

Plate 292. *A New Hall silver shape teapot stand decorated with a Chinese style blue printed border design. Enamelled centre in the style of the fashionable Chinese export market porcelains. 7½ x 6¼in. (19.05 x 15.88cm). c.1790-1800.* Godden collection

PLATE 293. *A New Hall coffee can (left) and a coffee cup decorated with a standard blue printed so-called 'Tobacco-leaf' design (after a Chinese original). This print occurs with various added enamel and gilt enrichments, as the unfinished cup (right). Patterns 272, 274, 360, 490 and 856 are based on the underglaze blue design. Cup 2¼in. (5.72cm) high. c.1800-10.* GODDEN COLLECTION

PLATE 294. *A rare early New Hall mug decorated with a hand-painted underglaze blue Oriental style landscape design. A different version is shown in Plate 108. 5½in. (13.97cm) high. c.1784-8.* GODDEN COLLECTION

or a border can be added to complete the design – as has happened in the case of the jug. This Chinese style pattern is very rarely found on New Hall porcelains, perhaps because it is seldom recognised. This jug, for instance, was catalogued by a leading London auctioneer as Caughley and was originally accepted as such. This rare form can occur with different handle forms and with blue printed designs as well as the even rarer hand-painted pattern.

A rather simpler hand-painted house, tree and fence design without the prominent rocks is found on some also very rare dessert wares, attributed to New Hall. It is here shown on a fluted dessert plate (Plate 295). Similar enamelled plates of this shape are shown in Plates 68, 195 and 204, but there is a slight element of doubt about the attribution of these blue painted dessert wares.

The oval moulded basket and stand shown in Plate 296 is generally considered to be New Hall, although again there is an element of doubt. It is painted with various floral sprays in underglaze blue and the moulded florets are also picked out in blue. At least two pairs of these baskets are known and are believed to have come from a dessert service. The stand to one pair has not been pierced; it shows only the moulded basketwork edge. I do not, however, know of any matching plates or fruit dishes.

Rare New Hall dessert wares are known with a moulded Sèvres style shell like edge. The moulding is accentuated with underglaze blue and gold but I do not consider this to be a true underglaze blue design. An

Plate 295. *A New Hall moulded dessert plate of the same form as the Duvivier decorated set shown in Plate 195, but painted in underglaze blue with a simple mock-Oriental landscape. Other early dessert service shaped dishes also bear this hand-painted design. Diameter 8¼in. (10.96cm). c.1787-92.* Godden collection

Plate 296. *A rare moulded and openwork dessert basket and stand, believed to be New Hall. Hand painted with flower sprays in underglaze blue. Other dessert wares should occur bearing matching blue floral sprays. Stand 10 x 8in. (25.4 x 20.32cm). c.1785-95.* Godden of Worthing

Plate 297. *A moulded (Sèvres style) dessert dish, matching examples shown in Plate 208, the moulding picked out in underglaze with added gilding. See Colour Plate 58. 10¾ x 8¾in. (27.31 x 22.23cm). c.1790-5.* THE LATE A. DE SAYE HUTTON

Plate 298. *A very rare New Hall sprinkler (for sugar or condiments) decorated in underglaze blue with simple floral sprays, rather in the Continental manner. 3¾in. (9.53cm) high. c.1785-95.* MERCURY ANTIQUES

example is shown in Plate 297; matching shapes were shown in Plate 208.

The Meissen so-called flowering onion pattern can also occur on New Hall porcelain. The only example known to me was included in a mixed group illustration used by Charles Rowed in his book *Collecting as a Pastime* (Cassell, London, 1920). The teapot with its typical clip handle is obviously New Hall, but this piece may have been made to match an incomplete Continental tea service rather than being a standard New Hall design. It is noteworthy, however, that it does not bear a mock crossed swords mark.

Simple floral spray designs which may or may not have been inspired by Continental imports can occur on New Hall porcelains of the 1780s or early 1790s. A very rare example is shown in Plate 298. It is strange how many early New Hall shapes are known only with blue and white designs.

The major pieces of a New Hall tea service painted with the 'Royal Lily' pattern, a design favoured at the Worcester factories, were sold by Messrs. Bonhams in December 2002. This gilt enriched, underglaze blue pattern bore the pattern number 281, showing it was a stock New Hall pattern although it had not been previously reported. The teapot and sugar bowl shapes were as Plate 168.

Other early New Hall blue printed and blue painted designs may well await discovery, but one should bear in mind that such blue decorated porcelains could have been made by other firms which were producing rather similar looking hybrid hard-paste porcelains towards the end of the eighteenth century. Such contemporary makers include the later Caughley, early Coalport, Chamberlain-Worcester, some late Liverpool wares, Wolfe porcelain and 'Factory X' which may be associated with Keeling, one of the first partners in the Tunstall enterprise – see Chapter II.

The New Hall story and the identification of its products is complicated. The eighteenth century examples decorated in underglaze blue have been rather neglected, at least by collectors of English blue and white porcelain. Examples in my own collection and illustrated in this chapter have been sold to me under various erroneous descriptions – Caughley, Worcester, Coalport and even Derby! There is therefore much scope for the knowledgeable collector or specialist. Although the number of known New Hall blue printed designs is small, the number of forms they may appear on is impressive.

The reader will be able to compare the New Hall blue and white wares and patterns with other types by consulting *Godden's Guide to English Blue and White Porcelain* (Antique Collectors' Club, 2004)

---

1. See David Holgate's Plate 107 in his 1987 *New Hall* book.

2. The leaf shaped dishes, like other objects, were made in various sizes, at least four. That shown in Plate 248 was the most popular.

3. The part set, David Holgate informed me, included two, unmarked, plates, the bowl part of a rice-bowl type sugar box which would have had an inverted saucer like cover and various teabowls, handled coffee cups and saucers.

4. If one accepts that the lion crest mark does relate to the Palatinate crest mark of the Frankenthal factory in Germany under Paul Antoine Hannog, then it should be borne in mind that my reading of the Continental authorities suggests that it was an early mark only used in the 1755-61 period. That is, as I understand the position, well before Nicholas (or Pierre) Berthevin attempted to sell the secret of transfer printing to the Frankenthal management in the subsequent Carl Theodor period, when an entirely different mark was used. There seems, therefore, no direct link between the lion crest mark and any experiments in printing at Frankenthal in or about 1770-2.

5. David Holgate has commented on my linkage of the Earl of Shrewsbury with this mark and has pointed out that the Earl was more concerned with affairs (!) in London than with Staffordshire manufacturers. See *Transactions of the English Ceramic Circle* Vol. 14, Part 2 (1991).

6. Another example in a private collection has the border design applied to the inside (not the exterior), leaving more room for the scenic print. It also has a gilt line at the rim.

7. The lion crest mark occurs on a grooved handle coffee cup in my collection. This could be New Hall, but the match is not certain or unique.

8. A very scarce major variation has been noted with two persons on the bridge – see page 294.

9. See *Liverpool Porcelain of the Eighteenth Century* by Dr. Bernard M. Watney (Richard Dennis, 1977), Fig. 374.

10. Ibid., Figs. 375 and 402-3.

11. As this design occurs on earthenwares and on porcelains that do not, in my experience, link with undoubted New Hall shapes, I have reservations regarding this print with the two figures on a bridge.

12. See Messrs. Phillips' Watney collection auction sale catalogue, Part I, of 22 September 1999, Lot 445.

13. In connection with the earthenware version, it has been suggested that the engraver was Thomas Rothwell. Could he have also worked at New Hall or supplied that company with their prepared copper plates?

14. Another example from the Watney collection is featured in Messrs. Phillips' auction sale catalogue, Part I, of 22 September 1999, Lot 441.

15. The teapot (ref. no. DW 2382) is on display; the other pieces are in the reserve collection.

16. This cup is of an unusual shape with a rounded foot. It has been suggested that it is not New Hall. Other shapes with this blue version are awaited to help identification.

CHAPTER VIII

The 'Cottagy' Oriental Style Designs

Collectors and authors have a great temptation to show off their finest pieces, their rare examples and, more especially, unique articles. This is very understandable, but it is not all that helpful to the new collector. This practice also grossly distorts the overall picture of the factory's products.

This is certainly the case with New Hall. The factory did not prosper for over fifty years by producing unique one-off pieces; it would not have existed for fifty days had it endeavoured to do so! A porcelain factory lives not on gateau but on bread and butter lines. Without its large sale of less expensive wares the management cannot pay its weekly wage bills or order the raw materials and fuel that are its life blood. The popular lines are largely popular simply because they are (or were) inexpensive or relatively affordable to a large proportion of the market, although masses of even nineteenth century households would have existed without a single porcelain tea service or perhaps any porcelain at all in their homes.

To ensure that your products or your porcelains are affordable in competition with the cost of other makes you obviously have to produce simple shapes, by the cheapest methods. You also should decorate them in an acceptable but simple manner, preferably with patterns that can be painted by semi-skilled, cheap, labour; in the ceramic industry this means by women, young girls or boys. You certainly do not add gilding, which necessitates an extra firing and then hand burnishing.

It also helps if the patterns (blue and white or equally the coloured designs) are a happy mixture of traditional Oriental designs, combined with English fashion, to produce a neat, almost Regency charm, attractive to the vast middle classes.

PLATE 299. *A typical grouping of New Hall teawares of the 1790s, decorated with an originally inexpensive Chinese export market type simple overglaze enamel pattern, without gilding. This was to be New Hall's pattern 171 but was also copied by other manufacturers. Teapot 5¾in. (14.61cm) high. c.1790.* GODDEN OF WORTHING

The New Hall partners in the 1780s did not invent the designs that are now associated with the name. Most of these designs originated in China and were there painted on the thousands of tons of Chinese export market porcelain that were imported into Europe in the eighteenth century. These designs painted for the white 'Foreign Devils' proved so popular that they were widely copied by our own manufacturers. Many of these Chinese designs were slightly amended so that few are exact copies of the original. Several so-called 'New Hall' patterns will be made up variations which manage to retain the spirit of the Chinese porcelains – not that 'spirit' is the right word for some of these designs are rather lifeless! Yet, they proved so popular.

It was probably the Anglo-Chinese style of decoration that Dr. John Aikin had in mind when he wrote in 1795: 'The china made at New Hall is very little, if at all inferior, especially in colours, to that of the East Indies...'.[1] By the East Indies he of course meant the Chinese porcelains imported (as a state-granted monopoly) by the English East India Company.

With the possible exception of Chelsea, all our eighteenth century porcelain factories produced a large range of Oriental-inspired patterns. Our underglaze blue designs were almost exclusively Oriental in feeling. This was simply because this style was what the buyers demanded. All manufacturers also produced Chinese figure designs painted in colourful overglaze enamel colours.

The formal floral designs, however, tended to become popular rather later in the century, by about the mid-1780s, continuing into the nineteenth century, in other words in the New Hall period. Perhaps the major producer of Chinese export market floral designs was the Lowestoft factory in Suffolk. Typical examples are illustrated in specialist books such as my *Lowestoft Porcelains* (Antique Collectors' Club, 1985). The Lowestoft porcelains are of a soft paste type containing calcined bones, quite different from the harder New Hall body.

The problem group of porcelains which I have termed 'Baddeley-Littler'[2] may be a class referred to by Josiah Wedgwood in 1786 when giving evidence at Whitehall being, he stated, 'empowered to speak in the name of the Potters and of the proprietors of Mr Champion's Patent and also in the names of Messrs. Baddeley Booth & Company, China Manufacturers...'. Porcelains of the 1780s which I tentatively associate with Baddeley's factory managed by William Littler are illustrated in *Staffordshire Porcelain*. Chinese formal floral designs are shown in Plates 45-9, 56 and 59 of that book and are in the general New Hall style – or, rather, in the popular style which came to be universally accepted as typically New Hall.

Other early types could be cited but by 1800 nearly all our porcelain manufacturers were producing simple Oriental style designs. The saleability of these English copies had been greatly helped when in December 1791 the Directors of the English East India Company decided to cease their bulk importations of the standard types of Chinese porcelains. It would be hard to underestimate the effect of this decision on the British 'Chinamen' (dealers in chinaware) and on the British manufacturers who were to find that their main commercial competition had been removed. The effect of this decision was delayed, however, as the Company held such large stocks of Chinese porcelain in their London warehouses, but no new bulk orders were placed in China after 1791. Some small quantities continued to be imported as the ship's officers' 'private trade' but this in the main comprised special orders for personalised items with the owner's armorial bearings or initials.[3]

The market was by the mid-1790s all but devoid of the popular and fashionable Chinese export market hard-paste porcelains of the type I have shown in Chapter I, Plates 1-7. This opened the floodgates to British manufacturers and helped successfully establish several new firms in the late 1790s, including Mintons. Other firms had already established themselves and were well positioned to take advantage of the lack of newly imported fashionable Chinese teawares. Prominent amongst these was, of course, the New Hall partnership.

However, by the the mid-1790s, when the effect of the cessation of imports from the East was being felt, the English porcelain manufacturers had moved on. Their traditional Oriental style patterns were being added to new style European forms. We had almost entirely progressed from the old type globular Chinese shape teapot to oval plan teapots based on our silver shapes. The covered sugar basins and creamers followed in general form the teapot shape, although some sets were still made with Chinese style handleless teabowls – see Plate 299.

It must not be thought that from the 1790s all new enamelled designs were of the Oriental type. In fact only a very small percentage of the designs drawn in any factory's pattern book would be in this style, yet in terms of the number of units sold they were very important. Obviously, far more teasets were sold at, say, £2 than richly gilt sets at £12. The market was large for this type of simple pattern which is why some New Hall designs introduced in the late 1780s were still selling thirty or

PLATE 300. *A New Hall oval teapot and its stand, decorated with a popular Chinese figure style design based on a printed outline. Coloured in by hand with slight gilding. See Colour Plate 59. Pattern number 425 but unmarked. Teapot 6¾in. (17.15cm) high. c.1797-1800.* MRS. P. LONGMAN COLLECTION

more years later, although after 1810 the demand for this type of pattern was decreasing.

The amount of Oriental-inspired New Hall (or New Hall look-alike) porcelains gave rise to the belief – still widely held – that all New Hall was decorated in this style. An internationally regarded postwar authority wrote of the New Hall products:

> The decoration tends to be limited to floral sprays, to copies of simple Chinese scenes derived from earlier factories, and less often to scenes copied from the 'Mandarin' patterns of contemporary Cantonese export-porcelain.

He was not alone in this belief.

I wish to discuss in this chapter both the Chinese style rather formal floral designs and the Oriental figure subjects – the highly popular types. If we examine the first thousand New Hall numbered patterns, or rather those that we know of, it is found that a mere fifty-five can be classed as comprising formal floral patterns in the conventional so-called New Hall style – that is slightly over five per cent. Possibly only three other new similar patterns were issued in the next thousand numbers because, after about 1810, fashions changed and in general the old Chinese style floral patterns were outdated. Few are found on the bone china body, certainly few new designs in this style.

The New Hall numbered patterns bearing formal floral designs are certainly not the earliest to be issued by the partnership. The first of the Chinese style designs seems to be number 67 (Plates 33, 33A and 112) and the most commonly found are numbers 121, which is usually unnumbered (Plates 34, 35, 109, 141 etc.), 171 (Plates 170 and 299), 172 (Plate 128) and 195 (Plates 48, 163, 175, 302-4 etc.) or 241 (Plate 174). These (with the exception of 121, which seems to occur only on early forms) were continued into the 1800s. An early figure subject design is New Hall's pattern 20 as here illustrated in Plates 91, 113, 127, 138, 148 etc. All English porcelain manufacturers seem to have issued Chinese style figure subject designs – clearly the style is by no means unique to New Hall. I do not consider floral pattern number 3 (Plates 28, 33A, 36, 38, 97, 98 and 107) to be a true Oriental style design, this appearing to me to be more European in its style of flower painting. Always bear in mind that most flower patterns are English or European in origin; it is only the very formally painted examples with obvious Chinese style border designs which are my concern in this chapter.

Regarding the Oriental figure designs, we know, by reference to David Holgate's specialist book *New Hall* and to the late Anthony de Saye Hutton's *A Guide to New Hall Porcelain Patterns* (Barrie & Jenkins, London, 1990), of eleven designs which are very clearly of this type. These are patterns given the numbers 20, 157, 421, 425, 431, 520, 621, 789, 1040, 1066 and 1172. Except for the last three, these patterns would have been originally issued on the hybrid hard-paste body. Even this dense body is very different from that used by the Chinese potters, but it is surprising how many casual (non-collector) owners of New Hall teabowls and saucers decorated with a mock Chinese design fondly believe they own Oriental examples. To many it is the surface decoration, the general appearance of the piece, that is all important. This was probably always the case, helped perhaps by the lack of a mark or the absence of a pattern number[4] on a New Hall Chinese style teabowl and saucer.

These formal floral and Oriental figure subjects are essentially British middle market designs. They strangely do not seem to have been favoured by Continental porcelain manufacturers or by the up-market English porcelain factories in the 1780-1810 period. They do not occur on Derby or on Flight period Worcester porcelains, for example.

I have already in previous chapters introduced illustrations of some Chinese inspired New Hall patterns. I could not have done otherwise because they are so typical of our factory's output. To many these designs are 'New Hall' and, indeed, I and other collectors were weaned on this type of New Hall. It was widely available when we started collecting and was quite reasonably priced. It also had a simple if 'cottagy' charm.

The charm or appeal of these simple floral patterns is very real. It is interesting to note that in the picture-book-cum-catalogue of an exhibition held at the Victoria & Albert Museum in collaboration with the Council of Art and Industry held in 1935, it was noted (by W.B. Honey in an unsigned introduction) that:

> The Staffordshire porcelain of the New Hall type also shows much simple but ingenious decoration, which makes it an excellent model for the modern manufacturer.

PLATE 301. *A group of New Hall teawares bearing a Chinese export market style floral pattern. Note the handleless teabowls and the smaller bowl serving as an open sugar bowl. Other more costly sets would have an oval covered sugar box, as Plates 168 or 172. Pattern number 354 on major items. Teapot 6¾in. (17.15cm) high. c.1797-1800.* SOTHEBY'S, SUSSEX

PLATE 302. *A moulded fluted New Hall coffee pot decorated with the popular and much copied Chinese export market style enamelled pattern known as the 'Knitting Wool' pattern, number 195 at the New Hall factory – see page 129. 10¼in. (26.04cm) high. c.1795-1805.*

S. STRONG COLLECTION

PLATE 303. *A hand-turned New Hall coffee pot of conventional shape with pierced knob, here shown with its circular stand. Decorated with the popular and inexpensive, non-gilt, 'Knitting Wool' design. Pattern number 'N. 195' on pot. 10in. (25.4cm) high. c.1795-1805.*

PRIVATE COLLECTION

It is still today the most available type of New Hall, simply because it was originally so popular and so much was sold. It is at the same time the class of porcelain that will present so many problems to the advanced collector. This is because, due to its popularity, most other 'middle market' English porcelain manufacturers copied the New Hall or Chinese designs. All tended to produce close copies of popular, that is saleable, designs. That is precisely why they were porcelain manufacturers – to make a saleable porcelain and earn a living!

David Holgate titled his first book (published in 1971) *New Hall and its Imitators.* In this he discussed some of the factory's contemporaries and illustrated a selection of Chamberlain-Worcester, Miles Mason, Minton, Caughley and Coalport porcelains, plus those then termed factories 'X', 'Y' and 'Z'. These sections opened one's eyes to the number of imitators or, as I prefer to call them, contemporaries of New Hall. Since then the position has become more complicated for we have now to consider several more rival makers of New Hall style porcelain patterns. It is a vast subject, touched on in the large book *Staffordshire Porcelain* (a multi-author work, published under my editorship in 1983, by Granada Publishing Ltd.). It was my original intention to include illustrations of such contemporary wares in this present book, but the subject is so vast and so complicated that I have decided to leave this to another book or books! The basic point, however, is that not all so-called New Hall patterns were produced by this one firm. It would probably not be exaggerating to say that there are more non-New Hall, New Hall style patterns on the market than there are true New Hall! The New Hall partnership was, however, from at least 1790 the market-leader in these Oriental style designs. It was the backbone of their production, the bread and butter of their diet.

I do not intend to list or discuss all the New Hall

PLATE 304. *Popular originally inexpensive New Hall teawares of the late 1790s decorated with that factory's pattern number 195, and so marked. Teapot 5¾in. (14.61cm) high. c.1795.* GODDEN OF WORTHING

designs that are in the general style of the late eighteenth century Chinese porcelains made for Europe. Yet one in particular is of special interest and serves to illustrate the several problems of attribution. A Chinese hard-paste original is shown in Plate 4, right.

This was copied as New Hall's pattern '195' which would have been introduced in the late 1780s. I illustrate it in this chapter under Plates 302-4. It is illustrated elsewhere in the book in Plates 48, 163, 175 and 310-1. This pattern is known to collectors as the 'Knitting Wool' pattern, on account of the wavy red line motif in the border.[5] Like most Chinese style patterns it also features various floral sprays arranged within the border design.

This pattern, which can easily be adapted to fit various shapes and sizes of objects, proved extremely popular. Yet Major Stringer's comment given in his 1949 book *New Hall Porcelain* has an element of truth. He stated: 'This freehand pattern is without character and its originator may have been a person lacking that desirable characteristic…'. Well, that person was probably Chinese,

Plate 305. *A New Hall obconical shape milk or cream jug of a popular shape (copied by other manufacturers) bearing an inexpensive floral design in the style of the imported Chinese teawares. Pattern number N 186. 4½in. (11.43cm) high. c.1795.* Mrs. W.A. Freeman

Plate 307. *A standard New Hall coffee pot enamelled with the Chinese export market style pattern, numbered 449. Decorative, but originally inexpensive. Painted pattern number N.449. 10¾in. (27.31cm) high. c.1795-1800.* Private collection

Plate 306. *A rare form of New Hall teapot decorated with the Chinese export market enamelled pattern, numbered 186. This and similar patterns were easily adapted to various sizes and shape of object – compare this with Plate 305. Pattern number 186. c.1808-13.* Private collection

Plate 308. *A standard New Hall silver shape teapot painted with a popular Chinese export market style pattern copied by other makers. Painted pattern number 172. 6in. (15.24cm) high. c.1795-1800.*
Godden Collection

for the painted pattern does occur on Chinese export market porcelain teawares of the approximate period 1780-90.[6] The New Hall partnership may have been the first English firm to have copied this Chinese design and to have entered it into their pattern book, under the number 195. The major pieces in a New Hall tea and coffee service will usually (but not invariably) bear this number written on the underside of the base. It may be rendered '195', 'N195' or 'No 195'.

I have a largish collection of pieces with this 'Knitting Wool' pattern, bearing pattern numbers from 2 upwards. Only those examples bearing the pattern number '195' will be from the New Hall factory. The Chinese hard-paste examples will not bear a pattern number but this simple fact should not be taken to indicate that all unnumbered examples are Chinese! John Turner (one of the early partners in this Staffordshire venture) or his son William issued this pattern on their own porcelains as pattern number 2. It was Thomas Minton's pattern 7.

Other contemporary English factories issued the same hand-painted pattern using their own different pattern numbers, such as 109, 124, 125, 145 or 189. Several manufacturers issued this popular inexpensive design without troubling to use a pattern number. All were in competition with each other producing this pattern on similar (but not identical) shapes and all striving to keep the price down to within a few pence of each other. That they were all reasonably successful in this shows the extent of the market for such simple formal floral patterns. All were producing complete tea services to sell for approximately £1. Some of the larger firms, such as the New Hall partnership, produced other objects such as bowls, jugs or mugs. These, however, are rarely found decorated with this inexpensive design.

Whilst New Hall's pattern 195 is the most often copied by other manufacturers it is wise not to regard any such Oriental-inspired formal floral or figure subject pattern as unique to New Hall. This leading firm may in most cases have been the first to use this pattern on English porcelain. Rival firms will have copied the most popular designs. To be New Hall the pattern number must be the correct one, although this will not appear on all pieces

Plate 309. *A New Hall, so-called punch bowl enamelled in the style of the popular imported Chinese porcelains. Such simple, formal, designs could be painted by cheap child painters. Diameter 11in. (27.94cm). c.1795-1805.* Godden of Worthing

(certainly not on cups and saucers!), the shape must be *exactly* right, as must the type of hybrid hard-paste porcelain and its glaze.

The examples made by other factories, in or outside Staffordshire, will be of a similar decorative nature and may well be interesting in their own right but they will not be New Hall – see Plate 48.

Turning to the New Hall patterns incorporating Oriental figure designs, the pattern later given the number 20 was the first to be introduced, in about 1783. This appears on an interesting range of early shapes – see Plates 91, 113, 127, 138, 148, 216 and 217. This design was entirely hand painted, in contrast to most of the later figure subject designs which were at least based on a printed outline. The early examples of this pattern, produced before about 1795, will not bear a painted pattern number.

I have previously illustrated versions of the design in Plates 310 and 311, a Chinese fashion large bowl. These are usually referred to as punch bowls, but they could have been used for fruit, pot-pourri, for any liquid or merely for display. This example (Plate 311) has the figure design, number 20, on the inside as well as on the exterior. It is always rendered in this naïve child-like manner. In this case the border of another popular pattern (195) has been used to decorate the inside of the rim. It is completely unmarked, as would have been a Chinese hard-paste porcelain prototype. The potting of the English copy is much thicker than a Chinese bowl and consequently it is heavier. The glaze on a Chinese example would be thinner and more uniform, lacking the mass of small bubbles usually present on New Hall examples.

Several versions of this pattern will be found and, being hand painted, some considerable differences in colours and in the detailing of the fence and other parts may be expected. A rare single figure variation is shown in Plate 312. As with other Chinese inspired designs, some non-New Hall examples may be encountered. It was a standard early design at 'Factory X', one of New Hall's early competitors.

A rather later but very popular New Hall figure pattern subject was number 421,[7] known to collectors as the 'Boy with the Butterfly' (Plate 313). The main aspects of this design, the figures in particular, have a printed outline to guide the young painters responsible for applying the quite broadly painted colours. The decoration at the sides and in the foreground was painted freehand. In this way the pattern could easily be adapted to suit different sizes and shapes of objects. This was intended as an inexpensive pattern. With this in mind it never has gilt embellishments and the shapes are of the simplest, without surface moulding. The teacups tended to be handleless teabowls except on the later post-1800 examples. The details of the faces have often worn away – if they were ever painted in. The teapot shown in Plate 313 illustrates these featureless faces.

Plate 310. *The exterior of the New Hall punch bowl decorated with the popular Chinese figure pattern design, number 20, in conjunction with an inner border of pattern 195. No pattern numbers. Diameter 9in. (22.86cm). c.1795-1805.* Godden of Worthing

Plate 311. *The interior view of the New Hall bowl shown in Plate 310, decorated with a combination of two popular, inexpensive, Chinese style designs, numbers 20 and 195. See Colour Plate 61. Unmarked. c.1795-1805.* Godden of Worthing

PLATE 312. *A New Hall saucer painted with a rare one-figure version of the popular normally two-figure pattern, numbered 20. Diameter 5in. (12.7cm). c.1785-95.* GODDEN COLLECTION

Another much more detailed Chinese figure design or 'Image pattern' was added to the New Hall pattern book just four entries later than 421, possibly in the same week. This is New Hall's pattern 425 of the late 1790s, a design now known to collectors as the 'Window Pattern' or 'the Boy at the Window' – see Plates 51, 221, 231 and 300. This was again a coloured-in printed outline design, but the tinting is usually more carefully accomplished than is the case with pattern 421.

John Wyllie, the London retailer, ordered sets of cup and saucers of this 'Imaged' pattern in the 1805-09 period. The brief published details[8] show that this New Hall figure design was then their most popular design, as far as Wyllie's middle-class business was concerned. 'Setts teas', comprising, I believe, twelve cup and saucers, were invoiced at 7s. with handles to the cups, 6s. without handles, that is teabowls and saucers, or only 4s. if slightly faulty 'seconds' were acceptable – which they obviously were as ninety-six sets were ordered in 1809. These prices for a 'sett' of cups were 7d., 6d. or 4d. per cup and saucer, respectively. John Wyllie ordered the 'full imaged' version on the new bone china body in 1812. This later version was usually enhanced with a gold edge and inner gilt line. This version on the new softer porcelain was given the pattern number 1066 and from this 1812 period the old pattern 425 found on the harder hybrid hard-paste body should have been discontinued.

The above statement makes commercial sense, but John Wyllie or his clerk was still ordering the old pattern number 425 in July 1815 and in January 1816, although there is a reference to the new bone china number 1066 in December 1812. The continuation of the old number may have been merely force of habit on the clerk's part or the New Hall factory might still have held stocks of the old harder bodied version three or four years after the change in porcelain and the introduction of the new pattern number.

It is, however, puzzling to find that on one entry under the date 'January 24th 1816' teawares of both the old pattern '425' and the later bone china number '1066' were being ordered or had been received. The prices were the same for both pattern numbers.

The Wyllie accounts suggest (if prices remained constant over the 1809-12 period) that the cost of the colourful Chinese figure pattern (numbers 425 or 1066) was much the same as the simple black printed landscape pattern (number 1063) with its black line (non-gilt) border. Although the figure or 'image' pattern is far more colourful and complicated, the painting in of the design over the printed outline could be carried out by child or apprentice labour at little cost. The design was cheap and cheerful, hence its popularity.

As with all printed patterns a large number of engraved copper plates had to be available to fit the different size of objects in a tea service or to suit the different forms that might need to be embellished with a popular design. Such rare items include mugs and jugs, both produced in different sizes, requiring different sized engraved copper plates. In the case of cups, teabowls and saucers, more than one copper plate could be required to speed production. Such articles are required in large numbers and several similar engravings would be in almost continuous use.

This coloured-in printed outline pattern which covers most of the surface of the article occurs, in my experience, only on plain shapes, that is non-embossed non-fluted surfaces. It occurs on standard simple forms, not on fancy shapes.

The Wyllie accounts, which feature this popular inexpensive pattern over several years, give us an idea of the standard charges for it (Plate 300) numbered 425:

'Image', 'Imaged' or 'Full Imaged'	
Teapots	4s. and 3s.6d.
Creamers	1s.

PLATE 313. *A New Hall late silver shape teapot with its stand, decorated with a standard and inexpensive Chinese style figure pattern known as the 'Boy with the Butterfly' or pattern number 421. Teapot 6in. (15.24cm) high. c.1795-1804.* PRIVATE COLLECTION

Pint basins	1s.6d.
Bread and butter plates	1s.6d.
Sugar boxes and covers	2s.
Sugar bowls (no covers)	1s.
Teabowls and saucers	6d.
Handled teacups and saucers	7d.
Coffee cans and saucers	8d.
Breakfast bowls and saucers	1s.
Bute shape teacup and saucers	1s.

The breakfast bowls and saucers were probably rather large versions of the teabowls. This inexpensive pattern was available with open sugar bowls (at 1s.) or with the oval (or London shape) covered sugar box at 2s. These prices seem to have applied both to the old pattern number 425 and to bone china teawares of pattern 1066.

Another Chinese figure pattern was given the number 789. This is of a higher quality with intricate scrolling and gilding. Presumably on account of its higher price, this was clearly not as popular as the less expensive pattern 425 and is consequently now much rarer. Originally it may have been introduced merely as replacements to a Chinese tea service and then added to the factory pattern book as a design available to all customers.

In general terms the inexpensive Oriental style formal floral patterns and the Chinese figure designs went out of fashion by about 1810. They were largely replaced by the printed English landscape and figure patterns produced by the bat-printing process. This is the subject of Chapter IX. They were novel, good looking and inexpensive, whilst the patterns in the style of Chinese export market porcelains really related to the eighteenth century. Nevertheless, these coloured designs formed the basis of the partnership's popularity and standing in the middle-class market. The designs were relatively inexpensive and the hybrid hard-paste New Hall porcelain was strong and durable. The wares were fit for their purpose.

I have in the next chapter explained the need to engrave (or purchase from specialist engravers) a long set of copper plates to match the size and shape of the various porcelain forms, if one seeks to produce printed tea services. With several of the figure subject designs (but not the formal floral and border patterns) these printed outlines were completed by hand labour, normally young children (mainly girls) who would colour in the printed outline – a reasonably simple task well suited to semi-skilled cheap labour.

These young paintresses were usually paid on a piece-rate basis, or as a team. The payment would be by the potter's dozen. This count varied considerably, the standard Staffordshire count to the dozen being for teawares:

The large bread and butter plates	12
Large teapots	18
Large (pint-size) slop bowls	24
Small teapots (2nd size)	24
Large milk jugs	24
Small slop-bowls (half pint size)	30
Teacups	36
Coffee cups or cans	36
Saucers	36

This scale relates to the size of the object and therefore the amount of work or time required to decorate each object. The smaller the object, the more to the dozen and therefore the more one had to complete to earn the payment for the potter's dozen.

This calculation was expressed in a different manner in the Chamberlain records at Worcester. The following list of payment units relates to the 1780s or 1790s and could well be applied to New Hall porcelains of the same period and to the payment of their painters and gilders. The Chamberlain piece-rate list reads:

Teapot 4th [large size]	3½
Teapot 3 and 2nd [sizes]	3
Teapot stand	1½
Spoontray	1½
Cream ewer	1½
Milk pot and cover	2
Sugar box and cover	2½
Slop bason, pint	2
- do - ½pint	1½
Tea canister and cover	2
Plate 2nd [large size]	2½
Plate 1st [size]	2
Saucer	1
Teacup	1
Coffee cup	1

This table could also be used in pricing. A 1s. per unit priced design would mean that the large teapot was 3s.6d., the stand 1s.6d. and so on. These payment and pricing lists could be applied across the whole range of a factory's pattern books, not only to the simple, popular designs discussed in this chapter.

With regard to Chamberlain's porcelain works at Worcester, its period is much the same as that for New Hall, in the case of Chamberlains from the 1780s as decorators and from c.1790-2 as porcelain manufacturers. Taking their first fifty numbered patterns, these ranged from £1.16s.0d. for a simple Chinese figure design – 'Common Image, no border' – to 10gns. for richly gilt teawares painted with fruit. Most patterns, however, fell into the popular price range of 2gns. to 4gns.[9] The Chamberlains and the New Hall partnership were competing for much the same market; both prospered.

The market for attractive but simply decorated and therefore relatively low priced porcelain tea services was certainly expanding as the eighteenth century drew to a close. Richard Champion's extended patent for the use of china stone and china clay in a translucent porcelain body expired in 1796 – see Chapter I. The New Hall partners no longer held sole rights to produce such hardish porcelains if, indeed, they ever enjoyed such a monopoly.

By about 1800 there were many different manufacturers of useful porcelains, mainly teawares. In the vast majority of cases the added designs are close copies of popular New Hall style simple floral patterns of the cottagy type discussed in this chapter.

These contemporary porcelains serve to underline the popularity of such simple patterns. The competition in the market must have been large and the profit margin very small, but the market was huge. Once the importation of the Chinese originals all but ceased in 1792, the New Hall partnership were the market leaders for such middle market tableware designs.

1. *Descriptions of the County from thirty to forty miles around Manchester* (1795).

2. See *Staffordshire Porcelain* edited by Geoffrey Godden (Granada Publishing Ltd., London, 1983).

3. The full story of the cessation of the East India Company's trading in Chinese porcelain and on the 'private trade' importations is told in my *Oriental Export Market Porcelain* (Granada Publishing, London, 1979).

4. Pattern numbers, as previously stated, occur only on the main pieces of a New Hall tea service, not on the cups and saucers.

5. Michael Berthoud in his *A Cabinet of British Creamers* (1999) acknowledged John Pinnick's observation that the so-called jumble of knitting wool represents a Chinese coin (a cash) suspended on ribbons and used in China as a symbol of good luck and prosperity. A nice thought, lost on the English copyists of this popular pattern.

6. It is possible, but unlikely, that the Chinese might have copied this design from a drawing or sample sent out to China from Europe. It seems, however, merely to be one of hundreds of formal floral patterns favoured by the Chinese because child labour could mass-produce the designs.

7. A variation of this design (given the pattern number 431) has the main figure dressed in yellow and mauve rather than in blue, as is the case with pattern 421.

8. 'A London Staffordshire Warehouse – 1794-1825', a paper by Ann Eatwell and Alex Werner published in the *Journal of the Northern Ceramic Society*, Vol. 8 (1991).

9. See my *Chamberlain-Worcester Porcelain 1788-1852* (Barrie & Jenkins, 1982).

CHAPTER IX

The On-glaze Bat-printed Designs

I believe that the importance, charm, quality and scope of the bat-printed overglaze New Hall designs has been greatly understated. The New Hall essays in tasteful bat printing would fill a book in its own right! These early nineteenth century porcelains are decorative, highly collectable and as a group probably represent the most inexpensive of the New Hall porcelains now available, although some designs are very rare. A large range of printed subjects occur on both the hybrid hard-paste porcelains and the post-1812 bone china examples. This chapter therefore serves both to link the two basic types of New Hall porcelain and to highlight the decorative New Hall bat-printed designs.

The New Hall partnership made better use of its hundreds of copper plate engraved designs than any other factory, Spode included. They were used printed in various single colours or tastefully coloured in with overglaze enamels. They also occurred in association with numerous different borders, ground colours or gilt trim. They were decorative, interesting and affordable. No wonder they were popular.

The overglaze printed designs (the underglaze blue prints have been discussed in Chapter VII) present some problems but at the same time they assist in solving others and they certainly appear on a wide range of attractive and interesting shapes. Bat-printed patterns were introduced in the earlier, or hybrid hard-paste period and continued apace, into the post-1812 bone china period. They seemingly went out of fashion in the 1820s, for they are seldom found on the later shapes.

Statistically, if we were able to examine the lost factory pattern books, the bat-printed designs would not appear of great importance. If we took a selection of just over six hundred New Hall patterns from, say, number 400 to 1040, we would find under thirty numbers allocated to printed designs! Yet these twenty odd New Hall pattern numbers for bat-printed designs encompass a wonderful range of floral, figure and landscape patterns. Hundreds upon hundreds of copper plates bearing finely hand-engraved delicate designs were in use.

Really only the Spode factory rivalled (or perhaps led) New Hall in the quality and number of bat-printed designs produced in the early 1800s. The Spode factory did not, however, favour the colouring in of its bat-printed designs. This was possibly because they employed several competent artists who could paint free-hand, without the need of a printed base. It is noteworthy that New Hall's main Staffordshire competitor in the middle-class market, 'Factory X' (with several others), hardly produced any bat-printed designs.[1] Printed designs were economic only if you had a large output, for the sets of copper plates were time consuming and costly to prepare, each being made up of hundreds or rather thousands of accurately placed dots or punched points of varying controlled size and depth.

The initial problem to consider is when did the New Hall partnership, under John Daniel's management, commence to produce on-glaze printed patterns? The technique or style did not suit the globular teapots or indeed the silver shape pots, for we do not find New Hall bat-printed designs on these forms. Nor do they seem to occur on the oval ogee shapes discussed in Chapter VI and shown in Plates 164-72.

They first appear in their true design form on the straight-sided oval teapots, sugar boxes and creamers of the shape we now call 'Old Oval'. This was the case also at the Spode factory.

It has been stated that New Hall bat prints date from

PLATE 314. *An oval New Hall creamer of quite rare form (as Plate 181) decorated with a bat-printed landscape design and gilt trim. The print is one of a large number used as pattern 462, usually on teawares. 4½in. (11.43cm) high. c.1805.* GODDEN OF WORTHING

1795. I do not think that this was the case. Other authorities have suggested c.1800 but 1805 might be nearer the mark. New Hall's pattern 423 is the earliest I know with bat prints. These are floral designs, very much in the style of Spode's pattern 500. New Hall's pattern number 462 marks the commencement of a rich series of landscape or rural prints – see Plates 314-5 and 321-2. These again closely follow Spode's popular 557 series of printed designs. It should be noted that the full trim on 462, as it appears on the main pieces from a tea service, will not appear on the cups and saucers or other small objects which have only line borders – see Plate 315.

Given the fact that the first two New Hall bat-printed series of prints, number 423 (flowers) and 462 (rural landscapes), very closely follow popular Spode bat-printed designs[2] and that the same 'old oval' forms were used at both factories, the dating of the Spode essays in this technique is very relevant. The two great authorities on Spode printing, David Drakard and Paul Holdway, in their joint book *Spode Printed Ware* (Longman, London, 1983), state that the Spode bat-printed series started in 1803. I do not think that New Hall examples preceded the Spode and therefore consider that the New Hall bat prints were introduced in the 1803-05 period.

They may not have been immediately popular, for the essays on the 'old oval' shape teawares are quite scarce. Most examples will be found on later teaware forms and also on dessert wares continuing into the bone china period and the advent of London shape teawares after about 1812.

So far in this chapter I have been writing about what I call true bat-printed designs, where the pattern is complete in its own right, even though different borders or gilt trim were applied. A form of printing was, however, also practised and was introduced before the

PLATE 315. *A low oval New Hall creamer decorated with bat prints and '462' pattern gold trim. Note the leaf-like gilt motifs appear only on the major pieces, as Plates 321-2, not on the smaller objects like the coffee cans. The printed designs will appear rather different on various shapes – compare this creamer with that shown in Plate 314. 3in. (7.72cm) high. c.1805.* E. RANDALL COLLECTION

PLATE 316. *An 'Old Oval' shape New Hall teapot, each side decorated with a finely engraved bat print with gilt border and trim design together making New Hall's pattern 466. Each piece in the set will bear a different view. Painted pattern number 466 with a small cross device. 6in. (15.24cm) high. c.1805.*
PRIVATE COLLECTION

advent of the true bat printing. I here refer to the printing of an outline that could be used as a guide to the enamellers. These outlines relate to Oriental style figure designs, the slight printed outline being all but covered over by the later enamelling so that the patterns often do not appear to be printed at all. This practice was an old and standard one in the industry. As such it is in no way restricted to the New Hall management.

New Hall's patterns 272, 274, 421, 425, 431, 490, 621, 789, in the hybrid hard-paste period, are of this type. Number 425, the so-called 'Window' pattern, and 421, the 'Boy with a Butterfly', were particularly popular being inexpensive Oriental-looking patterns that were over-painted by child or apprentice painters. These early printed outline designs can occur on late silver shape teapots, whereas the true bat-printed floral and landscape designs do not. I have discussed the popular Oriental figure subject designs, such as number 425, in the previous chapter.

It should be noted that very many of the bat-printed designs now to be discussed, although complete in their inexpensive versions, were sometimes coloured over, but in general the print was so detailed and complete that the pieces could be sold without added colouring. This is not the case with the earlier printed outline designs, where the print was merely intended as a guide for the young painters.

Bat Printing

Bat printing is an overglaze technique enabling delicately engraved or etched designs to be transferred from the sheet of copper by means of a pliable bat or pad, depositing oil on to porcelains or other surfaces without the need to heat the copper plates. It is a cold printing process, which can be carried out with the minimum of labour (one man rather than a team of three or four) and expense. No hardening-off extra firing is required and badly placed, faulty designs can simply be wiped away and a new bat applied to the surface in the correct manner.

From the original buyer's point of view the relatively low cost of such wares and the charm and variety of designs available obviously weighed favourably in their choice of purchase.

For present-day collectors and students, particularly of New Hall porcelain, the bat-printed designs have many advantages. The original charm and delicacy still apply, but also the process spans both the hard-paste and the introduction of the bone china body c.1812; some prints are to be found on both types. Furthermore, we have a most important datable event associated with the bat printing technique, the patent taken out by Peter Warburton in 1810.

As with any printed pattern, everything depends on the quality of the engraved pattern on the copper plates and on the taste and beauty of the composition and its association with the articles it is to enhance. The on-glaze bat printing technique as practised by several English porcelain manufacturers from at least the 1790s lent itself to a great delicacy of touch. The printers did not have to charge deeply engraved lines with a thick cobalt blue mix but rather merely rub on to the engraved sheet of copper a thin oil.

With a copper sheet engraved for bat printing you can hardly see the recessed design, so finely is the pattern worked into the surface. Most of the work, certainly the shading, comprises small punched dots, spaced nearer together or further apart depending on the shading required.

Because the detail is both finer and more complicated than that employed for the underglaze blue hot printing technique, the time required to engrave the designs on the various sized coppers needed to print a complete teaset is very considerable. I have a small copper recently worked by a modern master engraver at the Spode factory, Paul Holdway. The engraved area measures only 3 x 2½in. (5.08 x 6.35cm), but Paul tells me that he spent 'approximately fifty hours' in engraving this one small sheet!

Although the engraving was time-consuming and therefore the tooling-up for a new design was expensive, it happens that the newly introduced bat-printed patterns of the approximate period 1803-20 tend to be of a harlequin nature, that is a variety of related designs, landscape or figure subject will be used to enhance a service. A tea service may, for example, bear well over thirty different views whereas with the earlier underglaze blue or overglaze outline printed patterns the same basic design usually appeared on each piece but in a different size or close version to fit each shape.

Once the complete set of engraved copper plates has been prepared, either by the factory's own full-time engraving department or else purchased from independent engravers to the trade, and a stock of glazed blanks produced, one can proceed to transfer the designs. But first a supply of pliable glue-like bats has to be made. This is normally done the preceding evening so that the bats can be ready for the following day's work. Various recipes exist for the preparation of the bat. One contemporary example reads: '1 bl. of glue melted down with 1 gill of beer or sweet wort, when properly melted pour it off on an even surfaced dish and let it remain until cold.'

The most convenient 'even surfaced dish' was found to be a glazed meat platter, the liquid glue run in to a depth of about ¼in. (0.64cm) or slightly more. When cold and set, the bottom surface (that resting on the glaze) will have a beautifully clean, glossy, grain-free skin similar to that found in a jelly when it comes away from its jelly mould. The glue and beer mix should not set solid but remain strong yet pliable, like rubber. Once set this sheet of glue can be cut up into sizes suitable for the engraving to be worked and the pieces lifted off the dish. With this cold, bat printing system, where no presses or heat are used, the size of each design should not be larger than that which can be held in the palm of the hand – that is some 7 x 5in. (17.78 x 12.7cm). If large sizes are attempted the bending or movement of the glue bat will result in unwanted distortion of the design. In essence bat printing lends itself to the transferring of a series of relatively small compositions, not long border designs.

The mode of proceeding is very simple – when all is well! The engraved copper is charged with a special oil. One recipe for this reads: '1 gill linseed oil, 1 oz. Barbadoes tar or oil of amber – boiled to the thickness of treacle or until it burns a feather'. The surplus oil is then wiped off the surface of the copper plate so that it remains only in the recessed parts. A piece of the already prepared glue-bat is then taken in the palm of the hand (or alternatively placed on a mat-like small cushion held in the hand) and the glue-bat pressed upon (or rolled on to) the oil-charged copper plate. This pliable glue-bat will then take up the oil from the recessed parts of the engraving. The oil-charged bat is then lifted (or rolled back) from the copper and placed upon the glazed porcelain. In this way the faint oil impression is transferred to the article. The design is then accentuated by dusting very finely ground ceramic pigment of the desired colour over the oil. This dusting was normally applied or dusted down from a linen bag, the dusting sticking only to the oil and not to the glazed surface. The surplus pigment is then blown or otherwise cleaned away and the piece fired at a relatively low temperature in an enamel kiln or oven to fix

Plate 317. *An attractive New Hall bat-printed coffee can and saucer from a service of pattern 511. A set with such intricate gilding could not have been cheap but was saleable on account of the varied printed motifs. See Colour Plate 62. Can 6¼in. (15.88cm) high. c.1805.* W.A. Brown

the colour and burn off the oil. The glue-bat can be cleaned and reused or put aside to be melted down for reuse the following day. Any gilt border or trim is of course applied last by the gilders. This requires refiring and then burnishing.

The bat printing technique sounds simple compared with the hot method and the use of paper transfers but difficulties could still arise. It was important for the glue-bat to be in the correct condition; if it was too pliable it would bend and distort as it was applied, resulting in a blurred impression or crooked or curved lines. The temperature of the room or the dampness of the atmosphere could affect the result to a surprising extent. The mixing of the glue, the oil, the colour-pounce as well as the condition of the glazed surface could all affect the result. Care and expertise were essential.

When all went well the effect could be quite beautiful and as only the oil was applied to the copper plate the engraved design suffered little wear when carefully used. The same design could also be dusted with different colours or enhanced with different gilt or coloured borders, so that the range of patterns available from any one set of copper plates was very great.

I have previously stated that this process was employed at the New Hall works in the approximate period 1803-20 but, while these statements are correct, it is believed that the technique was also used elsewhere (but probably discontinued) in the middle of the eighteenth century for the decoration of enamels and perhaps some porcelains. Abraham Ree's early nineteenth century part-work *The Encyclopaedia; or Universal Dictionary of Arts, Sciences and Literature* wrote of bat printing as 'an improved method of printing, comparatively of very recent invention, was introduced under the direction of the late Martin Barr... and where economy is the object of the consumer, this style of decoration suits very well...'. The Worcester company under Martin Barr and subsequent partnerships produced some very elegant and high quality bat-printed designs. The fact that the main Worcester company and Spode made such a feature of bat printing illustrates its high regard in the trade. It was not merely a convenient inexpensive mode of ceramic decoration. It was novel and decorative as well as inexpensive to produce, once the sets of copper plates had been engraved.

Plate 318. *A part New Hall 'Old Oval' shape tea service decorated with bat-printed scenes and gilt border, New Hall's pattern 473. Some prints, as the teapot, will appear with different gilt borders under a different pattern number, see Plate 316. Teapot 10¾in. (27.31cm) long. c.1805.* Messrs. Sotheby's

My information on the process has been largely gathered from lectures and demonstrations given by Paul Holdway of Messrs. Spode, who still practise this art, but various published views and accounts of the process are available. William Evans' 1846 work the *Art and History of the Potting Business* contains a description of the process, as does the official catalogue of the 1851 Exhibition. Chapter XVII in R.W. Binns' book *A Century of Potting in the City of Worcester* (B. Quaritch, London, 1877) is also of considerable interest. A very full and interesting paper by Colin Wyman was published under the title 'The Early Techniques of Transfer Printing' in the *Transactions of the English Ceramic Circle* (Vol. 10, Part 4, 1980). There are also several magazine articles on bat printing including the late C. Williams-Wood's article published in *Collectors Guide* magazine of June 1976. However, the fullest and most expert account is given in *Spode Printed Ware* by David Drakard and Paul Holdway (Longman, London and New York, 1983). This book includes good illustrations of the various stages of bat printing.

The delicately engraved bat-printed designs were introduced by the New Hall management within a year or two of 1803. The earliest bat-printed subject noted so far comprises simple floral sprays and was given the pattern number 423. Next we find a series of related scenic designs which were issued under the numbers 462 (Plates 314-5 and 321-2), 466, 487, 511, 559, 709 (Plates 319-20) and 744. The different pattern numbers mainly signify different added gilt borders or other embellishments. The landscape designs are extremely varied and attractive; one could trace well over fifty scenic prints which occur on tea services with these numbers. Most of the pieces in such sets will bear a different design. The oil transferred designs could be dusted with different colours, not always black, although this was the least expensive or least troublesome colour.

The early bat-printed multi-scenic subject New Hall designs issued under pattern 462 appear to have been preceded by a rare hand-painted (non-identical) version in monochrome. My hand-painted teaset (Plate 193) does not bear a pattern number but I assume it preceded the printed version. This replacing of hand-painted patterns with an inexpensive but acceptable form of printing obviously suited the manufacturers and was the object of the cost-cutting exercise. Seen side by side with the hand-painted pieces the printed version comes out extremely well.

When first issued these bat prints were transferred on to the early hybrid hard-paste body and on to teaware shapes of the form now known as 'Old Oval' with 'Bute' shape teacups and straight-sided coffee cans. New Hall teawares of these standard but rather scarce shapes are shown in Plates 316-8. It must be stated that several other factories made their versions of these standard English teaware forms and in some cases quite similar prints were added to these non-New Hall wares. The New Hall bat-printed 'Old Oval' shapes are scarce, as they were soon superseded by new style forms, such as 'New Oval', but normally in the amended prow version, as Plates 320 and 325, before progressing to the shapes found in the post 1814 bone china body.

Several of the bat-printed landscape designs bear gilt borders or other embellishments, but one less expensive series has simple black printed line borders. These black edged printed teaware designs are New Hall's pattern 709, as Plates 319 and 320, but the treatment is by no means exclusive to this factory.

The Spode factory in particular produced in their bone china body similar teawares to those New Hall porcelains here discussed. Most of the early Spode porcelains bearing landscape subject prints were issued under the Spode pattern number '557'. Miles Mason's pattern 240 was of a

PLATE 319. *A New Hall coffee pot decorated with the inexpensive pattern number 709 comprising bat prints within black line edging and trim. Painted pattern number 709. 10in. (25.4cm) high. c.1810.*

MESSRS. CHRISTIE'S

PLATE 320. *A New Hall prow shaped teapot decorated with the crocodile bat print within simple enamelled line borders and trim, as pattern 709. Painted pattern number 709. 10in. (25.4cm) long. c.1805-10.*

PRIVATE COLLECTION

Plate 321. *A New Hall prow shaped teapot and stand decorated with a version of the crocodile bat print (from a different copper plate from that used in Plate 320) with gilt trim. A more expensive pattern than the non-gilt later pattern 709. Pattern 462 (as Plate 315). Painted retailer's mark 'Abbott and Mist. Fleet Street'. 5¾in. (14.61cm) high. c.1806-9.*

E. Randall

similar type. It should be noted that not all bat-printed designs found on New Hall porcelain are unique to this factory. Several designs occur on other wares, either directly copied from the New Hall examples or taken from the same published source such as an illustrated book or print. It could well be also that the New Hall management themselves copied other firm's designs, in particular those of the market leader – the Spode company. In all cases, however, slight variations may be found between the various versions.

As to the source of the ceramic prints, one must remember that there were, at least in the cities, many print-sellers. Prints for wall decorations were extremely popular and of course many books were illustrated with prints as were music sheets and suchlike material. The Staffordshire manufacturers did not have to send to London for prints to copy; the local *Staffordshire Advertiser,* for example, carried advertisements, such as that which appeared in the issue of 8 January 1814:

> NEW PRINTS
> T. Allbut, Printer, Bookseller and Stationer, Hanley ... has just received a large assortment of elegant Prints, consisting of landscapes, views, ... groups of figures ... &c. got up in a superior style, and well adapted for engravers, and enamellers of china and earthenware....

Similar advertisements would have appeared over a very long period or at least the print- and booksellers would have been happy to sell their wares to the potters. Some special printed source books such as the *Ladies Amusement* date back to the 1750s.

The bat-printed New Hall teawares which bear, together with their pattern number, the name of the London china dealers Abbott & Mist are important from a dating point of view. This partnership between Andrew Abbott and James Mist flourished in Fleet Street, London, within the 1806-9 period. The partnership was dissolved on 25 March 1809, so any marked examples should have been ordered, made and supplied before that date. New Hall's bat-printed scenic pattern 462 is recorded with the painted name mark of this partnership – see Plates 321-2 This series of prints was, however, well established in the market by this period; the pattern number was not new in 1809.

The New Hall patterns numbered 846, 887 and 888 are very interesting as these always, in my experience, occur bat-printed in gold – that is, finely ground gold powder was dusted on to the transferred oil impression. These patterns were produced under Peter Warburton's patent (number 3304 of 1810, which was dated 13 February and was enrolled on 11 April 1810).

The abstract of Peter Warburton's patent shows clearly that the process was exactly the same as that carried out with normal bat printing except that instead of black, brown, green or blue ceramic colour being dusted on, gold or silver was employed.

Peter Warburton (a member of the New Hall partnership) stated:

> I take an impression from a plate of copper or any substance on which an engraving can be made, in the following manner –
>
> The necessary oils are rubbed with a boss into the figure, landscape or design engraved on the plate. The plate is then cleaned with the hand or otherwise, in order to take off all the oils except what fill the part on which the figure, landscape or design is engraved.
>
> A substance, composed of glue and isinglass, called by potters and printers a bat is then applied to the (copper) plate and the impression is taken off by means of a boss or a roller. The impression is then transferred from the bat to the earthenware, china or glass intended to be decorated by means of a boss; after which such preparations of gold or silver as are employed by painters to produce the metallic appearances called burnished gold or silver lustre, being previously dryed and reduced to a state of powder, are laid on the piece of china intended to be decorated with cotton wool, or any substance fit for the purpose, the gold or silver adhering to that part only which has received the impression. It is afterwards cleaned with silk, cotton or a like substance and then put in the oven or kiln in the usual way.

Peter Warburton also described a second method using paper to transfer the oil from the engraved copper plate to the object, instead of the glue-like bat. He also wrote of printing with 'silver and platina [platinum], as are made use of by painters to produce the metallic appearances called ... silver and steel lustre and have hitherto been effected by painting only'. I have not seen any examples of such silver or platinum printing but Dr. Bernard Watney kindly reported a cup and saucer with bat-printed landscape designs which he informed me show by X-ray florescence that the metal transferred or dusted on the oil to make the pattern was platinum. He added the note 'perhaps other prints you have are platinum also'. However, Dr. Watney's tested example does not have the appearance of platinum; the design is in a dark grey-black! Platinum should remain bright as it does not tarnish.

Warburton's patented gold printing is found on New Hall porcelains of the approximate period 1810-1812. Such teawares usually bear, at least on the major pieces, a large boldly painted publicity mark. I here show a typical example.

I have only noted this mark and New Hall's gold printing on the hybrid hard-paste porcelain, not on the later bone

Plate 322. *A covered sugar bowl matching the 462 patterned teapot shown in Plate 321 but of course bearing a different bat-printed landscape design. Painted pattern number '462' with London retailer's name 'Abbott and Mist, Fleet Street', inside the cover. 4in. (10.16cm) high. c.1806-9.* E. Randall

PLATE 323. *A blue and gold bordered New Hall teapot with gold dusted bat print on each side and on the cover. Painted mark 'Warburton's Patent' No. 888 (under a crown). 5¼in. (13.34cm) high. c.1810-2.*

GODDEN OF WORTHING LTD.

china body. I have not observed the technique used on dessert services or on jugs or forms other than teawares. Perhaps the technique was too expensive to be used on dessert services and even the teawares are rare and must originally have been costly.

It seems strange to us now that this specially hand-painted mark includes only Warburton's name, with no indication of the manufacturer's name or the New Hall address. This fact, however, underlines the general policy of the firm up to about 1814 that no identifying mark should be employed. Indeed, this 'Warburton's Patent' mark has only in recent years been correctly attributed to the New Hall factory

As I have already noted (see page 152), Peter Warburton was a son of Jacob Warburton, one of the first partners in the so-called New Hall partnership. Peter had succeeded his father on the board of directors and it was therefore natural that Peter's patent was used on New Hall porcelains. What we do not know is whether Peter Warburton was also associated with the introduction of the normal bat printing process at the New Hall works and whether he was responsible for the engraving of the copper plates. It could well be that, having control of the printing department, he saw the potential of dusting the oiled impression with precious metals. I have not noted any signature or initials on the engravings and so far as I know there is no evidence regarding the printing aspect of the New Hall decoration.

The patterns I have mentioned – 846, 887 and 888 – are three of the very few to bear Warburton's gold-dusted engravings; but these pattern numbers relate to the underglaze blue and gilt borders or surrounds which I believe were especially designed to complement these more expensive gold printed patterns. We can therefore surmise that these patterns were introduced early in 1810 when the Warburton patent was being worked. They form a very useful time-check on the sequence of New Hall numbers. The first bat-printed pattern, number 462, was included nearly four hundred patterns before the 846 Warburton patent of early 1810. The pieces with this marking of the approximate period 1810-12 help also to pinpoint the dates of the progression of New Hall teaware shapes, see page 252.

Whilst these three patterns, with their deep blue and gold borders or embellishments, were seemingly special to the gold printing process, it also happens that the earlier copper plate designs were used for other gold dusted patterns. The same, shallowly engraved copper plates

Plate 324. *An oval teapot stand bat printed in gold under Warburton's Patent of 1810, within underglaze blue and gilt border. 5¼ x 3¾in. (13.34 x 9.53cm). c.1810-12.* Private collection

could be used no matter what colour or metal was to be dusted on to the oil. It could therefore happen that gold printed designs transferred under Warburton's patent could duplicate any of the bat prints introduced previously and still available and deemed to be saleable. It seems almost certain that the gold printed versions would have been more expensive than the standard coloured prints. Even if Peter Warburton did not require a royalty payment, the gold content of the mix would have to be taken into account and, more importantly, the gold needed to be fired and then hand burnished.

I should mention that the Spode firm produced gold printed designs of two basic types: one where the print was simply applied via the oil to the white bone china, the other where it was laid over a deep blue ground. This later type appears rather heavy and I do not think the gold printing is set off at its best, the design being perhaps somewhat too delicate. It is interesting to note that the Spode essays in gold printing do not bear the Spode name mark, nor do they bear any reference to Warburton's patent. It would seem however, that Peter Warburton's 1810 patent pre-dated the Spode essays in this style for the Spode management apparently did not contest the patent application which would of necessity claim to be a new

Plate 324A. *A close-up of the bat-printed design used on the teapot stand shown in Plate 324. All the copper plates used for the bat printing process are engraved or etched with dots, rather than straight lines.*

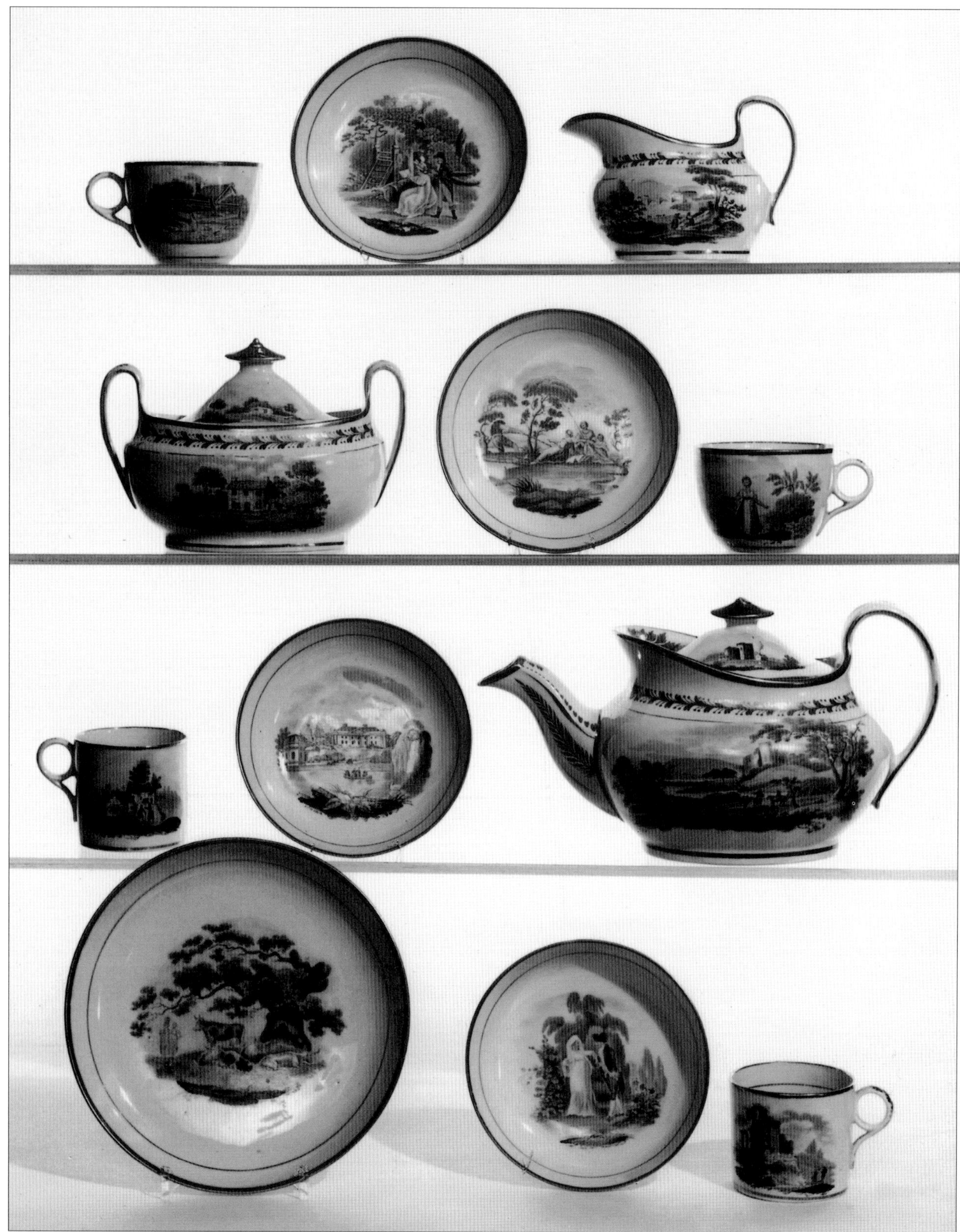

Plate 325. *A selection of New Hall bat-printed teawares in the hybrid hard-paste body with gilt trim and with hand applied over-painting. These teawares are New Hall's pattern 984, but note the full gilt border occurs only on the larger articles. Painted pattern number 984 on larger items, with tally marks. Teapot 6in. (15.24cm) high. c.1810-4.* Godden of Worthing Ltd.

PLATE 326. *Two New Hall hybrid hard-paste saucers with gilt borders, two examples from a service of pattern 466. Diameter 5in. (12.7cm). c.1810-13.* GODDEN REFERENCE COLLECTION

invention. Still, the Spode gold printed wares have the appearance of being nearly contemporary with the New Hall essays in this style. The Spode pattern numbers for gold printed designs include 1691, 1692, 1693, 1695, 1696, 1697, 1699, 1700, 1701 and 1703, but many pieces do not bear a pattern number. For information on the Spode bat-printed wares, both bone china and earthenware, the reader is referred to the two standard works – Leonard Whiter's *Spode* (Barrie & Jenkins, London, 1970) and David Drakard and Paul Holdway's *Spode Printed Ware* (Longman Group Ltd., London, 1983). The Spode gold printing usually occurs on their 'New Oval' shape teawares. See *Staffordshire Porcelain* Plate 153.

I have already mentioned that the New Hall bat-printed designs may be found in different colours. This applies also to the Spode examples and David Drakard and Paul Holdway's researches on the Spode pattern books and archives have suggested the following sequence of Spode colours: black and French brown c.1803; blue (on the glaze) c.1804; chocolate brown c.1810; gold c.1811; red 1817 (or earlier); purple c.1818; rose 1819; and green c.1821. We have no such factory guidelines for the New Hall bat prints, but no doubt the progression was much the same.[3] Colours which I have noted used for the dusted-on bat prints include black (the most common), brown, green, pink, blue and gold.

The New Hall gold printed porcelains produced by Peter Warburton's patent are of the prow shape, the teaware forms which probably superseded the 'Old Oval' and 'New Oval' shapes. It is, however, possible that the prow and the 'New Oval' were in production at the same period. The earlier 'Old Oval' shapes are shown in Plates 316-8, the 'New Oval' teapot in Plate 184, the prow shape in Plate 325. It would appear that the gold printed designs were only issued for a short period, perhaps for two or three years from 1810.

These standard shaped New Hall teawares were, of course, also embellished with a host of printed designs of a non-metallic type, not produced under Warburton's patent. The same shapes were also decorated with a large array of hand-painted designs.

As with other New Hall styles of decoration, the painted pattern number and also the 'Warburton's Patent' mark (when applicable) only occur in the main pieces of a service, not for example on the cups, saucers or coffee cans. It often happens, however, that a painter's or printer's tally mark was added by the pattern number or on its own. These tally marks can be quite helpful in identifying New Hall porcelains, especially as these devices can be found on the smaller items in a teaset, on articles that might not bear a pattern number. A selection of the more commonly found tally marks are reproduced in the mark section – see page 129.

Whilst writing of pattern numbers, it should be understood that these were by no means universally painted on the New Hall porcelains, not even on the

PLATE 327. *A Bute shaped New Hall teacup and saucer in the pre-1813 hybrid hard-paste body, delicately bat printed with a floral design within blue green border. Pattern number 934, but not marked, being a cup and saucer. Diameter of saucer 5in. (12.7cm). c.1810-12.* GEOFFREY GODDEN

PLATE 328. *A very rare New Hall eggcup stand with six eggcups and central container (for salt?). Each unit bears delicately engraved bat prints, with gilt trim. Pattern number 753. Diameter of stand 6¼in. (15.88cm). c.1810-2.* RODERICK JELLICOE

major articles. Many examples are unmarked.

Apart from the series of standard monochrome-printed landscape designs, the lucky collector can also find some attractive floral or fruit (pattern 753) subject prints. One pattern in particular is of superb quality and is to my eyes most attractive – I refer to pattern 934 illustrated on a teacup and saucer in Plate 327.

The Warburton's Patent New Hall teawares are, as previously stated, of the hybrid hard-paste variety, being produced in the 1810-12 period. It is important to note that the ring handles to the cups and coffee cans[4] have a circular aperture for the finger, as has the pattern 934 cup shown in Plate 327. These contrast with the more oval or egg-like handles which are found on the rather later, post-1812 bone china cups – see Plates 335-7, 341, 347-8, 350 and 351.

It must be remembered that the pattern number does not relate to the individual printed motif but to the general printed style and to the gilt border or other 'trim' – that is, the added border or borders or to the treatment of the print, plain or coloured in. This general rule I believe relates equally to any English factory – Spode, Minton, Machin, Ridgway or Factory Z, citing only a few of the better known porcelain manufacturers which produced bat prints.

Remember also that some popular printed subjects were used at factories other than New Hall. Nevertheless, some New Hall prints, especially when the correct pattern number is present, do enable the collector to identify some rare New Hall objects. Such a case presents itself in the eggcup stand shown in Plate 328. The simple floral bat prints represent New Hall's pattern 753.

This linking of bat-printed designs also enables us to identify the very rare New Hall coffee pot shape shown in Plate 329. In this case the pot, with its spout pressed back into the body to form an elongated lip, could have been used for hot water or indeed for any liquid.[5] The identification in this case can be confirmed by the pierced vase shape finial and by the body and glaze being typically New Hall.

Some New Hall bat prints which occur on typical New Hall teaware shapes, particularly on teapots with their large body area, are also found on dessert dishes and centrepieces. This duplication of use enables the identification of New Hall dessert wares to be confirmed and also enables some unusual, rare, shapes to be traced. This exercise is, however, mainly confined to the post-1812 bone china period.

It is possible that one or more of the several independent printers operating in the Staffordshire Potteries purchased New Hall blanks which they printed and sold on as a commercial venture. The existence of such mainly small firms is well documented in local directories.

I have seen some New Hall hybrid hard-paste teawares of the approximate period 1790-1810 which bear rather naïvely engraved non-New Hall overglaze prints, rather poorly applied. The additional trim also was poor, enamelled rather than gilt. The specimens seen do not bear a pattern number, although this lack of a number also relates to some factory decorated specimens.

Some of these rather strange prints comprise titled figure subjects within an oval frame. Titles or descriptions include 'Conjugal Felicity' and 'The Happy Fireside'. Others are not framed or titled and these include hay being loaded on a farm wagon. These rather crudely engraved prints can appear in a dark shade of black or in

Plate 329. *A very rare form of hybrid hard-paste coffee pot (or hot water jug) bearing a popular New Hall bat print with gilt trim. See Colour Plate 63. 9¾in (24.77cm) high. c.1805-10.*

Private Collection

Plate 330. *The reverse side of the coloured over bat-printed presentation jug also shown in Plate 437. This bone china jug bears the gilt date 1814. 6in. (15.24cm) high. 1814.* Godden collection

other colours. The effect is quite different from the finer, well-engraved New Hall factory printed designs.

The examples of New Hall bat-printed teaware so far discussed and illustrated in this chapter have been manufactured from the hybrid hard-paste body and I believe these date to the approximate period 1803-12. If a pattern number occurs on these examples it will be a lesser number than 1000.

The accounts of the London dealer, John Wyllie, importantly include, under the date 24 December 1812:

> 24 setts handled Black landscape china
> no. 1063 £7.4s.-0d.

These handled cup and saucers at 6d. each were followed by other matching items, such as:

14 teapots	at 3s.6d.
10 covered sugar boxes	at 2s.
12 cream ewers	at 1s.
16 slop bowls	at 1s.6d.
6 plates (bread and butter)	at 1s.6d.

also '12 setts teas full imaged, 1066 £3.12s.0d.'

As pattern numbers 1063 and 1066 are only found on New Hall's bone china teawares it would seem clear that this body and these patterns were available by the end of December 1812. As detailed in the last chapter, however, the earlier harder bodied version of bone china pattern 1066 (number 425) was still available as late as 1816 – see page 326.

It is also of interest to note that Wedgwoods took delivery of teawares of New Hall's pattern 446 in April 1812. In my experience this design (Plate 187) is found only on New Hall's hybrid hard-paste body. It seems probable, therefore, that the change in body took place between April and the end of 1812. Most but not all the new bone china teawares are the London shape, as Plates 336 and 337.

The dating of the introduction of the bone china body to c.1812 is confirmed in part by the dated 1814 bone china bat-printed jug shown in Plates 330 and 437. A dated 1811 jug is of the earlier hybrid hard-paste body – see Plate 228. At this point we can discuss and illustrate some New Hall bat prints which occur on the usually whiter and more thinly potted bone china, but this subject is mainly dealt with in the following chapter.

Bone China Bat-printed Designs, c.1812 onwards

Many of the earlier bat prints which were introduced on the hybrid hard-paste body continued to be used on the bone china because the designs were still popular and were selling. However, the range was enlarged, the new versions or completely new patterns being given pattern numbers in excess of one thousand. New shapes also came

Plate 331. *A New Hall bone china plate (one of two in each tea service) bearing a coloured over popular bat-printed design within gilt line borders. Painted pattern number 984. See Colour Plate 64. Diameter 8¼in. (20.96cm). c. 1814-6.* Godden collection

into favour, particularly in regard to teawares. The 'London shape' (copying popular silver forms) is shown in Plates 334, 336-7, 341, 344, 346 and 352. I believe all New Hall London shape teawares are of the bone china body.

There is, however, a quite rare transitional form of teaware which seems to occur in the hybrid hard-paste body (Plate 306) and also in bone china. I show an example of this teapot shape in Plate 332. This pattern (1147) has also been reported with the number 1162. Such bat prints include classical figure designs in the so-called 'Adam Buck' style of decoration and these figure subjects are mainly associated with the London shape teawares – see Plates 336-7. The pattern numbers are in the bone china range, that is in excess of a thousand. A Bute shape cup and saucer of this 1147 pattern also has the oval ring handle form associated with New Hall's bone china period – see Plate 335. Other teawares of these rare transitional forms are shown in Plates 359-61. Some examples have been reported as being of the hybrid hard-paste but examples I have handled have been in the bone china body.

Many most attractive bat prints comprise a lengthy series of figure subjects, not posed in landscapes but rather in an indoor setting and engaged in domestic pursuits – see Plates 334, 336 and 337. Although these now rather classic designs are sometimes referred to as 'Adam Buck' subjects, the source of these prints was probably very varied, not exclusively from Adam Buck prints or designs. These were produced at a time when prints by or after Bartolozzi, Cosway and Kauffmann were exceedingly popular and such attractive prints, often published by the London firm of Ackermann, are still readily available a hundred and fifty years or more after their issue

Most of these 'Adam Buck' type prints, as Plate 334, feature mother and child subjects. In the Wyllie accounts such patterns are referred to as 'Infant' as opposed to 'Landscape'. Often these different descriptions appear listed consecutively at the same price. I will not use the description 'Infant' as seldom or never do children appear on their own; the mother is the prominent figure in the composition. Most of these figure subject prints were added to the London shape teawares introduced in about 1812 – see Plates 336 and 337 for typical examples. This type of design has been aptly described as 'an enchanting marriage between Neo-classicism and Romanticism'. Similar figure subject prints were, of course, also used by other potters.

With the general introduction of the London shape in, or soon after, 1812, we find several innovations being introduced. As explained in Chapter III, in the marks section, we find a simple printed name mark 'New Hall' within a double lined circle being used. An example is reproduced below.

This device was used surprisingly sparingly and apparently for a relatively short period, perhaps c.1814-20. It is often cited as the New Hall mark but it was only used for a few years, in the bone china period.

We also find that several of the printed designs were issued in a coloured-in version. These obviously would have been more expensive than the plain versions printed only in one colour. Still the tinted-in versions were more realistic and might look like a hand-painted design. Wide coloured borders were also sometimes employed, again resulting in a higher price and therefore fewer sales! Examples are shown in Plates 338-340, 342-4, 346 and 348-358.

A new urn or vase shape form of New Hall coffee pot was issued in the bone china body and is sometimes associated with the London shape tea service. As with all porcelain coffee pots, they are relatively rare and were not issued with the standard tea services. Plates 338-340 show typical examples of these post-1812 bat-printed coffee pots. It has been noted that most examples bear bat-printed designs rather than hand-painted patterns.

Some New Hall patterns introduced in the pre-1814 hybrid hard-paste period can also be found on post-1812 London shapes in the bone china body. This is particularly the case with the popular and decorative printed landscape designs, issued under the number 984.

Plates 336-341 illustrate a representative range of New Hall London shape teawares, all decorated with bat-printed designs. The number of different landscape and figure designs is remarkable. A complete harlequin tea service comprised over forty pieces and it must be remembered that many units carried two different designs. This is the case with the teacups and the coffee-cans (or cups) as well as the teapot and covered sugar. A single waste bowl can be decorated with four different prints.

At a B.B.C. Antiques Roadshow at a very, very wet Lyme Park in Cheshire, I happened to be shown a bat-printed coffee pot. It bore only a pattern number, 1100. This baffled one of the other team members who brought it over to my table. I was in luck. I knew the shape was a New Hall one (it was as Plates 338-340) and I knew that

PLATE 332. *A rare early bone china New Hall teapot decorated with one of a series of popular figure subject bat-printed designs with gilding. Perhaps incorrect pattern number 1162, with tally marks. The usual number for this design is 1147. 6in. (15.24cm) high. c.1814-6.*

GODDEN OF WORTHING

PLATE 333. *The New Hall bone china stand to the teapot shown in Plate 332. Each article in a complete service would bear a different bat print. 5 x 3¾in. (12.7 x 9.53cm). c.1814-6.*

GODDEN OF WORTHING LTD.

pattern number was the correct one for New Hall. I also knew the prints which adorned the front and the back of the coffee pot and was consequently able to tell the lady owner that it was a rare and desirable specimen of New Hall porcelain, dating from about 1815.

This was all a matter of experience, knowing the shape, the pattern number and the prints. Such experience can be gained in the hard way over twenty, thirty or in my case fifty years of dealing in and collecting English porcelain – or, given a little time and access to the right reference books, the lady owner could have carried out her own research!

She may however, have experienced some difficulty, not knowing its age, or even its country of origin. Having been told it was New Hall this was in itself unhelpful as she had never heard of the factory and I needed to explain that it was in Staffordshire. She then happened to mention that it was but part of a large tea and coffee service, even

PLATE 334. *A bone china New Hall covered sugar box of the new fashion London shape, as Plate 336. Bat-printed figure designs and gilt trim, as pattern 1162 (Plate 332), but in this case marked 1147. 4½in. (11.43cm) high. c.1814-8.* GODDEN OF WORTHING

PLATE 335. *A New Hall Bute shape teacup and saucer, with bat-printed designs and gilt trim as pattern 1147. Note the oval handle shape and compare with the earlier form shown in Plate 327. Workman's tally marks. Diameter of saucer 5½in. (13.97cm). c.1812-5.* GODDEN OF WORTHING

PLATE 336. *Representative pieces from a New Hall bat-printed bone china tea service of pattern 1147. The main pieces of the fashionable London shape, the teacups and coffee can of the slightly earlier Bute form. Note the oval handle form associated with the bone china examples. Pattern number 1147 on major pieces. Diameter of plates 8¼in. (20.96cm). c.1812-5.* MESSRS. SOTHEBY'S

PLATE 337. *Representative pieces from a bat-printed bone china New Hall tea service with black borders. The main pieces are of the fashionable London shape. The cup is of the slightly earlier Bute shape. Painted pattern number 1109 on major pieces. Sugar box 4½in. (11.43cm) high. c.1814-8.* SOTHEBY'S SUSSEX

PLATE 338. *A New Hall coffee pot of the standard bone china form decorated with coloured over bat-printed designs and gilt trim, as pattern 1053. See Colour Plate 65. See Plate 339 for the reverse side. 9in. (22.86cm) high. c.1814-8.* GODDEN OF WORTHING

PLATE 339. *The reverse side of the New Hall bone china coffee pot shown in Plate 338. This side illustrates two further coloured over bat-printed designs used in the series numbered 1053. 9in. (22.86cm) high. c.1814-8.* GODDEN OF WORTHING

containing two teapots! This was most exciting. The owner had brought along, on a shocking day, a coffee pot to a Roadshow at which I happened to be present. It had originally been seen by another team member who could easily have all but dismissed the piece as a standard early nineteenth century Staffordshire bone china coffee pot, 'perhaps Spode, value about £100'. Luckily, it was referred to me.

I was able, at a later date, to follow up the coffee pot and was permitted to see the complete bat-printed, harlequin service – a rare treat. This set has over the years perhaps lost two teacups and two coffee cans, as only ten of each are now available. The remaining pieces of this pattern 1100 bat-printed and gilt New Hall service, which I would date to c.1815, comprised:

Coffee pot and cover (shape as Plates 338-40)
Teapot and cover
Teapot stand
A smaller teapot,[6] cover and stand
Sugar box and cover
Slop bowl
Creamer (or milk jug)
2 bread and butter plates
12 saucers (plus one extra)
10 teacups
10 coffee cans

PLATE 340. *A New Hall bone china coffee pot decorated with coloured over bat print and gold trim. The pattern number for this unframed scenic series is 984, introduced in the hybrid hard paste period. Painted pattern number 984. 9in. (22.86cm) high. c.1814-8.* PRIVATE COLLECTION

PLATE 341. *Representative parts of a New Hall bone china tea service. The teapot is of the revised London shape with a rather upturned handle. Standard bat-printed subjects with black enamel trim. Painted pattern number 1109 on major pieces. Teapot 6in. (15.24cm) high. c.1818-22.* GODDEN OF WORTHING

These various pieces bear forty-six separate main prints plus the smaller prints on the four covers and that inside the bowl. This totals fifty-one or fifty-nine if we include the prints on the four missing cups. Each one of these separate prints or scenes had to be hand engraved on copper plates, in the slow painstaking stipple technique needed for successful bat-printed designs. The different prints occurring on this and all the bat-printed services lead to the description a 'harlequin set'.

As one would expect of a New Hall tea service, only the main pieces bear a pattern number – merely, in this case, the numbers '1100' without a pre-fix 'N' or 'No'. The cups and saucers do not bear a number.

It is possible that the coffee pot originally had a stand but I have never seen a stand that was obviously made to accompany such a coffee pot.[7] It may be significant, however, that this set has thirteen saucers, rather than the expected twelve. Perhaps the extra one was used as the coffee pot stand. The two saucer-shaped bread and butter or cake plates were nearly of the same size (measuring 8in. and 7¾in. – 20.32cm and 19.69cm – in diameter). The earlier harder paste examples usually show a greater difference in their diameter.

The great surprise and pleasure was to find this set complete with a small London shape teapot. These rarely occur but very small pots were made also by other firms, notably by Spode.[8] These are often called bachelor's or 'one cup' teapots. In fact this charming example was found to contain (when filled to the spout-level) four teacups or five coffee can measures of liquid. This is exactly half the capacity of the larger, normal size teapot. The two major prints on the side of the smaller pot differed from those on the larger. The two teapot stands were of the same size.

The teacups in this 1100 pattern service were of the curved Bute shape (as Plates 336-7 and 341) and the coffee cups were of the straight-sided can shape. This may indicate that the service was of an early transitional period, having old traditional shape cups but a new fashion London-shape teapot, sugar box and jug. It is also likely that the old shape cups were used because they took the existing prints so well, far better than would the London shape cups with their smaller area (see Plate 352). By retaining the traditional cup form the existing, costly, engraved copper plates could still be used. It was not necessary to re-engrave copper plates to suit the shape and lower proportion of the London shape tea and coffee cups.

However, the cup handles have been remodelled, without affecting the surface area to be decorated. The earlier (c.1803-9) handles were usually of a simple loop form (Plates 315-8). By the time of Warburton's 1810 patent the handles were of the ring type, as illustrated in Plates 335-7 and 341.

With the advent of bone china in about 1812 these formerly circular ring handles had been remodelled to a more oval shape – see Plate 362.

Turning to the printed designs, eleven of the landscape views were titled suggesting that at least these were copied from a printed illustrated book or other source. The titles to bat-printed scenes are often difficult to read and some were trimmed off or partly wiped away if they overran the bottom of the object or the edge. The named views on this selection of designs, were:

A View from the Island in the Garden of (?) Hopkins Esq, near Cobham
Bush Hill Park
Coghill Hall
Leasowes
Newnham Court
St Albans
Twickenham Meadows
Upton House
View of Greenwich from Deptford
Woburn Abbey
Worfield Grove

These eleven represent only a small proportion of the named views to be found on New Hall porcelain. Over fifty titles have been recorded.[9] On this one service we found rather less than one in four engraved views bore a title. This might suggest (no more) that the total number of New Hall engraved landscape designs exceeded two hundred in total.

As these designs can be issued with various trims or added decoration such as borders, the sum total of possible New Hall bat-printed designs climbs easily into the thousands.

These basic prints occur firstly with enamelled, usually black, line edging. Such sets would have been the least expensive. New Hall's pattern 709 represents such a black-edged treatment – see Plates 319-20 in the hybrid hard paste pre-1813 period. A bone china version is pattern 1063 (similar to Plate 53 but with printed landscapes). John Wyllie, as previously stated, had ordered and received 'black landscape china no. 1063' in December 1812. The prices quoted for the individual examples are well below the lowest grouping in the undated factory price list.

In this the sugar boxes are quoted at 3s. and the cream ewers at 2s.6d. to give the total price of the least expensive forty-five piece teaset at £2.18s.6d. The price entered in the Wyllie accounts for black edged bat-printed landscape covered sugar boxes was only 1s. (a third of the price of that quoted in the factory list) and creamers also cost 1s. It can be assumed, therefore, that the least costly bat-printed complete New Hall tea services in the early nineteenth century were around £1. It was this version that was the one reordered time and again by John Wyllie. Presumably he found it saleable because it was so inexpensive and represented such good value for money. The New Hall printed teawares almost certainly were less costly than the Spode examples.

The New Hall partnership, however, issued these bat-printed teasets in several more expensive forms, the hand-

Plate 342. *The exterior of a New Hall bone china bowl richly decorated with coloured over bat-printed panels on a dark underglaze blue ground, with gilding. Painted pattern number 1277. Diameter 9in. (22.86cm). c.1815-20.* Godden of Worthing

Plate 343. *The interior view of the richly decorated New Hall bone china bowl shown in Plate 342. The inside includes panels of typical coloured over bat-printed designs. See Colour Plate 66. Diameter 9in. (22.86cm). c.1815-20.* Godden of Worthing

Plate 344. *Representative parts of a splendid New Hall bone china bat-printed tea service with light blue ground and gilding – see Colour Plate 67. Painted pattern number 1092 with decorator's tally marks, as Plate 345. Diameter of plate 8¼in. (20.96cm). c.1814-18.* Godden of Worthing

coloured gilt-enhanced pattern being number 984 – see Plates 325, 331 and 340. The surviving Wyllie accounts only list the less expensive version, patterns 1063 or 1109 (Plates 53, 337 and 341) with the black edging. The versions with gilding (as 1100) were obviously more expensive. Messrs. Chamberlain at Worcester issued as their pattern 347 teawares with New Hall (and Spode) type black printed landscapes with gold edging to sell at £3.3s.0d. In the New Hall price list the two lowest priced teaset listings were for sets selling at £2.18s.6d. and at £3.8s.3d. It would seem therefore that even when gilt trim was added to the bat-printed teawares, the cost was quite low. The hand-coloured printed designs were, one would expect, rather more costly. Not only were the prints neatly coloured but the enamel painting would require firing. Another process was involved.

While not all these compositions on English porcelain are unique to the New Hall firm, when a pattern number does occur on a piece this can link it to our factory or show that it is unlikely to be a New Hall specimen, as the case may be. The later post-1812 figure subject pattern numbers are 1109, 1147, 1178, 1236, 1277 and 1525. These numbers refer, as is usual, to the border or ground work rather than to the print itself which can vary greatly. Most other manufacturers' essays in similar style bear lower pattern numbers than these New Hall ones except for the Spode examples. For example, the Machin 'Mother and Child' prints are numbered 205 in the untinted version and 224 when coloured in. Strangely, the large Spode firm which produced such high quality bat-printed designs did not favour the Adam Buck type 'Mother and Children' domestic bliss style printed designs; nor did their great rival Minton. Indeed Mintons produced very few bat-printed designs.

These so-called 'Mother and Child' printed subjects are found on bone china rather than on the earlier hard china. I prefer not to continue the description 'Mother and Child' as by no means all the figure compositions include these delightful subjects. Some harlequin services that seemingly have been together since they were first sold have prints of varying subject, landscapes, for example, being mixed with figure subject prints. As previously stated, however, the different subjects could be ordered separately. A range of such domestic figure subject prints is shown in Plates 336-7 and 341 on shapes of approximately 1815-20. These shapes include some of the first version of New Hall's 'London' shape teawares, Plates 336-7.

In some cases these domestic figure subject prints are coloured over (that is, the print is coloured in by hand), as is the case with the magnificent blue ground and gilt punch bowl shown in Plates 342-3. These coloured-in printed designs include patterns numbered 1236, 1277 and 1525. The additional tinting may well have lifted the price of a tea service by some fifty per cent.

This over-enamelling of bat prints also occurs on most

PLATE 345. *Two upturned New Hall coffee cans showing the decorator's personal tally marks under the bases. Such differing marks are often found on New Hall porcelains. See page 129. Diameter of bases 2¼in. (15.72cm). c.1815-20.* GODDEN REFERENCE COLLECTION

PLATE 346. *Three bat-printed New Hall London shape milk jugs from tea services. These represent very many different designs and styles of finish employed at this one factory over a relatively short period. Left, pattern 1140; middle, 984; right, 1357. See Colour Plate 68. 4in. (10.16cm) high. c.1815-20.* GODDEN COLLECTION

PLATE 347. *A New Hall bone china Bute shape teacup and saucer, decorated with bat-printed figure subjects, within a decorative reddish-orange border. Unmarked but pattern numbered 1140. Diameter of saucer 5½in. (13.97cm). c.1815-20. See Colour Plate 68.* PRIVATE COLLECTION

PLATE 348. *A tastefully decorated New Hall bone china trio, decorated with coloured over standard bat-printed design and gold trim. Other prints from a tea service of this pattern 1053 are shown in Plates 349-51. Diameter of saucer 5¼in. (13.34cm). c.1815-20.*

GODDEN OF WORTHING

PLATE 349. *Saucers from a New Hall bone china tea service of pattern number 1053 showing a few of the popular coloured over bat-printed scenes employed at this one Staffordshire factory. Decorator's tally marks on some pieces. Diameter of saucers 5¼in. (13.34cm). c.1815-20.* GODDEN OF WORTHING

of the New Hall landscapes (such as pattern 984) and other subjects found mainly on bone china. In some cases ground colour (the bat prints appearing in reserved panels) was added as well as complicated gilt enrichments. The tea service shown in Colour Plate 67 and in Plate 344 would rival in magnificence most entirely hand-painted designs from any English porcelain factory. However, I prefer the more restrained simple treatment given to the trio shown in Plate 348. The richer service of pattern 1092 is enhanced with the bone china period series of landscape designs which include some named views.

These named New Hall scenic bat prints, which may be left as printed (pattern 1063) or tinted in, include:

Brecknock
Bruce Castle
Bush Hill Park
Cusworth
Edgbrook (?)
Edgecote Cottage
Fenwell Hall
Kirkham Priory Gateway
Pinxton Mill
View from Eltham
View of Greenwich from Deptford
Windsor Park
Winstone Cottage

These titles, which appear under the print, are often indistinct and when a gilt inner border has been added the print is often cut to a smaller diameter and the title is lost.

As I have previously stated, the early bone chinas bearing both bat-printed and other forms of decoration may bear the standard printed 'New Hall' name mark as shown on page 345.

It would appear that the use of this mark was limited to the approximate period 1814-20. Unlike pattern numbers, it can occur on saucers, but this mark is rarish rather than common. When it does occur with a pattern number it serves as an invaluable guide to origin and, to some degree, to the period of the piece.

Whilst I have been able to show particularly in this chapter a good array of tea services or the main parts of original services, these are seldom found today or, if found, are seldom affordable!

One can of course form a specialist collection of, say, teapots. These are the most popular article to collect but only one was in each set and they tend to be rather costly. I find cream or milk jugs just as decorative and interesting. They are also rare but generally not as expensive as teapots. Plate 346 shows a small group of New Hall London shape jugs, each with a different type of bat print and different border or gilt trim. Even less costly are the

PLATE 350. *A selection of New Hall bone china Bute shape teacups of (unmarked) pattern 1053, as Plates 348-9 and 351. Note the oval handle forms – see Plate 362. True London shape cups were seldom used in New Hall's bat-printed cup, as the coffee plates had been engraved for the larger surfaced Bute cups. Height of cup 2¼in. (5.72cm). c.1815-20.* GODDEN OF WORTHING

PLATE 351. *A selection of New Hall bone china Bute shape coffee cans of (unmarked) pattern 1053, as Plates 348-50. Note the oval handle form. The can shape coffee cups were favoured even when the main pieces were of the London shape, as the size and shape was easier to decorate with available bat prints. Height of cans 2¼in. (5.72cm). c.1815-20.* GODDEN OF WORTHING

Plate 352. *A rare New Hall bone china London shape teacup and saucer, decorated with coloured over bat prints, within blue and gold border. Parts of these fruit prints also occur in other forms, as pattern 1357, and were also used on dessert wares – see Plate 357. Diameter of saucer 5½in. (13.97cm). c.1820-25.*
GODDEN COLLECTION

cup and saucers, as twelve were in each complete service. These will show an even more diverse range of bat prints. Even the odd saucers, or odd teacup or coffee can, will show the New Hall bat prints to good advantage – see Plates 349-51.

Some New Hall bat prints are rarely found, some I have only seen once or twice in over forty years of collecting. Others may await discovery. Plates 352-3 feature two of many coloured-in prints of fruit compositions. These three pieces show three different but similar designs. The complete tea service may have featured forty or fifty different designs. Regarding the coloured-in fruit printed designs as shown in Plate 346 right, a lengthy teaset of this pattern number is in the Potteries Museum at Hanley.[10] It has been handed down through many generations. Each of these printed designs may help to identify other rare New Hall bone china shapes. Examples of this possibility are cited in the following chapter.

Up to this point I have been concerned with the bat-printed New Hall teawares, but several other types of article were also embellished with the same prints, notably, the dessert services. These are much rarer than the teawares, the latter being the standard output of the factory. Once the teawares have been identified by their characteristic forms, the added print, or by the pattern number or printed 'New Hall' mark, one can proceed to

Plate 353. *A cake (or bread and butter) plate from a New Hall bone china tea service with London shape cup and major pieces. Coloured over bat prints which were sometimes used in other forms. Pattern number not known but fruit prints occur in simpler forms as, for example, pattern 1357. See Colour Plate 69. Diameter 8¾in. (22.23cm). c.1820-5.*
PRIVATE COLLECTION

PLATE 354. *The footed centrepiece from a New Hall bone china dessert service. The centres of the various pieces decorated with various coloured over bat prints, within relief moulded borders. Length 10½in. (26.57cm). c.1815-20.* GODDEN OF WORTHING

PLATE 355. *A blue bordered New Hall bone china dessert dish, with typical relief-moulded border. The centre bears one of many available bat-printed scenic designs, coloured over by hand. 9¼ x 7¼in. (23.5 x 18.42cm). c.1815-20.* GODDEN OF WORTHING

link these patterns and prints to other articles which do not bear a mark.

Some of the larger prints found on teawares can also be seen on the rarer dessert services. The crocodile print (Plates 320-1, 376 and 409) is a case in point. When the bat prints appear on dessert wares the prints are coloured over, not left untinted. It can happen that the foreground is extended by hand-painting to fill the larger area of a dessert dish. This linking of prints and the rare addition of the printed 'New Hall' mark enable certain relief-moulded border designs to be identified, but again close copies were produced by other makers. Apart from prints found on tea services, some bat-printed floral and fruit subjects occur, mainly on the dessert services. A selection of these coloured-in dessert ware prints is shown in Plates 357-8. The usual dessert ware pattern numbers of this type are 1478 (baskets of fruit), 1706 (groups of fruit) and 2240 (groups of fruit), but many examples do not bear a pattern number – the landscape designs are usually unmarked (see Plates 354-6).

Apart from the decorative bat-printed dessert services (or nowadays the odd pieces from such originally complete sets), jugs and probably mugs were embellished with bat-printed designs, normally in a coloured-in version. A good New Hall bat-printed jug of pattern 984 and of typical bone china form is in the Potteries Museum at Hanley and is illustrated by David Holgate in his *New Hall and its Imitators* (Faber & Faber, London, 1971). Small scent bottles (Plate 406) have also been recorded and some rare component parts of breakfast services were no doubt embellished with bat-printed patterns from the standard tea service range. Such breakfast service articles included small plates, covered muffin dishes, preserve pots and eggcups. In addition,

PLATE 356. *A blue bordered New Hall dessert dish, one of several standard shapes. Coloured over bat-printed named view of Windsor. 9 x 7in. (22.86 x 17.78cm). c.1815-20.*

GODDEN OF WORTHING

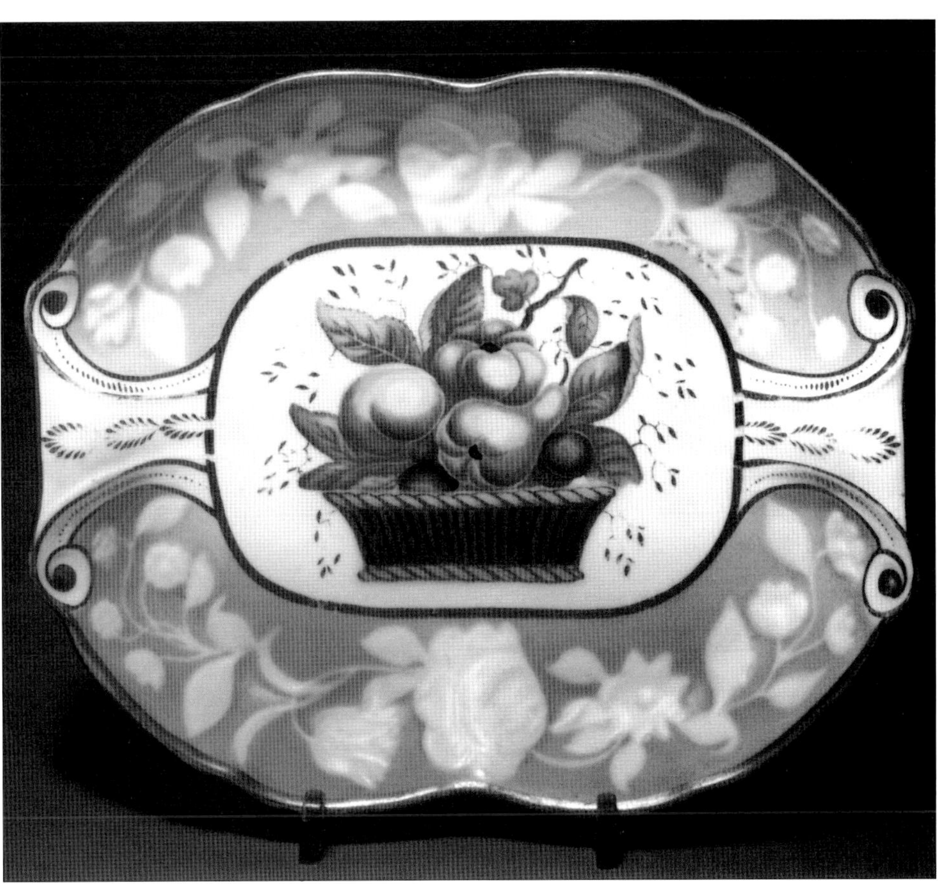

PLATE 357. *A similar shaped New Hall dessert dish to that shown in Plate 355 but with a bat-printed fruit design, one of many in the series – see Plates 410-2, pattern 1478. Printed 'New Hall' name mark in double lined border. 9¼ x 7¼in. (23.5 x 18.42cm). c.1815-20.*

GODDEN OF WORTHING

PLATE 358. *Representative parts from a New Hall dessert service with relief-moulded border. Decorated with various coloured over bat-printed fruit designs. Painted pattern number 1629. Oblong dish 9¾ x 6½in. (24.77 x 16.51cm). c.1820-5.* MESSRS. DREWEATT NEATE

David Holgate illustrates a rare double-handled chocolate cup with cover and stand as Plate 174 of his 1971 book. I show other forms in the following bone china chapter.

Some post-1820 New Hall bone china tea and dessert services bear prints that are more in the nature of simple outline designs intended to be filled in by young paintresses as the design would not be capable of being sold in an untinted state. These are discussed on page 324. The printed outline designs include 1357, 1511, 1659, 1742 and 2383 but, of course, such a printed outline technique was employed by all British porcelain manufacturers.

I regard the bat-printed New Hall porcelains, both the hard body and the later bone china examples, to be very neglected. They can be quite beautiful and charming while the sources of the design offer interesting lines of research. Particularly in the 1805-20 period, great care appears to have been paid to these printed designs which formed an important feature of the factory's production. The range of prints is great and the different manner in which each could be treated increases the scope. A very interesting collection could be formed of the New Hall bat-printed designs, a collection which could be enlarged by the inclusion of link pieces made by other contemporary firms.

---

1. However, 'Factory Z' (perhaps Wolfe's) produced some superb quality bat-printed teawares, including some subjects or styles associated with New Hall.

2. It is interesting to note that the Spode patterns were introduced at a far faster rate than the New Hall designs. New Hall's 423 and 462 are mirrored in about 1803 by Spode's 500 and 557, but by the period of Warburton's patent in 1810 New Hall's patterns 840 or 888 were matched by Spode's 1695 or even 1703. New Hall's range had increased by about 400, Spode's patterns by over 800 in seven or eight years.

3. John Wyllie's purchases of New Hall teawares in May 1814, however, include 'Purple landscape', but it is not clear if this written description without a pattern number relates to printed landscape designs.

4. Some probably earlier can handles are of a plain loop form – see Plates 315 and 317-8.

5. The pierced knob might just enable this pot to be used as an argyle.

6. It is possible that the moulds for the sugar box were used for these small teapots, a spout replacing the handle at one end and a vent-hole pierced into the cover.

7. I do not think that the Spode coffee pots of a rather taller, more slender form were issued with stands.

8. The small globular teapots were called at Spode 'Afternoon teapots', but no Spode bat-printed examples are recorded.

9. Dr. Joyce McCarthy recorded in 1993 fifty-seven named views on bat-printed New Hall porcelains. This specialist collector has also traced the source of several views – see the *Morley College Ceramic Circle Bulletin,* second series, no.2, July 1993. Strangely, very few Spode views carry titles.

10. Representative pieces are illustrated in issue 3 of *New Hall and Friends* (Spring 2002), the magazine issued by the New Hall Collectors' Society.

CHAPTER X

The Bone China Wares

The previous chapter spanned the two basic types of New Hall porcelain, the hybrid hard-paste porcelain and the later bone china wares. The original body was produced for about thirty years, from c.1782 to c.1812. The bone china period lasted for a rather shorter period, just over twenty years. Colour Plates 64 onwards illustrate a good range of the bone chinas.

The New Hall bone china wares have been little researched and, of course, by the 1820s the shapes and added designs bear little or no relation to the traditional New Hall products of the 1790s or even of the early 1800s. The later porcelains can be very decorative and collectable although from the 1820s they do not seem to bear a factory mark.

The pattern numbers well exceed 3000 and may even have reached the early 4000s by the time the factory was closed in 1835. One teapot bears an indistinct number that could be in the 5000 range. In addition some teawares of the late 1820s or early 1830s bear fractional pattern numbers, the main number being expressed under the numerator '4'. These high pattern numbers underline the long-standing of this Staffordshire concern and they enable us to almost positively identify numbered examples of the late 1820s and early 1830s. Apart from the very different Daniel and usually name marked Spode porcelains, no other as yet identified English porcelain factory produced patterns in the 3000-4000 range during the New Hall period.

We do not know precisely when the New Hall management decided to change the basic mix of their porcelain body from their traditional hard-paste or hybrid hard-paste porcelain related to William Cookworthy's eighteenth century patent to a revised mix incorporating calcined and then ground animal bones – that is, to produce a type of 'bone china' which had been introduced at the Spode factory in about 1800 and by about 1810 had almost entirely replaced other types of porcelain in the British Isles.

PLATE 359. *An early New Hall bone china teapot and stand, decorated with a coloured over bat-printed design, titled 'Brecknock'. Painted pattern number 984. See also Plates 332 and 360. 6in. (15.24cm) high. c.1814-6.* MESSRS. SOTHEBY'S

PLATE 360. *Representative pieces from a New Hall tea service showing early or transitional bone china shapes. See also Plates 332 and 359 for the teapot form. Underglaze blue, overglaze enamel and gilt pattern 1085. Pattern number on major pieces. Teapot 6in. (15.24cm) high. c.1814-6.* GODDEN OF WORTHING

In the case of the New Hall management the change of mix should have been relatively easy as they were already making a body comprising the basic ingredients of hard-paste porcelain – the china clay and china stone. To turn this composition into a bone china they only, in essence, needed to add calcined, that is burnt, animal bones, to their standard mix. The result is a high-class bone china, possibly a little harder than some other Staffordshire bodies of the 1812-35 period.

The new amended bone china mix resulted in a very strong stable and workable pleasant looking porcelain, whiter in colour than the British hybrid hard-paste mixes. It also matured at a lower temperature which reduced production costs. The change was made for good commercial reasons.

Most old reference books suggest that the change at the New Hall works took place in, or about, 1810. Modern authorities opt for a date nearer to 1815 but the exact year has yet to be pinpointed.

As I mentioned in the previous chapter, we have as a guide the presentation jug in my own collection (Plate 228). This beer jug was made, or at least decorated, to special order and is inscribed 'John Brown, Yoxall, 1811'. It was made in the hard-paste, pre-bone china, body. Another presentation jug in my collection bears the date 1814 and this was made in the bone china body.

To help narrow down this 1811-14 period of the change-over we have the surviving accounts of the small scale, middle-market London retailers John Wyllie and his wife, Ann.[1] Under the date 24 December 1812 we find the entry:

> 24 setts handled Black landscape, china
> No. 1063 £7.4s.0d.

Bat-printed black-lined bordered New Hall teawares of this pattern are in my experience only found in the bone china body. This new New Hall porcelain mix we can therefore assume had been introduced by this December 1812 date. It is often stated that any New Hall porcelain bearing a pattern number above 1000 relates to bone china. This idea could be revised to take account of patterns up to 1046 which has been reported on the earlier hybrid hard-paste body. The position is, however, complicated by the possibility that old stocks of hybrid hard-paste porcelain were decorated with early bone china designs with pattern numbers in excess of 1000. Stocks of glazed blanks would not have been broken up; they would have been decorated and put on the market.

PLATE 361. *A rare New Hall bone china jug, matching in form the teawares shown in Plate 360. Enamelled with early period pattern, numbered 22. Painted pattern number 3½in. (8.89cm) high. c.1814-6.* GODDEN COLLECTION

Also, one must not assume from my previous remarks that any New Hall article bearing a pattern number under 1000 must of necessity be of the earlier hard-paste porcelain for several popular designs first introduced in the hard-paste period were later added to the new bone china blanks. However, one can generally assume that New Hall pattern numbers in excess of 1000 will be in the bone china body.

I must at this point, however, note that the bone china

PLATE 362. *Left, a New Hall bone china Bute shape teacup with oval handle, here contrasted with the earlier hybrid hard-paste coffee can with its more circular handle. Both bear bat-printed motifs. Can 2⅜in. (6.1cm) high. c.1812-8.* GODDEN COLLECTION

mix was not constant for the period from c.1812 to the factory's closure twenty years later. Various amendments would doubtless have been made and even at any one time two or more mixes may have been employed for different types of article. In my experience, or rather to my eyes, the jugs seem to be of a harder body than teawares which are contemporary productions. My use of the words 'to my eyes' serves to make the point that we all look at these objects with different eyes and have differing experience of porcelain types. In other words, unless a piece is analysed (and this is an expensive process), the appearance of a porcelain body is individual and in most cases it is the covering glaze which we are viewing and which we touch and feel.

Nevertheless, the body may not have varied greatly, because the glaze had to 'fit' the body, expanding or rather contracting at the same rate in the firing and as the pieces cooled. The late Reginald Haggar published in the *Northern Ceramic Society Newsletter,* no. 26 of June 1977, a New Hall bone china formula, as used in 1824:

7 bls of bone
5 bls of china clay
5 bls of china stone
1½ bls of blue clay
2 grains of blue calx

A variation reads:

9 oz of bone
6 oz of china clay
4 oz of china stone
1 oz of blue clay
3 grains of enamel blue

These New Hall bone china receipts were contained in a small notebook once the property of Francis Emery. These copied entries were stated as being 'given by Jas. Wildin, 18th October 1824'. Francis Emery is believed to have been the decorating manager at the New Hall works in the 1820s. He may have undertaken some of the decorating himself and been employed as a painter or gilder at an earlier period – see page 188.

A marked 'New Hall' bone china teacup and saucer of pattern 1511 (Victoria & Albert Museum, Number C698.1920) was analysed in 1922. The following result was published by Herbert Eccles and Bernard Rackham in their booklet *Analysed Specimens of English Porcelain* (H.M. Stationery Office, 1922):

Silica	38.50
Alumina	18.22
Lime	24.88
Phosphoric acid	15.48
Magnesia	0.21
Soda	1.64
Potash	0.67
Oxide of Lead	0.88
	100.48

Plate 363. *A bone china London shape teapot and stand. Coloured over bat-printed subject in the 984 series – see also Plate 359. Painted pattern number with workman's mark. Teapot 5¾in. (14.61cm) high. c.1814-8.*
PRIVATE COLLECTION

PLATE 364. *New Hall bone china teawares showing London shapes. Underglaze blue and gold pattern numbered 1059. Painted pattern numbers on major pieces. Teapot 5⅜in. (13.65cm) high. c.1814-8.*
GODDEN OF WORTHING

Tea Wares

Perhaps the earliest New Hall tea service forms to have been produced in the bone china body from about 1812 are the rare shapes shown in Plates 359-61 and earlier in Plate 332. These forms occur in the earlier hybrid hard-paste body (Plate 306), but most examples seen by me have been in bone-china. The cup handles to the part service shown in Plate 360 have the oval finger aperture found on such later bone china sets rather than the rounder version associated with the earlier body (see Plate 362).

The rather ungainly milk or cream jug shown in Plate 361 would I think match these shapes. This example is particularly interesting as it bears the early pattern number '22'. It therefore serves to identify this pattern first used before the New Hall management had introduced their use of pattern numbers – see Plates 92 and 97. This design had seemingly been in use for nearly thirty years, from the early 1780s to c.1812.

This shape certainly does occur with earlier patterns, such as 984 (coloured-in bat-printed designs) which originally related to the hybrid hard-paste porcelains. I believe this is merely the continuation of a popular design

Plate 365. *A New Hall bone china milk jug decorated with bat-printed panels with an orange, red and gilt border design. Painted pattern number 1140 – see Plate 362 for the teacup. 6in. (15.24cm) long. c.1814-8.* Godden collection

into the bone china period, as was the case with the creamer, of pattern 22.

The hybrid hard-paste New Hall patterns issued before, say, 1813 are thought to be below the 1000 numbering. It can, of course, happen that early period pattern numbers were continued on bone china shapes when that pattern was still in demand. There seems to have been little or no difference in the price, whichever body was in use – see page 326.

This preceding, perhaps, transitional teaware shape leads us on to the very popular London shapes. These forms, as shown in Plates 363-71 will (if New Hall) certainly be in the bone china body. It was formerly thought that these forms dated from 1814 or 1815. I believe, however, that they were introduced in about 1812. As recorded on page 351, some teasets had an extra, small size London shape teapot.

The New Hall London shape teapots were produced (with the sugar boxes and jugs) in two slightly amended forms. The first, of c.1812-17 is shown in Plates 363-9. The top member of the teapot handle is almost horizontal or straight, not swept upwards as was the later version (Plates 371 and 376-8). The first London shape tea services were issued with the earlier Bute shape curved teacups and with straight-sided coffee-cans (Plates 362 and 364). The early covered sugar boxes have large ear-like handles, matching the larger single handle on the teapot, or the handle on the jug.

The pattern numbers, which still were only applied to the major pieces in the teaset, will be in excess of 1000 – providing the design was a new one, not an old design carried forward from the hybrid hard-paste period. The circular printed New Hall mark can occur on these London shape teawares, although not by any means on all specimens.

Within a short period the tea and coffee cup shapes were changed to the standard London shape with an angled body above a double concave turned foot. The old oval ring handles were replaced by the three unit curved handle form (Plates 366-70). Typical gilt trim on these handles is shown in Plate 367, but some other designs can occur.

The term 'London shape' may be confusing as its use was not confined to the London trade or market. It was the term used by the manufacturers for the new shapes introduced by the silversmiths.[2] The description 'London shape' appears in the Spode factory's turner's book showing the then contemporary (c.1820) shapes in production, with their sizes. The shapes are still being produced by this firm's present-day successors.

An outline history of these popular ceramic forms is given by Philip Miller in Chapter 15 of *Staffordshire Porcelain* (Granada Publishing, London, 1983). It was favoured by both the porcelain manufacturers and many potters over a very long period. Examples were even

Plate 366. *A New Hall bone china trio of London shape cups with their saucer, of pattern 1458. In these cases the main design is inside the cups. Several patterns are close variations on this formal floral design. Diameter of saucer 5½in. (13.97cm). c.1815-20.* Private collection

Plate 367. *A New Hall bone china London shape coffee cup (left) with a matching teacup. Blue, red and gilt pattern 1279. The gilt design shown on the coffee cup handle is very characteristic. 2½in. (6.35cm) high. c.1815-20.* Private collection

Plate 368. *Representative pieces from a New Hall bone china tea service, showing the first version of the London shapes. Underglaze blue, enamel and gilt pattern 1153. See Colour Plate 70. Painted pattern number on major pieces. Teapot 5¾in. (14.61cm) high. c.1815-20.* Godden of Worthing

Plate 369. *A selection of pieces from a colourful New Hall bone china teaset, showing London shapes. Underglaze blue, enamels and gilt formal pattern 1288. Painted pattern number on major pieces. Teapot 5¾in. (14.61cm) high. c.1818-22.* Messrs. Sotheby's

included in the 1851 Exhibition, although by that period very many new fancy shapes had been introduced. By the 1830s Minton had renamed their London shape 'Cottage'. This may well correctly indicate that by this period the rather old-fashioned shapes were reserved for the simpler styles of decoration, that is for the lower price range of designs. Nevertheless, New Hall up until the early 1820s produced very richly decorated London shape tea services (Plates 368-70, 378-9), although many were of a less costly nature. These included the attractive bat-printed tea services, either coloured in or left untinted – see Plates 375-6. Some lustre patterns can occur, including all-over Sunderland-type splash lustre. The lustre patterns do not seem to bear pattern numbers and the lustre may have been added by specialist firms.

It should be noted that the potters also used the description 'London' to denote the size of the cups, smaller or standard size. Other size designations were 'Irish' for large and 'Dutch' or 'Holland' for a smaller capacity cup or teapot. The London shape teawares were also made in the miniature sizes as toy sets. These miniature wares are obviously very rare; their identification is helped by the patterns and their correct high pattern number.

A slight amendment was made to New Hall's version of the London shape teapot at an unknown period but probably prior to 1818. First, the top of the teapot handle was swept upwards at its outer end, giving a better grip for the hand. This also applies to the jug handle, which became more curved – see Plate 371.

The old large ear-like handles to the sugar box were also replaced by smaller, more solid grips. These were far less prone to damage. The new form sugar boxes are shown in Plates 370, 373 and 378. These were not, however, unique to the New Hall teasets; Minton and a host of other manufacturers produced their own versions.

It is difficult to date these changes exactly, as the stocks of the old types would have been used up over a period

Plate 370. *Representative units from a matching New Hall tea and dessert service of pattern 1153, decorated in underglaze blue, overglaze enamels and gilding. This grouping suggests that the same series of pattern numbers was used for various types of porcelain. Teapot 5¾in. (14.61cm) high. c.1820-25.*

Messrs. Phillips, Bath

Plate 371. *Two New Hall London shape milk jugs. The right-hand example with coloured over standard fruit subject bat prints is the earlier version, with pattern 1357. The left-hand example with underglaze blue and gold pattern 1861 represents the slightly later version of this popular shape. Note the downward curve at the top of the handle. Painted pattern numbers. 3¾in. (9.53cm) high. c.1820-25.* Godden collection

Plate 372. *A London shape (with canted sides) bread and butter plate with basket moulding border. Pattern 1944 in underglaze blue with enamel painting and gilding. See Colour Plate 71. Painted pattern number 1944 in red. Diameter 8½in (21.59cm). c.1823-8.*

Private collection

Plate 373. *Representative pieces from a New Hall bone china tea service with basketwork moulding (not unique to this factory). Painted pattern number 1944 in red on major pieces. Teapot 5¾in. (14.61cm) high. c.1823-28.*

Bonhams

and fashionable patterns were applied to both types. I show, for example, pattern 1153 on the first shapes in Plate 368 and the same design on the new models in Plate 370.

This Plate 370 is also interesting as it shows that matching tea and dessert services were made. It also shows that the same pattern number was used for both tea and dessert services, in this case the colourful 'Japan' pattern 1153, incorporating areas of underglaze blue with overglaze enamel colours and gilding.

The few surviving accounts of the London retailers, John and Ann Wyllie, do not in most cases indicate the shape of teawares being ordered or received. Where no description is given the shape was, I assume, the standard London shape, from about 1812 onwards. However, when we come to 1818 and 1819 there are a few references to the 'Grecian' shape. I cite a few typical examples entered under the date 30 September 1818:

2 setts Blue Grecian burnished gold	£4.8s.0d.
2 setts Blue Grecian cans	£3.8s.0d.
12 sets teas Blue Grecian, not gilt	£3.0s.6d.
24 setts teas, Grecian, 1663, at 5s.4d.	£6.8s.0d.
24 setts Teas Grecian, no. 425 at 5s.4d.	£6.8s.0d.

PLATE 374. *An unmarked New Hall London shape teacup of pattern 1944 (as Plates 372-3) showing the basket moulding and a new handle form. 2¼in. (5.72cm) high. c.1823-8.* PRIVATE COLLECTION

Other items of this 425 pattern ordered at the same time included coffee cans, open sugar boxes or bowls and breakfast bowls and saucers.

Other entries seem to confuse rather than clarify the

PLATE 375. *A New Hall bone china new London shape teapot and stand of pattern 2383 (over four hundred higher than the similar shapes shown in Plate 373). The panel design is printed in outline and coloured in by hand. See also Plate 54. Teapot 10½in. long. c.1825.* GODDEN OF WORTHING

Plate 376. *A New Hall new London shape teapot with curved upper member to the handle. Printed with a rather more expensive version of pattern 709 (Plate 320) having gilt trim rather than black edging. Probably pattern 1100. 5¾in. (14.61cm) high. c.1820-5.* Private collection

Plate 377. *A New Hall bone china new London shape creamer, with curved upper member to the handle. Bat printed and gilt pattern 2120 over fawn band. Painted pattern number. 3½in. (8.89cm) high. c.1820-25.* P. Champion collection

Plate 378. *Representative pieces from a splendid New Hall bone china teaset of the new London shape, with standard London shape cups. Painted with panels of rustic figures (as found on some dessert wares) and flowers on a light blue ground, richly gilt – see Plate 379. Pattern number 2215 painted on major pieces. Teapot 5⅞in. (14.92cm) high. c.1825.* Sotheby's, New York

position. Standard blue printed designs seem to have been applied to the Grecian shape: '12 setts Blue Temple handled scalloped teas, Grecian shape' (October 1819) or '4 setts Grecian Blue handled teas, Brosley' (July 1819). 'Broseley' is the trade name for the popular mock-Chinese landscape and temple pattern, as Plate 383. The Grecian pattern teawares were available in a scalloped or reeded form, as well as plain. However, these slightly ribbed teawares with a wavy edge seem confined to the blue printed designs.[3] Also, this named Grecian shape was available in an embossed, or relief-moulded, variation: '12 setts Grecian handle china, embossed 1930' (July 1819).

I have not been able to trace an example of New Hall's pattern 1930 to help identify this shape. Bearing in mind that two standard rather cramped blue printed landscape designs (Plate 383) occur listed on the Grecian shape, although the cup forms may have been redesigned, I believe it is the upmarket name for the slightly redesigned old London shape. These forms seem to bear patterns from about 1900 up to about 2400 and must be regarded as the standard New Hall teaware form of the approximate period 1818 into the early 1820s, although other more ornate shapes may also have been in production within this period. Messrs. Wyllie was still receiving some 'Grecian' teawares in 1823.

The revised London shape with its rather upswept teapot handle and the new sugar box with its stubby handles certainly occurs in an embossed variation, that is with basket-weave moulding – see Plates 372-5. In the case of the more expensive designs, some of the moulding is picked out in gold – the panel outlines and the crossed lines – but in the less costly patterns this refinement was not applied – compare Plates 372-4 with 375. The New Hall cups have, I believe, distinctive handles – see Plate 374.

Excavations or building work at the Dudson factory site at Hanley, part of which relates to the earlier New Hall factory, brought to light in the 1990s a selection of New Hall bone china wasters or shards. Although the finds were mixed with other types, some have been very helpful in confirming a New Hall origin for some of the rare late New Hall relief-moulded porcelains. These recent finds include basket-weave moulded London shape teawares matching the examples shown in Plates 373-5. Later

Plate 379. *The smaller of two plates similar to the service shown in Plate 378. Note the style of colourful flower painting and the scroll design on the gilding. Painted pattern number '2215' – see Colour Plate 72. Diameter 8in. (20.32cm). c.1825.* Formerly Godden collection

reference to these wasters will refer to them as 'Dudson site wasters'. The Dudson connection is complicated and interesting for it would appear that Thomas Dudson was producing some porcelains for John Daniel and the New Hall Company. The pattern numbers given in a Dudson order book include 984 (a bat-printed design), 1600, 1696 and 1699.[4]

The moulded basket-weave London shape teawares were also produced by other factories, noticeably by Charles Bourne of Fenton, from about 1817. His examples often but not invariably have his initial 'C.B.' placed just above the pattern number. Most examples of the revised London shape now perhaps retitled 'Grecian' are of the plain shape, without the embossed moulding. These standard shapes permit the use of popular designs such as the bat-printed motifs (Plate 376) or other all over designs. With the moulded designs special patterns had to be devised, the main motif being confined to the reserve panels within the basketwork. The basket-moulded ground could, however, on expensive patterns be tinted with various colours.

With the Grecian shape it is the teapot which is slightly streamlined by the new more curved handle. This feature is repeated in the revised milk or cream jugs (see Plate 371). The jug itself stands rather higher than the earlier

Plate 380. *A boldly painted New Hall new London shape teapot, with enamel, not gilt, trim. Pattern number 1571. Painted pattern number. 5¾in. (14.61cm) high. c.1820-25.* Mrs. N. Wright

PLATE 381. *A revised London shape teacup and saucer of unnumbered pattern 1571, as Plate 380. Note the ring-handle shape. Diameter of saucer 5¾in. (14.61cm) high. c.1820-5.* PRIVATE COLLECTION

PLATE 382. *A New Hall trio bearing an intricately gilt pattern, number 1980, showing the graceful variation on the standard London shape. Diameter of saucer 5¾in. (14.61cm). c.1820-5.* PRIVATE COLLECTION

Plate 383. *A ribbed revised London shape New Hall teapot decorated with the popular underglaze blue printed 'Pagoda' or 'Broseley' pattern. This print was issued under various numbers – 1762, 2483 etc., according to the added gilt borders or trim. 6in. (15.24cm) high. c.1820-5.* Dr. G. Audley

Plate 384. *An elegant New Hall teacup and saucer decorated with the bone china version (pattern 1066) of the earlier popular hybrid hard-paste pattern 425 (see page 326). The basic design is a coloured in printed pattern. Diameter of saucer 5½in. (13.97cm). c.1820-5.* G.W. Page

Plate 385. *An intricately moulded bone china teapot of a rare form, believed to be New Hall, although similar moulded shapes and rose patterns were produced at other works. 10½in. (26.67cm) long. c.1825-30.*
Private collection

version and, as previously mentioned, the smaller, dumpy, handles appear on the sugar box (Plate 378). The cups and saucers, however, now present some problems to the collector. At this period some of the designs can be rather simple and therefore inexpensive, although one tends to seek the rather more expensive and decorative examples.

By this period from the mid-1820s the high pattern number ceases to be a reliable guide to attribution, although it can still be a helpful indication. Some other factories were using pattern numbers in the thousands, Samuel Alcock being one, and of course Messrs. Daniel of Stoke used numbers in the 3000 or 4000 range, as they continued (or started at) the former Spode numbering sequence.

A large variety of English porcelain London shape teapots are illustrated in Philip Miller and Michael Berthoud's joint book *An Anthology of British Teapots* between their pages 246 and 277. It is, however, extremely difficult to distinguish any minor differences in shape from small photographs. This work does, nevertheless, show well how popular these London shapes proved to be and that versions were produced by practically all British manufacturers.

Several simple and graceful New Hall cup shapes occur which approximately link to the London or Grecian form. I show examples in Plates 374, 382 and 384. The teacup and saucer of pattern 1571 (Plate 381) conveniently link with the Grecian pattern 1571 teapot illustrated in Plate 380. The ring handle, however, differs from the standard three unit London shape handle, as shown in Plate 366. Another version of the basic Grecian teapot and related objects may have concave lateral indentations around the body, as seen in a pattern 1571 jug illustrated by Michael Berthoud in his *A Cabinet of British Creamers,* Plate 664.

The well-moulded cup and saucer shown in Plate 386 may also fit here, although the pattern number of this floral design example indicates a rather later period, number 2502 of perhaps the mid-1820s. The intricate moulding on this cup and saucer can perhaps be seen to better advantage on the very rare New Hall teapot shown in Plate 385.[5] This is of a basic oblong form that could be linked to the earlier London shapes. The matching milk jugs have the same body shape and relief moulding and a smaller version of the teapot handle – see *A Cabinet of British Creamers* Plates 829-30. This moulding was found

PLATE 386. *A New Hall relief moulded bone china coffee cup and saucer, well painted with floral sprays, with gilt borders. Painted pattern number 2502. Diameter of saucer 5½in. (13.97cm). c.1825-30.*
GODDEN COLLECTION

on the Dudson factory site in the 1990s (see page 373).

It must be borne in mind that by this approximate period the New Hall partnership, or what was left of it, was running down. From 1820 attempts had been made to sell the factory. Well respected as had been their porcelains, these attempts were seemingly unsuccessful. Failing another attempt in 1831, the then management endeavoured to let the factory. Again they were unsuccessful, but in the autumn of 1835 they advertised the sale of the remaining stock – see pages 403-405. During this time it is reasonable to assume that fewer new shapes or designs were produced and that as much old stock as possible was being turned into cash – a rare commodity in the industry at that, or at any, time!

The New Hall partnership produced two, new low, circular plan teapot forms in perhaps the early 1820s. An example decorated with pattern 2784 and a lower wide teapot of pattern 2901 are shown in the *Anthology of Teapots,* Plates 1778 and 1779. The covered sugar and milk jug forms to accompany the first mentioned circular plan New Hall teapot as my Plate 387 are shown in Plates 388-9. The knob of the teapot and sugar bowl are in the form of a low, wide, flower or bud. These shapes have been called 'Etruscan', but some care is needed in using such names as different authorities and different factories may have used this description in referring to different forms. I have just mentioned a New Hall teapot of pattern 2784; one could usefully note that the Wyllie accounts mention sets of teacups and saucers of pattern 2789 ordered in 1824.

Typical teapots of the popular shape sometimes called 'Old English' are shown in Plates 391-3. Again, this was a very popular form and near variations can be found used by, for example, Ridgway, Rockingham, Hicks & Meigh, Daniel and Yates. Some of these, with others often unattributed, are shown in the *Anthology of British Teapots.* When numbered the New Hall examples usually fall into the 2900-3100 range.

Our review of New Hall bone china teawares is now approaching, or in, the 1830s – that is, we are concerned with the last five years of production. The examples can be heavily potted, made down to a price rather than up to a quality. This point is well made in the teapot and creamer of pattern 3203 (Plates 394-5). This ungainly shape of teapot has been recorded with patterns up to the 3900 range.[6]

This teapot form has a rather crudely modelled floral knob and a dolphin-like handle. At least two other

Plate 387. *A fine quality New Hall teapot decorated in red and gold. Some pieces on this service bear the indistinct pattern number 3247. 5½in. (13.97cm) high. c.1822-7.* Private collection

Plate 388. *A New Hall bone china covered sugar bowl of pattern 2903. This shape would accompany teapots as Plate 387 and jugs of the form shown in Plate 389. 5¼in. (13.34cm) high. c.1822-7.* Private collection

Plate 389. *A New Hall milk or cream jug of pattern 2903, incorporating two tones of underglaze blue with overglaze enamels and gilding. Painted pattern number. 3½in. (8.89cm) high. c.1822-7.* Private collection

Plate 390. *A New Hall cream or milk jug of the rather rare forms associated with teawares shown in Plates 387-9. Pattern number 2359, decorated in underglaze blue, enamels and gilding. 6½in. (16.51cm) long. c.1822-7.* Godden of Worthing

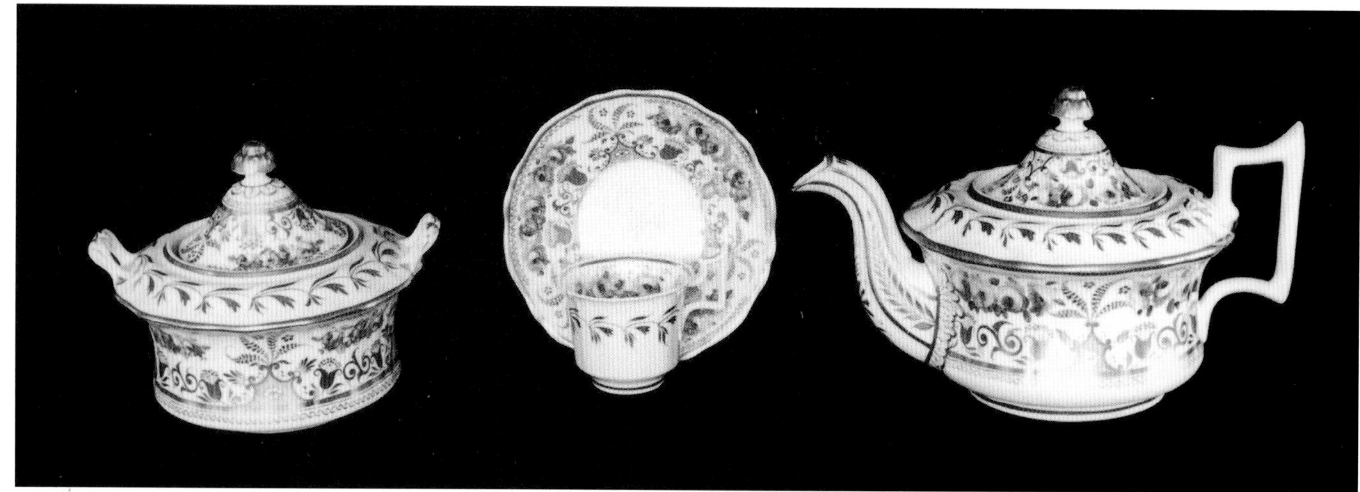

Plate 391. *New Hall teawares of pattern number 2901 but of forms that were closely copied at several other factories, including Ridgways. Painted pattern number on teapot and sugar bowl. Teapot 6¾in. (17.15cm) high. c.1825-30.* A. de Saye Hutton

Plate 392. *A good New Hall bone china teapot of pattern 3050, with underglaze blue border and richly gilt. See Colour Plate 73. Painted pattern number. 6½in. (16.51cm) high. c.1825-30.* Private collection

Plate 393. *A cream ground New Hall teapot of pattern 3324, including underglaze blue with enamels and gilding. Painted pattern number 3324. 6½in. (16.51cm) high. c.1825-30.* Godden of Worthing

factories – William Adams, who had a nearby pottery, and Hilditch at Longton – made a very similar shape. For a discussion of the possible links with the Adams the reader is referred to *Collecting Lustreware* by G.A. Godden and Michael Gibson (Barrie & Jenkins, 1991) Plates 59-61, pages 75-6. I am still a little unhappy about the attribution to New Hall of all such rather heavily potted teawares. Examples with pattern numbers well below 1000 may have been produced by Hilditch or other Staffordshire firms of the 1825-35 period. The specimens attributed to New Hall have the holes at the bottom[7] of the spout arranged in an inverted pyramidal form with holes pierced in rows, 4, 3, 2 and a single hole at the bottom. The reader should also consult the 1999 specialist book *Adams Ceramics, Staffordshire Potters and Pots 1779-1998* by David Furniss, J. Richard and Judith Wagner (Schiffer Publishing Ltd., Atglen, U.S.A.). These authors cite very high Adams pattern numbers, in the New Hall range.

New Hall teawares of this type were also decorated with light blue sprigged motifs. One such is shown in Plate 400 and similar applied modelled motifs were employed at many other factories in the approximate period 1825-35,

Plate 394. *A New Hall moulded teapot decorated with an inexpensive coloured over printed design, without gilding. Painted pattern number 3202. See also Plate 395. 6in. (15.24cm) high. c.1830-35.* Private Collection

Plate 395. *The moulded New Hall creamer of pattern 3203 to accompany the teapot shown in Plate 394. 3¼in. (8.26cm) high. c.1830-35.* Private Collection

Plate 396. *A New Hall moulded teapot (as Plates 394 and 397) with its stand. Painted with a middle price pattern, number 3639. 6in. (15.24cm) high. c.1830.* Godden of Worthing

Plate 397. *A moulded teapot similar to those shown in Plates 394 and 396 but in this case with a fractional pattern number, 4/3431. Underglaze blue cream and gold ornamentation. Painted pattern number. 10¾in. (27.31cm) long. c.1830-35.* D.R. Platz Collection

but examples of the forms shown in Plates 394-402 will almost certainly be New Hall, especially if they bear a pattern number over 3000. A rare variation of this shape teapot, but with a more conventional double curved handle, is illustrated in *An Anthology of British Teapots,* Plate 1780. A tea cup to match this 'pineapple' moulded pot is shown in *A Compendium of British Cups,* Plate 964.

These shapes of late New Hall teaware can also occur with a non-characteristic form of pattern number. The high, New Hall type numbers (usually in the 3000s) are expressed over numerators such as '2', '3', '4', '5' or '7', giving a fractional form of pattern number. This number may indicate the shape, i.e. number '4' shape. Shape '4' seems the most common or popular.[8] I show in Plate 399 a very decorative, finely painted, ground laid and gilt trio and matching jug of this class. The pattern number is 4 expressed over 3753. The highly interesting point is that one cup from this service bears the boldly incised year date '1831'. This neatly fits in with my dating of these late New Hall bone china teawares.

The cup and saucers recorded with the heavily potted dolphin-handled teapots are quite attractive and simple. A

Plate 398. *A decorative moulded milk or cream jug, with the fractional pattern number 4/3609. 3¾in (9.53cm) high. c.1830-5.*
Dr. and Mrs. G. Barnes

Plate 399. *A richly decorated, deep puce bordered jug with coffee cup and saucer, of fractional pattern number 4/3753. See Colour Plate 74. This cup has the incised date (?) 1831. Jug 3½in. (8.89cm) high. 1831.*
Dr. G. Audley

trio of coffee, teacup and saucer is shown in Plate 401 and a rather upmarket teacup and saucer in Plate 402. All these have 4- series fractional pattern numbers.

Other late New Hall bone china shapes may be represented by the fractional series pattern number jugs shown in Michael Berthoud's *A Cabinet of British Creamers,* Plates 853-4. Before discussing the New Hall bone china dessert wares and the jugs and related mugs, it is convenient to introduce a few of the rarely found New Hall porcelains of the post-1812 period. The pieces known to collectors, however, fall into the first fifteen or so years of bone china production, that is pieces made in the approximate period 1812-27. This may be partly due to the fact that the pieces are unmarked and difficult to identify, but it is also due to the fact that few, non-tea service objects were made. The partnership, like most porcelain manufacturers, concentrated on tea and dessert wares.

However, we must not forget the breakfast services which, although sold in small numbers, included covered butter dishes such as that of pattern 1934 shown in Plate 403. In this connection pattern 1930 in embossed teawares (perhaps similar to Plate 400) is featured in the Wyllie accounts in 1819. Basket moulded breakfast wares include covered muffin dishes, very small plates, or stands, and eggcups. Breakfast services traditionally include dishes and plates, upright milk jugs holding a half or full pint and even, in some cases, toastracks. Such rare breakfast services

Plate 400. *An unmarked covered sugar bowl and teacup of the basic shapes that would have accompanied teawares as shown in Plates 394-9 but with mauve tinted relief decoration and gilt trim. Cup 2in. (5.08cm) high. c.1830-5.* Dr. G. Audley

Plate 401. *A well decorated trio with underglaze blue border, flower painting and tasteful gilding. Fractional pattern number 4/3747 on teacup. Diameter of saucer 5½in. (13.97cm). c.1830-5.* Godden Collection

Plate 402. *A teacup and saucer with painted figure centre and gilt border, the gilding on the exterior being very similar to that shown in Plate 401. Fractional pattern number 4/3914. Diameter of saucer 5½in. (13.97cm). c.1830-5.* Private collection

Plate 403. *A rare New Hall covered butter dish on fixed stand, hand painted with landscapes and gilt. Painted pattern number 1934. 4¾in. (12.07cm) high. c.1810-20.* Godden of Worthing

Plate 404. *A rare New Hall bone china spill vase (originally one of a pair or even a set of three) bearing a New Hall bat-printed (coloured over) fruit design. This design also occurs in Plates 352 and 405. 5¼in. (13.34cm) high. c.1810-20.* Private collection

Plate 405. *A rare New Hall bone china two-handled cup of the type that had a cover and stand bearing a known bat-printed fruit motif. See Plates 352 and 404. The reverse side is shown in Colour Plate 75. 2⅞in. (7.3cm) high. c.1810-20.* Private collection

or parts thereof will be decorated with standard teaware designs. They are in essence enlarged tea services.

Most of the rare New Hall bone china shapes have been identified with the help of the bat-printed designs they bear. These designs can often be linked with known New Hall tea service shapes or even with pieces bearing the circular 'New Hall' printed mark. These bat prints include the several fruit groups and the several 'Mother and Child' designs.

Using such help we can almost certainly attribute to New Hall the elegant, unmarked, spill vase shown in Plate 404 and also the double-handled chocolate or caudle cup shown in Plate 405 which would have had a stand and probably also a cover. Note the oval apertures to the handles; these link with the handles on the bone china teacups. Similar handles made in the earlier, pre-1812, hybrid hard-paste body are of a more circular form.

The small scent bottles shown in Plate 406 are probably New Hall examples, but other manufacturers produced similar articles. A rare tumbler is illustrated in A. de Saye Hutton's *A Guide to New Hall Porcelain Patterns* as Plate 303. This specimen is embellished with gilt initials and the date '1815'. It also bears a 'Mother and Child' print.

A range of New Hall jugs and mugs is shown in Plates 436-57.

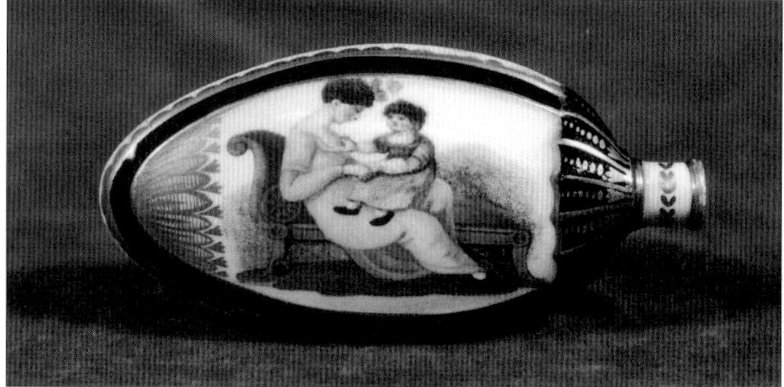

Plate 406. *Three views of two rare New Hall bone china scent bottles, bearing coloured over bat-printed designs. These would have been equipped with stoppers and perhaps metal collars. 3¾in. (9.53cm) long. c.1810-20.* Private collection

Dessert Services

New Hall bone china dessert services fall into four main moulded forms, although each can be decorated in many different styles. These basic forms and approximate periods are:

A. Relief-moulded floral borders. c.1814-20.
   See Plates 407-12.
B. Relief-moulded border with birds. c.1818-5.
   See Plates 413-8.
   I. These basic shapes but with basket-weave borders, not birds.
   II. These basic shapes, without relief-moulded borders.
C. Groups of relief-moulded flowers. The dishes usually have open ribbon like handles.
   c.1820-30. See Plates 420-30.
D. Thickly potted dessert wares with moulded edges and shell like, open work handles to the dishes.
   c.1824-33. See Plates 431-5.

As one might expect, these shapes were copied by (or had been copied from) other English porcelain or pottery manufacturers and consequently not all examples of these dessert forms will necessarily be New Hall. The pattern numbers used by this partnership will, however, exceed 1200 but will probably not be above 3800. This is a very large range considering the relatively short period under discussion, c.1812 to nearly 1835. Most patterns within this range will relate to teawares rather than to the rarer, more costly dessert services.

The make-up of a New Hall bone china dessert service probably varied more than that of a standard forty-five piece tea service. The number of plates could vary from the standard dozen to eighteen or even twenty-four, according to the buyer's needs or purse! The side dishes would be of three or four different shapes, with two or four of each. A footed oval centrepiece would be the largest article and in the more costly services this would be accompanied by a pair of covered tureens for sugar and cream. These may have been originally equipped with porcelain ladles.

Taking a Chamberlain-Worcester dessert service price list[9] as an example, we find that standard dessert services were three times the price of a tea service of the same pattern, a £5.5s.0d. tea service design equating with £15.15s.0d. for a twenty-four plate dessert service or £63 for a richly decorated dessert set decorated in a similar style to a £21 tea service. In a middle price dessert service selling for £21, each plate was 6s.6d., the centrepiece was £2 and the different shape fruit dishes averaged 15s. Pairs of tureens were £2.6s.0d. Whilst these prices were for Worcester examples, the New Hall management's prices would not have differed greatly from those of their Worcester rivals.

The New Hall dessert wares will when inscribed with a pattern number have this reference number quite boldly painted and in a four figure range. Pattern numbers on Daniel or Minton sets would have been rendered in a neater, smaller, manner. The Daniel pattern numbers would be high, like New Hall's, in the 2000 or 3000 range. Spode pattern numbers, too, could be high, but examples usually bear the 'Spode' name and the dessert shapes are different from those here illustrated as New Hall.

The dessert wares in the first grouping 'A' may also bear the printed New Hall circular mark, as used in the approximate period 1814-20.

Furthermore, some of these New Hall relief-moulded dessert wares may bear New Hall bat-printed designs that are also found on typical and accepted New Hall teawares, especially the teapots – see Plates 376 and 409.

The New Hall dessert services in the first grouping 'A', that is those with the flowing branch of mixed flowers moulded in relief, may be found with various coloured grounds. These borders show the reliefs in contrasting white porcelain and are most decorative. Such up-market patterns have gilt borders or handle ornamentation.

Less expensive patterns do not have the coloured borders and have less (or no) gilding and simpler decoration. Most but by no means all such New Hall dessert sets were decorated with bat-printed landscape or figure designs. In most cases these prints were coloured in by hand with overglaze enamels – see Plates 409-12.

The 'A' type relief-moulded floral bordered design incorporating a prominent rose and tulip with leaves and buds, in a repeated pattern, may have originated at the Chamberlain factory at Worcester; it is certainly not unique to New Hall. The Worcester centrepiece shape and the side dishes are of different forms from the New Hall examples, which are shown here in Plates 407-11. However, the Chamberlain plates are very similar to New Hall in their moulding. The Chamberlain factory also used this moulding to embellish their London shape teawares.

PLATE 407. *Representation pieces from a blue ground relief-moulded New Hall bone china part dessert service of pattern 1476. Out of thirty-four pieces, only nine have the painted pattern number and only ten bear the standard painted 'New Hall' mark – see page 385. Centrepiece 10½in. (16.67cm) long. c.1814-8.*
SOTHEBY'S, NEW YORK

PLATE 408. *A typical New Hall relief-moulded oval centrepiece from a dessert service, the painted pattern similar to 1476 (Plate 407) but not identical. Similar floral moulding can occur on non-New Hall porcelains. Circular printed 'New Hall' mark. 10½in. (16.67cm) long. c.1814-8.*
GODDEN OF WORTHING

The Swansea factory in Wales also used this relief-moulded floral border, employing similar shapes to New Hall. Such Welsh porcelains of the approximate period 1814-18 are illustrated in A.E. Jones and Sir Leslie Joseph's book *Swansea Porcelain Shapes and Decoration* (D. Brown & Sons Ltd., Cowbridge, 1988) on their pages 91 and 163. A plate is illustrated in E. Morton Nance's monumental work *The Pottery and Porcelain of Swansea and Nantgarw* (B.T. Batsford Ltd., London, 1942), Plate CXIV, C.

Very similar shaped relief-moulded bone china dessert wares were produced by Messrs. Mayer & Newbold of Lane End from about 1817. These examples can be marked with low pattern numbers, such as 60, expressed under the initial 'M & N'. Such a dessert dish is illustrated in my *Encyclopaedia of British Porcelain Manufacturers* (Barrie & Jenkins, London, 1988), Plate 270.

Similar forms occur in Lakin's[10] fine quality earthenwares. Some other good bone china dessert wares are also very, very close to the New Hall examples. These too can bear tinted bat-printed designs (including coastal

Plate 409. *A light blue bordered New Hall dessert dish with relief-moulded floral design, the centre decorated with a coloured over version of a popular New Hall bat print – see Plates 320 and 376. 9¼ x 7¾in. (23.5 x 19.69cm). c.1815-20.* Godden of Worthing

Plate 410. *A marked 'New Hall' relief moulded dessert dish of characteristic form, the centre bearing a coloured over bat printed design, pattern 1478. Circular printed 'New Hall' mark. 9 x 7in. (22.86 x 17.78cm). c.1815-20.* Godden of Worthing

Plate 411. *One of the handled dishes which were included in pairs or as a set of four, in New Hall dessert services. Coloured over fruit bat prints as pattern 1478. Printed circular 'New Hall' mark. 7¾in. (19.69cm) long. c.1815-20.* The Potteries Museum, Hanley

Plate 412. *A New Hall dessert plate with one of several much used fruit subject bat prints. These were usually coloured in by hand and most dessert sets are of pattern 1478 – see Plates 410-1. Versions of these prints also occur on teawares etc. – see Plates 352 and 404. Diameter 8⅛in. (20.64cm). c.1815-20.* Victoria & Albert Museum. Crown Copyright

scenes) in the New Hall fashion. The prints, however, are different and the pattern number (if present) is well below 1000. Such non-New Hall porcelain dessert wares could have been produced by Thomas Lakin (& Co.) of Stoke. The firm also traded as Thomas Lakin & Son and under the single name Thomas Lakin. These succeeding firms of the 1811-7 period are recorded as producing both earthenwares and porcelain. No marked porcelain has as yet been recorded.

A similar shape of dessert dish to Plate 409 without the

PLATE 413. *Representative pieces from a magnificent New Hall bone china dessert service, with relief-moulded border, believed to be unique to New Hall. See also Plates 358, 414-8. Pattern 1874. The large ice pails or fruit coolers are particularly rare, if rather ungainly. Pails 13in. (33.02cm) high. c.1818-25.*

FORMERLY GROSVENOR ANTIQUES LTD.

relief moulding has been attributed to the Pinxton factory in Derbyshire[11] but the probable date of this, c.1800, is some ten years or more prior to the date of the New Hall examples. The same source attributes a floral moulded version, as Plate 409, to the Swansea factory. Any Pinxton or Swansea pattern number will be very much lower than New Hall at this period, not above 1000.

A probably slightly later relief-moulded New Hall dessert border, which I term 'Type B', has attractive scrolling with birds in leafy branches (Plates 413-8). The relief-moulded border is perhaps unique to New Hall. The part dessert service shown in an old photograph as Plate 413 is unique in my experience in that this set includes a large pair of fruit coolers. Openwork sided fruit baskets with stands have also been reported with the birds in branches moulding, but I have not seen an example with a known New Hall design and pattern number. I have not noticed New Hall landscape bat prints associated with this border but coloured-in New Hall type prints of fruit certainly occur. These include patterns 1629 and 1706 – see Plates 416-7.

These same basic type 'B' shapes also occur (rather more rarely) with a moulded basketweave wide edge or border to give type 'B I'. This matches the moulded teawares illustrated in Plates 372-5. This version was usually used for the less expensive sets but some have a wash of colour over the basketwork moulding. Dessert wares of this type enhanced with floral patterns 2018, 2350, 2369 and 2449 (coloured border) are featured in *A Guide to New Hall Porcelain Patterns* by Anthony de Saye Hutton (Barrie &

PLATE 414. *A relief-moulded New Hall handled dessert dish of characteristic form. Painted with pattern 1874, as Plate 413. 7¾ x 6½in. (19.69 x 16.51cm). c.1818-25.* GODDEN OF WORTHING

PLATE 415. *One of a pair of small tureens (for cream and sugar) included in the more costly complete New Hall dessert services. This example, of pattern 1706, bears coloured over bat prints of fruit. The dishes and plates bear larger fruit groups, as Plates 416-7. Painted pattern number 1706. 5¾in. (14.61cm) high. c.1818-25.* GODDEN OF WORTHING

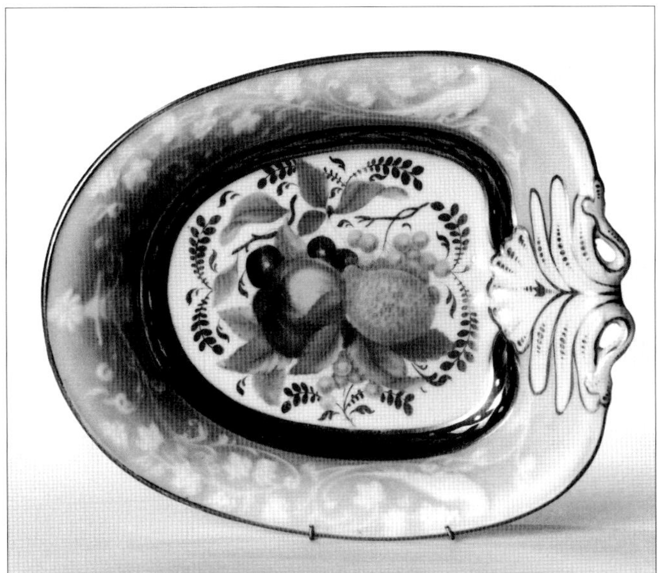

PLATE 416. *A New Hall handled dessert dish with pale blue and relief-moulded border. The centre has coloured over bat prints of fruit, being pattern 1706, as Plates 415 and 417. For this shape see also Plates 413-4. Painted pattern number 1706. 7¾ x 6½in. (19.69 x 16.51cm). c.1818-25.* GODDEN OF WORTHING

PLATE 417. *A New Hall relief-moulded dessert plate of pattern 1706, as Plates 415-6. Light blue border and coloured over bat printed centre. See Colour Plate 77. Diameter 8½.in. (21.59cm). c.1818-25.* DAVID GOLDING

PLATE 418. *A relief-moulded New Hall dessert dish of characteristic shape. This and other basic shapes also occur with moulded basketwork border and plain (devoid of any moulding). This hand-painted pattern is 1707. 9⅞ x 6⅝in. (22.54 x 16.83cm). c.1818-25.*

GODDEN OF WORTHING

PLATE 419. *A New Hall blue bordered dessert plate with raised gold borders and hand-painted centre, of pattern 2155. Dessert dishes of shapes similar to Plates 416 and 418 also occur to match this plate, with a plain border, devoid of moulding. Diameter 8½in. (21.59cm). c.1820-25.*

GODDEN OF WORTHING

Jenkins, London, 1990) – see his Plates 195, 210 and 214.

The same dessert ware shapes were used for the cheaper patterns. These wares did not include the relief moulding nor therefore the coloured edge. These I have termed type 'B II'. Simple floral designs were usually painted on these non-relief-moulded dessert sets. A printed outline floral pattern was number 1742. A dessert tureen of this type and pattern is illustrated by Anthony de Saye Hutton in his Plate 176.

The pattern numbers usually found on these type 'B' bone china New Hall dessert services, with shapes as shown in Plates 413-418, fall into the range 1600 to 1900. I would be doubtful about a New Hall attribution for any similar looking examples with pattern numbers below 1500, unless it was an accepted early New Hall design that had been reused on these later shapes. A few richly decorated plain (not relief-moulded) dessert sets are also recorded, such as blue bordered pattern 2155, with raised gilding, see Plate 419.

The next series of New Hall dessert services have relief-moulded sprays of flowers arranged around the borders. These shapes (my type 'C') are not unique to the New Hall factory, but the examples bearing pattern numbers in the approximate range 2000 to 2800 may be regarded as originating at our factory. The Dudson site at Hanley yielded several New Hall wasters of such dessert wares, some with the underglaze blue border (or ground) to the white reliefs.

Again, it is possible that some still saleable earlier patterns were applied to the new shapes. In most cases, however, new patterns were applied to the new moulded forms which date to about 1820-5.

Apart from the moulded flower sprays, several of the type 'C' shapes have openwork handles, like a bow tied in ribbon. Plates 420-30 show typical examples of these shapes. Amongst the factories that may also have produced these shapes are Messrs. Ralph & James Clews of Cobridge, in the Staffordshire Potteries. This partnership succeeded William Adams at their Cobridge factory in September 1817 and produced earthenwares and stone china as well as porcelain. Among dessert dishes with New Hall look-alike ribbon handles are impressed marked 'Clews' blue printed wares. Charles Bourne of Foley (Fenton) also produced moulded dessert wares of this moulded design from c.1817. Several other firms probably copied New Hall or Clews, but their products are unmarked.

The New Hall examples included coloured-in known New Hall bat-printed designs as well as some good figure subjects. The later include a series of paintings depicting

PLATE 420. *A New Hall dessert tureen with floral relief border (as Plates 421-30) on fixed base. Hand painted floral sprays and gilt trim. Painted pattern number 2226. 8¼in. (20.96cm) long. c.1820-25/30*
GODDEN OF WORTHING

PLATE 421. *A handled New Hall dessert dish with moulded border and hand painted floral sprays, and gilt trim. Unrecorded pattern number but probably 2226, as Plate 420. 8½ x 8in. (21.59 x 20.32cm). c.1820-5.*
PRIVATE COLLECTION

PLATE 422. *A New Hall dessert dish with moulded border. Hand painted with floral spray, as pattern 2371. This is a less expensive variation of pattern 2226, as the line edge and turn is in enamel, not gold. Painted pattern number 2371. 9⅛ x 7½in. (23.18 x 19.05cm). c.1820-5.*
PRIVATE COLLECTION

PLATE 423. *A blue bordered relief moulded oval dish from a magnificent dessert service, each piece hand painted with figures in landscapes. Painted pattern number 2229. 11 x 7½in. (27.94 x 19.05cm). c.1820-5.*
GODDEN OF WORTHING

the adventures of Dr. Syntax[12] – see Plates 424-8. These richly decorated, costly services often have coloured borders, usually a rich deep underglaze blue.

I have written previously of the high pattern numbers associated with New Hall bone china of the post 1812 period. I have quoted here dessert service patterns in the 2000 range. Such high numbers in use before, say, 1830 are not exclusively New Hall. Other factories that had reached such numbers at this period include Spode and H. & R. Daniel of Stoke. However, in both these cases the numbers would be written in a small, neat, script. In contrast the New Hall numbers are usually boldly written in rather a clumsy manner.

The next identified New Hall dessert service form is again not exclusive to New Hall. Regrettably all copyists, like the New Hall partners, did not favour a name mark.

In this case the type 'D' pieces are rather thickly potted and have a moulded, shaped edge. The handles include a

PLATE 424. *A decorative New Hall dessert dish with underglaze blue border and floral reliefs. The centre hand painted with figure subject from the Dr. Syntax adventures, popular subjects of the period – see also Plates 425-8. See Colour Plates 78. Pattern 2623. 12 x 5in. (30.48 x 12.7cm). c.1822-7.* W. KIRKBY

PLATE 425. *Representative shapes from a New Hall dessert service, hand painted with figure subjects taken from prints of Dr. Syntax's adventures, pattern 2623. Whilst similar forms were produced by other firms, such as Clews, the moulded border design does link with Dudson site shards – see page 390 and Plate 427. c.1823-7.*

MESSRS. PHILLIPS

Plate 426. *Further examples of New Hall's moulded edged dessert wares, hand painted with scenes from Dr. Syntax's adventures. These are often named or numbered on the reverse – see Plate 427. Pattern number 2623 on some pieces. c.1822-7.* Messrs. Phillips

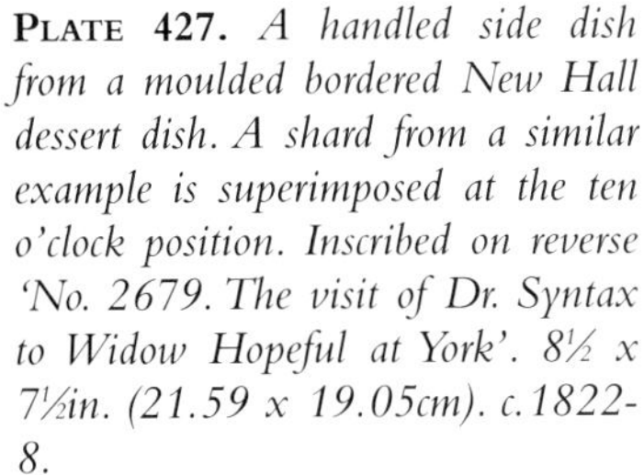

Plate 427. *A handled side dish from a moulded bordered New Hall dessert dish. A shard from a similar example is superimposed at the ten o'clock position. Inscribed on reverse 'No. 2679. The visit of Dr. Syntax to Widow Hopeful at York'. 8½ x 7½in. (21.59 x 19.05cm). c.1822-8.*

Plate 428. *A New Hall plate with relief moulded border, as Plates 420-7, but without the usual coloured border. Hand painted with Dr. Syntax subject and neatly gilt. Painted pattern number N.2810. Diameter 8½in. (21.59cm). c.1825-30.*

Plate 429. *A dessert plate with pale blue border and moulded reliefs, as Plates 420-8. The centre with coloured over bat prints of the type found on various New Hall tea and dessert wares as well as on other shapes. Pattern number 2240. Diameter 8½in. (21.59cm). c.1820-5.*

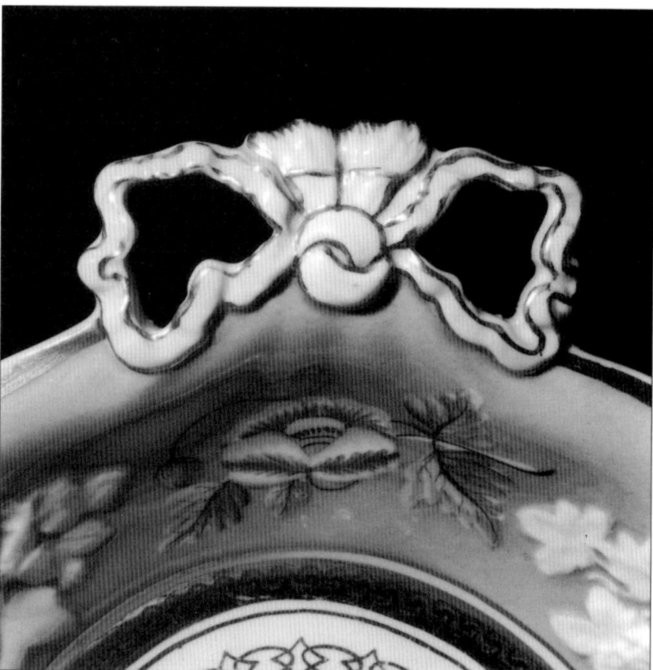

Plate 430. *A close-up of a New Hall dessert dish of pattern 2240, to show the relief moulded sprays and the moulded ribbon-like handle. Some other factories, including Clews, are believed to have produced close copies. The high New Hall pattern numbers, usually above two thousand on these shapes, is a helpful guide to origin.*

shell-like device with an opening on either side. I show typical examples in Plates 431-5. The New Hall patterns range from about 2900 to at least 3664. These dessert wares were seemingly in production for a long period, although examples are quite rare. Indeed these forms have only in recent years been attributed to New Hall. The Dudson site at Hanley yielded some wasters of these New Hall dessert wares. Various shaped dessert dishes will have been produced and footed centrepieces, some with a pierced edge. Sugar and cream tureens may also have been made as these were part of the more expensive dessert services.

Coloured and well gilt borders occur and some good, bold, flower painting appears on these sets of the late 1820s or early 1830s. One colour bat printing does not seem to have been used, as it had become outdated, apart from outline prints, such as the fruit designs which were coloured in by hand (see Plate 433). Some hand-painted designs, without coloured borders or intricate gilding (as pattern 3035), would have represented the low price range New Hall's dessert wares. Well gilt patterns such as 3030, 3664 or 3934 were, on the other hand, relatively costly.

Messrs. Samuel Alcock & Co. of Cobridge (and later at

Plate 431. *A New Hall dessert dish with deep blue border and hand-painted floral sprays. This and related shapes (shown in Plates 432-5) were also produced at other factories, including Mintons. The high New Hall pattern numbers prove helpful. Painted pattern number 2930. 8½in. x 8¼in. (21.59 x 20.96cm). c.1824-30.*

Godden of Worthing

PLATE 432. *A pale blue bordered New Hall floral painted dessert dish of the type shown in Plates 431, 433-5. Pattern number 2932. 9½ x 8¾in. (24.13 x 22.23cm). c.1824-30.*
GODDEN OF WORTHING

PLATE 433. *A thickly potted New Hall dessert plate, decorated with underglaze blue border with gilding. The centre with printed outline coloured in print of earlier type (see Plate 429). Painted pattern number 'No.3030'. Diameter 9¼in. (23.5cm). c.1824-30.*
GODDEN COLLECTION

PLATE 434. *A very decorative blue bordered New Hall dessert plate, with typical late flower painting and intricate gilding. Painted pattern number 3034. Diameter 9¼in. (23.5cm). c.1824-30.*
GODDEN COLLECTION

PLATE 435. *A superb quality New Hall dessert plate with pale yellow border and intricately gilt floral motifs. The centre painted with figures in landscapes. Painted pattern number 3664. Diameter 9½in. (24.13cm). See Colour Plate 79. c.1828-33.*
PRIVATE COLLECTION

Burslem) certainly produced this type of moulded edge dessert ware, as the shape is shown in a factory pattern book. The Alcock examples dating from about 1826 would have pattern numbers lower than New Hall and higher than the Minton numbers, in the approximate range 700-900.

The Minton version of these dessert wares is shown in *Staffordshire Porcelain*, Plate 189. These fine quality Minton bone china examples were produced in the second period of Minton's porcelain production, that is in the mid-1820s. They will bear low pattern numbers, almost certainly under 500, in contrast to New Hall numbers at this period which were well above 2000.

The New Hall dessert plates of this period appear rather clumsy in shape with four straight sections between the moulded shells. Two examples of contrasting patterns and price ranges are shown in Plates 434-5. Pattern 3664, with its superb quality gilt flower design, surrounding the figures in landscape centre shows the heights that the factory could still reach in the 1830s.

These New Hall dessert shapes are, however, the latest known to me and possibly they mark the end of the partnership's dessert service production. On the other hand, other shapes may await discovery or the correct attributions. It seems probable, however, that as the factory and its production was run down in the early 1830s, in the face of growing competition, few if any new dessert service shapes or patterns were introduced. Almost certainly the pattern number sequence did not climb above 4000.

The New Hall management seem not to have produced any dinner services and they were certainly not alone in leaving this costly aspect of ceramic production to other firms such as Spode, Derby or the Worcester manufacturers.

Jugs and Mugs

Jugs, for various liquids, had always been an important part of the New Hall range of products, as had to a lesser degree mugs. Jugs were produced in various sizes or capacities and they proved very suitable for presents. A good number are therefore found with individuals' names or initials, with sometimes a date being added. A few were decorated with special designs (Plates 438, 448-50), but most were of standard patterns or types. The New Hall management was, of course, not alone in producing jugs and mugs; they were a popular line made by most ceramic firms. Some saleable styles, such as the lilac or lavender

PLATE 436. *An unmarked New Hall bone china jug, bearing coloured over bat-printed designs of the type found on teawares of pattern 984 found on both the hybrid hard-paste body and the post-1814 bone china. The print on the reverse side is as shown on the coffee pot in Plate 340. 5½in. (13.97cm) high (other sizes would also have been produced). c.1814-18.* THE POTTERIES MUSEUM, HANLEY

PLATE 437. *A rare form of New Hall bone china jug bearing coloured over bat prints of the type seen on New Hall teawares. See Colour Plate 80. The reverse side, with gilt date 1814, is shown in Plate 330. 6in. (15.24cm) high. 1814.* PRIVATE COLLECTION

blue ground pieces with relief-moulded motifs, were standard products of the 1815-30 period. A selection of these are shown in Plates 439-44, 452-4 and 456.

Perhaps the earliest, post-1812, New Hall jug to be produced in the bone china body was of the form shown in Plate 436. These are, however, rarely found today, perhaps because they were soon superseded by new shapes. The also very rare shape shown in Plate 437 is of the same approximate period, but with a revised handle form. This example bears the date 1814 on the reverse side – see Plate 330.

The next form to be considered, the globular shape with a moulded handle emulating a series of moulded overlapping leaves (giving a good grip for the hand), proved extremely popular. This was seemingly the standard jug shape from about 1817 into the early 1820s. Several examples were especially inscribed, usually with initials and a date. There is a school of thought that disregards the given date on such presentation pieces, but I feel that nine times out of ten the date may be considered to record the date of the presentation or of the occasion. Certainly, the dates on these (and other) New Hall pieces link well with the probable date of manufacture and coincide with the style and form then in fashion. My earliest dated example of this globular, moulded leaf-handled jug is inscribed 'Wm.Williams, Loppington, Decber 27th 1817'. This jug (Plate 438) is most unusual because it is decorated with platinum lustre

PLATE 438. *A unique inscribed and dated New Hall jug, but of a standard form. Decorated with 'silver lustre' with printed outline arms. Inscribed on the front 'Wm. Williams. Loppington. Dec.ber27th, 1817'. 6in. (15.24cm) high. 1817.* PRIVATE COLLECTION

PLATE 439. *An attractive New Hall jug of a popular type with white reliefs on a pale blue ground. Note the moulded handle form. Dated in gold '1819'. 4¼in. (10.8cm) high. 1819.* PRIVATE COLLECTION

PLATE 440. *The reverse side of the presentation jug shown in Plate 439, illustrating companion relief motifs. These are not unique to New Hall. Inscribed in gold 'c.1819'. 4¼in. (10.8cm) high. 1819.*
PRIVATE COLLECTION

and bears a coloured-in print of armorial bearings. I know of a floral painted example personalised with initials and dated 1818.

PLATE 441. *A good and typical New Hall presentation jug, with tinted reliefs on the white bone china ground – the reverse effect of that shown in Plates 439-40. Inscribed in gold 'George Dighton Dishford'. 6½in. (16.51cm) high. c.1818-20 Later dates can occur.*
GODDEN OF WORTHING

The most popular form of decoration associated with such globular jugs is illustrated in Plates 439-43. These have what is termed 'sprigged' decoration, that is, motifs are produced from special moulds and then applied or 'sprigged' on to the unfired porcelain body before glazing, the exterior of the jug being lightly tinted – usually a lilac or lavender blue colour to display better the white reliefs. In general style such objects (which are not confined to jugs) seem to emulate the Wedgwood blue jasper wares with their classical white reliefs. Those were copied by various potters such as Neale, Turner or Adams because they were so popular. The glazed porcelain examples were easier to clean than the unglazed jasper jugs, but the sharpness of the relief moulding tended to be partly lost under the porcelain glaze.

Apart from New Hall these sprigged lilac or lavender blue ground porcelain jugs were produced by other firms, noticeably by Spodes, Ridgways and Davenports. The Ridgway porcelain examples may date from 1808 onwards, as examples are known which bear the early mark 'Ridgway & Sons' – see my *Ridgway Porcelains* (Antique Collectors' Club, 1985).

The Wyllie orders from the New Hall partnership, then trading as Messrs. Hollins, Warburton, Daniel & Co., record the purchase of different sizes of 'Blue Jugs' in April, June and October 1817 and in September 1818. This simply described jug most probably relates to the relief moulded 'sprigged' jugs. The simple designation underlines the standard and popular nature of the jugs, no greater description being required.

The sizes, expressed in the normal potter's manner, were given as '4s', '6s', '12s', '24s', '30s' and '36s'. The lower numbers were the larger jugs, the '30s' and '36s' the smallest, the count being the number of articles to the dozen! The prices were 15s. for the '4s', '6s' and '12s' and 18s. for the other sizes – that is for the largest jugs one received four jugs for 15s. and for the smallest one received thirty-six jugs for 18s., giving a price of 6d. each. These jugs were obviously standard types, not especially inscribed or ornately decorated examples.

The sizes quoted are merely those ordered in September 1818 by one London retailer. It would seem that the list is not complete as other, not mentioned, standard jug sizes were '8s' and '18s'. If, as seems probable, the New Hall partnership also made these sizes, the total number of sizes for this one jug shape was eight.[13] The New Hall porcelain jugs do not have the size numbers marked on the bases as was the habit within the industry at a later period.

Whilst quoting the jugs ordered by John and Ann Wyllie in 1817, it should be noted that in April 1817 various 'coloured jugs' were ordered or received. No other description was given, nor was a pattern number mentioned. These coloured jugs were probably the standard sprigged types but with the reliefs coloured over. I show such an example in Plate 446.

Plate 442. *Two typical New Hall bone china jugs with popular reliefs on a light blue ground. Note the different basic shapes and the border designs. 6¼ x 6½in. (15.88 x 16.51cm) high. c.1818-22.*
Godden of Worthing

Plate 443. *Two New Hall presentation jugs with 1820 and 1821 dates added in gold. The right-hand example has standard coloured over fruit bat prints; the left-hand example has standard reliefs of the type shown in Plates 439-42. 5½ and 6¼in. (13.97 and 15.88cm) high.*
Private collection

Prices per dozen were £1.1s.0d. (3s.6d. each) for the large jugs of size 6. Sizes 12 and 24 were listed at £1.4s.0d. and the smaller ones of size 30 and 36 at £1.7s.6d. a potter's dozen. 'Blue Jugs' received at the same time were invoiced at the same prices. Duplicate orders were placed by this relatively small London retailer in June 1817, when over a hundred such standard jugs were ordered, giving a total of nearly two hundred and fifty jugs in the April and June 1817 listings. These New Hall sprigged jugs were indeed widely popular.

Apart from the sprigged designs shown in Plates 439-43, the factory also produced examples with hunting scenes. The late George Stringer contributed a general paper on this type of bas-relief decoration, showing how one basic design was used by several potters. His paper 'Notes on Staffordshire Bas-Reliefs of the Eighteenth and Nineteenth Centuries' was published in the *Transactions of the English Ceramic Circle,* Vol. 4, Part 1 of 1957.

Mugs were produced to match both the standard New Hall types, the blue ground jugs with white sprigged motifs and those with a white ground but with painted reliefs (both styles are shown in Plates 444-5). These were generally of small size, the reason being that the mug held enough liquid for one person whilst a jug was a communal vessel.

The Wyllie accounts for August 1817 show the coloured mugs charged at £1.2s.0d. a dozen for size 24 and £1.4s.0d. for the smaller size, where one received thirty-six to the potter's dozen. The mugs, being smaller articles than the jugs, were slightly less costly. A larger variety of blue (ground) mugs was ordered in March 1819, the potter's sizes being given as '12s' for the largest, through '24s' and '30s' to the smallest which were '36s'. Today the New Hall sprigged mugs are rarer than the popular jugs.

Several different sprigged designs and combinations of motifs were used and some jugs may have been made in sets of graduating sizes and capacities. Various border motifs were also employed, as were different ground colours. In some instances the reliefs were picked out in enamel colours (Plates 445-6), but for my taste the white reliefs on a tinted lavender blue ground are by far the most attractive. Some examples have more gilding than others, depending on the selling price or on any special requirements from the ordering parties.

Whilst it is possible that some extra gilding or inscriptions were added to standard products by the larger retailers, some of whom employed gilders or decorators with their own muffle-kilns, the inscriptions appear to be of a matching type and I believe were applied by New Hall factory gilders. If this was the case, the special orders would merely have been sent by post to the factory as were regular orders by way of the retailers. The place names on some inscribed, presentation, jugs cover a very wide area within the British Isles. Many are from quite small towns or villages that would not have local gilders. These must have been supplied by the New Hall factory. They illustrate its large market.

These globular New Hall jugs of the 1817-20 period

PLATE 444. *A New Hall bone china mug bearing typical relief designs on a light blue ground. Inscribed in gold 'Thomas Spencer Leicester. 1818'. 3¼in. (8.26cm) high. 1818.* FORMERLY GODDEN COLLECTION

PLATE 445. *A small relief-moulded bone china mug, the reliefs picked out in enamel colours. Painter's tally mark 'V'. 2½in. (6.35cm) high. c.1818-25.* GODDEN COLLECTION

Plate 446. *A New Hall bone china jug with standard relief motifs picked out in overglaze enamels in the same style as the small mug illustrated in Plate 445. Printed circular 'New Hall' mark. 5½in. (13.97cm). high. c.1818-25.*

Plate 447. *The side view of a superb and large presentation jug, showing very fine quality flower painting. See Colour Plate 81. The inscribed scenic front is shown in Plate 448. 9½in. (24.13cm) high. c.1816-22.* Messrs. Bonhams

were sometimes hand painted with flowers or other motifs, as was the really superb example illustrated in Plates 447-8. Other quite rare examples were decorated with bat-printed views or other subjects such as the popular coloured-in fruit prints. One initialled and dated '1818' example is shown in Plate 451. Although this was seemingly a special order, it does not bear any gilding, only enamelled edges and trim. It is attractive but would have been modestly priced – a happy combination for the original purchaser.

John and Ann Wyllie's orders dated 20 March 1819 include 'Blue Jugs' in a 'New Shape'. These entries for two dozen size 24s and 36s may well relate to either of the forms shown in Plates 452-6. These are rarely met with in New Hall porcelain but the vertical sprigged leafage and cowslip designs are not unique to New Hall. The upswept handle to the jugs shown in Plates 453-4 is reminiscent of the revised handle to the second version of the London shape teapot – see page 373.

Two slightly different versions of this form are recorded. The one with the wider leaves (Plate 454) is the rarer and this has been recorded with the 'NH' raised initial pad mark – see page 131.

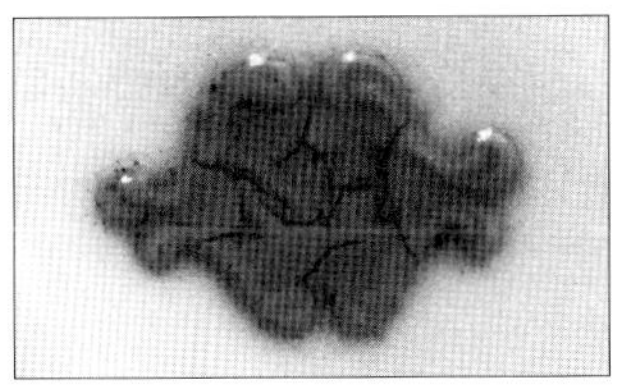

Plate 448. *The front of the New Hall jug shown in Plate 447. The rare cricketing subject helped the 1992 auction price to £4,000, being sold to an Australian cricket enthusiast. See Colour Plate 82. 9½in. (24.13cm) high. c.1816-22.* Messrs. Bonhams

PLATE 449. *A superb New Hall presentation jug with shipping scenes and armorial bearings on a standard jug form. See also Plate 450. 7¼in. (18.42cm) high. c.1820-5.* MESSRS. PHILLIPS

PLATE 450. *The side view of the New Hall jug illustrated in Plate 449. Here the new steam and paddle powered vessel is contrasted with the old sailing vessel. 7¼in. (18.42cm) high. c.1820-5.* MESSRS. PHILLIPS

The general form of the jug shown in Plate 452 proved very popular, especially at the Ridgway factories. Care must be taken in attributing porcelain examples to the New Hall factory.

I have been discussing moulded jugs with reliefs. It is also possible that simple moulded or turned jugs without raised motifs were produced. It is almost certain that miniature or 'toy' jugs were produced by the New Hall management, as they were by several other manufacturers, particularly by the Spode firm at Stoke and by Chamberlains at Worcester. The Wyllie-New Hall accounts, for example, include under the date 22 December 1823: '6 Toy jugs blue ground flowers and gold 16s.'.

What other miniature articles were produced, and were full size jugs made in the same rich style with a dark blue ground with perhaps panels of well-painted flowers and ornate gilding? Certainly such examples were popular, but most examples are attributed to other firms such as John Rose of Coalport.

Returning to the relief-decorated moulded jugs of full size, the relief-moulded jug shown in Plate 455 is I am sure a New Hall example. It certainly seems to be rare and is the only example known to me.

The moulded handle, however, links with a rather more common type of the mid-1820s which has coloured floral sprigging. A typical 'N.H.' initial marked example is shown in Plate 456. Spoilt 'wasters' relating to such jugs were found on the Dudson factory site – see page 373. Therefore there can be no doubt of the attribution of the initial marked examples, one such sprigged initial mark being found in 'waster' forms. However, the basic jug shape was also made by other firms in various sizes.[14] The

PLATE 451. *A standard shaped New Hall jug decorated with a bat print on a pale lavender ground. The edging and trim is in black enamel, not gold. Dated at front '1818'. 7¼in. (18.42cm) high. 1818.* PRIVATE COLLECTION

New Hall handle form as shown here is the most helpful feature when examples do not have the 'NH' sprigged coloured pad type mark.

Matching mugs were also produced, but these usually have the standard New Hall overlapping leaf type handle, as my Plate 445. David Holgate in his *New Hall* shows a floral pattern mug as his Plate 95, left.

It is possible that these relief 'sprig' moulded jugs proved so popular that they were produced into the 1830s when the factory was running down, leading up to the closure in 1835.

On the other hand new, as yet unrecognised, forms may have been introduced and await discovery. They are unlikely to be marked, they probably will not bear a pattern number and by the 1830s it is unlikely that their decoration will readily link with earlier New Hall styles. Moulded jugs of the type shown in Plate 457 could well represent a late New Hall basic form. Much still needs to be discovered about the little researched later New Hall bone china products.

This leads to the last recorded source of information on the possible products of the New Hall partnership in its later stages. It takes the form of advertisements for an auction sale of the 'valuable and extensive stock of burnished gold china' to be held early in October 1835. The advertisements appeared in the local *Staffordshire Advertiser* between 5 and 26 September. The last notice read:

NEW HALL CHINA MANUFACTORY. SHELTON
Valuable & Extensive Stock of Burnished
Gold China.
To Be Sold by Auction
By Mr Johnson.

On the Premises at the New Hall China Manufactory at Shelton in the Staffordshire Potteries, on Monday, Tuesday, Wednesday, Thursday and Friday, the 5th, 6th, 7th, 8th and 9th days of October 1835, and the following week, (if necessary);

ALL the very valuable Stock of Burnished gold and other CHINA, which consists of complete rich burnished gold tea services, in a great variety of shapes and patterns; also breakfast services to correspond. A very choice assortment of dessert and toilet services, with numerous modern and fancy-shaped jugs and mugs, chimney ornaments, &c. A very general assortment of Common China, Hawkers' Sets &c.

This will be found a most advantageous opportunity for Merchants and China Dealers, who may rely upon every liberality being exercised towards their interest as purchasers to sell again. Likewise Inn-Keepers and the public in general, who are desirous of supplying themselves with a small assortment for their own use will find this Sale well deserving their attention.

The New Hall Company are declining business, and have let the premises, which they now occupy, with immediate possession; a circumstance which makes it quite necessary that they should dispose of their Stock without reserve.

The sale will commence each morning at eleven o'clock.

The stock of remaining gilt tea services is to be expected. More surprising is the mention of matching breakfast services and dessert services at this period. Totally surprising is the mention of toilet services. Such items could have included large jugs, wash bowls, chamber pots, soap dishes and the like. It is admittedly rather early for

Plate 452. *An attractive relief-moulded New Hall bone china jug of a type produced by several English factories including Ridgway. Examples are rarely marked. Other shapes also bear these reliefs – see Plate 453. 7½in. (19.05cm) c.1818-25.* Private collection

Plate 453. *A New Hall bone china jug with standard relief motifs on a light blue ground as also seen in Plate 452. This jug form is quite scarce but was made in various sizes. 5¾in. (14.61cm) high. c.1818-25.* Godden of Worthing

large complete toilet services, but they had been produced at the Spode factory for well over ten years. There may therefore exist New Hall bone china toilet wares in the styles associated with the early 1830s.

It is also of interest that this 1835 closing auction was to include 'numerous modern and fancy-shaped jugs and mugs'. We know of very, very few jugs or mugs that seemingly relate to the closing years of the factory, but see Plate 457.

The sale announcement also mentions 'chimney ornaments'. It is now not clear what was intended. Small ornamental figures were sometimes described as chimney ornaments, but I know of no evidence that any porcelain figures were ever made by the New Hall partnership. A possibility is that these ornaments were small vases such as those made by all early nineteenth century porcelain manufacturers to hold spills. Earlier accounts of New Hall porcelains ordered by the Wyllies in London suggest that the chimney ornaments were indeed sets of spill vases. The Wyllie accounts dated 22 December 1823 include:

1 sett china ornaments, Japan pattern £1.1s.0d.
2 setts ornaments, 3 in a sett, Japan pattern as before £2.2s.0d.

The description three in a set strongly indicates sets of spill vases, possibly then of the flared shape shown in Plate 404. The centre vase in such sets (as made by most contemporary firms) was slightly larger than the flanking pair.

Our scant knowledge of the later New Hall porcelains of the post-1825 period suggests that the wares were quite richly decorated. However, this closing sale also included inexpensive wares. These were described by the auctioneer as: 'A very general assortment of Common china, Hawkers' sets &c.'

Innkeepers were also mentioned as being potentially interested in the sale. This short notice did not, however, mention a stock of white undecorated porcelains or of unfinished wares. One would expect that the factory would have included large amounts of unfinished blanks. Perhaps other arrangements had been made to dispose of such goods within the trade, perhaps to the next occupier of the factory – see page 409.

The announcement also does not mention the availability of a catalogue. A formal catalogue is unlikely to have been issued as even the duration of the sale was left open. The sale early in October 1835 was to continue into the following week 'if necessary'.

It is just possible that this sale included some non-New Hall stock, being goods submitted for sale by other owners. I think on balance, however, that this auction held

Plate 454. *A rare New Hall bone china relief-moulded jug with typical light blue ground. Although the basic shape is as Plate 453, the reliefs are different. Relief moulded 'N.H.' mark. 4¾in. (12.07cm) high. c.1818-25.* A. de Saye Hutton

Plate 455. *A rare form of New Hall moulded jug. The basic hunting design is not, however, unique to New Hall. Note the handle form and compare with Plate 456. 7½in. (19.05cm) high. c.1825-30.* Godden of Worthing

Plate 456. *A rare pad-marked New Hall jug with applied tinted reliefs. The basic shape and floral motifs are not unique to New Hall but the handle form is characteristic. Relief-moulded tinted pad initial mark 'N.H.' (see page 401). 8¾in. (22.23cm) high (other sizes would have been produced). c.1825-30.* Godden of Worthing

Plate 457. *A relief-moulded jug that could well represent an unmarked New Hall form of the 1830s. These jugs are recorded in various sizes and appear to witness New Hall characteristics. 7½in. (19.05cm) high. c.1830-4.* Private collection

in October 1835 relates to the remaining New Hall stocks and that it marks the closure of the factory. It had prospered from the early 1780s, that is for a period of over fifty years. The various changing partners produced a vast amount of interesting, decorative, sound porcelains that proved serviceable to their original owners and so collectable to later generations.

We can now turn to follow the history of the New Hall factory and its site in the middle of the Staffordshire Potteries.

1. 'A London Staffordshire Warehouse – 1794-1825' by Ann Eatwell and Alex Werner, *Journal of the Northern Ceramic Society,* Vol 8, 1991.

2. The cup shape may not have been all that new, in that a so-called London shape Chinese cup or drinking vessel is in the Burrell Collection, Glasgow and is attributed to the Tang dynasty, some eleven centuries before the Staffordshire examples were introduced!

3. See *An Anthology of British Teapots* by P. Miller and M. Berthoud (Micawber Publications, 1985). Plate 1541, pattern '1769' and my Plate 383.

4. See *Dudson a Family of Potters since 1800* by Audrey M. Dudson (Dudson Publications, Hanley, 1985), Chapter 6.

5. Once again this type of relief-moulded ground work is by no means limited to the New Hall factory. The Coalport and the Grainger managements are amongst those who produced similar moulded designs.

6. See *A Guide to New Hall Porcelain Patterns* by A. de Saye Hutton (Barrie & Jenkins, London, 1990), Plate 236.

7. See Mrs. Pat Preller's contribution 'Dolphin handled teapots' published in *The Hilditch Newsletter* (private publication of The Hilditch Collectors Group), number 5, October 2001.

8. See issue three (Spring 2002) of *New Hall and Friends.*

9. See *Chamberlain-Worcester Porcelain 1788-1852* by Geoffrey Godden (Barrie & Jenkins, 1982), page 125.

10. See 'Thomas Lakin, Staffordshire Potter. 1769-1821' a paper by Harold Blakey published in the *Northern Ceramic Society Journal,* Vol. 5, 1984.

11. See the *Pinxton Porcelain Society Newsletter* No. 5 (Spring 1998), page 4.

12. William Combe's 'Tour of Dr. Syntax In Search of the Picturesque' was first published in Ackermann's *Poetical Magazine* in 1809. It appeared in book form in 1812. The second tour was published in 1820, the third in 1821. The original illustrations were by Rowlandson.

13. Len Whiter in his specialist book *Spode* (Barrie & Jenkins, 1970) shows that that firm produced such jugs (termed at Spodes, at least, 'Low Dutch jugs') in eleven sizes up to one of four quart capacity.

14. Other possible makes include Daniel, Ridgway and Hicks & Meigh. Examples can be found with dates within the approximate period 1825-30. The non-New Hall examples have a straighter, more angular handle.

CHAPTER XI

Post-1835 Developments on the New Hall Site

It is of interest to take the opportunity to detail the later history of the New Hall works after the 1835 auction of stock and the closure of the old porcelain works. One can also see how potteries were let, relet or sold and sold again, amended, enlarged or divided into two or more parts until the original works became unrecognisable. In some cases the original name was retained, in other instances the trade name was brought up to date, so that all traditional links were lost. In the Staffordshire Potteries, too, road names were sometimes changed and old districts were absorbed by their larger neighbours. In this way the basic old New Hall address of Shelton is no longer in general use. It is part of Hanley, itself part of the present City of Stoke-on-Trent.

But first I wish to recap and record some information contained in an 1838 will relating to Ann Booth. This lady is not recorded in earlier accounts of the New Hall history, yet her will found by Mr. Harold Blakey in the local Newcastle Manor Court Rolls contains interesting information on the earlier history of the estate. The facts were no doubt gleaned from earlier documents including a previously quoted surrender of property in July 1779. but there is new information and some updating. I am grateful to Mr. Blakey for drawing my attention to this will, now in the Public Record Office at Kew, ref. DL30.510-3. The will is dated at Shelton 24 November 1838 and was proved on 31 January 1839 after the termination of the New Hall partnership.

The document, being drawn up in a legal manner, does not include punctuation and it is written as an entirety. I have for the sake of clarity and appearance broken it into paragraphs. The important parts follow the main will of Ann Booth and were written or signed by Thomas Fenton, the Steward of the Manor of Newcastle-under-Lyme and the relevant local authority for the registration of documents relating to land or property, hence the legal lengthy wording. The document dated 7 January 1839 relates to various

> 'Messuages, Dwellinghouses or Tenements Potworks Buildings, Closes Pieces or Parcels of land and other hereditaments with the appurtenances situate in Shelton...' previously owned by the Warburton family – Josiah ('late of Cobridge but now residing at Boulogne-sur-Mere'), Frances, Peter, Jacob and Mary. The property descending by Will from Peter Warburton, being:
>
> '...All That Copyhold or Customary messauge or Tenement situate in Shelton aforesaid with the Court Garden Outbuildings and Appurtenances to the same belonging And All Those several Erections or Buildings Potworks and Pot ovens also situate at Shelton aforesaid used as works for the Manufacturing of China and Earthenware and called or known by the name of the New Hall China Works'.
>
> And all Barns Stables Yards Outbuildings Ways Waters Watercourses and Appurtenances to the said last mentioned premises belonging which said Messuages Potworks and Premises were formerly in the holding or occupation of Samuel Boulton afterwards of Thomas Palmer and since of Messrs Hollins, Warburton, Daniel and Company.
>
> And all those several Closes pieces or Parcels of Land meadow or pasture situate near to the said messuages and potworks formerly in nine Closes and then called or known by the several names of The Little Croft, The Hall Meadow, The Middle Field, The Aslem Patch, The Cloven Field, Miles Meadow, The Near Bryans Wood, The Middle Bryans Wood and the Further Bryans Wood, but which were afterwards divided into seven closes and called or known by the several names of the Two Brick-kiln Fields (being what were formerly called the Little Croft, the Hall Meadow and the

Middle Field) The Meadow (which was formerly the Clover Field) The Upper Corn Field the Lower Corn Field (being the Closes formerly called the Aslem Patch and Miles Meadow) The Upper Bryans Woods and the Lower Bryans Wood (which comprised the Middle Bryans wood part of the same having been laid to each) and which said Closes Pieces or Parcels of Land were formerly in the tenure of occupation of the said Samuel Boulton afterwards of Humphrey Palmer or his under Tenants and since of Messieurs Hollins, Warburton, Daniel and Company and containing by estimation Twenty eight acres, one Rood and fifteen Perches thereabouts.[1]

To the entirety of which said Messuages Potworks Buildings Lands Hereditaments and Premises the said Peter Warburton and his then Partners in trade – Samuel Hollins, John Daniel and William Clowes constituting the firm of Hollins Warburton Daniel and Company were admitted Tenants in Common in the Fee on the surrender of Esther Palmer, Elizabeth Palmer and James Neale at the Court held in and for the said Manor on the Twenty sixth day of April One thousand eight hundred and ten.

And also of and in all that Plot or Plots or Pieces of land or Grounds situate in Slacks Lane in Hanley, adjoining on the West side of the said Lane to the Lands before described and containing by measuration from the North to the South ends thereof One thousand eight hundred and twenty five square yards to the entirety whereof the said John Daniel was admitted Tenant in fee in Exchange for certain Plots of land part of the Hereditaments before described on the Surrender of Jonathan Adams at a court Held on the seventh day of July One thousand eight hundred and twenty.

And also...all that Dwellinghouse or Tenement with the Stables Barn and Buildings standing near thereto situate in Shelton heretofore in the occupation of the said Samuel Hollins Peter Warburton John Daniel and William Clowes as China Manufacturers and Co partners and to the entirety whereof they or some of them were admitted Tenants in Common in fee under or by virtue of several surrenders made at Courts held in and for the said Manor on the fourth of February One thousand seven hundred and ninety three, the ninth of May One thousand eight hundred and five and the fourth of August One thousand eight hundred and fourteen And of and in All other the Copyhold a Customary Messuages Farms Lands and Hereditaments situate lying and being at Shelton aforesaid heretofore purchased by the said Peter Warburton and his before named Partners or the survivors or survivor of them for or on account of the said Partnership...

In Witness whereof I the said Thomas Fenton have hereunto set my hand and seal the Seventh day of January in the year of our Lord One thousand eight hundred and thirty nine – T Fenton (SS) signed Sealed and Delivered by the above named Thomas Fenton (being first duly stamped in the presence of Samuel Williamson Clerk to Mr E W Tomlinson.)

T Fenton, Steward of the Manor

Manor of Newcastle under Lyme.

The estate was a large one, enjoying the use of much land, but alas we have no description of the New Hall itself or reference to its use as a porcelain manufactory.

Our only evidence relating to the appearance of the 'New Hall' as it might have appeared early in the nineteenth century during the time of the New Hall partnership are some few earthenware models. These are variously inscribed 'New Hall Warehouse' or 'New Hall China Manufactory, Staffordshire, 1813'. The dated example, here reproduced from an engraving in Major Stringer's book, can be seen at the Potteries Museum at Hanley.

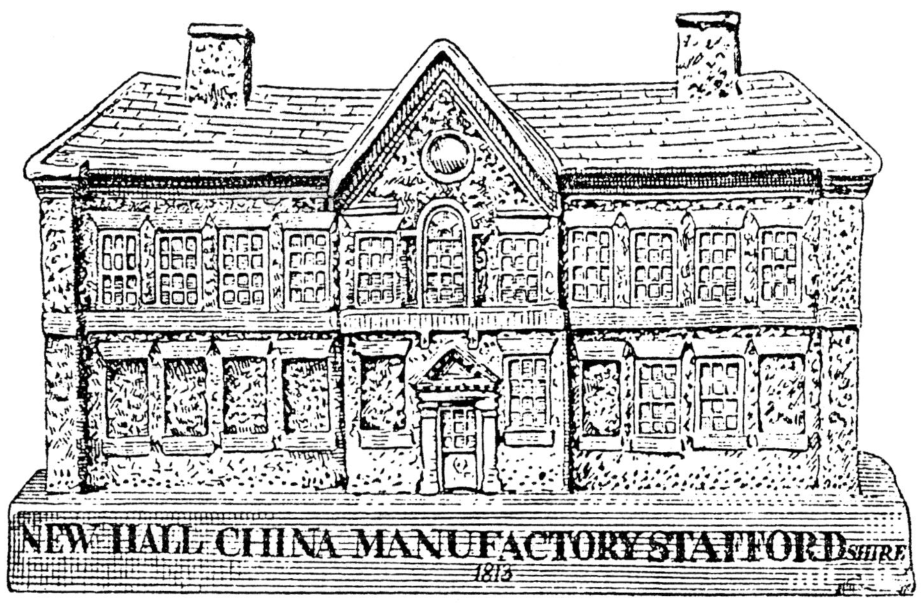

These models present several difficulties. First they are earthenware, not porcelain. Secondly, the period of manufacture is open to considerable doubt. George Stringer stated in his 1941 booklet that his inscribed and dated example was 'made by a workman employed by W & J Harding Bros (at New Hall 1864-1869)'. He later added to and amended the original brief note. His new information read:

> The model was given to me by Miss Lucy Harding as World War II 1939-1945 was drawing to a close. I had been invited to tea at Clayton House, which lies behind Clayton Lodge. Miss Harding was then well up in her 70's and was living quite alone which horrified me as the house was most secluded. She was the daughter of Joseph Bron Harding. It was an enjoyable visit. She knew my Aunts and all about me, and showed me her family treasures. In giving me the model she said 'I should like to feel it was in the hands of somebody who appreciated its interest'. She also lent me various 18th century documents including a deed of apprenticeship which is printed on p.81 of 'New Hall Porcelain'. Miss Harding must have told me that the model was made by one of her Father's workmen. It was obviously made in 1813 and by Hollins Warburton Daniel & Co. who were then in occupation of the factory.

Miss Harding could well have been correct, that it was made whilst the old New Hall works were occupied by one of the Harding earthenware partnerships, but admittedly the post-1850 date for the Hardings at New Hall seems too late for the style of these models. On page 43 of his 1949 book *New Hall Porcelain* George Stringer suggested that the models were made by the New Hall partnership to commemorate their purchase of the New Hall estate in 1810, but they are dated 1813. Stringer's views may have been influenced by his erroneous belief that the New Hall partnership produced both porcelain and earthenware.

It is interesting, however, that the building depicted in the earthenware models does not have the appearance of a pottery. No kilns or kiln chimneys are shown, no large opening for the delivery of raw materials is apparent, just a narrow residential doorway. Were it not for the inscription 'New Hall China Manufactory' or 'New Hall Warehouse' and the blocked-up downstairs windows, the model would pass for any large residence. I have earlier in this book suggested that the manufactory buildings were in the grounds of the old house, although the main property may well have served as a showroom, warehouse or housed some of the decorating shops. I do not know of any contemporary map or drawing that shows the New Hall or the pottery buildings as they were in the 1780s or in the early 1800s by which time they had probably been enlarged.

The New Hall estate, including the manufactory, had been advertised for sale in 1820, in 1825 and 1831 and, failing an outright sale then, the New Hall premises were available to be let in 1832. The 1831 sale details are reasonably detailed and may well be of interest. The sale announcement appeared in the *Staffordshire Advertiser* of 5 March 1831:[2]

> Staffordshire Potteries
> Extensive China Works, Steam Engine Flint Mill
> and valuable land for Building Purposes
> TO BE SOLD BY AUCTION
>
> By MR R JOHNSON.
>
> At the Swan Inn in Hanley, in the county of Stafford on Thursday, the 24th day of March 1831, at four o'clock in the afternoon, either altogether, or in the following lots, namely:
>
> LOT 1: - All the long established CHINA WORK, called NEW HALL, situate in Shelton in the Staffordshire Potteries, comprising the Warehouse and a plot of land fronting to New Hall Street, and the Dwelling House adjoining, in the occupation of MR JOHN TITTENSOR, together with the Workshops, Buildings and Yards, every requisite convenience for carrying on a most extensive business, the whole including an area of about 7,200 superficial yards. This lot is bounded on the south Side by New Hall Street, and on the West by Brook Street, and has a communication with Hope Street in the East. In addition to its great extent, from its central situation on the main line of thoroughfare through the Potteries, it possesses local advantages for business which can scarcely be equalled.
>
> LOT 2: - All the STEAM ENGINE MILL, with the valuable machinery and apparatus belonging thereto, used for grinding of flint and Porters materials, situate at Booden Brook in Shelton aforesaid, and in the holding of Mr Thomas Crockett together with the dwellinghouse, garden and yard adjoining, the whole containing about 6,715 superficial yards of land.
>
> LOT 3: - The several pieces or parcels of LAND lying between Great York Street, and Booden Brook and Brook Street aforesaid, and on the East Side of Great York Street, continuous to Lot 1, and also on the East side of Hope Street, fronting to certain New Streets already marked or laid out, and named Peers Street, Union Street, Cross Street, Trafalgar Row, Paddock Street, and Brian's Wood Street; the whole comprising 13a. 1r. 3p of LAND, presenting a variety of the most eligible situations for building purposes.
>
> Also, sundry BUILDINGS consisting of a Dwelling House, Barn, Stable and Hovel, with the yard about the same, situation on the south West Side of Brook Street, and containing about 448 superficial yards, which will form part of Lot 3.

> The above property is all copyhold of inheritance of the manor of Newcastle-under Lyme.
>
> A plan of the premises, showing the boundaries of the several pieces of land comprised in Lot 3, and the lines of the different streets intersecting the same, may be seen on application to MR JOHN TITTENSOR, at the New Hall Manufactory, who will attend the parties upon the premises.
>
> Further information may be obtained of MR LEWIS GEORGE HALES, Land Surveyor, Cobridge, or at the office of Messrs. TOMLINSON, Solicitor, Cliff-Ville.
>
> 2nd March 1831

Seemingly no buyer came forward to purchase the New Hall estate, as just set out and subsequently it was offered to be let. Again nothing came of this and the partnership under the management of John Tittensor seems to have continued trading, although probably on a reduced scale. The trading conditions were, however, difficult at this period and the New Hall Company would not have been the only one to experience problems. The concern apparently struggled on until the summer or early autumn of 1835.

The advertisement for the final sale of stock as published in the *Staffordshire Advertiser* of 5 September 1835 marks the end. It contained the following statement:

> The New Hall Company are declining business and have let the premises, which they now occupy, with immediate possession; a circumstance which make it quite necessary that they should dispose of their stock without reserve.

This 1835 letting may have been wishful thinking and claimed to help the auction of the stock, which did not seemingly include any working materials, engraved copper plates, etc. The New Hall Company paid rates on the property in its own name in 1835 and in 1836. Interesting information on the sale and commercial development of part of the New Hall estate, but not the main factory buildings, is given by Mrs. Audrey Dudson in Chapter 5 of her specialist book *Dudson. A Family of Potters since 1800* (Dudson Publications, Hanley, 1985).

The New Hall manufactory was occupied by William Ratcliffe from at least 1837. It was apparently again up for sale (or to be let) in 1841 when John Boyle, an experienced potter and the former partner of Herbert Minton, recorded in his diary:

> looked over the New Hall manuf, and found all the places in bad repair to such an extent indeed I do not consider it tenable in its present state. The ovens also are too large for the Hovels and all the saggar houses are small and inconvenient.

This report was made only six years after the New Hall porcelain company vacated the premises. It is also relevant to note that the succeeding firms after the original New Hall partnership produced earthenware, rather than porcelain, on the site.

However, in 1843 the old New Hall works formerly worked by William Ratcliffe were sold for the sum of £3,050. The buyer, William Lowndes, purchased it as an investment and the works were then let to William Hackwood & Son (also trading as William & Thomas Hackwood) at a rent of £225 per year.

The fourteen year lease from William Lowndes to the Hackwoods is an important document as it gives good details of the property at that period, less than ten years after the New Hall company ceased manufacture and at a period when we can expect that the premises had not been altered by William Ratcliffe, except that the schedule includes a 'new hot house' and an unnumbered 'new green house' which may have been the same place used for drying wares before their first firing.

This 1843 lease is in the William Salt Library at Stafford (Folio number D1798-536-5-13) and was published by David Holgate as part of his Appendix II. Dated 7 January 1843, it gives the following basic information: William and Thomas Hackwood leased

> All that capital earthenware Manufactory called the New Hall Manufactory consisting of five Hovels [kilns], three Sliphouses and two hardening hovels together with all and singular the warehouses, Workshops, Machine House and other buildings and erections thereto belonging and together also with the Marl Bank, Clay yards and other lands and grounds hereditaments and premises thereto also belonging situate at Shelton within the said Manor of Newcastle-under-Lyme in the county of Stafford and late in the tenure or occupation of William Ratcliffe. Together with all and singular the fixtures and articles comprised in the schedule hereunder written. The schedule lists twenty-nine places which contain fixtures and articles. These comprised:
>
> No 1 Large Warehouse. No 2 Best Warehouse. No 3 Warehouse. No 4 Biscuit Warehouse. No 5 Dipping House. No 6 Lead House. No 8 Painting Shop. No 9 Printing Shop. No 10 Printers Hot House. No 11 Throwing House and Soaking room. No 12 New Hot house. No 13 Turning house. No 17 and 18 White sliphouse. No 19 Squeezing house over the Biscuit Saggar house. No 20. No 21 the room over the last. No 22 Flagged Chamber over Saggar-hot-house. No 23 Saggar makers hot house. No 24 Saggar makers place. No 25 Dish makers place. No 26 room over Clay cellar and the Greenhouse. No 27 Saucer makers place and rooms for squeezers, Dish Makers place. No 28 Clay Cellar near New Green House. No 29 The Clay Cellars under the Printing Stove and Hot house.

In about 1850 the New Hall works passed to Thomas Hackwood and in about 1856 it was let to Cockson & Harding, then to W. & J. Harding (c.1863-9). Thomas Hackwood had purchased the estate in the 1850s for in March 1872 he sold it to John Aynsley of Longton for £4,100. Later that year Aynsley, who did not work the pottery, seems to have divided the property. On 26 November 1872 he sold Shelton Hall (the so-called 'New Hall') with its stables and barns to Henry Hall, a metal mounter of ceramics, who was already a tenant. John Aynsley later sold off other sections of New Hall land, which were subsequently developed. Llewellynn Jewitt recorded in the 1878 edition of his *The Ceramic Art of Great Britain* that the back portion of the old New Hall works had been let 'to its present occupiers, Messrs. Thomas Booth & Sons. The entire front of the New Hall works was purchased by Mr. Henry Hall, metal mounter of jugs, teapots, sets, so that the manufactory became divided into two distinct properties'. The property was reunited in the twentieth century by the New Hall Pottery Company.

The back portion of the Victorian New Hall manufactory (not Shelton Hall itself) was interestingly reported on in the local *Staffordshire Times* of 2 October 1875, just before it suffered a serious fire. The report on Thomas Booth & Sons' works and products read, in part:

> ...the manufactory is an old one, and has a history peculiar to itself. The style of building and arrangement has all the characteristics of our early pot manufactories. Built in an age when machinery was little known and the desire to economise or save labour less appreciated, it presented few facilities possessed by our more modern manufactories.
>
> The workshops, the offices and the warehouses seldom running higher than two storeys and presenting a very primitive appearance. Especially is this noticeable in the workshops, which are low with their cross-beams and ancient style of hot-houses, or, as they are called by the potters, stoves. The works in its original state was divided into two yards – one for the making of the clay, and for the first stages of forming the ware, the saggars and for firing the biscuit. The other was devoted to glazing, decoration, warehouses and offices. The front of the manufactory was built to run parallel with the old coach road and the archway and gates[3] which from Boothen Lane (Brook Street) seems to have been the entrance for all raw materials.
>
> The more pretentious range, formed on the angle of the road and joined to the office and the main building by a primitive-looking brick arch, which is utilised to the purpose of a bridge, was in the early history of the place the principal warehouse, decorating department and show-room ... Not much of the old appearance of the works remains for since it fell into the hands of the present occupants, Messrs Booth & Sons, great alterations have been made. The wide yards have been filled up by modern buildings, to increase the producing power ... the erection of kilns, workshops, etc. In this respect the manufactory is very interesting.
>
> We see, the transition from the rude style of planning when human hands were everything and machinery nothing ... Here let us consider briefly the history of the works. The manufactory was built by Mr James Whitehead, ... and it was called the New Hall, from the fact of its being built near a hall which stood here in former times ... The ruins of the hall yet stand, and are a most interesting *relique* ... After the cessation of the New Hall company in about 1835 the works were now taken by a gentleman named Ratcliffe, who was formerly a colour maker at Hanley. Under this management the place came to grief and silence and poverty reigned within the walls... With the manufacturing demise of Ratcliffe, the place was taken by Mr Hackwood, 1842 (or 1843) who removed from a works held by him near Joiners Square. Mr Hackwood, who was the son of the famous modeller... Under this management the New Hall attained a reputation and its productions were much esteemed in the continental markets.
>
> In 1856 the manufactory again changed hands, becoming Cockson & Harding... On Cockson withdrawing, the firm remained Harding Brothers, who for some time continued the works. On the place being given up by the Hardings, it was entered up by the present firm, Booth & Sons.'

Here followed a lengthy account of the Booth products of the mid-1870s – mainly earthenwares, stoneware jugs, metal-mounted teapots, jugs etc. – and concludes 'The house is about to embark on the manufacture of jasper... china is also contemplated, when the ancient mark [name?] of the first company will be revived ... The works are under the management of Mr Charles Heath... since the above was written the manufactory has suffered from a severe fire. The men are however, expected to resume work next week.' This report appeared on 2 October 1875.

Jewitt, in his 1878 *Ceramic Art of Great Britain,* was therefore able to report that the 'portion of the old New Hall works occupied by Messrs. Booth, having been burnt down has been rebuilt'.

Thomas Booth had during the approximate period 1864-71 occupied the Britannia Pottery, High Street, Hanley, producing mainly moulded jugs and teapots, many of which were of registered designs. On taking over the back portion of the old New Hall works c.1872, he took his two sons, Walter and Henry, into partnership, leaving them to continue the business when Thomas retired in September 1874. As stated in the 1875 *Staffordshire Times* report, Messrs. Thomas Booth & Sons were then intending to use the old New Hall name as a mark. It does in fact occur as an impressed, misleading mark on Booth's earthenwares or moulded stonewares of the 1875-79 period, although some examples bear earlier design registration marks relating to Thomas Booth, when at the separate Britannia Pottery.

The back portion of the divided old New Hall works was rebuilt after the 1875 fire. The subsequent history of the new works does not really concern us here, but it is of interest that the next occupier – Ambrose Bevington & Co. – produced some china as well as earthenwares using the address 'Newhall Works' within the approximate period 1880-91.

We can now continue the story of the earlier front portion of the New Hall works, the part that had not suffered a fire. A late Victorian engraving featured in the advertisement shown opposite can, however, hardly be related to the size or appearance of the original pottery a hundred years previously.

The front portion had been purchased by Henry Hall in 1872. His main business had been as a mounter of metal covers on jugs and similar ceramic objects that were at this period fitted with pewter or Britannia metal covers. He may also have produced some earthenwares and majolica type wares as a manufacturer. This 'entire front of the New Hall works' was then occupied by Messrs. Creyke & Boulton who carried on the mounting business but also produced standard types of inexpensive earthenware. Their trade advertisements of the 1894-5 period featured 'special lines in decorated Toilet Sets, Sets jugs, Cheese Stands, Teapots, Kettles, etc. Largest variety of metal-covered jugs, teapots, etc. in the Trade'. The Creyke & Boulton partnership continued until c.1900 when it was succeeded by G.M. Creyke trading alone, mainly as an 'earthenware decorator'. The trading style then became G.M. Creyke & Sons.

Even in this relatively recent period the history of the New Hall site and history is difficult to unravel, possibly because the original site had become divided and perhaps then reunited. George Stringer, writing of his first-hand knowledge in his 1949 book, on pages 42-3 stated:

> when I first came to New Hall in about 1907, the building depicted by the model (titled 'New Hall China manufactory…') was not in the ownership or the occupation of the Company which operates at New Hall today (the New Hall Pottery Co Ltd.); in 1907, the building was owned and occupied by Messrs G M Creyke & Sons who were metalmounters… Mr Dyson was making his commercial travellers very comfortable in his temperance hotel; William Johnson was busy cutting appropriate texts on gravestones and on the little parcel of land that was left, Mr Chatfield was busy keeping sound roof over the heads of the living.

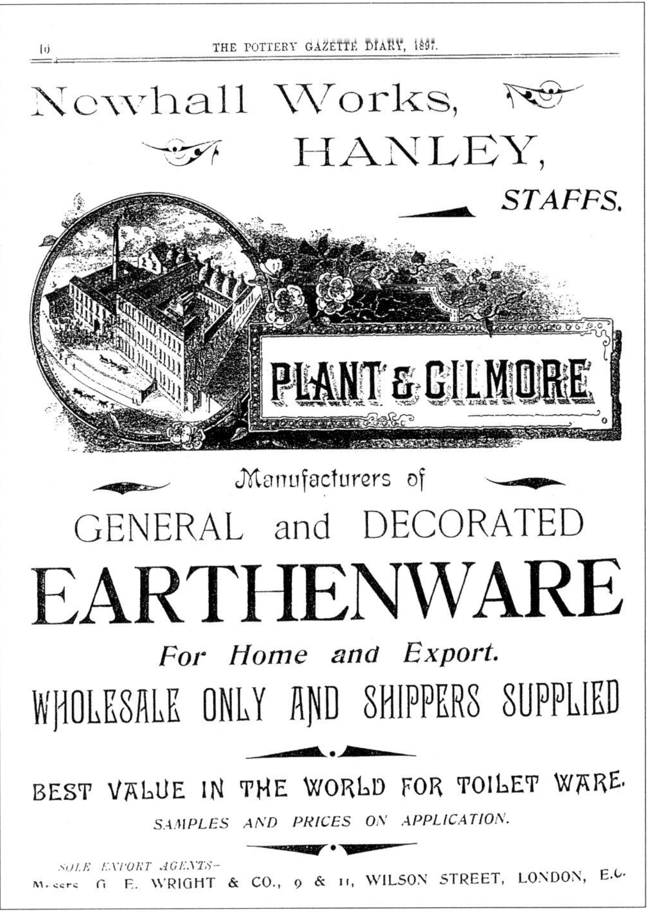

Stringer later returned to mention these folk (see page 413) but first I have to record that the new 'New Hall Pottery Company' was formed in 1899 and that the site had previously been occupied and worked by Messrs. Plant & Gilmore. This partnership moved from the Providence Pottery, Chell Street, Hanley to the New Hall pottery in 1895. They were manufacturers of inexpensive types of earthenware, specialising in toilet wares. I reproduce part of their 1896 trade advertisement, which features an engraving of the New Hall pottery as it was at that period. Seemingly this was quite unlike the old New Hall porcelain works as it was before the 1835 sale.

The next stage, the reversion to the old New Hall trade name, is neatly recorded in an announcement dated 28 August 1899 and published in the trade magazine *The Pottery Gazette*. It was stated that Messrs. Plant & Gilmore[4] of the New Hall Works, Hanley, had been purchased by John Copeland and Robert Audley and that the 'works will be started immediately under the supervision of Mr F.J. Plant, late of the old firm, under the style of the New Hall Pottery Company'.

The new company took a full page advertisement in the 1900 *Pottery Gazette Diary,* which was prepared, printed and on sale late in 1899. This read:

> THE
> NEW HALL POTTERY CO.[5]
> (Late Plant & Gilmore)
> manufacturers of specialities in
> TOILET WARE, TEA WARE and JUGS.
> NEW HALL WORKS. HANLEY. STAFFS
>
> August 28th, 1899.
>
> Having purchased the estate of Messrs. Plant & Gilmore, we the under-signed, intend carrying on the business as the NEW HALL POTTERY CO.
> The whole of the work will be under the personal supervision of Mr F.J. Plant, of the late firm of Plant & Gilmore.
> By the prompt execution of orders, excellence of goods and moderate prices, we hope to receive the same support as extended to the late firm.
> It is our intention to introduce from time to time new shapes and Designs, which we hope will lead to a largely increased trade.
> Yours faithfully
> R Audley,
> J Copeland.

History in a sense was repeating itself. Here we have two new adventurers[6] taking over an existing firm, putting in a manager and endeavouring to save or expand the business, little different from the backers who had sided with Richard Champion in 1781. The new company continued from the middle of 1899-1956, almost exactly the fifty-four year duration of the original New Hall company, c.1781-1835. Whilst as far as I am aware the twentieth century New Hall earthenwares are not collected (as yet!), George Stringer as a director or owner of the new company did much to advance the study of and interest in the old New Hall porcelains when he published his pioneer book *New Hall Porcelain* in 1949. Like many pioneer works it contains several theories that have not stood the test of time, but more good than harm has arisen from its publication.

Before leaving the awakened New Hall Co., it is of interest to see from the full page advertisement in the *Pottery Gazette Diary* of 1901 how the company quickly established itself and its specialities. The advertisement drawn up in 1900 reads, in part:

> Manufacturers of Earthenware for Home and Export.
> Cheese Stands, Bread Trays, Jugs, Teas, Butters, Teapots &c. &c.
> Best Value in the World
>
> For
> TOILET WARE
> Special quotations for 10,000 or more sets, Upwards of 15,000 toilet sets were included in our stocks on December 30th, 1899...

Cox's Potteries Annual and Year Book of 1924 contains a full page, neat advertisement for the New Hall company (see page 413), showing a perhaps enhanced engraving of the then enlarged factory site with mention of the London wholesale showrooms in Hatton Garden. This 1924 *Year Book* also includes a photograph of Robert Audley, the managing director, with a brief resumé. If only similar publications had reported on partners and directors of the 1790s, 1810s and 1820s! For future ceramic historians I repeat the 1924 notice:

> **Mr Robert Audley,** the managing director of the New Hall Pottery Co., Ltd., Hanley, is a stalwart in that section of the pottery trade which caters for the needs of the masses. The factory over which he presides has a very historic reputation, and is one of the very oldest of the Staffordshire 'pot-banks'. Under Mr Audley's control, however, it has been considerably extended and modernised. A 'Shaw' chamber gas-kiln, which was erected a few years ago at a cost of many thousands of pounds, is today helping to solve the problem of mass production, and Mr Audley will have the satisfaction, when the time arrives for him to hand over the administration of the factory to a younger generation, of knowing that he has left a good deal on record which will redound to his fame. As an old commercial traveler, Mr Audley became the President of the N.S. Commercial Travelers' Association in 1919. His record in connection with Freemasonry would require columns to relate...In 1922 he passed through a serious illness, from which happily, he has since recovered.

To return to our study of the late history of the original New Hall factory site, George Stringer has recorded in a little privately published 1941[7] booklet on the New Hall factory how the works and perhaps the original Shelton Hall were gradually rebuilt in the twentieth century. Writing of the Hall he recalls that one small part could have survived in two world wars:

> It is possible that today there is still a small portion left of the original pottery in the shop that is known as 'Dick Welsby's Shop' (Dick being the dishmaker operating the oval jolley). During the Great War of 1914-1918 a third of the potting shops on the pottery were burnt down and one of the first jobs I did on my return from the war was to make a potters shop for Dick and his pals out of a glost warehouse, and the oak adze-hewn dowelled and pegged trusses are still there supporting the roof, for it was impossible to obtain new timber for some time after the war ended.
> Many alterations have been made at New Hall during my lifetime. The first large reconstruction was made in 1912,

New Hall Pottery Co., Ltd.

SPECIALITIES:

TOILET WARE, TRINKET SETS,
TEA WARE, :: JUGS, :: ::

Works:
NEW HALL STREET, HANLEY, Staffs.

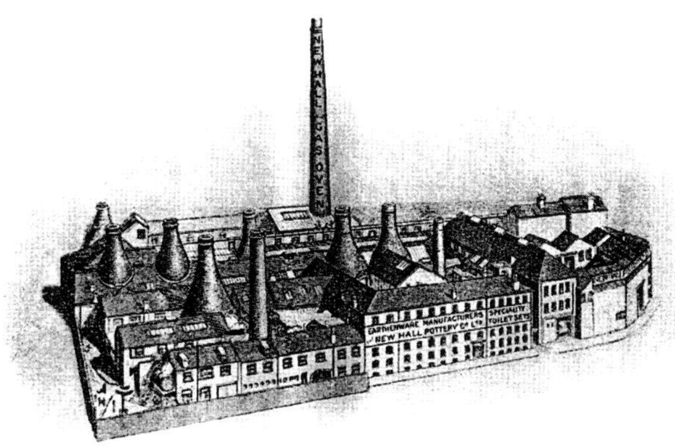

LONDON SHOW ROOMS: 34, Hatton Garden, E.C.
WHOLESALE ONLY.

FLOWER POTS,
VASES,
CHEESE STANDS,

STEAK DISHES,
BREAD TRAYS,
BUTTER DISHES, &c.

when two new biscuit ovens, a new biscuit warehouse and potters shops were built. In 1914 and 1915 two new Climax kilns were built and in 1919-1921 three of the four bottle-neck glost ovens were pulled down and the Shaw kiln and the three-decker shop containing the packing house. In building this shop we first of all had to pull down Creyke's Metal Mounting Works... and in pulling down the metal mounting works we pulled down what was in my opinion the original façade of the Pottery, which faced south and looked on to Chatfield's builder's yard, which also must one time have formed part of the estate, as all the old deeds say that the estate was bounded on the south by New Hall Street.

In his slightly later and more detailed book *New Hall Porcelain* (Art Trade Press Ltd., London, 1949), George Stringer recounted:

I well remember the interior of Shelton Hall (New Hall) when it was in the occupation of G.M. Creyke & Sons; the first floor consisted of one long room with a deeply curved cornice, into which had been let at intervals circular bosses – these bosses at one time supported gas brackets...
During the First World War, the late Mr Robert Audley, the founder of the present New Hall Pottery Company, restored the ancient boundaries of the New Hall China Manufactory and New Hall is once more bounded on the south by New Hall Street, as it was in 1813. Today Mr Dyson's hotel [see page 411] contains our offices and showrooms; Mr Johnson's offices and showrooms; Mr Johnson's office is let to a ladies hairdresser; Mr Chatfield's builders yard is our crateyard, but alas, the site of Shelton Hall (New Hall) is covered by our packing house.

1949, the year in which George Stringer's pioneer hard-back book was published, marked the fiftieth anniversary of the establishment of the new (!) New Hall company. The trade journal *Pottery & Glass* in the issue of July 1949 included an interesting article to mark the event. This included a good aerial view of the factory,[8] now on a large triangular site, and some interior shots. After a historical resumé, the story was brought up to date. The old toilet sets and jug lines were finally dropped in 1924 when tablewares were introduced along with hotel wares. In 1949, after four years of peace, the New Hall factory gave employment to some 450 persons. Production of decorated wares was still restricted to export markets – Canada, New Zealand, South Africa and, of course, the United States of America. Production even then could not keep up with supply; the management looked forward to being able once again to supply the home market when restrictions were lifted. These far reaching restrictions on home supply of various articles was to enable as much as possible to be exported and so earn foreign currency and to assist the balance of trade difficulties that remained for many years after the war.

The tasteful streamlined teawares shown in this 1949 article bear simple broadly painted floral sprays within simple borders, designs that in their way are strangely reminiscent of traditional late eighteenth century New Hall porcelain.

Another good brief outline of developments up to the 1950s and nearly to the closure of the concern is given by Cyril G.E. Bunt in his 1959 book *British Potters & Pottery Today* (F. Lewis Ltd., Leigh-on-Sea, 1956). Largely using material supplied by the then Chairman of the New Hall company, George Stringer, this pleasing work gives the following authoritative account of the developments:

...'Turnover' was his yardstick from the first; and, in 1913 (when King George V and Queen Mary visited the Potteries) it was authoritatively asserted that 'the Company is known all

> over the world as the largest manufacturers of cheap toilet sets and jugs.' In 1908 the Company produced and sold more than 50,000 toilet sets of the Waverley shape alone…
>
> The war over sweeping constructions took place, for an important part of the factory had been burnt down and left in ruins for lack of building material. At this period Shelton Hall was still standing. It was now demolished and replaced by a well-designed three storied building designed to house the packing department, the glost drawing warehouse and decorating shops. Three old intermittent glost ovens were replaced by a recuperative and regenerative chamber kiln of 23 chambers. At the time when this was lit off (1921) there was probably no other factory in Staffordshire doing its glazing by gas. It is still in use (It should be explained, perhaps, that in this 250 ft long kiln the fire moves through the stationary wares, whereas in modern tunnel kilns bogeys carry the stacked wares through stationary firing zones).
>
> After the war Robert Audley took into partnership his two sons-in-law Albert Cook and Harold Clive. The latter was an expert potter and a man of foresight. He realised that the demand for toilet sets[9] was being killed by the growing popularity of fixed lavatory basins and that milk and beer bottles were supplanting jugs for certain everyday uses. He therefore turned his attention to dinner and hotel wares.
>
> The economic situation during the decade 1926-1936 was one of peculiar difficulty and anxiety for all the potteries, including New Hall. There was no coal and no work for months at one period. Mr G E Stringer, Chairman and Director, to whose published account we are indebted for much information, has summarized the situation in the following words: 'This year [1926] hastened, if it did not entail, the financial crisis of 1931, when our customers could not place their orders owing to a lessened demand and mounting stocks. The ordinary channels of trade were moreover being diverted into shops called chain stores with an immense capacity to sell a cup and its saucer for three-pence…tuppence for the cup and its handle and a penny for the saucer… In order to sell something, men pretended to give away something else, and the so-called gift scheme affected every trade – silver, glass, leather and particularly pottery. The quantities required by these schemes were fantastic and in 1936 New Hall purchased the New Pearl Pottery to enlarge its capacity'… since the war a certain amount of reconstruction of out of date workshops resulted in improved conditions. The factory has been repowered and relit and many new machines installed… Today [in the mid-1950s], in the many excellent new patterns and the consistently high quality of the New Hall productions, is embodied the testimony that the company at the present time is worthily upholding the traditions[10] which have been associated with Shelton Hall [New Hall] for so many industrious generations.

Alas, as these words were being penned or published, the 1899 company was about to cease business.

It is, however, relevant to recall that the New Hall Pottery Co. Ltd. was still taking full page advertisements in the *Pottery Gazette* trade journal in the 1950s and that it had agents in Argentina, Australia, Belgium, Canada, Chile, Denmark, France, Holland, New Zealand, Norway, South Africa, Sweden and Uruguay. The New Hall Company ceased trading in April 1956 and Robert Audley (the grandson of a founder director) died just previously, having acted as Sales Director. In April 1957 the *Pottery Gazette* reported that the Royal Art Pottery of Longton 'have acquired all the hotel ware moulds previously owned by New Hall Pottery Co. Hanley'.

In May 1962 the same trade journal in a general review of post-war Staffordshire pottery firms noted:

> Shock of New Hall–
>
> Possibly the most famous manufacturer to have closed down during the period under review – it certainly caused a big shock at the time – is the New Hall Pottery Ltd. Which produced a very high quality earthenware that was remarkable for very high technical standards and finish that were virtually of fine china standard. The factory, which closed down in 1956, is today derelict.

The two standard present century New Hall Pottery company printed marks are reproduced below. That on the right was used from c.1951.

c.1930-51

c.1951-56

Strangely these later wares at present seem rarer than the original porcelains of the pre-1835 period, but then their commercial value has not brought the later New Hall utilitarian earthenwares to the market or salerooms. Perhaps their day will come.

In the early 1990s I endeavoured to discover the fate of the factory and the famous site. Mrs. Pat Halfpenny, at that time Keeper of Ceramics at the nearby then City Museum and Art Gallery at Hanley, wrote:

> I lived in Hanley most of my life and Kathy's [Mrs. K. Niblett, then of the Ceramic Department] grandmother lived just below the site of the New Hall factory. All either of us can remember are large advertising hoardings shielding the site. I can find no documentary evidence but our guess is that the buildings were demolished and the site lay fallow through the 1960s…

In fact a series of photographs in the extensive Warrillow Collection in the local Studies Department of the Keele

University Library include views of the pottery prior to demolition (Ref. Warr. 1482, 1529 and 1532) and one of the site in the midst of demolition. This photograph (Warr 1359) bears the caption 'Hanley, New Hall Pottery Demolition, Marsh Street. 1963.

The site seems to have remained empty[11] for some twelve years surrounded, according to Mrs. Halfpenny, by advertising hoardings. As to its redevelopment, a brief note was included in the *Northern Ceramic Society Newsletter* Number 14 of March 1975. It was rather negative:

> The New Hall factory site, Shelton (now Hanley) is being redeveloped. As a consequence very deep and widespread excavations have taken place. In spite of a careful watch nothing of any ceramic consequence has been found.[12]

I understand that this mid-1970s redevelopment included a multi-storey car park and Tesco Store being built to replace the old New Hall pottery. Both serve the city, as did the New Hall ceramic products. The New Hall porcelains give more lasting pleasure – on a world-wide basis!

The world has certainly changed since Champion sought to bring a new type of porcelain manufacture to the Staffordshire Potteries. As he wrote to James Fox in August 1781, of the introduction of porcelain: '...when it becomes general in Staffordshire, which is part of the plan...'.

The plan has borne fruit. This centre of the British pottery industry is now rightly considered the porcelain capital of the kingdom – if not of the world.

---

1. Earlier documents quote larger land holdings suggesting that some parts had been sold off, as happened at various periods.

2. Discovered and published by the late Reginald Haggar, see *Northern Ceramic Society Newsletter* Number 26 of June 1977.

3. No such archway or gates are depicted on the various ceramic models of the building which is described as the New Hall manufactory or warehouse.

4. The Gilmore brothers then took the Fountain works at Fenton trading as 'Gilmore Bros' – 'Toilet Ware and Jugs a speciality. For Home and Export.'

5. The new company became a Limited Liability Company c.1901, giving rise to the amended title New Hall Pottery Co. Limited.

6. Mr. Copeland was a mineral water manufacturer, Mr. Audley was his friend. Between them they put £1,500 into the business allowing Plant to pay his creditors 6s.8d. in the pound. Mr. Plant took £5 a week out of the new company. *(Staffordshire Advertiser* 29 March 1902.)

7. Rodney Hampson has kindly drawn my attention to a slightly amended and updated copy of this work, in the Hanley Reference Library under the reference P738.942464. These amendments were made byGeorge Stringer in the 1956-7 period.

8. A similar good aerial view was reproduced by G.E. Stringer in his *New Hall Porcelain,* Plate XIII. He dates the photograph to 1921, but the factory can hardly be related to the pre-1835 days.

9. Some old type toilet services remained in use to well after the 1939-1945 war, particularly in colleges.

10. Some traditional old patterns such as number 172 – the mauve ribbon border design – were reissued in the post-war period.

11. David Holgate believed that the site was used as a car park, but perhaps not on a large, or official, scale.

12. Later, as recorded on page 373, some New Hall factory wasters or spoilt pieces were found on part of the Dudson factory which originally comprised part of the New Hall estate.

APPENDIX I

The Patents

I give in this Appendix the text of the patents that were to form the claimed basis for William Cookworthy's Plymouth porcelain (c.1768-70) and subsequently for Richard Champion's Bristol porcelain. It was this 1768 patent which Champion sought to sell in Staffordshire in the 1780-1 period – see Chapter I.

COPY OF SPECIFICATION OF PATENT GRANTED TO WILLIAM COOKWORTHY OF PLYMOUTH. IN THE COUNTY OF DEVON. CHEMIST. 17TH MARCH 1768 FOR MAKING A KIND OF PORCELAIN. NEWLY INVENTED.

To all people to whom these presents shall come, I William Cookworthy, of Plymouth, in the County of Devon, Chemist, send greeting.

Whereas, His Most Gracious Majesty King George the Third, by Letters Patent bearing date at Westminster the Seventeenth day of March now last past, did give and grant unto me, the said William Cookworthy, my executors, administrators, and assigns, his especial license, full power, sole privilege and authority, that I, the said William Cookworthy, my executors, administrators, and assigns, and every of us, by myself and themselves, and by mine and their deputy or deputys, servants, or agents, or such others as I, the said William Cookworthy, my executors, administrators or assigns, should at any time agree with, and no others, from time to time, and at all times thereafter during the term of years therein expressed, should and lawfully might make, use, exercise and vend 'A KIND OF PORCELAIN NEWLY INVENTED BY ME, COMPOSED OF MOOR-STONE OR GROWAN, AND GROWAN CLAY' within that part of His Majesty's Kingdom of Great Britain called England, his dominion of Wales, and town of Berwick-upon-Tweed, in such manner as to me, the said William Cookworthy, my executors, administrators, or assigns, or any of us, should in our discretion seem meet, and that I, the said William Cookworthy, my executors, administrators, and assigns, should and lawfully might have and enjoy the whole profit, benefit, commodity, and advantage from time to time coming, growing, accruing, and arising by reason of the said invention, for and during the term of years therein mentioned, to have, hold exercise and enjoy the said license, powers, privileges and advantages thereinbefore granted unto me, the said William Cookworthy, my executors, administrators, and assigns, for and during and until the full end and term of fourteen years from the date of the said Letters Patent, next and immediately ensuring, and fully to be compleat and ended according to the state in such case made and provided; in which said Letters Patent there is contained a provisoe as or to the effect following (viz.) that if I, the same William Cookworthy, should not particularly describe and ascertain the nature of my said invention, and in what manner the same was to be performed, by an instrument in writing under my hand and seal, and cause the same to be inrolled in His Majesty's High Court of Chancery within four calendar months next and immediately after the date of the said Letters Patent; then the said Letters Patent and all libertys and advantages whatsoever thereby granted should utterly cease, determine, and become void, as in and by the said Letters Patent (relation being thereunder had) more fully and at large it doth and may appear.

Now know ye that I, the said William Cookworthy, in pursuance of the said recited provisoe, do, by this my Deed in writing, declare and make known the nature of my said invention, and the quality of the materials, and manner in which the same is performed, which is as followeth (that is to say):-

The materials of which the body of the said porcelain is composed are a stone and earth or clay. The stone is known in the countys of Devon and Cornwall by the names of Moorstone and Growan, which stones are generally composed of grains of stone or gravel of a white or whitish colour, with a mixture of talky shining particles. This gravel and these talky particles are cemented together by a petrified clay into very solid rocks and immense quantities of them are found in both the above-mentioned countys. All these stones, exposed to a violent fire, melt without the addition of fluxes into a semi-transparent glass, differing in clearness and beauty according to the purity of the stone. The earth, or clay, for the most part lies in the valleys where the stone forms the hills. This earth is very frequently very white, tho' sometimes of a yellowish or cream colour. It generally arises with a large mixture of talky micae, or spangles, and a semi-transparent or whitish gravel. Some sorts have little of the micae, or spangles but the best clay for making porcelain always abounds in micae, or spangles. The stone is prepared by levigation in a potter's mill, in water in the usual manner, to a very fine powder. The clay is prepared by diluting it with water until the mixture is rendered sufficiently thin for the gravell and micae to subside, the white water containing the clay is then poured, or left to run off from the subsided micae and gravell into proper vessels or reservoirs; and after it has settled a day or two, the clear water above it is to be then poured or drawn off, and the clay or earth, reduced to a proper consistence by the common methods of exposing it to the sun and air, or laying it on chalk. This earth, or clay, gives the ware its whiteness and infusibility, as the stone doth its transparency and mellowness; they are therefore to be mix'd in different proportions, as the ware is intended to be more or less transparent; and the mixture is to be performed in the method used by potters, and well known (viz., by diluting the materials in water, passing the mixture through a fine sieve, and reducing it to a paste of a proper consistence for working in the way directed for the preparation of the clay) this paste is to be form'd into vessells, and these vessells, when biscuited, are to be dipp'd in the glaze which is prepared of the levigated stone, with the addition of lime and fern-ashes, or an earth called magnesia alba, in such quantity as may make it properly fusible and transparent when it has received a due degree of fire in the second baking.[1]

In witness whereof I, the said William Cookworthy, have hereunto sett my hand and seal this Eleventh day of July, in the Eighth year of the reign of our Sovereign Lord George the Third, by the grace of God of Great Britain, France, and Ireland, King, Defender of the Faith, and so forth, and in the year of our Lord One Thousand Seven Hundred and Sixty-eight.

WILLIAM (L.S.) COOKWORTHY.
Signed, sealed and delivered by the within-named William Cookworthy in the presence of
GEORGE LEACH,
J. STOVE.

And be it remembered that on the aforesaid eleventh day of July, in the year above mentioned, the aforesaid William Cookworthy came before our said Lord the King in his Chancery, and acknowledged the Specification aforesaid, and all and everything therein contained and specified in form above written. And also the Specification aforesaid was stampt according to the tenor of the statute made in the sixth year of the reign of the late King and Queen William and Mary of England, and so forth.

Inrolled the fourteenth day of July, in the year above written.
SAMUEL CHAMPION, a Master Extraordinary.

EXTRACT FROM CHAMPION'S SPECIFICATION OF PATENT FOR MAKING PORCELAIN.

'The raw materials of the above porcelain are plastic clay generally found mixed with mica, and a coarse gravelly matter. It is known in the counties of Devon and Cornwall by the name of growan clay. The other raw material is a mixed micaceous earth or stone, called in the aforesaid counties moor stone and growan. The gravel found in the growan clay is of the same nature, and is used for the same purpose in making the body of my porcelain, as the moor stone and growan. The mixture of these materials to make the body of the porcelain is according to the common potters' method, and has no peculiar art in it. The proportions are as follows: - The largest proportion of the stone or gravel aforesaid to the clay aforesaid is four parts of stone to one of clay. The largest proportion of clay to stone is sixteen parts of clay to one part of stone mixed together. I use these and every proportion intermediate between the foregoing proportions of the stone to the clay, and the clay to the stone and all this variation I make without taking away from the ware the distinguishing appearance and the properties of Dresden and Oriental porcelains, which is the appearance and are the properties of mine. The raw materials of which the glaze is composed are, the stone or gravel aforesaid and the clay aforesaid, magnesia, nitre, lime, gypsum, fusible spar, arsenic, lead and tin ashes.

The proportions of our common glaze are as follows, together with every intermediate proportion, videlicet: -

'Growan gravel	128 parts	)	
Growan or moor stone	112 parts, and	)	The materials
I vary it from 96 to 144		)	ground and mixed
Magnesia	16 parts, and	)	together with
I vary it from 14 to 18.		)	water.
Gypsum	3 parts	)	
Lime	8 parts	)	

'But I also use the following materials for glaze:

Growan Clay	128 parts	)	
Growan or moor stone	112 parts, and	)	
I vary it from 84 to 140 parts		)	
Magnesia	20, and	)	
I vary it from 16 to 24 parts.		)	The materials ground
Lime	8 parts, and	)	
I vary it from 6 to 10 parts)		)	and mixed together
Nitre	1, and	)	
I vary it to 2 parts		)	with water.
Fusible spar	20	)	
Arsenic	20	)	
Lead and tin ashes	20 parts, and	)	
I vary it from 16 to24			

I have decided truly and justly the raw materials, the mixture and proportions of them which are used in making my porcelain, which has the appearance and properties of Dresden or Oriental porcelain, and which porcelain may be distinguished from the frit or false porcelain, and from the other pottery, or earthen, or stone wares as follows:-

The frit or false porcelain will all melt into a vitreous substance, and lose their form[2] and original appearance, in a degree of heat which my porcelain, agreeing in all properties with Asiatick and Dresden, will not only bear, but which is necessary for its perfection. My porcelain may be distinguished from all other wares, which are vulgarly called earthen or stone wares, which can sustain an equal degree of heat by the grain, the colour of the grain, and by its semi-transparency, whereas the earthenwares such as Staffordshire white and yellow earthenwares and all other earthenwares which sustain a strong heat without being fused, are found when subjected to the most intense heat to appear cellular or otherwise, easily by the eye to be distinguished from the true porcelain.'

RICH. (L.S.) CHAMPION.
(Inrolled fifteenth September, 1775)

An Act passed in 1775 (15 George III. Cap. 52) entitled, 'An Act for enlarging the terms of Letters Patent granted by his present Majesty to William Cookworthy, of Plymouth, Chymist, for the sale use and exercise of a discovery of certain materials for making Porcelain, in order to enable Richard Champion, of Bristol, merchant (to whom the said Letters Patent have been assigned), to carry the said discovery into effectual execution for the benefit of the public.' It is as follows:

'Whereas his present Majesty King George the third has been graciously pleased to grant his Royal Letters Patent under the Great Seal of Great Britain unto William Cookworthy, Chymist, in the words or to the effect, following: that is to say; George the Third by the grace of God of Great Britain, France and Ireland, King, Defender of the Faith, and so forth, to all whom these presents shall come, greeting; Whereas, William Cookworthy, of Plymouth, in the County of Devon, Chymist, has by his petition humbly represented to us that he hath by a series of experiments discovered that materials of the same nature as those of which the Asiatic porcelain is made are to be found in immense quantities in our island of Great Britain, which ingredients are distinguished in our two counties of Devon and Cornwall, by the names of moor stone, and growan, and grown clay; that the ware which he hath prepared from these materials hath all the character of the true porcelain in regard to grain, transparency, colour and infusibility, in a degree equal to the Chinese or Dresden ware; whereas, all the manufacturers of porcelain hitherto carried on in Great Britain have been only imitations of the genuine kind, wanting the beauty of colour, and the smoothness and lustre of grain, and the great characteristic of genuine porcelain sustaining the most extreme degree of fire without melting; that this discovery hath been attended with great labour and expense, and, to the best of his knowledge and belief in regard to this kingdom, is new and his own, the materials being even at this time, applied to none of the uses of pottery but by him and those under his direction; and that he verily believes this invention will be of great advantage to the public. He, therefore, most humbly prayed us that we should be pleased to grant him our Royal Letters Patent for the sole making and vending of the new invented porcelain, composed of moor stone or growan, and growan clay, within that part of our kingdom of Great Britain called England, or dominion of Wales, and the town of Berwick-upon-Tweed, for the space of fourteen years, according to the statute in that case made and provided; we, being willing to give encouragement to all arts and inventions which may be for the public good, are graciously pleased to condescend to the petitioner's request. Know ye, therefore, that we, of our especial grace, certain knowledge, and meet notion, have given and granted, and for these presents our heirs and successors do give and grant unto the said William Cookworthy, his executors, administrators, and assigns, our special licence, full power, sole privilege and authority, that he the said William Cookworthy, his executors administrators, and assigns, and every of them by himself and themselves, or by his or their deputy or deputies, servants, or agents, or such others as the said William Cookworthy, his executors, administrators, and assigns shall at any time agree with, and no others, from time to time, and at all times hereafter during the term of years herein expressed, shall, and lawfully make take, use, exercise, and vend his said invention within that part of Great Britain called England, our dominion of Wales, and the town of Berwick-upon-Tweed, and in such a manner as he, the said William Cookworthy, his executors, administrators, and assigns or any of them, in their discretions seem meet; and that the said William Cookworthy, his executors, administrators, and assigns shall, and lawfully may, enjoy the whole profit, benefit, commodity, and advantage from time to time coming, growing, accruing, and arising by reason of the said invention for and during the term of years herein mentioned, to have, hold exercise, and enjoy the said licence, privileges, and advantages hereinbefore granted, or mentioned to be granted, to the said William Cookworthy, his executors, administrators, and assigns, for and during to the full end of the term of fourteen years from the date of these presents next and immediately ensuing, and full to be completed and ended according to the statute in such case made and provided, and to the end that he, the said William Cookworthy, his executors, administrators, and assigns, and every of them, may have and enjoy the full benefit and the sole use and exercise of the said invention, according to our gracious intention hereinbefore declared; we do by these presents, for us, our heirs and successors, require and strictly command all and every person and persons, bodies politic and corporate, and all other our subjects whatsoever, of what estate, quality, degree, name or condition soever they be, within that said part of Great Britain called England, our dominion of Wales, and our town of Berwick-upon-Tweed aforesaid, that neither they nor any of them, at any time during the continuance of the said term of fourteen years hereby granted, either directly or indirectly, do make, use, or practice the said invention or any part of the same so attained unto by the said William Cookworthy as aforesaid, nor in anywise counterfeit, imitate, or resemble the same, nor shall make, or cause to be made, any addition thereunto, or substraction from the same, whereby to pretend himself or themselves to be the inventor or inventors, deviser or devisers thereof without the licence, consent, or agreement of the said William Cookworthy, his executors, administrators, or assigns, in writing under his or their hands and seals, first had and obtained in that behalf upon such pains and penalties as can or may be justly inflicted on such offenders for their contempt of this our Royal Command; and further, to be answerable to the said William Cookworthy, his executors, administrators, and assigns according to law for his and their damages thereby occasioned; and moreover, we do by these presents, for us, our heirs, and successors, will and command all and singular the justices of the peace, mayors, sheriffs, bailiffs, constables, head boroughs, and all other officers and ministers whatsoever, of us, our heirs, and successors for the time being, that they, or any of them, do not, nor shall at any time hereafter during the said time hereby granted the said William Cookworthy, his executors, administrators, or assigns, or any of them, or his or their deputies, servants, or agents, in anywise molest, trouble, or hinder the said William Cookworthy, his executors, administrators, and assigns, or any of them, or his or their deputies, servant, or agents, in or about the due and lawful use or exercise of the aforesaid invention or anything relating thereto: Provided always and these our Letters Patent are and shall be upon this condition, that if at any time during the said term here granted, it shall be made or appear to us, our heirs, or successors, or any six or more of our or their Privy Council, that this our grant is contrary to law, or prejudicial or inconvenient to our subject in general, or that if the said invention is not a new invention as to the public use and exercise thereof, in that part of our Kingdom of Great Britain called England, our dominion of Wales, and town of Berwick-upon-Tweed aforesaid, or not invented or found out by the said William Cookworthy as aforesaid, then, upon signification or declaration thereof to be made by us, our heirs, and successors, under our or their signet or Privy Seal, or by the lords of our or their Privy Council, or any six or more of them under their hand, these our Letters Patent shall forthwith intents and purposes, anything hereinbefore contained in anywise notwithstanding. Provided also, that these our Letters Patent, or anything herein contained, shall not extend or be construed to extend to the privileges of the said William Cookworthy, his executors, administrators, or assigns, or any of them, to use or imitate any invention or work whatsoever which has heretofore been found out or invented by any other of our subjects whatsoever, or publicly used or exercised in that part of our Kingdom of Great Britain called England, or dominion of Wales, and town of Berwick-upon-Tweed aforesaid, unto whom the like Letters Patent or privileges have already been granted for the sole use, exercise, and benefit thereof, it being our will and pleasure that the said William Cookworthy, his executors, administrators, and assigns, and all and every person or persons to whom the like Letters Patent or privileges have already been granted as aforesaid, shall distinctly use and practice their several inventions by them invented and found out, according to the true intent and meaning of the said Letters Patent and of these presents. Provided likewise, nevertheless, and these our Letters Patent are upon this express condition, that the said William Cookworthy, his executors, administrators, or assigns, or any person or persons which shall or may be at any time or times hereafter, during the continuance of this grant, have or claim any right, title or intent, in law or equity, or of in, or to the power, privilege, and authority of the sole use of the said benefit hereby granted, shall make any transfer or assignment, or pretended transfer or assignment, of the said liberty and privilege, or any share or shares for the benefit or profit thereof, or shall declare any trust thereof to or for any number of persons exceeding the number of five,[3] or shall open, or cause to be opened, any book or books for public subscriptions to be made by any number of persons exceeding the number of five[3] for such or the like intents or purposes, or shall presume to act as a corporate body, or shall divide the benefit of these our Letters Patent, or the liberty and privileges hereby by us granted, into any number of shares exceeding the number of five,[3] or shall commit or do, or shall procure to be committed or done, any act, matter or thing whatsoever, during the time such person or persons shall have any right or title, either in law or equity, in or to the said premises which shall be contrary to the true intent and meaning of a certain Act of Parliament, made in the sixth year of the reign of our late royal grandfather King George the First, entitled, 'An Act for the better securing certain powers and privileges, intended to be granted by his Majesty by two charters, for the Insurance of Ships and Merchandize by Sea, and for laying money out upon bottoming, and for restraining several extravagant and unwarrantable practices therein mentioned,' or in case the said privilege or authority shall at any time hereafter become vested in, or in trust for, any number of more than five persons[3] or their representatives (reckoning executors or administrators as for the single person whom they represent, as to such interest as they are or shall be entitled to in right of such testator or intestate), that then, and in any of the said cases, these our Letters Patent, and all liberties and advantages whatsoever hereby granted, shall utterly cease and become void,[3] anything hereinbefore contained to the contrary thereof anywise, notwithstanding. Provided also, if the said William Cookworthy shall not particularly describe and ascertain the nature of his invention, and in what manner the same is to be performed, by any instrument in writing, under his hand and seal, and cause the same to be enrolled in our High Court of Chancery within four calendar months next and immediately after the date of these our Letters patent, that then these our Letters Patent, and all liberties and advantages whatsoever hereby granted, shall utterly cease, determine, and become void, anything hereinbefore contained to the contrary thereof in anywise notwithstanding. And, lastly we do by these presents, for us, our heirs and successors, grant unto the said William Cookworthy, his executors, administrators, and assigns, that these, our Letters Patent, or the enrollment of the exemplification thereof shall be in and by all things good, firm valid, sufficient, and effectual in the law, according to the true intent and meaning thereof and shall be taken, construed, and adjudged in the most favourable and beneficial sense for the best advantage of the said William Cookworthy, his executors, administrators, and assigns, as well in all our Courts of Record as elsewhere, and by all and singular the officers and ministers whatsoever of us, our heirs, and successors in that part of the said Kingdom of Great Britain called England, our dominion of Wales, and town of Berwick-upon-Tweed aforesaid, and amongst all and every the subject of us, our heirs, and successors whatsoever, and wheresoever, notwithstanding the not full and certain describing the nature of the said invention, or of the materials thereto conducing and belonging, in witness whereof we have caused these our Letters to be made patent; witness ourself at Westminster, the seventeenth day of March, in the eighth year of our reign.

And whereas the said William Cookworthy hath by an instrument in writing, under his hand and seal, described and ascertained the nature of the said invention, and the manner in which the same is to be performed, and hath caused the same to be enrolled in His Majesty's Court of Chancery within the time and in the manner directed by the said Letters Patent; and whereas by a deed of assignment, bearing the date the sixth day of May, One thousand seven hundred and seventy four, the said William Cookworthy (for the consideration therein mentioned) hath assigned all his interest, benefit, and property, in the said Letters Patent and invention, unto RICHARD CHAMPION, of Bristol, merchant, his executors, administrators, and assigns, and whereas the said Richard Champion hath been at very considerable expense and great pains in labour in prosecuting the said invention, and by reason of the great difficulty attending the manufacture upon a new principle, hath not been able to bring the same to perfection until within the last year, and it will require further pains, labour and expense, to render the said invention of public utility, for all which trouble and expense the said Richard Champion will not be able to receive an adequate compensation unless the term granted by the said royal Letters Patent be prolonged. To the end therefore that the said Richard Champion may be encouraged to prosecute and complete the said invention, may it please your Majesty (at the humble petition of the said Richard Champion) that it may be enacted, and be it enacted by the King's most excellent Majesty, by and with the consent of the Lords spiritual and Temporal, and Commons, in this present Parliament assembled, and by the authority of the same, that all and every the powers, liberties, privileges, authorities, rights, benefits and advantages, which in and by the said Letters Patent were originally given and granted to him the said William Cookworthy, his executors, administrators, and assigns, and no further or greater than he or the said Richard Champion would have been entitled to if this Act had not been made, shall be, and the same are hereby given and granted, to the said Richard Champion, his executors, administrators and assigns, and shall be held, exercised, and enjoyed by him the said Richard Champion, his executors, administrators, and assigns, for and during the present term of fourteen years granted by the said Letters Patent; and from and after the end and expiration of the said term of fourteen years thereby granted, and for and during the further or additional term of fourteen years, in as full, ample, (and beneficial manner, in all respects, and to all intents and purposes whatsoever, as he the said Richard Champion, his executors, administrators, and assigns, could have held and enjoyed the same under and by virtue of the said Letters Patent for the term thereby granted, in case of the said Letters Patent had been originally granted to him the said Richard Champion, his executors, administrators, and assigns.

Provided always, and be it further granted and declared by the authority aforesaid, that if the said Richard Champion shall not cause to be enrolled in the High Court of Chancery, within four months after passing this Act, a specification of the mixture and proportions of the raw materials of which his porcelain is composed, and likewise of the mixture and proportions of the raw materials which compose the glaze of the same (which specification is now in the hands of the Lord High Chancellor of Great Britain); or if the same shall not be a true and just specification of the mixture and proportions of the said materials, then this Act shall cease, determine, and be absolutely void, anything hereinbefore contained to the contrary notwithstanding.

Provided also that nothing in this Act contained shall be construed to hinder or prevent any Potter or Potters, or any other person or persons, from making use of any such raw materials, or any mixture of mixtures thereof (except such mixture of raw materials, and in such proportions as are described in the specification hereinbefore directed to be enrolled), anything in this Act to the contrary notwithstanding. And be it further enacted by the authority aforesaid, that this Act shall be adjuged, deemed, and taken to be a public Act, and shall be judicially taken notice of as such by all judges, justices, and other persons whomsoever, without specially pleading the same.

This extended Patent for the manufacture of hard-paste porcelain and for the use of Cornish 'moor stone' and growan clay (china stone and china clay) within the prescribed proportions for the manufacture of translucent ceramic bodies was that asset which Richard Champion sought to sell on to a consortium of Staffordshire potters and investors. As with all English patents of this period there were, however, various restrictions relating to the selling on of shares or on the setting up of a Company.

It is not now known if the new owners, the more than five partners in the Staffordshire firm, attempted to enforce any patent rights that they may have purchased from the holder, Richard Champion. It is noteworthy that no mention of patent rights appeared on their marks or bill-head and I have not traced any attempt to restrict the use of the vital raw materials, by other persons.

Certainly several then contemporary English porcelain manufacturers produced porcelains that appear to be as hard or nearly as hard as the early New Hall body. I have added to this Appendix a few notes and analysis which show the close relationship, at least in terms of the chemical make-up of some ceramic bodies of the hybrid hard-paste type.

Over the years several analyses have been published of New Hall bodies and of a few of the contemporary hybrid hard-paste type porcelains. Some of these tests were carried out in the 1920s and most later ones have been undertaken by different persons, probably using different apparatus or techniques. Comparisons taken from these differing analyses, therefore, may well not be very helpful or exact.

In an effort to overcome these difficulties and to furnish myself with an analysis of a piece from the corrugated class of porcelains (see Chapter II), I had seven specimens tested by Messrs. Watts Blake Bearne & Co. Plc. of

Newton Abbot, a firm recommended to me by Dr. W. Ryan of the Department of Ceramic Technology and Geological Sciences at the North Staffordshire Polytechnic, Stoke-on-Trent.

The following analyses were carried out by this professional firm, using the same apparatus and techniques for all specimens. The results, it will be noted, differ slightly from other previously published analyses such as those given on page 45 of David Holgate's 1987 book *New Hall*. These variations may result from different methods being employed or merely from the variable mixes used over a period at any eighteenth (or early nineteenth) century factory. It is unlikely that any two pieces of Bristol porcelain, for example, will give an exactly similar result.

The pieces tested are:

1. Bristol (hard paste) cup. c.1775
2. Corrugated class (New Hall type tea bowl). c.1781. See Plate 46, left
3. New Hall waste bowl, pattern 171. c.1790.
4. Early 'X' class (type) cup, pattern 11. c.1785+.
5. Chamberlain Worcester gilt cup, pattern 55. c.1790.
6. John Rose period (hybrid hard-paste) site waster from the old Caughley site, c.1800.

I have been unable to include here comparisons of mixes of the later bone china type which would contain phosphate as the X-ray fluorescence method employed in Messrs. Watts Blake Bearne & Co.'s laboratory does not determine phosphate. Here we are concerned with the earlier (hard-paste type) mixes of the 1775-1800 period.

	1 Bristol	2 Corrugated	3 New Hall	4 X Class	5 Chamberlain	6 Coalport
Silica	73.20	68.80	71.90	71.40	68.61	74.50
Alumina	22.80	24.00	20.80	21.70	23.52	19.90
Iron	0.45	0.40	0.29	0.34	0.34	0.25
Lime	0.32	1.58	1.37	1.19	1.14	0.46
Magnesia	0.25	0.25	0.18	0.19	0.16	0.14
Potash	2.43	3.51	3.40	3.70	3.61	2.84
Soda	0.29	1.09	1.71	1.27	1.27	1.61
Titanic Oxide	0.03	0.03	0.05	0.08	0.02	0.06
Loss	0.24	0.10	0.28	0.15	0.34	0.20

No earth shattering discoveries can be gauged from these analyses. These different types of hard-paste and hybrid hard-paste porcelains show remarkably similar percentages of the main ingredients – Silica and Alumina – while the New Hall percentages nearly match the 'X' class Staffordshire mix.

Many readers may well be surprised by the apparent difference in make-up between the Bristol and the early Staffordshire corrugated formed porcelains which were reputedly made from the same basic raw materials to the same recipe. Seemingly the mix was amended by the new Staffordshire owners of the original patent. Again, one would have thought that the analyses for these corrugated shaped porcelains would have been rather close to that given for the true New Hall specimen. The corrugated class seems, on the evidence of these professional analyses, to be the odd one out. One can also remark on the similarity of make-up between the New Hall specimen and the other classes of hybrid hard-paste porcelain tested including the 'X' class and Coalport.

As to the probable firing temperature necessary to mature the New Hall porcelain body, Paul Rado working at the Worcester Royal Porcelain works has suggested from tests in the Worcester kilns that the required temperature was rather less than 1250° centigrade. This compares unfavourably with hard-paste Bristol, Dresden or Chinese porcelains which withstood a temperature of about 1400° centigrade. George Stringer told of similar results on his pages 102-3. Nevertheless, we can consider the pre-bone china mix to be a type of hard-paste or a hybrid hard-paste body, a modern term explained on page 15. The New Hall partnership favoured, on their bill-head, the description 'Real China'.

1. This 1768 description relates to a low first firing and a higher firing to vitrify the porcelain after it has been glazed. This is the sequence for true, or Chinese type, porcelain. The New Hall partners reversed the sequence and may thereby have nullified the patent.

2. This fact has more recently been confirmed by firing tests carried out for me at the Worcester Royal Porcelain Company's works. See page 421.

3. See page 91 for my quotation of Roger Pomfret's comments on these points.

APPENDIX II

The Land Tax Returns

I have transferred the details of the Staffordshire Land Tax Returns from Chapter IV to this Appendix as the details are now very confusing and would have tended to have delayed my discussion of the early New Hall porcelains if such information had been retained in the main section of this book. The basic difficulty is that the various properties are not described; only the owner and the tenant's name is given, with a rateable value.

The following Shelton Land Tax returns, that is those completed in 1784, 1786, 1788, 1789, 1790, 1791, 1792, 1794 and 1795, all list the occupier of what I assume to be the New Hall premises (owned in trust by James Neale) as Thomas Heath. At this approximate period (as I have previously noted) some local directories include the firm of 'Heath Warburton & Co.'. It would now appear that the first-named principal partner could have been Thomas Heath, not as has previously been believed, Joshua Heath, who is named in the 1803 agreement. Thomas Heath is not mentioned in connection with the New Hall partnership in other books and my discovery presents its own problems, which I will shortly return to discuss.

James Neale is listed as the owner of the New Hall estate until the return of 5 April 1801, although several different spellings are used – Neal, Neil and Nale. I have given all correctly as Neale. There is no return available for 1802. The 1803 return lists the owner as Miss Palmer and this name is repeated to 1808, although she had died in 1805 or 1806. The Shelton returns from 1809 to 1822 list the owner as John Daniel & Co. (or rarely as John Daniel), reflecting the partners' purchase of the property which they had previously rented. Mrs Dudson,[1] on her page 32, states that in August 1814 the partners surrendered the title to John Daniel, their manager, and that the firm's trade name then became the New Hall Porcelain Company. The 1826 Land Tax returns on a new style printed form gives the ownership of the 'Land and Manufactory' as the 'New Hall Co.'. This ownership continues to the last available return of 1832.

Transferring our attention to the column in the Land Tax returns listing the occupier of the premises we find Thomas Heath named up to the 1795 Shelton return. The return for 1796 is missing but the next, that of 1797, lists the new occupier as John Daniel, who was the manager of the New Hall china works. He remains listed as the occupier until 1805 after which the name was slightly amended to John Daniel & Co., a style also listed as the 'Proprietor' of the land. From 1826 both the ownership and occupiers are given as 'New Hall Co.'. There are no returns available in the Staffordshire County Record Office after that for 1832.

In my research in these records I have assumed, unless there was evidence to the contrary, that all the Thomas Heath entries in the 1783–1812 records relate to the same person, although obviously this may not be so. The Land Tax returns are divided into three basic columns, giving the name of the land (or property) owner (The 'Proprietor'), the name of the occupier at that time and the amount of the assessment or tax to be paid at the rate of 4s. in the pound, that is twenty per cent.

The Thomas Heath entries, which I believe relate to the Shelton or New Hall estate (I have lettered these for future reference), are puzzling and the 1783 additional notes are not clear. However, I take the 1783 return to read:

	Proprietor	Occupier	Assessment
A.	Thos. Heath for Marshes	Himself	13s.10d.
B.	Thos. Heath for Childs	Himself	1s.4½d.
C.	Thomas Heath	Himself	£1.3s.5d.
D.	Thomas Heath	Himself	3s.2d.
E.	Lord Gower	Thos Heath	17s.6½d.

The next or 1784 return, that for the year 6 April 1783 to 5 April 1784, has the interesting additional Thomas Heath entry relating to property owned by James Neale:

F. James Neale Thomas Heath £1.19s.3½d.

This replaces the entry found in the 1783 returns:

James Neale (no other occupier listed) £1.19s.3½d.

This important assessment I believe relates to the New Hall estate at Shelton, then (as explained on page 144) in the name of James Neale, the London dealer and former partner of Humphrey Palmer.

Now to recap, in regard to the first 1783 entry 'A' – I am not sure if the indistinctly written words 'for Marshes' refer to marsh or swampy land or whether he was holding the land for other persons named Marsh? This entry, however, seems of little consequence to our further study of Thomas Heath.

Likewise, 'B' is probably of little direct relevance. The proprietor or owner is listed as Thomas Heath for Child. This relates to a person of that name. The entry possibly indicates that Thomas Heath was listed as the owner as he was acting as the agent for John Child who is mentioned in a document dated 9 June 1785, referring to land – Pump Meadow, Little Hollies, Ball's Meadow, Stonary Bank etc., – transferred from Thomas and Sarah Heath to John Child. The Land Tax returns predate this official transfer by a year or so.

The next assessment 'C' is of greater importance, for not only is Thomas Heath listed in his own right, without added notation, as the owner and occupier, but the amount of the tax is relatively large signifying a large parcel of land or an important building. The assessment is given as £1.3s.5d. at a time when very few entries were for sums greater than £1. For comparison, note that the Shelton or New Hall potteries, outbuildings and considerable surrounding land was assessed at £1.19s.3½d.

It is of interest to follow through this entry on subsequent returns. In 1794 the occupier is given simply as 'Marquis', but in 1797 the owner of the land is given more fully as the Marquis of Stafford with Thomas Heath as the occupiers. This is continued to 1808 with the owner being described in various ways – in this year as 'Lord Granville Gower', that is the Marquis of Stafford, about which more later. After 1808 Thomas Heath's name is not mentioned in regard to this assessment and his name is replaced by that of Richard Hicks.

'D', which appears in the records after the large £1.3s.5d. assessment just mentioned, most probably relates to Thomas Heath's separately valued residence. This supposition is strengthened by the fact that the 1794 record for this assessment has the addition 'Gent' after Thomas Heath's name and in 1795 the rather fuller description 'Gentln' was used. Such courtesies were extremely rarely used by the assessors or their clerks writing up these records.

We now come to the interesting entry 'E'. This relates to land or property owned by 'Lord Gower' (the Marquis of Stafford) and occupied by Thomas Heath and valued at 17s.6½d. This entry commences in the 1783 return. The title of the proprietor changes somewhat over the years – Lord Gower, Marquis of Stafford, Right Honble Marquis of Stafford or Lord Granville Gower. In about 1804 a slight amendment occurs in that the notation is 'John Sparrow Esq's land' and in 1806 John Sparrow Esq is listed as the owner instead of the Marquis of Stafford, although Thomas Heath is still listed as the occupier.

In the 1812 returns two points arise. First, Thomas Heath's name is not given as the occupier of this land or property which still retained the original assessment of 17s.6½d. Lord Leveson Gower is now given as the occupier of John Sparrow's property. After the death of Thomas Heath in February 1812 the Land Tax returns show amended entries for 'Heath widow' or 'widow Heath' replacing Thomas Heath.

It is interesting that Thomas Heath was so closely linked with the first Marquis of Stafford on these Land Tax returns. Thomas Heath was occupying two separate parcels of land owned by Lord Leveson Gower (1721-1803) and subsequently by his son (1773-1846). His Lordship, with his county seat at nearby Trentham, was a most important and well placed personage, a one time Lord of the Admiralty, Chamberlain of the Royal Household, etc., etc. Lord Gower was one of Josiah Wedgwood's great friends at court and a leading figure, with the Duke of Bridgwater and Wedgwood, in their plans to extend the great canal system and to link the Staffordshire Potteries with the important port of Liverpool. Lord Gower called their group 'the Amicable Society of Navigators'. At an early meeting of the proprietors of the Trent and Mersey Canal (the Grand Trunk) Lords Gower, Anson, Gray and other leading spirits elected Josiah Wedgwood treasurer of the great enterprise, one that was to prove so vital to the growing prosperity of the potters.

Eliza Meteyard, in her two volume work on *The Life of Josiah Wedgwood* (Hurst & Blackett, London, 1865 and 1866), records many visits by Josiah Wedgwood to his

Lordship at Trentham and London, while Lord Gower and his family often visited the Wedgwood works or the London showrooms. Miss Meteyard refers to Wedgwood consulting his 'unvarying friend Earl Gower'. Josiah Wedgwood also produced a portrait medallion of Earl Gower. Miss Meteyard makes the following, perhaps typically rather over-stated, comments on the Marquis of Stafford:

> The earl was a fine specimen of the old Whig nobility. His face, as thus preserved to us in cameo, makes us feel that he was a scholar and a gentleman, and yet one who perhaps shone more as lord of his county, in promoting canals and highways, in patronising agriculture, in presiding at great public meetings, than even in his ministerial capacity as Lord Privy Seal, Lord Chamberlain and Lord President of the Council, popular as he was, even when in coalition with the Opposition under Lord North. He always met Mr Wedgwood on the simple footing of man with man, and seems never to have been so happy as when at home amidst his neighbours. His name is constantly appearing in Mr Wedgwood's letters to Bentley...

My brief account of the local Marquis of Stafford, Lord Gower, may be out of place, but at an early stage in my research on this hitherto unrecorded figure in the history of New Hall porcelain, I thought that Thomas Heath might have been recorded as occupying these two relatively highly assessed properties in Shelton as an agent for Lord Gower. If this was the case, he could also have been acting for his lordship whilst listed as the occupier of the New Hall estate. It would have been a happy thought if Josiah Wedgwood had recommended Lord Gower to Richard Champion as a possible purchaser of shares in the projected new enterprise to bring the manufacture of 'real china' to the Staffordshire Potteries – a district in which the Marquis of Stafford was so obviously interested. What might have become of the new company had Lord Gower with all his wealthy friends become financially interested in the concern? Wedgwood thrived on such friendly contacts, but the New Hall management had to be content to produce mainly teawares for the middle classes. Alas, I cannot state that Lord Gower was directly involved in the company.

Part of the Thomas Heath mystery was, however, solved when I happened to read the Shelton Land Tax returns of the 1820s at a period long after Heath's death. Here in the 1822 and later returns, which are rather more detailed than the earlier ones, I found that the property still assessed at 17.6s.½d. (item 'E' on page 422) was clearly described as a 'colliery'. Pursuing this line of inquiry, I found a passing mention to the Heath family's interests in mining included in the Burslem section of *The Victoria History of the County of Stafford,* Vol. VIII, page 140: 'The Adams family of Birches Head and the Heath family of Hanley and Burslem were mining at Cobridge...', this and the following information having been extracted from *A History of the Adams Family of North Staffordshire* by Percy W.L. Adams (The Saint Catherine Press, London, 1914). Documents in the Stoke Reference Library confirm Thomas Heath's interests in mining. One dated 20 December 1786 relates to mineral rights at Cobridge, another of 5 January 1803 relates to the 'extinguishment of mine rent (£263.17s.10d.) in Sneyd Green' when Thomas and John Heath released the property to John Turton. A William Heath may have taken up the family interests in the colliery business as Holden's directory of the 1809-1811 period includes 'William Heath, engineer and Agent to the collieries, Hanley'.

1. *Dudson, A Family of Potters since 1800* by Audrey M. Dudson (Dudson Publications, Hanley, 1985).

Closing Notes

As I treated myself to some opening notes, I should perhaps conclude with brief closing notes before proceeding to the two part bibliography. The first part lists the hard-back books that relate to my subject and this is followed by a listing of articles, learned papers, catalogues and suchlike helpful material that normally is published in a flimsy form or as part of a magazine or journal.

Over the years, indeed even in recent times, much nonsense has been published on New Hall porcelain and the history of this important partnership. Books can easily become out of date and at best they only reflect the opinion of that author or of his current beliefs. Authors often wish they could correct or up-date their published works, but this is seldom possible.

It could well be that in the future some statement made in this book will, in turn, be questioned and corrected. I would welcome such rechecking and delving for this is the only way that our knowledge of the true facts relating to the establishment of the New Hall partnership over two hundred years ago may be reconstructed and its subsequent developments be fully understood.

My first brief quote is representative of the type of overboard, general statement which tends to be made by journalist type writers. These persons have no deep knowledge of the subject but have been given by their editor, or chosen for themselves, a collecting subject to write about in, say, twelve hundred words!

> ...New Hall wares are easy to identify – they are usually domestic wares made of a greyish paste that has a yellowish tone, glaze is skimped. The finer styles of decoration were not used. Shapes are typical and easy to identify, teapots were made in the style of the silver ones with straight sides and were boat-shaped. The cream jugs match them. In 1810 hard paste was discontinued and for about fifteen years bone ash was used instead...

These misleading and unhelpful statements appeared in the old *Antique Finder* magazine of June 1970. I have no idea where the writer gleaned such superficial knowledge. We need not waste too much time over these views or question which of the many forms of New Hall teapot the writer had in mind in the muddled description 'in the style of the silver ones with straight sides and were boat-shaped'. All cream jugs from whatever factory broadly match the teapots in general shape and of course in their added decoration.

Most, if not all, authorities would suggest that the glazing was generous rather than 'skimped'! The hard-paste type body was continued after 1810 and the factory closed in or about 1835, not 1825 as is suggested. I have been collecting New Hall porcelains for well over a quarter of a century and still do not find 'New Hall wares are easy to identify'. If I did I might not be so interested in them and I most certainly would not feel the necessity to write this book.

Do remember that not everything that appears in print is gospel! Look to the authority and his or her depth of knowledge and research. Bear in mind the market at which the account is aimed and the period of publication. Much new information has been unearthed in the last twenty years and older accounts, while reliable in some instances, have been overtaken by later research.

Llewellynn Jewitt, for whom I have the greatest respect, wrote an important early contribution to our understanding of New Hall porcelains. This was published under the title 'New Hall China' in the *Art Journal* magazine of January 1864, as one in an interesting series on British pottery and porcelain. These articles were later expanded and used in Jewitt's great work *The Ceramic Art of Great Britain* (first published in 1878 with a revised edition in 1883).

Jewitt's 1864 pioneer article, the first to illustrate New Hall porcelains, repeated an even earlier error in stating that Richard Champion of Bristol sold his patent rights to the new Staffordshire partnership in about 1777. Simeon Shaw in 1829 had opted for this date. The 1781 date now seems reasonably certain, see page 91.

I, for one, would doubt Jewitt's statement that:

> The ware made at this period will, on examination, be found to be precisely similar in body and glaze to that of Bristol, to which, from the fact of some of the same artists being employed, it bears also a marked resemblance in ornamentation

The New Hall porcelains in general do not seem all that similar to the earlier Bristol porcelains. Few, if any, former Bristol painters seem to have been employed and Richard Champion had left Staffordshire before the partnership moved from Tunstall to the 'New Hall' at Shelton.

Many authors have stated that the original New Hall Company made earthenware as well as porcelains. I and most present-day authorities do not believe that any pottery was produced. This partnership was formed to produce porcelain in a pottery district. It would have been foolhardy to compete with all the already successful earthenware firms. I have not noticed any earthenware directly linking with New Hall porcelains, in shape, pattern number or engraved design.

Very many unhelpful comments, brief or detailed, have been made regarding the so-called silver shape teapot (as Plates 138-9, 141-6, 149, 151-7 and 161-2). *The Concise Encyclopaedia of English Pottery & Porcelain* (A. Deutsch, London, 1957) states 'a distinctive silver-shape teapot is peculiar to this factory'. This form, however, is not all that distinctive. Several versions were made by the New Hall firm and many (twenty or more) other contemporary manufacturers also made silver shape pots which are very close imitations of the New Hall specimens.

The late T.A. Sprague wrote a series of four interesting articles on New Hall and related factories in the *Apollo* magazine in 1949 and 1950. The first of these, published in the June 1949 issue, incorrectly attributed some pieces to Bristol. Some 'Bristol' examples, such as his Figures III, IV, VI and VII feature undoubted New Hall pieces of the mid- to late 1780s. In a way they further extend the old belief that simple New Hall type patterns (of the post-1785 period) were made earlier at the West Country factory, giving rise to the misleading description 'Cottage Bristol'. Hopefully, this misleading term has now gone out of favour.

It is unfortunate that the first book to be devoted to New Hall should have, in hindsight, contained so many errors of attribution. This pioneer book, *New Hall Porcelain* by George Eyre Stringer (Art Trade Press Ltd., London, 1949), is valuable on many counts and the historical background had been well researched by this then owner of the New Hall Pottery Company Ltd.

On his page 32 George Stringer noted that 'so far as my knowledge goes at present, there are few instances in which New Hall gilded its real china'. The author goes on to explain that for this reason he rejected a fine tea service of pattern 196 – 'the set was not purchased because of the gilding'. This service was, of course, New Hall and it should be noted that the more expensive classes of New Hall porcelains may be very richly gilt. Some of the earliest designs are tastefully decorated only with gold – see, for example, Plates 89, 93-4, 96 or 100.

Several of the illustrations included in George Stringer's book are not now considered to be correctly attributed. The following articles are, I believe, not New Hall, although I have not had the opportunity to handle the pieces:

Plate XVI
Plate XVII
Plate XVIII
Plate XIX
Plate XX
Plate XXI
Plate XXXVI, all examples

Apart from the errors relating to New Hall porcelains, he also stated that the Minton factory at Stoke did not produce porcelain before 1824, whereas it was probably doing so before 1800, and certainly the Minton factory pattern book includes several New Hall type simple floral patterns, of the type featured in my Chapter VIII.

I could list many further points and errors in now old reference books, but I have probably cited enough to encourage the reader to consult as modern a work as possible and to double check so-called facts. Best of all, he or she should carry out their own research and add to our general fund of knowledge. However, the researchers will need to know what has previously been written on this or any other subject, hence the following Bibliography.

It should be noted that the New Hall concern was one of the few in Staffordshire that produced only porcelain for the whole of its fifty or more years' history. This contrasts with the mixed output of such firms as Spode, Minton or Ridgway. The New Hall output of porcelains of a useful nature was huge. At the great exhibition of Staffordshire porcelain held at the Hanley Museum in

1979 New Hall held pride of place with forty-two entries compared with twenty-five for Spode and eighteen for Minton. The scope for the New Hall collector is vast. Examples can still be found to suit most budgets. Often the humble teabowl and saucer of a standard pattern is visually more pleasing than a unique museum piece, where rarity alone sets the price!

I should also point out that not everything offered for sale by dealers or auctioneers as 'New Hall' is necessarily so. New Hall is now a fashionable and collectable factory and its name gets affixed to all sorts of porcelains (even to earthenwares). Many factories of the 1780-20 period produced New Hall type patterns and similar forms because they were in demand. I hope one day to publish a book on New Hall 'look alikes', but it will be a very large work! In the meantime, reference to *Staffordshire Porcelain* (Granada Publishing, London, 1983), under my editorship, and to my *Encyclopaedia of British Porcelain Manufacturers* (Barrie and Jenkins, London, 1988) should alert you to the difficulties! However, these New Hall style pieces can be very interesting and collectable, and even costly! It is merely that they were not produced at the New Hall factory.

Lastly, it may be helpful to list some of the events that took place within the approximate period of the New Hall story, starting in the 1760s with William Cookworthy's patent to produce true porcelain after the Chinese fashion. This table should help to chart the more important landmarks.

RESUMÉ OF KEY DATES

1760	Accession of George III. The population was about seven and a half million.
1766	Commencement of canal system linking the Staffordshire Potteries with the Port of Liverpool and other commercial centres.
1768	William Cookworthy's patent to produce true or hard-paste porcelain using Cornish raw materials. Experiments at Bristol and Plymouth may have preceded the patent. See Chapter I.
c.1770	Transfer of Plymouth venture to Bristol, where Cookworthy later assigned his patent to Richard Champion. See Chapter I.
1775	Establishment of the Caughley porcelain manufactory, in Shropshire.
1776	Declaration of Independence by the Americans.
1777	Completion of Trent and Mersey Canal system linking the Potteries with the Port of Liverpool.
c.1781-2	Richard Champion (of Bristol) seeks to sell his patent rights and know-how to a group of Staffordshire earthenware potters and investors. See Chapter II.
c.1781-2	Porcelain production commenced on a small scale at Anthony Keeling's pottery at Tunstall, initially with the help of Richard Champion. See Chapter II.
c.1783-4	Anthony Keeling and John Turner left the new partnership. Production was transferred from Tunstall to the 'New Hall' at Shelton (Hanley). See Chapters II and IV.
1784	Duty on tea reduced leading to increased consumption and demand for tea services.
c.1784-5	Increased duty on silver leading to more expensive silver teapots and other silver articles.
1786	Ratification of Anglo-French Trade Treaty, resulting in lower duties on imports and exports. Increased importation of French porcelains into the British Isles.
c.1787	Fidelle Duvivier, the talented Continental ceramic artist, employed by the New Hall management. Decorated costly, highly decorated, porcelains. See Chapter V.
1790	In November 1790 Fidelle Duvivier wrote to William Duesbury of the Derby factory, stating that his engagement at New Hall had expired and that the proprietors do not intend to do much in the fine line of painting. See Chapter V.
c.1790	New Hall's pattern numbering system introduced. Numbers will, however, only be found on some examples and not on small objects such as the cups and saucers. See Chapter III.
1791	The Directors of the English East India Company resolve to discontinue their bulk importations of the standard types of Chinese export market porcelain. However, the large stocks held in the company's London warehouses lasted for several years until the mid-1790s.
1793	Great Britain and France at war again. Trade conditions were extremely bad at this period.
1796	Richard Champion's extension to William Cookworthy's original patent came to an end. This brought to an end any monopoly which the New Hall partnership might have enjoyed.
c.1800	Introduction of the perfected bone china body by Josiah Spode, to be followed by most Staffordshire firms. The New Hall partnership retained their standard hybrid hard-paste body until c.1812.
c.1803	Bat-printed designs introduced. See Chapter IX.
1810	Peter Warburton's patent process for printing in gold, some examples being marked 'Warburton's Patent'. See pages 129-131. In April the four remaining partners Hollins, Warburton, Daniel and William Clowes purchased the New Hall estate for £6,800.
c.1812	New Hall partnership changed to a whiter rather softer bone china. See Chapter X. London shaped teawares introduced at this approximate period but common to all English porcelain manufacturers.
1813	Mason's Patent Ironstone China introduced. These colourful, durable and reasonably priced wares must have affected the sales of New Hall porcelain. Tea services would have been less affected.

1815 Peace again, Treaties of Vienna, but trade was poor, prices low and great unemployment.

1820 Death of George III. Succeeded by George IV, the former Prince Regent. The population of the British Isles had risen to approximately fourteen million.

1820 New Hall partnership, Messrs. Hollins, Warburton, Daniel & Co., advertised the manufactory to be sold by private contract, with stock of china, working utensils and materials. It did not find a buyer and was re-offered at various times in the 1820s and early 1830s. See page 408. The number of porcelain manufacturers in the Staffordshire Potteries had greatly increased in the past twenty years. Competition was fierce.

1830 Death of George IV, accession of William IV. Opening of the Liverpool-Manchester passenger railway.

1833 Factory Act regulating working hours and conditions. Various enquiries and report followed.

1835 Sale in October 1835 of the 'valuable and extensive stock of Burnished Gold China' at the New Hall works. It was also stated that 'The New Hall Company are declining business and have let the premises'. At later periods various (mainly earthenware) manufacturers occupied and worked the (divided) premises. See Chapter XI. This 1835 period, however, marks the end of the New Hall porcelain story, from a production point of view.

1864 The collecting and appreciation of New Hall porcelain may be said to have commenced in January 1864, when Llewellynn Jewitt's article on 'New Hall China' appeared in the influential monthly magazine *The Art Journal.* In this he wrote '...historically speaking, few works have played so important a part in the history of the fictile art of this country, or formed so interesting a link in the chain which connects the present high state of excellence and prosperity of that art with the olden days of patient trial and profitless experiment...'

Yes, indeed, and what pleasure and interest it has given to countless collectors and students of 'old china'.

Selected Bibliography

This listing includes the main sources of information or of quotations given in the main text. Most of the earlier, pre-1960, books are difficult to locate outside major reference libraries and they may well be costly to purchase.

It should be remembered that some of the opinions given in the older works are at variance with present-day thoughts. Because a book is old it does not mean it is reliable, but of course interesting or helpful points might be made and can be accepted *once they have been rechecked.*

This Bibliography is given in chronological order. It is not necessarily complete, particularly in regard to directories or trade papers. I have not here listed every such issue, but where such works have been quoted in the text, the source has been given in full.

First I list the hard-cover books, followed by articles or papers included in magazines or the *Transactions of the English Ceramic Circle* or the various publications of the Northern Ceramic Society.

A Survey of the County of Stafford by William Tunnicliffe (privately printed, 1787)

History of the Staffordshire Potteries by Simeon Shaw (privately printed, 1829)

The Borough of Stoke-on-Trent by John Ward (W. Lewis & Son, London, 1843)

Relics of William Cookworthy by John Prideaux (Lidstone, 1853)

Memoir of William Cookworthy by George Harrison (Cash, 1854)

Two Centuries of Ceramic Art in Bristol by H. Owen (Bell & Daldy, London, 1873)

The Ceramic Art of Great Britain by Llewellynn Jewitt (Virtue & Co. Ltd., 1878, single volume revised edition 1883)

Contributions Towards the History of Early English Porcelain by J.E. Nightingale (Bennett Brothers, 1881)

Analysed Specimens of English Porcelain by H. Eccles and B. Rackham (Victoria and Albert Museum, London, 1922)

Cookworthy's Plymouth and Bristol Porcelain by F. Severne MacKenna (F. Lewis Ltd.,1946)

Champion's Bristol Porcelain by F. Severne MacKenna (F. Lewis Ltd., 1947)

New Hall Porcelain by G.E. Stringer (Art Trade Press, London, 1949)

Jubilee Souvenir of the New Hall Pottery Company Ltd by G.E. Stringer (privately published, Hanley, 1949)

British Potters & Pottery Today by C. Blunt (F. Lewis, 1956)

Victoria History of the County of Stafford, contributions by R.G. Haggar. (Vols. 1 and VIII, University of London 1967 and 1963)

English Blue and White Porcelain of the 18th Century by Bernard Watney (Faber & Faber, 1963, revised edition, 1973)

English Porcelain 1745-1850 edited by R.J. Charleston, New Hall chapter by G.E.A. Grey (E. Benn Ltd., 1965)

Master Potters of the Industrial Revolution – the Turners of Lane End by Bevis Hillier (Cory, Adams & Mackay, 1965)

New Hall and its Imitators by David Holgate (Faber & Faber, London, 1971)

William Cookworthy 1705-1780 by John Penderill-Church (Bradford Barton, 1972)

Cookworthy 1705-80 and his Circle also titled *Cookworthy – a Man of No Common Clay* by A.D. Selleck (Baron Jay Ltd., 1978)

Godden's Guide to English Porcelain by Geoffrey Godden (first edition Granada Publishing Ltd., London 1978, with subsequent revised editions)

An Anthology of British Cups by Michael Berthoud (Micawber Publications, 1982)

Staffordshire Porcelain edited by Geoffrey Godden. New Hall chapter by David Holgate (Granada Publishing Ltd., London, 1983)

Eighteenth Century English Porcelain, A Selection from the Godden Reference Collection by G.A. Godden (Grafton Publishing Ltd., 1985)

Dudson, A Family of Potters Since 1800 by Audrey Dudson (Dudson Publications, 1985)
An Anthology of British Teapots by P. Miller and M. Berthoud (Micawber Publications, 1985)
New Hall by David Holgate (Faber & Faber, 1987)
Encyclopaedia of British Porcelain Manufacturers by G.A. Godden (Barrie & Jenkins, 1988)
A Guide to New Hall Porcelain Patterns by A. de Saye Hutton (Barrie & Jenkins, 1990)
A Compendium of British Cups by M. Berthoud (Micawber Publications, 1990)
British Teapots and Tea Drinking 1700-1850 by Robin Emmerson (Her Majesty's Stationery Office, 1992)
English Porcelain 1745-95 by Hilary Young (V. & A. Publications, 1999)
A Cabinet of British Creamers by M. Berthoud (Micawber Publications, 1999)
A partial reconstruction of the New Hall Pattern Book by Pat Preller (privately published 2003)
Godden's Guide to English Blue and White Porcelain by Geoffrey Godden (Antique Collectors¿ Club, 2004)

Articles, Papers, Catalogues, etc., relating to New Hall

'New Hall China' by L. Jewitt *(Art Journal,* London, January 1864)
'New Hall China' by F.A. Rhead *(Connoisseur,* Vol. XLVI, December 1916)
'Fidelle Duvivier: Ceramic Artist' by W.H. Tapp *(Apollo,* December 1940 and March 1941)
'Histories of the Old and New Hall Potteries...' by G.E. Stringer (privately published Hanley, 1941, with later updates and corrections added to the copy in Hanley Reference Library)
'At the Source', unsigned trade resumé of the New Hall history and their current wares *(Pottery & Glass,* July 1949)
'Hard Paste New Hall Porcelain' by T.A. Sprague *(Apollo,* June 1949; also July 1949, August 1950, October 1950)
'New Hall – the Last Phase' by R.G. Haggar *(Apollo,* November 1951)
'Hard-paste New Hall Porcelain' by T.A. Sprague *(Transactions of the English Ceramic Circle,* Vol. 3, Part 3, 1, 1954)
'Black Transfers on Bone-Paste Porcelain' by T.A. Sprague *(Apollo,* March 1956)
'The End of Bristol. The Beginning of New Hall' by R.J. Charleston *(Connoisseur,* April 1956)
'Notes on Staffordshire Bas-Reliefs of the Eighteenth and Nineteenth Centuries' by G.E. Stringer *(Transactions of the English Ceramic Circle,* Vol. 4, Part 1, 1957)
'New Hall Porcelain' by Mrs. Kit Holgate *(Antique Dealer and Collectors Guide,* October, 1965)
'New Hall Porcelain' Mrs. Kit Holgate *(Antique Collecting,* August 1967)
'Some Interesting New Hall Patterns' by Mrs. Kit Holgate *(Antique Collecting,* Part I May 1970, Part II August 1970)
'New Hall Hard Paste Porcelain' by G. Grey *(Transactions of the English Ceramic Circle,* Vol. 8, Part 1, 1971)
'Further thoughts on New Hall' David Holgate *(Journal of the Northern Ceramic Society,* Vol. 1, 1972/73)
'The Total look of New Hall', related articles by Mrs. Kit Holgate and by Geoffrey Godden *(Antique Dealer and Collectors Guide,* April 1971)
'New Hall China' by R.G. Haggar *(Northern Ceramic Society Newsletter,* No. 26, June 1977)
'Hard-Paste Porcelain', Lecture Meeting by David Holgate *(Northern Ceramic Society Newsletter,* No. 27, Sept 1977)
'New Hall Seminar' by Diana Darlington *(Northern Ceramic Society Newsletter,* No. 28, December 1977)
'Porcelain – Some Thoughts on English Hard Paste Porcelain' by Maurice Hillis *(Northern Ceramic Society Newsletter,* 31 September 1978)
'New Hall Porcelain. Bicentenary Exhibition 1781-1981' by David Holgate (Catalogue of exhibition held at the Stoke-on-Trent City Museum & Art Gallery, April-June 1981)
'Fidelle Duvivier Paints New Hall' by David Holgate *(Transactions of the English Ceramic Circle* ,Vol. 11, Part 1, 1981)
'New Hall: An Assessment' by Reginald Haggar *(Northern Ceramic Society Newsletter,* No. 43, September 1981)
'William Cookworthy and the Plymouth Factory: an Updating' by F. Severne MacKenna *(Transactions of the English Ceramic Circle,* Vol. 11, Part 2, 1982)
'New Hall Niceties' by Mrs. Kit Holgate *(Antique Collecting,* October 1983)
'New Hall: A Champion Broadsheet and some Advertisements' by David Holgate *(Journal of the Northern Ceramic Society,* Vol. 5, 1984)
'A New Hall Postscript' by David Holgate *(Northern Ceramic Society Newsletter,* No. 59, September 1985)
'An Urn amongst the Flowerpots' by Mrs. Kit Holgate *(Journal of the Northern Ceramic Society,* Vol. 6, 1987)
'The Lion of Lane End' by Roger Pomfret *(Journal of the Northern Ceramic Society,* Vol. 6, 1987)
'New Hall Early Patterns and Shapes' by R. and J. Carter *(Ceramic Index,* February 1988)
'Origins of some New Hall Bat-prints' by Joyce McCarthy *(Northern Ceramic Society Newsletter,* No. 70, June 1988)
'An Enterprising Factory' by Kit and David Holgate *(Collectors Guide,* July 1988)
'New Hall, some Interesting Nuances' by David Holgate *(Transactions of the English Ceramic Circle,* Vol. 14, Part 2, 1991)
'A London Staffordshire Warehouse – 1794-1825' by Ann Eatwell and Alex Werner *(Journal of the Northern Ceramic Society,* Vol. 8, 1991)
'Closer to the Bone' by Robert Copeland *(Journal of the Northern Ceramic Society,* Vol. 9, 1992)
'New Hall at Keele' by Roger Pomfret *(Northern Ceramic Society Newsletter* No. 86, June 1992)
'New Hall – what we Know. A Brief History' by Philip Miller (privately published notes, relating to a lecture given in May 1993)
'Procurement of Raw Materials by the Spode-Wolfe Partnership' by Trevor Markin *(Journal of the Northern Ceramic Society,* Vol. 11, 1994)
'The Lion Mark Revisited' by Roger Pomfret. *(Journal of the*

Northern Ceramic Society, Vol. 12, 1995)
'Introducing New Hall' by M. Berthoud *(Ceramic Bulletin,* No. 5 Micawber Publications, 1996)
'Some thoughts on Obconical Creamers' by G. Godden *(Northern Ceramic Society Newsletter,* No. 103, September, 1996)
'Mirror Images and Thoughts on Obconical Creamers' by Barry Lomax *(Northern Ceramic Society Newsletter,* No. 105, March. 1997)
'Obconical Creamers at New Hall' by David Holgate *(Northern Ceramic Society Newsletter,* No. 108, November, 1997)
'A New Hall Dessert Service' by David Holgate *(Northern Ceramic Society Journal,* Vol. 15, 1998)
'Variations on a theme of New Hall's Pattern 3' by David Holgate *(Northern Ceramic Society Journal,* Vol. 16, 1999)
'New Hall – the Enigma Variation' by Roger Pomfret *(Northern Ceramic Society Journal,* Vol. 16, 1999).
'The Watney Collection', Auction Sale Catalogues, Part I, 1999, Parts II and III, 2000, compiled by John Sandon (Messrs. Phillips, London)
New Hall and Friends, illustrated magazine issued to members of this New Hall collectors group, 2001 onwards. Joint editors Mrs. Jean Barratt (Riverside Cottage, Mill Lane, Lower Tean, Staffs, ST 10 4LL) and Mrs. Rosie Cooke.

Where to see New Hall Porcelains

Many museums will include some porcelains at least attributed to the New Hall factory. Examples may not necessarily be on display; some may well be in storerooms and such stores will most probably only be available by prior appointment.

The main museum collections are the Victoria and Albert Museum and the British Museum in London. In Staffordshire there is a large holding at 'The Potteries Museum' in Hanley but only a token selection may be on display. Other holdings are at Norwich Castle Museum (mainly teapots), the City of Manchester Art Gallery and the National Museum of Wales.

Leading dealers should have a selection of well-attributed examples and most of the vetted antiques fairs, in particular the specialist ceramic fairs, will include specimens in various price ranges. Specimens also turn up in the major auction rooms. The major firms issue well-illustrated catalogues with sound attributions – not that they guarantee their descriptions; read the printed 'Conditions of Sales'. This is not to imply that fakes abound; the main danger is in optimistic attributions!

The Godden collection, representing many pieces featured in this book, is currently on loan to The Potteries Museum at Hanley.

Checklist of Illustrated Marked Patterns

Recorded New Hall patterns which are illustrated in this book are given in the following checklist. Other patterns may be found in A. de Saye Hutton's *A Guide to New Hall Porcelain Patterns* (Barrie & Jenkins, 1990) or in Pat Preller's *A partial reconstruction of the New Hall Pattern Books* (privately published, 2003).

Many patterns are not recorded and several New Hall designs, mainly of the pre-1800 period, do not seem to have borne pattern numbers. As a good general rule pattern numbers will not occur on New Hall porcelains made before about 1790. The numbers will only occur painted on (or on some of) the major items in a tea service, not, for example, on cups and saucers. The exception to this rule occurs in the later years, in the 1820s or early 1830s.

The specimens here associated with the first few years when the partnership was centred at Tunstall, before moving to the New Hall at Shelton, do not bear a pattern number. These unmarked porcelains are illustrated in Chapter II.

Also specimens decorated solely in underglaze blue, the subject of Chapter VII, do not bear pattern numbers. However, some blue printed designs that were additionally embellished with gilding can bear a pattern number – this will relate to the gilt design, not necessarily to the blue design.

The rich or special designs associated with the Continental ceramic artist Fidelle Duvivier (see Chapter V) do not bear a factory pattern number. They were special designs or in some cases may have been produced as private commissions (or as independent work), not as standard factory products. However, some few Duvivier painted pieces bear low numbers which may relate to his personal design books or records. Certainly in the early period, or before 1800, more New Hall porcelain will be found without a pattern number than with one!

New Hall porcelains of the pre-1800 period which have enamelled or gilt designs without known pattern numbers are here listed. These may originally have been known by names or descriptions, rather than by a fixed number. This point was made on page 104. No New Hall factory pattern book or original list seems to have survived. Unrecorded pattern numbers are featured in Plates 87-8, 90, 93-6, 100-6, 110-1, 118, 124-5, 133, 135-6, 155, 157, 172 and in Colour Plates 1-3, 6-23, 26-7, 32, 39-46, 48-58, 60, 69, 80-2.

Examples here illustrated with painted pattern numbers are in the following checklist but in practice the early numbers under about 100 do not as a general rule bear these numbers. In this case most of the pattern numbers have been identified by collectors or authors by reference to the numbers occurring on later examples. A typical example is the bone china jug of c.1815, shown in Plate 361, which bears the early pattern 22 which would have been introduced over thirty years previously.

Collectors have as yet succeeded in tracing or identifying less than half of the patterns that were introduced by this long-living series of partnerships at New Hall. This statement assumes, of course, that the original pattern books contained designs numbered in a continuous sequence from 1 to well over 3,000, without gaps.

NUMBERED PATTERNS ILLUSTRATED

3. Colour Plates 4-5, 25, 28. Plates 28 (and versions) 33A, 36, 38, 97-8, 107, 117, 120
12. Colour Plate 26, left. Plates 99, 119, 121
20. Colour Plates 24, 29, 47, 61. Plates 91, 113, 127, 138, 148, 216-7, 310-1
22. Colour Plates 25, 30. Plates 92, 97, 123, 361
52. Plate 216
64. Plate 89
67. Plates 33, 33A, 112
78. Plates 112, 122, 144-5
81. Plate 173
83. Plates 130, 134, 150
84. Plate 131
89. Plates 153, 173

90. Plates 139-40
119. Plates 127, 149
121. Colour Plate 31. Plates 34-5, 109, 141-2, 146-7
122. Plate 143
139. Plate 132
142. Plate 154
148. Plate 165
152. Plate 47
153. Plates 47, 172
154. Plates 116, 151
160. Colour Plate 33. Plates 137, 156
167. Plates 115, 126
171. Plate 170, 299
172. Plate 128, 308
180. Plate 174
186. Plates 305-6
195. Colour Plate 34. Plates 48, 163, 175, 302-4, 310-1
198. Plates 152, 164
213. Plates 159, 232
233. Plate 166
241 Plate 174
270. Plate 167
274. Plate 168
280. Plate 169
353. Plates 160, 194
354. Plates 161, 301
421. Plate 313
425. Colour Plate 59. Plates 51, 221, 231, 300
436. Colour Plate 50. Plate 223
446. Colour Plate 36. Plates 50, 187
449. Plates 176, 307
461. Plate 192
462. Plates 314-5, 321-2
466. Plates 316, 326
472. Plates 180-1
473. Plates 234, 289, 318
478. Plate 184
484. Plate 188
511. Colour Plate 62. Plate 317
540. Plate 177
568. Plate 183
570. Plate 178
571. Colour Plate 37. Plate 189
621. Plate 222
638. Plate 185
660. Colour Plate 35. Plate 162
661. Colour Plate 38
709. Plates 319-20
753. Plate 328
839. Plate 179
888. Plate 323
917. Plate 190
934. Plate 327
984 Colour Plates 64, 68. Plates 325, 331, 340, 346, 359, 363
1045. Plate 52
1053. Colour Plate 65. Plates 338-9, 348-51
1059. Plate 364
1066. Plate 384
1085. Plate 360
1092. Colour Plate 67. Plate 344
1100. Plate 376
1109. Plates 53, 337, 341
1140. Colour Plate 68. Plates. 346-7, 365
1147. Plates 334-6
1153. Colour Plate 70. Plates. 368, 370
1162. Plates 332-3
1277. Colour Plate 66. Plates 342-3
1279. Plate 367
1288. Plate 369
1357. Colour Plate 68. Plates 346, 371
1458. Plate 366
1476. Plates 407-8
1478. Plates 357, 410-2
1571. Plates 380-1
1629. Plate 358
1706. Colour Plate 77. Plates 415-7
1707. Plate 418
1861. Plate 371
1874. Plates 413-4
1934. Plate 403
1944. Colour Plate 71. Plates 372-4
1980. Plate 382
2120. Plate 377
2155. Plate 419
2215. Colour Plate 72. Plates 378-9
2226. Plates 420-1
2229. Plate 423
2240. Plates 429-30
2359. Plate 390
2371. Plate 422
2383. Plates 54, 375
2483. Plate 291
2502. Plate 386
2623. Colour Plate 78. Plates 424-6
2679. Plate 427
2810. Plate 428
2901. Plate 391
2903. Plates 388-9
2930. Plate 431
2932. Plate 432
3030. Plate 433
3034. Plate 434
3050. Colour Plate 73. Plate 392
3202. Plate 394
3203. Plate 395
3247. Plate 387
3324. Plate 393
3639. Plate 396
3664. Colour Plate 79. Plate 435

Fractional Pattern Numbers

4/3431 Plate 397
4/3609 Plate 398
4/3747 Plate 401
4/3753 Colour Plate 74. Plate 399
4/3914 Plate 402

Acknowledgements

A great many people have helped in the preparation of this book. Alas, as this research has taken place over a very long period, several of these kind helpers are no longer with us. Nevertheless, their names should be recorded and my gratitude expressed.

Whilst in such listings I do not normally single out any special persons, I must in this case acknowledge the sterling assistance offered by my late fellow collector and author David Holgate. David kindly read, corrected and helpfully commented on the many batches of typescript which I (by his invitation) sent to him. The finished book is so much better for his kind and scholarly advice, although any remaining faults must be at my door. This book has been rightly dedicated to David, who sadly died in December, 1999.

Other folk have generously lent me their treasures to study or to have photographed professionally. Others have supplied photographs of rare or interesting examples. Leading members of the trade and the auctioneers have been particularly generous in this regard. It should be noted that the illustrations are credited to the person or firm owning the example at the time of it being photographed and that they may not now be the owner. This obviously applies particularly to credited auctioneers and dealers who supplied or made possible the photograph and applies to pieces accredited to my late firm Messrs. Godden of Worthing Ltd. Some private owners have asked that their pieces be merely recorded as from a private collection. Their collective help is however gratefully acknowledged.

The majority of the illustrations have been taken by my local professional photographers, Messrs. Walter Gardiner, Photography (of Worthing). Other photographers are not known to me by name. Likewise personnel from acknowledged auction houses, museums or libraries are not always known to me by name. My thanks to all such helpful persons is most sincere. I am also most grateful to my ever patient typists who have turned my long-hand scrawl into a presentable typescript. Thank you Janet Belton and Mrs. Jan Welch.

I trust that I have included in the following list all those who have helped in the preparation of this book. My apologies are offered to any others, where perhaps the length of time has occasioned a lapse in my memory. Please forgive me for any omissions.

Dr. Gary Audley
Horace Barks Reference Library, Hanley
Dr. and Mrs. G. Barnes
Michael Berthoud
Mr. and Mrs. Harold Blakey
Dr. & Mrs. Stephen Brant
British Broadcasting Company, Bristol
British Ceramic Research Limited
British Museum
Bristol Museum
Ceylon Tea Centre
R.J. Charleston
Charnwood Antiques
Messrs. Christie's
Robert Copeland
T. Cuncannon
Miss Diana Darlington
Peter Davis
Mrs. Sheila Davis
Messrs. Dreweatt Neate
Mrs. A. Dudson
Roger Edmundson
Robin Emmerson
Robert Finan
Flintshire Record Office
Dr. J. Gold
Miranda Goodby
Jonathan Gray
Alan Green
Geoffrey Grey
Grosvenor Antiques
Guildhall Library
Reginald Haggar
Mrs. Pat Halfpenny
Mr. and Mrs. Rodney Hampson
Martin Harrison
Robin Hildyard
Mr. and Mrs. David Holgate
The late Mrs. Kit Holgate
David Hollis
Jonathan Horsfall-Turner
Mollie Hosking
Mr. and Mrs. A de Saye Hutton
Charlotte Jacob-Hanson
Roderick Jellicoe
Keele University Library
J.P. (Pat) M. Latham
Mark Law
Christopher Lewis
Lichfield Record Office
Terry Lockett
Barry Lomax
Sue London
Stafford Lorie
Trevor Markin
Iain MacPhail
Dr. J McCarthy
Messrs. Mercury Antiques
Philip Miller
Norfolk Museum Service
Arnold Mountford
Diana Edwards Murnaghan
National Museum of Wales
Elizabeth L. Pettitt
Messrs. Phillips
D.R. Platz
Roger Pomfret
The Potteries Museum, Hanley
Mr. and Mrs. Preller
Public Records Office, Kew
Paul Rado
E. Randall
Mrs. L. Richards
Miss Gaye Blake Roberts
Peter Roden
Miss Letitia Roberts (Sotheby's New York)
William Salt Library
Henry Sandon
John Sandon
Mrs. Debbie Skinner
Alan Smith
The Smithsonian Institution
Messrs. Sotheby's
Cyril Staal
Messrs. Stockspring Antiques
Staffordshire County Record
George E. Stringer
Sun Alliance Insurance Group
Hugh Tait
University of Keele
Victoria & Albert Museum
Mrs. Sadia Walsh
Dr. Bernard Watney
Messrs. Watts, Blake, Bearne & Co. Plc.
Trustees of the Wedgwood Museum[1]
Len Whiter
Mrs. Wildish
Dr. Michael Witherick
The Worcester Royal Porcelain Co. Ltd.
Worthing Public Library
Mrs. N. Wright
Hilary Young.

1. The full acknowledgement in this case is 'By Courtesy of the Trustees of the Wedgwood Museum, Barlaston, Stoke-on-Trent.

Index

Page numbers in bold type refer to illustrations and captions

Abbott and Mist, 336
Adams, W. (& Co.), 92-3, 149, 380, 390
Alcock, S. & Co., 142, 377, 394-6
asparagus servers, 267, **293**
Audley, R., 411-2, 415
Aynsley, J., 410

Baddeley Booth & Co., 317
Baddeley-Littler, 10, 16, 65, 276, 317
Baddeley, M., 151
Baddeley, R., 144, 146
Bagnall, C., 10, 91, 93, 150, 155, 166
Bagnall, S., 155
baskets, **261, 313**
bat printing, **54-7, 63,** 136-42, 329-60, **330-1, 333-44, 346-50, 352-60**
Bevington, A. & Co., 411
Billingsley, W., 123-4
Blackwell & Dillons, 156
blue and white, **50-2, 72-5,** 84-5, **85, 87,** 134, 267, 277-315, **277, 279-81, 283-314**
Bolton, S., 144
bone china, **54-64,** 344-60, **344, 346-50, 352-61,** 361-405, **361-84, 386-405**
Bone, H., 186-7
Booth, A., 406
Booth, E., 94-6, 145, 149
Booth, H., 144, 149
Booth, L.M., 123-4
Booth, T. & Sons, 131, 410-1
Bourne, C., 390
bowls, **53, 56, 116, 284, 324-5, 352**
breakfast wares, 255-6, **342, 383**
Bristol, 13, 73, 75-87, **76-7, 79, 81, 83-7,** 126
Britain, J., 78
Brocas, T., 154
butter boats, 199-200

Caughley, 278
Chamberlain (Worcester), 93, 183, 328, 385
Champion, R., 10, 13, 15, 65-7, 73-88, 102, 277
Chatterley, E., 151
Chelsea, 160-1, 181
'Chelsea' ewers, **194-5,** 195-6, **197**
Child, T., 95, 423
china earth, 70, 72
china stone, 13, 68
chocolate cups, 275, **275,** 384
Clewes, Ralph, 126, 222
Clewes, R. & J., 390
Close, V., 93
closing sale, 142
Clowes, A., 156
Clowes, W., 91, 93, 154-6
Clowes & Williams, 155
Cockson & Harding, 410
coffee pots, **34, 54-5, 137, 214-5, 233, 249, 309, 320, 335, 349**
colliery interests, 157
'composition', 93
Cookworthy, W., 13, 66-7, 70-6, 88-90
Copeland, J., 411-2, 415
corrugated porcelains, **17-21,** 99-101, **100-5, 107-116, 118**
cottagy, cheaper patterns, **37, 52-3, 128, 137, 214-5, 221, 224-8, 237, 242, 244-5,** 316-28, **316, 318-27**
Cotton, E., 132, 156
cream ewers, 194-6, **197-9**
Creyke, G.M. & Sons, 411, 413
Creyke & Boulton, 411
Cristall, J., 187

Dalton, A., 144, 146
Daniel, A., 154, 166-70
Daniel, J. (& Co.), 89, 91, 93, 145-8, 153-4, 164, 167-73, 257, 422
Daniel, S., 164, 166, 168
dessert wares, **23-5, 41-5, 52, 61-3, 169-73,** 256-66, **257-66, 358-60,** 385-96, **386-96**
Dillon, F. & N., 156
Dr. Syntax subjects, 391, **391-3**
Duché, A., 72
Dudson, Mrs. A., 144, 409
Dudson, T., 373-4, 402
Duesbury, W., 160, 182
Duvivier, F., **22-30, 40-4,** 159-186, **159, 162-80, 184-6,** 204, 212, **257-61,** 257, **264**
Duvivier, H.J., 160

East India Company, 15, 68, 71
Egan, R., 65-6, 132
Emery, F., 188
errors by earlier writers, 425-6
Exley, C.L., 123-4

'Factory X', 98, 124
firing temperatures, 15, 68, 79-80
flasks, **267**
Fletcher, T., 189
Fogg, R., 134

Gerverot, L-V., 164, 182, 287
gilders' numbers, 121
Giles, J., 182
Gilmore Bros., 415
Gower, Lord, 423-4
Gray, T., 168-171
Grey, G., 9. 98-9, 112-3, 116

Hackwood, W. & Son, 409
Hall, H., 410-1
hard paste porcelains, 15, 68
Harding, Miss L., 408
Harding, W. & J. (Bros.), 408, 410
Harrison, G., 90
Heath, C., 410
Heath, J., 10, 144-6, 148, 150
Heath, T., 10, 91, 95, 148-50, 422-4
Heath Warburton & Co., 89, 93, 144, 148, 422
Heath, Warburton, Daniel & Co., 145
Hendra Company, 151, 153
Henshall, Williamson & Clowes, 155
Hingston, R., 72
Holdway, P., 334

Holgate, D., 6, 13, 16, 66, 99, 106-7, 114, 183, 186, 262, 265, 409, 421
Holgate, K., 102, 115, 287, 291
Hollins, J., 10, 91, 150-1
Hollins, S. (& Co.), 10, 91-3, 95, 145-7, 150-2
Hollins, T., 152
Hollins, Warburton, Daniel & Co., 133
Hutton, A. de Saye, 9
hybrid hard paste, 15, 66-7

Jewitt, L., 146, 166-8
jugs, **25, 32-3, 46-50, 54, 63-4, 118-9, 122, 164-5, 267-74,** 268-73, **280-1,** 396-402, **397-9, 401-5**

kaolin, 13, 68-72
Keeling, A. (& Co.), 10, 66, 91-8, 124, 144, 148, 276
Keeling, E., 95, 149
Keeling, J., 188
knife handle, **298**
'Knitting Wool' pattern, **320-1,** 321-4

Lakin, T. (& Co.), 386-7
Land Tax Returns, 422-4
Leach, B., 16
leaf dishes, **287**
lion crest mark, 126, 285-92, **289, 295,** 315
Littler, W., 10
London shape, **348, 350, 352, 354, 357, 364-75,** 368
Longton Hall, 10
Loosdrecht, 160, 182
Lowndes, W., 409
lustre, 380
Lygo, J., 65, 132, 143

marketing, 131-3
marks, 125-7
Meigh, J., 154
milk jugs, 194-5, **199-201,** 200-1, **203-7,** 206, 238-44
Minton, 396
Morgan, T., 182
Mortlock, 188
Moseley, J., 154
mugs, **22, 100, 120, 162-3, 175, 180,** 273-5, **274-5, 292, 400-3**
museum collections, 431

'N' incised, 126
Neale, J., 95, 144, 147, 149, 157, 182-3, 422
New Hall, 66-7, 93-4, 143-8, 193
New Hall Company, 10, 15, 65-6, 147
New Hall factory, 406-14
'New Hall' marks, 131, 310, 345, 384-5, 414
New Hall Pottery Co. (Ltd.), 131, 410-5
New Hall site, 40
'New Oval' shape, 335
'N H' pad mark, 131, 148

'Old Oval' shape, 246, **246-9,** 329-35, **331**
Oriental porcelain, **68-73,** 68, 134, 191, 235, 277, 305, **305,** 317, 328

Palmer, H., 144-7, 149
Palmer, M., 145-7, 151
Palmer, T., 144, 146
patent, 10-3, 66-7, 76, 80, 88-9, 91, 416-21
pattern numbers, 126-9
Perry, S. (& Co.), 149, 155
petuntse, 13, 68-72
Pinxton, 123-4, 388
Plant & Gilmore, 411
platinum lustre, 252, 276
Plymouth, 73-5, **74-5**
Pomfret, R., 91, 184, 288
prices, 133-142
printing, 278-9

Rado, P., 421
Ratcliffe, W., 409
'real china', 15, 144, 157, 421
retailers' marks, 132-3
Rogers, H. M., 8
Rothwell, T., 315

scent bottle, **384**
Schreiber, Lady Charlotte, 126
seconds, 136
shares, in company, 11-3, 92
Sheen, C., 106
Shelley, T., 149
Shelton Hall, 144, 157
Shorthose, J., 149
Shrewsbury, Earl of, 288, 315
'silver shape', **30, 36-7, 184-5,** 221-5, **221, 224-7, 229-37,** 236-8
silver lustre, 252, 276
Smith, J., 95
Smith, T., 144

Smith & Swift, 95
Solon, M.L., 16
spill vases, **384,** 404
Spode, 341
spoontrays, 217-8, **218-9, 223, 286, 296, 302**
Stringer collection, 158
Swansea, 386
Swift, P., 95

tally marks, 129, 212
Tansley, J., 133
tea, 191
tea canisters, **197,** 215-6, **217, 283, 295-6**
teawares, **17-21, 25-40, 51-4, 56-6, 68-71, 73, 76-7,** 78, **79, 81, 83-4, 86,** 101-5, **107-118, 123, 125, 128, 130,** 133-4, **135, 137-9, 166-7, 174-9, 184-6, 190, 192-221, 223-37, 239-55, 279, 316, 318-23, 327, 330-1, 333-44, 346-50,** 349, **352-57, 361-83**
Thomas, F., 160
Tittensor, C., 156
Tittensor, J., 155-6, 409
Tournai, 160, 181-2
Tunstall, 96-7
period, **17-21,** 88-124, **100-5, 107-20,** 191-3
Turner, J., 10, 65-6, 91, 93-4, 98, 144-8, 160, 287
Turner & Abbott, 65
Turner & Newbury, 65

Warburton family, 406
Warburton, J., 10, 91-4, 152
Warburton, P., **130,** 131, 152-3, 336-9, **338-9,** 343
Warburton's Patent, 129-31, **130,** 141, 252, **338-9**
Wareham, J., 187-8
Wedgwood, J., 10, 71, 88, 92, 132, 134, 143, 147, 151, 251, 282, 317
Wedgwood, R. (& Co.), 183
Whiter, L., 120
Wildin, J., 188
Williamson, H.H., 146, 156
Wilson, D., 156
Wilson, R., 147, 150, 157
Wirksworth, 263
Woolliscroft, C., 153, 186
Wyllie, J., accounts, 135-42, 326-7, 351-2, 371, 373, 398-401